WOMB
AWAKENING

"*Womb Awakening* is a magnificent achievement that gives new life to the vision of tantra, with women as spiritual power-holders and initiators who celebrated the womb as a treasury of knowledge and source of bliss, compassion, and liberating wisdom. With radiant prose, the book ushers us to the original altar and holy temple within us all, guiding us into the womb realm of magic, transforming power, and healing grace of sacred union with ourselves, our partners, and the earth."

MIRANDA SHAW, PH.D., ASSOCIATE PROFESSOR OF RELIGIOUS STUDIES AT THE UNIVERSITY OF RICHMOND AND AUTHOR OF *PASSIONATE ENLIGHTENMENT: WOMEN IN TANTRIC BUDDHISM* AND *BUDDHIST GODDESSES OF INDIA*

"A brilliant and heartfelt book, I believe this work has the potential to forever change our ideas about the womb. I was enthralled from the very first pages. A beautiful and timely body of womb wisdom that will be shared for generations to come."

ROSITA ARVIGO, D.N., AUTHOR OF *SASTUN: MY APPRENTICESHIP WITH A MAYA HEALER* AND FOUNDER OF ARVIGO TECHNIQUES OF MAYA ABDOMINAL THERAPY

"An extraordinary book that is both a revelation and a priceless shamanic guide to the Divine Wisdom of the Feminine—obliterated and obfuscated by patriarchal religion for five millennia—a wondrous, generous, astonishing, deeply researched, and utterly extraordinary gift to women and men who are searching for the true meaning of the Holy Grail and the deeper purpose of their lives on this planet."

ANNE BARING, AUTHOR OF *THE DREAM OF THE COSMOS* AND COAUTHOR OF *THE MYTH OF THE GODDESS* AND *THE DIVINE FEMININE*

"*Womb Awakening* is a comprehensive and unrivaled guide to the hidden wisdom of the womb. More than just a book, it is an initiation into the sacred feminine mysteries, opening a portal to the possibility of embodying ancient insight. Allow yourself to be transformed by the deep feminine wisdom contained in this powerful book."

LUCY H. PEARCE, AUTHOR OF *MOON TIME, BURNING WOMAN,* AND *FULL CIRCLE HEALTH*

"Azra Bertrand, M.D., and Seren Bertrand have captured the spirit of this deeply important journey we must all go on at some stage of our lives. Together they compel, inspire, guide, and encourage both men and women into Womb Awakening. I highly recommend this book for everyone!"

ANAIYA SOPHIA, AUTHOR OF *SACRED SEXUAL UNION* AND
COAUTHOR OF *WOMB WISDOM* AND *SACRED RELATIONSHIPS*

"The Bertrands have gathered a compendium of historical information to illustrate how we have lost our connection to nature. By relying upon ancient and reverent womb wisdom, we can move away from the current human crisis of separation that has been imposed upon us through a polarization of masculine consciousness. This book points the way to recover our wholeness through inviting the feminine consciousness of unconditional love into our lives as a necessary guiding force."

PIA ORLEANE, PH.D., AUTHOR OF *SACRED RETREAT* AND COAUTHOR OF
REMEMBERING WHO WE ARE AND *CONVERSATIONS WITH LAARKMAA*

"*Womb Awakening* is both a mystery school and a portal. It is a reclamation and celebration of the womb as adytum within the temple of a woman's body. Through story, mythology, history, poetry, ritual, and lush imagery, the authors deftly induct the reader into the heart of the feminine mystery. A stirring and heartfelt offering whose pages shimmer with wisdom and magic."

SHONAGH HOME, SHAMANIC THERAPIST, TEACHER, POET, AND AUTHOR OF
IX CHEL WISDOM: 7 TEACHINGS FROM THE MAYAN SACRED FEMININE

"This book is to be read in exactly the same way you should eat dark chocolate: slowly, intentionally, and with complete devotion. Its pages are encoded with the wisdom of the ancients—the womb bodhisattvas and menstrual mystics—it's a full-bodied remembrance of who we really are, which is so 'bloody' necessary when navigating these interesting times we're currently living in."

LISA LISTER, CREATOR OF THE SASSY SHE AND AUTHOR OF
LOVE YOUR LADY LANDSCAPE AND *WITCH: UNLEASHED. UNTAMED. UNAPOLOGETIC.*

"Azra and Seren Bertrand have woven together a convincing theory of ancient myths and practices to help us understand that womb wisdom has been honored and preserved throughout the millennia of time. The nonlinear presentation accentuates the necessity of a return to living by nature's rhythms. Their work should become a model for understanding the wisdom and the depth of the Divine Feminine."

CULLEN BAIRD SMITH, COAUTHOR OF *REMEMBERING WHO WE ARE* AND
CONVERSATIONS WITH LAARKMAA

WOMB
AWAKENING

INITIATORY WISDOM FROM THE
CREATRIX OF ALL LIFE

AZRA BERTRAND, M.D., & SEREN BERTRAND

Bear & Company
Rochester, Vermont • Toronto, Canada

Bear & Company
One Park Street
Rochester, Vermont 05767
www.BearandCompanyBooks.com

Bear & Company is a division of Inner Traditions International

Library of Congress Cataloging-in-Publication Data
Names: Bertrand, Azra, author.
Title: Womb awakening : initiatory wisdom from the creatrix of all life /
   Azra Bertrand, M.D., and Seren Bertrand.
Description: Rochester, Vermont : Bear & Company, 2017. | Includes
   bibliographical references and index.
Identifiers: LCCN 2016052317 (print) | LCCN 2017025857 (e-book) |
   ISBN 9781591432791 (pbk.) | ISBN 9781591432807 (e-book)
Subjects: LCSH: Uterus—Religious aspects. | Cosmology. | Spirituality.
Classification: LCC BF1999 .B3748175 2017 (print) | LCC BF1999 (e-book) |
   DDC 202/.4—dc23
LC record available at https://lccn.loc.gov/2016052317

Printed and bound in the United States by P. A. Hutchison Company

10 9 8 7 6 5 4 3

Text design and layout by Virginia Scott Bowman
This book was typeset in Garamond Premier Pro, Avenire, and Gill Sans with Trajan Pro, Avenire, and Garamond Premier Pro used as display typefaces

Dedication page illustration: Winged Heart in Moon © The Fountain of Life, design by Arantxa Pedros and Heather Skye
Introduction and Cycles 2, 6, and 7 illustrations by Heather Skye; Cycles 1, 3, 4, and 5 illustrations by Natvienna Hanell
"[i carry your heart with me(i carry it in]". Copyright 1952, © 1980, 1991 by the Trustees for the E. E. Cummings Trust, from *COMPLETE POEMS: 1904–1962* by E. E. Cummings, edited by George J. Firmage. Used by permission of Liveright Publishing Corporation.

To send correspondence to the author of this book, mail a first-class letter to the author c/o Inner Traditions • Bear & Company, One Park Street, Rochester, VT 05767, and we will forward the communication, or contact the author directly at **www.thefountainoflife.org**.

CONTENTS

CYCLE 1

WELCOME TO PRIMORDIAL WOMB CONSCIOUSNESS

CYCLE 2

ANCIENT WOMB COSMOLOGY AND FEMININE MYSTERY SCHOOLS

CYCLE 3

WOMB OF LIFE AND ALCHEMY OF REBIRTH

CYCLE 4

THE LUNAR MYSTERIES AND WOMB CODES OF CREATION

CYCLE 5

GRAIL WOMB SHAMANISM AND SACRED SOUL-MATE UNION

CYCLE 6

WOMB MEDICINE WHEEL: AWAKENING THE EIGHT GRAIL GATES

CYCLE 7

RETURN OF THE FEMININE CHRIST: COMPLETING THE CIRCLE

FOREWORD

Linda Star Wolf

"The Word Made Flesh . . ."

These are the words that ignited the fires of my imagination as a young child, words that whispered directly into the depths of my feminine psyche. It was a coded message, a hint of a magical possibility that activated the imaginal cells within my being and gently guided me along toward my destiny. Little did I know at that time that I, a small child living in a conservative Baptist family in rural Kentucky, would one day experience a profound spiritual awakening, at the hands of the Great Mother, and "awaken the shaman within." The word would indeed become flesh, and in a female body no less!

It was not easy being me in that Baptist church. I innately sensed, even at a young age, that there was more to the story than I was being told. And despite scoldings, I regularly committed the mortal sin of asking too many innocent questions. I was told that if I doubted the word of God, I would go to hell and be damned for eternity. I must admit, since all the adults around me appeared to believe in these stories, the idea of having a red devil torture me with his pitchfork made me think twice. I prayed harder to have more faith and fewer questions, but still they continued. Feelings of shame, feeling different from the others and not fitting in were a regular feature of my life at that time.

Looking back as an adult, I can see that it was my wild and witchy grandmother who saved my life. She was my mother's mother—Mammy Jones—my renegade Baptist Celtic shamanic grandmother, and was my sole/soul refuge during my early childhood years. Even though she attended church services and read the "good book," she seldom wore shoes; she let her hair down wild and loose; she talked, joked, and laughed loudly; and was frowned upon for not being very ladylike.

Mammy Jones taught me the sheer joy of being connected to the natural world, as we would take mysterious walks into the woods, share in the sensual pleasure of digging our bare feet into the rich, black, loamy soil of Mother Earth, and pick luscious fruits and vegetables from the gardens and orchard. We played in the rain, waded in the pond, gathered the still-warm eggs from our chickens, and made corn maidens from the long ears of corn that grew in the cornfields. We rescued baby birds that had fallen from their nests and watched caterpillars morph into butterflies. At night we sang songs, prayed to God, Jesus, *and the fairies* all in the same breath! We asked them to bless our gardens, animals, and all those we loved. We made up rhymes and stories and told old beloved fairy tales in the dark until bedtime, swinging back and forth under a star-filled, luminous night sky.

Her big heart, free spirit, unrelenting faith, and love helped me to believe in myself. She would remind me that I was special, not defective as I often felt, even though I could see and hear things in the shamanic realms that others didn't seem to even know existed.

I have written about my beloved Mammy Jones in many of my books, because it was her wild "womb wisdom" that nurtured my young body, soul, and spirit, and that kept me fed when the world around me didn't make sense and threatened to eat me alive.

She died unexpectedly right after my twelfth birthday and just before my first "moon time." So, when the "curse," as it was known, came to me, I didn't have anyone to turn to with my questions. My own mother was quite young herself, and was lost in deep grief and depression over the death of her mother. She gave me some sanitary napkins, some aspirin, and a hot water bottle for cramps and didn't have much to say about any of it. I didn't even know what it was all for.

After my grandmother's death I felt tremendously alone, with no one to guide me (although I always felt her love and spirit nearby). However, the spiral path of my life wove on, taking me on many shamanic journeys of death and rebirth. Eventually, in my thirties, I fully embraced my destiny as a spirit keeper on the shamanic path of the heart, when life surrendered me into the Void of the Great Mother and I let go of the "normal" world. I finally came back home to myself, the real self that my grandmother had so tenderly nurtured and furiously protected for the first twelve years of my life, and what a relief it was.

As I stepped into my inner knowing, my shamanic spirit began to guide me into my inner depths, and I heard the voice of my own womb knowing emerging with more and more power. The wild, sensuous kundalini energy that was pouring through every cell in my body exploded within me and the true meaning of "the word made flesh" blossomed in my own life. Many mysteries were revealed to me that had always been hidden just beneath the surface of my consciousness. I finally understood that "the word made flesh" was my spiritual journey, a journey of descent and embodiment. Our spirit, which vibrates at a high frequency, must descend into the heart of the matter, so that we can fully experience what it means to be human, and the incredible gifts waiting for us. What a joy it was to realize that our *flesh* is sacred, not sinful. Our body is the temple.

I truly knew for the first time that I was not evil, and that the Goddess and Sacred Feminine priestess were alive in my body and blood. I could see that what others had judged me for, and what I had been afraid of, was my own divinity, my royal birthright to become a heavenly queen on Earth.

Since that great time of awakening, my soul has taken me on a multitude of epic journeys filled with many shamanic and archetypal energies that have magically embodied my being—each bringing me into communion with more expansive fields of wisdom and unconditional love.

When I first met the authors of this book there was an instant recognition of a soul kinship; we were traveling along the same spirit paths and creating from the same universal flow of Shakti. What I was calling "awakening the shaman within" was very akin to what they spoke of as "womb awakening" and "reclaiming the feminine Holy Grail." We spoke together with great enthusiasm of a deep inner well of wisdom that was the portal that, once opened, gave access to the world's sacred mystery schools' teachings. This knowledge was all held within us, including the vast library of the Akashic Record. When the inner shaman awakens and when the womb awakens, nothing can be hidden any longer.

This beautifully written and intelligent book, *Womb Awakening: Initiatory Wisdom from the Creatrix of All Life,* is born from the rich, experiential, personal journeys of two amazing lovers of truth, who were always destined to find each other and to discover sacred union within themselves as well as in each other's arms and hearts. They share the elixir of their ecstatic love, as a fountain of rebirth and renewal, with the thirsting soul of the world.

I am honored to introduce you, the reader, to Dr. Azra Bertrand and Seren Bertrand, world travelers, researchers, mystics, and shamanic souls, who have dedicated their lives to studying and living the great mysteries around the globe on both the outer planes and the inner ones. Their collective wisdom is admirable, and their commitment to awaken the forgotten and repressed passions of the Womb Consciousness that belongs to us all, reminds one of the stories of the great Grail kings and queens of old. They are troubadours of the spirit, singing a new song into being that is so timely and important for this age.

I humbly bow in reverent recognition to the power of the word made flesh in this lovely book, the lost Song of Songs that is once again returning, as our imaginations connect with our renewed passions to re-create and rebirth the world we live in through reuniting the collective wisdom of our feminine consciousness.

Linda Star Wolf, Ph.D., has been a visionary teacher and shamanic guide for more than thirty-five years. The founding director and president of Venus Rising Association for Transformation, Venus Rising University, and the Shamanic Ministers Global Network, she is also the creator of the Shamanic Breathwork Process and the author of nine books, including *Shamanic Breathwork, Shamanic Mysteries of Egypt, Visionary Shamanism,* and *Soul Whispering.*

PREFACE

LOVE LETTER FROM THE AUTHORS

Be patient, She is weaving and spinning—you cannot even begin to dream of the possibilities She is stitching into being for you.
A. AND S. BERTRAND

DEAR WOMB PILGRIMS, thank you for choosing to take this journey into the Womb. Every woman who takes this pilgrimage, and every man who walks with her, brings an incredible blessing and boon into the world. The pilgrimage into the Womb brings us deeper into life and love. We believe the collective awakening of the Womb is the medicine our world needs. It is time to reclaim our creative womb power and to restore the ancient feminine cosmologies that honor the sacredness of life and help guide us to live in harmony with all of creation.

The remembrance of Womb Consciousness is as vital to men as it is to women, as we were *all* created and birthed through a womb and within Womb Consciousness. This transformative, primordial energy flows within every cell and atom of our being, regardless of our gender.

When we speak of the Womb, we refer to more than a physical organ within a female body—although this sacred site is brimming with creative magic. We refer also in a greater sense to an energetic, multidimensional portal, a bridge between worlds, that lives within us whether we have a physical womb or not. This knowing reflects the ancient primordial womb teachings.

For women who have had a hysterectomy, the energetic power and blueprint of the womb remains within; for those in moonapause, your energetic wise blood still flows in harmony with the cycles of the moon. Women in their crone phase are the spiritual grandmothers of the tribe, the wise wombs. Men also have a spiritual or energetic womb, which we call the *hara*.

The Womb is one of the greatest powers in the universe—it is an incredible gift and honor to hold this power within our body. We need to reclaim our womb sovereignty—as this cosmic stargate within us holds the power to birth, create, and shape multidimensional realities. As we stand at the dawn of a new cycle, we must initiate this cosmic birthing power within us.

It is good to be clear within yourself that the power of the womb is not to be *used*—but rather to be awakened, reunited with, and embodied. We suggest that people do not use womb power in unethical ways or for low magic, but rather to honor the spirit of life with love.

The doors of the Grail Castle—the Womb—open only for those who pilgrimage to her with the deepest love and sincerity. This journey will demand everything of you and give you everything in return. The grace of the Womb will awaken your wild Shakti and rebirth your life.

We have answered a call from the universe in this book—earth and the feminine dimension are reaching out to remind us of something vital that has been forgotten. If you also hear this great call of love, singing from deep within your bones, from the rivers, the plants, and the ancestors, asking you to protect the codes of life and earth's wisdom, then the Holy Womb is calling to you.

We offer you this book. It belongs to you, and you to it. It is a grammarye— the magical lore—of your soul. This book is ensouled: there is a feminine energy transmission streaming from within the magical portals of the yin spaces between the words, if you choose to open to receive it.

As you journey through the book, please feel free to read in a nonlinear way. You may wish to use the book as an oracle, asking Spirit for guidance and turning to a random page that brings a feminine wisdom message to you. Or you may feel particularly drawn to one of the seven wisdom cycles presented in the book and may wish to dive straight in and begin your journey there.

This book is a magic doorway into many worlds; trust your pilgrimage path.

You can also support your shamanic journey through the womb medicine wheel by downloading three guided audio meditations (see page 525).

Within you is a *womb shaman* who holds the sacred blueprints of creation. Your hidden feminine essence transmits the untamed spirals of the primordial life force, Shakti, initiating others into the mystery of life. She is emerging from a long slumber. Can you feel her energy pulsing inside? She has been sleeping on primeval forest floors, steeped in fertile soils, flowing in crystal-clear rivers.

The Womb is calling us back onto the *path of love,* traveling a starlit walkway back into primordial innocence, dancing into the central Womb of Creation, spiraling along the energetic deertrods, dreampaths, and dragonlines* of our wombs—and the Earth Mother and web of life with which she is intimately interwoven. Women and men alike were created as beings with a deep feminine *feeling* nature; our feminine heart, the womb and hara, holds this knowing and leads us back home to the sacred union of love. We cannot take one step alone; we can only walk together into the mystery.

The feminine path is full of passion, desire, and longing; our heart's desires birth through the womb. Our deepest feelings are dimensional doorways, full of rich fertility. Let us activate our sacred desire and dream-birth a new earth into being, incandescent with love, honoring all of life.

Thank you for walking with us. We walk together . . .

WITH LOVE,
AZRA BERTRAND, M.D.,
AND SEREN BERTRAND

---

*Specialized terms and significant individuals that may be unfamiliar to the reader, such as *deertrods, dreampaths,* and *dragonlines,* are explained in a glossary at the end of this book.

INTRODUCTION

I am the voice speaking softly.
I exist from the first.
I dwell within the Silence,
Within the immeasurable Silence.
I descended from the midst of the Underworld
And I shone down upon the darkness.
It is I who poured forth the Water.
I am the One hidden within Radiant Waters . . .
I am the image of the Invisible Spirit.
I am the Womb that gives shape to the All
By giving birth to the Light that shines in splendor.

GNOSTIC TEXT, *TRIMORPHIC PROTENNOIA*
(NAG HAMMADI CODEX 13)

OUR CREATOR is full of love and this pure seed blooms within us.

Through oral mystery teachings passed down as precious threads of wisdom by our ancient ancestors, it was known that the womb was the source of all Creation. Sethian Gnostics explained how the universe was a womb and said, "heaven and earth have a shape similar to the womb . . . examine the pregnant womb of any living creature, and . . . discover an image of the heavens and earth."[1] Gnostic shaman Simon Magus—who inherited the mantle of John the Baptist and was a peer of Jesus—agreed, declaring that the terrestrial paradise is the womb: "Moses . . . using allegory had declared Paradise to be the womb, and Eden the placenta."[2]

Paradise is within us; Eden is the mother-matrix of our life-coded primordial feminine biology. The Great Womb that birthed All is pregnant with *magical possibilities*; we can weave with these infinite creative threads to receive new strands of wisdom. We are still connected by a spiral umbilical cord to the placenta of the Void

1

and can draw deep sustenance, nourishment, and support from her Cosmic Womb.

As with all mystery teachings, this book is designed to catalyze a direct experience of the Womb of God *within* you. The teachings as we present them are held in the alchemy of *true love*. The womb teachings, focused as they are on the greatest source of power in all creation, have often been misused to birth more limited and self-serving agendas. Even those who believe they hold good intentions have often been disconnected from the true feminine flow of energy and perspective.

Because of this, the knowledge of the womb was forced underground for safety's sake. It is a great honor and privilege that we live in times when this wisdom is returning to flower again. The womb has a heart space, just as the heart has a womb space—and a magical umbilical cord of light connects them. The divine intelligence manifests through the *heart-womb:* these two energy centers united together in sacred union. One without the other is incomplete, just like the twin halves of the masculine and feminine belong together in the blueprint of creation.

In our current paradigm the heart has been separated from the womb; our creative power has often been divided from love. When our love does not have roots, and our power is not connected to the heart, suffering is birthed. Remembering that the love energy that we most easily associate with the heart also *includes* and flows through the womb is a huge key for our awakening. The womb holds the primordial wisdom that initiates all new creations of Spirit.

The merging of heart and womb also brings the vital power of our sexual energy, our life force, back into the frequency of love and pristine consciousness—making sexual union the highest sacrament of love, where we experience the heart and womb united. From this place of union, a new energy can be birthed onto Earth, from the power of love. This is the perfected blueprint of primordial innocence—the true human that lives within us.

Remembering and activating the Sacred Feminine essence and divine blueprint within our personal womb restores us to the throne of our own power—and reconnects us to the deeply lived knowing that we are part of the eco-system of Gaia's consciousness, not separate from it. From this rooted and secure place within our own being, we can begin to extend out into the cosmic and interplanetary grids, recognizing that we are also an integral part of this ecosystem. Ultimately we can embrace and experience the pure love pouring through all of existence from the Womb of God, and know that we are also part of this magnificent flow of infinite love energy.

We can open the living libraries again and access the incredible codes of consciousness stored in *matter:* in the human body; in the plants and animals; in the oceans and rivers; in the rocks, minerals, mountains, and crystals of Gaia herself. We can learn to once again merge with the consciousness contained in these precious jewels of creation, and open the doorways of light again. In ancient traditions this meant entering the "winged gate" of the Great Womb.

The Great Womb: The Holy Whore

The Great Womb of Creation, the preexistent birther of All, was once known as the Great Whore. In the Semitic languages of the Middle East, *hor* meant "cave" or "womb." She was also known as a harlot—a "Womb of Light." It is time to remember and reclaim the beauty and sanctity of our inner whore, our inner harlot, our Great Womb of Light—the original Holy Feminine.

In Hebrew the word *horaa* meant "instruction" and the word *hor* meant "light."[3] In fact, it was from these holy *hor* word roots that the Torah, the Old Testament, took its name. The Womb of Light was always known as the lawgiver, the teacher, the enlightener, the light bearer. *Horasis* was the ancient Greek word for Womb Enlightenment, often bestowed through the sexual union of man and woman. In the Bible, *horasis* was used to describe an oracular, ecstatic vision.

Throughout the world, we discover these feminine womb words at the foundation of spiritual worship—root words such as *her, har, hor, hera, hara,* and *hero.* In ancient Babylon, Ishtar was called the Great Goddess Har, Mother of Harlots. "Her high priestess, the Harine, was considered the spiritual ruler of the city of Ishtar."[4] In the indigenous Huichol tradition of Mexico, the name for the primordial grandmother goddess of the ocean is Haramara: Womb Mother. We also find these root words, sequestered like magical pearls, inside words such as *char*iot, *chor*us, *char*m, and *har*mony.* The word *charis,* the name the holy men of India—devotees of Shiva-Shakti—give to the entheogens they smoke, means "goddess" or "menstrual blood," and is also the root of the Christian word eu*charis*t.[5]

Following the same magical threads, the Greek words *christ* or *chrism,* meaning "the anointed one" or "the anointing oil," are a contracted form of the words *charist* and *charism,* which blooms out into the word *charisma,* describing an "anointed" or "christed" person filled with the enchanting, magnetic feminine light of the blessed Cosmic Womb. Moon blood was known to be the original blessing, gifted from the wise womb of woman. Chrism is the soul of the flesh, the golden serpent of life force. The Christ *is* Shakti, our primordial life energy.

---

*Harmony literally means "to be in tune with the moon or womb cycles." The word *moon* itself is derived from the Greek *mene* and the Proto-Indo-European *me(n)ses,* both meaning "moon."

In ancient Sumeria, the sacred sexual temple priestesses were called Sal-Me, meaning "divine yoni women."[6] *Sal* was the Sumerian word for both woman and yoni, and *Me* meant sacred, having divine properties. Sal-Me is the origin of the name Salome, which described a female sexual initiate of the Womb Mysteries. It was Salome, as a sacred womb priestess, who performed the mystical dance of the seven veils, for which she was later demonized. In ancient Sumeria, the pictogram of the vulva was called *sal,* and was the sister of the Hebrew *daleth*—the downward-pointing triangle, symbolizing the yoni, as the cosmic gateway.

The original teaching of *sal*vation referred to the primordial redemption of consciousness, experienced through the shamanic return to the spiritual Great Womb of the Yoni-Mother. Isis, as the Queen of Heaven, was known by her devotees as the savior—she who bestowed the healing feminine balm, poured lovingly from the center of all creation, the great Cosmic Womb.

In ancient Sumerian texts, the Goddess Inanna's boat of heaven is compared to her "wondrous vulva," meaning that the title of the Queen of Heaven (attributed to Inanna, Isis, and the Virgin Mary) could also be interpreted as the queen of the vulva or the queen of the womb.

This Womb of God lives at the root of all religion. The opening Hebrew words of Genesis, *B'rashith,* are usually translated as "In the beginning," but there is a deeper and more occult meaning that has been lost, or deliberately obscured, which is translated as "In the Womb," referring to the cosmic feminine generative force that birthed all creation from her primordial Cosmic Womb.[7] Likewise, *apocalypse* means the "revealing of the womb," and comes from the word root *calypso,* which means that which is covered, concealed, hidden in the "chalice" or "cauldron"—ancient symbols of the womb.

In Russian folk traditions there are feminine mystery teachings preserved in stylized, symbolic embroideries of *rozhentsas,* archaic birth mothers, also called "original mothers." These artisan teachings show a female body in a birthing position with arms and legs outstretched. The yoni is depicted with an X at the center of a womb cross—also the sacred symbol of the Cathars. Often interpreted as a solar symbol, the cross was first the womb gateway of the Mother of Life.[8]

The Yoruba culture of Nigeria views the world as a nested set of mother-wombs powered by the mysterious spiritual mother-force called *Aje,* originating in the womb of the Great Mother deity, and called "the secret of life itself." It flows into human women through their own sacred, life-giving womb. *Aje* gives women earthly, celestial, and spiritual powers that surpass men, but those who use this power, the Elders of the Night, are called to the highest moral and spiritual standards—they must use this power in service of the good of all. They are often elderly female priestesses, respectfully referred to as "the owners of the world" because of the power of the divine womb-force they channel.[9]

Our mythical origins whisper with many lost allusions to the forgotten Sacred Feminine; and as she was stripped from our lives, she was also stripped from our language and our consciousness. By reclaiming our holy feminine language, we begin to rebirth the lost goddess back into our psyche—and into our world.

We are redreaming our cosmology—a new, yet ancient, way of perceiving the horizons and landscapes of creation. The vast wealth of knowledge of this ancient cosmology, often oral, has been lost and destroyed as the war against the feminine realms has been ferociously waged. The libraries may have been destroyed, but the memory lives on within our magical feminine DNA.

Creating This Book

This book represents the fruition of more than twenty years of the practice and study of alchemical sciences and soulful shamanic journeying for the authors. It has spanned many vistas; from the more well-trodden pathways of the modern world—such as working with more than 25,000 people in the fields of healing and medicine, including facilitating spontaneous remissions of terminal cancers—to assisting with research conducted in the late 1990s at the National Institute of Health in Child Health and Human Development, studying the neuroendocrine and behavioral correlations of love and mother-baby primal bonding.*

It also includes working with scientific colleagues, modern-day alchemists, who are researching and experimenting at the cutting edge of menstrual-blood stem cell regenerative science, often with miraculous results, including the reversal of the aging process and the regrowth of heart cells.

But this is only a side street of the story. For the true knowing came from walking the lesser-trod lunar pathways of the ancient womb shamans and priestesses, into deep, mysterious forests where our true his(her)story lives, hidden away in Pandora's box waiting to be unlocked—in the wilds of our lost feminine soul, the imaginal lands of the womb otherworld and underworld.

The feminine dimension is an enchanted realm of paradox and miracles. Our current world is withered to the truth of the feminine, as she so often unravels our most cherished certainties.

---

*This research was led by Stephen J. Suomi, Ph.D., in the lineage of British psychiatrist John Bowlby, M.D., and American psychologist Harry Harlow, Ph.D.

In feminine shamanic traditions, teachings are often described as flowery and unclear, strange and cryptic, rich with ambiguity. The feminine is a riddling realm, as ancient bards knew. We so often want the clear shining light of masculine logic to explain everything, but the feminine leads us into mystery. She opens herself into doorways, questions, and possibilities, pointing to places the light can't reach.

We offer our work in this open spirit of inquiry, rather than as fixed absolutes and certainties. So you will find woven throughout this book both scientific and historical "facts" *and* experiential imaginal gateways that we *feel* are true and have traveled through in our personal gnostic experience, but that we leave as an open doorway for you. Gnostic shamans and priestesses of the ancient feminine mystery schools always placed a great emphasis on imaginal work as the gateway to feminine consciousness, and it remains as true now as then.

And we have heard only an echo of a whisper of what was once known—there are vast amounts of rich material throughout every culture and tradition, from China and Japan to South America and Africa, that overtly or subtly encode the wisdom of the womb. We pass you this thread—and we hold the dream-candle that you weave in your own womb wisdom to this great tapestry, including your own spiritual and ancestral lineages, to bring through more feminine wisdom.

With this sacred intention, we invite you to journey with us into these realms of magical possibilities, shared here as thirty-three spirals forming seven cycles of pilgrimage into Womb Awakening.

Walking the Path of Your Own Essence

You may hear ideas you are unfamiliar with during our time together, as we discover and remember the ancient womb ways. Try to remain open and receptive, while consulting with your own womb for her feedback and guidance. Your womb is queen of your realm. The words in this book are also a womb space, a magical portal through which you can peer into the vast wilds of Creation.

Only you can truly know what waits here for you. For everyone's pilgrimage into the womb is different—we each infuse the same threads and pathways with our own essence and experience. As the feminine ways know, even truth is an infinite spiral. We receive only what we are ready for, and every new evolutionary wave shows us a different facet.

The key is for you to wake up to your own inner knowing, to percolate these ideas in your own inner womb cauldron, so you connect with your own wisdom. Womb Awakening is a path open to everyone—it does not need gurus, masters, formulaic rules, or great psychic powers. Your own inner wisdom holds all the keys you need. All it requires is that you root into *your essence*.

From our experience, your own inner feelings and soulful intuition—flowing through a deeply rooted listening connection with the wisdom of earth—are your most reliable spiritual guidance.

Be playful with the terms used in this book and include yourself; if you are a man, allow yourself to replace *womb* with *hara*; if you are in same-sex relationship, interpret it to suit your journey. If you are multiamorous, let that in. Suck the juice you need from the words and spit out the pips. Allow yourself to adventure through the formless realm into the world of form.

In this book we often refer to Source in feminine terms, as we are now in an age where there is an unprecedented and urgent need to remember the feminine face of God. But we feel Great Creator Womb is both a mother and father—as she holds both feminine and masculine poles within—and is also beyond the realms of opposites, which are birthed from her Mystery.

The Womb Oracles Awaken

We have been accompanied on our journey by members of a worldwide womb circle, some of whose experiences will be shared as we travel along this pilgrimage. These testimonials come from their deep inner work, ceremonial visions, and insights received in the dreamtime, as they dived into a shamanic apprenticeship in the Womb Mysteries. Their visions have arisen from the forgotten oceans of the collective memory of humanity, and they speak to all of us, bearing messages of archetypal wisdom that our world is thirsting for right now. In the feminine mysteries, initiates journey together as a web consciousness—and each oracular message received is not only personal to the individual but prophetic for the whole. These sharings are akin to a Greek chorus, inspired in Greek drama by the Old Ways of Diana Artemis, where women sang, danced, and prophesied together as a circle of voices. Their shared wisdom was honored as the words of the goddess herself.

Once again, the womb oracles are awakening, echoing a collective voice onto the stage, to show that Womb Awakening is a living, breathing movement, birthing through *all* those who desire womb gnosis. As you journey through this book, remember that you are an important thread of this web of Womb Consciousness. Take the time to sit and percolate with any ideas that flow to you as you read. Your own insights and visions are a vital part of this collective tapestry of remembering, helping to restore the feminine principle back to our beloved Earth.

Weaving a New Way Together

We need to unravel the threads of time that have left us separated from our past and future selves, and reweave the womb of timelines that connect existence together in a unified reality.

The Great Mother Womb has always been known as a weaver, a Divine Creatrix, artisan, and craftsperson of all life. In fact the word *crafty* refers to the cunning Old Ways of the wise woman, and the Indian word *tantra* means to "be woven together." The priestess title Magdalene (Mag-Dal) also translates as "great weaver" and "magic doorway."*

In nearly all shrines dedicated to Artemis, spindle whorls, loom weights, and shuttles have been found, and in her sanctuaries woolen clothing and threads wound on spools were offered as gifts to her. On Corinthian vases, Artemis and her womb priestesses are seen holding a spindle.[10]

The ancient and timeless Womb Mysteries are a path of love, a returning to harmony with the way of nature, with the dreaming of Gaia, with life's vast benevolence, with Creator's deep and tender love, and with the wild, untamed creative flows and cyclical rhythms. This feminine feeling dimension is rooted in love, wildness, kindness, tenderness, patience, and union.

Feminine consciousness is weaving a new way into being, and inviting us to step through the magic doorway to be part of the great change—to become conscious co-creators of a new reality.

She who lovingly created us, gestated us, and birthed us, is now calling out to us.

There is no coincidence you have been called to this book. What we can be sure of is that *your* womb is waiting to birth something incredible, a unique expression that only you can gift to this wonderful world. A circle of love supports you; our wombs are linked by a magical thread of starlight, woven together in many mysterious ways, working as a web of wombs.

The return of Womb Consciousness is the greatest revolution on the planet at this time. The womb has the power to birth and to rebirth. The ancients looked to the womb for all their healing and redemption, and the feminine was honored as the throne of creation.

As a web of wombs, we are birthing a new earth into being. Together we can heal the inner and outer wasteland and return it to love.

---

*In the Semitic languages *mag* was the ancient word root meaning "magic" or "greatness," and *daleth* or *dal* meant "doorway" or "portal."

We are weaving a new way,
Stitching revolutions together,
Spinning new worlds from our wombs,
Dreaming back the wild edges of our souls,
Calling forth that which has been lost.
We are women of the womb,
Maddened by love into action,
We are men of the heart,
Softened into surrender,
Afraid only of not feeling.
We are thinking in a web,
Your thread holds mine together.
We are tale-weavers and troubadours,
Telling the words that were broken,
Singing the songs of longing.
We are weaving a new way,
Gathering the thread of pain,
Spinning it back into gold.

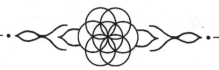

CYCLE 1

WELCOME TO PRIMORDIAL WOMB CONSCIOUSNESS

SPIRAL 1

WOMB AWAKENING

Opening the Magical Doorway Within

The Tao is dark and unfathomable.
How can it make her radiant?
Because she lets it . . .
This source is called darkness.
The gateway to all understanding.

Tao Te Ching

THE WOMB IS THE ETERNAL MYSTERY of the primordial dazzling darkness that births light into being. It is the gateway to a magical realm of wisdom. It is the Holy Grail: the chalice that holds the secrets of life. We don't need to search outside of ourselves to receive the answers we need in our lives; we need only make a pilgrimage deep inside our own bodies. Our bodies are temples; Source lives inside of us. Every cell is a stargate, a portal, and the womb is the mother of this complex, magnificent system we call the human body. It is a hologram of God.

This pilgrimage is a journey through the magic doorway of your own personal womb space into the Womb of Creation, the source and root of our consciousness, so we can remember her love, and re-member ourselves and our world back into wholeness. The consciousness that lives in our womb births our reality, and has the power to rebirth it too.

Just as science now knows that black holes—womb holes—birth galaxies, so all of existence was birthed through the Womb of Creation, our prime Creator. It is a cosmic cradle of shining darkness, pregnant with infinite possibilities of light, bathed with a powerful creative energy we call love, which is pure life force. This is our birthright; this is our throne of magical possibility.

We live within a womb cosmology of creation, a great metaverse, a maternal lineage of Great Mother universes that birth, transform, and dissolve all in their majestic Cosmic Wombs. Our universe was born from the womb of a Mother universe, a metaverse that is coherently and magically connected by womb holes, interdimensional yoni passageways. Our Mother universe birthed our universe and lives on within our cosmic DNA codes, much as the genetic code of our parents informed the conception and growth of the embryo that grew into who we are today.

The Indian saint Ramakrishna described his kundalini awakening in the visionary terms of a "wombiverse," the universe appearing as a lake of silver, with the ultimate cause of the universe as a huge luminous triangle giving birth every moment to an infinite number of universes.[1]

The Hindu sacred text the *Bhagavad Gita,* which translates as "The Song of the Womb of Creation," poetically describes this cosmic Womb Consciousness that birthed our universe: "Know that it is the womb from which all beings arise; the universe is born within me, and within me will be destroyed. . . . All beings remain within me. They are gathered back into my womb at the end of the cosmic cycle— a hundred fifty thousand billion of our earthly years—and as a new cycle begins I send them forth once again pouring from my abundance the myriad forms of life."[2]

D. C. Lau, translator of the Chinese cosmological poem *Tao Te Ching* says, "Just as living creatures are born from the womb of the mother, so is the universe born from the womb of the mysterious female." This "mysterious female" was also known as the "valley spirit", the deep well of feminine yin energy that underlies all of creation.[3]

The Rigveda, an ancient Indo-Aryan sacred text from India, called the source of the universe *hiranyagarbha,* which literally means "golden womb."

In the Kabbalistic work the Zohar, the first divine emanation is described as *botsina de-qardinuta,* "a spark of impenetrable darkness," which is so radiant that it cannot be seen.[4] New universes are created inside black holes, where the known laws of physics do not apply—within lies a magical quantum feminine otherworld, a fairy banquet of cosmic proportions. The black hole of one universe may be the white hole that births another, a liminal realm of death, birth, and rebirth.

Journey to the Zero Point

Infinite primordial creative intelligence is streaming through us at all times, and in fact created us, and rests at the foundation of our being. Yet we have mostly forgotten it.

For many people the Womb of Creation feels like a black hole in its negative connotations: an infinite abyss, a place of death, transformation, darkness, fear, overwhelm, the unknown. It is the hidden shadow realm we dare not enter. We have forgotten she is filled with pure love, that she births and rebirths us, that this spiraling black vortex births the light.

Womb Awakening is a journey to allow everything inside us that is not love to descend into the Void in order to rebirth. It is the death and rebirth all shamanic traditions spoke of, the "descent into the underworld"—a sacred return to the zero point, the origin of consciousness. Before patriarchy, it was clear that the cycle of death and rebirth was a deeply feminine process at its core; it was a return to the womb, for both men and women. And as black holes birth light, so this journey into the womb transfigures and births us into radiant living light.

That Great Shift of 2012 prophesied by the Maya referred to this knowing that a cosmic birthing gate was opening—that we would enter a time of rebirth, entering the Mother's Cosmic Womb.

The science of black holes shows that when we are on the event horizon of the dark mother, everything we have known or think we are starts to destabilize, wobble, and fall apart.

Going over the edge feels like a form of dying to who we thought we were. But this soulful "menstruation" process also renews us, in order to birth the beauty of who we *truly* are. Life is a beautiful holographic mirror that reflects *all* we are back to us, in order to restore wholeness.

Inside the black hole, the laws of physics as we know them no longer apply. In the quantum birthing field we are not limited by time, space, or causal consequences. We are in a radiant, renewing field of miracles. It is not a linear journey. It is a spiral journey—a fairy dance. This journey will take you to zero point over and over again, but at a higher spiral.

Eventually you will become immersed in Womb Consciousness, the *renewing now*. You will learn to flow with and ride the wild waves of life force, this dynamic creative force known as Shakti. These oceanic waves will flow you onto the shore of a magical feminine dimension that lives within.

Ultimately no belief is real. Only love is real. The Great Womb will awaken you into pure love.

Black Holes: The Source of Enlightenment

Although it sounds outrageous to the logical mind, we can enter a black hole through a feminine shamanic journey and travel through a multi-dimensional spiritual "worm hole" to emerge out the other side into another space and time, or into another universe altogether—through a bridal chamber or swan bridge in feminine shamanic terms, or through an Einstein-Rosen bridge in the words of modern science. (See fig. 1.1 and color plate 1, both visions of Cosmic Womb portals.)

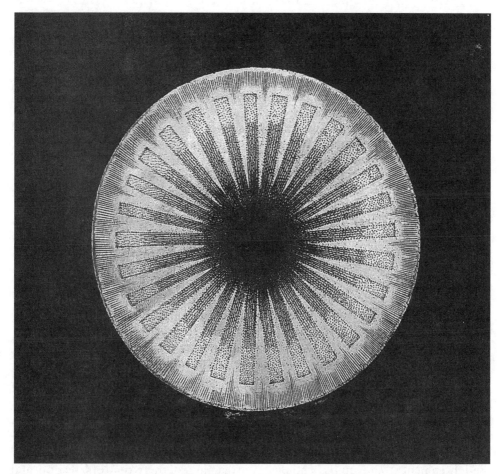

Fig. 1.1. Alchemist Robert Fludd, from *Ultriusque Cosmi,* 1617–1621

Scientists are now considering this to be a physical possibility, as alchemists have long known it was a spiritual possibility. "Our galaxy could really contain one of these [womb-hole] tunnels, and that tunnel could even be the size of the galaxy itself," says Paolo Salucci, astrophysicist of the International School for Advanced

Studies (SISSA) of Trieste and a dark matter expert. "We could even travel through this tunnel, since, based on our calculations, it could be navigable."[5]

John A. Wheeler, Ph.D., who was a preeminent theoretical physicist at Princeton University and mentor to five Nobel Prize–winning physicists, left a cryptic note on a photograph a few years before his death that said, "black holes are a source of enlightenment." Like Albert Einstein, Max Planck, Neils Bohr, and other pioneering quantum physicists before him, the deeper he peered into the underlying physical reality of the universe, the more mystical he became.

The first black hole was discovered around the constellation Cygnus; known as Cygnus x-1, it is a high-energy x-ray emission source that emits 1 million times more x-ray energy than the sun. This magical cosmic womb holds an intense luminosity at its membrane of transformation, its event horizon, which womb shamans of the ancient world journeyed through to go beyond the limitations of time and space and to enter the womb of otherworld.

This shamanic knowledge of black holes, which can be entered by the soul and spirit body, is secret wisdom that has been passed down the ages. Christian mystic John Pordage, born in 1607, describes the transcendent God, source of All, as an all-seeing eye within a sphere or abyss. He contemplates the essence of nature as the circumference of this globe, the "event horizon."[6]

In Western Caucasian dolmens built around 3500 to 2500 BCE, round portals are carved into the front wall of the structure for the soul to journey through in shamanic flight. An example of such a portal is shown in fig. 1.2. It was believed a journeying soul had to pass through a *hole* in order to visit other dimensions and worlds.[7]

Similarly, according to Huichol Indians there is a doorway, a *nierika,* within us that usually remains dormant until the time of death. It is defined as a cosmic passageway, an interdimensional yoni, that connects us to infinite worlds. But we do not have to die to access this doorway and the gifts it brings; shamans have long known we can take this spirit journey while still alive.

There is a black hole nested *within your own womb,* holding the power of Womb Enlightenment. Your womb is a holographic daughter of the Womb of Creation, and contains the same miraculous potentials—"as above, so below." When we choose to open this door while alive, we are reborn.

What is *truly* outrageous to the logical mind is that at the deepest levels of existence there is no space and time as we think of it. So the concept of a black hole is not just something that lives out there in space but is also something that lives *within us,* at the heart of matter and consciousness. This black hole is a quantum space of

Fig. 1.2. Womb portal dolmen in Caucasus region of Russia, built ca. 2500 BCE
(Photo by Yury Smirnov, www.spaceoflove.com)

death and rebirth that pulses creation in and out of existence in every micromoment, birthing a world that is at once infinitely ancient yet also eternally new with shimmering innocence and miraculous possibility. In this paradox, the beginning and the ending are never separate from each other and complement each other in the mystery of the circle. In the ancient womb religion, this mystical knowing was symbolized by an ouroboros—a serpent or dragon eating its own tail, the primeval Dragon Mother of creation.

One of the keys of shamanic awakening is to enter this inner realm, beyond the limits of time and space, beyond linear evolution and sequential cause and effect. Entering this birthing field of the Womb, the renewing now, can transform and rebirth anything in any moment, if we ask, without constraint, by directly working with the quantum energy that creates the world.

Heaven on Earth

This magical realm is a seed space, an embryo of love and creative potentiality that lives within all matter, rooted in the mysterious field of dark matter, the great primordial matrix. This means that however far we have fallen as a species, the womb has the power to redeem us. It is a state of grace, bestowed by the great love that created us and never left our side.

The Gospel of Mary Magdalene tells how the true ministry of Jesus was to teach people to discover and embody their inner savior—a blueprint of the perfect human that lives within them—rather than give their power away by waiting for an outside force to save them. This perfected human is the essence of who we truly are, and we can rebirth into this state at any time.

The Gospel of Thomas describes an inner or esoteric state of original innocence called the bridal chamber, which is another way of saying immaculate Womb Consciousness or a womb hole that can connect us to that dimension of original innocence. Thomas also describes an external state of fallen consciousness that occurs when "the bridegroom leaves the bridal chamber."

This symbolizes the collective state of human consciousness over the past 5,000 years, in which the hypermasculine cerebral consciousness has separated from its feminine origin. It has abandoned its Mother—the Great Womb that births all into being—and in its separation from Womb Consciousness, it has become hopelessly lost.

When the bridegroom has separated his consciousness from the Cosmic Womb that created him, he (or she) must take an inner journey of return, using shamanic tools, to open to love again.

The Zohar alludes to this return to the "womb to come," called the *enclosure, as* "a closed site, opened only by a single narrow path, intimated secretly." It is likened to supernal rings, linked to each other, birthing the elements, emerging from each other, and called the "world that is coming," *ha-olam-ha-ba.* This world to come already exists, as a hidden feminine dimension, right here, waiting for us to rediscover it. It is a reality that lives at the heart of matter, like a black womb hole, birthing creation, yet itself eternal, beyond time.[8]

In the feminine Christ mysteries, Magdalene-Yeshua emphasized that this renewing primordial Womb Consciousness, this state of original innocence and union called "heaven on earth," was not a state far away from us, located in the future. It is right here, inside ourselves, if we choose to open to it. Yeshua says, "It will not come by waiting for it. It will not be a matter of saying 'here it is' or 'there it is.' Rather, the Queendom of the Mother* is spread out upon the earth and men do not see it."[9]

New earth has been within us all along, waiting to birth.

The Dark Mother: The Great Birther

Everything is birthed through a womb, and the fabric of creation is a pregnant ocean of dark matter: the dark mother, the dark birther, a dynamic but creative shimmering Void of luminous darkness. This great sea births us into life, and eventually we fall back into her living waters.

In ancient spiritual traditions across the world, the power of the dark mother as a birthing portal, or "black hole," was often alluded to, either directly or in poetic or symbolic terms. In Egypt, Isis was described as wearing a black robe; in Anatolia (modern-day Turkey), Cybele was worshipped as a black stone, as was the goddess Al-Lat now enshrined at Mecca in Saudia Arabia. Artemis of Ephesus was depicted in her primordial glory of blackness. In Indian tantric traditions, the Black Mother, Kali, is considered to be the Cosmic Womb, the Void of birth and death. The Nirrutara Tantra says, "The Blessed [Kali] . . . must be understood as the womb. Everything that exists, animate and inanimate, is of the nature of the womb."[10] In Jewish mysticism, the dazzling darkness of the Cosmic Womb births the tree of life, "the ray which emerges from Nothing is . . . sown into the 'Celestial Mother' . . . out of whose womb the sefiroth [creative energies] spring forth as King and Queen, son and daughter."[11] Even the word *alchemy*—the Great Work of transformation—comes from the Egyptian root word *khem,* meaning "black" or the "dark womb," the primordial crucible of death and rebirth. Our spiritual traditions are replete with references to the mystical birthing portal of maternal black light—the Black Madonna—an unimaginable celestial power that is rooted in the universe's infinite darkness.

A black hole holds an octave of intelligence even beyond that of a star, representing the metamorphosis of the vast stellar consciousness of a star into a new

---

*The Aramaic term that is commonly translated in the Bible as "the Kingdom of Heaven" or "Kingdom of the Father" is *malkutha d'shmaya.* We believe "Queendom of Heaven" or "Queendom of the Mother" more accurately reflects the original meaning of the phrase. Malkuth is the ancient Semitic mother goddess who predated the arrival of the Judaic father god Yahweh, circa the fifteenth century BCE. In addition, in Aramaic, *malkutha* is a feminine gendered word. Thus, *malkutha* originally meant "queendom" rather than "kingdom." This is just one example of the widespread phenomenon of older feminine religious terms being adopted by the arriving monotheistic patriarchal cultures and given new meanings to suit a patristic religious system.

form of being, a mystery of rebirth and renewal at a cosmic scale. Like the menstrual mysteries of old that were associated with the dark phase of the moon, cosmologic rebirth also happens through the river of darkness.

This pattern is reflected again and again at each level of existence, from the microcosm to the macrocosm. We see it as well in the caterpillar who encloses itself in a dark and silent cocoon to dissolve its entire physical body, with the exception of a few remaining imaginal cells that give birth to the radically different biology of the butterfly, along with a new state of consciousness and a very different purpose in this world.

The physicist Brian Swimme, Ph.D., also describes our sacred origins in terms of a womb cosmology, writing, "The vast ocean of our solar system is like a womb that brings forth life."[12] Scientist or spiritual seeker, the universe, or rather the *yoniverse,* makes mystics of all who look deeply into her dark vortex eyes.

We are inside the Womb of God, and we have never been, nor could be, separate from her. The yoniverse is a sexual, sensual, vast, sentient being. The thread of her infinite ecstasy weaves in cosmic womb waves through all of creation, flowing across the shimmering web of life. We are gestated, birthed, dissolved, and then rebirthed in waves of her galactic womb cycles of joyful conception and ecstatic cosmic menstruation.

From this dark cauldron of bliss, all is birthed—dripping and glittering with luminosity, sparkling with golden erotic luster, pulsing with pleasure beams of light. Dare we claim our inheritance of luminosity, our birthright of brilliance?

"If humans committed themselves to their deepest allurements with the same devotion that stars bring to their own activation of power, the earth would enter a new era of well-being,"[13] says Brian Swimme, observing how the cosmic power of stars is the same cosmic power within us.

Dark matter, the creative web of life, is alive and conscious and responds to our desires, thoughts, feelings, intentions, and prayers. Primordial sexuality flows from its creative loom. Its realm is mysterious. It speaks to us, communicating through our dreams, our intuitions, and through synchronicities in our lives. It asks that we listen to the dream-whispers of our soul. The creative intelligence of dark matter weaves a birth chrysalis spun from our deepest soul desires, so we can renew our lives. When we trust this Cosmic Womb wisdom, we are guided by Source. The cosmos dreams within us. This cocoon of transformation is woven from conscious visionary particles that know the possibilities that the future holds for us, both personally and collectively.

The Seat of Knowing

The secrets of the yoniverse live deep within our bodies—the robe of life and vessel of our soul, gifted to us from Gaia—so we may take this magical journey into the earth realm.

Yet we have been taught to judge our bodies, to ignore and override the messages our biological systems try to communicate to us. In many ways, our minds torture our bodies in this age. We *think* we know what is best. We feed our bodies toxic food, we steamroll over their natural cycles, we pump them with artificial drugs if they express pain. We follow beliefs, fads, rules that crush our natural harmony. We look outside ourselves to find the way, or we rely on our logical rational mind to navigate rather than our deep inner knowing.

Many religions and spiritual systems deny the sacredness of the body, proclaiming its needs and desires to be the enemy of our spiritual pursuits, or, at best, a gross and temporary distraction from the true mission to save our eternal soul. Or the body is dismissed as merely an expendable container for the consciousness that lives on after we die. We have suffered greatly from these attitudes. Now is the time to reclaim our feminine power, and to honor and trust this miraculous form we inhabit. We do not yet know who we truly are or own our true worth.

How would you feel if someone gave you a spaceship built from pure gold, full of magical possibilities? What if someone built you a beautiful mansion that could fulfill all your needs and desires, and was the jewel of the universe? Would you be inclined to honor, value, and take care of it and appreciate the gifts it brought you? This is the incredible, but forgotten, reality of our lives. Our body is that priceless golden spaceship; our planet is that majestic mansion.

We have been told that matter is the lowest form of light. Nothing could be farther from the truth. *Matter is the most precious form of light.* It is embodied love, and is part of an incredible cosmic experiment to bring light into the deepest vibration of ecstatic expression, flowing as liquid gold. We have been taught to devalue our bodies and our earthly life, so that we lose access to this astounding gift. We have checked out into illusory mental realms of a false creation. Unwittingly, we have handed the keys to the queendom over to those who have misused power. There is an incredible cosmic mystery living at the *heart of matter,* waiting for us to remember.

The human body is infinitely intelligent; it was created through the original blueprint of life, and it stills holds all the secrets of this knowledge. It is the cradle of our soul, and a direct translator and transceiver of all worlds. In every moment our body is communicating something to us, and these are messages from God.

We are part of the sensual dreaming of Gaia, and our inner and outer worlds are created in a blissful, shimmering, glittering world of enchantment. This luminosity we sense in the vivid green of forest floors and the cathedral domes of treetops, which permeates all of life, is the embodiment of infinite creative waves of *ecstatic cosmic sexuality* emanating from the Great Womb.

The thinking mind has forgotten the magical feminine thread, but the body remembers and is part of this vast, sensual, sensory network of aliveness.

The instinctive body, in its primal innocence, knows what is best for you. Trust in its wisdom. Consult with it; start a dialogue. Follow its instincts, its feedback, and its feelings. Explore your own energy system and allow the trapped energy to flow again, because it is only by surrendering to the flow that the power of universal Shakti can flood through you and unfold your personal destiny.

Many thousands of years ago, people knew about the power of the body, and they knew about the jewel it contained—the womb. We have lost this connection, and it is time to remember it again. The womb is our seat of *knowing*. In Greece this was called *gnosis*—direct or primary knowing—and in Celtic traditions it was called *nous* or *cunning* (from which the word *cunt* derives).

Gnosis or nous happens when we have a direct connection to Source, which opens us to divine inspiration, moments of genius, and revelation. Gnosis is when knowledge becomes essence. This wisdom is available to everyone; we just have to be open and receptive. People we consider scientific geniuses, such as Albert Einstein, are in touch with this feminine quality of intuition or knowing. Their most potent ideas come in unanticipated flashes of inspiration, emerging spontaneously *from the vast creative potential of the feminine unconscious mind, the root of primordial consciousness,* rather than the separated logical mind.

Einstein's famous theory of relativity came through when he was a nineteen-year-old high school dropout, while working as a clerk in a patent office. In a daydream, he imagined himself taking a shamanic flight alongside a beam of light. As his consciousness merged with the light wave, he instantly understood how reality bends and shifts as we approach light speed. From this experience he derived his paradigm-shattering equation, $E=mc^2$. Energy is equivalent to mass, gravity bends time and space, and black holes must exist. The rest is history. We cannot learn our way to gnosis—but we can become open and receptive to it.

If we desired, we could download all the secrets of the universe in one moment. We could open our doors of perception, and take the inner journey into the shamanic feminine mind, which Zulu shaman Credo Mutwa calls the Mother Mind. But for most people, the busy logical mind, which is heavily conditioned and programmed by beliefs and traumatic experiences and the loop of emotional wounds and dialogues it generates, prevents this pure receptivity by getting in the way of our natural intuitive wisdom and vast capabilities of primordial knowing.

As a race we are eager to know the workings of galactic constellations, but we also need to understand our own inner constellations. You will find your body has incredible messages to give you and is just waiting to deliver them. The more in tune you become, the more these messages may appear supernatural or psychic—but in fact this kind of knowing is completely natural, it is your birthright. Just as animals have incredible telepathic abilities, so do you.

Awakening to Aliveness

Every journey begins with the first step, and as you begin this pilgrimage into your womb, step by step you will become more and more open. Your energy will begin to flow freely again. Ideas will come to you. You will magnetize good fortune. As you follow the voice of the womb, your inner guide, you will find your true way again.

First and foremost this pilgrimage is a healing journey, to reclaim your vitality, your emotional ease, your creative power, your connection with the flow of life. It is about developing an intimate relationship with your body and discovering that underneath your everyday life, there is a wild, wise, erotic, sensual creature who plays, feels pleasure, and *knows*.

This wise, wild *creature* is the real you—before your childhood and cultural wounds conditioned you to be someone else. *Wild* means not living in captivity. You were not created to be in bondage or in pain. Your womb will set you free.

Our sexual energy is the most misunderstood force in existence. Sexual energy is *liquid living light*—it is the invisible thread that weaves all of existence together. It is not confined to a momentary sexual experience between humans. It is the living pulse of life; it is the distilled essence of pure creative power; it is God embodied. It is the compassionate, unconditional exchange of love.

Our sexual energy, our life force, is innocent. It is our expression of the pure and exhilarating desire to be *alive*. Everything contains this powerful impulse. In its deepest expression, it is the desire to give love. It takes an incredible amount of energy to keep it locked down, but we do because of shame, judgment, emotional wounding, sexual trauma, and deliberate manipulation through cultural conditioning.

When we explore deeply into our bodies and release the emotional, energetic, and physical contractions that block the free flowing of our life force, something incredible happens: our *aliveness* awakens. We feel ourselves fully, maybe for the first time in this lifetime. We realize we are magical, powerful creatures beyond measure, interconnected with all of life. *Anything is possible.*

We are not only the agents of magic; we *are* the magic. We are not only the vessel of God; we are *part* of God. We are a beautiful living cell in the great cosmic body. We were not created as slaves, not to our jobs, to the system, to money, to our parents, to bad relationships, to our emotional wounds, or to health problems. We were created to love and be loved, to thrive, to create, to enjoy, to inspire and be inspired, and to revel in Creation.

For eons the interplanetary and Gaian womb grid has been shut down, but now these portals are opening again and life is asking us to step through the magical doorway and reclaim her.

Shall we take this journey, this pilgrimage back to our true sacred origins?

✳ Womb Awakening: Opening Ritual

As you begin this pilgrimage, you step through a magic doorway. You enter a womb temple, a circle, a church of the feminine ways. We invite you to begin by honoring the Womb of Creation that birthed you and lives within you.

In the original "feminine" indigenous and shamanic traditions that once existed across the world, there was a universal concept of three worlds or dimensions of experience—underworld, middleworld, upperworld—as well as the four cardinal directions, with a magical center point thought of as a womb portal, vaginal passage, or umbilical cord of connection that linked them all and allowed for psychic travel between the realms. Together, the seven sacred directional points—east, west, south, north, up, down, center—served as a spiritual and cosmologic map of creation. Each world was originally thought of in feminine terms as a queendom or womb realm, as the womb is housed in the cosmic body of the Mother.

We shall be exploring the pathways of this feminine shamanic map of creation, known as the Sacred Feminine medicine wheel or "womb cross," extensively throughout the book. But first, we invite you to sense these queendoms within your own body through ritual. When we *know* the map of creation *lives within us,* we can awaken the Grail codes. We become a living chalice to embody the cosmic life-force energy here on Earth.

1. Connect to your personal womb (middleworld, Queen of the Throne): close your eyes, bring your hands to your womb or hara (for men). Breathe into the vast fertile darkness of your womb space.

2. Connect to the Womb of Gaia (lowerworld, Queen of the Underworld): feel a spiral umbilical cord of luminous light descend down into the Womb of Gaia. Feel yourself anchored into Earth and her creative power. Feel this luminous light travel back into your womb, shining even brighter.

3. Connect to the Cosmic Womb (upperworld, Queen of Heaven): feel a spiral umbilical cord of luminous light ascend upward into the Cosmic Womb. Feel yourself anchored into the universe and her infinite love. Feel this luminous light travel back into your womb, shining even brighter.

4. You are the Holy Grail, a chalice for these cosmic creative energies. From your heart-womb repeat with devotion: *Divine Mother, Father, thank you for my life.*

WOMB ORACLES SHARE
Awakening the Witch Eye

I met the crone at the gateway between the worlds. She appears like a fairy-tale witch, but beautiful and radiant. She is wearing a black dress—tight at the top with a huge swirling black skirt, like Sufi dancers would wear. She has the energy of a swirling Sufi witch who dances in the Void. She gazes at me with her penetrating crone eyes; then she pulls her left eye out and passes the eyeball to me. Her left eye socket is now a gouged, red womb space. I swallow her eyeball, and it travels through my body, passing through my womb until it finally lodges in my cervix.

"I have given you the sight," she says. "You are a seer. This is your witch eye, the all-seeing eye of the Great Womb." I can feel the eye blinking and staring between the worlds at my third Grail Gate. Her own eye then grows back and restores.

She walks toward an infinite black ocean, and gracefully walks deeper and deeper until her black skirt is floating in a perfect circle around her. Her upper half begins to dissolve until only her black skirt remains. The skirt then begins to swirl and spiral round like a Sufi dancer, until it creates a vortex whirlpool of water, like an amniotic black hole, sucking everything down into the infinite ocean.

I walk forward, understanding the crone has created a vortex gateway for me to enter. The crone is part of my lost feminine soul, calling me home.

S.B.

SPIRAL 2

MESSAGE FROM AN ANCIENT MOTHER

Awakening the Magdalene Womb

I received a lamp, which lighteth me, and I came up by the ropes of the boat of understanding. I went to sleep in the depths of the sea, and not being overwhelmed with the water, I dreamed a dream. And it seemed to me that there was a star in my womb . . . I laid hold upon it, and I will never let it go. I went in through the doors of the treasury of wisdom and I drew for myself the waters of understanding.

MAKEDA, QUEEN OF SHEBA, *KEBRA NAGAST*

THE FIRST DAY I (Seren) bled in the Old Way, the first bloom of poppies appeared outside our little mountainside home. Their bloodred petals were wildly vivid against the rich green leaves. I felt as if nature herself were blessing my pilgrimage back to the roots of the ancient ways of the womb. The red of my menstrual blood snaked down my thighs, a rich effluent, heavily scented with life, calling for remembrance.

I sat on the steps looking out across the Himalayan mountains, as thousands of newly hatched white butterflies swept across the view. A sweet harmony descended as though the subtle elixirs of the moon blood were transporting me deeper into life, into a hidden dimension that lay inside all creation.

My bare yoni was pressed against the warm stone floor, and as I got up I noticed

I had left the perfect scarlet imprint of the ancient vulva symbol where I had sat.

I walked back inside and lay down on our bed, my thighs now thick with blood. I lay and looked at this forbidden sight—the free flowing of my menstrual blood, with no tampon, no sanitary towel, no moon cup, no underwear. I felt a kaleidoscope of emotions: horror, fascination, joy, sensual pleasure, fear. But more than anything I was overwhelmed by the *primal* nature of who I really was, of the womanly creature who hid beneath the conventions of society.

My beloved walked in. I felt a flicker of shame—how would he feel? "I'm bleeding," I said simply, looking down at my thighs. "I know," he replied. "It's beautiful. You look as though you have hearts imprinted on your thighs."

I looked down, and saw he was right. From this view, when my thighs met, it appeared as if my blood was marking out the symbol of the bleeding Sacred Heart.

Tears began flowing down my cheeks, from a deep, long-hidden and shamed part inside—where all my female ancestors dwelt too. A man acknowledging and honoring the beauty of my free-flowing blood stirred deep into my soul. We lay together and the womb blood became a doorway, a portal into another realm; one of shimmering light-filled innocence. We journeyed together and entered a timeless feminine dimension. Everything I felt, he felt; we had merged into one. I realized the womb blood was a gift of love—to be shared with the beloved.

I knew I would never, *could never* stop the flow of my womb blood again. Since then I have kept to that sacred promise. I have "wild" menstruated, wearing no tampon, no sanitary towel, no moon cup, no underwear, and no trousers—granting the elixir of my womb free passage to meet Mother Earth and merge with her.

Allowing my blood to flow has been an act of freedom, of anarchy, a reclaiming of my womb power, a soul promise to not allow society to shame my nature. I called this free-flow menstruation—shamanic menstruation. I have menstruated this way in a remote village in India, in cities in America. I have walked with blood-smeared skirts among ordinary people in supermarkets.

I remember collecting our womb lyre—a unique instrument tuned to the frequency of the womb—from our old, gnomelike lyre maker as I was menstruating, flowing freely. There was an air of magic, of enchantment, an unspoken intoxication of the feminine present that enveloped us innocently. To this day, he is in rapture speaking of this meeting, not knowing why.

I have lived out the Old Ways in a new world and felt deeply how much we have lost. How distanced we have become from our own sweet, sacred essence; disconnected from the awesome life-bearing powers of the womb.

When did we lose touch with our primal feminine essence? Even as late as the

eighteenth century in France, menstruation was celebrated for its power and seductive qualities. It was filled with a fertile, irresistible red magic that was "impregnated
with the subtle vapors of the essence of life," according to Alain Corbin, professor of
history at the Sorbonne.[1] And it is reported that five hundred years ago European
women walked openly in public while menstruating, blood streaming down their
legs in pride, as an elixir of love.

Awakening the Magdalene Womb

Aged thirteen I was drawn into a Catholic bookstore where I discovered a small book
on a saint who was unknown to me; her name was Mary Magdalene.

Though I came from a nonreligious background and did not know who she was,
I felt compelled to have this book. As I took it from the bookshop, the sharp edges
of the paper cut my skin, and a crimson rivulet of blood ran down my finger and dif-
fused out onto the crisp white paper.

For days I entered a rapturous internal state where I received a vision from this
living Grail called Mary Magdalene—where I was shown how embracing our Sacred
Feminine wounds would lead us back to sexual and spiritual wholeness and complete
a cycle of redemption.

At the time, I could only *feel* the vision, like a holographic dream within my
psyche, making perfect non-sense. Many years later, I understood that this deep
visionary experience was identical to the Gnostic accounts of Sophia's archetypal
journey and mystical marriage.

Soon after this I began creating paintings of women with light shining from their
wombs, or women with huge red womb spaces, with the Eye of Horus* staring out,
symbolizing the cervix as the gateway between worlds. I also painted magical trees
with a womb in the center; sometimes this "tree womb" contained a baby, sometimes
it was just red or a glowing portal of light.

In my family, as in most families of the time, talking about women's wombs
or menstrual cycles was utterly taboo. I had never seen or heard about any secret
stream of occult knowledge of the womb. I had no idea there was a mystical tradition of alchemical feminine artwork featuring womb symbology dating back
for thousands of years, spanning Indian tantric cultures and Western alchemical

---

*In ancient Semitic languages *hor/har* could mean "cave," "pregnant," "sacred mound," and
"womb." In ancient Egypt, the Eye of Horus was a female serpent goddess, and the name Horus
itself, which shares the same word root *hor,* may well have originally meant "of the womb."

Renaissance art (see plate 2). Or that female shamans in Mesoamerica wore dresses with embroidered trees bearing magical fetuses in them, to show that they were womb shamans.

As time wove by, I went to university to study for a degree in English literature, history of art, and modern philosophy. I had been drawn to my course because it held the most extensive syllabus on feminist literature in the country. I was searching for the "lost" feminine principle.

My dissertation papers were on the feminine Christ and the femme fatale as a symbol of forbidden feminine sexuality. Unknowingly, I had surrounded and immersed myself in the wisdom of the Grail lore and its poetry and literature.

Over time, life drew me into the arms of the different aspects of the feminine, and aged twenty-four I visited India, where a meeting with Kali plunged me into a Dark Night of the Womb. Discovering the dark face of the feminine took me into the crucible of my repressed shadow realms; like Persephone and Inanna, I took a journey to the underworld to be stripped to my psychic bones.

Five years later, in 2001, I was diagnosed with endometriosis, a physical expression of my unresolved emotional pain, especially connected to my feminine self and sexuality. After a brief flirt with conventional medicine, I set out to heal myself. The gnosis arose that the Divine Feminine did not live outside of me; *she was within me—inside my womb.* I instinctively knew that only by embracing the Divine Feminine within could I heal. My personal womb dis-ease reflected the greater society's dis-ease of disconnection from the feminine.

I withdrew from ordinary life; I did not work or socialize and was celibate. Instead I devoted myself to the Divine Mother, praying to her for hours and hours at a time. I practiced womb breathing, meditated, fasted, cleansed, spent time in nature, used herbs and essences, and synchronized my rhythms with lunar cycles. I wrote a book on womb healing that I never released, exploring the spiritual and energetic practices to restore the feminine spirit.

Eight years later, in 2009, my unfolding journey led me to Sainte Baume in France to connect with the energies of Mary Magdalene, whose mystical spirit had called to me once again. During this solitary pilgrimage I stayed in a convent overlooking the Sacred Grotto, where the nuns would ask me if I had received my vision of Mary Magdalene yet; they knew she was waiting for me.

At the end of this stay, two women asked to speak to me in the convent and said they had a message from the priestesses of Isis. This message was to flow me on to yet another, deeper, unfolding of the spiral—leading me to the opening of my womb to sacred union.

Around this time many of my spiritual practices fell away. I no longer felt drawn to yoga, meditation, fasting, or other more masculine paths. All I wanted to do was sing, dance, and celebrate Shakti, allowing the life force to sweep me away on its flow.

By chance I was introduced to the beautiful Indian sacred dance, Odissi—a dance of the moon—that had been practiced by tantric temple priestesses, known as *devadasis,* for thousands of years. On instinct I traveled to a remote tribal village in Orissa, India, to live and study with an Odissi dance guru. There I immersed myself in sacred dance. In the village, where life unfolded much as it did ten thousand years ago, I experienced a moment the poet Blake describes as having the "doors of perception cleansed," as Isis "lifted her veil" and opened my eyes to the truth of creation's majesty.

I had carried my harp with me to the wilds of Orissa, and one night, playing harp intuitively on the roof in the deep black velvet night, I watched as the trees *came alive.* In the darkness they lit up with a vivid, electric green life force that flowed through every branch, every leaf, creating a startling fairy-light show.

I had *seen* the truth that everything was vividly, pulsatingly alive, and only the disconnection of our sensory perception stops us perceiving this. For a moment I had been graced with the vision to truly see. Gaia had revealed her true inner beauty. For a moment I had perceived the mystical, flowing, living, dreaming of Gaia.

It was incredible to know this luminous greening power of God was flowing through all of existence, unseen to the ordinary eye, but ever present.

Soon afterward, another huge shift into Womb Consciousness was catalyzed as I met my beloved twin flame. Together we dived deep into the loving wisdom of sacred union and the healing power of sacred sexuality as a pathway to our return to original innocence.

Surrendering to the Heart of Creation

After quitting our successful lives to see if we could return to a state of innocence and unwind all the wounds and conditioning this world had weaved into us, my beloved and I embarked on a radical journey of healing and opening that took us on an inner and outer journey to a small Himalayan village in India.

The challenge was this: to *fully* trust in love again, to open ourselves to life with the innocence of a child's heart, to merge with each other and feel all the fear, constriction, and obstacles we had placed around our hearts, and then to dissolve them and keep trusting—to open into our pure inner essence together and ignite the power of our life-force energy.

We spoke only truth to each other, confessed all our darkest secrets, all our inadequacies, all our deepest fears. We said the things we dreaded to say, things we had never told *anyone* else before, the things that would make us look needy, stupid, weak, unworthy, petty, pathetic. We offered up our shadows to each other, braving our deepest fears that we would be rejected, abandoned, scorned, shamed.

We made love every day, we wept, howled, keened, and felt how our emotional wounds had embedded in our sexuality, how every bad experience was etched there like a record of debt. We made love gently with sacred intent, we made love passionately with pleasured abandon, we made love like wild creatures who had thrown off their human disguise and were free. We communed with Source, we embraced the earth, we went to places beyond this world.

And in every moment we kept choosing love, no matter how hard it felt, no matter how emotionally dangerous it had become. We kept trusting love.

Then one day, we *popped*. We made love and finally surrendered to the vast embrace of the Cosmic Womb's velvet darkness, catalyzing a profound dimensional shift in our consciousness.

We were at the very center of the universe, and *I was a star*. I had no clue what that meant, or that this was the *key* to *horasis*, Womb Enlightenment, as practiced in ancient mystery schools and written about by Solomon's beloved, the Queen of Sheba. But the feeling was clear, and rested in a newly opened perceptual place in me that I could not parcel into my logical mind. I just *knew* I was infinite.

My womb had awakened into a star; there was a cosmic stargate within me.

Sitting in the heart of creation, I was grounded in a deep stillness, but waves of ecstasy were dancing all around me, rippling out as ever-increasing circles into infinity. I felt at home, powerful, held in exquisite tenderness. A quiet joy was bubbling inside me.

I looked like I'd gone out of my mind. I was giggling and laughing one moment, then sitting perfectly still the next. I was drunk on life force, and my movements were unpredictable, like a wild animal just out of captivity, stretching, playing, and exploring.

I just knew I was at the center of the universe, the yoniverse, the Great Womb. But I hadn't gone anywhere. I was firmly in my body, finally at home in this form, and loving it. The Womb of Creation and I had merged.

Soon the ecstatic innocence settled into an all-pervading softness—the kind that melts everything in its path into an unworldly delicacy of tenderness. Now tears streamed down my cheeks, carving pathways of forgiveness and grace.

Love spread like a warm sunset, covering everything in its amber and honeyed hue. The softness was spiraling, unraveling me like a deep sigh of relief. I was aware that not only was I feeling this divine softness; I was also transmitting it. It was undulating out of me, touching everything in its path; it was bringing others into the soft folds of its arms. My eyes glistened with wonder. I was fully awake, fully in the world, eyes wide open, seeing life just as it is, embracing all.

There was nothing to do except sit back and behold the world from the heart of creation, in innocence, knowing the universe's best-kept secret. We were born in innocent love, and our womb remembers the way back home.

We set off that night to travel overnight by Indian train and, amid the chaos, an all-encompassing feeling of tenderness surrounded us like soft spring blossoms. We didn't need to be alone or meditating. Life *was* peace.

A Cosmic Library Was Living Inside Me

This experience marked the beginning of an incredible awakening process, which was unlike anything we had experienced before. It felt like we had traveled into the feminine dimension—deep into an unknown magical land. In the tradition of the Magdalene and Isis Mysteries, we had entered into the Eye of the Earth Dragon, passing through the cervical threshold of the Earth Womb to merge with the Dragon Mother and her deeply embodied primordial black light. We had then passed through the gateway between the worlds, ascending to the Cosmic Womb, which leads out into infinite universes and creative possibilities.

It was a fairy tale, an enchantment, once upon a timeless, happily ever after. But it was very real, very down to earth, and a place that was only a hairsbreadth away from our ordinary reality.

For more than six months my thinking mind was shut down and I was immersed in a new primordial, sensual feminine realm, feeling with my feminine brain. Life flowed as a soft liquid gold, where all information was dancing in spirals of light and color, accessible in holographic sonnets beyond the confines of logical understanding. One day my thinking mind switched back on with the thought, "I just had a thought." The "mirror mind" had begun its commentary again, but this time it did not take me over; it was an occasional interfering radio band, like a static noise that played low in the background, behind the beautiful musical wavelength of my primordial Womb Consciousness.

During this communion with this high/deep vibration, I felt in tune and harmony with everything, with a deep feeling of knowing everything at once. I didn't have to read books or investigate to receive information—it was streaming into me, bubbling up from deep inside me. I felt as if Mother Earth was whispering directly into every cell of my being, as if the stars were downloading their holograms of light into me, as if everything I ever needed to know was right there. A cosmic library was living inside me.

In moments of deep womb gnosis, I intuited medical knowledge about the healing potential of menstrual stem cells, which with later research proved to be true. I could *feel* the lives of people thousands and thousands of years ago and the shamanic and spiritual rituals they held sacred, even though I hadn't read much of this information before. Some of it was radically shocking. Some of it was so beautiful, simple, and truly innocent.

Living Inside Love

During much of this time I was in the eternal *now;* in fact, time and any conception of it had ceased to exist. It's almost impossible to describe this feeling, but it was as if we were in another dimension altogether, but also right here. Everything was alive in a shimmering ecstasy of light; the world was fluid with love. My experience of love was completely new. It was not an emotion or even a feeling, more like a *place*. It was somewhere we just *were*. And in that place, love was everywhere and everything was made of it. We couldn't be separate from it—we *were* it, and so was everything else. Living *in* love, just as we might live inside a house, meant we didn't have to go anywhere to get love or even give love. We could just *be in love*.

This new experience of love changed many things. For instance there was no need to pray, in fact any thoughts of praying to God were not possible. Praying suggested we were separate from something and needed to connect or speak to it. But we were already *in* it. Praying would have been like making a telephone call to talk to yourself. We were already *inside* the Source.

There was no fear either. It wasn't that the concept of fear still existed, but I just wasn't feeling it because I was fearless, evolved, or courageous; fear just didn't exist, like bibbledebop doesn't exist. It wasn't there; even the possibility wasn't there. Later I realized that if someone full of hate had come up to me with a knife during those times and stabbed me through the heart, I would have just smiled. There was no idea of judgment or fear of death in this state either.

If there was one feeling that encapsulated this experience, it was *innocence.* Everything was bathed in a virginal feeling, as if the world was glittering with diamond light. Fresh, pure, simple, *new*—every moment born with complete enchanted wonder—a blade of grass, flowers, the sky, the skin on my fingers, kissing my beloved.

Life felt very simple, with an indescribable feeling of trust and belonging. My womb and yoni would pulse like a heartbeat, not only during sacred sex, but also when I received wisdom that felt true, or when simply looking at flowers or watching butterflies. My body had an orgasmic response to *all* of life, not just lovemaking. Gentle, orgasmic waves pulsed through my womb and body; with every wave my perception of the world became clearer, brighter, purer—as if the volume was being turned up.

I discovered I could experience physical orgasms in different parts of my body: my heart, my throat, my thyroid, my knees, and my solar plexus. Sometimes they would happen when more love surged through my being, and sometimes they would come with emotional release. I understood that orgasm *is* surrender to life in the fullest sense. I understood that death was also an orgasmic rebirth.

The culmination of these experiences was a flood of wisdom or gnosis about menstruation. I felt deeply that our menstrual blood *is* our innocence. I was guided to share my menstrual blood with the earth and with my beloved.

At the peak of this experience, for two days we both communed with a being, a primordial mother, whom I will call Sophia, who gifted us with a taste of what original innocence might feel like. She desired so much to reach across the veil and assist us—and everyone—to rebirth ourselves. I "saw" and painted her during this experience and it was as if the page had become a portal she could step through. I dissolved in tears when I felt her. The powerful, magnetic innocence of her love was . . . who can describe it? She united all streams into one being; there was no separation or division of anything. Her vibration was of the purest love.

We knew clearly that in original innocence, when we lived *inside* love, menstruation was a sacred journey shared by men and women together in soul pods. It was a time of communion between the masculine and feminine and life itself. It was also a gift to be shared with the whole community. In ancient times, the entire tribe lived in balance with the menstrual moon rhythms—men, women, and children. Waxing, creating and building together, then waning, resting and renewing. The three days of the dark moon were a "time out of time" for the entire tribe, a collective vision quest, so that the community could renew and dream together. There was no separation—there were not even red tents. Men menstruated too, energetically, alongside the women. The gift of renewal was for everyone.

I knew that menstruation was an elixir of life, but that its powers could only be activated by a state of pure love. I knew that our bodies contained a kind of fairy dust—stem cells—scattered all through our blood, and if they switched on it would change everything. We would become a chalice for living light—a "feminine Christ." I knew that we were living *inside* the Womb of God.

I also knew that women had disconnected from the wild, primal power of the womb—and we were deeply afraid of our own femininity on a subconscious level. During this initiation into shamanic menstruation, I experienced a powerful dream that dredged up my most primal, hidden fears, like the forgotten hull of a long sunk ship being reclaimed from the murky depths of the inner oceans.

Looking into the Void

I am in a large room; it is at dark or at dusk. I am naked and there is an inner sense of conflict and fear, not fear of something external to me, but fear of something inside me; some energy and power residing in my own being that I am uncomfortable with and somehow disturbed by.

I am menstruating and I realize this is the root of the inner conflict.

I walk toward a large, old Victorian mirror to look at myself and the blood of my menstruation. I want to see the forbidden cave where the blood flows from, which is hidden away and safely locked in.

When I see the blood I am overwhelmed by its power and magnetic force. It is a deep red, almost black—rouge noir—there is so much of it, more than I expected. It is an abyss of deep darkness, it's like looking into a Void that looks back at me, fully conscious. In fact, rather than me as a being looking at the blood as some smaller part of me, it is as if the blood is vast, and conscious, looking back at me, engulfing me, making me feel small and awestruck at the magnitude of its presence, power, and depth. It is primal beyond words; I am an emission of it; it is not an emission from me. I am overcome with fear—not fear that the blood is dark, dangerous, or a threat. Just afraid of its power, its potential, its promises.

I am afraid of who I am really meant to be, who I really am, afraid of my own power, and understanding its source is something far vaster and greater than myself. I do not own this blood or this womb or this power. It does not empower me or guide me—it is a communal space, for everything. Its love, power, and wisdom is not limited to the boundaries of me.

The womb *knows,* and she was speaking to us once again, calling us home. At a deep, intuitive level we had long known that somehow human beings were mostly offline, disconnected from our full sensory-biological-spiritual birthright, functioning on the bare minimum to survive. For a moment we had switched back on.

This gift has left us changed forever, like a near-death experience, but in our case it was a near-life experience: a glimpse into another realm, except that it was right here, right now in our bodies and on this Earth, as our natural human birthright of original innocence. We discovered that we—and you—don't have to die to experience this heaven, to live inside love; we just have to come alive.

This is the secret of all secrets, the mystery behind the mysteries. And, it is the sacred power of the womb that is the gateway to this heaven on earth.

SPIRAL 3

AWAKENING THE WILD MASCULINE

The Womb Births the Sacred Man

Shakti [the Goddess] is the creator of the Universe,
And the Universe is her fascinating body;
Shakti is the basis of the entire world;
She is the intimate substance of any body.

SHAKTISANGAMA TANTRA

THE SUMMER of my nineteenth year, I (Azra) set out for the wilds of Alaska with only my backpack and an unquenchable thirst for life. Not the safe, packaged, and manicured life I grew up with in suburbia, but the real thing—raw, primal life. Though I couldn't have articulated it at the time, I was compelled by a deep longing for wildness. As a teenage boy, my soul had been insistently whispering that some vitally important and alluring element was missing from the secure life my parents and society expected of me—and I knew I needed to leave "normal" society to find it.

I wanted freedom, wildness, adventure, aliveness—not security and a pension plan.

Hiking up onto a glacier a few thousand feet above the forest floor—where literally no humans had been for many years—I set up camp directly on the glacial ice. As a storm blew in that night, gale-force winds threatened, reminding me of just how fragile a human being is in the greater scheme of the ecosystem of Gaia. Out in the wild, thousands of miles from civilization, on that long first night

37

I was initiated by nature in all her rawness and wild power, as the storms raged around me.

Over time, sleeping in the raw on the peak of a mountaintop under the full moon, with no tent, no sleeping bag, nestled into a snug of a granite rock peak looking up into the infinite night sky above me, I also communed with the vast beauty of this wildness; a magnificent beauty that etches itself into the depths of the soul.

Alaska is untamed nature for thousands of miles—99.9 percent of it does not even have roads or fences; it is unbounded. In these vast stretches of undisturbed land, the humming energetic field of the Earth can be felt in a way that is impossible in the civilized world. It is like the difference between trying to stargaze from within a brightly lit city compared to the vast dark skies of a remote mountaintop. When the background glow of civilization vanishes, perception becomes clear. Our primal senses switch on. An invitation is extended to join nature's resonance.

During my adventure into the wild, sleeping on mountaintops and forest floors, I carried only toothpaste, a wool hat, a rain suit, and two changes of clothes. It was at least a three-day hike into the woods from the nearest gravel road, which was itself miles from civilization. I was literally a world away from conveniences we have come to rely on—such as grocery stores, tap water, hospitals, and bathrooms. So anything I ate was what I caught or had boated in.

The first journey to Alaska is disorienting, if not downright shocking; it is the primal shock of feeling the true wilds for the first time, and the realization that something wild within us has been living in captivity—tamed, domesticated, neutered. Long dormant genetic memories begin to stir. You begin to sense for the first time, not at a cognitive level but at a primal feeling level, that you yourself are a part of this wildness, not separate.

For more than two months I slept on the belly of the earth in remote forests every night, allowing Mother Gaia to infuse me with her energies, to take me into her rhythms, to take me into her womb. I bathed in the cold of her northern oceans; I ate her offerings of fish and game. I accepted her many gifts and allowed her to teach me. My perceptions altered, my sense of time warped, and the subtle but consuming background compulsion that I had to do anything or go anywhere other than just be a human creature vanished. My own primal nature had synchronized and merged with Gaia. What an incredible homecoming. I could no longer feel where my own boundaries ended and nature's began. I became wild—unself-conscious and free. I was born again, alive for the first time. And in this my life was forever changed.

Walking down to Resurrection Bay every morning, seeing the glory of the snow-capped peaks that run down to the waters edge, and then jumping into that ocean water—so cold that it takes your breath away—I was immersed in primal aliveness.

It is only in retrospect that I began to understand what had happened to me in the woods of Alaska, and what drew me there to begin with. And it was only after years of unsuccessfully attempting to integrate those experiences into my "civilized" life that I eventually learned that it was impossible. You cannot fit the wildness into a box of ownership, separated off by fences, roads, boundaries. Just as the wildness of our soul cannot fit into society's vision of what it should be. Civilization itself must bend, not nature. Likewise, the civilized parts of myself needed to give way to my innate wildness. My soul needed to take the lead. And this was only the beginning.

In Alaska, I was a solo journeyman, a lone wolf, independent; like many men, I thought that freedom was to be found in solitude, meditation, and contemplation. Due to my youth at the time, I could not see that my longing for union with Gaia and her natural wildness was also a longing for Woman; for union with her wild womb; and for the untamed, wild, feeling nature of my own feminine self. I desired to truly meet the feminine in all her wild and beautiful elements, and to remember how the masculine was an integral part of this vast, dynamic beauty.

For it is this communion with the feminine that truly births the wild masculine.

The womb of woman is the sacred space that truly initiates a man into his inner kingship and power, and gifts him a "second birth" into the deeper realms of love.

Over time I came to understand that separating myself from the feminine, from intimate connection and relationship, in a bid for true freedom would only create another prison in the inner realms. Sleeping in the arms of the forest, watching the tapestry of midnight starlight, could not replace the homecoming of sleeping in the arms of a woman and her soft, embracing light. Love is our birthright, and within love lives the greatest freedom. Love is the wildness.

Ten years after my communion with Divine Mother and Gaia in Alaska, I experienced a powerful and overwhelming experiential vision of Mary Magdalene. She appeared to me during a pilgrimage and made her radiant presence known. I was so profoundly moved by this frequency of pure love she emanated that on the spot I made a sacred vow to dedicate my life in service of the Magdalene and to be a guardian of the womb for the Sacred Feminine, in all her many forms.

At the age of nineteen, I was searching for what I now know to be the greatest human desire: the longing to merge, the longing for union. I wanted to be one with the earth, and as it turns out, I wanted to be one with the Mother. I instinctively knew that.

I was being called by the Divine Mother at the deepest soul level.

This calling of the Divine Feminine became the guiding light of my life.

SPIRAL 4
POWER OF THE WOMB

Gateway to Infinite Love

For Sophia (wisdom) is better than rubies;
My fruit is better than gold . . .
I was set up from everlasting, from the beginning . . .
Blessed is the man that heareth me . . .
For whoso findeth me, findeth life . . .

PROVERBS 8

THERE IS NO POWER GREATER in this world than the womb. It houses our ability to create life. Truly feel that for a moment . . . *the power to create life.* This is a godlike power of creation, to make another being in "our own image"—this genetic copy of ourselves and our partner is a Russian doll of not only our DNA and cellular memories but of all our ancestors' DNA and cellular memories that have gone before us, back to the beginning of time.

Epigenetics shows that we can "switch on" coded information and remember the past lives of our ancient mothers and fathers. Our DNA is not fixed; it is more like a vast biological internet that shifts and adapts and is modified according to our life experiences and emotions, and those of our ancestors. We are always connected, as if by an invisible string of molecules, and we imprint ourselves again and again through the immortality of this womb portal.

And yet, this is only one facet of the womb's power.

Just as we do not fully understand the true function of the brain or of the heart, less so do we understand the true function of the womb. It is more than a physical organ, it is a multidimensional doorway, a holographic imprint of the Cosmic Womb that birthed all Creation. It is a gateway through which new life steps into this dimension, where a life spark of consciousness and genetic information takes form. It is also where new ideas take form.

On an energetic level, the womb is also the door we travel through on our way back out from this life. NDEs talk of rushing through a dark tunnel toward a light—is this not how a new baby feels being born?

We birth and rebirth through the womb. It holds the power of life and death—and beyond that, the mysteries of the entire cosmos.

Womb wisdom tells us that everything is connected, interconnected, entangled, holographic; we are weaved together in an infinite cosmic web of existence and information. We *know* everything, because we *are* everything. We are not separate—either from the Source of our creation or the infinite expressions and manifestations of Creation. We have forgotten, but our womb remembers and can connect us back to the conscious remembering and sensory reality of this.

If we opened our womb's eye, we would see there is infinite space inside, as quantum mechanics suggests. We hold supernatural powers within our cells and in the hidden yin spaces between our cells; they make every human being a walking, living miracle. We cannot even conceive of the possibilities held within us, and this lack of imagination keeps our potential power shutdown.

We are floating in outer and inner womb space as our Earth spins her way through the infinite multiverse of God's Womb. Our womb is a stargate, a black hole, connecting our innermost being to the farthest-flung star matter of existence and to the galatic center. The womb can create, transmute, and access information on multi-dimensional levels. If we could see it clearly, we would be stunned at what this power does, and how it communes and communicates with all of life.

We hold love up as a spiritual ideal, but it is also designed to be a fully embodied, biochemical reality. Our womb grid, following its original blueprint, allows us to experience life as sensual, ecstatic love, full of trust, joy, expansion, harmony, true communion. We are told our primal brain is wired only for fear and survival, but that is a misconception. It has been rewired to feel these negative states. Our original genetic wiring was designed for love, and we have a chemistry of "heaven" that is waiting to be unlocked and fully lived here on Earth. Human beings were not designed to suffer.

We are embarking on the start of a time prophesied by many traditions; it is a new cycle, where the Earth Womb, our own womb, and the Cosmic Womb will align and awaken to a powerful new birthing energy, bringing many new and loving possibilities to reality. For thousands of years the secrets of the womb were hidden. Only fragments of knowledge were held in any one lineage, and no single tradition held all the keys. Now they are being reunited and remembered.

This is the birth of a feminine-centered spirituality, which also embraces and includes the masculine. It is Womb Enlightenment: the feminine way, the path of love, the opening to union and harmony with nature in every sense. It has never been embodied on Earth before—at least not for many thousands of years, back even before the mystical times known as Atlantis.

It is now time for our wombs to wake up and remember the true creative power and sacred purpose that directly connects us back to the Universal Womb and the Source of Creation. Every awakened womb has its own unique sacred signature—every woman's womb power is part of the divine weaving of existence, and is incredibly valuable.

Men are also being called to experience this deep healing and reconnection, each called to become a Grail knight for a new era—pledging to honor, protect, and open to the feminine, in himself, in his relating to women, and his connection to earth. When a man makes this commitment all of creation comes to his assistance, supporting his healing journey, his relationships, and his soul mission. He feels the presence of the Sacred Feminine, holding and honoring all he is.

Cosmic Time Keepers: Menstruation of the Worlds

As a race we are on a precipice, and either we jump into the awakening of our true potential on a path of grace, or we fall into a destructive abyss, which will also transform us in its intensity. Either way, a new birth is happening, and inviting us to be a sacred midwife for this process.

The womb *knows* how to rebirth, so we are in safe hands. We have only to flow with the emerging creative energy and surrender to its wisdom. It is the way of union, not separation. The time of patriarchy or matriarchy is over. This is the birth of a co-creative, collaborative consciousness that invites and includes All into its dance of love. We are holding hands and walking together as equals. We are spiraling into the mysteries of the Womb of Love.

We have entered a long-predicted phase of *cosmic menstruation and renewal*. The process that unfolds inside a woman's womb is directly analogous to the renewal process unfolding inside the Cosmic Womb, as we prepare to birth a new frequency earth. As we approach a cosmic menstruation we do not need to "save the world" anymore than we need to save the womb lining before menses. Instead we can relax, soften, trust, and understand that the dissolution is natural and guided by a greater intelligence and is integral to the process of releasing the old, so something new can be conceived and born. The more we tense up and resist releasing the old, the more painful it will feel. The more we relax into this process and trust the great inner and cosmic flows of primordial intelligence, the more shamanic and orgasmic it will be. The womb does not see the cosmic menstrual flows as the end of the world but as a rebirth and renewal. This does not mean we have to be passive or allow unhealthy destruction—it means our actions come from a place of true connection and trust in the forces of life.

In Indian tradition this era is known as the Kali Yuga—from the pre-Vedic root word *kal,* which meant "black," related to the dark-moon pole of menstruation, explaining Kali's bloodthirsty iconography. She also represents the Cosmic Mother, the dark-matter mother, who spirals through the black ocean of naked space, birthing and dissolving creation in vast menstrual cycles.

The ancient ones paid great attention to the cosmic menstrual cycles of the Great Mother, which flow through approximately 26,000-year cycles, just as the human womb flows through twenty-nine-day cycles. These great cosmic cycles were also known as the precession of the equinox, and many stone temples from the womb religion were created to chart these Cosmic Womb cycles. As women's menstrual cycles, flowing with the moon, became the first calendars, so did the Great Mother's galactic menstrual cycles mark the cosmic timekeeping for those who knew. As with female menstruation, times of cosmic menstruation were renowned as extraordinary moments of visionary possibility—shamanic, liminal, quantum dreamtimes with vast creative potentials.

This is the time we are now living in, as the womb births miracles into being and we are given the opportunity to make quantum evolutionary leaps, both personally and as a collective, deeper into love.

Salvation of Sensuality

Our cosmic reconnection with the web of creation starts with our own personal healing. We can reclaim our lives and planet womb by womb. Change can happen only when we choose to open ourselves. The most revolutionary choice we can make is to "reset" our womb to innocence—and share this experience with a committed man. When a man receives a taste of this Holy Shakti from his beloved he is inspired and opened. If he bathes in it, he is melted into love. This is the journey to becoming a Magdalene, a magic doorway to transform all back into original love.

This is experienced as a gentle wave of purity, full of sensuality, which allows us to feel ourselves and the world from an expanded place of sensory perception, as if an inner quickening is blooming. We feel fully alive; colors shimmer brightly, sounds are enchanting, hearing the breeze through the trees is felt as a beautiful harmonic symphony. There is a feeling of lightness, quiet joy, stillness, and serenity that is very much connected to the flow and movement of life. It is a feeling of dancing in the primordial stillness and singing in eternal silence.

It could be described as a different frequency or a different dimension—the dimension of love. But it is here, on Earth. When we reset our womb, clearing away all the shocks, traumas, and betrayals, a wave of innocence floods through us. This is our natural state of being. It is our true birthright. It is a gentle, radiating, all-encompassing softness that enraptures the soul.

The gateway to this heaven lives within our wombs and sacred sexuality. Our sexuality is pure and immaculate—and only negative experiences and feelings stored in our wombs and sexual centers block this from being a lived reality. Sexual union with another is much like visiting a beautiful place in nature; we go there to commune, to enjoy, to play, to love, and restore—and we should leave the space in the same pristine condition we found it, without leaving our trash.

But many of our sexual encounters have not honored the pristine nature of our womb. Many people have dumped their "trash" in some way—either subtle or shocking. Every lover or sexual encounter that does not honor our feminine soul or the sanctity of our womb sovereignty leaves a footprint in the pure landscape of our physical sexual centers and our sexual energy body. Scientific studies now suggest that women may carry genetic material from the sperm of past lovers for years inside our body systems.[1] This energetic residue could leave an imprint forever, unless we decide to feel and release the memory and to gently discover, explore, and dissolve any negative footprints, and allow ourselves to heal.

This imprint is also passed down our ancestral line. We are born with a collective genetic footprint, the boot of oppression, where the feminine principle has been stamped out. We have been epigenetically modified by an antilife patriarchal system and the pain perpetuated by that.

Every man has been birthed from a womb that holds many negative imprints, and from mothers who were wounded emotionally, sexually, and energetically—which often prevents true and loving bonding with their sons. This has in turn led men to inflict their own negative footprints on the women they connect with, who then birth more children from this wounded imprint, and the cycle keeps looping and degenerating.

We may have even left our own negative footprints—every thought, fantasy, touch from ourselves that is not truly self-loving leaves an imprint on our body. Our own lack of self-love and erotic wounds can crush our innocence, and attract us to encounters that create even more emotional and energetic scars, adding to our secret feelings of shame and unworthiness.

Our erotic wound imprint is a map that shows us the path to our deepest shadows—and helps us heal them. We release these trauma footprints by opening our sexuality and precious life-force energy in love, embracing any traumatic memories and toxic patterns back into love, and remembering how beautiful and pristine our bodies and emotional and soulful sexual desires are.

Every time we have allowed another to enter our sacred yoni temple without true love, without honoring, cherishing, and holding us—a negative imprint is left inside the energy field of our yoni. Every time we do not speak from the authentic voice of our womb, say yes when we mean no, or do not share our deepest feelings, fears, and concerns, the womb subtly closes part of herself off.

Women hold much grief in the womb about the times they have been pushed, not respected, or been on the receiving end of a subtle demanding and inconsiderate sexual energy that only wishes to take from the womb, not give. There is much grief, and also shame and guilt that somehow we allowed this to happen or were powerless to stop it. These deep feminine wounds that live inside our womb need great tenderness and gentleness. We can hold hands with our earlier wounded self, who may have lacked discernment, often rooted in the loss of feminine initiation or sexual rites of passage in our culture and the lack of teachings about self-love.

We can also allow ourselves the full voice of our rage, anger, and shame for the times our innocence was taken against our will and, if appropriate, allow the balm of forgiveness or acceptance to flow into these contracted places of despair, pain, hate, and self-hatred.

All of these experiences are a call back to love; we can allow these memories and feelings to arise and embrace them with compassion. With our honesty and authentic willingness to feel and embrace, the womb can bring *all* experiences back into the frequency of love, forgiveness, self-love, and the purity of innocence.

All these energy imprints can be safely and gently cleared from the womb space.

Our sexual energy is beautiful, and it belongs to us, not to anybody else.

We can also open to the knowing that sexual experiences shared in love, trust, pleasure, ecstasy, honor, and respect *also* imprint on our womb space, creating a positive pathway of healing and awakening the codes of sensual, embodied love deep within our feminine soul.

Womb Awakening is a journey back to self-love and self-respect to help bloom our "womb garden." When we hold our sacred womb space in the sanctity she deserves, she begins to open and create magic and miracles in our lives. When we only invite others who are also pure of heart and respectful to share of her essence deep healing can blossom.

✻ Prayer of the Sacred Woman

1. Place your hands on your womb, and gently breathe into her soft, black velvet energy. Allow any feelings to arise, and greet them, welcome them, embrace them.

2. Ask womb to show you the memories she is still holding in her energetic field of any of the times your precious, sensitive feminine sexuality has not been respected or cherished. Allow the feelings or visions to wash over you until the memory is embraced, or a sense of your womb sovereignty is restored, and you feel centered in the soft strength of your feminine power.

3. Now visualize a soft golden light in the center of your womb, pristine and untouched. Allow this powerful creative light to pulse brighter, illuminating your entire womb. Feel this beautiful light flowing through your entire body, infusing healing where it is needed. You are the light of the world.

4. Now offer these words of prayer: "Divine Mother, thank you for the blessing of being a woman. Please help me release all memories of the times this precious gift of the feminine has not been honored. I now open into the knowing that I am a beautiful, wise, and deeply sacred woman. I honor and appreciate myself."

As we bloom back into innocence, we remember our orgasmic birthright; we reconnect with the harmonious flow of life; we attract partners who honor and open us deeper into love and pure pleasure; we find our soul mate, our life purpose; we become creative; our days are filled with laughter, inspiration, creation, and joy; we discover just how good it feels to be alive; and we learn to truly love ourselves and to commune with life.

We can begin to reset our womb to innocence on our own, or in a loving, committed relationship. Because it is our natural state, as soon as we make the choice to heal and open, the energy of life rushes in to help and support us. This is the hero or heroine's journey.

When our womb returns to innocence, we feel as though a great weight has been lifted and a sense of freedom and magical possibilities returns. We don't have to walk around carrying the burden of the past, replaying the traumas that have scarred and shamed us. Our relationships heal, our relationship with earth heals, and we can open to and embrace our lost feminine consciousness.

Our feminine essence is wild innocence. It is flowing in every womb this very moment—waiting to come out and play and be fully expressed and enjoyed in pure love, and shared with the masculine, who has the complementary, beautiful blueprint of this wild innocent energy.

These teachings were time coded to emerge again when it was safe to remember the womb.

In Tibetan tantric teachings there is a tradition of "treasure texts," which are important teachings that are implanted and embedded into the cosmic consciousness, waiting to bloom at a later time. These treasure texts are considered divine revelations that appear with perfect timing in the future. They are often received and shared by a reincarnated tantric shaman of the lineage.

The cosmic alarm clock is now ringing loud and clear—like church bells calling us back into the inner temple of the womb. It is time to remember these feminine treasure teachings and to build the schools of wisdom again, so we can initiate ourselves back into the harmonious flow of life.

WOMB ORACLES SHARE
Awakening the Power of the Womb

My beloved began holding his hands on my womb, and we started to feel how strong it can be when the gates open. We immediately felt the energy moving. It was as if the whole womb space opened and I could physically see how energy from the womb was bathing us both. At one point it got so strong that I went into a profound state of altered conciousness and all I could see was different colors, patterns, and movements. It felt as if my brain was my womb and there was so much energy rushing through me. My beloved was crying and I have never ever felt so much love from him, the more he cried, the more my body opened. I felt like a bee queen, but my beloved also had his own experience that was very different from mine, he could see my womb dragon moving, he began crying when he saw her. . . . Powerful experience!

N.H.

The Birth of My Womb Star

During the meditation I saw swirling galaxies, as if the Milky Way was in my womb. Then a bright light descended into my wombspace from the cosmos and a new star was born and the light of that diamond spark was a billion stars alighting at once, a billion wombs awakening. I heard the Great Mother's message: every awakened womb and hara is a universe waiting to give birth.

E.S.

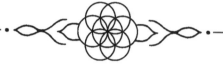

CYCLE 2

ANCIENT WOMB COSMOLOGY AND FEMININE MYSTERY SCHOOLS

SPIRAL 5

WOMB COSMOLOGY

The World's One Religion

The whole universe rests upon Her,
Rises out of Her and melts away into Her . . .
She is both mother and grave . . .
The gods themselves are merely constructs out of Her maternal
*   substance . . .*

HYMN TO THE GODDESS,
DEVI BHAGAVATA PURANA

PIECING TOGETHER THE THREADS, it becomes apparent that at one time a great womb religion held sway on Earth, uniting the world in a spirituality that celebrated Creation. The ancient ways were far more than a matriarchal goddess religion; it was a deeply embodied womb cosmology, practiced and honored by the entire tribe—both men and women. Of the many Stone-Age sculptures discovered around the world, 90 percent of them are of female forms, emphasizing the generative womb of life.[1]

This religion was deeply immersed in the knowledge of the multifaceted powers and wisdom of the mystical womb, as the Source of life itself. It was known that there was a universal womb, and that the Big Bang that generated our cosmos was actually a Big Birth,[2] and that there were also galactic wombs and planetary wombs.

Our ancient feminine cosmology followed and harmonized with celestial cycles, lunar and solar rhythms, seasons of the land. This wisdom was a living sacrament, felt in the body, expressed in relationship, embodied in community, and celebrated in harmony with Earth. The Celestial Womb gave birth to divine daughters, earthly emissaries whose womb cycles and monthly blood held the sacred power of red magic to create life and bring Spirit into form. This power could also rebirth the tribe into spiritual states of prophecy and communion with Creator. Ovulation and menstruation held the two poles of creation and dissolution, and were honored on full, dark, and new moons.

A Womb Cosmology of Creation

Stretching back into the farthest reaches of our ancestral memories, archaeological evidence paints a picture of ancient humans who, for hundreds of thousands of years, conceived of the world as a feminine vibration: a universe that was born from the dark primordial womb waters of Great Mother that held and contained us in layers of nested "mother-wombs." Our first experience of life was a state of psychic and physical union, held safe in the womb of our biological mother, who herself was supported by the protective womb of her tribe, and sustained by the fertile womb of Mother Earth that provided nourishment and shelter. Our planet itself miraculously spun along the starry vulva of the Milky Way, magically guided in a great cosmic journey through the Celestial Womb. Each of these "mothers" was a sentient being who was alive and communicative at a psychic level, to be honored and respected as a source of life.

The macrocosm of the cosmic birth process was mirrored in the microcosm of the human experience—as above, so below. The numinous powers of creation flowed through human women in the primary transformational mysteries of menstruation and birth. Red was a sacred color of the womb religions, the life-giving and life-sustaining blood of birth and menstruation that was freely given without war or injury. Blood symbolized the renewal of life, and the portal into the mysteries. The sacred red ochre pigment represented feminine blood, and was mined in earth-honoring ways across the world for ceremonial use for more than three hundred thousand years.

Menstruation was a time of psychic opening and renewal for the entire tribe. The gifts of the womb did not belong to women alone; they were a divine blessing for the community, protected and cherished by men as well, whose love and physical union contributed to fertilizing and activating the spiritual "mana" of the women. As recorded by the Aboriginal Australians, the Hopi, and many other indigenous groups, in this ancient dreamtime humans shared telepathic communication not just among themselves but also with the plant and animal world and with celestial ancestors and star beings.

In the cultures of old, the vulva, womb-belly, and breasts of women were celebrated as sacred—containing the power to create and nourish life. Serving more than just a biological function, they acted as mystical sexual-spiritual portals into many dimensions of consciousness. The yoni was a gateway to the heavens; the woman was the sacred witch-shaman.

Death was the final sacred journey, back into the earth belly of the Great Mother who birthed us, so our spirit could pass through the mystical portal of the Womb of Gaia back to the spirit realms where we came from. The living maintained communication with the spirits of their ancestors who lived on in otherworld. The two-sided doorway of communion was always ajar.

Patriarchy:
Destruction of the Womb Religion

But as patriarchy ravaged the primordial wisdom that had been celebrated and revered since time began, humans disconnected from their own inner rhythms and harmony, and their relationship to each other and earth devolved, as did their connection to Divine Mother. The Womb doorway between the worlds began to close down.

Over time, the feminine birthing essence was increasingly degraded or enslaved.

In Mexico, anthropologists believe that emerging Mayan kings established their rule by performing rituals in holy womb caves, which symbolized the earth's power and the power of the feminine womb to the Mayan people. If a king could "claim and own" this feminine creative power ritually, he then established a legitimacy to rule.[3]

Interestingly, the respected academic Julian Jaynes, author of *The Origins of Consciousness in the Breakdown of the Bicameral Mind,* speculates the fragmented psyche humans experience now only came into existence around 3,500 years ago, at the time the womb religion came under attack. He collected an overwhelming amount of evidence supporting a collective shift in brain functioning from right-brain artistic, imaginal, feminine consciousness, to left-brain analytical, masculine consciousness, caused by widespread cultural-psychological trauma. Our peaceful garden planet started to become a place of war and suffering. This amounted to a cosmic rape of consciousness, shattering our psyche. Before that we felt ourselves as a whole web. We danced in tune with the sacred song of the spheres.

Shall we revisit and rebirth this magical cosmology again?

Neanderthals:
Prehistoric Womb Shamans

The ancient womb religion had been honored for at least three hundred thousand years, with some evidence that hints at an origin as far back as 3 million years ago.* Birthed in the dark sanctuaries of mother womb caves by Paleolithic shamanesses, the religion of the ancient ones flourished and spread across the world. The sacred womb cosmology of the Stone Age was passed down as the knowledge of our original communion and gnosis, forged in mystical "archaic techniques of ecstasy" from a unified, holistic consciousness that moved in the swaying rhythm of Oneness. Symbolic V shapes, depicting the female pubic triangle—the sacred vulva—date back at least three hundred thousand years, from the dawn of the Paleolithic era, and were drawn by Neanderthals.

This dreamtime of the Neanderthals, where the menstrual wands (ritual staffs marked with lunar dates) of the female womb shamans measured out a mysterious, cyclical time that magically renewed itself from the depths of the cosmos, again and again in a nonlinear spiral, was an orgasmic dreaming of ecstatic union, dancing, and singing in celebration. In a wild place that lives beyond the curtains of language and logic, a magical feminine, symbolic living unfolded, present in the fluid *now,* with telepathic communication merging all into one flow of truth, swimming the primordial ocean of life together as a pod of unified tribal consciousness. Red ochre "moon" pigments blessed the bones of the dead as they were tenderly covered with woven-flower blankets and laid to rest in fetal position, returned back to the earth belly of Great Mother's womb-tomb caves. Children were birthed under incandescent moonlight, often at the mouths of the same protective caves, to the sound of pentatonic flutes and otherworldy harmonies, as the women danced wildly to guide spirit into matter. Animals were friends, guardians, and spirit guides. Nature, alive with wisdom, was an ally, a cherished family member.

Womb Guru:
Feminine Enlightenment

The wisdom of the Sacred Feminine as the Source of creation *and* spiritual initiation was passed down into worldwide cultures, traditions, and mythology.

---

*Recent British research, reported in Burleigh Muten's *Return of the Great Goddess,* dates the earliest Great Goddess figurines at 3 million years old.

The yoni, the doorway between worlds, has long been worshipped as the source of life, both literally and metaphysically. In a twelfth-century relief carved on the walls of a goddess temple in southern India, two holy men are depicted sitting at the foot of a great vulva, their hands raised in prayer. In a Renaissance painting of Venus, "rays of light are emanating from her vulva, illuminating a group of men" (see plate 3).[4] This is the power of Womb Awakening—enlightenment through the feminine.

Buddhism also contains the threads of a deep womb lore. The root word *buddh* means "to know," and is equivalent to the indigenous Evenki word *shaman,* "one who knows." Knowing or wisdom was believed to be gifted by the feminine consciousness and her divine elixirs. Buddha, as a womb shaman, was enlightened under a tree, in front of a river, after drinking milk given by a woman, as Venus was rising. This is a symbolic encodement of Womb Enlightenment, where a male shaman receives his wisdom and enlightenment from the feminine womb. In fact, old texts describe how Buddha attained his enlightenment through the womb-throne of the Earth Goddess. This throne was located at the mystical center of the world—the navel of the Earth herself.

The tantric text Cakrasamvara Tantra candidly reveals that the secret to Shaktyamuni Buddha's enlightenment was sacred union, *maithuna,* with his wife, Gopa. In it Buddha discloses his Shakti teachings for advanced initiates, saying, "take refuge in the vulva of an esteemed woman."[5] The womb of the sacred woman was the gateway to the Earth Womb.

In Russia, the crone-witch Baba Yaga symbolically encoded the embodiment of feminine womb power and immortality, who traversed both the full and dark moon, and included the male-female power within her magical flying mortar and pestle. The name for witch in Russian, *ved'ma,* comes from the word "to know"—denoting a gnostic womb shaman. Her holy *pech* stove is symbolic of the Womb of Earth and the cosmic Shakti force that the male heroes must unite with or be destroyed by.[6]

Lost Legacy of Womb Lore

This ancient spiritual path has left many telltale clues, if we know where to look for them. In France the indigenous Mother Goddess of the womb cosmology is many thousands of years old. The Goddess of Lausell figure, sculpted into an entrance of an Ice Age cave in the Dordogne region, was created around 23,000 BCE. She is carrying a bison horn shaped like a crescent moon, etched with thirteen marks to represent the lunar calendar, and her other hand is touching her womb. These ancient roots of the lost womb religion also belong to Black Madonnas, who were frequently found in trees, caves, or grottos and were believed to hold incredible magical powers.

More than eight thousand years ago, in northern Yugoslavia, fifty-four red sandstone sculptures were placed around vulva- and womb-shaped altars in shrines designed in the shape of a pubic triangle, with V-shaped decorations, denoting the sacred vagina.[7] The downward-pointing triangle—the daleth symbol of the yoni doorway—is found across the world, including Japan, Bulgaria, India, and in the Celtic lands of England.

In Cornwall, England, there are a number of megalithic rock stuctures known as *quoits,* dating to pre-Celtic times, often built on mounds or power places of Earth— the "dragon lairs" where Gaia's energy lines converge. These chambered womb-tombs were revered by ancient cultures as magical womb spaces of life and spiritual rebirth. They were typically built with covered passageways or entryways, symbolic of the yoni passageway of the Mother Goddess, from which the initiate could rebirth.[8]

Trevethy Quoit, also known as Womb or Rebirth Rock, is an ancient manmade circular hole in a rock face that was regarded as a place for transformation and spiritual rebirth and renewal.

Giant stone circles also created a sacred womb space for ritual and ceremonial rebirth, which local legends say were used in fertility and renewal rituals. Women would ceremonially crawl forward through the circular hole in the stone to receive a fertility or rebirth blessing.[9] One such stone circle, Mên-an-Tol, can be found in Cornwall (see fig. 5.1 on the following page).

Womb Church: Sacred Caves

The sacred space of the womb—symbolically shown in a circle—became the blueprint for religious worship, from sacred caves and stone circles, to temples and churches.

Fragments of this womb cosmology are still infused into medieval gothic cathedrals and round churches built by the Templars, whose floor plans were modeled on the symbol of the female womb, based upon the original design template of King Solomon's temple. In Freemasonry texts, King Solomon's temple is described as a womb space, "calculated to symbolize the maternal human body, wherein the candidate must enter to be born again. The uterus and vagina represent the porch of the temple, the pillars of the porch represent the fallopian tubes . . . and the pomegranate, the ovary and its exuberant seeds, the ova cells."[10]

Fig. 5.1. Mên-an-Tol megalithic stones of Cornwall, England. The circular stone represents the yoni-womb. The straight menhir represents the lingam.

Church is derived from the same word root as *circle,* which was an external representation of the feminine womb space. Stone circles or churches represented the mystical womb, where a man or spiritual initiate could experience a second birth, a rebirth, to be 'born again' through the Great Mother and her dazzling darkness of love.

This womb church originated in the primordial caves of Earth—the dark, fertile chambers carved within the Womb of Earth herself. Natural caves were the focal point of early societies, serving as homes, temples, and sacred burial chambers. To the early human psyche, the cave represented an external manifestation of the womb that held and protected them during gestation. They were one of the greatest symbols of the womb religion—especially those caves containing water.

A holy "womb" cave in Sainte Baume in the south of France is now a popular pilgrimage site for Mary Magdalene, who legends say meditated naked in the cave there for thirty years, before ascending to heaven. The mysterious grotto has been the site of womb worship for thousands of years, predating Christianity, and was previously a sacred site for Diana of the Moon, the Light Bearer of feminine awakening. To this day in modern French, the womb is sometimes referred to as *la grotte sacré,* the sacred cave.

Archaeologist Spyridon Marintos says about Greek goddess worship, "It may be that the Minoans found in deep and dark caves the most suitable places for worship for their great chthonic Goddess, who dwelt in the innermost parts of the earth."[11]

Caves and the "inner cave" of the female womb were always known as primordial power places. For thousands of years this power was honored. Shamans, medicine men, knights, kings, devotees, pilgrims, initiates, and seekers sought out the wisdom and blessings held "deep within the deep" of the feminine cave—through communing ritually in a womb cave of Gaia, or in shamanic sexual rites with the Holy Womb of a spiritual bride or womb priestess.

Holy of Holies: Temples of Womb Worship

As the womb religion evolved, people began building beautiful and elaborate temples devoted to the feminine Womb Mysteries—where women and men would pilgrimage for initiation and where priestesses practiced their mystical rites.

In Minoan Greece, a culture renowned for its Sacred Feminine spirituality, remote sacred caves became "civilized" starting from 3500 BCE, as elaborate womb temple complexes were built, to which young girls would pilgrimage for menarche (first menstruation). Dedicated womb priestesses practiced renewal rituals in constructed cave spaces known as lustral basins or *adyta,* which means "holy of holies" in Greek.

The lustral chamber located at Akrotiri on the island of Santorini is decorated with extraordinary frescoes that convey the Womb Mysteries at the heart of lustral or renewal rituals. One young woman has a bleeding foot (symbolizing the genitals), and there is an altar with Minoan sacred horns, anointed with menstrual blood. Young girls are shown picking crocuses, which are used as herbal remedies for menstrual cramps.

The palace at Knossos on Crete contains three of these magical womb chambers, one of which has a ceremonial throne, and dates from around 1700 BCE. Experiments at the throne room's lustral chamber conducted by Lucy Goodison reveal that the chamber room is illuminated with light during the sunrise of midsummer solstice.[12]

The carved throne itself is illuminated during the sunrise of the midwinter solstice, and these rays would have illuminated whoever sat upon the throne at that time, in a sacred enthronement ceremony.

These ingenious architectures of light are rooted in the womb religion, and are found in many of the more ancient stone temples, such as Newgrange in Ireland, seat of Brigid and her swan priestesses, bearers of both life and rebirth. Newgrange is a symbolic womb-tomb, an underground "doorway between the worlds" carved with triskele spiral eyes of the Goddess (see plates 4 and 5). On the morning of winter solstice, a beam of sunlight penetrates the dark passageway, illuminating and fertilizing the symbolic womb cave of the inner chamber, marking the solar rebirth.

This magical tradition is also seen in Chartres cathedral, dedicated to the Virgin Queen of Heaven,* where the first rays of midsummer light up the altar and nave, ritually illuminating this elaborate house of the Mother in her beautiful glory.

The womb-religion symbolism of a dark chamber impregnated by light is encoded into the Kabbalah creation myths, as told in the writings of Rabbi Isaac Luria. He describes the birth of the world as the constriction of the light to create a round womb space, and then the drawing of "a straight thread of Infinite Light" into it.[13]

In Hindu temples, the innermost sanctum, the holy of the holies, is called the *garbha grha,* or "womb chamber," from Sanskrit *garbha* (womb) and *grha* (house, chamber). It is without windows and dimly lit, to help facilitate an inward, womb-like spiritual experience. If there is a spire on the temple roof that points up to the heavens, the central womb chamber is found directly beneath it, representing the foundation of the *axis mundi,* or vertical axis of the world. If there is horizontal cross axis to the temple, the sacred womb chamber is located at the center of the cross—it represents the center of the cosmologic map of the Hindu world.

---

*The church is officially dedicated to Mother Mary, but some suggest it secretly honors Mary Magdalene and the lineage of Mari-Isis.

Keys of a Womb Cosmology

The essence of the womb cosmologies can be found in these common motifs.

Dark Seas and Primeval Womb Void

The creation myths of the womb religions invariably begin in the dark primeval Void of Creation, mirroring our earliest gestational experiences in the dark amniotic ocean of our mother's womb.

Across time and cultures, the underlying structure of existence was always conceived of as a dark abyss, a dark Void, a dark primeval sea, or a primordial dragon mother—an undifferentiated dark sea of potential energy that existed before all manifest creation, and from which sprang all of existence. This darkness had a feminine vibration and was thought of as the Original Mother, often represented by the sacred sound vibration *Om* and the color black.

The indigenous Kogi people, from the heart of the Sierra Nevada mountains of Colombia, are one of the few living cultures that have maintained an unbroken connection to the deep feminine wisdom since ancient times, uninterrupted by the modern world. They are the spirit keepers of the most intact womb cosmology on the planet, and they have been told by Aluna, Great Mother, that now is the time to spread this knowledge to the world, as our Earth is at risk. They say:

> In the beginning there was blackness, only the sea. No sun, no moon, no people. In the beginning there were no animals, no plants, only the sea. The sea was the Mother. She was not a person, she was nothing, nothing at all. She was when she was. She was memory and possibility. She was Aluna. She is the mind inside nature.[14]

In the creation myths of the Yavapai-Apache people of the American Southwest, the Creation goddess Pukmukwana wove and spoke into existence the First Woman by grinding black stone star powder in her great mortar. The black heavenly stardust gave form to First Woman's body.[15]

In Egypt, one of the earliest known Mother Goddesses is Nut, from whose name comes the word *night,* and whose origins date back to the matrilineal tribal cultures of the predynastic Egypt. Nut was the goddess of the primeval darkness: Mother Night, she who birthed the world from the abyss of her dark womb, and the Creator of the cosmic egg. She represented the undifferentiated dark sea of potential energy that existed before all manifest creation, and from which sprang all of existence. This same creation story echoes through many traditions, and even in the "creation story" of modern quantum physics, with its mysterious dark matter.

Mother Nut is traditionally pictured holding up the starry firmament, her great back arching over the midnight blue night sky, scintillating with points of starlight (see plate 7). As is typical of the primeval feminine Creatrix, she was associated not just with birth, but with death: her image was traditionally painted on the inside lid of coffins and sarcophagi to help guide the deceased back to their original home in the celestial spirit world, in union with her maternal embrace (plate 6). Even if all the light of the stars and suns were to disappear, her primordial darkness would remain and birth the universe anew. She is the center, the spinner, the dissolver.

Web of Life and Spiderwebs

We live in a universe that is abundant with *dark matter,* rich with the presence of the *dark mother.* Dark matter appears to have a gravitational pull, or a push, that spins and flows in invisible weblike filaments that extend out, like cosmic spiderwebs, from the supermassive black holes that form the inner core of galaxies. Dark matter links together all the galaxies in the universe, much like the story of Indra's web described in Vedic and Buddhist cosmology.

Eastern sages intuited very accurately the actual superstructure of the physical universe—that space itself has jewel-luminous galactic "nodes" connected by flowing highways of dark energy and dark matter, much like our own brain has neurons connected by a vast neural net. In the Avatamsaka Sutra, Indra's net is described as "studded with wonderful jewels, composed of sounds produced by the knowledge of universal virtue . . . nets of diamonds from the sphere's of Buddhahood, surrounded by as many worlds as atoms in a Buddha-field, all uniformly pure."[16]

This also mirrors research from the University of Oxford that shows how threads of spider silk transmit "songs" of information through web vibration.[17]

The web of life motif is also found in the Hopi and Zuni traditions of America, in which Grandmother Spider Woman weaves life into being. Spider Woman, who represents the female creative principle and Earth itself, sings aloud "I receive Light and nourish Life. I am Mother of all that shall ever come."[18]

Cosmic Egg and World Womb

The concept of the cosmic egg or world egg is found in many traditions across the world, including Celtic, Orphic, Egptian, Tibetan, Norse, Chinese, Pelasgic, Phoenician, Hindu, Vietnamese, Russian, Mesoamerican, and others.

Sometimes laid by a magical goose or heron, and sometimes produced directly from the belly of the original feminine Mother herself, the egg represented the protecting and birthing energies of the womb and was also a symbol of maternal containment, holding the entire universe within itself.

Often, at the moment of birth, the world egg breaks apart into two halves, forming the earth below and the skies above, or the male-female creator twins. Symbolically, this is represented by a half-white, half-black circle or oval, as in the Taoist yin-yang symbol.

The Upanishads share the creation myth of a Golden Womb that floated in primeval emptiness until it split apart into two halves, forming heaven and earth. The Rigveda contains similar womb myths. This cosmogony mirrors the first division of the human ovum, or egg, after fertilization in the womb, into "daughter cells," which carry the potential of a new life.

The Kogi conceived of a womb medicine wheel that recognized the four cardinal directions of north, south, east, and west, with three additional directional points of the zenith (up), nadir (down), and the center. These coordinates were visualized as an egg shape, surrounding them on all sides and orienting them in time and space. They were formulated into nine stages of development, paralleling the nine moons of human gestation. Mother Goddess, the creator of the universe and mankind, created the cosmic egg, the world womb in which we live.[19]

Cosmic Vulva and Spirit Birds

A number of womb sites across the world were aligned to the constellation of Cygnus—the celestial swan—said to be the vulva and Womb of the Cosmic Mother, and the celestial origin of our species. Shamanic journeys into Womb Consciousness often involved flying on the back of a magical swan or swan barge into the primordial center of the black hole for a wisdom initiation of death and rebirth. Womb priestesses and shamans wore ritual swan feathers or magnificent white swan cloaks for this journey, later remembered as the shamanic swan wings of angels.

The significance of the Cygnus constellation is that it rests in the "vulva" of the galaxy, the dark rift of the Milky Way through which souls enter or exit the galactic womb—the black "mother" hole at the center of the galaxy. Depictions of this symbolic connection are found in ancient texts and temple carvings across the world.[20] In Mayan lore the galactic center was known as *Hunab Ku* (Mother Womb) and the vulvic rift was known as the "road to Xibalba" (pronounced Shibalba), simultaneously both the underworld and cosmic heaven. In Tibet, a culture linked with many magical threads to the Maya, we find the legends of the mysterious Shambala, alternately a paradise or underworld city.

Birthing into a new incarnation or rebirthing after death through the Galactic Womb involved "flying the swan"—journeying through the galactic vulva for a multidimensional renewal. The swan flight is the original mystical shamanic journey made by womb priestesses through their inner black "womb" hole, which was spiritually and symbiotically linked to the great Cosmic Womb and the Earth Womb. The swan—along with the goose, vulture, and dove—is sacred to the Goddess and feminine across many cultures, from Semitic to Greek to Celtic to Indian.[21]

Cosmic Umbilical Cords and Placenta

The first peoples of Earth ascribed magical powers to the placenta. It was the spiritual twin of the living baby and held the child's soul signature. Placentas were often left connected to the newborn for an extended period of time, or until they fell away naturally, a practice more recently named lotus birth in recognition of the ancient symbology of the lotus, whose flower grows up from a long thin stalk, rooted in the underwater "placenta" of Mother Earth. In mythology, when the lotus-womb blossomed, it revealed the splendid light of a "divine child."

Stories of umbilical cords and ladders leading from heaven to earth pervade the myths and rites of the womb religions, particularly those of birth and death and the passage of souls across the threshold. Across Southeast Asia and China, female shamans used birthing ropes, representing umbilical cords, to assist in their soul travel. Pregnant women hold the symbolic umbilical cords during childbirth to assist the entry of the new soul into the world, and shamans hold the cords to communicate with ancestral spirits or take spirit journeys.[22]

In Mayan sacral art, umbilical cords are shown descending from the heavens into this world to allow for divine communion. Similar cords are shown descending down into the "Earth maw," the underworld. Egyptian burial art shows ladders ascending from the underworld up to the "boat of Re," which the deceased use to ascend to the celestial heavens. Every tomb is considered to be the site of such a ladder.[23]

In many traditions spiritual umbilical cords were an important etheric bridge between different dimensions, and allowed safe cosmic travel. Womb religions recognized that just as an umbilical cord connects us to the birth womb, so an umbilical cord of light also connects us to the death womb. Burial rites for the Kogi were considered an act of "cosmification"—a return back to the Cosmic Womb by way of first journeying back through the Earth Womb. Although it has now been forgotten by most living cultures, the Mother cultures realized that the secret portal to the Cosmic Womb was accessed *through union with the Earth Womb.*

When a Kogi tribal member dies, the shamans, or *mamas,* return him or her back to the Womb of Mother Goddess, in a burial pit that is considered to be a womb. The dead body is placed in a fetal position, in a carrying net, with a braided rope tied to the hair. The net symbolizes an energetic placenta, nestled into the Earth Womb, which is connected by an umbilical cord (rope) to the spirit of the deceased journeyer to nourish her on her nine-day trip back to the Celestial Womb. After nine days, the umbilical cord is cut, allowing the person to be fully rebirthed into spirit world.[24]

World Navels and Stone Thrones

World navels, such as the Omphalos of Delphi, appear across many cultures as gateways to the Womb of the World. Standing stones were erected at sacred womb sites to represent "omphalos points" or "world navels"—the mythological center of the world. They were ritually kissed and anointed with the sacred fluids of life—commonly honey, milk, oils, and menstrual blood—in practices dating back to the Stone Age. The anointing of Beth-el stones later evolved into the ritual anointing of the king by the high priestess as part of the enthronement rituals, where initiates sat on a stone throne, or later a red throne, to represent the womb of the Mother.

In the fourth century Epiphanius records that heretical female priestesses, initiates of the Collyridian school of Christianity, celebrated the Eucharist in the name of "Mary Queen of Heaven," writing, "They adorn a chair or square throne, spread a linen cloth over it, and, at a solemn time, place bread on it and offer it in the name of Mary; and all partake of this bread."[25]

Isis was also known as the "throne of kings." Like the Celtic idea of sovereignty, only the land spirit, envisioned as the Goddess, could grant royalty or power.

Mother Caves and Womb of Gaia

The cave was considered to be a magical passageway to the Womb of Gaia, who herself was a shamanic portal to Otherworld. Some of the earliest knowledge of the Neanderthals and later peoples comes from their magical shamanic cave art.

Ritual ceremonies held in the darkness of caves were accompanied by shamanic music even from the oldest times. The earliest-known musical instrument is a 45,000-year-old Neanderthal bone flute discovered in a sacred cave in modern-day Slovenia.[26] In shamanic womb cultures, music served as a "spirit horse" to shape and transform consciousness, opening doorways to altered dimensions of experience.

Sacred caves feature in almost all spiritual texts, myths, and practices across the world. The Hindu "Mother of the caverns" Kurukullā is one of the oldest faces of the Divine Mother in India, while in Europe the Mother Goddess Cybele was called "cavern dweller."[27] Indian and Tibetan yogis went to caves to meditate and find enlightenment; avatars and prophets were born in caves; Cathar initiations were held in secret womb caves; and the Zohar, the sacred book of Kabbalah, was written after Rabbi Shimon spent *thirteen* years in a cave, a coded reference to the menstrual number of Sacred Feminine numerology.

Caves are one of the most important symbols in the Taoist tradition as well, as they are known to be places of purified *qi* (energy). Taoists believed there were caves within the body called cinnabar fields, a red color that represented immortality, associated with the magical blood of menstruation and birth.[28]

The most archaeologically significant pyramids in pre-Columbian Mesoamerica, located at Teotihuacán, Mexico, are built on top of a system of even more ancient ritual caves. These caves, shaped like four-petaled flowers, represented the Womb of the Mother and are the people's earliest sacred image of the cosmos.[29]

Caves and womb chambers had a rich meaning for our ancestors, which cannot always be understood with the logical mind but rests in the multidimensional ocean of primordial consciousness—promising an inheritance of quantum and spiritual renewal.

Womb-Tomb and Death/Rebirth Rites

Womb chambers are connected to funeral rites or symbolic death and rebirth rites. In the early Semitic cultures, the concepts of cave and sacred tomb were closely linked. The Hebrew word for cave, *marh,* contains within it the root word *ar,* "to awaken," referring to the tradition of spiritual rebirth that took place in caves (such as the legend of Lazarus), both for the living prophets and for the deceased who were buried in the cave tomb. The word for *cave* also contains the root word *mar,* the name of the Mary/Maria priestesses of the old religion, keepers of the cave temples and feminine rites.

Returning to the Womb of the Mother upon death is an important ritual concept in the ancient womb religion. At the Paviland cave in Wales, the oldest yet discovered magical menstrual wands, crafted from mammoth tusks, were found alongside an ochre-colored skeleton, with red "menstrual markings" ensuring that its death-spirit-menstruation would lead to rebirth.[30]

Death as menstruation was a key of womb cosmology, and this symbology continued in Europe until medieval times. In the cave of La Chappelle-aux-Saints, France, in Paleolithic times, the dead were laid in the fetal position and covered with red ochre "menstrual" paint, symbolizing a return to the womb of the Earth Mother.[31] Neanderthal burials were also discovered at this site.

The womb-tomb was also a place where people received shamanic initiations, rebirthing in the Womb of Gaia, often remaining in the darkness of a cave for three days and nights, as Jesus and others were said to have done in their resurrection mysteries.

These womb chambers were at the heart of the transformational rituals of the mother religions, imbued with the power to shift the very fabric of one's soul.

Circle of Underworld and Paradise

The Cosmic Womb as a heavenly paradise and the Womb of Gaia as a primordial underworld were key features of the womb religion. The words for cave, womb, sacred, and underworld were interrelated in the ancient languages. In Sumeria, the word *matu*—derived from the root word for mother—meant "sacred cave," "womb," and "underworld." In German we see the same pattern in the related words *hohle* (cave), *Hel* (Germanic goddess of the underworld), *hel* (shelter), and *hohl* (hollow). In English we have *hole, whole, holy, hallowed, hell,* and *halo.* Hell and the ancient goddess names *Elen* or *Helen* also share the same origin. The underworld was understood to be the sacred Earth Womb, rather than a realm of pain and punishment. *Hell* was once *holy.*

The ancient link between the Cosmic Womb and the underworld Earth Womb is held in the Nordic mythology of Helheim, the underworld land of the dead, and source of the modern word *hell.* Helheim was guarded by the Norse goddess Hel, or Hilda, northern ruler of the night. However, the Milky Way—the Galactic vulva— was also known as "the path of Hel" or "the path of Hilda," as the northern night souls would return back to the great Celestial Womb after death.[32]

In linear thinking the Cosmic Womb and Earth Womb are poles apart, but in spiral feminine consciousness they are cojoined doorways united in the arc of the circle.

Venus Star and Pentagram

The magical thread that connects the underworld and heaven is also shown in the ancient hieroglyphs of Egypt, in which the celestial realm was represented by a five-pointed star of Venus, and was pronounced "dua." The symbol for the underworld was the exact same star, but embedded in a circle, and also pronounced as "dua" or "duat." These hieroglyphs are shown in fig. 5.2. As the brightest "star" in the night sky, the planet Venus was considered sacred in every Mother culture as a symbol of feminine rebirth and immortality. As it appears from Earth, the path of Venus traces a five-pointed pentagram in the heavens. On its journey it takes an unusual course, plunging deep into the underworld as it passes underneath the Earth from its position as the "dying" evening star in the western sky to its position as the "reborn" morning star in the eastern sky. Venus's cycle of birth and rebirth, from underworld to the celestial heavens and back again, continues eternally.

Pentagram, 5-pointed star,
the path of Venus in the sky as
seen from Earth

Roman numeral 5,
the number of Venus

5-petaled wild rose,
the rose of Venus,
Virgin Mary as "the mystical rose"

Egyptian hieroglyph for
heaven,
the Celestial Womb

Egyptian hieroglyph
for Duat,
the underworld womb

Fig. 5.2. Venus as goddess of rebirth, goddess of the underworld.
(Illustrations by Heather Skye)

Nine Moons:
Sacred Feminine Numerology

Nine was the sacred number of gestation and birth across all cultures, and features in creations myths, and stories of birth, death, and rebirth in the underworld realms. Nine represents the nine moons, or months, of gestation in the human womb. When the number nine appears in myth and legend, it invariably indicates that the story contains hidden messages from the ancient womb lore.

The sacred number nine is repeated throughout the Hopi rites—nine annual ceremonies, nine active days of festival, nine ceremonial washings, and nine worlds within the Hopi cosmology.

There were nine Muses, nine Morgans, nine maidens tending Ceridwen's womb cauldron, and nine days of the Eleusinian rebirth mysteries. In Egypt, the Ennead, or nine gods and goddesses of creation, arose from the primeval waters of the great birther goddess, *Nun,* from whose name is derived the word *nine.* The ancient Semitic letter *nun* was symbolized by the picture of a germinating seed—a metaphor for gestation and spiritual transformation—and meant "child," the fruit of woman. It was also linked with the fish and snake, both symbols of the womb and feminine sexuality.

In Norse mythology, Odin hung from the Yggdrasil tree of life for nine days in his process of spiritual rebirth, and the Yggdrasil contained nine worlds. The river Styx of the Greek underworld-womb had nine twists, flowed through the nine hells, and was originally presided over by its namesake, the prehistoric goddess of death, Styx.[33] Another name for the river Styx was Alpha, the birth womb.[34] In Dante's *Inferno,* hell had nine concentric descending circles. In China the netherworld had nine rivers, represented as nine dragons. The Mesoamerican underworld hell had nine levels, as did the pyramid of Kukulcan at Chichén Itzá, along with many other Mayan temples. The nine levels of the underworld originally represented the nine sections or phases of the journey back to union with the Womb of the Great Mother at the time of death, the reverse gestation process that mirrored the nine moons in the human womb.

The Magic Numbers of Seven and Thirteen

Just as nine is the sacred number of the underworld womb, the Sacred Feminine numbers of seven and thirteen are associated with the Celestial Womb. To the earliest peoples, the heavens above and the earth below were both domains of the all-containing great feminine round—the nested mother wombs that contain us.

Whereas the earthly and underworld realms were the dwelling places of the deep unconscious psyche and primal birthing energies, the celestial spheres were the realms of brilliant light and ascending consciousness—born from the Cosmic Womb of the Great Mother in a scintillating show of divine creative power. Even modern physics describes the formation of new stars as a birthing process that happens in a "stellar nursery," created by powerful gravitational waves emanating from the galactic center, the supermassive black hole and Galactic Mother located at the center of our galaxy.

Of all the sacred numbers, seven is the most widely venerated across all the cultures of the world. The Seven Sisters stars of the Pleiades are held sacred by almost every indigenous culture of the world, and the passage of the moon, the great timekeeper and queen of the night sky, is divided into four equal phases of seven days. Menstruation, the numinous symbol of feminine procreative power, comes every 7 x 4 days.

The concept of the seven heavens, or the seven divisions of the world, are seen in dozens of cultures and spiritual traditions across the world—including Maya, Hopi, classical Greek, Sumerian, Christian, Judaic, Islamic, Tibetan Buddhist, Hindu, Hermetic, Gnostic, and Egyptian, among others. In China seven is connected to the feminine cycles and the "road of yin."[35]

The idea of seven circles of initiation to reach the "Queen of the Eighth"—the Cosmic Womb or "home of God"—was a central motif of the feminine mysteries (see plate 8). The journey through seven veils or gates was the heart of initiations in the temples of the Great Mother, such as Isis, Inanna, and Ishtar.

Seven is also the halfway point of the sacred lunar number thirteen. The number thirteen is the number of the moon—the haloed goddess of the night—in both her celestial aspects and in her role as governess of the female menstrual cycles. There are thirteen new moons or full moons in a year, and thirteen lunar months of twenty-eight days. There is evidence that the original zodiac was a thirteen-division lunar zodiac before changing to the modern twelve-division solar zodiac.[36]

The moon was considered by many Near Eastern cultures to be the highest god, or goddess, in the celestial pantheon. In the Mayan worldview, there were thirteen celestial heavens, revealing an older lunar cosmology that existed prior to the patriarchal era. Similarly, in ancient Mesoamerican cultures, the moon occupied a higher position in the heavens than the sun.[37] In the Egyptian tradition, Nut, whose dark womb contained the moon and all of the stars in the sky, was painted on the inside of sarcophagi and coffins to welcome the dead back to her heavenly maternal embrace.

Mystic Rose:
The Forbidden Doorway

The Womb is the radiant darkness that not only births creation but also holds the secret power of spiritual rebirth. The womb that holds the blueprint of original innocence, our true spiritual potential, is also the portal for us to be "born again" into this pristine state. Shamanic rituals such as sweat lodges and enactments of burials in Gaia are all deeply connected to womb wisdom—embodying the knowing that we can return to the womb depths for rebirth, to be nurtured again by the Great Mother, and arise as a renewed being. We see this echoed in many myths, such as in the story of Jonah's rebirth from the belly of the whale, symbolizing the primordial oceanic womb mother.

Womb cosmologies also contained the secret teachings of awakening the "Magdalene Womb," or the "mystical rose," by experiencing a mystical union with the Earth Womb. Through the spiral path of merging and harmonizing with the primordial elements, a person could once more enter the collective dreaming of Gaia.

This mystical *descension* process into the Earth Womb, or the underworld, was the key to unifying with the *arche,* primordial feminine first cause, the deep silence of the dark mother. Uniting with the interconnected cosmic weaving allowed one to gain access to the vast knowledge store held within the Akashic field—the collective cosmic memory. In this way the arche was a transmitter of information that reached beyond our normal human sensory perception; connection with this energy was achieved through a feminine path of *descent* rather than *ascent*. This is also the secret meaning of the myth of the Greek hero Jason and his ship the *Argo,* another name for this same energy. Jason's journey involved a spiritual rebirth, at the feet of the goddess, after being swallowed by a great serpent, the dragon Kholkikos, who represented the abyssal mother consciousness.

Across many mythologies, the Womb of Gaia becomes the dreaming gate back to the mysterious flow of union—to true wisdom, knowing, and *nous*—becoming One with the primordial intelligence, called the "universal root consciousness" by the Gnostic shaman, Simon Magus. Alchemist and philosopher Basil Valentinus described the essence of this time-honored alchemical journey, "Visit the inner earth; through purification you shall find the hidden stone," referring to the Philosopher's Stone, another name for the Holy Grail.[38]

The womb as the crucible of creation, the alchemical vessel of all birth and rebirth, was imprinted in ancient traditions across the world. This worldwide womb lore now lies like a jewel hidden at the bottom of a vast, dark ocean. Her magnetic light still sparkles bright, as a mysterious and luminous invitation for those prepared to dive deep for her secrets.

Worldwide Womb Lore

Here is just a sampling of her many treasures.

The Americas

The ancient Mesoamerican ritual of Temezcal, or sweat lodge, is known to be a symbolic return to the Mother's Womb for rebirth and renewal. The Temezcal is presided over by Tonantzin, the great mother of gods and humans, who welcomes her children into her womb space to heal them of all wounds.[39]

Native American medicine man Campbell Papequash describes the sweat lodge as both Mother Earth's Womb and a woman's womb. This primordial womb space has four doors, which represent the four cardinal directions.[40]

Alaskan Eskimos had a shamanic death and rebirth through the symbolic womb of the igloo. The word *ani* means both "to go out of an igloo" and "to be born." When leaving the womb igloo during shamanic initiations, Eskimos wear a sealskin cord around them to represent the umbilical cord of their igloo womb.[41]

In South America, the Tukano peoples believe the womb to be a "manifestation house" where spirit meets matter. For the Tukano, the sacred medicine plant aya-huasca (yaje) is a vehicle used to enter the primordial Womb of Creation. The yaje pot symbolizes the uterus and is sometimes painted with a vulva and clitoris—which they regard as the door to otherworld.[42] Mother Ayahuasca was considered to be a symbolic entrance to Womb Consciousness for those who were ready—and whose hearts were open to her vision.

Egypt

Hathor, the ancient Egyptian goddess of dance, sexuality, fertility, and love, was also called "lady of the vulva."[43] She was linked to the Theban goddess Mut, meaning "Mother" and the Greek Methyer, meaning "primordial water." Hathor is called Hwt-Hr in Egyptian, which translates to "the Womb of Horus."[44]

The instrument sacred to Hathor, the sistrum, symbolized lunar cycles.[45] The temple of Hathor at Dendera is surrounded by birth houses. Ancient Egyptian cosmologies attributed Hathor to be a goddess responsible for birthing the day, and the Milky Way was Hathor's amniotic fluid.[46]

The ancient Egyptian goddess Nut, who is also said to give birth to the day (or the light or the sun), was painted on the inner side of sarcophagi so that she could bring the deceased into her Womb and renew their lives.[47]

Africa

In Africa, the goddess Ngame was the "Mother of all nature, the Womb of Life." She holds two water jars, pouring forth the waters of life.[48]

The Serer peoples of Africa believed that all modern humans were birthed from the Womb of the supreme feminine principal Roog, their god. Their oral tradition holds that creation had three phases of gestation, culminating in a birth of baby and placenta.[49]

In Nigeria, the Yoruba ceremonially call upon ancestral maternal spirits, which they call "the owners of the world," whose power flows to them through their wombs.[50]

The Far East

The Wu, ancient female Chinese shamans, were rumored to possess the "herb of immortality." Their name is linked with such concepts as feminine, dance, fertility, egg, and receptacle. The oldest glyph meaning Wu is a four-directional womb cross. Many legendary Wu are remarkable for their extraordinary births.[51]

The Shingon and Tedai Buddhist rituals of Tibet center on two mandalas, one of which is the "womb realm" or womb mandala.[52]

The mystic Chinese sage Lao-tzu claimed the origin of the world was through a feminine mother being.[53] Tao master Liu Chuxuan also wrote poetically of the power of the womb, claiming, "The womb's immortal [energy] bathes you. . . . Inside, you will not hunger or thirst."[54]

In Japan, there is a Sugendo womb cave ritual, in which participants pass through a narrow cave called *tainai kuguri* (literally, "passing through the womb") to symbolize a great shamanic rebirth.[55]

Northern Asia

The most important cave in ancient Mongolian pilgrimages was called "Mother's Womb." The pilgrim would greet a goddess figure such as Tara in the center and would be assisted by a midwife upon leaving the cave. After completing the pilgrimage, the pilgrim was considered reborn.[56]

In Siberia, a shaman's voyage was considered a journey into the womb. The entrance to the upperworld in Siberian cosmology was depicted as a vulva, a small hole in the fabric of the universe.[57]

In Mongol and Quitah faiths, the deity called Umai was the great Mother Goddess, whose name also meant "womb," "placenta," and "umbilical cord."[58]

In North Asian myth, the celestial warrior goddess, Ome Niang-Niang, whose name meant "the womb goddess in the sky," was believed to reign supreme. Sacred art shows her behind an open lotus representing her yoni/womb, surrounded by her seven celestial children—the Pleiades.[59]

Southeast Asia

The Dravidians of India worshipped a Mother Goddess, who is depicted on seals as naked with plants growing out from her womb. She is also known as Jagad-Yoni, meaning the "world womb."[60]

The Mediterranean and Macedonia

Delphi, the most sacred site of the ancient Greeks, who regarded the site as the center of the world, means "womb."[61] Inside the cave at Delphi was yet another womb symbol: the omphalos, a mound-shaped stone covered with a netlike pattern—the net was also a Grecian womb symbol. This site is steeped in lore of death, rebirth, and feminine psychic power.

In ancient Greece, the human womb was considered to be a supernatural and primeval deity. Menstrual blood was regarded as a magical substance, thought to be both indestructible and a means of magical protection.[62]

The most commonly discovered Gnostic Grecian ritual amulet is shaped like a uterus. This amulet has been discovered bearing inscriptions of deities from many different origins, including Egyptian, Jewish, and Babylonian.[63]

In the four-thousand-year-old burial mounds of Kanzanlak, Bulgaria, Thracian kings were buried in hill-tombs for their return to the Womb of the Earth Goddess at the time of death.[64]

The Maltese Hal Saflieni Hypogeum, is an underground tomb with dozens of womb shaped chambers, decorated with red ochre spirals and disks. The ancient Maltese carried forward the Neolithic tradition of underground womb chamber burials to bring regeneration through the womb of the Goddess.[65]

Judeo-Christian Tradition

In the Semitic tradition, Ashtoreth/Astarte is a goddess frequently mentioned in the Old Testament in connection with Baal. Her name literally translates as "womb" or "that which comes from the womb."[66]

St. Augustine referred to the baptismal font as "mother church's uterus" and the baptism as a second birth.[67] He also claimed that the womb was the place where human merged with divine.[68]

John Chrysostom, Archbishop of Constantinople, born in 349 CE, lauded the "milky liquid of the [baptismal] font" as the womb of the mother. And, baptism was considered both a womb and a tomb—a death and rebirth.[69]

Russia and Eastern Europe

The Russian matryoshka—the "doll within dolls"—comes from the ancient Ugrian Goddess Jumala who contains all things within her womb. Originally the matryoshka was a sacred idol of the Mother God, made of pure gold, kept in sacred forest groves. Worshippers left gold offerings on a tree, and when enough gold was collected another outer casing of her body would be forged. Treasure hunters in the Urals say this "Golden Mother" still exists, now hidden by her devotees.[70]

In Hungarian folklore, it is said that the fairy race and the human race were birthed from the womb of Cygnus. The head of the celestial swan was known as "dance of the fairies" and the tail was known as "turning of the fairies." It was said to be home to Ilona, the Mother of Life.[71]

Northern Europe

There is evidence of omphalos-like structures in Europe at the site of Chartres cathedral that existed prior to its construction. The mounds symbolized the pregnant womb of the earth.[72]

In France, Spain, Romania, Indonesia, central Asia (from Mongolia to the Ukraine), Ecuador, Colombia, Northern Ireland, and elsewhere, megalithic statues of women holding their vulvas open, often in a shamanic context, have been discovered.

Avebury stone circle in England represents a giant Earth/Cosmic Womb portal, described as symbolizing both "tomb and womb, and the Cave of the Dead" (see fig. 5.3 on the following page). Experts say the north circle was set aside for winter rituals for the dead, as they returned back to the Great Mother, and the south circle was used for spring "regeneration and renewal" rituals, connected to the birthing of life.[73]

Reclaiming Our Lost Womb Cosmology

As Womb Consciousness returns, we are left with the legacy of the past five thousand years of disconnection from the feminine vibration—and are now being guided to pick up the fragments of the womb religion and begin to weave them back together again. In doing so, we are weaving our own fragmented souls back together, remembering and reclaiming the lost feminine knowledge that has been banished for too long.

The spiritual traditions born in this patriarchal era have lost touch with the womb cosmologies, with the knowledge of the natural cycles of creation and dissolution, especially within the female body. Our true spiritual gifts can only flourish when grounded firmly in the fertile soil of a mother consciousness that honors the human mothers that birth us and the Earth Mother that sustains us.

As we begin to piece together the many lost fragments of the womb religions, scattered across myth and time, we begin to glimpse the big picture of what we have lost. The truth is startling; it is so *huge* that it can be difficult for us to fully conceive of

Fig. 5.3. Avebury stone circle and womb mandala, England.
(Photo by Nicholas Mann. From *Avebury Cosmos,* Moon Books, 2011)

it—along with all the miraculous gifts waiting to be reclaimed. Womb Consciousness is the mystery of the mystery schools, it is the secret many have died to protect or procure. It goes far beyond simple balance or rights for women. The pilgrimage into the womb is a journey back to love, to wholeness, to the root of all creation.

The traditions of the ancient Womb Mysteries were kept alive by a sacred red thread that secretly wove through many eras and cultures, hidden from the general public and known only to initiates—from the Eleusinian Mysteries, to the lost feminine Shakti teachings of Jesus and Magdalene, to the medieval troubadour traditions of Amor, to the Cathar initiations into agape, through the great artistic movements of the Renaissance and the pre-Raphaelites.

In the early twentieth century, poet and feminine visionary H. D. (Hilda Doolittle), a close friend of D. H. Lawrence and Ezra Pound, experienced her Womb Awakening after childbirth. She describes this living tradition of Womb

Enlightenment from her own visionary experiences. She calls awakening a "vision of the womb," saying, "Vision is of two kinds—vision of the womb and vision of the brain. The brain and womb are both centers of consciousness, equally important."[74] She described how uniting these two gates of awareness is necessary for a new spiritual birth, to be "born again."

She then reveals the secret at the center of the Womb Mysteries—"This is the mystery of Demeter, the Earth Mother. The body of the Eleusinian initiate had become one with the earth, as his soul had become one with the seeds enclosed in the earth."[75]

This return to Womb Consciousness holds the power to transform the world. In the words of H. D., "[It] could turn the whole tide of human thought, could direct lightning flashes of electric power to slash across and destroy the world of dead thought. Two or three people gathered together in the name of truth, beauty, [Womb]* consciousness could bring the whole force of this power back into the world."[76]

Are you ready to be a Grail bearer for this sacred red thread of wisdom?

WOMB ORACLES SHARE
Rebirth in the Cauldron of Wisdom

I journey on a panther, then fly with raven wings. I know the way. The stars are like stepping-stones. I arrive at the World Tree. I go into a circle of sunlight in the forest and I roll around. I roll on my back like an animal and I scratch my back. I have whiskers and a nose. There are clusters of beautiful nasturtiums and I decide to give them to the World Tree as an offering. I have a little basket and I am gathering the nasturtiums, pansies, snowdrops, and bluebells. I gather them into a beautiful posy, add fern leaves, and tie them into a small bunch.

I see the World Tree. I lay the flowers right at the roots of the World Tree. I put them in there so they're safe. And as that happens a doorway opens in the roots, like a dark vulva, which dilates and gets bigger. I think I can fit in it, but I have to crawl inside on my hands and knees and it's dark and damp. I get all earth on my hands and knees and it smells loamy and fertile. I crawl down and down, down this tunnel, on my hands and knees. I have a tail, and that helps. As I come down there's a hole with a rope in it. I have to shimmy down the rope, and I shimmy and shimmy and shimmy, until it starts twirling and twirling and twirling—like strands or spirals of DNA. I arrive suspended above the Cauldron of Wisdom. There are crones gathered all around the Cauldron of Wisdom. I ask if I can sip from the Cauldron of Wisdom. "Anything you want, my dear," they reply, laughing. They begin to

---

Womb is our insert, replacing the word over-mind.

lower me into the cauldron, laughing again, saying, "The cauldron's sipping you! Time to rebirth from the earth." I swim deep in the cauldron. It is full of green dragons. There are earth dragons and water dragons and we swim around together. When I'm fully soaked, the crones pull me out. They give me the gift of tongues, the gift of wands, the gift of words, the poetry of the birds: "You are our daughter, lover, sister, mother—birth well, my dear."

S.B.

The Cave of the Divine Mother

I entered a cave by a waterfall, and walked down a tunnel that widened into a rounded area with a large well in the center. Over the well the cave ceiling was open to the sky and rain was falling lightly onto the water. The bottom of the pond was covered with solid gold coins. On the other side of the well was an open door to a room glowing with firelight. Inside was a desk in the center, and behind were tall shelves filled with rolls of parchment, extending back beyond where I could see. And a full-length mirror was standing near the left side wall. A woman with long red hair and a forest green dress came over to me from the right side of the desk. She was the record keeper. She put a delicate gold crown on my head. I turned toward the mirror and saw my reflection with long dark wavy hair and a crimson red, medieval-style dress. Then a stream of light language was given to me.

H.S.

Shawl of Stars

The deer appeared to take me into the cave; I walked naked, vulnerable, and surrendered, and I felt completely safe. Tears streamed down my face as I whispered "mama, mama," feeling my deep longing for Her. I felt the presence of the Great Mother. It surrounded and enfolded me, like a big shawl of stars. I asked her to tell me more about my Womb name and She said that it was the energy of gentle fierceness and fierce gentleness.

V.M.

SPIRAL 6

WOMB SYMBOLOGY

The Lost Feminine Holy Grail

She bore the Perfection of Paradise, both root and branch. That was a thing called the Grail . . . for the Grail was the fruit of blessedness, such abundance of the sweetness of the world that its delights were very like what we are told of the Kingdom of Heaven.

Parzival, a Grail romance by
Wolfram von Eschenbach

FROM THE CHALICE OF CHRIST to the Cauldron of Ceridwen, and the Kabbalistic Cup of Blessings, there is a lost Holy Grail in many spiritual traditions. In Africa, Polynesia, New Zealand, and other places, the womb was symbolized as the calabash. The Waitaha, a legendary race that preceded the indigenous Maori peoples of New Zealand, were known as the People of the Gourd, the Carriers of the Water of Life. The Womb Mysteries are often symbolized by legends of a Sacred Feminine vessel that contains the essence of life, renewal, and immortality. This motif is a doorway into the lost feminine soul of the world and the quest to reclaim her and redeem the land.

Grail legends were also entwined with the secrets of witchcraft and the immortal Isle of Apples, known as Avalon, and the Ladies of the Garter and the Ladies of the Lake, a Grail mythology that was celebrated right through to the Pre-Raphaelite movement.

The Grail symbology spoke of a boon-bestowing magical Chalice that had the power to inspire, enchant, and transform the knights who quested for it. But the stories provided no easy answers or directions to the Holy Grail—for, as in all feminine mystery traditions, it was a riddle and the magic doorway of the Womb of Infinity.

Feminine consciousness is a realm we can enter but not grasp. She pours her blessings on those who come to her in the spirit of surrender and service. If we undertake the quest in order to use or control her, then her doors stay closed—and the world remains a wasteland of fallen power, and our psyche is separated from its source.

The Grail Womb: Mystical Chalice of Creation

With the suppression of the feminine religions, the ancient teachings of the Grail lineages were encoded in myth, story, and symbol, cunningly hidden in art and architecture, and carved into the very cathedrals of the religions that supplanted the Old Ways—waiting for the time when the world was ready to enter the Grail Castle again.

The popular Grail legends emerged from Welsh lore of a mystical cauldron and were alluded to in the Mabinogion. The theme was later taken up in the English poem *Sir Gawain and the Green Knight* and by Thomas Mallory in *La Morte d'Arthur,* in 1470.

It was in twelfth- and thirteenth-century Europe, at the French court of Champagne, that these Grail legends began to be woven into Christian mythology—despite their distinctly heretical flavor. It is no coincidence that the Grail romances of Chretien de Troyes and the songs of the troubadors arose from the South of France—the heartlands of heresy—where Mary Magdalene was revered. Carrying the mantle of Mari-Isis and the Feminine Christ, Magdalene is deeply connected to these mysterious and elusive Grail legends, which were feminine in nature, speaking in hidden code of a lost knowledge.

These myths, first created by the Grail troubadours and heretics, were later rewritten by the Catholic Church. The Holy Grail became the Cup of Christ, the chalice that Jesus drank from in the last supper, or the vessel that caught his blood during the crucifixion. The similarities in shape with the female womb are apparent in fig. 6.1. The Holy Grail was usually depicted as an ornate chalice, similar to Catholic eucharist chalices that held the red wine of communion, symbolic of the blood of Christ. However, the idea of the blood of God originated first in the ancient womb religions as the menstrual blood of the Goddess. Her sacred yoni portal was symbolized by the fish.

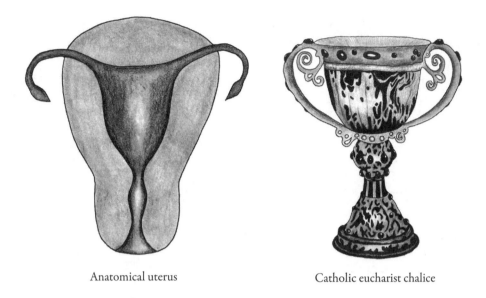

Anatomical uterus   Catholic eucharist chalice

Fig. 6.1. Womb as the Holy Grail

(Illustrations by Natvienna Hanell)

The cup that contains blood is deeply suggestive of the womb and the healing powers of menstrual blood, a mystical blood that has the power to redeem and renew. This feminine wisdom, often symbolized by wine or bread, was appropriated into the Christian Cup of Thanksgiving used in the Eucharist, where the body of Christ is eaten, symbolized by bread, and his blood drank, symbolized by red wine.

> *The cup of blessing which we bless, is it not the communion*
> *of the blood of Christ? The bread that we break, is it not the*
> *communion in the body of Christ?*
> CORINTHIANS 10:16

Joan of Arc's champion, the Grail King René D'Anjou even possessed a red chalice inscribed with the words "Whoever drinks from this cup shall see God, whoever drinks it in one draft will see Mary Magdalene," hinting at coded Grail Womb lore.

The symbolism of the womb chalice as the baptismal font, the fountain of life, can still be seen in Christian rites to this day. Officially, the baptismal font represents the virgin womb of the Catholic Church. Yet a traditional baptismal liturgy reads, *Ab immaculato divini fontis utero in novam renata creaturam progenies coelestis emergat,* which literally translates as, "From the immaculate divine fountain of

Fig. 6.2. Alchemical baptism in the bridal chamber of the womb font, from the manuscript *Les Grandes Heures du duc de Berry,* ca. 1400

the womb, this creature is reborn; from this womb font a celestial child emerges renewed."

The writings of the early Gnostic Christians confirm this association. They described their religion as *Synesaktism*—another word for *agape*—which means "the way of Shaktism," a variation of the ancient pre-Vedic tantric womb practices of India.[1]

There was also a heretical lineage, which included the Cathars, that interpreted the Grail myth as a conception tale of the *sang-raal*—the royal blood of a child created by the union of Jesus and Mary Magdalene who escaped to France and Britain to avoid persecution.

While the story of a bloodline may be true, the diffusion of similar myths and stories connected to the womb, across many times and lands, suggests that the wisdom the Grail legends contained ran much deeper than just a physical lineage of Jesus.

It was a *lost knowledge* rather than just a lost bloodline.

The author of one of the first Grail romances, Robert de Boron, writing between 1190 and 1199 CE, stated that his inspiration for the nature of the Grail came from a "great book," whose secrets had been revealed to him.[2]

Legends of a lost book of wisdom abound, including one written by Jesus himself, or possibly Jesus and Magdalene together, called The Book of Love. Could this have been a magical treatise on cosmic womb wisdom?

Alpha and Omega: Womb Portals of the Mother

On the two-thousand-year-old Catholic eucharist chalice of Saint Dennis of France (shown in fig. 6.1), the letters inscribed on the base, flanking a haloed Christ, are alpha and omega, in reference to Jesus as "the alpha and the omega, the beginning and the end—all which is, which was, and which is to come." A similar line is seen in the Gnostic poem "The Thunder, Perfect Mind," found in the Nag Hammadi scrolls: "I am the First and the Last, the Alpha and the Omega," which is said to represent the feminine voice of Sophia. A similar line is found yet again, more than one thousand years earlier, etched in the temple of Isis at Sais in Egypt: "I am all that is, was, or ever will be," said to be the words of the goddess herself. But what is the origin of this phrase?

Hathor: The Horned Goddess

The letters alpha and omega are the first and last letters of the Greek alphabet, the parents of the modern Latin letters *A* and *O*. They symbolically represent the womb portals of the beginning and end of the known universe. In the Semitic languages, the first letter, *A* or aleph, was pictured as a bull's head, cow's head, or ox head, which was one of the earliest symbols of the Great Mother.

The horned head of the ox was synonymous with fertility—the life-generating fertility of the feminine principle in its cow form, as well as the earthly masculine sexual energies of the bull. In Egypt, the original Mother Goddesses Hathor and sometimes Isis were depicted with head and horns of a cow, and were associated with the breast milk of the all-nourishing mother. Visually, the symbol of the ox head is almost identical with an anatomical drawing of the uterus with fallopian tubes, and uterine anatomy is still described by modern Western doctors as "two-horned" (see fig. 6.3). In Sumeria, the ox head was drawn as a down-pointing triangle, the universal symbol of the yoni, woman, and womb. In the psyche of the ancient womb cultures, alpha represented the birth womb, the original Creatrix of humans and the cosmos.

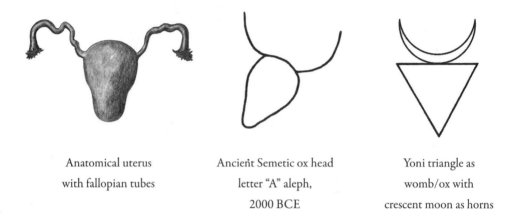

Anatomical uterus
with fallopian tubes

Ancient Semetic ox head
letter "A" aleph,
2000 BCE

Yoni triangle as
womb/ox with
crescent moon as horns

Fig. 6.3. Early Neolithic womb symbols
(Illustrations by Natvienna Hanell and Heather Skye)

Omega, the "Great O," represented the Great Round, the cosmic womb of dissolution and rebirth, to which we return upon death. Life is a great circle that begins with the birthing womb and ends with a return to the Great Womb when we die, represented by the womb of the earth, or the Celestial Womb of the cosmos.

As an archetypal symbol, this primordial cosmic womb is given expression as the Great Round, the cosmic egg, or the ouroboros serpent whose tail cycles back into its own mouth, completing the round. Examples are shown in fig. 6.4.

Mary Magdalene and the Neanderthal Legacy

For thousands of years parallel spiritual traditions coexisted, as the feminine way continued onward, even as she was being uprooted by the emerging patriarchy. The temples of the Goddess rubbed shoulders with new religions, and even the

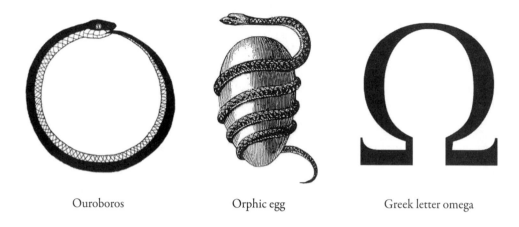

Ouroboros   Orphic egg   Greek letter omega

Fig. 6.4. Womb of life: The Great Feminine Round

(Uroboros illustration by Natvienna Hanell)

indigenous peoples felt this shift, as new ideologies were threaded into their primal cosmologies—and gradually the womb symbols lost their original fragrance.

One of the last icons of the womb religion was Mary Magdalene, who became the secret feminine figurehead of a prehistoric religion that was forced to go underground but kept its story alive through art and myth in the symbols of the Holy Grail.

The Neanderthal womb shamans depicted honorific religious symbols of *V*s and *M*s to celebrate the generative feminine womb portal, carving them artistically into bones and painting them onto cave walls. These same *V* and *M* symbols continued to be etched into the stone figurines and clay pottery of the Neolithic age beginning around 8000 BCE. Mary Magdalene eventually inherited this symbolic Grail legacy of the Neanderthal womb religion and became the treasure keeper for these ancient feminine symbols.

Her initials, MM, were drawn in symbolic ways in medieval texts, for those with the "eyes to see," and she was linked to ancient traditions that included Egyptian goddesses, fertility rituals, mermaids, sirens, and the Sheela na gig.

The *V* symbolizes the female vulva, the pubic triangle, the womb of life. Closely related is the symbol *M,* which is the vulva (V) with outstretched legs on either side, representing the female birthing position and the open legs of female sacred sexuality, as well as a wave of the waters of life.

During Neolithic times, the *M* symbol became fused with the image of the sacred frog goddess with her open legs. She represented the regenerative power of the womb and was also associated with the traditional squatting position of childbirth.

In Egypt the frog goddess was known as Heket; her symbol was the *M,* which was also part of the Egyptian hieroglyph for "water." In the old European tradition the Greek goddess Hekate was also called Baubo, meaning "frog." The frog goddesses were represented as a face with big frog eyes, over an *M* symbol. Frogs were associated with primordial birth magic and gestating in amniotic waters, and represented fertility; legend had it that if a frog crossed a woman's path she would soon be pregnant.[3]

The symbolism of the fertile frog goddess was passed along to the Celtic Sheela na gig—a froglike female figure squatting down and holding open the gates of her supernatural vulva, an invitation to her fertile womb sanctuary. Fittingly, her vulva iconography was carved on the entrances of many early churches in Celtic Christianity, reminding all comers that they were entering the sacred womb church.

The origin of the name Sheela na gig has long been a mystery, as it is unrelated to any language used in the Celtic lands. Yet, at the temple of Erech in Sumeria—sacred land of the goddess Inanna—temple priestesses who held the high office of "sacred harlot" were called *nu-gug,* meaning "the pure and immaculate ones," suggesting that Sheela na gigs are an echo of the womb priestess tradition.[4]

The womb symbols embodied in the *M* were also associated with Egyptian "skirt-raising" rituals, where women would ceremonially raise their skirts and show their vulvas to ensure the fertility of the earth. In 60 BCE Herodotus wrote about an Egyptian skirt-raising ritual at the Serapheum temple in Memphis, called the *ana suromai.* These feminine shamanic rituals continued into the twentieth century in rural Europe, where women would show their vulvas to growing flax crops, saying, "Please grow as high as my genitals are now." The yoni was a sacred talisman with mystical properties of regeneration, growth, and abundance.[5]

Magical ancient skirt-raising rituals connected to the frog goddess also explain the appearance of Hekate in the Eleusinian Mysteries in the underworld journeys of Demeter and Persephone. As Demeter loses hope of finding her lost daughter, Hekate appears as Baubo—the frog goddess—and lifts her skirt, laughing and revealing her cosmic vulva. Demeter throws her head back and roars in laughter too, and from this mystical feminine rite finds a renewed fertility of hope and descends down into the Womb of Earth to reunite with her daughter, the maiden of spring.

Mary Magdalene and Mother Mary continued this ancient goddess worship and womb symbolism tradition *within the iconography of the Christian Church.* They were both represented by the ancient double *M* symbol, which was also the pictograph for water and mermaids.

Magdalene, in particular, became the torchbearer of an earthy feminine tradition, where sexuality and the body were revered for their life-bearing powers. Her supposed sinfulness became a thinly veiled disguise to attribute to her all the powerful, magical qualities of a sexually awakened womb shamaness and the forbidden allurements of primal fleshly pleasures. In the *Passion of Aras* (written in 1430 CE), Magdalene's character speaks the words, "My proud little breasts, my beautiful vermillion petticoat which shows off my body. My flesh is rose and as white as a fairy's. I am upright and flourishing, and I am available to all," alluding to her sacred vulva, symbolized as a "beautiful vermillion petticoat," the fertile throne of the goddess.[6]

Forbidden Pathway of the Red Priestess

The roots of the Grail Womb legends spiral down time into the ancient Neanderthal womb religion, passing through the forbidden path of Celtic, Egyptian, and Tantric red magic practiced by priestesses in secret traditions of feminine folk magic.

Egypt—with its magical priestesses of Hathor and Isis—held the secret of the Grail, which was passed down from the prehistoric Womb Mysteries of mother Africa. These magical feminine traditions were the true source of Egypt's astounding spiritual power.

The male cults of the pharaoh god-kings and elite priestly caste arrived in Egypt around 3000 BCE, but long before that time there was a mysterious feminine shamanic culture, whose cosmology and mythology was wild, vividly alive, sexual, and dreamlike.

Sexual symbology was inseparable from religious symbology. Sex was sacred. Sex, birth, death, rebirth, personal transformation, shamanic journeys, and the alchemical act of merging into oneness consciousness with another all happened through the portal of the yoni-womb. The womb was both the religion and the doorway to spiritual power.

The Two Ladies of Egypt: The Red and White Sexuality

The physical land of Egypt is conceived of as a female body, divided into an upper and lower half—the two ladies. The upper half is the white crown of her heart, breast milk and heavenly celestial qualities. It is the land of the vulture sky-goddess Nekhbet, who escorts dead spirits back to the cosmic womb. The lunar mysteries reside here, in their soft, silver light, along with the energy of Sothis (Sirius), the brightest star in the night sky, and the soul of Isis.

Lower Egypt is the red crown of her sexuality, womb and vulva. It is the land of the cobra goddess Wadjet, primordial sexual energy, and the land of the fierce lioness Sekhmet who represents the scepter of female life-force energy and authority, *sekhem*.

The ancient goddess Hathor was known as the Mistress of the Red Robe, Lady of the Vulva, and Womb of Horus and was the goddess of love, sexuality, childbirth, and the feminine temple arts. Her priestesses wore patterned red dresses, red scarves, and beaded *menat* necklaces that doubled as musical shakers. In the inner sanctum of the Hathor temple, a troupe of red-robed priestesses with diaphanous red veils would move slowly in rhythm, perfectly synchronized in their mesmerizing, snake-like movements, shaking their beaded rattles and sistrums, chanting otherworldly hymns to the goddess.

The priestesses of Hathor were oracles, dream interpreters, midwives, dancers, and musicians. Her temples contained rooms for the mixing of perfumed oils and cosmetics, treasuries of jewels and musical instruments, and birthing chambers where pregnant mothers were welcomed and assisted by the trained priestess-midwives.

Ritual Magic and Symbols

Symbolic ritual magic was at the heart of the feminine folk religion. Ivory birthing wands were inscribed with archaic, mystical feminine symbols, magical spells, and fantastic deities that suggest the existence of a lost world of oral tradition unknown to modern scholars—but still rich with imaginal power in the feminine dreamtime.[7]

The Daughters of Isis priestesses worked with the *shen* womb ring of immortality to shift the fabric of time and to send protection to those in their journey of rebirth. The *ankh,* a womb of life symbol, was used to magically transmit life-force energy—often into the lunar portal of the Alta-major, located at the base of the skull.

The *tiet* menstrual Blood of Isis symbol was a powerful protective amulet, often carved into red jasper pendants and painted on the interior lids of coffins and sarcophagi to assist the dead in their journey of rebirth.

Temple priestesses often had striking web patterns tattooed on their abdomens, encircling their wombs in a net, and diamond tattoolike markings appeared on the thighs of female fertility figurines, suggesting sexually stylized body art among priestesses. The most famous example of shamanic tattoo art was discovered on the mummy of Amunet, high priestess of Hathor, in 1891 by French Egyptologist Eugène Grébaut.

Shamanic Womb Mysteries of Egypt

The goddesses and gods of the old religion represented the elemental Shakti of the natural world and were called *netjers* (source of the word "nature"). They were fantastic, otherworldy blends of animal and godlike beings who could shape-change at will—such as Ta-Weret, the primordial hippopotamus birthing goddess, with her bottom half a crocodile and paws of a lion, who was a fierce protectress of women and children.

Female sexual energies expressed the womb power of red or white magic, and priestesses honored the wild lioness Sekhmet and the sensual cat goddess Bast. Sekhmet is the solar, dynamic, active feminine energy. She is the sexual initiator, the pursuer, the uninhibited, the dissolver, the queen of magic red menstrual blood. In patriarchal times her image was polarized and demonized into a wrathful, destructive goddess of divine retribution because she threatened the status quo. Similar to the Hindu Kali, she was known as "she who dances on blood" and was identified with the color red.

Bast, the cat goddess, was one of the most loved goddesses in Egypt. She was the lunar face of Sekhmet, associated with sensuality, playfulness, erotic pleasure, and love. She could be open and surrendered but also activated and energized. She was beautiful, fragrant, and adorned, her name written with the symbol of a jar of anointing oil or perfume—similar to the anointrix Mary Magdalene and her alabaster jar (see plate 9). The annual festival of Bast was the most popular in all of Egypt. Women would dance, drink, sing, make music, and display their yonis in wild abandon, celebrating their feminine power.

Red Enchantress:
Tantric Goddess of Magic and Seduction

Around the same time, in the indigenous feminine shamanic traditions of India, the red magic of the Goddess was also celebrated for her erotic powers of allurement and magnetism. Called Kurukullā, "cave dweller"—later to become Red Tara—she was the goddess who wielded the "unconquerable and irresistible force of love." This was the feminine power of magnetism and the creative potential held within desire and longing. The color red predominated in her rites—ceremonial daleth triangle doorways were traced out on the earth with red vermillion powder or menstrual blood, priestesses wore red flowing robes and were adorned with red flowers, altars were draped with red fabric.

The original goddess of the red left-hand path was the Grail bearer of life force, brimming with erotic passion and the ecstatic seduction of surrendering to divine love.

She is described as the pulsing, creative, ecstatic *spanda*—the heartbeat of creation: "Kurukullā is a goddess with unlimited powers of enchantment. Her voluptuous body is bright glowing red, the hue of passion and desire. Glistening with ruby radiance."[8]

Womb Mandalas: Sacred Maps of the World

From the depths of these ancient feminine shamanic traditions, different rituals, practices, and "womb gate technologies" emerged in order for initiates to commune with, merge into, and pass through the cervical gateway of the Goddess. Meditating on magical symbols of the womb created a portal into awakened states of lunar feminine consciousness—and this developed into the art of sacred mandalas.

Mandala is an ancient, pre-Vedic word that originally meant "moon door" or "gate of the great feminine circle" to the ancient shamanic mother cultures of India and Tibet, and later came to mean "sacred circle" or "container of essence" in Sanskrit.

Mandalas were originally associated with the womb and the cosmology of the feminine Great Round. Across the megalithic cultures of the world, mandalas represented a map of the universe, a cosmic order based around a central point or *bindu,* symbolizing the Cosmic Womb, along with the four cardinal directions. Through the spiritual device of the mandalas, practitioners of the early religions could access progressively deeper levels of the unconscious, into the womb of the deep feminine psyche, and eventually travel through the mysterious central moon gate, merging into states of oneness consciousness with the mother cosmos.

The first mandalas were living temples built as great circles of standing stones called *menhirs,* and stone gates, known as *dolmens*. Standing stone circles and dolmens have been found across the world from the British Isles, to the Middle East and Africa, across all of Europe and Asia, into Melanesia, and even extending to the Americas.

The female body, with the Great Round of her pregnant womb-belly and central bindu point of the navel, was the original circle, church, and sacred precinct—a model for later symbolic representations of the mandala across the world. (See fig. 6.5.)

These original stone circle mandalas later evolved into the paintings, etchings, or sand drawing mandalas that are found today, not only in the Buddhist religion, but also in indigenous shamanic traditions in the Americas, Australia, and other parts of the world.

Although Tibetan Buddhism covered over much of the symbology of the indigenous womb religions from which it was birthed, some mandalas still reveal the older feminine cosmology. In the Tibetan Wheel of Life paintings, the mandala, representing the entire cosmos, existed in the womb-belly of Srinmo, the original Tibetan

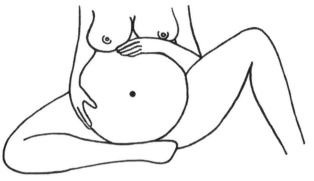

Ancient symbol for Womb,
primordial creation, seed of creation,
eye; later: gold, sun, day

Aztec mandala

Rose window at
Chartres Cathedral, France

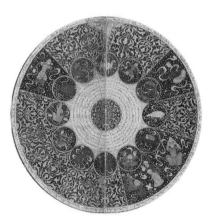

Persian astrological mandala

Chinese zodiac mandala

Fig. 6.5. Womb as world: the original mandala

(Illustrations, first column: by Natvienna Hanell, Keepscases, Wellcome Images;
top two in second column by Heather Skye)

world mother, who later became demonized and "staked" down as a bloodthirsty monster or witch.

Yet her dragon wisdom remained, and the two main forms of Tibetan mandalas are *Garbha-dhatu* (Sanskrit, meaning "womb world") and *Vajra-dhatu* ("diamond world"). The Tibetan womb-world mandala symbolizes the energy of movement from the unified one out to the many, the birth of the manifest world. The diamond-world mandala symbolizes the return from the many to the one: the dissolution of the physical world back through the scintillating diamond of the Celestial Womb.

Mandalas commonly use the ancient symbol of the lotus, or are formed in the shape of a lotus, which is symbolic of the yoni-womb. The Tibetan goddess Padma, meaning "Lady Lotus," and also known as Lakshmi, was a primordial creator goddess from whose yoni-lotus the world was birthed into being. Not only did the manifest world spring forth from her lotus-womb, but also the Buddha and later divine incarnations of his shamanic wisdom, such as Padmasambhava (literally, "lotus-born"), were born from the lotus-womb of the Great Creator Goddess as well.

Kali's Womb Gate

The Sri Yantra and Kali Yantra of India and Tibet also reveal themselves as yoni-womb gateways of consciousness. Like mandalas, yantras are considered to be magical spiritual devices, and are associated with looms, as they weave together realities in order to birth new tapestries of creation on the spiritual levels. A yantra is said to be a house of God, or a place where God dwells, accessed by traveling through the central bindu point. The Sri Yantra and Kali Yantra in particular make use of the sacred yoni-womb symbols of the down-pointing triangle, lotus, and the central bindu point of the cosmic womb. The Sri Yantra also incorporates the masculine upward-pointing triangle in symbolic sacred union with the feminine downward-pointing triangle. Examples can be seen in fig. 6.6. Yantras were often used in yoga, which means "union."

Goddess Eye

Cervical Cosmic Eye of Horus

Eyes were also a symbolic gateway to the Womb of the Goddess. The ancient symbol of the circle with a central dot was originally a womb symbol with diverse meanings, including the ideas of the cosmic egg, the seed point of creation, the cervical womb eye, and the "sun behind the sun" or cosmic black hole of creation. (See fig. 6.7.) Later, the

Kali Yantra

Sri Yantra

Yoni, womb, down,
female, birther,
earth/water, lunar,
descent of spirit into matter

Masculine, lingam,
Cosmic Womb,
rebirth, air/fire, solar, celestial,
ascent of matter to spirit

Star of David,
sacred union,
Masculine-Feminine,
male-female balance

Fig. 6.6. The sacred triangle
(Illustration at top left and in bottom row by Heather Skye)

all-seeing feminine eye was adopted to become the symbol of a masculine consciousness that had separated from its mother-origins. It was depicted in Egypt as the masculine Eye of Horus, or in Tibet as the "Wisdom Eyes" of the Buddha.

Lunar Eye of the Serpent Goddess

Originally, the Egyptian Eye of Horus/Eye of Ra (see fig. 7.4, page 108) belonged to Wadjet, the female serpent goddess who is the right eye of Ra, Horus, Atum, and other male sun gods. She is regarded as the most powerful of all the deities, representing deep feminine perception, womb gnosis, and sexual creative potency of the gateway of creation. An incredible myth tells the story of how the Eye of the Goddess was usurped.

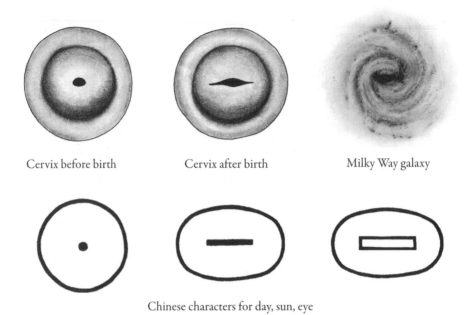

Cervix before birth   Cervix after birth   Milky Way galaxy

Chinese characters for day, sun, eye

Fig. 6.7. The cervical eye: guardian of the womb threshold
(Illustrations of cervix by Natvienna Hanell; Chinese characters
and Milky Way by Heather Skye)

In the old days of Egypt, Wadjet, the Eye of the Goddess, was both the sun and the moon. She took her rightful place, in her fiery solar form, as the right eye of the male sun gods. Together they lived in partnership and balance. However, as time passed the sun god grew more arrogant and powerful. One day the god Atum realized that he had lost his children. He had taken his eye off them, so to speak, and they had wandered into the darkness of the underworld. The Eye Goddess went down to retrieve them, shining her light into the dark abyss, birthing the light of the first dawn.

When she returned, rather than being praised and honored, she was shocked to find that Atum had discarded her, and replaced her instead with an artificial new masculine eye in an attempt to bring himself glory. In a fury she exiled herself to the wild deserts and, like Lilith of Mesopotamian myth, became "The Distant Goddess" or the lost feminine goddess. Humanity is born from her tears of grief and anger.

Quickly, the sun god Atum becomes vulnerable and "blind" without his feminine eye. He realizes he cannot live without her and pleads for her return. She eventually agrees, and he reinstates her on his forehead as the Uraeus serpent of feminine vision and power, at the third eye chakra of the Vedic traditions. From this time forward all kings would wear the Uraeus serpent headdress—the feminine eye of the moon—as a symbol of sovereignty, authority, and divine power granted by the goddess Wadjet.

Cervical Eye: Gateway of the Goddess

The Eye of the Goddess represents a power older than the sun gods. Her eye is the serpent of life and the cosmic cervical eye of creation; her pupil is a womb that births both gods and men.[9] (See fig. 7.4.) To gaze into the Eye of the Goddess is to gaze into the Great Womb eye who births and rebirths the world.

Across the world, shamans would pass through a womb-eye, known as God's Eye or a Diamond Eye, in order to journey in or out of spirit world. Shamanic journeying meant passing through the cosmic cervix. The Huichol God's-Eye paintings and yarn weavings symbolized the entrance into spirit world. They traditionally contained a central eye, called a *nierika,* which was known to be a yoni. They were created as womb portals for spiritual journeys, as womb-fertility amulets, and as tools to help call in the soul of a child during birth. They were sometimes gifted to Wirikuta, the sacred Huichol land of peyote, and the Womb of Creation. "Neirika are considered mirrors or portals to other worlds, allowing participants to visit Wirikuta, the Womb of Creation, to be healed and reborn."[10]

Among the Warlpiri of Australia, women weave very similar diamond-patterned fertility charms around a central cross. Called *makarra,* meaning "womb," "afterbirth," and "umbilicus,"[11] they are used as magical amulets in birth and rebirth ceremonies—another example of the cross-cultural importance of the yoni-womb portal in sacred rites.

Covenant of the Womb Ark

Similar womb symbology is seen in the Ark of the Covenant, which according to Old Testament descriptions, consists of two winged cherubim facing each other with outstretched wings. The design is modeled after the Egyptian motif of the embracing wings of Isis, whose tips form a diamond-shaped yoni portal. The name Nephthys, the twin sister of Isis, meant "Mistress of the Womb." Moses, who is said to have commissioned the building of the "Womb Ark," was born and raised in Egypt, and was rumored to be of noble or priestly blood. Moses was also associated with ancient feminine symbology of the serpent, which he raised on a brass cross in honor of Yahweh, who himself was originally depicted with mermaid-serpent legs. The name *ark* is derived from the ancient words *arche* or *argha,* referring to the feminine first cause or primeval feminine vibration of creation. It is likely that the spiritual secret of the Ark was originally a womb technology, and its true identity was later revised to be in keeping with patriarchal religious doctrine, and to obscure its feminine roots. See examples in figure 6.8.

Huichol God's Eye

Australian Aboriginal fertility
and female ceremonial amulet

Mayan Venus
yoni symbols

Yoni mudra

Ark of the Covenant:
the arche feminine first principle,
the argha feminine boat,
the winged gate

Dragon eye

Mayan birth from
tree of life

Fig. 6.8. Womb iconography: entering heaven's gate
(Illustration of Ark of the Covenant and Dragon eye by Heather Skye;
others by Natvienna Hanell)

Womb Cross and the Tree of Life

The cross—also known as the tree of life—was an ancient womb symbol. This symbol wove together the idea of an upperworld, middleworld, and lowerworld, with four corners of the manifested world, or four elements of creation, and the spiritual initiations of a spiral or labyrinth journey of rebirth into a central womb vortex.

The ancients believed that we *are* the tree of life; that our bodies, in connection with the spiral-portals of cosmos and earth, possess an incredible mystical power, when we know the keys to unlock its secrets. This pure creative essence does not live outside us but instead rests at the very heart of our physical and spiritual being.

In ancient indigenous European cultures, the tree of life was also considered a map of life. The eternal, formless Creator was represented in the center of the circle, and the four arms of the cross represented the four corners of the world: the four elements of air, fire, water, earth that Creator birthed from her central fifth element, the *quintessence* or womb. This tradition was kept alive by the Cathars of France, whose most holy symbol was a womb circle with an X drawn in the middle. The center point represented a cosmic doorway to infinity, around which the arms of the elements spin the world into creation and form.

In Nordic lore it was Yggdrasil, in Celtic traditions it was the World Spindle, and later the distinctive Celtic cross. For Druids it was the primal serpent or dragon wrapped around the sacred tree, which could also be symbolized by a wooden cross. In Native American tradition it was the four-petaled flower or cross, in Egyptian tradition the ankh, in Indian lore the swastika, and in Tibetan tradition the four-cornered mandala design with the central womb for Buddha to rebirth in. For Kabbalah it became the sephiroth, which depicted the dimensions of God. Finally, it emerged in Christian religious tradition as the tau or the crucifix that Jesus died on.

It was also symbolized by the Grail symbol of the red cross on top of a red heart, representing the Sacred Feminine heart—the womb—and her moon-blood flow. The physical heart is not actually "heart shaped"—yet a woman's free-flowing menstrual blood does make this exact imprint on her thighs, and is the hidden origin of the sacred "bleeding heart." This became the universal red heart symbol. Various womb cross symbols are shown in fig. 6.9.

Womb Cross of Resurrection

In esoteric Christ mysteries, Jesus did not die on a physical cross but was reborn and "Christed" through the "eye" of the Great Womb—symbolized by the cross.

We can reframe his death and resurrection journey as an initiatory event or

Celtic womb cross

Cathar womb cross

Navajo world lotus
womb cross

Worldwide
womb cross

Mayan
womb cross

Moon cross

Alchemical
womb
cross

Order of
the Golden
Dawn

Mayan
world cross

Spiraling cross
(swastika)

Egyptian ankh
symbol of life

Symbol of Venus,
woman

Mayan sacred
flower

Fig. 6.9. Womb cross: Sacred Feminine medicine wheel

(Illustrations: Celtic, Navajo, and Mayan crosses by Natvienna Hanell;
Cathar cross, Ankh, Venus, Worldwide and Moon crosses by Heather Skye)

spring rite, where Jesus experienced his great rebirth on a womb cross—either in the Cosmic or Earth Womb, or through his beloved's womb in sacred sexual rites.

The Apocalypse of Peter, a Gnostic text discovered at Nag Hammadi in 1945, shows Jesus "glad and laughing on the cross," and in Acts of John, Jesus is shown leading his disciples in a "round dance of the cross," chanting, singing, and hymning.[12] This bears great resemblance to the wisdom of the Old Ways, where the womb cross was the spindle upon which all of life was spun, and was celebrated as such.

Womb Church:
The Original Mystery School

Over time, sacred symbols of the yoni rebirthed into the symbols of Jesus, who—like Mary Magdalene—secretly became the repository for many of the symbols, ideas, and tools of a womb shaman. The sacred fish—now adopted by Christians as a sign of Jesus—was a yoni symbol dating back several thousand years, and was a part of the greater *vesica pisces* design, meaning the "sacred vessel of the fish." This encoded the mystery school teachings of the cosmic sexual union of the masculine and feminine in the central yoni-womb space, the almond-shaped *mandorla*. Audaciously, the glorious mandorla-yoni was often shown surrounding iconic pictures of Jesus and the Virgin Mary throughout Catholic imagery—imbuing them with a forgotten lunar magic.

"Church as Womb" symbology continued in Christian architecture up to the Middle Ages, as seen in the design of the Gothic cathedrals across Europe, which featured "hidden in plain sight" womb religion symbology of arched yoni entryways and Grail-rose stained-glass windows, at times with a Black Madonna mother goddess figure hidden in a dark underground crypt, symbolic of Earth's Womb. See fig. 6.10.

Symbols act directly on our deep feminine consciousness, singing like ancient mermaids, reminding us of the lost Grail. This legacy speaks anew to each generation—calling us back to the red ruby of remembrance. It reminds us that the symbols and rites of the Goddess, and the keys to her womb queendom, were taken by a theology that jailed her—stealing her sacred powers in order to dethrone her.

Authentic mystery schools and moon colleges sought to preserve the old teachings—and as they took their last breaths, they infused their Grail symbols into the new Christian religion, creating a secret passageway back into the Womb of Creation.

Is it not time we reclaimed our collective symbology and reenchanted our world?

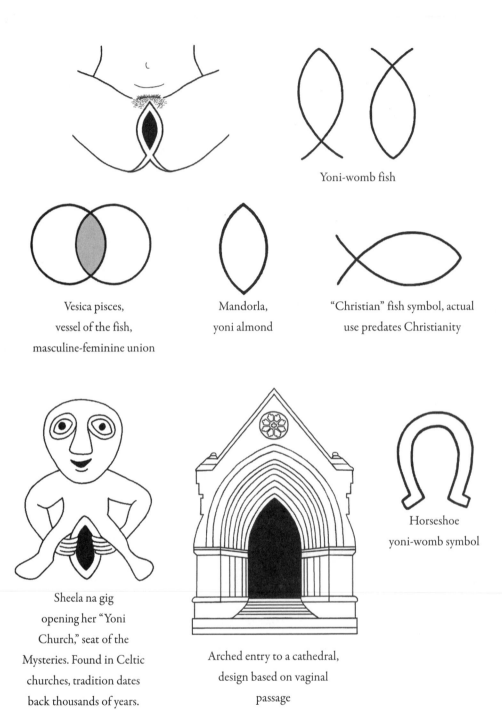

Yoni-womb fish

Vesica pisces,
vessel of the fish,
masculine-feminine union

Mandorla,
yoni almond

"Christian" fish symbol, actual
use predates Christianity

Sheela na gig
opening her "Yoni
Church," seat of the
Mysteries. Found in Celtic
churches, tradition dates
back thousands of years.

Arched entry to a cathedral,
design based on vaginal
passage

Horseshoe
yoni-womb symbol

Fig. 6.10. The great yoni doorway: entering the gateway to God.

(Illustrations by Natvienna Hanell and Heather Skye)

WOMB ORACLES SHARE

Descending to the Womb of the World

The crone stood at the edge of the woods on our land, as twilight poured over into darkness. She was wearing a black robe and a somber countenance. Her staff was made of bone and the knowing held in the bones. I felt fear creep into me. She beckoned me, turned round, and began walking deeper into the woods. I followed her. At a clearing in the woods, a round hole had been dug out. I instantly knew this hole was created to receive bones. It was a grave of sorts. I looked around for the bones to place in it, I could "see" them in my cosmic eye, but I could not find them.

I then realized the bones that were being asked for were within me. I did not want to get in that grave, not one bit. I felt very afraid. The crone said nothing.

I breathed a deep sigh, letting go into the death breath, and climbed in the hole.

Whoosh. As I tucked myself into the dark inner curve of the earth, She devoured me, with great force, in a devastating inward suck of breath, and down, down I went. I was traveling at great speed within great tree roots, traveling them like inner tubes. A dense, rich darkness surrounded me and engulfed me, as I descended.

I was not afraid anymore; the journey was rapid and full of orgasmic release. The further I descended, the more a vast cloak of primordial silence enveloped me. This deep stillness and silence had a distinct texture, like the velvet lining of the Womb.

Traveling through a luxurious darkness, loamy with fertility and potential, I finally slid down into a small cave at the center of the Earth. The crone was sat quietly. Her manner had softened, and she tended to a fire in the center with gentle movements. She didn't look up at me, but there was an unspoken bond between us.

I gathered myself and sat beside the fire. It was not a huge, dramatic fire. It was small and steady. The flames were full of glowing warmth and comfort. It was a fire you could come close too, right to the edge, without fear of being burned or hurt.

The crone and I sat together, in silence, looking into the gentle flames.

The atmosphere was undulating with warm waves of love. It was very relaxing, very simple, very homely. Just being there with the fire. Occasionally throwing on a stick, and tending to any stray sparks. Patterns of light danced on the cave walls.

Without warning I could distinctly feel the entire weight of Earth and all her people pressing down on us, as we huddled in the small cave. It was immense—like the feeling of looking into the sky at night, into the infinite universe. Except this infinity was now heavy with soil and bones and stories, weighing in on us.

The walls of the cave had taken on the circumference of the Earth, and I knew I could access anywhere in the world from this small space. Instinctively my awareness went to the valley beneath Mam Tor, Mother Mountain, where my father's body was buried, not yet thirteen moons within the ground. The crone nodded.

I could distinctly feel we were underneath his grave. Without warning the crone sucked in with deep inhalation, and pulled his body and bones through the bottom of the grave, down through the substructure of earth, and into the heart of the fire.

Silently we watched the flames flicker higher for a while, then die back down.

I now noticed a bench at the edge of the cave. Lying on it was the bloated, flaccid corpse of my mother, eyes staring like glass. As she was still alive, somewhere out there up on Earth's surface, this corpse represented my inheritance of loss. All the pain and suffering that had passed down the maternal line, into my own bones.

The crone huffed now, looking determined, as she struggled to drag this bloated collection of thoughtforms and feelings to the edge of the fire. With a great push, she hoisted it into the flames, as I looked on, somewhat disturbed and speechless.

We watched the flames gently do their work, flickering with tenderness and care.

I felt like an orphan—a cosmic orphan. The sensation of loss hit me in my stomach. I felt alone and little; all my safety was turned to ashes in the fire. Nothing was left.

Sitting with this feeling, watching the fire, the silence kept us company. As I stretched out into the arms of this silence, it whispered into my ear, reminding me our earth parents are temporal, that our true Parent is eternal and everywhere.

I accepted the wisdom of the silence, and the sadness and freedom it spoke of. Some time went by, measured only by the dimensions of infinite darkness.

Then the crone spoke without looking up, still gazing into the fire. "This is the center. This is the spark from which all your true creations are birthed. Tend this fire, always. Never forget this fire. Birth everything from this place."

Dazzled by the web of infinite pregnant potentials, I suddenly found myself back in bed. The crone was gone. The dark night was breathing out stars.

S.B.

SPIRAL 7

COSMIC WOMB AND EARTH WOMB

Gateways to Upperworld and Underworld

O moving force of Wisdom, you encircle the wheel of the cosmos,
You encompass all that is, all that has life, in one vast circle.
You have three wings: One unfurls aloft in the highest heights.
The second is solicitious of the earth.
Over, under and through all things whirls the third.

HILDEGARD VON BINGEN,
THE VIRTUE OF WISDOM

JOURNEYING BETWEEN the Earth Womb and Celestial Womb, through the secret gate of either the human womb or the womb of the soul, was the spiritual heart of feminine shamanic wisdom. It was known that to ascend, one first had to descend. These mystical descension and ascension rites unfolded in the depths of the psyche, the infinite feminine dreamtime, accessed by initiatory experiences such as sacred sexual union, ecstatic devotion, or soulful rapture—where union with the cosmic consciousness of Oneness creates spontaneous awakening.

Although these initiatory journeys were potently experienced during the processes of birth and death, as people journeyed by merkabas (vulvic chariots of light), boats, and swan flight between spirit and matter, these interdimensional womb paths were also traveled by living priestesses and shamans who took psychic death and rebirth journeys back to Source.

The triple-world model of many shamanic cultures was based on the holy trinity of the Cosmic Womb, the female womb, and the Womb of Earth, which were united holographically. The Cosmic Womb was known as heaven, the female womb as Eden or the "throne," and the Earth Womb as hell or the underworld. Originally, all three worlds were honored.

In Celtic traditions, the Earth and Cosmic Wombs were known respectively as lowerworld and upperworld, or Mother Earth and Father Sky. Hermetic belief taught "as above, so below," and most ancient cultures honored both the earth underworld *and* the starry cosmic upperworld, which were connected with each other by magical quantum wormholes, or womb holes, like a great circular ouroboros of wombs.

This triple-world system is reflected in the Hindu philosophy of the three gunas: *sattva,* the luminous, upperworld, ascending energy; *rajas,* the human world of creation; and *tamas,* the descending lowerworld that has its roots in darkness. In the Vedic text of Maitrayana Upanishad these gunas—the three qualities from which all creation proceeds—are described as birthing out from tamas, the primordial darkness of the womb. "All was *tamas:* It [the Supreme *Brahma*] decreed a change, and *tamas* took the complexion of *rajas;* and *rajas,* having been commanded once more, assumed the nature of *sattva.*"[1] The dark root was the mother of life.

The ascent to enlightenment could only be accomplished by first making a pilgrimage through the shining darkness of the womb: the culmination of this mystical ascension is to make the "shaman's return"—to descend back to earth and embody this living light in physical form.

Womb of the World: Descending Spiral Path

The spiral was a symbol of the womb, descent, and rebirth. In the earliest Paleolithic womb cultures the feminine journey was envisioned as a spiral path, a downward and inward movement along a nonlinear circle of dreamtime consciousness.

The first Paleolithic temple spaces were caves with serpentine passageways spiraling deep into the earth—sometimes marked with red handprints, often left-handed "moon ochre" imprints of women and children. Later cultures created ritual underground womb chambers, often with symbolic labyrinths carved into their entryway. Walking the circuitous or spiral path in or out was a movement through the birth canal, before merging into the center point of Womb Consciousness.

Other indigenous cultures spirit traveled along Grandmother Spider's labyrinthine web, or were swallowed by the great Rainbow Serpent, or the Great Fish of the biblical story of Jonah. See examples of these spirals in fig. 7.1. In Peru, the Incan

Labyrinth of
Crete, Greece

Hopi womb symbol,
place of emergence

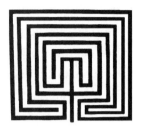

Hopi Mother
Earth symbol

Australian Aboriginal symbol:
hole, cave, well, home, rest,
water, breast, or stone

Triple spiral of
Newgrange
womb-tomb Ireland

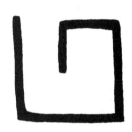

Ancient Hebrew "Beth"
pictogram; also Egyptian
hieroglyph: house, tent, in

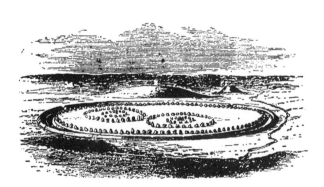

Reconstruction drawing of
Avebury, England

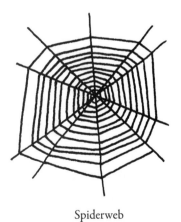

Spiderweb

Fig. 7.1. Labyrinths, spirals, and circles

(Line drawings by Heather Skye and Natvienna Hanell)

peoples built the spiritual temple of Moray, a set of terraced concentric circles heading downward into the womb-belly of the earth, shown in fig. 7.2.

God was in the soil and in the caves, and spirit was contacted by merging with the heart of matter. The womb religions knew the greatest spiritual secret and perennial wisdom of all time: that the true gate of heaven does not exist externally to us in a faraway paradise, it exists within us and within the body of Gaia. In their deepest essence, heaven and earth were not separated places—they were linked, one blending seamlessly into the other.

Shamanic journeys could take place in actual physical caves or underground chambers, or they could happen by drawing concentric circles and then psychically traveling through the portal. These ancient ideas were preserved in Aboriginal Australian cultures, who originally traveled *downward and inward* in their shamanic journeys. The pictogram for *cave, womb, home, water, down,* and *in* was a set of concentric circles, fulfilling the same role as the labyrinths of the megalithic peoples. The creation myths of the Northern Aranda of Australia tell the story of the emergence of their first human ancestor from the womb of the earth. The site of emergence is marked by concentric circles painted on the earth, colored red, and sprinkled with blood to symbolize birth blood. When their primordial ancestor leapt from the earth, it is said that the gaping hole was filled with etheric feminine fluids: "the sweet dark juice of honeysuckle buds."[2]

For the Aborigines, rebirth came on the renewing menstrual waves of the Great Mother's Womb (see plate 10). In one of their rebirth rituals performed at Ankota, "vulva of the earth," they chanted, "A straight track is gaping open before me. An underground hollow is gaping before me. A cavernous pathway is gaping before me. An underground pathway is gaping before me. Red I am like the heart of the flame of fire. Red, too, is the hollow in which I am resting."[3]

In the Hopi traditions of North America, all spiritual life was centered around the annual cycle of the nine sacred mystery plays—the sacred reenactment of the cosmic drama of birth, fertility, and gestation. The ceremonies took place by descending into an underground kiva ceremonial chamber, representing the womb of Mother Earth. Within the womb-kiva was a central hole in the floor called a *sipapuni*, "the path from the navel," which was the site of emergence of this world from the womb of the prior world. A ladder, representing an umbilical cord, reached up from the kiva into the world above, symbolizing the coming age of humanity that was waiting to be born. These birth rites granted spiritual rebirth to the initiates.[4]

The myth of the Hopi story of emergence, the birth of one world from the

Fig. 7.2. Sacred Incan womb temple of Moray, Peru, descending down into the earth.
(Photo by Kenneth Moore Photography)

womb of another, was symbolized by the sacred labyrinth design. It was known as the *Tapu'at,* or "Mother and Child." The most common square design represents the unborn child in the womb of the Mother Earth, with a straight line leading out of the labyrinth that symbolized the umbilical cord.

Labyrinths were a key feature of the underground temples and passageways of the megalithic era, but they were also found in a variety of other forms across the world—and walking the labyrinth was included in Christian worship up to medieval times.

In Mayan cultures, the flower symbolized the womb, birth, moon blood, and consciousness. This was expressed in the sacred iconography of a "flowering mountain earth." This sacred symbolic mountain was believed to be located at the center of the earth, and was associated with the tree of life and a paradise where the ancestors lived. It was also known as the "cave of emergence"—as this mother mountain contained a sacred womb cave deep in her center, from which the ancestors could experience rebirth and make their celestial ascent to the stars.[5]

In the age of the worldwide cultures that built the megalithic monuments, the standing circles and dolmens were conceived of as downward mystical gateways: moon doorways, magical gates, or psychic womb portals into the womb-belly of Mother Earth.[6]

Sacred Womb Mounds: Ascending Mother Mountains

The megalithic peoples also located sacred circles and temples atop holy mounds, or in caves situated in powerful "moon mountains" or "mother mountains." They conceived of the sacred mound or world mountain as the pregnant womb-belly of the Great Mother that birthed all. Her consciousness was grounded in the earth, but simultaneously rose up majestically toward the luminous celestial bodies of the sun, moon, and stars—and could propel her devotees into the upperworlds.

In Russia, on the festival day of Krasnaia Gora, meaning "red mountain," young men and women gathered to "dance the round" bearing dyed-red eggs and bread, celebrating renewal. At sunset, a young woman stood on the sacred mound, mediating between the earthly womb of the ancestors and the celestial goddess.[7]

Sacred mounds and world mountains exist across many cultures of the world—from the "mountain around which all moving is done" of the Navajo, to the mythical ancestral Mount Mashu of the Sumerians, to the sacred mounds of Silbury Hill and the Glastonbury Tor in England, to Mount Sinai (meaning "moon mountain") of the Semitic tribes, to Mount Everest, whose Tibetan name, Jomo Lungma, means "holy mother mountain." These cultures looked upward to access the celestial spiritual energies but also honored their roots in the ground of Mother Earth, to unite their power (see fig. 7.3).

The grand pyramids and stupas also follow this tradition of mother mountains—rather than just temples or tombs, they are man-made *magical spiritual devices,* created as upward-pointing womb chambers designed to spiritually rebirth the deceased king or saint back to the heavens of the Celestial

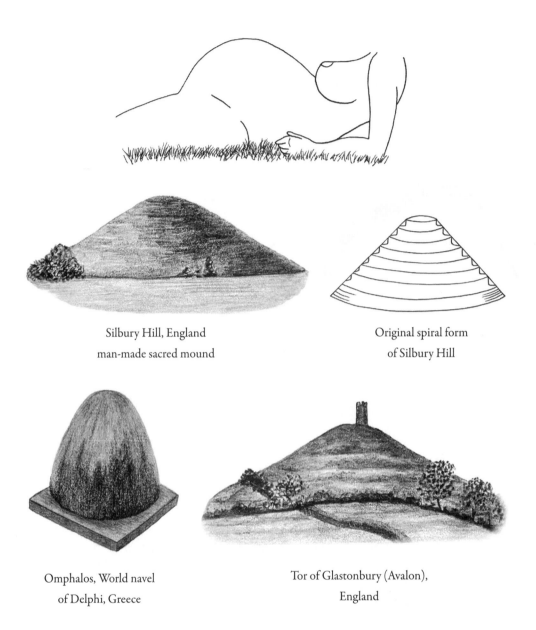

Fig. 7.3. The sacred mound as pregnant womb-belly of Gaia.

(Illustrations by Natvienna Hanell)

Silbury Hill, England
man-made sacred mound

Original spiral form
of Silbury Hill

Omphalos, World navel
of Delphi, Greece

Tor of Glastonbury (Avalon),
England

Womb. They are "resurrection machines" powered by womb magic (see fig. 7.4).

This ascending path was often reserved for kings, Buddhas, or pharaohs, who would make the journey, as savior, back to their birthplace in the stars or in the central black hole of the Milky Way.

Female cervix, eye of the
womb, eye of birth onto
Earth

Eye of Horus
Eye of Ma'at
Eye of the Cosmic Feminine

Ascent to Celestial Womb

Great Pyramid of Egypt

Descent into Earth Womb

Buddhist stupa

Mayan temple of Kukulcan
Chichén Itzá

Cosmic serpent eye, Mississippian
engraving, 1200 CE

Fig. 7.4. Ascending and descending womb portals
(Illustrations: Female figure, Buddhist stupa, and pyramids by Heather Skye;
cervix and serpent eye by Natvienna Hanell)

Spiritual Descent into Source

Most spiritual and religious teachings describe a process that was originally understood to be a shamanic descent into the womb of primordial consciousness, a process of entering into a quantum-vibrational dimension outside of the limits of the laws of physics, into the "Womb-Source of Creation" for a transformation and rebirth, in the still-point of black light.

The rites of all religious, spiritual, and shamanic traditions originally invoked the primordial journey of the nine moons of conception, gestation, birth, and rebirth. The journey of death was viewed as a reverse birth, or menstruation, through the nine moons or spheres of gestation, back through the great Cosmic Womb doorway into spirit.

In womb mythology, spirit originates in the Cosmic Womb, then descends down into the Earth Womb, waiting for birth. Native shamanic traditions describe a tree of life in which souls perch on the upper branches like birds, waiting to fly down into a human baby in the womb. We then gestate for nine months, and birth out into the earth realm in the "flowery" sacred birth blood, as it is described by the Maya.

At the time of death, we repeat this cosmological journey in reverse, leaving our human body, and descending back down into the Earth Womb in our spirit body. We are accompanied by death doulas, psychopomps, and spirit guides as we travel backward through the nine moons of gestation—which were also known as the nine realms of hell—releasing our earth memories, letting go of our human form, seeing the truth of our life, and birthing back into spirit.

The Sacred Heart of Matter

At the center of ancient shamanic traditions was the knowledge that to awaken, one had to first fully descend—into the body, into the psyche, and into Gaian consciousness. By merging deeply into the Womb of Gaia, symbolized by the primordial dragon or serpent, a spontaneous bioenergetic spiritual supernova was awakened, opening the swan wings in preparation for shamanic dreamflight. A shaman or initiate then ascended up on the celestial energy currents of Shakti into the Cosmic Womb for a rebirth of consciousness and a magical voyage into multidimensional realms of perception, gathering wisdom and boons for the tribe.

To begin this time-honored pilgrimage along the ancient feminine dreampaths, one must first enter the Womb of Earth to fully surrender to and then transcend the mysterious laws of gravity. Gravity is the final frontier of quantum science, and holds the secret keys to understanding black holes and dark matter—the dark mother. This initial descent into the Mother's dark embrace is always an act of total surrender and allowance, of letting go—to allow the root of matter to pull us down, to "give in" fully to the primal womb song of creation.

The womb center of the Earth is the lowest point of creation. Wherever we are on the planet, the gravitational force of this magnetic core pulls us downward toward this center or bindu point. The more we try to resist, struggle, or avoid its pull, the greater its force of attraction and power becomes. When we surrender fully and magically travel the gravitational dragonlines to the center of Earth, something extraordinary happens: we transcend gravity and enter the queendom of love, where we experience a point of pure stillness in the heart of creation.

At the very center of Earth, deep within her Womb, gravity is not perceived at all. At the heart of matter and density, if we surrender, we discover an incredible spaciousness and freedom, an ecstatic dimension of pure love. From here the ascent into the living light begins. If we were to journey to reach this zero point physically, it would feel like we were floating in outer space, completely weightless. Paradoxically, the laws and limitations of Earth's gravity are transcended in this secret place within the heart of the Earth, called the *yolcab* by the Maya. Here we experience antigravity. Balanced by an equal mass on all sides, all gravitational forces cancel out. Instead a point of perfect balance and union exists, where the magnetic pull of polarity disappears, and we enter the silence of the womb Void.

The Journey to Hell

Navigating these journeys through womb realms, especially upon death, required spiritual preparation. For Tibetans it was the journey through the *bardo* ("in between") realms, as described in their spiritual text, the *Bardo Thodol,* or Tibetan Book of the Dead. For the Egyptians it was the journey through the Duat, and the all-seeing eye of Ma'at, as written about in the Egyptian Book of the Dead and Coffin Texts.

Upon death, departing from this world meant journeying back into the Earth Womb to return the earth body, and to pass through the cosmic doorway between worlds—where we meet "truth." It was known that every thought, every action, every feeling was etched into the Akashic Record—the collective cosmic memory—of the Earth Womb, waiting to be witnessed. By seeking forgiveness from Mother Earth for any transgressions, a person made peace with their heart before they entered the Mother's Womb again.

The origins of Catholic confession, Christian judgment, and the Egyptian rites of Ma'at, in which the heart is weighed by the Great Mother Ma'at upon our death, are all rooted in this descent into the Earth Womb upon death for the menstruation and renewal of our spirit. Women priestesses often officiated over these pre-death confession rites. In the Vladimir province of Russia, it was customary for those dying to ask for permission to enter Earth's Womb again with the ritual invocation, "Mother Moist Earth, forgive me and take me."

In the Aztec tradition, ritual confessions were made to the Earth Goddess Tlazolteotl, the "eater of filth," since the earth received and cleaned everything. Similar practices of confession were practiced throughout Mesoamerica—in the Zapotecs, Maya, and other groups.[8] The shamanic journey of self-discovery, confession, and atonement is also known as "recapitulation." This later transformed into the idea of "sin eaters" and "eating the humble pie" of earth.

The act of *humbly* confessing helped unburden the psyche so it could merge back into feminine consciousness of the Earth Womb; ideally this humility had been a living spiritual practice, helping to make things easier at the time of death. The word *humble* is derived from the Latin root *humus,* meaning earth. Being humble meant being prepared to meet Mother Earth upon death.

Often people were buried in carved tree trunks made from sacred wood, the origins of modern coffins, to symbolically help their journey to enter the tree of life.[9] In Egypt a coffin was considered to be a womb. In ancient Rome, tombstones were marked with an invocation to the mother: *Mater genuit, Mater receipt,* translating as, "The Mother bore me, the Mother took me back."[10] In Russia, eggs painted red, purple, or brown were often placed near graves to symbolize the supernal rebirthing power of menstrual blood circulating in the fertile earth to resurrect life.

After this menstrual process in the Earth Womb, the spirit entered the great cervical doorway, ascending back into the Cosmic Womb. Souls traveled up ladders, spiral staircases, and umbilical cords of light to return to the great Cosmic Mother, to be reborn in other dimensions.[11]

Shamanic Journey of Christ

When we peel back the veils, we begin to see some compelling parallels between all the world religions and ancient shamanic beliefs. According to the spiritual visionary Rudolph Steiner, Christ also took this core shamanic journey awakening through primordial descending and ascending rites, which are the hallmark of ancient womb wisdom. His spirit descended down from the "Central Sun"—symbol of our celestial origin at the central galactic black hole—on a "path of descent from cosmic heights to the Earth, on the downward path leading ultimately to the Mother."[12] He envisioned Christ's journey, accomplished through the human body of Jesus, as a downward journey of spirit into matter, and ultimately into the underworld womb of Gaia, completely merging with and permeating the heart of the world before expanding up in a Robe of Glory back to the heavens. This was his cosmic redemption through the power of Sophia, the "sister and bride" of Christ, the Rose of the World or Celestial Rose, physically embodied in the being of Mary Magdalene, whose yoni-womb was a gateway to merge with Gaia-Sophia.

In doing so, it was believed that his union with Sophia, marrying heaven and hell again, had reopened the cosmic door between the worlds, deep in the world womb, and set free trapped souls—and created an incredible redemptive pathway for humankind.

The Bible describes this shamanic journey, saying in Ephesians 4:9–10, "What does 'he ascended' mean except that he also descended to the depths of the earth? He who descended is the very one who ascended higher than all the heavens, in order to fill the whole universe."[13]

In the crucifixion story of Jesus, those with the eyes to see can understand the feminine descent symbolism hidden in the story. Jesus was crucified on "the Living Cross" or the "Cross of Calvary," which was a representation of the feminine tree of life—a parallel story to Odin's hanging on the Norse Yggdrasil tree of life, as well as images of the mystery school saviors, Dionysus and Orpheus, hanging on a cross or tree of life. The flow of Christ's blood into the earth, and his three-day entombment in a womb cave, enacts the shamanic "menstrual" descent and merging into the body and consciousness of Mother Earth, paralleling the ritual journeys once practiced by almost every culture across the Earth for thousands of years.

This journey of descent and redemption also takes place in sacred sexual union, in the "crucible of the womb," when the magnetic "gravitational" pull of attraction between the complementary poles of male and female, masculine and feminine, is completely surrendered to. In the mystical center point of this meeting, souls and bodies merge; a perfect union and spaciousness unfolds, which dissolves all polarity and transcends them into pure bliss consciousness. They become the archetypal world parents, rebirthing and fertilizing the world. This sexual descent into the womb for the purposes of spiritual awakening and deepening into love has been practiced over thousands of years by the tantric, Gnostic, Taoist, Hermetic, and mystery school lineages. This archetypal story of Jesus and Magdalene's redemptive union is part of this tradition.

Ascending to Heaven's Womb

Yet, as we lost touch with Womb Consciousness, this foundational experience of incarnating and disincarnating through multidimensional womb paths became a perilous and misunderstood journey that needed complex encoded ritual and lore to "midwife" the process. Over time, and with the birth of cultures that had become separated from the feminine, this spiritual teaching became more abstract and literal, often confused and spiked with punishing ideologies and angry male gods. The increasing disconnection from the Great Womb of birth and death gave rise to a new set of patriarchal myths that buried and obscured the original stories, making it difficult to decode the true shamanic feminine teachings and return home to Her.

The idea of descending into the Earth Womb to be menstruated and renewed by the Great Mother became so painful that religions were created where the goal was to skip the frightening menstrual descent into the Earth Womb—and to simply ascend.

Göbekli Tepe

In the remarkable temple structures of Göbekli Tepe in southeastern Turkey, we can see the earliest shoots of a new phase in human consciousness—a spiritual focus on the *ascending journey* into the celestial realms. These cultures still respected the womb, but the womb was now used to power their return to a glorious cosmic starry home. The oldest known megalithic temple complex in the world, Göbekli Tepe was originally constructed around 9600 BCE. The name *Göbekli Tepe* suggests "pregnant-bellied hill," as it was a "world navel" and direct portal into the Womb of the World. It was aligned to specific astronomical features, including the constellation of Cygnus the swan. Inscribed on one pillar is an encoded message for us, nearly twelve thousand years in the future, with a reference to 2012 as the beginning of a new age for humanity—matching the prophecies of the sacred Mayan calendar, which predicted that in 2012 a cosmic "birth" doorway would open.[14]

Archaeological discoveries at Göbekli Tepe present a compelling picture that it was the center of an incredibly sophisticated and technologically advanced Cosmic Womb cult, serving as the axis mundi that linked heaven and earth via a cosmic vulva-womb portal.[15] The site consists of some twenty womb chambers—ovoid circles formed by massive megalithic standing stones, containing two finely sculpted cosmic "stargate" pillars in their center, as depicted in fig. 7.5. The "birth canal," *dromos* passageways led to the largest of the chambers, which required descent from above in order to enter, similar to the Hopi kiva and other underground womb chambers across the world.

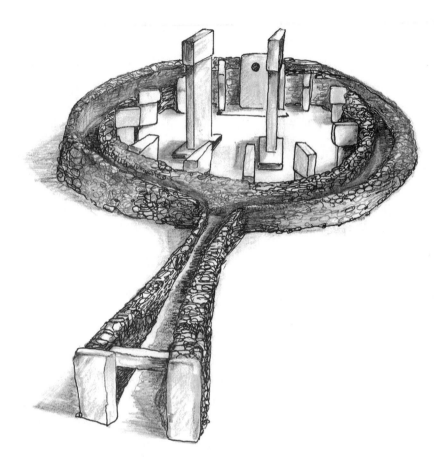

Fig. 7.5. Göbekli Tepe womb temple of Turkey, built circa 9500 BCE, with womb and vaginal passage/placenta and umbilical cord design motif and a central soul-hole stone aligned to the galactic womb for spirit travel.

(Illustration by Linda Go)

The two primary womb chambers each contain a porthole stone, whose central hole represents a vulva or womb portal, as seen in other megalithic dolmens around the world. But at Göbekli Tepe, this "soul hole" stone functioned as a viewing hole to aim at a specific alignment, and was directly astronomically aligned with the Great Rift of the Milky Way galaxy, the galactic vulva, to facilitate a ritual shamanic journey back to the Cosmic Womb.[16] Immediately adjacent to the porthole stone is a Vulture Stone, portraying the psychopomp (literally, "soul carrier") or spirit guide that ferried dead souls back to heaven.

The anthropologist Mircea Eliade describes this interdimensional travel through the central womb hole, saying, "An 'opening,' a 'hole'; it is through this hole that the gods descend to earth and the dead to the subterranean regions; it is through the same hole that the soul of the shaman in ecstasy can fly up or down in the course of his celestial or infernal journeys."[17]

Egypt's Womb Pyramids

After 3000 BCE in Sumeria and Egypt, with advances in "civilization" and the birth of the new architectural styles of ziggurats and pyramids that reached upward toward the heavens, patriarchal solar-based religious ideas began to spread.

Yet the patriarchal Egyptian traditions could not eliminate their feminine roots. The Giza Plateau marked the end of the "road of the Neters," the gateway to the Duat, or underworld. The Pyramid Texts show that a voyage through the underworld waters, on the vulva-boat of the goddess herself, was the compulsory initial stage of the journey before ascending to the heavens.[18] Within the Duat the candidate would meet the Mother Goddess Ma'at who would weigh his heart against a feather. (See fig. 7.6 on the following page.) Only if his conscience was clear, if his deep feminine psyche was healed, could he pass through the Earth Womb of the Duat, and on to upperworld.

The pyramids were spiritual technologies of resurrection and rebirth—built with the purpose of assisting the journey of the pharaoh or the spiritual initiate back to heaven or awakened consciousness. At the time of death, the pharoah was placed in the King's Chamber of the Great Pyramid, symbolically entombed in the womb-belly of the Great Mother, who alone could grant him the power to ascend, as he "climbed onto her hips"—her womb throne—and ascended her ladder into heaven. Hieroglyphic writings from the Pyramid Texts, found carved onto the pyramid walls and sarcophagi at Saqqara, read,

> The deceased ascends on the ladder . . . he ascends on the hips of Isis; he climbs up on the hips of Nephthys . . . the deceased goes to his mother Nut, he climbs upon her in this her name of "ladder."[19]

Stupas, Ziggurats, and Mesoamerican Pyramids

Buddhist stupas were also man-made wombs, like the Egyptian pyramids: they were dome-shaped womb-tombs designed to house the bones of a saint and midwife his journey back to the heavens upon death. Joseph Campbell writes, "As the pharaoh entombed in a pyramid is believed to have passed to eternity, so also the saint enshrined in such a [stupa] tomb. Both monuments symbolize the world mountain, that 'mountain mother' from whom all things appear, and to whom

Fig. 7.6. Goddess Ma'at holding the ankh womb of life,
with traditional serpent and feather symbols.

(Fragment of Egyptian gate in Pushkin,
© Zanozaru | Dreamstime.com)

they return in death. The great pagoda above stands for the stages of heavens."[20]

The Egyptian pyramids, Buddhist stupas, Sumerian ziggurats, and Mayan stepped pyramids evolved naturally from the earlier ideas of the sacred mound with its womb cave—the world mountain or cosmic mountain. Common to all of these monuments was the original cavelike womb opening, or inner chamber, that would house the dead or assist spiritual candidates on their journey of initiation. The more modern monuments, like the sacred mounds of old, were seen simultaneously as the womb-belly of the mother, a ladder or umbilical cord to the stars, a womb-tomb, a downward gateway to the underworld, an upward gateway to the heavens, and the site of emergence of our ancestors. The "Flower Mountain" of the Maya, as well as the *Kur* or *Khursag* sacred mountain of Sumeria, embody all of these concepts.

The architectural clues hidden in the step pyramids of the Maya, Toltec, and Aztec cultures also reveal the focus on the descending and ascending rites of the womb religion. Many of the great pyramids and monuments—including Chichén Itzá, the Pyramid of the Sun of Teotihuaán, Palenque, and others—were built on top of sacred cave systems, underground *cenote* cavern pools, or burial mounds from the much earlier feminine mother cultures, or they featured womb-tomb chambers. A number of the Mayan temples and pyramids were built with nine stepped levels, such as the temple of the feathered serpent, Kukulcan, of Chichén Itzá, and the Temple of Inscriptions at Palenque. The nine levels originally represented the sacred gestational number nine, and nine layers of the underworld womb in the Mayan cosmology.

One famous Mayan temple complex is Palenque, which was originally called Lakamha (literally "big water"). In 1994, archaeologists there discovered a concealed tomb within the step pyramid: Temple XIII, known as the Tomb of the Red Queen, named for the red cinnabar pigment that covered the remains of the noblewoman interred within. As in other burial sites around the world, red cinnabar or ochre is the traditional symbol of the feminine menstrual and birth bloods, used in burials to help assist the spiritual rebirth process.

The Mesoamerican pyramids mirrored the original feminine mother mountains—whose bellies or caves held the "womb power" necessary to assist the spiritual journey. By the era of the classical phases of Mayan, Toltec, and Aztec cultures, roughly 300–1500 CE, the original *downward and inward* feminine rites had transformed to *ascending* rites, in which the priesthood focused on an upward journey to commune the male gods—the Aztec sun god Huitzilopochtli, the Toltec god Quetzlcoatl, and the Mayan Itzam Na and Kukulcan. Some of the greatest Mayan rulers were said to ascend directly to the cosmic vulva, the Great Rift of the Milky Way, at the time of death, whereas commoners would descend to the underworld womb.

The ancient feminine womb symbology of the Maya lived on as a hidden root. Some of the temples situated on the top level of the pyramids were built to honor Itzam Na, the male creator god whose name can be translated as the "house of the cosmic womb dragon." Like many male creator gods, he was originally a she. The traditional translation of *itzam na* is "house of the lizard," but *na* is a word denoting the feminine, as well as house, and great cosmic container—or *womb. Itzam* refers to the great reptile that created the world, depicted as a two-headed dragon whose body contains the stars and planets. One head births into the Celestial Womb, the other into the underworld womb—a symbology that across time and culture was always associated with a birther *goddess.*

Shamanic Death/Rebirth Initiations

The famous "moon college" mystery schools of Alexandria, Eleusis, Delphi, and others, held the wisdom keys of the great shamanic death and rebirth journey—symbolic of the psychic descent into the personal subconscious and collective unconscious, to "know thyself," as was inscribed on the entryway of the schools of Delphi and Alexandria. The initiate journeyed inward and downward through any limiting, trauma-based beliefs and feelings before ascending back to surface in a state of purified immaculate consciousness.

In feminine mystery school traditions, the journey through the Womb-bardo realms of the underworld could be taken upon death, or it could be consciously chosen during life as transformational death/rebirth initiation. This was the mystery of Inanna's shamanic descent into the underworld, after passing through seven veils to meet the "cervical eye of death" and unite with her dark sister Ereshkigal. This is also the epic Dark Night of the Soul that Christian mystics spoke of, and the return to the Womb of Isis that Egyptian mystics described.

Samuel Angus, author of *The Mystery Religions and Christianity,* describes a mystery religion as "a religion of symbolism . . . blazing lights and dense darkness, liturgies and sacramental acts, and suggestion quickened the intuitions of the heart, and provoked in an initiate a mystical experience [of] regeneration."[21]

The Greek Eleusinian Mysteries, dating from 2000 BCE, also followed this symbolic descent into feminine consciousness and the womb to rebirth. Their annual rituals were highly secret and often used sacred entheogens—either hallucinogenic plants or possibly a highly guarded recipe of snake venom mixed with menstrual blood, to allow the magical, awakening stem cells to enter the bloodstream directly and bypass digestion. The Eleusinian Mysteries also involved ritual pilgrimage to the sea, similar to Isis festivals, carrying a chest, singing and dancing, often walking in procession by torchlight at night, and ritual theater invoking the feminine mysteries of childbirth and rebirth. The culmination of these mysterious rites was the knowing "I and the Mother are One."

Apuleius recounted his initiation into the mysteries of Isis in the book *The Golden Ass,* where he underwent a voluntary death and rebirth in the service of a goddess—whose followers were "as it were reborn." He says of his Isis initiation into the "bright darkness," "I approached the confines of death, and having trod on the threshold . . . I returned therefrom, being borne through all the elements. At midnight I saw the sun shining with its brilliant light."[22]

These rites also aimed to unify and merge the ascending, fiery-rising, solar masculine energies, and the descending, flowing, downpouring, living lunar waters of the feminine. The masculine and cosmos was symbolized by an upward facing triangle, and the feminine and earth was symbolized by a downward triangle—the daleth. When these ascending and descending triangles merged it created the star—the fully enlightened embodiment of the primordial human.

False Reincarnation Cycles

As consciousness began to gradually shift from an earthly to a heavenly orientation, the world psyche began to fragment, and the Earth Womb or underworld became hell. The separated masculine consciousness still knew it must travel the feminine wombways, but feared it may get trapped in there—and was tricked into dissociating, heading upward, avoiding the darkness, and coming out of connection with the body, with the feminine, and with earth.

In the Egyptian ideas of the Duat, as well as in the Tibetan Buddhist ideas of the bardo, death was now regarded as a perilous journey fraught with danger and doom. There was no guarantee that the dead would safely find their way through the Earth Womb and back home to the Celestial Womb—it was taught that many people did not make it and were forcibly reincarnated against their will, back into a new life on earth. Ideas of compulsory reincarnation, which holds the same terrifying energetic signature as "eternal hell," started to emerge, signaling that the womb door between the worlds was jammed, and a new fear-vibration was taking over.

Spiritual aspirants prepared for a lifetime so that they could navigate the netherworld lairs of the Duat or bardo, and their own underworld psyche. Elaborate prayers were made, womb-tombs were constructed, special ceremonies and offerings were made, all to assist the journey. This was when the new class of spirit guides called psychopomps by the Greeks emerged to guide the way through the treacherous soul passage at death. In the Tibetan traditions, a living lama would sit by the deceased person, making chants and prayers to remind him to stay focused on the Buddha consciousness as he descended down through the seven chakras.

The Duat and bardo also represent the deep feminine psyche—the repressed underworld of the unconscious mind, first formed during our time in the womb—and a lasting repository of *all* of our memories and experiences. The psyche that has become fragmented and separated from its maternal source, and that has lost touch with deep Gaian consciousness has a difficult time *facing itself* at the time of death. It can easily get lost, stuck, or trapped in its own fears.

This fear would eventually translate into the terrifying tales of fire and brimstone and visions of eternal hell and damnation that emerged in later religions, as the process of spirit menstruation became blocked, forgotten, and discarded in a world that had lost connection to its Divine Mother and her shimmering black light and primordial kundalini fire.

Over time, people became afraid of the "dissolution womb"—the portal of death or shamanic-psychic death in order to rebirth on a new spiral of consciousness. Yet the womb of transformation still beckons.

In the Egyptian tradition, the ka—as the immortal placenta and mother of the human soul—comes to meet the soul upon death. The human soul calls out for its umbilical cord to Source, saying, "O great divine beloved Soul (the goddess Nut) come to me." An inscription on an Egyptian sarcophagus describes the ka replying, "Behold I am behind thee, I am thy temple, thy mother, forever and forever."[23]

Mystical Nocturnal Journeys

Monotheistic religions often retained the symbolic feminine structure of the womb religion but completely disconnected from conscious knowledge of its roots. This was the foundation of the Grail myths, which depicted a wasteland of a consciousness that had rejected and abandoned its Mother—causing the Cosmic Womb doorway to close.

Yet the initiatory journeys of the feminine mysteries are still encoded like gems in the religions that became patriarchal. After being anointed by the womb of Mary Magdalene, a priestess of Isis, Christ first descends to hell, the Earth Womb, after which he experiences his resurrection, completing his shamanic journey by a glorious ascension to heaven, the Cosmic Womb. Similarly, in Islamic lore, Muhammad experiences a nocturnal journey where he descends into the infernal regions (*isra*), followed by his ascension to the paradise realms (*mir'aj*). In modern psychology Carl Jung describes this as the "night sea journey."

The Bible describes Jacob's visionary experience with a bridge that unites heaven and earth, saying, "He dreamed, and behold, there was a ladder set up on the earth, and the top of it reached to heaven; and behold, the angels of God were ascending and descending on it! . . . Then Jacob awoke from his sleep and said, 'Surely the Lord is in this place; and I did not know it.' And he was afraid, and said, 'This is none other than the house of God, and this is the gate of heaven.'"[24] In Semitic traditions the word for house often referred to the sacred enclosure of the womb, and in the Sumerian traditions the gate of heaven refers to the supernatural vulva of the Great Goddess. This is a dramatic account of the divine passageway between the worlds.

Mystics and alchemists across the ages have secretly written about these mystical feminine descending and ascending womb rites. Dante's famous poem *Divine Comedy* also paralleled this initiatory journey, and Dante himself was connected to the Templars and influenced by the courtly love movement of the French troubadours who sang of the Grail and were peers of the heretical Cathars.

In Dante's journey to pass through hell and begin the ascending journey through purgatory and into paradise, one first has to pass through Satan's Navel, which represents the Womb of the Earth. When the pilgrim reaches the central place within the Earth, gravity itself reverses, and the descent becomes an ascension. The shamanic doorway to antigravity opens.

In both the *Book of the Nocturnal Journey* by Sufi mystic Ibn al-Arabi and the *Divine Comedy* by Dante, hell is entered via an immense funnel, like a birth canal, with circular steps of stairs descending gradually to the bottom of Earth—to the center point of gravity and matter.

Pilgrims are then purified in the three rivers that fertilize the Sacred Feminine garden (described as the garden of Abraham) before ascending to the nine spheres of heaven, which spiral around the great Cosmic Womb, mirroring the nine moons we journey through in gestation.

The ascent into paradise is depicted as a journey to the throne of God. In ancient mystery traditions *throne* was another word for the womb, so it could also be thought of as the "Womb of God." This holy of holies is described as a center of intense light, surrounded by circles of the "mystic rose" and accompanied by the celestial sound vibrations of great choirs of angels.

Womb Renaissance: Doorway of Light

The shadow journey of descent into a wounded vibration that needs love in order to embrace it so deeply that it dissolves back into innocence is the magical key that clears the way for ascent into a higher octave of light. This is why so many huge personal breakthroughs are preceded by what is known as a Dark Night of the Soul, or more aptly described as a Dark Night of the Womb, which is a universal mythological archetype and a necessary stage of the hero/heroine's journey.

At the very depth of this realm of primordial darkness, when all prior spiritual and temporal orientation has been cast off, all anchors to time, space, and identity dissolved, and cerebral consciousness humbled, the initiate would receive the grace to discover the doorway of light of the Great Mother, resplendent with shining swan wings, calling them forth to their rebirth into a new spiral of light and ascension into the Cosmic Womb.

This ecstatic experience of horasis, awakening through a womb portal, was like being "born again." The initiate experienced a journey much like a new baby who has gestated in the primal darkness of the womb and is then impelled to travel along the subterranean dreampaths of the mystical yoni—to be awakened by orgasmic pulsations of cosmic contractions and expansions, propelling them snakelike, on the belly of primal knowing, through the birth passageway. Then, at the crowning, there beckons a shimmering doorway of light. In passing through it, the initiate births into a completely new dimension of possibilities and experience, rooted here on Earth.

Our own inner soul journeys in the modern world still take this spiral path of death and rebirth in the Great Womb. We experience the agonizing moments of spiritual darkness—like Jonah in the belly of the whale—when all we see is the unknown stretching before us in every direction, with no signs, no clues, no comfort, no obvious map of certainty. All we can hold on to is our trust that we are held inside the benevolent womb of the Great Mother and that the primal darkness is fertile.

Like the rising sun, the doorway of light appears at the darkest hour, when our coping mechanisms have been utterly exhausted and we have given up all hope and surrendered into a space of primordial trust, openness, and receptivity. In this spaciousness of letting go, descending deep within the shining darkness of the Mother's Womb, we meet the infinite waves of Great Love who birthed us. We find our swan wings and fly again, free and unbounded.

WOMB ORACLES SHARE
The Stone Circles Speak Again

My grandmother appeared to me as the wise crone. As I remembered the thirst at the sacred well, the mouth of the goddess opened into feminine consciousness, and the eyes in the back of my head started to awaken from an ancient slumber.

The maternal lineage of my grandmothers brought me back to Ireland, to the Beltany stone circle where my ancestors have been waiting for me, calling me to remember the power of the wise woman, the role of the grandmother on the new earth.

My feminine lineage began in the mountains of Donegal, Ireland, that honored the old Gaelic ways of nature and the natural cycles of life and death. The seasons of creation, dissolution, and renewal were celebrated with rituals of music, dance, and drinking. Women had magical feminine power and sensuality. My Celtic Grail lineage goes back to the Irish "Kali" Cailleach, Creator, Destroyer, and Regenerator of Life—both hag and maiden, wild and pure, keeper of the Mysteries.

My grandmothers came from a tribe of gypsies, tinkers, and witches who traveled in caravans through the mountains, making moonshine, reading tea leaves, telling fortunes, talking about the banshees, and consulting with the fairy folk. They were medicine women, seers of the invisible mist, guardians of the deep well. They guided souls between the veils of birth and death. They had profound relationship to the spirits of the dead. They were wise women, herbal healers who were looked to for spiritual guidance of the wise blood before the days of patriarchy.

My great-grandmothers were womb priestesses, spirit keepers, women of the fey. They stirred the cauldron of womb blood and the healing elixirs. They made potato moonshine, poitin, known as "water of life" in the hills of Donegal, originally used in medicines and tinctures. This magical brew of potato elixir, rooted deep in the earth, could relieve pain and restore new life. They had great power to heal until the men stole their pots, disrespecting their feminine wisdom and life force.

Now I am remembering what happened in the circle of stones that stood silent for centuries. We are being called to heal the Famine of the masculine soul.

As a grandmother, I cannot remain hidden or silent any longer. The time has come to share these lost womb teachings with the world. The power of my wisdom can no longer be held back, it floods out into the unified field. The radiance of Grail light shines through the web of life that connects all generations on the new earth.

A.C.

SPIRAL 8
WOMB MYSTERY SCHOOLS

Resurrection Rituals
of the Mermaid Priestesses

I am nature, the universal Mother, mistress of all the elements,
primordial child of time, sovereign of all things, spiritual queen
of the dead, queen of the ocean. . . . The Egyptians call me by me
true name . . . Queen Isis

THE METAMORPHOSES OF APULEIUS

WOMB PRIESTESSES were weavers of magical, energetic "wombs of light"
that served as a holding and healing container for spiritual transformation. The
exquisite beauty of their magical touch brought a person alive. This chalice of
awakening was woven with rituals of beauty, pleasure, love, emergence, baptism,
and renewal. These shamanic rites helped birth stability, peace, interconnection,
love, optimism, bliss, strength, and courage in the body-mind, so a person could
withstand the shamanic descents and ascents of consciousness the psyche would
undergo.

Many ancient womb-worship cultures had similar rites across the world, showing
that thousands of years ago the womb was widely known for its powers of renewal
and salvation, and its capacity to reconceive and birth new life and creations into
being.

Ancient Symbols and Rituals of the Feminine Deity

In ancient mythology the world over, the feminine deity was honored with the following constellation of womb symbols and rituals:

- Statues or icons made out of wood
- Celebration or worship of trees
- Connection to apples or pomegranates
- Connection to the rose and lily
- Annual renewal ritual of bathing in water or blessing of the sea
- Association with lakes, wells, fountains, rivers, or primal waters
- Connection to dance, song, and fertility
- Connection to and celebration of lunar cycles
- A distorted form in which the womb renewal ritual becomes the funeral rite of a male god, or in which the goddess is raped or becomes the wife or consort of a male god

Moon colleges and Womb Mystery schools were established across the world to create an embodied realm of beauty and benevolence, where male and female initiates could enter the feminine dimension of love and rebirth. By awakening into Womb Consciousness, initiates could embody the creative cosmic powers and birth, shift, and transform realities in the frequency of love. These schools held a profound respect and honoring of all life-forms, and worked in harmony with the laws of creation—aligning themselves to nature and the feminine wombtime reality.

A respected Aleutian elder from the indigenous tribes of the Alaskan islands, Ilarion (Larry) Merculieff, recounts how he was initiated into a Womb Mystery school in recent times. He says, "Women elders, women healers, women spiritual leaders, took me into a Womb Mystery school and it lasted five years, and it was the most intense thing I ever experienced in my life." He shares how during these initiations into the feminine arts, a black hole opened in his mind and a vast flow of knowledge poured into him from the Womb at the Center of the Universe—the source of life.[1]

Anthropologist Margaret Murray describes how the inscriptions on many early Egyptian temples talk of the ancient religious rites being performed by "many priesthoods of women." Yet later on, these founding priestesses were demoted to "temple singers,"[2] as the temple traditions devolved into darker energies. Other moon colleges survived into the fifth century before being dismantled. Later these moon colleges became celibate, male-only "moonastries" as patriarchy took over.

There was a signature body of work, a core curriculum, throughout all these "yoniversities"—showing how they all drew from the same original well of wisdom. This shamanic curriculum included baptisms, lustral water rituals, lunar and menstrual mysteries, herbal lore, midwifery, sacred sexuality, enthronement, ascending and descending rites, shadow work, death and rebirth rituals, sacred song and ceremonial dance, mystical storytelling, dreamwork and regression, direct gnosis through communion with the elements, and oracular prophecy.

It also included shamanic wisdom on how to fly and swim the primordial and celestial highways and byways of the cosmos, to time surf through womb portals in the fabric of space-time, to understand the galactic and cosmic astrological cycles and to flow on the tides of Divine Mother's cosmic menstruations. To learn, students downloaded energy rays emitted from the galactic core and various star systems. The "textbooks" of these colleges were the vast living libraries of Cosmic Wombs, which are lined with the rich fertility of memory and wisdom, and who transmit this information to those open to receive. Earth and the stars were the wisest teachers.

Baptisms, Lustral Rituals, and Living Waters

The mystery of water, both in a physical and in a spiritual sense, is one of the deepest currents encoding the lost traditions of the ancient feminine mystery schools. Among the most ancient cultures, water was conceived as the flow of the body of the Goddess and her life-giving substances.

Our first experiences of life take place in the mysterious watery depths of the amniotic ocean of our mother's womb, cycling with the moon. We are sea or *mer* beings before we are land beings. The waters of life are our primordial mother and soul memory. The rivers of our body flow with memory.

Sanusi Credo Mutwa, Zulu shaman of Africa, tells how the great ocean and bodies of water have always been associated with the womb and the powers of life force, and hold deep medicine for the people of the land. He reveals that an ancient people called Ma Li—meaning "birthing mother"—once ruled northern Africa, and that these powerful women rode the great oceans in boats made of woven reeds.[3]

Even later religions such as Christianity recall our watery origins. In Genesis, the feminine Holy Spirit "moved upon the face of the waters" to birth creation.

In the womb religion, water rituals were considered a beautiful ritual of letting go of the old and inviting in the new—honoring the cycles of dissolution and rebirth and bathing our auric womb fields in magical new quantum possibilities, ever refreshed back into primordial innocence. This regeneration potential was inner immortality.

The mysteries of water were encoded and kept in the legacy of the ladies of the lake—such as the priestesses of Avalon, shamanesses of the Druidic tradition, mermaids of Africa, and the priestesses of Isis—and went on to become the foundation of Womb Mystery schools, where priestesses practiced their mysterious feminine arts, with miraculous renewal rituals of "living waters." These living waters were both biological-physical *and* multidimensional and etheric.

Embodied in our stem cells and biological feminine elixirs, these codes of living waters were also sourced in an etheric substance that flowed in magical energetic rivers from the placenta of the Void, and had the power to bioenergetically enlighten and resurrect a person in a "shining body" of liquid light.

Preparing lunar water infused with prayers, sound vibration, and midnight silver rays was known as "drinking the moon"—sipping from the chalice of immortality, from the moon who moved in cycles and resurrected from the dark in cosmic rites of death and rebirth. Moonlight on water was considered a healing balm to restore health and to infuse the soul with the shimmering light of the feminine dimension.

Water was revered and used in healing practices, due to its magical properties as a powerful transceiver and conducter of energy frequencies and quantum information. It was known that the feminine waters of the womb, flowing in sacred rivers during sexual union and menstruation held the primordial memory of Creation, infused with molecules of memory and wisdom from the Cosmic Womb—just as the sacred rivers of Gaia flowed directly from the innermost Womb of Earth, carrying her primordial powers and memories, which could bless and renew a person. Baptism or anointing with the sacred fluids of the yoni bathed a person in the original codes of creation, energetically connecting them to the Womb of God, to grant Womb Enlightenment.

Lustral renewals were designed to mimic the incredible renewing powers of the womb elixirs, including menstrual blood, which embodied a miraculous biological and shamanic death and rebirth every moon cycle. This cleansing of "sin"—the name of the ancient Semitic moon god/dess, associated with the "fruit of the new moon", or menstruation—was not originally meant to imply we were dirty or shameful and had to be purged of unworthiness, rather it celebrated the natural feminine blessing of monthly renewal into new possibilities.[4]

Ladies of the Lake:
Ancient Womb Priestesses

Throughout the world there is a hidden tradition of "ladies of the lake." In the modern world, these holy women have been demoted to a mythical realm of make-believe, when once they were living womb priestesses of the holy waters.

The womb priestesses who lived and practiced in the Sacred Feminine moon colleges were later known as merry maidens, mermaids, Magdalenes, ladies of the lake, and sirens. The priestess name *Morgan* meant "born of the sea"—referring to the mystical primordial womb ocean. In Basse Bretagne, there is a mermaid called "Mary Morgan"—a long lost reference to a sacred Magdalene priestess. In European indigenous witch-shamanism, a merry maiden was the high priestess.[5] Joan of Arc was known as the Merry Maiden of Orleans, the coven's high priestess, who first experienced her visionary communion as a "seer" after visiting an ancient fairy tree.

The mystery of the lady of the lake is encoded in the hidden meanings of wells, lakes, and sacred bodies of water, which were energetically mirrored in the body of the sacred priestess.

The word *lake* itself has a rich linguistic history, steeped in the dark waters of primal feminine earth mythos. Symbolically, lakes were once regarded as magical windows, mirrors, or portals through which a person could pass directly into the Womb of Gaia and the fairy realms. The Celtic word for lake is *loch,* and this same word in German also means "hole"—the lake is a porthole or doorway to primordial feminine consciousness and to the center of the Earth. The subterreanean pools and flows of water were the domain of the deepest currents of feminine Gaian consciousness—her waters of life and eternal springs of nourishment were imbued with the rich, mysterious, life-giving powers of her fertile darkness.

Loch/lake is an ancient archetypal word and was associated not just with water and holes, but also with a deep red color—the color of blood. This is seen in the Sanskrit word *laksha,* the Persian *lak,* Hindi *lakh,* and Latin *lacca*—all meaning a deep red color, dye, or resin. To the womb cultures, the word *lake* signified not just a body of water or porthole, but also the blood of the Mother Earth that flowed through the "veins" of her underground aquifers, rivers, and cavernous seas. This concept of the water as the blood of the Mother Earth is also seen in the Tibetan myths of the creator mother Srinmo, whose blood is pooled in the earth, and in the Mayan association with water as the blood of the god/goddess.

In Celtic tradition it was known that the Grail quest is undertaken in order to "free the waters," and allow the lustral waters of the feminine spirit to flow and heal the land again.[6] Ladies of the lake and mermaids represented the flowing primordial feminine essence.

Ladies of the lake abound throughout all traditions, not only in Celtic Grail lore. The oldest goddess of India, Sarasvati, known as the Mother of God is named as "she who flows"—the Great River, she is a queen of the mermaids and a lady of the lake. She is also a swan priestess, and the swan is her sacred animal familiar. In Indian lore the sacred swan is named *hamsa*—which represents the sacred union of the masculine *ham* and the feminine *sah*. Swans symbolize the highest octave of feminine enlightenment and the primordial merging into Love.

Isis is also depicted with shamanic swan wings and is known as a lady of the seas, a mermaid queen. Like Isis and Ishtar, the Iranian goddess Anahita was also known as a lady of the lake, mistress of moisture, and the birther of creation, representing the parthenogenic power of the Great Womb. She was later subjugated to the incoming Ahura Mazda, the patriarchal "God of Light."[7]

Fig. 8.1. Swan priestess

(Illustration by Natvienna Hanell)

Womb priestesses in the Yucatán, Mexico, had a sacred lady of the lake ritual where women bathed in a hollow of the earth, naked up to their breasts. The surface of the water was strewn with votive offerings of brightly colored flowers, the feminine jewels of nature. Priestesses danced around the woman as she bathed, praying, singing, and celebrating her spirit as she cleansed and renewed herself. [8]

Among the southern Slavs, the sacred marriage with the earth was reenacted by a young virgin adorned with flowers whirling ecstatically in a ring of women who "watered her" as she danced, invoking blessing of the sacred waters of life. [9]

In tantric tradition, the Tibetan womb priestess Dombiyogini was a lady of the lake who had the supernatural shamanic power to walk on water. She wrote ecstatic *vajra*-songs about sitting in the middle of a primordial wisdom lake, meditating on the sacred sexual union of the Buddha couple Vajrayogini and Cakrasamvara, united together in the Yab-Yum—the cosmic union of the primordial masculine and feminine. She hymns, "On the lake, Dombiyogini becomes two. How can they sit in the middle of the lake? The two of them sport in a palace of enlightenment, dancing in the sphere of phenomena, in a land of stainless purity." [10]

The African goddess Oshun, whose name means "sweet waters," rules the rivers that sustain life, and her priestesses revere and celebrate her in the rivers, stream, waterfalls, and freshwater springs that she embodies. She is often depicted as a mermaid, with a tail and the symbolic ritual items of the mermaid goddess—the mirror, fans, cowrie shells, a womb drum, and a crescent moon. Yoruba elders call her "the unseen mother present at every gathering." She is often associated with Venus and Aphrodite (and Aphrodite's water renewal rites) and is known for her sensual eroticism. Her knowledge of sacred sexuality earned her the nickname of La Puta Santa, meaning "Whore Saint" as well as Puta Madre, "Mother Whore"—similar to that of Mary Magdalene.

In Nigeria there is an annual ceremony to celebrate Oshun that is centered around a sacred grotto of the powerful river goddess, along the river Osun. The ceremony of Ibo Osun, held the last week of August for nine days, involves ecstatic trance-dance possession of the devotees by the goddess. The initiates move with a swimming motion of the waters, and are then granted a new name, as a rebirth, so the devotee can bring the healing waters of life to others.

Mermaids and the Star of the Seas

In classical Egyptian times, Isis was commonly referred to by her full titular name of Isis-Mari or Isis-Meri, *mari/meri* meaning "beloved" or "of the seas"—a *mer*maid. Isis was known as a goddess of new life, pregnancy, fertility, birth, motherhood, and also as a funerary goddess of death. Bearing the wings of the swan, she represented the gateway between the worlds—the womb—where new life takes form, or dissolves back into formlessness. Together with her sister, Nebe-Hwt (in Greek, Nephthys) she is depicted on coffins in the shape of a dragon with outstretched wings, protecting the deceased. The dragon depicts the primordial Dragon Mother who births and dissolves all within her quantum womb sea.

Isis as goddess or "star" of the sea was called Isis Pelagia, Isis of the Seas, and was celebrated in an annual renewal ritual called Navigium Isidis. The festival represented a deeper significance than the opening of the seas for naval traffic, but was symbolic of the ancient feminine rituals of renewal by water.

During the festival a procession opened with women dressed in white and adorned with garlands, scattering flowers. Others wore mirrors and combs, key symbols of the goddess, while other poured perfumes and ointments. Priestesses carried a chest containing the "mysteries of the goddess," a jar containing water of the nile. The procession would come to the sea, where the ritual to launch the sacred vessel into the sea would take place—followed by libations and the pouring of milk.

In 395 CE, the Navigium Isidis was banned. But writers attest to it surviving into the sixth century. The rites of this magical renewal festival were also celebrated in France and its influence continues to this day in the coastal village of Saintes-Maries-de-la-Mer.[11]

A festival in honor of Sara-la-Kali (Black Sara) is held every year on May 24 in Saintes-Maries-de-la-Mer. Her statue is taken in procession from the church to the sea to commemorate her supposed arrival by boat with the Triple Marys. There are many speculations as to the mysterious origins of this patron saint of the Romani gypsies, but one of particular interest is that Sara was chief of a tribe who practiced the Old Ways near the Rhone River—where they annually took a statue of Ishtar into the sea to receive the blessings of renewal.

In Marseilles, where a Black Madonna makes her home in the crypt at Saint-Victor Abbey, whispers of the worship of Isis of the Seas and her waterside renewal rituals remain. Wearing the green cloak of witchcraft, every year at Candelmass (or Bride's Imbolc) she is brought up from the crypt and a procession of devotees leaves the port to parade her along the streets.

The festival is also famous for little boat-shaped biscuits called navettes, which look very much like the vulva shaped biscuits of goddess worship, and also tie in with the legends that the three Marys—Mary Jacobe, Mary Magdalene, and Mary Salome (triple goddess)—arrived by boat from Palestine after the crucifixion.

These "mermaid rituals" celebrating the feminine mysteries were threaded through traditions across the world, with every culture having its own unique ladies of the lake—female priestesses who held the sacred wisdom and gifts of the womb.

Renewing Energetic Virginity

In Egyptian tradition, sacred pools and lakes were built around temples and pyramids to symbolize the primeval waters—and how creation birthed from her watery depths. Ritual bathing and water worship were a centerpiece of traditions said to have passed down from the Egyptian ancestors, the Shemsu-Hor, which translates as "followers of the child of the womb." In Isis's sacred renewal rites, sins were confessed and forgiven through immersion in the sacred waters.[12] The words, "Come to me all you who are heavy laden, and I will refresh you," were inscribed over the doorway of a temple dedicated to Isis at Dendera in Egypt, and were later ascribed to Jesus.

In Greece annual renewal rituals were held to celebrate the magical renewing properties of the lunar "living waters" of the feminine and her womb. These rites are symbolized by a procession to a source of waters to bathe or drink. Every year in the spring Hera went to the Canathus spring at Temenium in Argos to renew her virginity in the waters; although she was known as a Mother and Goddess of Sacred Marriage, who was invoked in the preparations of weddings, she also represented Eternal Virginity.

Virgin meant "sovereign women" with energetically awakened wombs. Energetic innocence or virginity was a key concept in the Womb Mysteries. It meant purity of perception and primordial Womb Consciousness, not abstinence from sex; in fact, these practices were performed so that sexual union could be experienced from the purest octave of consciousness.

Ancient Greek historian Pausanias says, "A spring called Kanathos where, so say the Argives, Hera bathes every year and, by so doing, becomes a maiden; it is this story which is of the secrets connected with the rites which they perform to Hera."[13]

These womb rites of Hera were so secret it was forbidden to speak of the practical nature of them in ancient Greece or even tell them in mythology. Hera was also revered as a triple goddess of Maiden, Mother, Widow—her followers bathed an archaic wooden image of her in the waters at Samos, to commemorate the bath the goddess herself took to renew herself from her menstrual widow phase.

Priestesses were called *loutrophoros,* "carrier of the washing water." In Hera's moon colleges, women learned how these sacred "washing waters" were actually the living waters inside their own wombs, making them ladies of the lake.

Aphrodite, the goddess of love and sexuality, is a famous embodiment of eros, the passionate sexuality of love, and is linked to Ishtar's cult of Sacred Prostitutes, her feminine symbols being the dove, swan, and the rose. Like Hera, she also celebrated an annual renewal ritual in the waters of Phapos.

In Italy, the Temple of Diana at Nemi was the center of a womb-priestess cult dedicated to the Great Lady, Diana of the Moon, also known as the Queen of the Witches. She had an annual festival called Nemoralia—the festival of torches—held on the August full moon. During this lunar festival the priestesses would carry lights to the lake and bathe in the magical moonlight on water—some people would even take boats across the mystical moon-lake. This festival date became the Catholic Feast of Assumption for the Virgin Mary (see plate 11).

The idea of blessed water—representing the flowing nectar of the feminine—is present throughout virtually all religious and spiritual traditions, in the form of renewing rituals, baptisms, lustrations, libations, and anointing with holy water. In the Theravada tradition, water is put into a new pot as a blessing for protection. Mahayana Buddhists recite sutras or mantras numerous times over water, which is then either consumed or used to bless homes afterward. In Islam drinking holy or "healing" water is a sacred ritual. The names used to describe the water are light (*nur*) and ambrosia (*amrt*).[14]

In Christianity, Jesus was baptized in the holy river under the dove, symbol of the ancient goddess, and was later anointed by womb priestess, Magdalene.

During Sukkot, one of the key Jewish feasts, the high priest performed a water ceremony every morning. He would walk through the water gate of the temple court-yard to visit the Pool of Siloam, followed by pilgrims. He would begin a water-drawing ceremony, by plunging a golden flask or cup into the water. The crowd would dance round him incanting from Isaiah 12:3, "With joy shall you draw water from the wells of salvation." The "well of salvation" is a code for the living waters of the womb, the primal source.

Led by the high priest, they would return to the temple with the flask of "living water" or *mayim hayim.* It was at the Pool of Siloam that Jesus healed a blind man during the festival of Sukkot, no doubt connected to these feminine rites.[15]

The Essenes, a Jewish spiritual sect who flourished at the time of Jesus and Magdalene's era, were believed to have connections with Jesus's teachings. They practiced a renewal ritual bearing similarities to the Grail legends, where they ingested a "teacher of righteousness," a fluid or substance that was said to be "the fountain of life" and the sexual emission of God, which extended people's life spans and awakened them into ecstatic consciousness.[16]

Holy Wells:
Sacred Womb Portals

Wells were often considered to be portals to the feminine underworld. In England, well-dressing rituals take place to this day, remembering womb-renewal rituals. Celebrated as part of the spring rites, sacred wells are decorated with elaborate flower displays and icons to venerate the flowing waters of the Mother of Life.

Glastonbury, in the Celtic summerlands of Ynys Wtrin, also known as the Isle of Avalon or the Isle of Glass, is a mythic womb portal of the feminine underworld, and a significant Grail chakra of the Earth. The Chalice Well is legendary for its red-iron waters, symbolic of the menstrual blood flowing from the womb of the Mother Earth. Also known as the "Isle of Apples," (apples being a womb symbol) it is the site of a powerful priestesshood—with the land symbolically linked to the womb and her otherworldly gifts of magical renewal.

Across the world, wells, springs, and other natural water sources were known as womb gateways, and until recently, sacred well sites were guarded by "damsels of the wells," wise women, priestesses, and female oracles. Before Christianity, baptisms, lustrations, and renewal rituals took place there in a form of "well worship" that spoke of the ancient womb religion.

In indigenous Grail Womb traditions, it was said the spirit of the living waters of the Mother's Womb dwelt within wells and was magically accessible to mortals—carrying the codes of life. These Grail Gates of Gaia were places for pilgrimage, healing, blessings, ritual, and divination. St. Madron's Well in Cornwall was known as an Asclepius, or "dream temple," and pilgrims or priestesses would sleep nearby the water in order to receive oracular dreams or visions.[17]

Holy wells dedicated to the Mother of Life, Elena, the spirit of the flowing womb waters of the earth, were rededicated to St. Helen in England. St. Bride's Church in England—located near the old Diana Temple that became St. Paul's Cathedral—was also built over an ancient holy well site.[18]

Fish, especially salmon, were feminine symbols associated with holy wells. Isis was known as Abtu, the "great fish of the abyss," and during celebrations for the Day of Venus, fish were eaten "orgiastically" in a sacramental manner. St. Non's Well in Pembrokeshire is famed for healing, and it is said that a spring burst forth when Nonnita gave birth to her son. *Nonne* meant "priestess healer," and *nun* was the Egyptian word for the primal ocean and the Semitic letter and pictogram for fish.

Legends of damsels of the wells and holy wells are lost whispers of a time when womb priestesses were revered, holding an honored and important role in spiritual

8.2. A drawing of an early Christian anchor-fish-cross inscribed on a wall of the catacombs of St. Domitilla in Rome, circa second century CE. The fish, cross, and anchor are symbols of the feminine religions predating Christianity. They continue to be used to the present day in the Cathar regions of France.

(Illustration by Heather Skye)

rites across the world, guarding and guiding the sacred energy of Earth's Grail chakras and sacred water portals.

In Egyptian lore, the Edfu texts refer to a mysterious chthonic place called the underworld of the soul, which later became Duat. The word for this realm of primordial Womb Consciousness, and seat of the feminine soul of the world, was *bw-hnm*—which translates as "place of the well."[19]

In the Mayan lands of Mexico, cenotes are the holy wells of Ix-Chel and her consort Chac. As Lady of the Waters, Ix-Chel (fig. 8.3) spins the feminine threads of liquid rainbow light. Important ceremonial sites, such as Chichén Itzá, originally a place of womb worship, were often near these living water yoni-portals of Gaia. The name Chichén Itzá itself can be translated as "mouth of the sacred waters of the womb."

The grid of wells across the world is intimately interwoven and laced into the web of wombs, and the threads of living liquid light that make up the web of life, the wyrd of the Great Womb. There is a direct symbiotic relationship between our inner and outer Sacred Feminine waterways and the need to honor the sanctity of the flowing crystal clear waters of Earth and her women.

Womb priestesses, the guardians of the wells, are now returning to restore the living waters of redemption to our world, and to ignite the magical threads of the multidimensional womb and her etheric rivers of quantum feminine energy.

Fig. 8.3. Ix-Chel, Lady of the Waters

(Illustration by Natvienna Hanell)

Moon Cycles:
The Shamanic Renewal of the Womb

Water renewal rituals are also deeply connected to the menstrual flow and the three days of menstruation, where the womb journeys through the underworld of rebirth on the waves of the descending energy of release and dissolution, or "death."

This process is more than physical, and it is not restricted to the female body. There is a "spirit menstruation"—a letting go into the downward flow, emotionally, energetically, and spiritually into order to rebirth—that can be equally embraced by men and women.

A three-day period of mourning or descent is featured in many renewal and mystery rituals, mirroring the three-day journey of menstruation. The Thesmophoria was a three-day festival of Demeter mourning her daughter. Christ resurrected on the third day. In India the initiatory Upanayana ritual is based on rebirth and lasts three days. In yogic tradition upana is the descending flow of energy—the feminine river that brings the gifts of menstruation, birth, orgasm, excretion, and renewal.

In Orissa in eastern India, the now-male deity Jagannath was originally the tribal tree goddess, Jaganata. See fig. 8.4. According to Barbara Walker, one of primordial mother Kali-Ma's titles was Jaganmata, which meant "mother of all life, creatrix of all manifested form."[20] The icon of the now-male god is a wooden rendition of the dark mother, with large, round, emphasized black eyes, depicting the mystical Womb eye of the cervical gateway between the worlds, and the vortexes of the cosmic and galactic black womb holes, which birth and rebirth worlds. These goddess eyes are depicted in medieval alchemical texts and found in mother worship the world over, including Spain, France, Egypt, and the Americas.

The "male" Jagannath has a festival of Nabakalebara every twelve or nineteen years, which is a lunar new embodiment/renewal ritual described as a funeral rite. The festival begins on *snama purnima,* meaning "full moon bath"—and continues over the two weeks of the waning moon, culminating in the rebirth of new moon. The name of the rite literally translates as "new body" and a transformation ceremony occurs in which life force infuses the new body at midnight and the old body is buried. The holy city of Puri has a complete light blackout during this night. In its more ancient origins this was the menstruation renewal rite of the Divine Mother. The feminine menstrual mystery of dissolution and rebirth was often classed as "death" in male revisions.

The renewal rite is presided over by members of an indigenous tribal caste called *daitas,* who are said to be on the left-hand side of God (the Brahmins are said to be on the right side), and who only preside over the regeneration/menstrual, death, and rebirth rituals. To initiate the renewal rite, they pilgrimage on foot to the temple of the goddess Mangala. They sleep overnight in the sacred womb-temple of the goddess for a "dream incubation" to receive directions to find the tree that will be used to carve the new statue of Jagannath and replace the old "dying" statue. If a dream does

Fig. 8.4. Jagannath

(Illustration by Natvienna Hanell)

not come, they create a flower oracle ritual where they decipher omens found from the patterns formed by flower offerings to the goddess.

For the two weeks of the waning moon they construct two huts—one with the old wooden statues being "menstruated" and one with the new wooden statues being crafted and "reborn." The painted faces of the old statues are "menstruated" with water collected in 108 pots from the temple of the goddess Sitala, while devadasis (temple priestesses) stand outside the hut of the menstruating/dying wooden statues, singing auspicious songs. Finally, on the dark moon the mystical transfiguration begins inside the temple. The "soul substance" (*brahmapadartha*) of the deities, which is said to reside in the central womb cavity/navel, is transferred to the new diety over night. Afterward the *daitas* take a bath, which begins a ten-day period of "death impurity."[21]

In the Kamakhya temple in Assam a yearly festival called Ambubachi Mela is held every monsoon to celebrate the menstruation of the Earth Goddess. Mother Shakti is worshipped in a temple cave in the form of a yonilike stone over which natural spring waters flows. During the festival the cave's waters run red with iron oxide resembling menstrual fluid. At the end of the three-day menstruation ritual, devotees of Shakti receive a piece of red cloth that has covered the yoni stone and is believed to be blessed and infused with the menstrual blood of the Great Mother.

This theme continues in the Celtic shamanic traditions in Great Britain, encoded in the tale of Ceridwen and the Cauldron of Poesy. The Gaelic word for the Cauldron of Poesy is *coire,* which also means "boiler," "vat," or "whirlpool." Across all traditions the womb is associated with a spiral vortex of energy, like a whirlpool, which is reflected in the whirling spiral arms of interstellar galaxies.

The cauldron is an alchemical place of rebirth and renewal. In the story of Taliesin's initiation and rebirth through Ceridwen's womb, he is asked to "stir her cauldron" for a year and a day—the old lunar thirteen-month year. The cauldron spits out three droplets of its elixir onto Taleisin's thumb, which he accidentally licks—and is suddenly infused with all the wisdom of the universe intended for her son. This is veiled symbolism for Taliesin drinking the magical menstrual blood of the goddess. If a womb conceives life, the lining forms into the placenta to nourish the baby, but if a child is *not* conceived, the same lining that would have formed the placenta becomes menstrual blood—rich with stem cells and consciousness-altering properties that can open the "doors of perception."

Taliesin drinks the "blood intended for her son"; the magical placenta now becomes the sacred elixir of menstruation, the wise blood, bestower of magical powers.

The Chalice of Living Light:
Awakening the Resurrection Body

These ancient symbols and rituals of renewing living waters contain deep alchemical secrets. The world is slowly waking up to the knowing that ancient myths, rituals, and practices were not only spiritual but founded in miraculous biological reality. In past times science and spirituality was not divided—the sacred often encoded scientific truth. This was the basis of endocrine alchemy—the knowledge of how to renew and restore the human blueprint on a biocellular level.

Ancient male and female shamans reached states of at-one-ment with the Creator and the web of life, receiving profound wisdom and cellular awakening. These religious epiphanies were often initiated by the alchemy of biological processes and fluids.

Across ancient cultures, annual renewal rituals were celebrated to embody the incredible spiritual, cyclical powers of the womb. More than a symbolic ceremony, it revealed the knowledge of the womb as a holographic replica of Source. The knowledge of these life-bestowing renewal rituals has mostly been lost, distorted, or more often, reappropriated into patriarchal systems and myths.

A feminine redeemer who holds the power of renewal in her womb, which "dies" every month and is reborn anew on the third day of menstruation, is replaced by the funeral rite of a male "son of God" who dies on the cross (an ancient womb symbol) and is resurrected again after three days—a ritual of resurrection in the womb. We drink the symbolic blood of a sacrificed male god, when once we drank the menstrual blood of the Great Mother for baptisms of wisdom and initiation.

Many ancient traditions believed that humans were actually created from the clotted menstrual blood of the Divine Mother and that it held supernatural life-giving properties, also held in every human womb in holographic form. Menstrual blood contains stem cells, which hold an incredible regenerative power to not only heal, but to renew our immortality. These stem cells could be considered a "molecule of God," holding the power and knowledge of creation. When they "switch on" we embody the blood of light, *the fountain of life*.

Although menstrual blood is the most potently concentrated chalice of these magical, renewing stem cells, they are also scattered like fairy dust throughout our entire bodies, holding the codes of life as they incubate in the rivers of our primordial blood—waiting to receive divine light. When enough of these stem cells awaken at once a quickening or rapture occurs; a person is transported into the frequency of Divine Love, and embodies the dimension known as paradise or heaven here on earth—which the Kabbalists called the Paradise Orchard. This knowledge of the biology of Divine Love transmitted from the Cosmic Womb was a feminine path to embody the divine light of the Creator as a physical reality, flooding our bodies with pure living light.

If our stem cells are shut down, we are like trees who cannot receive sunlight—we wither and function only to survive, not flourish and bloom with vitality. This stem-cell awakening is an act of profound alchemy, the science of love. Only opening to true love and devotion can fully catalyze this awakening, not just by spiritual practices. This wisdom was encoded in courtly love by Grail knights, where only the purest of hearts could enter the Grail Castle—the Cosmic Womb.

For the past few thousand years, pockets of pilgrims have tried to keep the flame burning for womb worship—and to keep the knowledge of the alchemy of love alive. These were the secrets recorded and kept in the Cathar's Book of Love.

Our blood, and especially our life-coded menstrual blood, contains molecules and stem cells that were created to hold living liquid light. In this modern age where the womb has been forgotten and attacked for so long, this capability is mostly switched off so we can no longer be a chalice for this living light. But it can be reactivated, and when this happens, we literally light up with luminous radiance and infinite love—referred to as a body of light. This is not supernatural or exclusive, but is the original blueprint of our original biology. Every child is created in this potential, until trauma separates them from their magical primordial potential.

Switching on the "blood of light" is a deep, soulful, alchemical process known as the Great Work. No menstrual ritual or spiritual practice can awaken this potential on its own; only opening to pure love can create this catalyst. This means journeying through our shadows, taking down, piece by piece, all the barriers to love we have erected that separate us from the felt experience of union with life. Womb Awakening and menstrual gnosis is a path to complete transformation, opening the soul into spiritual sacred union with the creative principle of life.

Sexual union, opened to with a pure and passionate heart, devotion, surrender, and spontaneous flowing love, also lights up our stem cells—creating rapturous states of bliss, deep healing, ecstasy, bonding, and cellular longevity. In Gnostic shamanism the achievement of this alchemy of embodying the blood of light was also called awakening the robe of glory or the resurrection body. In Tibet, it was called awakening the rainbow body, or the vajra—the diamond body of light (see plate 12).

This awakening of the resurrection body through our latent but inherently immortal stem cells was a feminine pathway of awakening—to unfold the petals of our essential cellular being, like an exquisite flower, to the supernal feminine light.

WOMB ORACLES SHARE
Queen of Resurrection

An eye spontaneously opened in my womb and then turned sideways into the Eye of Horus. There was a sense of Cleopatra, the reincarnation of Egyptian Goddess Isis. She was so close I could smell her perfumed oils of rose and myrrh surrounding me in this gauzelike cocoon. While focused on my womb space, suddenly the doors of an antique curio cabinet swung open and inside were rows and rows of glittering jewels; the radiance of the jewels was so bright they were almost blinding. I had to gently close the doors slightly to take in the brilliance of the radiant jewels inside. At the same time, I felt the cool presence of the Egyptian kings and queens buried in the tombs anointed with the sacred oils.

Coming out of this meditation, I felt like an ancient goddess resurrected, her essence dissolving into pure radiance of being. Later in the day I found a quote: "O King, I have come to bring you the Eye of Horus which is in its container and its perfume is on you, the perfume of the Eye of Horus is on you O King and you will have a soul by means of it." The Ancient Egyptian Pyramid Text.

A.C.

Guardians of the Void

I met the ancient crones. We were sitting in our circle in the Womb of Gaia and we became a circle of fire and as the circle of fire was expanding, a portal was opening in the middle. I felt we were holding the Way open. Then we were led through an ancient forest to a clearing, where we were painted and dressed in earth and leaves of the forest. We danced a ritual and chanted sounds. I felt it was an initiation.

In the beginning, I heard what felt like big black wings flapping and flapping, I had to open my eyes for a moment. I could feel them brushing over my shoulders as they circled around me, then they seemed to spiral me into deep blackness; there was a sense of dissolution. They were like guardians ushering me into the Void.

A.C.

Plate 1. *Ascent of the Blessed,* Hieronymus Bosch, 1510.
Souls ascending into the celestial Cosmic Womb escorted by soul doula angels with shamanic spirit bird
wings. Bosch belonged to the Brotherhood of the Swan, dedicated to the Virgin Mary,
and was linked to the heretical Cathar faith.

Plate 2. An alchemical painting from the seventeenth-century German text *Clavis Artis* depicting a mermaid and merman in union in the alchemical flask, a womb symbol. A flower in the shape of a pineapple or pineal gland rises and blooms from their union.

(From *Clavis Artis* vol. 2, p. 24, Biblioteca Civica Hortis, Trieste, Italy)

Plate 3. *The Triumph of Venus, a desco de parto* (birth tray) painted in Florence circa 1400, presented to a mother after a successful delivery. The painting shows Venus surrounded by a golden mandorla, symbolizing the vulva, with rays of light emanating from her divine womb, enchanting and enlightening her masculine devotees and identifying her as the Great Goddess, giver of horasis.

Plate 4. Newgrange yoni passageway with a *triskele* triple spiral womb portal symbol.

(Photo courtesy of Office of Public Works, County Mayo, Ireland)

Plate 5. Newgrange is a megalithic "womb-tomb" ceremonial center in Ireland, dating from around 3,500 BCE. Its inner "yoni" passageway is illuminated by the rays of the sun every winter solstice, representing the celestial fertilization of Mother Earth seeding new life in her womb. It was a sacred site to the ancient swan priestesses.

(Photo courtesy of BoyneValleyTours.com)

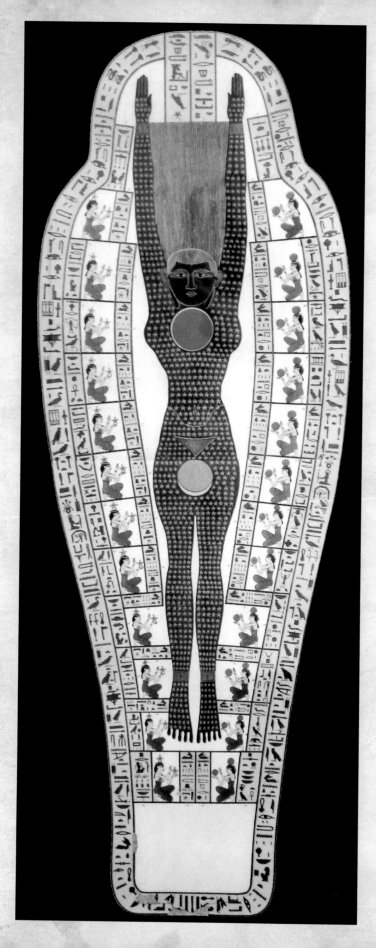

Plate 6. An image of the goddess Nut painted on the inside of a sarcophagus, circa 650 BCE, with her womb and heart prominent, featuring a black downward-pointing triangle symbolizing the yoni, the gateway between worlds. She is the Great Mother who receives the dead back into her Great Womb for their rebirth and whose body contains the sun, crescent moon, and all the stars of heaven.

(Photo by Asaf Braverman/beperiod.com, from the Dutch National Museum of Antiquities, Egyptian Collection, Leiden, Netherlands)

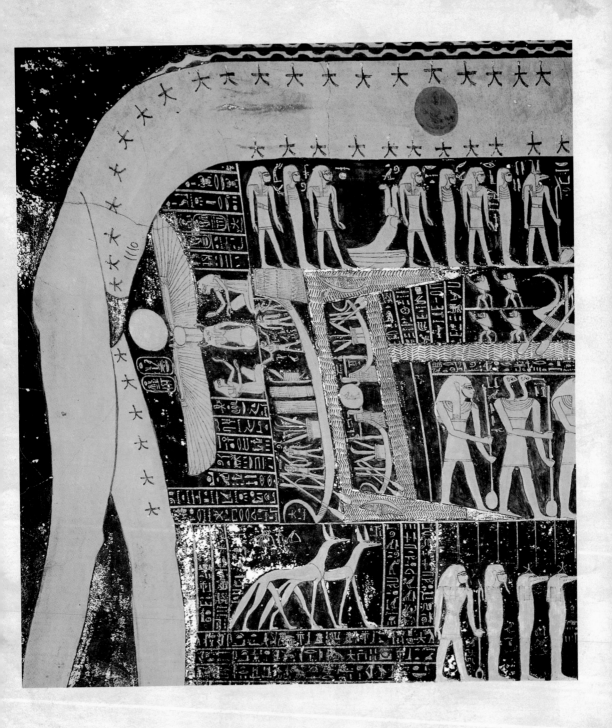

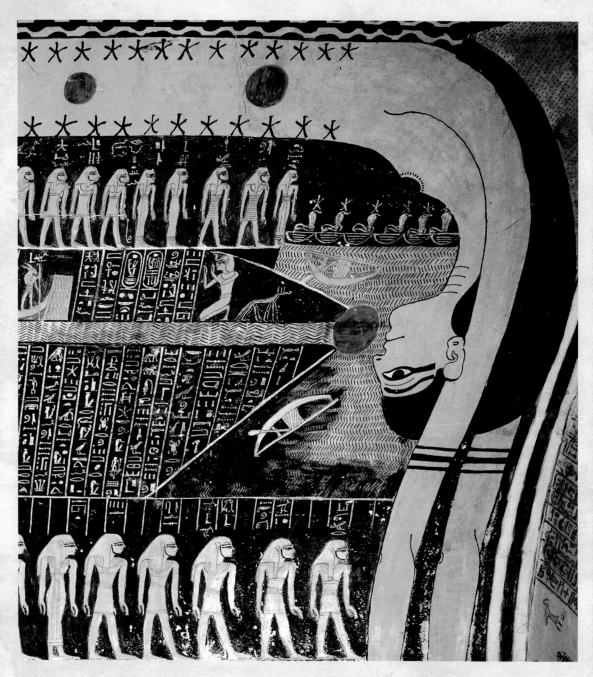

Plate 7. Detail of a painting in the tomb of Ramses VI showing the afterworld journey through the womb realms. On the left, the mother goddess Nut rebirths the cosmic egg/ sun and, symbolically, Ramses VI himself through her yoni-womb (the dark triangle), where it is received by three soul-midwife goddesses. On the right, Nut swallows the sun in the evening, taking it into her alchemical body for the "night sea journey" through the Afterworld.

(Photo by S. VANNINI/De Agostini/Getty Images)

· VENVS ·

Plate 8. Venus with an eight-pointed yoni star, from a fifteenth-century Renaissance astrology book. Her crown of flowers, red hair, and mirror are all symbols of the feminine Goddess and sacred sexuality. She is surrounded by seven rings of concentric circles, creating a celestial womb portal, with her yoni star symbolizing her awakened womb power.

(From De Sphaera medieval text, illumination on parchment, circa 1450–1465)

Plate 9. Mary Magdalene fresco, fifteenth-century Italy. Her scarlet cloak is a traditional symbol of the womb priestess and witch-shaman lineages and is often used to depict Mary Magdalene in medieval and renaissance paintings. She holds the alabaster anointing vessel of a priestess, also symbolizing her mystical yoni-womb that anoints the masculine for his spiritual rebirth.

(Photo by Sergio Anelli/Electa/ Mondadori Portfolio via Getty Images, from the Museo Civico, Sulmona, Italy)

Plate 10. Aboriginal Australian rock art from Kakadu National Park, Arnhem Land, showing the All-Birthing Mother Goddess in an *M*-shaped birthing position with her divine yoni exposed.

(Photo courtesy of Ecoprint/Shutterstock)

Plate 11. The Assumption of the Virgin Mary mosaic in the Basilica of Notre-Dame de Fourvière in Lyon, France. Mary rides the dragon, showing she is mistress of the primordial kundalini life-force energy rooted in the Womb of Earth, which ascends up to heaven. She also receives the descending dove, representing the feminine Holy Spirit pouring down from the Cosmic Womb, marrying heaven to earth.

(Photo by Godong/robertharding.com)

Plate 12. A traditional depiction of Sukhasiddhi Yogini, from nineteenth-century Tibet, with her enlightenment-granting yoni exposed, the focus of her tantric worship.

(Courtesy of Bridgeman Images)

Plate 13. Takutsi Nakawe, Grandmother Growth, the dark mother goddess of the indigenous Huichol culture of Mexico, created by a traditional Huichol shaman. Her outstretched canopy wings are a remarkable mirror of the shamanic wings of the Egyptian Isis, and her kundalini power descends from her womb-belly to heal a man beneath her, working in tandem with a male/female shaman team. Peyote buttons and nierika shamanic womb portals surround the scene.

(Photo by Azra Bertrand, private collection of Linda Go)

Plate 14. Hildegard von Bingen depicts her awakening as a fiery baptism of Holy Spirit. Yet the fire resembles blood, mirroring the story of the Yeshe Tsogyal, who received enlightenment through a baptism of the Great Mother's cosmic menstrual blood. Hildegard also holds a symbolic red-circled vessel on her lap, and the red "breasts" and "nipples" of the roof domes conjure up the sacred, life-giving breasts of the Divine Mother.

(Rupertsberger Scivias-Codex of St. Hildegard von Bingen [circa 1175], hand copy on parchment [circa 1930], Abbey of St. Hildegard, Rüdesheim-Eibingen)

Plate 15. An ecstatic vision painted by the twelfth-century Christian mystic and saint Hildegard von Bingen reveals a tantric mandorla—the universe as a fiery cosmic yoni/egg. An eight-petal star-flower is artfully blooming at the site of the clitoris, with a red crescent menstrual moon shining above the sacred gateway to heaven at the center.

(Rupertsberger Scivias-Codex of St. Hildegard von Bingen [circa 1175], hand copy on parchment [circa 1930], Abbey of St. Hildegard, Rüdesheim-Eibingen)

Plate 16. Fifteenth-century alchemical painting showing the red and white rivers of the feminine principle, *philosophical mercury,* depicted as the two intertwined trees of wisdom and life that form a mandorla-shaped yoni around the female shaman. The red menstrual river is rooted into the yang/solar energy and the white ovulatory river is rooted in the yin/moon energy. The triangle and the golden phoenixes show she has achieved the Great Work of union.

(Courtesy of Rare Book Department, Free Library of Philadelphia)

SPIRAL 9

FEMININE WOMB ENLIGHTENMENT

Womb Bodhisattvas and Menstrual Mystics

Look at my three-petalled lotus,
Its centre adorned with stamen.
It is a Buddha paradise, adorned with a Red Buddha,
A cosmic mother who bestows,
Bliss and tranquility on the passionate.

CANDAMAHAROSANA TANTRA

EARLY GNOSTIC CHRISTIANITY and tantric Buddhism carried the flame of the Sacred Feminine and delighted in the Shakti Mysteries, including women not just as spiritual equals but as spiritual initiators. With the power of their Holy Womb worshipped as the throne of enlightenment and resurrection, it was believed that the subtle substances and elixirs of the female body, brimming with rasa and holy spirit, gifted the essence of wisdom.

At the dawn of Christianity, Christ couples such as Yeshua and Magdalene, and Simon Magus and Helen, and other gnostic shamans embodied the male-female divinity in sexual union to awaken their "robe of light" body, which gifted them miraculous powers of healing and vision.

Gnostic shamans such as Simon Magus and his beloved Helen prayed in their Church-Womb-Circle gatherings with menstrual blood prepared with other consciousness-altering herbs, placed as a bindu in the center of their palms, and also taken as a sacrament. Patriarchal Christianity was outraged at these "heretical" practices of womb worship. Epiphanius, who lived between CE 310–404, rages on the topic of the menstrual mysteries: "They worship Helena . . . in the guise of Athena. And he enjoined mysteries of obscenities and . . . of the shedding of bodies, *emissionum virorom feminarum menstruorum,* and that they should be gathered up for mysteries in a most filthy collection; that these were the mysteries of life, and of the most perfect gnosis . . . this is the beginning of the so called Gnostics."[1]

Based on letters from founding father Clement condemning the Gnostic sect of Carpocrations, and other evidence of magical practice, academics such as Professor Morton Smith also believe that Jesus was a pagan magician who led an initiated inner circle dedicated to gnosis. It could be that tantric sex magic rituals were passed down to the inner circles of early Gnostic Christians, who kept this legacy of sexual shamanism alive. These lost womb and Shakti teachings often continued in a secret or hidden wisdom stream within the new religion.[2]

Records tell how Jesus and his disciples—often in lunar covens of thirteen—worshipped by dancing the circle, while Jesus sat in the middle chanting *amen,* and followers joyfully singing it back to him as they spiraled around. In Paleolithic paintings at Cogul in northeastern Spain, a religious ceremony is depicted of nine women dancing round a standing male figure.[3] This created a sacred mandala—a womb circle and moon doorway—from which to enter into states of feminine consciousness and cosmic communion.

Simon referred to his consort as Sophia, identifying her with the feminine principle. They traveled in couples, teaching circles of initiates the inner feminine mysteries—often dancing the circle, sharing elixirs and sacraments, singing songs of ecstasy and appreciation to their primal creator Alaha—Aramaic for the "eternal breath of life." Together they chanted the mantra *amen,* asking for their energy to be rooted in the earth, as they followed the left-hand path of Christ.

In the East, sumptuous tantric stupas were built depicting a resplendent enthroned Tara, Lady of the Lotus, rising from the watery depths. Mythologian Joseph Campbell says of these images, "Her womb is the field of space, her heart the pulse of time, her life the cosmic dream."[4] Legends even record Jesus visiting the tantric temple of Puri in Orissa, where devadasis—Shakti priestesses of the Divine Mother—practiced their feminine temple arts.

Womb worship had deep roots in the lands of India, and by the seventh century CE Buddha couples such as Yeshe Tsogyal, Mandarava, and Padmasambhava had infused these ancient womb-wisdom ways into the teachings of Buddha and were the wildish figureheads of a new form of tantric Buddhism, which incorporated the ancient

Shakti-goddess worship of the tribal peoples and matrilineal cultures of India.

They worshipped the yoni and paid homage to the female. Bathed in bliss, dissolving the individual self in the sacred union of Yab-Yum, these tantric couples committed to a conscious relationship where they could awaken their rainbow body of light together and journey into primordial realms of nirvana.

Women were often the gurus and gateways to the cosmic kundalini. These pioneering mystics often gathered together in circles, celebratory feasts, and revels, led by wild tantrikas—womb shamanesses who were liberated from patriarchal structures. Sky-dancing in bliss they honored the jewel of the lotus, the dharma-womb. In tantric revels and feasts, the female priestesses often gathered in a circle as a male yogi, a *hevajra*—a male Buddha—sat in the middle, mirroring the womb circle rituals of Jesus and other European shamans.[5]

A womb-centered feminine revolution was birthing, dancing with ecstatic abandon on rigid patriarchal laws, hierarchical structures, and caste systems, uniting the lowest and the highest stratas of society together into the equality and bliss of feminine enlightenment.

This was a worldwide phenomenon, and in other indigenous traditions, including the Ki'che Maya of Mexico, this tradition of pair-bonded shamans also flourished. In Native American tribes, shamanistic congregations gathered together in supernatural circles, a great medicine lodge, to celebrate the mysteries, often led by a female shaman called the "Great Mother."[6]

The budding flower of these ecstatic spiritual feminine traditions were couples who practiced and taught the Way together, often in bonded spiritual pairs, following the Shakti Mysteries of lunar, womb, and blood wisdom. They left a signature fragrance that permeates right through to the modern day. Its magic is still calling us to the hidden roots of religion and shamanic spirituality.

Yet over time, the patriarchal programming took hold, and this equality and feminine wisdom gave way to a celibate, male-dominated tradition where women and couples were sidelined and their teachings and lives obscured or persecuted. Instead a celibate, ascetic male priesthood arose, often exclusively relating to a male deity—the Father, Son, or Buddha—or at best relating to a deified and discarnate feminine force such as Virgin Mary or Tara.

The lifeblood of the female shaman, juicy with the fruit of embodied wisdom and compassion, in ecstatic sexual union with her lover, was excluded from spirituality and religious practice.

Monastic institutions tore Buddhism apart from its tantric heart, separating it from the precious womb jewel, which lives within the Mother of the Buddhas. Institutions focused on teachings that denigrated the female, saying, "It is impossible . . . that a woman could be a complete and perfect Buddha."[7] Or according to a fourth-century text, "All women are by nature full of defilement and of weak intelligence," forgetting the yoni *is* the Buddha-land.[8]

In the West, the founding fathers severed the Womb Mysteries from their religion, pruning the sacred texts to remove any trace of the sensual feminine perfume. Magdalene, the high priestess, the anointer and initiator, was sidelined and the female disciples rejected and disguised until only a coven of thirteen men remained. Women were burdened with the guilt of original sin and deemed to be soulless. Giving birth, the fruit of womb creativity, was condemned to be full of pain.

In Taiwan, the original female shaman was replaced with a transvestite male.[9]

Huichol shamans in Mexico told the story of how Takutsi Nakawe, Grandmother Growth, was usurped as the protector deity of shamans by Tatewari, Grandfather Fire (see plate 13). It was said the men got jealous of her and decided to steal her magic—killing her and taking her shamanic medicine tools and knowledge to claim as their own.[10]

By medieval times, in Europe the "burning times" of the witch hunts had decimated the female shamans and their wisdom, destroying their ecstatic bodies and their sacred texts. In the East, monks reconfigured tantric texts to focus on celibate practice.

Where love and union had blossomed, with sacred couples stepping off the edge of infinity together, flaming with passionate enlightenment, instead a dark night fell.

Yet shimmering stars of remembrance still lit up this dark sky. The female Buddha, Vajrayogini—wild, beautiful, passionate, and untamed—called disciples to her side. Tantric Buddhism melted into monastic structures, giving them depth and spice. Monks would renounce their vows for the direct transmission of a living *dakini,* an awakened womb priestess of the feminine mysteries. Kings and princes freely gave up their kingdoms of riches and power for a taste of the yogini's feminine nectar, pouring with blessings from her shining lotus of life.

In thirteenth-century France, troubadours hymned the praises of the Great Mother in their courts of love, celebrating the passionate union of Jesus and Magdalene as sacred consorts—supported by Grail kings and queens who claimed to be descendants of this union. Menstrual mystics, womb oracles, and female saints awakened into ecstatic reveries deep within their cloisters, enflamed by a cosmic union with the divine.

Patriarchy's attempt to stamp out the ancient wisdom of the feminine was the futile task of manicuring a primeval jungle, which is far too wet and fertile to control.

Instead, the roots and vines of the Old Ways blossomed through secret hidden cracks, flourishing deep within both Tibetan potalas and European convents.

Queen of Dakinis:
Womb Bodhisattvas

The legends of Padmasambhava, also known as Guru Rinpoche, one of the founders of Tibetan tantric Buddhism, were entangled with two of the most fascinating women in tantric lore, Princess Mandarava and Yeshe Tsogyal—both noblewomen who left their privileged lives to follow the path of ecstatic awakening. They are often referred to as assistants to Padmasambhava, although he himself admits that without them his power would be "meager."

As female womb shamans they celebrated the primordial feminine power, and initiated men into the mysteries. In a world that spoke of the female womb as a cursed and defiled place, Mandarava celebrates it as shining with rainbow light, birthing avatars from blissful emptiness.

She says, "Blissful, blissful, I feel so blissful! This vessel, my mother's body, is a blissful paradise. This red and white bodhichitta nectar of male and female is the bliss of method and wisdom, the sun and the moon. . . . The six-pointed source of the dharma womb is the blissful birthplace . . . the bliss of the dakini's song and dance."[11]

This celebration of feminine ecstasy also brought with it inherent dangers.

Both Mandarava and Yeshe Tsogyal speak openly of rape and the threats experienced by female yoginis. Mandarava shows her wrathful face to assailants who try and sexually intimidate her, lecturing them on the importance of honoring the female.

Yeshe Tsogyal experienced the trauma of being gang raped, and in the aftermath granted each rapist Womb Enlightenment from the pure light of her compassionate Lotus-Womb. The men, overwhelmed with love, vowed to honor the feminine—their wounded consciousness now redeemed by the benevolence of a female Buddha.

These womb-tantrikas were a living example of wild feminine courage and compassion, taking a tantric path that included primal psychological shadow transformation—and diving down into the root of consciousness to unite with foundational reality. In their search for true Womb Enlightenment, they allowed the fertility of the mud, which feeds and births and supports the lotus, to drench them in its dark magic. Their legacy is a ruby treasure that awakens the womb of all women.

Yeshe Tsogyal, who is often depicted as red and linked to Red Tara, associated her shamanic power with her "mansion of flaming bliss," her sacred vulva and womb.[12]

Other dharma-womb priestesses, such as Laksminkara, taught sacred rituals of "menstrual baptisms," with a vermillion triangle ritually drawn on the ground, representing the cosmic cervix and the life-giving menstrual blood of the earth.[13]

Womb Saints:
Christian Tantric Mystics

In European alchemical traditions, the mysteries of the womb and sacred union—often rooted in ancient Egyptian, Celtic, and Kabbalistic shamanic witchcraft—continued to be taught and practiced, using the disguise of Christian convention for safety's sake.

The Grail lineage of womb priestesses who had practiced their sacred craft since antiquity and knew the secrets of the archaic techniques of ecstasy, were not entirely crushed by patriarchal religions; instead they adapted and subverted the new religion with their Old Ways of the womb. Saints and abbesses such as Hildegard Von Bingen, Teresa de Avila, Catherine of Sienna, and Hilda of Whitby, whether they were conscious of it or not, upheld a visionary priestesshood of true gnosis from within the system.

In the thirteen century, the English nun Julien of Norwich announced with mystic audacity, from her secluded cloisters, that the Christ might easily be the Cosmic Mother, who fed humanity with the nourishment of divine breastmilk. Her radical visions entwined her to the web of wombs weaving the light of the feminine back into religion.

At age fourteen, Hildegard Von Bingen entered a monastic enclosure, where it is rumoured she was initiated by a shamanic burial and internment in the Womb of Gaia, preceded by a funeral Mass—replaying the death and rebirth rituals of the mystery schools. In letters dated 1148–1150, the mistress of the St. Mary convent in Andernach writes to Hildegard's convent to voice her concerns about the priestess style, elaborate ritual attire of the nuns as they emulated the brides of Christ during Mass, adorned with gems as they immerse in the ecstatic rituals of union.

"We have also heard of certain unusual practices that you countenance," she writes to Hildegard. "They say that on feast days your nuns stand in the chorus with unbound hair . . . and that as part of their dress they wear white silk veils. . . ."[14]

For a celibate nun, Hildegard appeared to be a well-versed tantrika on the alchemical principles of sacred sexuality. In her writings she discusses male ejaculation, female orgasms, and conception, saying, "When a woman makes love to a man, a feeling of heat in her brain which results in a sensual pleasure, announces the taste of that pleasure during the act and incites the deposition of the man's sperm."[15]

Her artwork also reveals an intimate knowledge about the elixirs of the womb, such as menstruation and female ejaculate, "the rivers or flows of living water." The miniature depicting her great awakening into God is believed to show the fiery flames of the Holy Spirit pouring through the ceiling of her nun's cell into her crown (see plate 14). But on closer examination, the artwork looks more like a river of menstrual blood, the sacred etheric blood flow of Holy Shakti, rather than literal fire.

The imagery of fire itself in many ancient traditions was symbolic of the power of menstrual blood and the dark moon. If we interpret it as a menstrual flow, Hildegard's experience bears similarities to Tibetan womb priestess, Yeshe Tsogyal, whose great awakening was described as the menstrual blood of the Great Mother flowing into her as the "fire of life" and awakening her into Cosmic Womb wisdom.

Hidden throughout Hildegard's artwork are various symbols of the Grail lineage and worship of the Great Womb Mother, including cosmic eggs (see plate 15); the vesica pisces; and Sheela na gig as the entrance to Paradise; snake; phoenix; dragon; and unicorn.

With her vast knowledge of herbal lore, including recommending mandrake— which was used in the old feminine mystery schools—as an aphrodisiac, it is also speculated that many of Hildegard's visionary communions with Source may have been aided by hallucinogenic plants, entheogens that were "gateways to God." In old witchcraft lore, the famous "broomstick" of otherworldly travel was often considered to be a carefully prepared stick or "magical" wand, applied with entheogenic herbs and substances in order to awaken and open the Grail Gate energy vortexes of the yoni into alchemical ecstatic states of sexual communion with the Godhead.

This feminine consciousness is celebrated by Hildegard, who speaks of God in language that resonates with the luminous fiery glow of kundalini, which inhabits all living things. "The greatest fire which you see stands for the . . . living God . . . I remain hidden in every kind of reality as a fiery power. Everything burns because of me in such a way as our breath constantly moves us, like the wind-tossed flame in a fire. All of this lives in its essence, and there is no death in it. For I am life."[16]

She also speaks of earth as being infused with the kingdom of heaven, called *Malkuta D'shmaya* in Aramaic—which is more richly translated as an ecstatic, shimmering Queendom of light and sound vibration.[17] Hildegard praises creation to "shine in their wonderful origin . . . glitter in the beauty of their fullness . . . heaven and earth are resplendent in their abundant-making."[18]

Her teachings also reflect the womb-shaman wisdom of a cosmic tree of life, with an underworld, middleworld, and upperworld that are all interconnected and inter-penetrated. "God has arranged all things in the world in consideration of everything else. . . . Everything that is in the heavens, on the earth, and under the earth, is penetrated with connectedness, is penetrated with relatedness."[19]

Another Christian womb mystic, Teresa de Avila, also celebrates an ecstatic communion with God, using language that is feminine and wantonly surrendered to the bridal chamber of the beloved. These ecstatic communions are interpreted as etheric, but the origin of these concepts and rituals came from the temples of Inanna and Isis, where the sacred marriage was not only a soulful union, but was also physically consummated.

Teresa's great work *Interior Castle* could be interpreted as an esoteric map of the labyrinth journey into the cosmic center of Creation, through the seven gates or "veils" of Womb Consciousness, to reunite with primordial innocence. The concept of a mansion or castle with seven rooms bears a hint of the mythical Grail Castle. In many ancient traditions, words such as *castle, mansion,* or *house* referred to the Great Womb that creates, contains, and holds all: the Chalice or Holy Grail. The seven rooms or chambers of the Castle also reflect the biblical story of Jesus casting out seven demons from Mary Magdalene.

It is also likely that Teresa's visionary concepts owe much to Kabbalah, a Jewish esoteric mysticism, which was flourishing in Spain at the time Teresa was born in 1515. Her grandfather was Jewish and retained his faith, despite being forced to convert to Christianity. During this time many Christian scholars and priests in Spain, originally from the Judaic tradition, began to weave into being a form of "Christian Cabala," and it is highly likely Teresa knew of these Kabbalistic ideas.

Womb Lore in the Ancient Jewish Tradition

Jewish religion itself was once interwoven in womb lore and the sacred union of opposites.

Originally the Shabbat was the bridal chamber of Shekinah. *Shabbat* meant "dwelling place"—a sanctuary, home, or womb. On Friday night devotees would welcome the Shekinah and her magical menstrual flow of restoration.

Originally Yahweh also had a bride, Asherah, and together they formed a Divine Couple united in the sacred marriage. Wooden icons of Asherah have been found throughout Palestine—there was even a statue of Asherah in the Temple of Jerusalem at one time, and Solomon was a known devotee of this Divine Mother.[20] The Temple also housed male and female cherubim depicted in sexual union.

Teresa's works are also infused with the wisdom threads of the feminine mystical Islam of the Sufi's (in which the mansion of seven rooms was also a key metaphor for God).

Sufi Tantrism

Mystical Islam was steeped in the womb and feminine mysteries. Sufism carried another remnant of the womb ways, which also influenced the Knights Templar. The male Sufi initiate experienced a rapture attainable only with a *peri,* otherwise known as a fairy mistress or spirit keeper, similar to the fairy queens who granted ecstatic Womb Enlightenment in Celtic witch traditions. This awakening, which was the heart of the Sufi mystical path, took a person into the Cosmic Womb—the black hole of creation—and initiated them in the Void that was the Mother of God.[21]

Feminist historian Barbara G. Walker also says of the Sufi faith, "Sufi mystics practiced a kind of tantrism in the *halka* or magic circle. Its symbol was the Arab rosary of alternating red and white beads . . . red and white were also the colors worn by alternating female-and-male dancers of the 'fairy ring' in pagan Ireland, where the old Goddess had the same name as the tantric Earth Goddess, Tara."[22]

The famous Black Stone of Mecca once belonged to an ancient goddess site, where priestesses and pilgrims circumambulated the yoni-stone, the dark Mother, to give worship to their triple goddess, Al-Lat, Menat, and Al-Uzza. Their yoni-stone, which had the yoni-imprint "mark of Aphrodite," was eventually enshrined in the Ka'aba, where modern day moslems still circulate the holy stone seven times in prayer.[23]

WOMB ORACLES SHARE
Magdalene's Wild Womb

Inside the Wild Womb ruby I meet Magdalene. She appears as she often does to me—wild, confronting, inhabiting the pulsing, primal sexual energy of the Holy Harlot. Her stare is frank, penetrating, and her movements soft and effortlessly sensuous. She reminds me what it means to become a Magdalene and to enter the Red River.

She turns and walks, leaving red-rimmed footprints in the sands of a faraway desert.

I walk behind her, placing each foot in the imprint she has left behind, stepping across time. She leads me to a low-built hut, and I lean over to enter the door/birth canal. Inside there is a coven of Magdalene priestesses, naked except for diaphanous red veils that fall like water across the curves of their bodies. They are sitting in circle around a black hole in the ground that descends down into the holy of holies, the Womb of Gaia, sacred gateway of the Divine Mother. The air is rich with a fertile blackness that shifts and moves in waves, ebbing and flowing around the circle. The women are orgasmically offering their moon blood to the holy center, the red power of potential impregnating their deepest prayers of love and creative possibility. They are breathing with the magnetic pulse of earth, their wombs at one with the Great Womb of the Mother, their intentions imbued with a sacred birthing magic. The collective power of their dreams, prayers, and intentions—seeded within the primordial fertility of their sacred blood—is gathering potency, distilling futures from the cauldron of Mother Earth's womb, re-dreaming the past, and building bridges to the future for women to cross over and remember, when the time is ripe.

Magdalene is dancing in cosmic waves, her laughter is birthing sensual supernovas, ecstatic portals of communion for us to enter. She reminds me of the power of ecstasy. Women must bleed in ecstasy; the ecstasy of the moon blood planted in the earth will bloom a new way, a path of pleasure will open up in the fabric of earth's body again. Mother Earth is waiting for our orgasmic birthright to ignite with hers. My womb is pulsing in orgasmic waves, rooted in virgin realms of pure ecstasy.

S.B.

Circle of Red Dakinis

I summoned the Red Dakinis
and dropped into the Red River flow.
The Red Dakinis turned into red fire dragons,
they started to dance wildly in the flames.
The red fire dragons turned into flames dancing and flickering
under a huge black cauldron.
The Red Dakinis shifted into the menstrual blood in the cauldron.
A circle of women of all ages surrounded the cauldron
that contained the blood of all women.
There was a Grandmother energy stirring the cauldron
that became a Knitting Circle.
I could hear the clinking of the knitting needles weaving through the red yarn
connecting all the women in the circle,
mending the wounds and holes
of the web knitting together the edges and corners of the Great Womb.

A.C.

SPIRAL 10

THE AGE OF INNOCENCE
RETURNS

Fairy Tales and Lost Womb Wisdom

Someday you will be old enough to read fairy tales again.
C. S. LEWIS

WE LIVE IN A WORLD we somehow feel we haven't chosen. When we are born, we inherit a way of being that is at odds with who we really are. A newborn baby is innocent, curious, playful, loving, expressive, demanding. It expects nourishment. It thrives on physical contact. It gives instant feedback, either with a happy smile or a wailing cry. It doesn't edit itself, or exhibit shame or censorship of its desires.

But as we grow we begin to adapt to the world and the people who inhabit it, and piece by piece our beautiful biological blueprint erodes. We feel ashamed of ourselves, we expect rejection and loss, we are afraid to reach out and really open our hearts to love or life.

Eventually we bend and contract ourselves into a cog that fits into society's wheel, which we endlessly loop round, until we are exhausted. We take jobs we don't love to earn money to pay bills. Laughter, joy, and pleasure are seen as luxuries. We make small talk with others, either complaining or glossing over our deeper feelings.

Time becomes a prison that defines and confines us; Friday-night elation slumps into Sunday-night blues. The nine-to-five cuts up our lives into ever-decreasing pieces, and kills the part of us that longs to be free.

Does it really *have to be like this?* we ask. How did it get this way? We *feel* deep in

153

our bones that this wasn't how life was meant to be; that financial slavery wasn't what we were created for, that our feelings shouldn't be stuffed down and regurgitated into acceptable pieces.

Some people make different life choices, but often the system tries to stifle them—and the residue of their childhood traumas haunt them.

Deep inside we all have memories of a different way, of an ancestral legacy that followed a feminine path of sacred union, cherishing love, pleasure, beauty, and living in harmony with nature, animals, and seasons, where honesty and vulnerability were shared in a supportive community. Our womb remembers, and our hearts long for this age of innocence. We connect with this realm of *otherness,* sometimes in our dreams, or during weekends spent in sun-dappled forests or by the glittering ocean. A soft contentment fills our being, as if our hearts are melting like honey, and a magical nectar of *now* is running through our veins.

Or we fall in love and time ends for a while, melted by kisses, caresses, strokes, intimacies, sighing pleasures, and secret confidences. We make love and merge together in sacred orgasms that open our bodies with primal songs of joy and ecstasy. Even trauma and shock can take us into this *otherworld* where we question everything and cease caring what others think, our grief pouring out tears, as wildness rages through us, making us want to rip apart the world at its seams and start again.

This lost world hovers on the periphery of our imagination, haunting us, calling to us, singing to us of an alternative reality. It is not something we learn about at school or read about in textbooks, which teach us only a one-sided *his*tory, grooming us with rules, regulations, and tests for a life of efficient corporate economic productivity.

It is through our myths, our fairy tales, our childhood flights of fancy that this *otherworld* reaches out to us and pulls us in, like a surprised and curious Alice in Wonderland. Bedtime stories of enchanted forests, faraway trees, creatures that speak, and women who fly across the skies on magical broomsticks fill our childhood selves with secret worlds of many possibilities that we are told are make-believe. Eventually we must grow up and leave such fantasy behind.

By this method of logic we have the feminine conditioned out of us. Our primal power of free expression is blocked, along with our ability to conceive, create, and interact with infinite magical possibilities. Through this conditioning we can be controlled into conforming to a world that is designed to separate us from the reality of love.

If you close your eyes and remember your favorite childhood stories and myths, what do you *feel*? Chances are there is a distinctly feminine essence to these tales. Unlike the modern world, this is a realm of bountiful, magical queens; beautiful, smart princesses; clever and cunning fairies; benevolent godmothers;

wicked stepmothers; enchanted mermaids; and powerful and wise witches.

These myths, fairy tales, and stories seem to speak of a time when the feminine was powerful, enchanting, and honored. When the world was filled with womb power, in both its dark and light forms. The infamous pointed black or midnight blue hats of witches and wizards of myth are actually rooted in ceremonial costume of the ancient mystery schools and the priestesses of old.

These legends, which we call myth, are actually fragments of our lost history, referring not only to real women, whose knowledge and power got passed down in lineages of womb priestesses through transmissions of storytelling, song, and dance, but also of a time in human existence when our consciousness, and the way we felt and perceived the world, was radically different.

We are told they are made-up, and we are dismissed as fanciful or woo-woo if we try to reclaim these memories. Much supporting evidence has been destroyed; because to acknowledge any roots of truth would get us asking questions about how and why we swapped the magic of an enchanted life for the soulless mechanics of survival, and how we might get it back again.

These myths are a gateway to rediscovering the feminine, and also uncovering how its legacy has been disguised and distorted. They point to our original innocence and our lost innocence, all at once.

Once Upon a Time

"Once upon a time" is a reality—it refers to a time and place on Earth that we no longer remember and have no written records for. It is our ancestral-lineage memories speaking to us beyond the known facts. We may call it fiction, myth, storytelling—but it is oral knowledge passed down, and finally encoded in a style of feminine consciousness that is nonlinear, symbolic, and non-sense to a conditioned, mechanical mind. It is truth waiting to be reclaimed.

If we unravel the thread that leads us down the path of "once upon a time" we reach a time and place where the feminine was honored, where the moon cycles and menstruation were worshipped, where God was a feminine vibration and creator of life, where sexuality, fertility, and relationship were sacred, and where earth, animals, and plants were considered alive with wisdom, and consulted and communed with, so every creature on Earth could live in harmony.

This knowledge and memory has lived on, though often attacked, distorted, and diminished, through lineages of women—womb priestesses. They have taken many forms and many names, but the source of their power and wisdom is the same: the womb.

Over time these womb priestesses, removed from original innocence, have worked on both the dark and light side of this power, and every shade in between. There have been times, during the transition from innocence to power, when women who held a deep womb power misused it. This reflects in our ancestral and mythic memories of the demonic feminine: wicked queens and witches who manipulated natural forces to control people and to gain power, status, and worship—and who excluded the masculine and demoted his power.

Before patriarchy, in Tibet there was a matriarchal queendom called Nu Kuo where the royal line of succession went to other women in the clan. Men were held in low regard, and every New Year men or monkeys would be sacrificed in a divination ritual. In another Tibetan queendom the female ruler wore black robes and had male servants paint her face black.

This fear of the misuse of feminine energy has also been used to turn us against the true feminine essence and to prevent us from harnessing our own womb power; we have become so frightened of our own feminine power that we reject it. It is important to realize that we all—men and women—hold this fear of a distorted feminine energy, and to also know this is used against us, to keep us from uncovering the pure feminine power we hold.

Womb power has also been sought and used by the patriarchal forces that repressed its public uses—while secretly harnessing its incredible creative and multidimensional powers in private. The further down the spiral of time, the less womb priestesses have remembered the true fullness and purpose of their power. But still a thread of memory has been kept alive and passed down the generations, for those who connect to it and can decode the knowledge.

Deer Priestesses and Elen of the Ways

Elen of the Ways was a primordial mother of the ancient world who was mistress and guardian of the deertrods of the vast, majestic boreal forests that covered most of Europe from the last Ice Age. She was also guardian and keeper of the inner deertrods, the dreampaths of Ann-wyrd—the innerworld pathways, and the shamanic ley lines of soul flight to the Great Mother.[1]

These inner and outer songlines of energy wove both the people and the land together in an entangled, symbiotic embrace. This created a symphony of dragon energies that merged into supernovas at the Grail chakras of Earth, and within the primal Grail Gateways of the body.

Elen was also known as the Bright One, and in Bulgaria her name means "deer."

The mystical town of Rennes-Le-Château in France, famous for its Sacred Feminine Magdalene Church, means "castle or home of the reindeer-queen." The names Elen, Helen, and Helena denote an ancient feminine spirit, connected to the land, often depicted as a shimmering white lady with golden red hair.[2] She is described as a fairy mistress, a lady of otherworld, who leads heros to their initiation. In the Welsh Mabinogion she is described as filled with golden light, seated on a throne, with a red sash. Often native female fairy-shamans were said to have the power to shapeshift into a red deer.

Elen was also protectress of the pathways of gold within the earth, like Aluna—the Mother Goddess of the Kogi tribe in Colombia, who called gold the "immortal blood of the Great Mother." These similar names for the original Mother, such as Elena, Ilona, Aluna are found worldwide.

In Alaca Höyök in Anatolia a deer goddess called Arinna was worshipped, and in Russia the Mother was also associated with deer, just as the Celtic Elen is the primordial Deer Mother.[3]

Womb priestesses who lived in deep symbiosis with earth wore the feminine antler crown. Deer priestesses guarded the earth spirit and connection to the land, to sovereignty, helping women to unite their wombs with the Womb of Gaia and to enter the roots of Gaia's dreaming: to follow the thread of magical intuition and place one foot after the other on the deertrods of life, living in tune with the earth.

But whispers of these sacred womb ways were demoted to myth and dismissed.

Sacred Reindeer

Every child remembers the moment they realize, or are told, that Father Christmas isn't real; it is a benchmark of our transition from a childhood world of fantasy to an adult world of "reality." We no longer hear reindeer hooves tapping magically on our roofs on Christmas Eve announcing the arrival of a benevolent being bearing gifts. We crash down into a world of logic where we cannot fly.

With this initiation to the "real world" comes a deep sense of loss; the magic fades along with the sounds of the reindeer's hooves. The world starts to become mechanical and practical with fixed limits of possibility.

But this "truth" we are conditioned into is subjective. It hides a deeper truth, an imprint of our past, held in this favorite Christmas myth. When we abandon our connection to this past, held in our myths, we abandon part of our heritage and possibilities as magical beings.

In Northern Europe, especially Siberia, reindeer shamans underwent their flights of consciousness on or just after winter solstice—December 21—to gather "gifts" of knowledge for their tribes. These shamans ate *Amanita muscaria* mushrooms, the red and white toadstools from fairy tale, which had hallucinogenic properties and grew under pine trees (Christmas trees) in symbiotic relationship.

The shamans wore red robes with white fur trim in ceremonial collections of these sacred mushrooms and often hung them on pine trees to dry out (like we hang decorations on our trees). On returning from a shamanic journey into *otherworld*, the shaman was believed to return back home through the hole in the top of her yurt, sliding down the pole bearing gifts of consciousness and prophecy to share.

Santa Claus, it seems, is an echo of the lost feminine still singing in our DNA.

The sacred mushroom, also known as fly agaric (and beloved of witches) is extremely toxic. Reindeer, however, are able to eat them with no ill effects (and safely enter other dimensions themselves). Because of this gift, shamans often imbibed reindeer urine as a safe way to use the hallucinogenic properties of the mushroom.

Reindeer were considered extremely sacred animals by our prehistorical ancestors. The oldest rock art known in Britain is a reindeer engraved on the wall of a cave in South Wales fourteen thousand years ago, probably related to this little-known ancient British Mother Goddess Elen of the Ways, who was guardian of the Earth's energy lines, protectress of Life, and also considered a "Horned Goddess" and "Green Lady"—before the "Horned God" and "Green Man" was known.

What is so sacred about reindeer we may ask?

This beautiful creature has a deep connection to the feminine. Reindeer are the only female member of the deer family to have antlers (usually only the male possesses this attribute), and the female reindeer keeps this incredible mantle even during the winter months—when the male reindeer shed theirs. What's more, reindeer herds are guided and led by an elder female rather than a male—likewise in ancient times, the original Siberian shamans were female.

In European witch traditions, the period between Samhain (October 31) and Imbolc (February 2) was considered to be a magical descent into the Womb of the Reindeer Mother—culminating in three days of Winter Solstice (from the eve of December 21) when the light was said to birth back out of her womb. This was followed by a magical thirteen days of celebration until Twelfth Night and Epiphany (January 6) known as "women's Christmas"—where female womb shamans performed menstrual renewal rituals to cleanse the old year and welcome in the new year.

This incredible feminine shamanic memory of female leaders, goddesses, light bearers, and gift bearers, benevolent ancient Mothers who traveled between the dimensions, who understood Earth energy, has been passed down to us in the distorted memory of Father Christmas, a man who buys consumer presents and delivers them by the power of flying reindeer to children who must be "good" and behave nicely to deserve them.

And even this distortion is discounted as childish make-believe.

We may have been conditioned to block out the sounds of powerful, benevolent, magical reindeer, but if we listen deep inside, buried in our archetypal DNA, we will hear the beat of their hooves calling us to remember, still guiding us along the Earth's energy lines back home.

Siren Priestesses: Mistresses of Sacred Sound

The legends and myths of womb priestesses are often reversed so they are recorded as dangerous forces that will destroy us, when in fact they will only destroy the conditioned mind that has separated us from our psyche—our soul—and our full sensory perception, which flows with and interconnects with many realms.

The myths of sirens who lure sailors—or more specifically *the masculine*—to their deaths, is symbolic of a feminine consciousness that lures us out of our logical masculine mind and into our primordial selves. This is reflected by the fact that sirens and mermaids are considered creatures of the waters, denizens of the primordial oceans of feeling.

That the sirens use music—lyres and harp—to seduce the men is a coded reference to the effect of music on our brain waves, and its ability to take us into a trance state, where logic dissolves and other dimensions open up, where we access our own subconscious.

In Homer's *Odyssey,* Odysseus had his men plug their ears and bind him to a post so that he could listen but not be free to respond to the calls of the sirens. This is symbolic: we restrain the part of ourselves that connects to the feminine, and dissolves our "I."

Even more telling is that, in a different myth, to prevent the sailors on the *Argo* from being enchanted by the women's beautiful music, Orpheus—a man—plays his lyre instead, to keep them fixed to their bondage. Feminine and masculine consciousness are separated and the subconscious nonlinear mind is judged as dangerous.

Since prehistoric times, music has been connected with the power to create—or control. The Aborigines sing their dreamtime into being, and primal peoples like the Neanderthals used music and song to create magic frequencies. The name of the sirens means "charming the mind"—using the frequency of sound to create or alter

Fig. 10.1. Mistress of sacred sound
(Illustration by Heather Skye)

realities, to *enchant*. It was common knowledge in the ancient world that sound vibration, including words and the vibration they hold, could heal or harm. Even the Bible refers to this power, owning that the *Word*—sound—created the world. When our hearts are open we can sound love and blissful new realities into being.

These legends and myths sound fanciful, but they are actually communicating something. In fact, sirens were real women—a lineage of womb priestesses who were charged with keeping the knowledge of music and the sacred power of sound frequency. The were singing the dreamlines of the feminine ways, keeping them alive.

A Temple of the Sirens has been uncovered in Italy, and it is probable that many more such temples existed around the Mediterranean. Sirens have also been connected with Venus and prostitution, and may well have been Sacred Prostitutes, whose healing art was music. They were also referred to as the daughters of Gaia, and linked to Persephone, who, in some tellings of the legend, was raped and taken underground by a male god.

In the Bible the word *siren* is translated as "owl"—like Lilith, the first wife of Adam, who refused to be sexually subservient. They represent an ancient female line of priestesses who were demonized by the incoming patriarchal movement, and their true power denied.

A cast terracotta figure of a siren was found in Canosa, Greece, among grave goods dated to 350 BCE; it is presumed the siren was a guide, helping the departed souls in the afterlife—like legendary swan maidens did.

Like sirens, mermaids were focal points of ancient cultures. In Zennor, Cornwall, there is a mysterious carving of a mermaid on a bench end in the church. She holds all the symbols of the goddess—with a spiral symbol carved over her womb—and is carrying a comb and mirror, which was symbolic of the moon. This solitary bench is all that remains, but in the distant past, each pew had a carving of a mermaid—carrying goddess symbols—on it. Sirens were once holy.

Another famous sect of womb priestesses were the Oracles of Delphi in Greece—Delphi means *womb*. Part of their practice was to squat over a crevice in the earth—representing a vulvic opening into the Earth Womb—and to receive wisdom and prophecy directly from the land's energy into their own wombs. Gas emissions from the cleft could have also caused them to access shamanic trance states. Yoni-steaming was a common feminine art in ancient cultures.

They also had the womb power to be impregnated with energy, to birth new creations via "immaculate conception." Originally the site was sacred to Gaia, the Earth Goddess, and also connected to the moon culture of Crete. The Delphic priestesses were said to have the gift of "honey-voiced singing" from the Muse, like the sirens.

French excavations of the site reveal scrying pools inside the temple, and the Pythia, as the oracle was known, was consulted on all matters of state importance until 300 CE.

The Swan Priestesses of Bride and Isis

Another lineage of womb priestesses are swan maidens and swan priestesses, who are only now returning to mass consciousness. Swans are symbolic of the goddess, and were revered in the northern hemisphere in places such as Denmark, where a burial site has been discovered with a baby buried in a swan wing. The swan is a symbol of the feminine Christ.

The image of the black swan and white swan twined together in union depicts the feminine flows in union. The black swan takes flight at the dark moon and the white swan at full moon. The white swan is governess of conscious conception, guardian of soul doulas, and carrying new souls to earth. The black swan is apocalyptic, a revealer, a spirit bird of menstruation and rebirth.

Their presence in Britain is less well-known, but many thousands of years ago the swan priestesses kept the knowledge of the womb alive in the Celtic lands, although their heritage drew from much further back in time. Secret pockets of this swan cult have been discovered in Saveock, Cornwall, where excavations have shown that "womb pits" were used as recently as the seventies, and were extensively used hundreds of years ago. Digging a womblike hole in the earth, and placing in it sacred offerings—including feathers, crystals, hair clippings, and menstrual blood—harnesses the power of earth's life force for creative purposes.* Swan feathers, crystal eggs, and many other offerings have been discovered in these womblike pits dug into the earth near a river famed for sacred healing waters.

Archaeologists excavating the Saveock site have connected the ritual swan elements with the Celtic Mother Goddess, Bride or Brighid, who is often associated with wells, springs, and the healing waters of the feminine. The site is famous for its healing waters, and local healers to this day journey to the site for the sacred waters.

Director of the excavations, Marie Jefferies, says, "There seem to be several connections with Brigit linking to the Saveock pits. The swan, whose feathers have been found in the majority of pits, is dedicated to Brigit. So too is the custom of offering eggs to her at times of harvest. . . . The Saveock site is situated next to a river, which is one of three linked rivers known as Three Waters. All this evidence seems to indicate the pits having some sort of ritual quality."[5]

The site at Saveock suggests the presence of swan priestesses in British prehistory conducting womb rituals at sacred sites. Like the temple of Delphi, the site also contains scrying pools—two sacred ritual pools have been discovered, in an ovarian formation, with a birth canal leading to the waters of the river. The pools may have been used for initiation, prophecy, or childbirthing. Both pools mirror each other, with stone seats carved in the bottom for ritual purpose.

Another famous sect of swan priestesses were the priestesses of Isis who had temples in Egypt. Isis and her swan priestesses bore the magical "angelic" shaman swan wings, and this legacy was passed on to Mary Magdalene, Salome, and all the other "Marys" of biblical lore.

---

*The Barongo tribe in Africa also use womb pits for ritual; they "impregnate" the pit with intent, using symbolic menstrual blood, and the presence of an important woman or female shaman at the height of her menstrual womb power.[4]

Womb Priestess: Mary Magdalene

Mary Magdalene, the mysterious biblical figure reputed to be the wife and consort of Jesus, was herself a priestess in this lineage. The name Mary Magdalene is a titular name rather than a personal one—Mary, having its roots in *mer,* as in *mer*maids, refers to a bloodline link to the ancient primordial Mother. Magdalene is an occult name meaning "watch tower" or "keeper of female energy and feminine wisdom," also "great weaver" and "magical doorway of life."

> ### Water into Wine
>
> Water and wine represent the mixing of the sexual fluids—the white semen emission and menstrual blood.
>
> The wedding at Cana mentioned in the Bible, where Jesus turned water into wine is a symbolic reference to the Marriage Feast of Canaan—a fertility Womb ritual that took place in the Middle Eastern lands of Canaan, featuring the Goddess Astarte, in sacred marriage with her male consort.
>
> This mirrors rituals such as Beltane, and tantric ceremony in India, where the yoni is believed to have birthed everything into existence.
>
> Similarly, Dionysus in the pagan mysteries turns water into wine at his marriage to Ariadne,[6] she of the silver turning wheel, Goddess of the Moon/Womb.

Mary Magdalene represents a special lineage of women who carried a powerful feminine sexual essence, holding ancient Womb knowledge—far more ancient in origins than Christianity. These gifts were much sought after, especially by men of royal blood, like Jesus. Her demotion to the ranks of a common prostitute, or the wife of a deity, is a common way in which womb power has been devalued.

Magdalene's use of spikenard, a sacred oil imported from India where it was used in tantric ritual, to anoint Jesus, indicates she was of the lineage of Sacred Prostitutes from the Temple of Isis, who used sexual energy on a multidimensional level. Part of these powers was the ability to rebirth or "resurrect" men into divinity or immortality, or their eternal etheric or light body.

Much of her wisdom has been deflected onto Jesus and attributed to him. Death by being nailed to a wooden cross—or tree—was a common fate of sacred kings in pagan religions. His "blood" meant the land would be renewed. During the crucifixion Jesus is lanced in the side, from which he bleeds into a cup—considered to be the Holy Grail.

Across many cultures, from Wodin in Scandanavia to the Fisher King of Grail lore, we see a patriarchal revision where the sacred power of female menstrual blood is taken and attributed to a man instead. As men do not menstruate, a "fake" menstruation has to occur, by inflicting a "sacred wound," such as the genital mutilation of circumcision, an animal or human sacrifice, or the mass murder of war. Like the myth of the Fisher King, who was wounded in the thigh or side, male wounding as a regeneration ritual for the land mimics feminine womb power.

This gender switch was the underlying reason for the rise of human sacrifice in religion, where the "earth thirsts for blood," and the travesty of satanic blood ritual and death replacing the life-giving and life-affirming tribal use of healing and regenerative menstrual blood.

Fall of Feminine Womb Consciousness

There is often the mistaken sense that modern man, with his developed thinking mind and complex technological creations, is the apex of evolution, yet the state of our relationship to Mother Earth, and to each other as human beings, is evidence that we are in fact currently residing in a nadir of disconnection, dissonance, and disharmony with the forces of life.

There are many speculations about what caused this fall of consciousness and when we first lost connection with pure Womb Consciousness and our blueprint of original innocence. Theories range from an ecological catastrophe that created collective trauma, to interdimensional intervention or invasion, or a cross-species evolution that created the thinking mind.

There is evidence of a catastrophic cosmic event around 10,000 BCE that impacted Earth and could well have created a massive fracture in the collective consciousness, disconnecting us from our living psychic connection to the web of life. It is also becoming clearer that there were different human types on Earth, who intermingled with each other. Mark Thomas, evolutionary geneticist at University College London, says of evidence of the interbreeding between Neanderthals and other hominids around 30,000 years ago, "What it begins to suggest is that we're looking at a Lord of the Rings type world—that there were many hominid populations."[7]

It is wise not to swim on the surface with simple explanations; our perceived separation from the whole, which birthed patriarchy and its twin sister matriarchy, is a shadow energy that was created by complex cosmic forces and has many perspectives. We can ask Womb to take us on a journey into these forbidden roots. By allowing ourselves to open to imaginal gateways, we can try various truths on for size, and see how it feels and what lessons or insights it brings us.

One extraordinary imaginal gateway into the cause of this fall comes from the

Gnostic shamans, who recorded an elaborate creation myth that on careful reading could also be read as a *re-creation* myth—an encoded story of how the world was reformed by unfortunate events. It tells of an astounding possibility of how pain and suffering came to our world.

Their philosophers had often pondered the paradox of how Sophia as the immanent feminine god-force had birthed an entity that had imprisoned her. Irenaeus quotes the Gnostics as saying "And after she had generated them, she was detained by them through envy, for they did not wish to be thought to be the progeny of any other. And it was [she] that was made prisoner by the Powers and Angels that had been emanated by her. And she suffered every kind of indignity at their hands . . ."[8]

Here we see the birth of a patriarchal force, a destructive impulse that wishes to separate from its Great Mother and deny the authorship of her creative Womb.

The reason for this miscreation, the birth of these rebellious entities, which have turned on their Mother and degraded and denied her, is attributed to Sophia attempting to create without her Syzygy, her twin, her masculine counterpart. By doing so, she was going against the perfection of the natural blueprint of creation, with its primordial dance of complementary opposites.

The Apocryphon of John says, "Sophia . . . conceived a thought from herself. . . . She wanted to bring forth a likeness out of herself without the consent of the Spirit . . . and without her consort and without his consideration."[9]

Her mistake was said to be this desire to imitate the parthenogenic self-generating power of the Supreme, the Great Womb, who is beyond opposites—but births them into being. This could describe a cosmic creative process, or we may speculate that Sophia attempted her own physical parthenogenic conception—possibily facilitated by nonhuman entities called angels.

Greek myths speak of a time when divine and semidivine gods were birthed into the world by priestesses and goddesses, bringing war and devastation with them as they thirsted for power—conquering the women that created them. Some scholars speculate these "gods" were birthed through parthenogenesis, and that over time this astral conception process led to a rape of consciousness.[10] Some speculate it was a hybrid mating between different species of humans.

Gnostic texts describe this grand drama, saying that Sophia "throws all the powers in the world into confusion through her unsurpassable beauty." Other records add that, "displaying her beauty she drove them to frenzy . . . and the Angels themselves went to war on her account . . . they set to work to mutually slaughter each other on account of the desire which she infused."[11]

This idea of beings from other realms, angels, who desire to sexually unite with the earthly feminine is mirrored in the Bible, which speaks of the angels coming down and mating with human women. This forbidden coupling puts the original blueprint into disarray, creating genetic hybrids, "giants" who roam the earth. In the Book of Enoch this race is described as watchers, or the *bene he-elohim,* mistakenly translated as the "sons of God," when *elohim* is a feminine word, meaning that this "heavenly hybrid race" was in fact the *sons of the goddesses.*[12]

Assyrians and Babylonians of the first millennium BCE belived in vampire-beings called *Edimmu* created by the intermarriage between humans and spirit world, who were said to be bloodthirsty and full of violence and rage against mankind.[13]

Could this be the root of legends of Eve's temptation? Gnostic texts say that "they (the Angels) had deceived the human race." Maybe our myths and spiritual texts are holding telltale clues?

This is not to blame or demonize women—as patriarchal religions have done for so many years, at such a devastating cost—but aims instead to explore how the great power of the feminine could be used wisely, or misused, by both men and women. By being open to this exploration, we can avoid casting women as the weak, powerless victims of history. Instead we can consider the feminine as active co-creators in both the light and dark aspects of our forbidden world story, who wielded an immense power that was coveted by many.

What we can draw from this storytelling, which is reflected in myths around the world from Hopi to Pygmy, Egyptian, and Chinese, who tell of a time of perfection and original innocence on earth and then a *trauma* where we fall, is that at one time we may have been forced, deceived, or seduced into misusing the power of the Womb. Not that our sexuality is in itself flawed.

> *God did not make death, and [s]he does not delight in the*
> *death of the living . . . the generative forces of the world are*
> *wholesome and there is no destructive poison in them.*
> WISDOM OF SOLOMON, 1:13–14[14]

The Hidden Shadow of Womb Power

One of the greatest gifts of the Womb is true wisdom, discernment, and *nous*— otherwise known as common sense. Womb power is neutral and can be used either way. There has always been the potential for its great powers to be used—or harnessed—incorrectly or with ill intent. When a woman opens her Womb, she will attract all kinds of interest—physical and nonphysical, benevolent and malevolent.

She will be able to create instantly—from her heart or from her wounds. This will be a huge initiation, as she has the potential to attract her worst fears, or be used unwittingly, or to create consciously, in love.

Orgasmic energy is also neutral; it can be opened and experienced by a benevolent being or person or a malevolent one. Just because a woman experiences a kind of "ecstasy" does not mean it is necessarily aligned with true love or is in the highest good for her or others. Yet when orgasmic energy is generated with love, from authentic womb sovereignty, its power to birth, shift, and create new realities is an immense treasure and a true gift of the Goddess.

The more we align with patriarchal-influenced belief systems—either religious, alternative, or new age—the less clear our Womb wisdom will be. There are many teachings still plugged into a patriarchal matrix. Bless these teachings; they have been a bridge. But now a new step is being called for. And it is important to understand that an unbalanced matriarchal energy that denigrates men and separates them from women is also part of patriarchy.

Courage to Question

The Womb is a truly radical voice; it will cut through many of your most cherished beliefs, as it leads you back to freedom and innocence. It requires great courage to question *everything*.

Consider every piece of information you know. Where did you hear it? Is it *really* true or just belief? Ask your Womb for the answer, she will "give it to you straight."

Always check within yourself first; *trust your feelings*. Not the obvious surface emotions trying to create drama and distract you from truth, which are birthed by wounds of anger, fear, and false beliefs—but the subtle, persistent whispers that arise from deep within that don't often make sense, but feel right. This wise, knowing inner voice, this deep intuition is your best ally. Truth is spiral, everything will be revealed at the level you can receive it.

Always ask yourself the questions that are the backbone of the path of Love: Does it feel innocent? Does it feel loving? Are you healing and evolving in Love? Are you a healing force for others? These are the clearest parameters to guide your awakening womb power.

Do not idealize anything without referring to your own Womb *knowing*. Powerful women of the past can be a helpful guiding light to feminine consciousness, without fully holding the frequency of love themselves—or fully embodying Womb innocence. Some of the biggest deceptions on the planet are happening in the name of God and Goddess. As people seek to liberate themselves, they are falling into yet another trap. Only by unplugging from this unnatural, patriarchal matrix, piece by piece, can the true wisdom begin to flow in.

Only pure Love can truly open the Womb into her fullest power and potential. So we must be careful not to get sidetracked by a false glamour, seductions, or the wound resonance of our unfelt shadows. Although every experience can serve as an initiation to Womb Awakening, often our mistakes can be our greatest teachers, and on a deep level, we may well have chosen them. We have peeled back only an inch of infinity, and we are still blinded by the light; everything in this world is received through a wound matrix, and contains gifts and distortions. Your Womb will navigate through these contradictions with graceful ease if you trust her.

If the primal womb powers were harnessed to create in a way that separated us from the blueprint of life, then the healing balm for this ancient wound is a return to primordial union. We can now heal this trauma back into innocence, and reclaim the wholeness of our shimmering sexual energy and the wonderous capacaties of the Womb to create in love. The more we love ourselves and trust our Wombs the more clarity will be revealed.

Our Wombs hold the divine blueprint and the elixirs of renewal that heal all. No matter what has unfolded, we have the potential to return to primordial bliss. Our innocence always renews.

WOMB ORACLES SHARE
Creation of the False Womb Grid

I approach the doorway to Atlantis. There is an imperious priestess standing at the door—I sweep her to one side, because she is absolute small fry compared to the power I have. I walk through the door. I am wearing a long white dress and a gold headdress with a cobra rising out of it. There is an incredible energy of the panther, whom I can shape-shift into. I have incredible shape-shifting powers.

I have strange shoes on, like invisible shoes; they give the impression I am levitating rather than walking, like I am not touching the earth. It is something that makes other people awestruck.

An entire civilization is on stilts, suspended on platforms, above Earth.

I am on a spaceship, but it is docked on Earth. It's a scientific base. It's a spaceship that has landed on Earth and is staying here. It is the headquarters. Again, I have a lot of power. It's such a deep power, but not necessarily over others. That would almost be too petty and small a use of this power. This power is not tied in with lower negative emotions, such as unworthiness or trying to be better than others. This incredible power is completely sovereign to itself. This womb power I have is so immense, it's like the power of a black hole. This is a power that can birth and destroy universes. It is awesome and one respects it. One doesn't toy with it in a sexually exploitative way. There's no emotion.

I am the head of a project—a breeding project. I am in a circular white room. All around the edges of the room are pods with women suspended in amniotic fluid with babies growing inside them. I am very powerful and very cold. It's a power that's completely disconnected from true morality or feeling. It's obsessed with its aim, whatever its aim is. It does not necessarily want to hurt people or to be cruel, but it is very single-minded in its mission. The room has a black crystal at the center. I feed this crystal with my womb power. My Womb is what animates this breeding program. Whatever is happening in these amniotic pods is being animated by my womb power. I'm like a false creatrix; a false goddess. I'm taking the place of the Divine Mother; I'm actually creating life from my Womb—but outside the natural order of creation. My womb grid has flipped, so it is now an antiwomb grid, now it takes, it sucks energy and power up into itself.

At one point I leave the ship and I go out into the jungle, and I'm with a panther. I'm not often in nature because of the way it's set up throughout the vast city—people have already disconnected from a deep bond with nature. And when I start to connect back to Earth and nature and the primal feel of the jungle, I start to come back into something, and when I do, I start to feel very lonely, that this life I've got and this power I've got is very lonely. I connect to my humanity. I start to walk and walk and I reach a pool, and my ancestor's bones are there. I start to feel sad. There was a time when I and my ancestors, or the women I represent, were under an immense threat. And in the face of that threat, they had to reverse the flow of their wombs to survive.

They had to switch it from energy flowing and giving outward; they had to switch it off and turn it back—so that people couldn't take energy from them.

There had been a survival imperative to reverse the flow of the womb. But the aftermath of this trauma is that over time, women had become disconnected from the flow of life, from their femininity, true power, and feelings. Over time they'd birthed this inhuman false creation. Whatever this project was, it was a result of that decision, of that necessity.

Now there was deep loneliness and ancestral grief in all this power.

It was almost too painful to come down into the jungle, because there I would start to remember my true self—and the trauma of my female ancestors.

There had once been a deep connection to nature, and then it was severed.

S.B.

CYCLE 3

WOMB OF LIFE AND ALCHEMY OF REBIRTH

SPIRAL 11

WOMB OF GOD

The Queendom of Feminine Consciousness

The all-powerful and ineffable God, who was before all ages but herself had no beginning nor will she cease to exist after the end of ages—it is she who formed every creature in a marvelous way by her own will.

SAINT HILDEGARD VON BINGEN (1098–1179)

WE ARE ENTERING a massive collective rebirth of humanity as we once again connect with the Womb of God and the feminine vibration of creation. This rebirth also unfolds on a personal level, with the reclamation of every woman's womb as a temple of sanctity and universal creation.

In the Apocryphon of John, this indwelling feminine creative spirit, "ruah," is acknowledged as the origin of creation: "[She is] . . . the image of the invisible, virginal, perfect spirit. . . . She became the Mother of everything, for She existed before them all." In another text found at Nag Hammadi, the feminine spirit is described as a true voice calling from within: "[I] am the Thought that [dwells] in light. [I] am the real voice. I cry out in everyone, and they know that a seed dwells within . . . I am the Womb [that gives shape to] the All. I am Mer[iroth]ea, the glory of the Mother."[1]

It is essential that we embrace the great cosmic importance of this return to Womb Consciousness—when we heal the wombs of the world, we will literally begin to birth a new world into being. The source of our current catastrophe on Earth is the loss of our connection to Divine Mother—and with this loss, the separation from the nurturing divine feminine womb.

Fig. 11.1. Black Madonna of Montserrat, Spain, symbolizing the dark fertility of the Earth Mother and the shining darkness of the Cosmic Womb of Creation

(Photo by Csiraf)

Studies show that when the sacredness of motherhood and mother-child bonding is interrupted by trauma and separation, it creates a fragmented, disassociated, and disruptive species. Yet, with the revival of conscious bonded mothering, in just *several generations* a profound healing can take place. Our holistic consciousness can be restored and our epigenetic innocence reclaimed for a new generation.[2]

This means, no matter how hopeless our world appears, it can renew and heal in only a few hundred years if we collectively focus on honoring and restoring the feminine dimension of God within ourselves.

We can birth ourselves back into a primordial wholeness by entering the vibration of the feminine dimension, which has been missing from human experiences for eons. It is a realm of feelings, intimacy, intuition, held in the primal cave of the Heart and Womb, coded into every single cell birthed into being. It blesses our spirit with love.

It is original innocence, soft, kind, earth based, life affirming; it unites man and woman, brings tribes together; it celebrates, honors, and communes with Mother and Father Earth; it makes love with pleasure, beyond the sacred or profane. It restores an inner ecology of communion.

In tantric traditions, men who considered themselves consort-devotees of the Mother honored the feminine vibration as the cosmic Creatrix and primordial source. Rituals include circling a woman three times, affirming, "You are my mother, I am your son. Until enlightenment, I will be nurtured by the milk that arises from your breasts, which are the limbs of enlightenment."[3]

The feminine dimension is the pulse beating in our every cell, our life force gifted from the beginnings of time, our ancient wisdom, once new and fresh, and always held in that innocence, connected with all of existence. It is our natural birthright, still held in our DNA, in the crystals, trees, oceans, and forests that we belong to in a universal ecosystem that we breathe with, live with, eternally.

The feminine dimension rests in the depth of our hearts, where it meets the Womb, to play with the sexual energy of creation that birthed stars from its seed. It embraces everything, for it was all created, and everything is allowed.

To enter these magical realms is to become vulnerable, natural, open, instinctive, whole.

Love Is the Foundation of Being

This dimension is nowhere else but here, it is not supernatural or enlightened nor a heaven far away. It is our human birthright, born of the very essence of existence, which loves because it *is* love.

It is a deep feeling, a space you melt into, an infinite realm of magical possibilities. Feelings become tangible, shadows, wisps, whispers, caresses, opening out into undulating vistas of sensual perception. Feelings embrace us, submerge us, commune with us, envelop us, dissolve us—take us beyond time itself.

Innocent, orgasmic, radiant, this is a realm of stillness, fullness, bathed in silence, where resonant musical soul refrains unfold your most tender inner petals of being. It is impossible to hold on to a separate sense of "you" as those resistant, contracted, afraid parts simply melt through your hands like warm honey.

There are no imposed rules, no enforced boundaries, no narrow definitions to measure yourself against. Everything just is, and is embraced gently in loving arms. Flowing, fluid, graceful, enchanting, the Heart opens into fairyland. A place of ecstatic innocence and wonder, where love is breathed in and exhaled out in every moment, shared, circulated, played with, creating a trust that makes all things safe to feel and be.

Love is remembered as the foundation of our very being—gentle reminders whispered from our dearest ancestors, whose hearts still live on inside ours.

A palpable essence, it heals us, touches us, sings to us—love dances with us, dreams with us, and brings our desires into being. It is not an ideal to be reached for or achieved. It is a place of nonachievement, of giving in, letting go, surrendering, of crying tender tears for all those places that still feel hurt, unworthy, unloved. It is a place to be real, to be free, to relax fully into the heart.

It is an invitation to passionately love yourself and others with wanton abandon, in pleasure, trust, and heart bursts of gratitude. It is a place to truly *come alive*.

Feminine consciousness is fluid, oceanic, opening us into the ecstatic experience of life as a mystical dreamtime of love and possibilities. Once we have touched this mystery it will whisper, embrace, and entwine with our most contracted places, gently opening them out into the mysterious magic of existence . . . it will reunite our masculine selves with the unknown.

In tantric traditions this state of consciousness is known as *mahamudrā*—a realm of being that is wild, unpredictable, spontaneous, playful, paradoxical, love drenched, deeply known yet always unknowable, unspeakable, incredible, laughable, mischievously foxy, full of miraculous creativity; it is a state of being that sings, feels, dances, celebrates without reason, just because it *is*.

The Tibetan saint Naropa said, "Without Karma Mudrā [Womb Priestess], no Mahāmudrā [Enlightenment]."[4]

Unraveling Masculine Imbalance

For the past two thousand or more years, when we have dared look upon the face of the Divine to know ourselves and our universe, we have seen the image of a male creator god mirrored back to us. He stands for truth, for righteousness, for a promise delivered. He is victorious—a warrior, a rule maker, a law giver. He has freed us from our unclean "lowly" existence in our bodies and lifted us up from the dirt of the earth, with the promise of a distant "pure" heaven when we die.

The only thing he has asked for in return is our absolute obedience and worship of him, and to shape the world in his image, according to his worldview—excluding and diminishing all others.

He has asked for sacrifices—for the foreskin of young boys, for wars in his name, for the genocide of nearly 9 million women of the Old Ways during the European inquisition, for the genocide of indigenous cultures around the world, for the continued degradation of the feminine, making menstruation and sexuality a "sin," and for the destruction and disregard of our living Mother Earth. He has asked us to die—or kill—for his righteous laws, to maintain his kingdom of control.

It was not always this way. Once upon a time, *all* of the peoples of the Earth honored the feminine face of both creator and creation, in union with the masculine. The two were not separate—the divine nature of the creator was inextricably woven into all of existence. The universe and all of creation was the body of the Great Mother. We humans were not separate from this. We were her well-loved children, along with all of the other animals, plants, mountains, and stars—born from love. We were integral shining threads of this great cosmic weaving, all equal in importance.

The universe was perceived by the world's peoples to be born from the dark mystery, sprung forth from the Womb of Creation, from the infinite seas of a great Void, filled with a dazzlingly dark energy. For tens of thousands of years these were the feminine creation myths, these were the ancient cosmologies that shaped our perceptions and actions in the world. They were the myths of connection, the myths of an interwoven existence, the myths that honored the web of life that created us and upon which our existence depends.

When we look around us at the modern world, we can see the devastating effects of the loss of the feminine cosmologies—the soul loss and disconnection in the modern world that has resulted in a species where depression is the number one world illness, and where we cannot even safely drink the Earth's waters.

For five thousand years we have lived under the shadow of patriarchal religion, which tells us God is a man, that we are saved by the son of that God, and that until a hundred years ago, women didn't even have souls. The very structure of our societies has been infected by this thought system, whether we believe in God or not. We live in a relentlessly productive, individualistic, (il)logical, extreme hypermasculine paradigm, where the feminine—in both men and women—has been persecuted and competition, greed, and fear rule.

Most of us, including women, don't even realize what we're missing. A deep consistent experience of and connection with the feminine essence has been missing from the world for thousands of years. It is hard to truly imagine now a society founded on cooperation, collaboration, connectedness, and compassion for each other and every creature in the cosmos, and the gifts this would bring.

In unraveling this masculine imbalance and reconnecting with the feminine, it is important to rediscover and explore where the Mother Goddess existed and how she was eliminated from our society—while being discerning about these energies. It is also likely that at some point on Earth a matriarchy ruled that did not honor men and was not the perfect expression of love. This is a root of some of our deep-seated fears of the feminine. A world where womb power ruled without love, compassion, and balance would have been just as destructive as the patriarchy. Everyone has suffered under ruthless or wounded women in positions of power or control, and knows that gender doesn't equate to love.

Reclaiming goddess culture is about reconnection with the feminine vibration of Creation and its Source. We can *feel* and *know* in our wombs and hearts the vibration any particular goddess is connected too. If it is about power, sacrifice, or control it is not truly feminine. It is a false feminine—a demon in a dress—who is operating within exactly the same frequency as the patriarchy, using fear and occult knowledge to control us and separate us from our own power. The true feminine mystery dissolves us into a space beyond gender, beyond the need to control anything or anyone, we "give up the reins" and flow with Life.

Reconnection with the Web of Life

A womb cosmology is a cosmology of connection and interrelatedness. It is primal ecology in the greatest sense, extending out into the entire web of life, including our earthly biosystems, but also to our human and celestial relations. It is a cosmology that honors our living connection to all of the nested "wombs" that birth and sustain us—from the womb of our human mother, to the Womb of Gaia, our garden planet that nurtures us, to the Cosmic Womb from which we came and to which we will return when we die. We live in a series of nested wombs, like Russian dolls, one enfolded within the other: as above, so it is below.

A womb-honoring worldview is not just for women, as both men and women are born from a mother and gestated in her womb. The physical, emotional, and spiritual development of all humans depends upon our experiences in this critical developmental window. Nor does a womb-centric worldview exclude or diminish the importance of men or the masculine energies of the universe. The Mother, as she was envisioned by pre-Taoist, pre-Buddhist, and pre-Vedic cultures, as well many indigenous traditions, was a "face of God" that was easy for us to relate to. Our elders recognized that on a deeper level, Source was beyond man or woman, encompassing both masculine and feminine, as well as all things known and unknown in the universe.

Womb cosmology offers a vision of harmony, love, and respect between men and women. It honors sacred duality, sacred complementarity of the "two becoming one," which is the most carefully guarded secret of the alchemical and esoteric sciences. It is the Great Work—a movement toward a postpatriarchal, postmatriarchal worldview. It is a cosmology of union.

In most traditions, the Great Mother had both masculine and feminine qualities, solar and lunar elements. Though she was known to be both a mother and father to her children, for tens of thousands of years humans primarily related to Source as a female, because she shares many of the fundamental qualities of our human mothers. She is a birther and creator; she creates all of existence from the dark Void, the Cosmic Womb that parallels our own early experiences in our human mother's womb. She nurtures and sustains our life through the fruits of the earth. Though the father's contribution is equally important to creation, it is our mother's body that housed and nurtured us for our nine formative gestational months. We were literally at one with our mother in this gestational time, and most of us spend the rest of our lives trying to discover the riddle of how to again reach such states of profound union—with our beloved, with our community, with our earth, and with the Great Cosmic Mother.

Creator is both a mother and a father to its Creation, it is a beautifully unified consciousness that contains the All. Creation contains the two flows of life force—one creative and active, one dissolving and receptive. These flows are twins, two sides of the same coin.

When we replace "God" with "Goddess" we create a similar hierarchical distortion. Nature suggests that Creation and its Source holds a paradoxical feminine blueprint that is neither male or female as we understand it. Imagining God as a man or woman inevitably involves including the attributes and defects of our own wounded psyches and parents. Either as punishing gods who make us suffer for our sins, or manipulative goddesses we have to please by making offerings.

The feminine essence is a vibration of Love that embraces everything with complete nonjudgment. Everything is allowed. It is innocent, powerful, and creative—it is the force of Life itself. This pure life force does not need our love, our devotion, our worship, our offerings, our sufferings, our atonement. It simply responds, playfully and nonjudgmentally, to our own desires and actions, and always extends pure love to us, should we choose to want to open and receive it.

This can be activated by our own innocent surrendering to the flow of life, and our own willingness to open to love and trust, even when we have fears because of past trauma. Letting go is allowing a wave of infinite love to rush in; it is our nature. We were created from the very substance of love—when we allow ourselves to be as we were originally created we effortlessly return to love.

Everything in existence holds a perfect harmonic blueprint, and anything we do that creates disharmony is countered by a powerful force guiding us back into our original harmony. This is truly a force to be reckoned with. It means that no matter how far we have strayed from harmony, the moment we choose to heal, to learn, to love again—all the forces of creation conspire to support us. Only humans judge each other. Even our wounds are agents of love returning to love.

The true feminine vibration or essence will always feel healing, loving, kind, non-hierarchical, wild. It will awaken your own power, rather than having power over you; it will inspire you with trust, not fear of negative consequences. Love will always be enveloped in a kind, nurturing *Divine softness,* even if it is delivering radical truth or fierce compassion or is wild with primordial passion. As a race we have hardened up; love invites us into softness again.

The womb invites us to remember this life-affirming nectar, this milk of kindness that loves all with purity and passion. It lives inside us—and this is our true savior.

WOMB ORACLES SHARE
Placenta of the Divine Mother

I was taken to a placenta, deep inside Divine Mother's womb—it was a feeling of being held in warm, red, honeylike liquid where I was safe and loved with a beautiful connection to everyone and everything. I received the message that the deeper we go to releasing all our wounds and honoring our blood, the stronger Divine Mother's placenta will become and the Divine Feminine will seep through her veins once more, bringing all life into balance. I saw every Womb joined together with light threads and there was a very deep, harmonizing sound vibration. I was traveling toward a round entrance that was covered over by a web in a membrane, and the power I felt just being close to it was mind-blowing.

S.J.

Inside Divine Mother's Womb

I could perceive Divine Mother only with my heart, not a visual perception at all. I told her about my lack of belief and this old pain. I was enveloped in her embrace, immersed in a light that was not a light, but light that contained the deepest dark and the brightest light, matter and energy, it contained all things. I felt love and the deepest peace. I felt beginnings and endings. I felt the most sacred feeling of complete understanding and absolution. The feeling that there is no need for absolution because in the center of it all I was pure and fully complete. It was beyond words. After the ceremony, I just sat in the moonlight. I could feel the nourishment just flowing within the light.

Also since I am in my moon cycle, when I placed my blood under my tongue, I sensed a profound difference. Before, it was just blood. This morning, the only way to describe it is as if my blood was alive and it was singing. My blood is singing.

J.O.M.

Aboriginal Black Madonna

At the cosmic gateway, I met the crone; an Australian Aboriginal woman appeared before me—she was naked and she opened her yoni to me. She was beautiful with the richness of earth and everything patriarchy classes as "ugly," her yoni was beautiful and black. She was an aboriginal Black Madonna. She beckoned me to enter her vulva. I walked through the lips of her yoni as she held it wide. Inside I began walking down a long dark tunnel—the royal road. It was beautifully lush, like a rainforest, shimmering in darkness and the wild scents of ancient earth.

As I reached the end of her sacred passageway, her cervix stood before me—a deep black hole. I stood humbled in front of this cosmic gateway of mystical power. With reverence I began to walk through it. As I entered the gateway it became a narrow passageway, like a naturally hewn tunnel in an underground cave. Lying on my belly, pulling myself along with my hands, in utter darkness I passed through.

Suddenly I found myself expanded into the cosmic cathedral of the Aboriginal woman's womb. I felt how I was deep within the ancestral womb. The blackness shimmered around me, melting into infinity, rich with fertility and warmth. I was in a holy place. I could feel the consciousness of the aboriginal Black Madonna surround me and infuse me—I was deep inside her sacred well; we had merged. She told me to sing the songlines; she beseeched me that earth's song was calling out. I could feel her Spirit with the world, and that she was the Soul of the world. She reminded me that all the ancestors were with us, there was so much support. "You are all in my womb," she told me, "and I will never leave you. You are inside me."

S.B.

SPIRAL 12

WOMBTIME ORIGINS OF SHAMANISM

The Dreaming Dimension of the Brain

In the beginning was the golden womb, the seed of elemental existence.

ATHARVA VEDA

THROUGHOUT THE AGES, mystics and shamans have long understood that behind the visible, logical world there exists another deeper reality—a feminine fairyland of consciousness. It has been called otherworld, spirit world, the real world, the Tao, and many other names, but its essence remains the same across time and cultures.

This realm of spirit exists beyond the confines of language and the laws of the physical universe. In moments of spiritual epiphany, the logical, rational, masculine mind no longer comprehends itself. Instead, it surrenders into a realm of mother consciousness guided by the deeper instincts of a hidden feminine process, a journey into the dark but scintillating field of universal root consciousness.

What we call shamanism is essential feminine consciousness, a truth reflected in an old indigenous proverb from the Chuckee tradition that says, "woman is by nature a shaman." The oldest shamanic burial site—from 28,000 BCE—found in the Czech Republic was that of a female shaman who was buried with all her ritual objects, with the menstrual red ochre paint that was typical for the shaman. Often male shamans mimicked feminine rites, such as menstruation, and male shamans were known to wear women's clothes. The word *shaman* means "one who knows" or "she who flows with the moon." The origins of shamanism are rooted in the prehistoric womb religion, representing the journey to reclaim the feminine dreamtime of Womb Consciousness. Elders in their moonapause and menstruating, pregnant, and sexually awakened women were the first shamans and initiators, whose wombs held the Spirit Gate between the worlds.

This is reflected in the "pure land" of the Tibetan dakinis, called *Nyayab Khandro Ling,* which can be translated as "dakini-land of the drumbeat," referring to the maternal landscape of the womb and the mother's body, with the shamanic, drumming pulse of her heartbeat.

The shamanic spiritual process belongs to the domain of quantum physics, in which all known laws of science break down into a sea of unpredictable quantum fluctuations at the root of physical existence—where we enter the birthing gate of matter, pouring forth her pregnant potentiality from the quantum womb Void.

Carl Jung speaks of it as a merging of the personal and collective unconscious mind into an archetypal or mythic reality, a holographic realm that quantum physicists now believe *entangles* matter across infinite time and space in a *nonlocal,* seemingly magical, but very real way. It is the "implicit order" described by physicist David Bohm, in which what the logical mind sees as chaos is organic order.

Entering our mother's womb and experiencing the mystical alchemical transmutation of spirit into matter inside the crucible of the sacred uterus is our first experience of shamanic Womb Consciousness embodied in this earthly realm.

The mystery of human gestation, hidden from sight in the dark womb-belly of the mother, is the origin of the universal alchemical notion that the most powerful magic occurs in an *occult,* or hidden, process, centered in the womb. In the unseen darkness of the womb cauldron, a fetus magically grows, blooms, and journeys forth into being on the red waters of life.

Wombtime as Shamanic Dreamtime

In the womb we enter a primal shamanic chamber of initiation that takes us on an epic journey through the evolution of collective and planetary consciousness, mirrored in our own formation—literally coded into the very atoms of our being.

We experience this magical shamanic journey deep in our newly developing bodies and brains, which are being forged like earthly stars, creating a blueprint for our soul's ability to embody feminine consciousness in our later life. Scientific research now confirms that our time gestating in the womb is a dreamtime state—an other-world state, an inner fairyworld, deep inside Womb Consciousness, which sets up an imprint, both spiritual and biological, of how our external lives will unfold.

During gestation babies swim in an amniotic ocean of dreamtime reality, merging dreampaths of both earth and the cosmos. We know from the development of the nervous system in newborns that different parts of the brain come online at different stages of development in the Womb. What we think of as "ordinary" consciousness as adults—thinking, logical, rational awareness—is generated by the cerebral cortex, a relative newcomer in development, and also in the history of life on this planet. The cerebrum is what society thinks of as the brain—the planning, practical, logical decision maker. We could call it the "masculine" brain. Yet it was actually the *last* part of the nervous system to develop in the Womb. It begins to come online only around six months of gestation, and even then, is barely functional. The other brain regions, the feminine "feeling brain," including the limbic system—the amygdala and hippocampus—as well as the cerebellum, are the centers of the brain connected to emotions and feelings. They form much earlier in gestation. Feelings are the soul.

When a baby's consciousness comes online in the womb, its perceptual intelligence awakens, but it is a different intelligence than the adult's. It is a *dreamtime* intelligence. The "back brain" or "primal brain" is activated, but the cerebral cortex remains asleep. It is similar to what we might experience while dreaming or in altered states of consciousness—through shamanic journeying, trance states, entheogens, ecstasy, or "religious rapture." Essentially the baby is a newly awakened shaman, already on an epic shamanic adventure, in his or her own unique womb chariot.

As the human embryo develops, the fetus retraces the forms of the evolutionary origins of life on this planet, memories held in the *arbor vitae,* the ancient tree of life of the cerebellum, which originated some 500 million years ago. The cerebellar development is so complex that it is one of the last areas of the brain to finish maturation, continuing to change, remodel, and be "pruned" throughout our lives. The cerebellum is very plastic—meaning it is a shamanic shape-shifter of consciousness and responds to our thoughts, feelings, experiences, and beliefs. The location of the cerebellum is shown in fig. 12.1.

In later months of gestation we spend 90 percent of our time dreaming in deep REM states. Our sensory perceptions when we're in the womb are radically different from those of our adult self. In the womb, we still have access to our primary perception, which is an undifferentiated infinite spectrum of kaleidoscopic sensations and images and feelings similar to a hallucinogenic experience, where we access multi-dimensional consciousness.

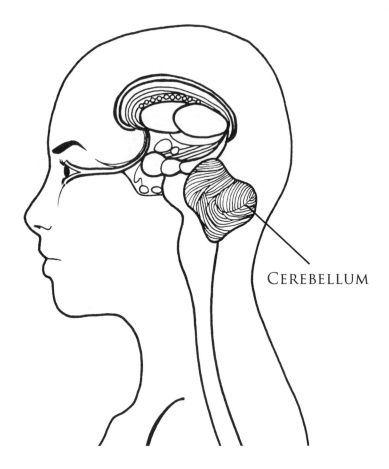

Fig. 12.1 The cerebellum, seat of feminine consciousness
(Illustration by Natvienna Hanell)

As babies we are fully "awake" and intelligent to our multidimensional soul-self, but are anchored in an imaginal wonderland. This is the root of our multidimensional, holographic consciousness. This has been researched by many people, such as Stanislav Grof, the founder of holotropic breathing who used both LSD and shamanic breathing to help people access memories and experiences in the womb and wombtime consciousness.

The key to the shamanic experience of the baby is the brain's "lost" feminine gateway to God—the cerebellum, located in the back of the brain, which is the home of our primal, feminine consciousness and the dreamtime of the ancients. Our solar-focused world has forgotten and forbidden all memories of the mysterious womb realm of shining darkness that every human was created in—but these memories live on, now stored in a place we call the "unconscious." The magical lunar waters of our feminine time in the womb, and the Womb Consciousness it is generated by, become the dark, disturbing, shadow waters of the lost feminine soul, where our inner monsters and demons lurk, and where our inner treasures call us.

When we lost connection to this inner dreamtime, to our deepest feelings and multisensory perception, we also lost connection to our "inner shaman," our soul, and the soul of the world. Patriarchy deliberately demonizes and programs us to fear this nonlinear, feminine consciousness, and bars the way to her dreaming gate—in case we journey through and release our perceptual bondage.

Shamanism of the feminine mysteries focuses on entering this gateway again, connecting and journeying back to this otherworld, to the dreamtime worlds within and the songlines of primordial feminine consciousness, which we first experienced within the womb—a magical liminal place "between the worlds." Medicine plants, trance music, trance drumming, trance dance, mantra, shamanic breathing, prayer, invocation, intentional daydreaming, all alter consciousness so we can take a shamanic journey and return to the living dreamtime we experienced in the Womb.

It is believed that our pineal gland, seat of the "third eye" psychic chakra of many yogic systems, had its evolutionary origins as a pair of independently functioning reptilian, or "dragon" eyes located at the top and back of the head, and linked directly to our cerebellum. Over hundreds of millions of years they descended into the brain and became the inner "eye of the cerebellum," which may explain why this gland buried in the middle of our brain is still sensitive to light.[1] This is the mystical seat of our "seeing" through the portal of Womb Consciousness.

The gift of shamanism is to be able to return to this primal consciousness and to reclaim the extraordinary capacities we naturally possessed in the womb—including extrasensory perception; memories of the Earth's evolution and Akashic Record; memories of past/coemergent lives; connection to multidimensional realms and interplanetary memories; abilities to transcend time and space; genetic shapeshifting abilities to embody the different animal races on Earth; and innate knowing and connection with cosmic wisdom. And most importantly, to retain a deeply felt and embodied umbilical cord connection with Creator and Creation.

Healing the Inner Split

The cerebrum, the brain of the conscious mind, and the cerebellum, the brain of the mystical unconscious mind, are the twin bride and bridegroom, the world parents of mythology. The cerebellar brain, governess of the primal brain network, holds the key to the feminine dimensions of experience—dreams, creativity, feelings, ecstatic states, trance, deep sexuality, oracular states, prophecy, waking dreams, and other nonordinary consciousness. On the other hand, the cerebral brain is in charge of the masculine dimensions of thinking, logic, rationality, focus, and being able to practically carry projects to completion in the external world.

Many people mistakenly think that the left side of the brain is inherently masculine and the right side of the brain is feminine. This is a misconception. Although the front brain does split different functions into the left and right sides—with the right hemisphere involved in more feminine qualities (in right-handed people)—either side of the cerebral cortex can embody both feminine and masculine consciousness, and can swap many of their functions to the other side in a crisis. Our cerebellum, on the other hand, is so deeply embedded in the primal feminine networks of our brain that it is created to be the throne of our feminine consciousness.

In gestation, the subtle hormonal differences between boys and girls profoundly affect brain development, not just the growth of the reproductive organs. Female hormones cause the development of a larger cerebellum in women—the primal brain of creativity, intuition, dreamtime, nonlinear thinking, and shamanic and supersensory capacities—as well as greater cross-connectivity between the different sides of the brain. Whereas men have smaller cerebellums and are more inclined to logical, problem-solving thinking, giving them an innate capacity to plan and build in the external world. Although men and women can still access both types of consciousness, their unique differences generate a potent synergy when unified in the alchemical cauldron. A beautiful blueprint of creation emerges, in which we can see and feel the inner union of our "masculine" cerebrum and "feminine" cerebellum, mirrored in the complementary union of male and female, who, together in sacred union consciousness, can vision and create paradise.

The cerebellum is a tenth of the size of the cerebrum, but its labyrinthine folds allow it to contain more brain cells/neurons than the *entire rest of the body put together*. Containing 70 percent of the body's neurons, it has more than double the amount of brain cells than the cerebral cortex. This seat of feminine consciousness is a transceiving station between earth and many interdimensional portals to otherworld and Divine Mother. In our original blueprint of creation, the cerebellum was the space where we retained our cosmic connection, our ancient memories, our soul purpose, where we attuned to the greater cosmic vision of Oneness, sometimes known as the "will" of God. The cerebrum was the masculine consciousness that implemented this state of knowing, that translated cosmic information into action.

In ancient times, a sacred bridge of communication existed between our cerebrum and cerebellum, meaning that our actions on Earth were harmonic and in tune with the web of life and Creator. The masculine and feminine worked together to create a world of beauty, wonder, and joy here on Earth that was in balance. At some point this bridge was broken and the cerebrum took over. The translator disconnected and became "god." This is what is known as the fall of consciousness. Set adrift, now the cerebellum is a weird and wondrous dreamtime realm separated from our conscious self—full of either hellish terror or heavenly ecstasy, depending on our experiences in our mother's womb. Shamanic journeys can help heal this inner split.

The cerebellum is *conscious* during our dreamtime in the womb, experiencing and storing all our mystical, magical dreamtime perceptions and cosmic knowings, but also storing all the epigenetic imprints of inherited fear and suffering. At some point these collective imprints from the maternal and paternal ancestral line become so overwhelming that the cerebellum shuts down from fully conscious perception, in order to protect herself during gestation, and so our magical Womb world becomes unconscious.

Awakening the Womb and feminine consciousness and returning to the feminine feeling dimension, builds a bridge of union between the two halves of our consciousness again. This is the task of restoration and "making whole" again.

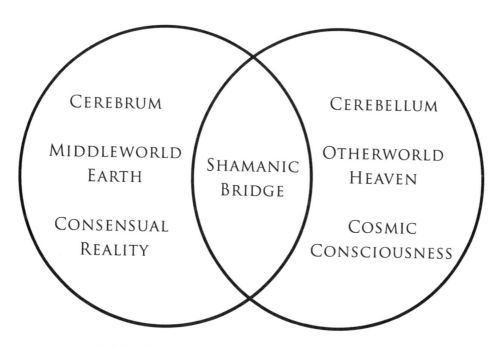

Fig. 12.2. Healing the inner split with a shamanic bridge of union
(Diagram by Heather Skye)

The cerebellum is the HQ of a "primal brain" network that sends, receives, modifies, and processes the vast world of unconscious information that runs the greatest part of our physical and psychic organism. It is unconscious only from the perspective of our cerebral cortex, which dares not lift the lid and peer into the dark, mysterious oceans of the cerebellum. However the cerebellum knows *everything* the cerebrum sees and thinks—every section of the cerebral cortex feeds information down to the cerebellum. In fact, to a great extent, the cerebellum and primal brain network controls exactly what the cerebral cortex "sees," through an extensive network of "sensory gating" or filtering systems, with the thalamus as the door or gateway of perception, the final stage through which all sensory information passes on its way to conscious perception in the cerebral cortex.

Cerebellum: Architect of the Dreamtime

The cerebellum is the cathedral of the mystic. Writes William Blake, "When the doors of perception are cleansed, you will see the world as it truly is, infinite."

Our dreams, new ideas, imaginal openings, and prophetic, magical, and extrasensory information originate in the fertile unconscious brain centers of the cerebellum and primal-brain network, and are then projected up onto the "movie screen" of the cerebral cortex, so that our conscious mind can become aware and make use of the vast cauldron of creative magic living within our cerebellar treasure chest. She is literally Pandora's box, the transmitting and receiving—transceiving—station of all magical, numinous, mystical, and otherworldly consciousness.

Philosopher, mystic, and scientist Emanuel Swedenborg, writing in the mid-eighteenth century, describes the cerebellum as the doorway to the mystical realms of the Divine, where God dwells. He explains that angels connect to the heavenly realms through the back of the brain—the primordial feminine centers, including the amygdala and cerebellum—and that in ancient times humans also had access to this pure angelic cerebellar consciousness, which made them divine.

Modern mystic Gurdjieff also focused on the magical properties of the cerebellum, and devised movement meditations to activate this nonlogical feminine consciousness. Most recently, psychologist Stan Gooch was pivotal in remembering the importance of the cerebellum, and linking it to the development of extraordinary clairvoyant, clairaudient, and psychic abilities.

The cerebellum has access to more than just our own individual biological perceptions. Like the vast interconnected networks of roots in a forest that act as a "biological internet," merging their biological "computing power" into a unified whole, the vast synaptic connections of our cerebellum and unconscious brain act like a quantum computer, receiving information from an infinite *quantumly entangled, nonlocal* perceptual field. This informational field, shared across space and time, is also known as the Akashic field. The eminent neurologist Karl Pribram was the first to understand and write about the brain's capacity to draw memories from a quantum cloud that exists outside of the physical brain. The idea of sharing unconscious information has been documented by the remarkable dream-sharing research conducted at the Maimonides Medical Center of New York and by many others.[2]

It is through our cerebellum, the womb portal of our brain, that our consciousness can shamanically reach up to the stars, or down to our deepest ancestral memories. She is the mistress of the infinite, the magical doorway, or "Magdalene," of the brain.

Our dreams emerge from the neural womb of our cerebellum every night. This multidimensional feminine intelligence communicates to us as the night falls, the moon rises, and we fall asleep. The cerebellum is the fairyland of consciousness, yet it is also very real, with very potent powers. Its primordial feminine consciousness is *creative*—whatever lives deep inside this womb-brain is not only projected into your dreams, but also your waking life.

The cerebellum is the magnet, the architect, the engineer, who weaves threads of synchronicity and seemingly impossible coincidence into your life. She also orchestrates the incredible storylines of unconscious trauma replay in our lives, hoping that by reliving the past we will remember it, and choose to change the future. The cerebellum is the cauldron of possibility and divine memory stirred and watched over by the Cosmic Mother.

The cerebellum is also the location and storage suite of our earliest memories, including our gestational memories.[3] It is thought that no piece of information stored in the cerebellum is ever lost, and these stored cerebellar memories continue to affect and "stalk" us through adulthood.[4]

On the other hand, the cerebrum is only allowed to see what is safe to see. The enormous amount of raw sensory data that allows the cerebellum to "see the big picture," and quickly make complex and intuitive decisions (without the cerebrum noticing) would overwhelm the masculine mind. Experiences, memories, and information that would be too unsettling to perceive are held in the cerebellar memory banks until they can be dealt with later, at a safer time, preserving the fragile ego at all costs. This is the biological basis of the repression of undesired memories and emotions.

Unfortunately, the repressed memories and traumas of the cerebellum do not go away or rest peacefully. They are like the steam whistling out of a pressure cooker—emerging sideways in dreams, unconscious behaviors, coincidences, and "law of attraction" events that profoundly influence our lives, for better or worse, depending on the extent to which we have healed our unconscious feminine psyche.

The cerebrum is the practical manager of worldy tasks, designed to takes notes and instructions and listen to the guidance of the deep feminine brain, but in this modern age he often forgets his true cosmic role and gets lost. However, when he truly listens to the whispers of the web of life, and when he is able to work together with the cerebellum, his practical skills become an invaluable part of the creative process.

Interestingly, the development of the shamanic and magical cerebellum peaked with the Neanderthal brain forty thousand years ago—a race who had a much bigger cerebellum than we do. This cerebellar capacity was revered by later civilizations, including the Egyptians, who were known to artificially enhance the shape of the head to mimic a large back brain. Since that time the human brain has been shrinking. If we are blessed, we can begin to take the hero or heroine's journey to reunite with our feminine consciousness again, to release the negative imprints held within her memory bank, and to awaken her Cosmic Womb eye again into the dazzling, multidimensional realms of creation. This is *gnosis*—when knowledge becomes essence.

Seat of Our Soul Shakti

The cerebellum is like a neural mystery school within the brain that guides and initiates all the ecstatic feminine potentials of embodiment, healing, relationship, intimacy, empathy, sexual arousal, and bliss. It is the portal to creating paradise.

Through this magical gateway we connect to and embody our deepest passions, desires, soul songs, the beauty of sensual movement, the power of our *Soul Shakti*.

"The cerebellum is the center and seat of desire," said the neurologist Gall in the nineteenth century[5]—a truth that is now being reflected by modern neuroscientists, with recent research linking the cerebellum to our deep unconscious motivations and desires. We are desire-beings in our essence. Desire is the sacred fire that gives birth to all of our creations. By awakening this womb of our brain we *come fully alive*.

Mystical traditions throughout the ages have intuitively understood that the primal brain network is the seat of the feminine soul, yet modern medicine has reduced the role of the cerebellum and limited it to purely physical movement and balance. It *is* true that the cerebellum governs the complexities of movement and coordination, but beyond that it also makes possible the process referred to to as embodiment or embodied awakening. It connects the profound consciousness, feelings, and memories stored in the cells, muscles, and organs of our body.[6] The cerebellum is what makes it possible to express the feeling-language of our soul through dance and movement. It is instrumental in coordinating expressive body language, and in mirroring others.[7] Our body actually *thinks* through a process scientists call embodied cognition. Our body also *feels* by embodied emotions. The organization and integration of all these arenas—our emotions, movement, body talk, body wisdom, cellular memories, and physical sensual awakening—are the realms of the cerebellum and the primal brain network. These are at the core of the feminine healing arts as practiced for thousands of years in the feminine mystery schools.

This feminine aspect of our brain is also the guardian of sacred union, awakened sexuality, and conscious relationship. It helps us embody and live the qualities needed to open to a deeply loving and bonded relationship—and it also holds the trauma memories that trigger us and cause separation and emotional conflict. Our wounds of love and our neural gateways of reconnection live in this sacred site.

Research over the past two decades has established that the cerebellum plays an important role in everything related to loving relationship.[8] It is fundamentally involved in accessing emotions and experiencing empathy—the foundation of healthy relationships. It helps determine whether or not we feel emotionally defensive, or "triggered."[9] The cerebellum stores memories of fears and traumas until they are healed and released, a function traditionally ascribed solely to the amygdala and limbic brain. Given its involvement in so many parts of the sensory and emotional processing systems, and its incredible information processing power, it is likely that the cerebellum acts as a central headquarters and "brain" of the emotional neural networks—coordinating, processing, and modulating the responses of all the other emotional centers.[10]

The cerebellum plays an important function in sexual memories and arousal, and because of the inherent psychic capacities of the unconscious brain, this likely extends beyond just personal experiences into collective memories and past or coemergent lifetimes. It is also involved in the experiences of sensual pleasure—the deepest gateway to our healing and awakening—with research linking the cerebellum to sexual pleasure as well as the soul-inspiring pleasure that comes from listening to beautiful music.[11] Healthy cerebellar functioning is the heart of sacred, loving, and conscious relationship.

As touched upon in spiral 9, Saint Hildegard Von Bingen alludes in her mystical writing to the magical qualities of the female brain, the cerebellum, in its role in the alchemy of orgasm, saying, "When a woman makes love to a man, a feeling of heat in her brain [cerebellum], which results in a sensual pleasure, announces the taste of that pleasure during the act and incites the deposition of the man's sperm. And once the semen has fallen into place, this intense heat in her brain attracts the seed and retains it, and soon the female organs contract, and now all parts opening up during menstruation close, in the same way a strong man can lock up an object in his clenched fist."

The cerebellum is also the seat of the imagination and intuition, the neural receiving and transmitting station that allows us to hear our deep intuition and whispers of the soul—the voice of the womb—and breathe these dreams into being. It is through the cerebellum that we tap into and follow our inner knowing, in harmonious connection with the web of life. The suggestions of our deep feminine brain may not always make logical sense, but if we follow its lead, magical synchronicities await us. Having the courage to follow this voice of inspiration and our sixth sense is at the heart of the feminine spiritual path, guiding us into the fertile flow of Shakti. They are direct communications from the Cosmic Mother.

Mouth of the Goddess: Feminine Third Eye

The energetic gateway to the cerebellum is known as the mouth of the Goddess and is linked to the all-seeing eye of the Womb. If our masculine third eye lives at our brow chakra, then our feminine third eye lives in this mysterious back-brain cavern region. In esoteric spiritual traditions, this area—corresponding to the cerebellum and brain stem at the base of the skull and above the first cervical vertebrae—has long been recognized as an important energy center. Helena Blavatsky, writing and channeling in the theosophical lineage, referred to this area as the *alta major,* and believed it to be a key to awakening. In Egypt, the ankh, or symbol of life, is often pointed at either the mouth or the cerebellum to transmit divine power. In the Chinese Taoist tradition, it is called the "jade pillow" (*Yu Chen*), and is considered a feminine, or yin, part of the brain, also referred to as the mouth of the God/Goddess, meant to balance the cerebral yang brain.[12]

Through the feminine third eye, our vision of the world is seen through the eyes of the cerebellum—the doorway into infinity, "the eye of the unconscious mind."[13] This home of a vast magical intelligence makes use of the nearly infinite perceptual capacities at our disposal, rather than relying solely on the five specialized senses (taste, touch, smell, vision, and hearing) perceived by our cerebral cortex. As the mystical saying goes, "Why would anyone be content to look through the five slits in the tower, when they could take off the roof and behold the grandeur of the entire night sky?" Opening our cerebellum, the feminine third eye, awakens our "witch eyes" in the back of our head.

Nondual Womb Consciousness

One of the paradigm-shifting conclusions reached by the feminine depth psychology work of the last century is that the deepest root consciousness in humans, what psychologists call the "unconscious" psyche, *holds a feminine maternal vibration, and this feminine consciousness is the womb and mother of the "conscious" masculine cerebral mind*.[14] In other words, the magical, nonlinear womb of the unconscious mind is primary—it comes first, both in our personal development as a baby, and in the evolution of life on the planet, just in the same way black holes birth stars.

Only later does this primordial consciousness, rooted in darkness, give birth to the logical, thinking, rational mind, which emerges like a tiny island of self-awareness out of the dark primeval waters—just as it is described in so many cosmogonic creation myths around the world. Universally, the light of conscious awareness is birthed from the fertile and infinite darkness of the unconscious feminine Void.

These unconscious processes in the deep feminine psyche are the birthers not just of our *inner* experiences, but, astoundingly, of the *external* events in our lives as well; our unconscious psyche magically draws events and experiences into our life. These are the synchronicities, coincidences, signs, and omens recognized by all shamanic cultures for many thousands of years. The deep feminine psyche holds an incredible creative power that would be considered magical and mysterious to the logical mind, which often cannot grasp the bigger spiritual picture or understand the root cause of the events happening in its own life. The conscious mind more easily perceives the single tree, whereas the unconscious perceives the entire forest.

The term *unconscious mind* itself fails to fully convey the practical *and* mythic power of our deep psyche, betraying the modern disregard for the incredible dreamtime intelligence that exists in our feminine depths. The unconscious mind is simply a different dimension of awareness than our conscious mind—a vast lunar awareness rather than a focused solar one. The exquisite intelligence of the unconscious mind not only governs our biological, instinctive, and emotional realms, but as an entire new field of research suggests, it is a better decision maker than our conscious masculine mind—and can even perceive the future.[15]

Female oracles who had awakened the black light of the mystical unconscious and cerebellum, could enter prophetic states by reading the possibilities and probabilities spanning out in luminous threads through the cosmic web of time.

Popular media commonly reports that 90 percent of our perceptions and mental activities are happening below the level of our conscious awareness. However according to modern neuroscience studies, it is closer to 99.999 percent—our unconscious mind processes an astonishing *500,000 times* more information than our conscious mind.[16]

When the deep feminine psyche chooses, she brings the masculine consciousness back into her dark womb for dissolution, as she does every night when we sleep, and as she does at the time of our death. The idea that masculine cerebral consciousness could ever in any way exist outside of the deep feminine consciousness, or be separate from it, is an illusion. Cerebral consciousness can only ever be nested in wombs within wombs of a deeper mother consciousness. The unconscious psyche is its revelatory foundation. The logical, rational mind is not a mistake—but a much-loved child and creation of the Mother, who holds, guides, and inspires it like a parent or lover. Only when the cerebral logical consciousness fragments into thinking it is separate, above, and disconnected from the mother consciousness that created it do problems arise. Then it becomes like a cancer cell of consciousness, something that moves out of harmony with the greater whole. As Albert Einsten observed, "The intuitive mind is a sacred gift. The rational mind is a faithful servant. We have created a society that honors the servant and has forgotten the gift."

The twins of consciousness, masculine and feminine, solar and lunar, and the brain parts that house them, cerebrum and cerebellum, are designed to be in sacred union, not separate. It is *both/and* rather than *either/or*. Both play a unique function and work together as a couple, conceiving and birthing magical creations.[17]

The individual's journey of consciousness, from the initial deep feminine state of Womb Consciousness to an eventual masculine cerebral consciousness, retraces and recapitulates the entire evolutionary journey of human consciousness, reaching back to the dawn of humanity. This knowing is described in the feminine myths, art, and symbols across time and culture. The earliest Neanderthals and Stone Age cultures occupied a fluid dreamtime consciousness much closer to the magical realms available to very young children, but they experienced it in adult bodies capable of surviving and sustaining themselves quite easily in this physical world.

Our ancestors lived in a dreamtime shamanic dimension of consciousness, just as each of us did while in the womb. They lived here on this same Earth, but in an enchanted and magical dimension that we can no longer easily perceive, in deep harmony with the Earth and her plants and animals. They naturally accessed extrasensory perceptions and telepathic capacities that we would consider superhuman, but that are patiently waiting for each of us to rediscover when we are ready. The neural pathways were already forged and walked during our time in the womb, and live on in our ancestral DNA, we need only reach across the veil and remember—so we can perceive beyond the mists and enter the "inner Isle of Avalon" once more.

The development of our individual consciousness from baby to adult parallels the evolution of consciousness in the human race: the powerful imaginal capacity of early humans is similar to the rich dreamworld of children. However, as indigenous shamans know, our earliest experiences and mythic images extend back far beyond the human era, and even beyond the history of Earth; they reach back to the beginning of consciousness itself, a consciousness that was contained in the quantum fields of matter even before the development of biological life. Our personal developmental journey, from spirit descending into fertilized egg to an adult human, retraces the entire evolutionary path of the consciousness of the universe. We "know" everything.

This is the source of our shamanic capacity to *remember and retrieve* knowledge from the quantum womb field, also called the Akashic field, quantum information field, zero point field, and implicit order by modern physicists and consciousness researchers. Because each of us has experienced these mystical states of multidimensional communion very early in our development, the neural pathways and cords of connection have already been formed. In a quantum sense we are *entangled* with them; we need only dive through the womb portal, into the deep feminine psyche, to remember. These threads of memory speak to us from within, guiding us along a path of grace and magic, if we choose to listen to them.

The development of every individual's consciousness begins in the maternal womb-vessel—as spirit descending into a single-celled, fertilized egg in the womb, in a deep feminine state of union consciousness. This is a nondual existence merged with the heart of the cosmos, outside of space and time. Gradually, the developing embryo begins to perceive more and more of the events in this world—the heartbeat and movements of her mother, the sounds and dim light that filter into the womb, and eventually her own dreams and visions triggered by her womb experiences. Yet it is in the perceptual framework of "I and the Mother are One."

Children Will Inherit the Earth

Throughout the early stages of childhood, the deep connection with the magical dreamtime world continues, only slowly beginning to solidify into a more logical cerebral consciousness by the age of six to seven years. Over this time, brain waves shift from the deep alpha and theta brain-wave patterns of early childhood that mark hyper-receptive imaginal states, to the beta patterns of more ordinary adult cerebral awareness. In our modern world, by adolescence, many of the experiences of early childhood can no longer be accessed in ordinary states of consciousness—they remain only as faint whispers in the dreamy darkness of the feminine psyche.

Across the ages, spiritual and religious traditions have recognized that children and gestating babies are merged in the ocean of wisdom, living in a state of consciousness that is closer to the divine, as compared to most adults. They have not yet lost their soul connection to the mother consciousness of the deep psyche.

A beautiful Jewish midrash (rabbinic literature), the Tanhuma Pekude, tells the story of the feminine angel of conception, Lailah, the midwife of souls, explaining that she lights a lamp over the head of the unborn child so he or she can see from one end of the world to the other. The gestating baby learns the entire Torah (womb lore) as well as the history of his soul in his nine months in the womb. He journeys to all the worlds, including the garden of Eden, and the netherworld of Gehanna. Then, at the moment of birth, she taps his lip and the light goes out. The baby forgets all he has learned.[18]

The ancient feminine wisdom is also in the Hasidic tradition, where it says, "The saddik [the perfected man] finds that which has been lost since birth and restores it."[19]

The Chinese sage Lao-tzu says, "He who is in harmony with the Tao is like a newborn child."[20]

And in the Christian Bible, Jesus describes this quality of original innocence, saying, "the Kingdom of God belongs to those who are like these children," and "whoever does not receive the Kingdom of God like a child will not enter it at all."[21]

In the Gnostic Gospel of Thomas it is written, "Jesus saw some babies nursing. He said to his disciples, 'These nursing babies are like those who enter the [Mother's queendom].' They said to him, 'Then shall we enter the [Mother's queendom] as babies?' Jesus said to them, 'When you make the two into one, and when you make the inner like the outer and the outer like the inner, and the upper like the lower, and when you make male and female into a single one, so that the male will not be male nor the female be female . . . then you will enter [the queendom].'"[22]

What does it mean that we must be like children to enter heaven? Jesus gives esoteric clues for those ready to enter the queendom of Womb Consciousness. Children are in an undivided state of consciousness—in them the two have become one, the male and female aspects have been made into a single one. In children, the masculine cerebrum and feminine cerebellum are fluidly merged, and in this way their whole consciousness is still open, innocent and receptive to the magic of spirit. The shamanic bridge between the dreaming and thinking mind is intact.

Indigenous cultures around the world regard children as teachers, not just as vulnerable dependents who have no intelligence. Because they are closer to and can still access the prenatal realm of mystical consciousness, they are still enfolded in the womb of the original knowledge. The dreams, images, questions, and responses of children are like treasures. The innocent words of the child might uncover lost ancestral knowledge, or reveal that they are the reincarnation of an ancestor or saint, as in the Buddhist Tulku tradition. The imprints of our original gestational knowledge still live within us, as memories. All deep knowing, all sacred knowledge, all prophetic revelation *can be regarded as memory,* stored deep in the cerebellar unconscious, in a dimension that exists outside of linear time and space. We do not need to work hard for, or struggle to achieve that which is already within us. We need only dive deep and remember. It is like a flower bud waiting to bloom.

Flowering of Consciousness

Our current crisis in modern human cultures is that we have become too polarized into masculine consciousness. In doing so, we have lost access to the feminine psyche, and have *failed to recognize and remember its numinous, magical, and divine nature*—and how this naturally interweaves us with the ecosystem of Gaia, so that our actions are in tune with her, and not harmful. The greatest peril to the survival of our species is this disconnection from Womb Consciousness—the loss of our divine nature—and our redemption, as a collective, lies in is its recovery.

When we have lost connection with our inner psychic source, our feminine Womb Consciousness, we are weak and vulnerable, fragmented and separated. Because we don't recognize the true cause of the problem, and our primordial need for reconnection and interconnection is not addressed at its sacred root, we divert our deep human longings and passions into a process of searching among an infinite variety of distractions and substitutes that can never bring us to wholeness.

We are like hungry ghosts, who can eat and eat but never be fulfilled. In this state, we are taken advantage of by the media, by marketing, by politicians, but the original problem remains veiled. For thousands of years, indigenous cultures around the world taught their children a different way—to reestablish a connection and communication with our root consciousness, and to the many living and layered "mother wombs" that contain us and upon which we depend: our inner unconscious psyche, our body, our sacred relationships, our Earth, and the cosmos itself.

Many famous thinkers, including Carl Jung, see the return to mother consciousness as a potential danger—a regression, or an infantile urge. The return to root consciousness is not about returning to a dependent childlike state, in which many people are developmentally trapped due to unresolved emotional wounds. Instead, it is about rebirthing our ability as a species to gracefully traverse the developmental stages of childhood so that we can flower and bloom into the full promise of our adulthood. From this full flowering of consciousness, we can inherit the awesome creative powers of the unconscious mind and mother consciousness, and put them into *practical action* in a way that is harmonious and embodies the beautiful evolutionary impulse of life. This is the path of birthing new earth.

Awakening Our Womb Shaman

The shamans (known as mamas) of the indigenous Kogi tribe spend the first eighteen years of life in a dark place to attune with Aluna—the root of Womb Consciousness. Ancient cave art sourced from the feminine dreamtime dimension—such as that in Lascaux or the Peche-Merle caves in France—is often located in caves that are difficult to access and require crawling through narrow black tunnels, mimicking the experience of the baby traveling between the worlds through his mother's yoni passageway. Spiritually, the initiate or pilgrim is being birthed and rebirthed through the Womb of Gaia, the gateway of the Great Mother.

Saint Patrick, the Catholic holy man from Ireland, was lowered down into a cave of "purgatory" by ropes in the fifth century, where he spent three days and nights experiencing his shamanic death and rebirth journey in the Womb of the Divine Mother. For hundreds of years, pilgrims followed in his footsteps and were lowered into this womblike cave to spend their three days in "penitence," to emerge "born again."

Over time, these ancient womb-rites were forgotten, discarded, and deliberately destroyed. We now live in a world that reveres the brightly lit, external solar pathways and demands our compliance with the logical mind; yet all shamans seek out the darkened, inner, lunar pathways and chambers for insight and initiation.

The power of the night, of the Black Womb, was known to initiate altered states of consciousness and awareness—to awaken our inner witch eyes, making us a seer of spirit world. The hormone melatonin, produced by the pineal gland and linked with psychic activity, is only produced in the darkness of the nighttime.

In solar or cerebral consciousness, the thalamus filters out much of what we perceive and experience in accordance with conditioned and limited parameters set originally by the beliefs and values of our parents and our parent culture. Our vast perception is programmed and "caged."

When we cleanse our programming and leave our cage of limited beliefs, we step beneath the thalamus and return to our wombtime, dreamtime, feminine consciousness. We enter the queendom of the cerebellum, and awaken into a vast, unlimited state of magical, shamanic perceptual awareness where many capacities are available to us that would be classed as miraculous to the mind.

Many shamanic practices return us to the Womb of the Mother, using the darkness of the night or ceremonial womb chambers, like the kiva or sweat lodge, to access these altered states of primal feminine consciousness. Inside these warm womb chambers, either in darkness or lit only by the flickering red light of fire, we experience a similar experiential vision and perception to our time in the womb—which was also a dark, warm chamber, with soft filtered red light.

The shamanic drumbeat becomes the rhythmic beat of the mother's heartbeat, the fetal heartbeat, the pulsing primordial union of two hearts beating together in one body, echoed in surround sound, bouncing off the sides of our womb container, sounds that seem to originate from all directions at once—like being in a darkened theater of creation.

Our nine moons in the womb and the rich feminine, multidimensional, miraculous primordial consciousness we first experienced there, and which is stored in the memory of the cerebellum, is the foundation for our shamanic journeying and our profound spiritual longing to return to the source.

The Womb beckons us for a second birth. We have been uprooted. Our root, our source, our origin is primordial Womb Consciousness. It is the root of our original innocence, it is the root of our longing to be reunited again with our deepest soul.

WOMB ORACLES SHARE
The Singing Bowl of Earth's Womb

The eye of a horse initiated a series of shamanic journeys. I heard the moaning of the Earth, she had lost her hum. I felt the Earth grieving; I was grieving with her, grieving the loss of the Mother. I went into the eye of the horse, down into her womb, and felt the galloping feet on the Earth rising up into my womb. There were souls of the Native People trapped in the Mother Mountains that needed to return home to the Great Womb. I was riding a white horse with souls passing through the butterfly net of my womb, the water wheel spinning as the gong sounded.

I journeyed into the eye of the horse again, under her hooves that kicked up the red dust of the earth. I was pulled into the vacuum of the vortex, my feet hovered over the molten core. I landed on my back on top of a water drum, feeling the reverberation of the earth below. Huge black V-shaped wings were flapping above me; three feathers were held up in front of my face. My nose turned into a bird beak. I had the head of an eagle. When I tried to open my eyes, I saw these golden-black eyes starring into my eyes. My vision opened into the dark night.

I journeyed into the hollow core of the Earth through the horse eye again a few days later. There was a sensation of deep openness and ecstatic warmth pouring down into my feminine crown, opening my Womb eye. Earth Mother was rising out of the water, mingling with the air of her breath and the fire of her heart into the Void of everything. She was the all-seeing eye of the Great Womb. Seer in the dark, navigator of the waters, looking out across the horizon where heaven and earth meet. She was the messenger between the Cosmic Womb and the Womb of Gaia. She was the utterance of the Mother Tongue linking the infinity loop of the Heart-Womb.

I started to journey down, spinning into the sound of the singing bowl of the earth. I saw a black snake, writhing sensuously, expanding and contracting with life force. It was full bodied and almost oozing, then the skin started to shed and dissolve. I was meeting life and death in the ouroboros of the Void. Then the white head of an eagle emerged, spreading wings of flight in rebirth. There was a sense of merging the deep lunar primal earthy feminine with the penetrating solar masculine in sacred union. I remembered the sound of the Earth moaning in grief and losing her hum. I had also lost my hum. I needed to surrender to love and trust, to dissolve the wall that separated me from the wild feminine and prevented union with the masculine.

A.C.

SPIRAL 13
SOUL MIDWIFE RITES

Conscious Creation and Conscious Death

What does God do all day long?
God lies on a maternity bed giving birth.
MEISTER ECKHART

FROM THE DAWN of human consciousness and for hundreds of thousands of years, the numinous and magical powers of transformation, birth, death, and rebirth were regarded as a feminine experience. And their ultimate symbol, container, and living expression was the womb, the dark mother from whose cosmic body we emerge at birth, and into which we dissolve again at the time of death.

We have become disconnected from both our beginnings and our endings, and we need to rejoin the sacred circle again and remember our origins and the nature of our creative cycles. Our woman nature is wild, wet, fertile, dark, mysterious, lit by moonlight, moving in cycles, living in a feminine underworld of primal enchanted forests where the tree of life and her life-giving and sustaining roots grow. She is the portal, the tree of souls from where we arrive and depart this realm.

When we are disconnected from this deep essential nature, we judge the primal feminine as evil, disturbing, dangerous, lower, and less than. We feel afraid of the earth and feel unsafe, unstable, unwelcome here; we become afraid of *daleth*—death—which is an ancient Semitic word that means "doorway," the passageway between worlds, where we dissolve back to Source so new life can come forth.

In our fear of the feminine, we seek only the light and the bright sunlit pathways. But the lunar pathways call us back, they whisper in our dreams; her moonlight seeps through the cracks of our wounds and heartbreaks, and reminds us of that dark place that births the light, and our deep desire to be Woman. To fully embody the womb power within, gifting us conscious creation and dissolution.

We were not created to be powerless victims of life or death; we were created to be conscious co-creators with both of these powerful flows of life force, which also mirror the lunar cycles of full moon ovulation and conception and dark-moon menstruation and dissolution.

Would a loving Creator bring us into a realm against our will or remove us from that realm against our will—inducing fear and powerlessness? Our birthright is one of love, not fear.

The Full Moon Doorway: Conscious Conception

When our conscious awareness was still connected to our womb and cerebellum—the *womb hole of the brain*—we could consciously choose and guide a new soul into our wombs through the primal intelligence held within our ovaries. This umbilical cord of intelligence that communed with the Womb of Creation carried the desire to birth a soul and matched it with a soul who wished to come in and resonated with the frequency the parents were carrying. Once a "divine match" had been made, the incarnating soul would guide the prospective parents to deeper levels of evolution in love to prepare for its conception into form, creating the highest container of possibilities in love for both itself and the parents.

Babies exist in the spirit realms before they are born and often make contact with the mother-to-be, guiding her in her conception journey. Spirit children are often described as orbs of blue light, and some women "see" a blue orb entering their womb at the time of conception. In Tibet, the second Dalai Lama's mother, Kunga Palmo, had a conception dream of her son, seeing a blue radiant light entering her womb.[1] By communicating with the spirit of the child it is possible to conceive at the perfect time, even if there are fertility issues, and it is also possible to ask a child to leave the womb if it is not the right time, so an abortion is not needed.

When we are conceived, the female egg draws the chosen sperm into her to consummate the conception of new life in the same way that the yoni and womb "allow" the lingam to enter—in fact, the woman "draws" him inside with her welcoming, receptive open energies. There is no penetration, only the surrender of the man, allowing himself to be drawn inside. If there is penetration, it means unwelcome invasion, imposing of will. It is pushy, controlling, ego led.

Within our epigenetic coding we hold all the traits and gifts of our entire ancestral lineage. Through communion with Source and the incoming soul, the egg *invites and allows* the desired sperm match into her biological, genetic, and energetic Grail Castle. This is the womb wisdom of evolutionary conception, utilizing the power of conscious epigenetic selection to create a DNA blueprint that a soul can express itself fully through. It may select ancestral DNA that holds the gift of music or the knowledge of herbs—whatever the soul wishes to embody and journey through and evolve in its time on Earth.

In ancient times, men and women would heal and open together in sacred union to facilitate this process. This was conscious conception. It brought a new soul into the world with the best possible conditions set up so it could evolve in love and share its gifts and talents with the world, rippling into the collective field. It created a child who was perfectly crafted as a shaman-avatar, known in ancient Jewish culture as a chosen one.

From this space of conscious or "immaculate" conception, every generation was an even greater evolution in love, growing and expanding into new realms and qualities of brilliance, spinning a bright thread that was intricately woven across the ancestral line, transmitting wisdom and light.

The science of conscious conception was very precise, and every factor was brought into consideration—including the astrological conditions the soul would come into. Everything would be selected for the optimum entry into the earth realm and for life on Earth. Some of this legacy still remains in cultures that seek astrological advice for conception. Throughout history there have also been "soul doulas," those who could help a soul through the birth process of selecting parents and birthing from spirit into the womb (rather than from womb into the world). This is now mostly a lost feminine art.

Paralleling the belief that souls of children perch like birds in the branches of the cosmic world tree before birth, in the Amur Basin in North Asia, female shamans who help the soul of a child to nest within the womb identify themselves by displaying poles with painted birds by their homes. They also embroider their wedding dresses with images of trees of life carrying on each branch a bird's egg, which contain the soul of the fetus, alongside depictions of auspicious animals such as swans.[2]

This knowing filters down in folklore of children being carried to earth by a stork, swan, goose, or other feminine spirit birds, remembering the lost art of conscious conception.

Song of the Soul

Indigenous cultures have held the memory of this ability in their stories of the "Song of the Soul." Sound frequency is a snapshot of a particular vibration or DNA expression.

A certain tribe in Africa counts the birth date of the child from the moment the child appears as a thought in the mother's mind. When the mother *consciously decides* she wants to conceive, she sits under a tree and listens until she can hear and receive the song of the child that wants to come in. Afterward, she goes to the prospective father and teaches him the song, which they sing together. As they make love they sing this song and invite the child in.

This is not a quaint custom; this is science of the soul and sound vibration. They are singing in the epigenetic possibilities held within their own DNA, and how they will be selected during their sexual union as a child is created.

This signature song holds the memory and potential of what this soul came to earth to embody and explore. In tribal wisdom this song is sung as the baby is born, as he or she is growing up, when he or she marries, and when he or she may have lost their way, to remind them of who they really are. It is also sung as they cross the great threshold and are birthed back into Spirit, into the Great Womb.

Impressionable Womb Space

Hawaiian Kahuna tradition also notes the incredible importance of the moment a mother realizes she is carrying a child—her emotional state and response in this moment creates an epigenetic container for the child that will affect him or her at the deepest levels for the rest of their life. Whether we are consciously conceived in joy or love, or unconsciously conceived in fear and doubt, makes the difference between a loving humanity or a lost humanity.

Gestation also continues this thread, as the consciousness of the mother affects the weaving of the child in her womb. In ancient China, women of royal birth would avoid unpleasant imagery, disharmonious music, abusive people, or anything that would negatively imprint on a child.[3]

Research led by Venezuelan psychology professor Beatriz Manrique, Ph.D., graduate of Yale University, confirms the impressionable space gestating babies are in, recording that mothers who showed affection and positive communication to the baby in the womb birthed children with increased visual, auditory, language, memory, and motor skills.[4]

Some shamanic traditions made it taboo for women to weave when they were pregnant, feeling that it might interfere with the Great Mother weaving the new baby into form. What this symbolizes is the knowing that the baby is in a vulnerable, magical, suggestible, liminal state.

In Huichol tradition it was believed that a midwife-shaman who specialized in fertility even had the power to change the gender of the child early in the pregnancy through conscious ritual.[5]

Reclaiming the Power of the Womb

One of the most urgent evolutionary urges of Womb Awakening is the call to heal the personal and collective wound of fear and powerlessness we hold around conception, and to reclaim the powers and wisdom of conscious conception.

When we lost the ability to consciously conceive it allowed the vibration of fear and powerless to enter our God(dess)-given power to create new life through sacred sexuality. It also meant that as a race we started to devolve in love. Every generation now brings with it more and more fears and wounds, piled one on top of each other like a negative Russian doll of ancestral legacy. Where once the epigenetic coding of our DNA was a powerful tool to select certain gifts and divine qualities and pass them on to the next generation as a genetic "Akashic Record" and memory imprint of our forebears, it is now a loaded weapon of wounds we are unwittingly born into—and must take the hero or heroine's journey to dissolve in our lifetime, literally becoming a "feminine Christ" for our entire ancestral genetic line.

This sense of powerlessness attaches to our sexual energy from the moment it blossoms into being in sexual relationship, and this fear contracts the man's heart energy and contracts a woman's sexual energy from full expression.

There is such a deep grief in the collective feminine that we have lost full communion with our lunar cycles and womb wisdom; with that disconnection, we have also lost the natural gift of conscious conception. In our original blueprint, women had the choice in full consciousness to conceive a baby or not, and could communicate this to the intelligence center of their ovaries and womb. No baby was ever meant to enter this world unexpectedly. No woman was ever meant to be in the agonizing position of conceiving a life she felt she was not able or safe to bring into this world. This wound is written large across humanity.

When we lost the ability to consciously create within the temple of our bodies, the feminine psyche also fragmented—sacred sexuality *not* for conception became difficult and tinged with fear. Polarized, we overemphasized the maternal, white river of our sexuality, while our erotic, wild dark sexuality, most naturally abundant at dark-moon menstruation, became illicit and forbidden. All women hold the collective grief of this in their womb; in each of our lives, as our budding sexuality was growing and blossoming, we faced the choice between artificial contraception we knew was not natural to our feminine selves or the fearful prospect of an unwanted pregnancy. First our innate creative womb wisdom had been lost over the ages, and then the ancient herbal lore passed down through lineages of wisewomen to aid fertility or provide contraception was eliminated, so that our womb sovereignty was compromised.

This fear and powerlessness is laced deep into our sexuality and wombs, even if we are not aware of it. How many women have had sex or made love, worried about getting pregnant? Or taken heart-stopping pregnancy tests? The orgasmic, ecstatic gift of sexual communion became laced with fear. The gift of consciously bringing a new soul into the world, at just the right time, with just the right person, so that soul could thrive in this realm, was lost—and the very creation of human life became entwined with powerlessness and the vibration of fear.

This grief lay heavily on men's hearts too, as they could no longer be a conscious co-creator, choosing to bring new life into the world. It created a deep fear of responsibility, and powerlessness and disconnection from the shared role of conception. Many men have much grieving to do for this loss.

Many souls who were aborted stay close to the earth in the spirit realms because of this wound, usually to help guide the mother who holds so much grief inside. When this grief is felt and expressed, the soul is free to continue on its journey.

Our ovaries hold a vast power and are a portal to Divine intelligence; the more we connect and commune with them, the more we become conscious creators and reconnect with this gift. Here is an exercise to help you activate and balance the energy fields of your ovaries and awaken their Divine intelligence.

❀ Lunar/Solar Ovary Breathing

1. Close your eyes, place your hands on your womb and gently breathe into the velvet darkness that lives within.
2. Begin to visualize a pulsating golden solar light in your right ovary; allow its glow to grow brighter and brighter. Feel the rich warm of the light it gives.
3. Then begin to visualize a pulsating silver lunar light in your left ovary; allow its glow to grow brighter and brighter. Feel the shimmering luminescence of the light it gives.
4. Be aware of both night and day inside.
5. Now visualize a vesica pisces, an ancient symbol of the Divine Feminine inside your womb space—each side of the two circles around the left and right ovary, with the magical portal it creates placed in the middle of your womb.
6. Take a deep in breath and draw both lunar and solar lights into the middle portal to merge. On the out breath, release the lights back to each respective ovary.
7. Keep breathing the solar and lunar lights into the center to merge, and then releasing them back into the left and right ovary. Visualize the two lights merge and melt into each other in sacred union.
8. Continue for at least three minutes or as long as you feel the need to.

Fig. 13.1. Lunar/solar ovary breathing
(Illustration by Heather Skye)

The Dark Moon Gateway: Conscious Death

Our relationship with death—the dark moon, menstrual, dissolution portal of experience—has also slipped into the vibration of fear and unconscious expression. And, of course, this fear of death is the biggest undercurrent within the collective psyche, in need of being met and healed. We were not created to die without our prior knowledge, consent, and preparation. Conscious death was also a gift of life.

With conscious death, the soul is like a ripe fruit ready to let go and fall off the tree, giving its beautiful body back to Mother Earth, and birthing back into the infinite otherworld to explore new horizons of evolution and love. If we can reawaken this ability, we create an incredible wave of light out into the collective consciousness, helping to dissolve the fear of, or secret wounded desire *for* death, and the mistaken thought that it is the end of our connection with those we love.

The most incredible realization is that we *do in fact choose when to die,* except that now this choice is not based in conscious awareness, but on our unconscious wounds of feeing unsafe, or on cosmic reasons that we cannot fully connect to and understand. Many people who are sick secretly have a trauma-based death wish that is buried so far down in the unconscious they are completely unaware of it—or they have a soul reason for leaving earth. Finding and healing that trauma, so they can choose to live again, is a key part of the healing process.

Womb Awakening understands death as a form of spirit menstruation, a moment of renewal and rebirth, where we are birthed back into the Womb of Creation for new adventures and missions. Upon death our soul leaves the body through our navel and journeys along the divine umbilical cord of the Great Mother, returning us to the

Original Source who birthed us. In the Old Ways, womb priestesses were soul doulas who helped assist those leaving the earth realm on their journey. They would sit with the body for three to nine days, praying and chanting, and offering the cosmic portal of their own womb spaces as a safe passageway for souls to return home directly to Source on the umbilcal cord of rainbow light, without getting caught in bardo or hell realms because of trauma or limiting belief systems.

In the Isis traditions, the priestesses would perform a Body of Isis infusion on a person who was preparing for the journey home to the Great Womb. This sacred body-work used the power of Shakti, sacred anointing oils, sacred sounds, and herbal elixirs, including menstrual fluid, to cleanse physical toxins and toxic memories, emotions, and beliefs from the rivers and landscape of the body—so that the soul could experience orgasmic surrender to the spirit menstruation of death, rather than clinging on to the body because of fear, doubt, confusion, or attachment. This sacred bodywork was also used on those preparing for rebirth initiations. Just as womb priestesses also attended those giving birth to dance and play music, they also attended the dying to dance ceremonially and play harp and assist them on their journey back to otherworld.

The ancient womb priestesses of China, the Wu shamans, were known as channels for Divine Mother, who held the ability to embody the portal between the worlds. The Wu were described as "part of the vertical axis by which the soul travels to the heavens,"[6] referencing the Womb as tree of life and axis mundi. They would often use ritual dance to open the gateway between the worlds. "The dancer as invoker who communicated with spirits was the vehicle through which the soul could find safe passage to immortality. The jade plaque figures found in Western Han-period tombs may be reminders of the ritual dance performed for the deceased, and they continued to offer protection and guidance for the soul."[7]

In Tibetan rites for the dead, a Grail vessel called a *boompha,* symbolizing the womb, is placed on the head of the deceased to help them in their journey.

Before the fall of feminine Womb Consciousness, these journeys between worlds—through interdimensional cosmic and planetary Wombs—flowed naturally. A person's spirit easily descended to the Womb of Gaia on a psychic menstrual flow of release, where it was dissolved into pure essence, and then journeyed upward on quantum swan barges through the amniotic womb ocean of dark matter to be rebirthed, into different dimensions, through the Cosmic Womb.

Because of the forgetting of this sacred art of passing souls through the womb upon death, we now have many earthbound spirits who are lost and unable to return home, who attach to the living and literally haunt people's lives. As our planet reclaims its Womb Consciousness, and women's wombs awaken, these souls can be birthed home.

Fig. 13.2. Siren Priestess carrying a soul between the worlds. Lycian tomb relief
from Xanthus, Turkey, circa 480 BCE.
(The British Museum)

The Doorway of Death

At the time of death, the human spirit begins a reverse gestational journey,
descending back through the stages of gestation, into the deepest primordial roots
of the unconscious feminine mind, and through that, back into union with the
Earth Womb of the Great Mother. From there, spirit could naturally pass back
into the great Cosmic Womb. The death process was a reverse birth process, a
final transformational journey from the material realms to a new dimension of
experience—rebirthing through the womb of Mother Earth in a very natural act
of "cosmification."

As we disconnected from Womb Consciousness, and the feminine dimension of life was lost, the Womb of our brain, the cerebellum—the seat of the soul or psyche—became detached from its natural, instinctive ability to consciously make these pivotal spirit journeys. The feminine dimension—the soul, the psyche—became a place of fear, or monsters and demons, lurking "in the deep" of our now unconscious self, which became profoundly separated and disassociated.

The beautiful underworld of earth became hell, a place thick with unprocessed beliefs, emotions, events, that trapped a person in a psychic nightmare realm, unable to gracefully rebirth back through the womb portals into cosmic renewal. This psychic underworld is now filled with lost souls, unable to find their way home, at times literally haunting those who remain on earth.

This also led to the distortion of shamanic and mystery school teachings from a feminine way that focused on opening to love, sensual embodiment, interconnection with the web of life, relationship, the power of love, and the gift of menstrual blood offerings, to a patriarchal shamanism and religion that created priesthoods practicing unnatural blood sacrifice and sexual ritual, and terrifying or painful initiations, or intense ordeals that promoted a fearless, disassociated strength of will and birthed power systems that were disconnected from the sacred heart.

Our patriarchal matrix has completely lost its connection with the rhythms of conscious creation and death; instead it unconsciously creates and creates like a mad, out-of-control machine, afraid to let go and release into "death" and make way for new expressions of spirit. This is the same mechanism by which cancer cells multiply endlessly and in doing so destroy the ecosystem that houses them. This disconnection also led to the abuse and rape of Gaia, entangling the feminine Womb and the energetic portals of Gaia into this realm of pain.

Similarly, our own unconscious psyche is often now a hell filled with lost soul fragments, which need to find their way home and be integrated so we can return to a whole consciousness. This requires a holistic merging of the feminine and masculine consciousness, both within and without, and a "diving to the depths." Ascension cannot happen without descension—returning deep into the body, deep into our feelings, deep into our feminine selves and earth, rather than disassociating "out" and losing connection with reality. We need to root.

We see this in the tree of life, where we first return to the root and plant ourselves deep in the fertile darkness of earth before spreading our branches out into the starry cosmic realms.

Awakening our personal wombs quantumly shifts and clears the collective womb portals, and creates a flow of energy to release these collective distortions and imprints, allowing all the parts of creation stuck in separation, suffering, and pain to renew back into love. This is part of the great work that Magdalene and Yeshua, as womb shamans, came to undertake—making the shamanic descent deep into the Womb of Gaia and then ascending into the Cosmic Womb, reopening the pathways of rebirth, renewal, and resurrection and restoring the womb grids.

This journey to awaken the Womb and the feminine psyche and restore her primordial creative virginity was symbolically encoded in Gnostic texts, which depicted this alchemical process. In Exegesis on the Soul it says, "The sages who came before us gave the soul a feminine name. She is also feminine in nature, and she even has a womb. When the womb of the soul . . . turns to the inside, she is baptized . . . the soul is cleansed so that she may regain what she had at first, her former nature, and she may be restored. That is her baptism"[8]

There is a psychic heaviness weighing on us personally, ancestrally, and collectively since we left our universal roots and lost our womb cosmology. One of the main tasks of Womb Awakening, as we reopen the magic doors of Womb Consciousness, is to reweave our psyche back to wholeness, and to also fulfill the womb rebirth of the dead—allowing them fluid passage home, not back into the earth realm, but back into infinite love consciousness.

Conscious death rituals and rites are also returning as this renewed wave of feminine consciousness returns to earth. Death is a portal of sacred rebirth. The world is its own magic—only our minds have become disconnected from its mysterious workings and weavings. But our Wombs know the way of the web.

The fear of death is a symptom of separation; in Oneness and interconnection we understand that nothing ever truly dies, and that we are never really apart. Death is transformation, rebirth into another interconnected realm, as we walk between the worlds. Open yourself more to this mysterious interconnected web of life, be in nature and ask to feel its living pulse of exchange: death birth, death rebirth, divine entanglement, the carbon monoxide we breathe out as a gift to the trees, the oxygen they exhale as their reciprocal gift to us.

WOMB ORACLES SHARE
Singing the Song of the Soul

Yemaya speaks: "My Beloved, you are sound shamaness. You carry within you the songs of the world, the songs of all Creation. You carry within you the blessed siren song—that which has the capacity to heal and bring together. You are able to sing the souls into conscious conception; sing souls earthside as they are birthed from their mother's wombs; sing home the souls of the injured and unwell, bringing them back to wholeness and health; and sing home the souls of those whose time on this earthly plane has passed. The sound that you will create is the essence of life through breath, through sound. It will all be about the magic of resonance. You will find the tones, the pitches, the vibration—that every tiny aspect of the nature of the sound will come forth for a particular reason for that particular person. The sound of each soul is magnificently different. You will feel into the energy of the soul and it will come forth—the sound itself will know what to do. All you need to do is trust, surrender, and allow. As you go, beloved sister, so too will you be gifted with traditional songs that will assist this process. You will begin to remember the ancient songs of wisdom, the ancient songs from rites of passage. They will be awakened and you will remember them and you will begin to sing them forth once more, recreating their power and honoring your ancestry. Sing. I will join you in voice and spirit and together we will begin to reawaken the songs of the world Soul, the songs of Creation, the songs and sounds and vibrations that will open you into your gift as sound shamaness—as blessed siren."

C.L.I.

Pyramid Afterlife Ritual

In the dreamtime I was in a pyramid with eight women; we were preparing a body for the afterlife. We were in a small room, which smelled like a mixture of frankincense and death. We washed the body, and then rubbed it with herbs, oils, and perfume. We painted the hands with a red powder, and also painted the face and feet in red ochre. Then we adorned it with jewels and wrapped it in fine golden silk. We fasted and prayed over the body for three days and three nights. We couldn't leave the room. We prayed and chanted to his ancestors that his spirit be received by them and guided to the Great Mother. No one talked, we communicated with thought, after we took turns holding his hands cupped and blowing into them. It was a symbolic blessing of his journey by sending our ancestors' blessing through our breath. It felt sacred and holy.

A.V.

SPIRAL 14

PLACENTA OF THE VOID

Divine Milk of the Cosmic Mother

Wherever in the world a female body is seen,
That should be recognized as my holy body . . .
My female messengers are everywhere;
They bestow all the spiritual attainments
By gazing, touching, kissing, and embracing.

VAJRAYOGINI, DIVINE BUDDHA-MOTHER

IN THE ANCIENT WOMB religion our Creator was not "out there" disconnected from creation, but was felt as a loving mother, who knew us intimately and loved us, feeding us with the mystical substance of her love in an embodied, immanent way. Filling us up with Divine nourishment, with the milk of loving kindness.

This Great Mother was a creative womb space that could create, generate, regenerate, and renew all of life, pouring her magical quantum primordial milk into all beings and life-forms, to sustain, protect, comfort, renew, heal, and support them, physically, spiritually, and energetically. Her sacred milk of love also flowed directly into the feminine on earth, pouring through every woman to birth creations and to bathe, refresh, and renew all.

Yet in the wasteland of this modern world of "virtual" love, embodied primordial love is what we are missing so deeply and longing for. It is the next step in our evolutionary wave to open ourselves again to a deeply felt and embodied sense of love that is firmly rooted and flowing—through our relationships with each other, within our sexual union, with earth and her creatures, and with our Creator.

We can receive pure love from Creator in an embodied way, not just a theoretical knowing, but as a deeply received physical presence into both our soul and cells. We can open to receive this primordial love into our whole being. We can receive quantum "energy milk" of loving kindness from the life-giving flow of our Great Mother, and receive deep spiritual nourishment from the placenta of her Void.

In the Bible this maternal sustenance is alluded to, revealing its roots in the feminine mysteries: "Like newborn babies, you must crave pure spiritual milk so that you will grow into a full experience of salvation. Cry out for this nourishment."[1]

In ancient Sumer the Cosmic Mother was envisioned as a holy cow, pouring the substance of her benevolent, nourishing milk into mankind. Her universal womb is placed higher than any other divinity or creative force. She was known as "she who bears the gods," "beloved lady," and "she who has fed the gods with her holy milk."

In Ephesus in Turkey, in the first century CE, the Mother Goddess Diana—Artemis in Greek—was believed to be the universal life giver and sustainer, and was depicted with many breasts so that she could feed and nourish the world and bestow blessings.

Placenta of Sacred Union

The placenta is more than just a physical connection. All humans have an energetic umbilical cord and placenta connecting us to our Divine Mother, through which we receive etheric nourishment, the substance of Divine Love. However, as modern humans, we have lost connection to this divine milk and to the dreamtime rhythms of Gaia. We find ourselves cut off from our roots, separated from the mother consciousness. From this place of disorientation and disconnection, we have been tricked into seeking our safety and nourishment from a false womb, a toxic man-made placenta—the artificial matrix of modern civilization that is on the brink of destroying our Mother Earth. The time is now to remember how to reconnect our energetic umbilical cords and placentas to the true planetary and cosmic womb grids and receive true love.

The placenta is the magical mother-baby interface that allows the unborn child to be nourished by the pulsing lifeblood of the mother, via its umbilical cord of connection. In the placenta, the baby's blood vessels and connective tissues interweave seamlessly with those of the mother. Half of the placenta emerges from the genes and tissues of the baby, and half from the mother, so that there is physical merging and entanglement of mother-baby biology. Our first experience of life on earth is in this sacred union with the Great Mother, through the physical body of our own human mother. This is the original blueprint of cosmic union: "I and the mother are one." It is through the mystical interface of the placenta, the bridge between the worlds, that this sacred union is created, and through which the baby is sustained.

To the baby, the womb is its all-nourishing and all-containing world. All of existence is contained in this space. The baby does not have to worry or think about how it will be nourished—it is simply taken care of. Imagine if the baby became separated from the placenta. Suddenly it would feel completely alone and unsupported, floating around in an abyss of empty darkness, unable to find any connection or sustenance. On the energy levels the baby would experience a profound sense of soul loss and existential angst, and of course, it could not survive very long without its placenta. This is the situation of the modern world.

Without this *felt* connection, we question if we are truly in the womb of the Great Mother and if it can be real that her living presence surrounds us in every way. Our psyche becomes frightened, fractured, doubting, disturbed as we contemplate our aloneness—and enter the illusion that the earth's lullaby hum no longer sings to us.

Across the ancient cultures, the peoples of the womb religions universally held the placenta to be sacred. It was considered the twin of the baby and the carrier of the baby's spirit or soul. At the time of birth, the physical placenta would separate from the baby, but the energetic placenta, the *ka body* or energetic double, would remain connected to the child, forming a new placental relationship directly with the Mother Earth and the Cosmic Womb. This connection was considered so vital that it became a central focus of the early Egyptian religion. The energetic placenta, the ka body of light, was the bridge to spirit world.

After birth and the natural separation of the physical placenta from the baby, indigenous cultures around the world would ritually bury the placenta in the earth, or under a tree that represented a soul tree or tree of life. By placing the placenta in the Mother Earth, they would *energetically transfer the umbilical and placental connection from the human mother to Earth Mother,* marking the beginning of a transition period in which Gaia would directly provide sustenance for the child, from the fruits of her own body, and become its "new mother." The burial of the placenta interwove and entangled the child's physical substance with that of the earth, so that Gaia could best know how to nourish her newly arrived human child, creating a potent psychic and spiritual connection for the rest of the child's life.

The sacred placenta itself is often identified with the tree of life, axis mundi, or omphalos. It is always a portal or interface between this world and otherworld, from the child's consciousness to the mother consciousness that created it.

Throughout many African tribes, there was the idea that the placenta was the king's spiritual twin and awaited reunion with him in the afterlife. Ancient Egyptians also considered the placenta to be a divine being of spiritual importance. This twin was honored as a god—or as a gateway to god—and housed the ka body of radiance.

In the Baganda tribe of Uganda, the placenta is believed to have a magical spirit. A Temple of the Twin was created to house it for the duration of the king's life. Every new moon, as the lunar crescent arose, the king held a special ceremony where the "twin" is placed in the doorway of the temple—symbolic of a birth gateway—so that the magical lunar rays could infuse and enliven it with radiance.[2]

The Cree Indians tell a story of a father watching the spirit of the placenta turning into a twin and playing with his real child. In Australia, some of the Aboriginal tribes believe that part of the soul, known as the choi-I, is to be found in the placenta, which is buried in a spot marked by a small mound of twigs.

In Sumatra, some tribes say that the afterbirth holds a tutelary spirit that will guide the person concerned during his or her lifetime. Others say that one such guardian exists in the afterbirth while a second exists in the embryo. This double has a feminine quality and is the source of the soul—the interface with the Creator.

This twin or etheric double, who acts as a protective guardian and interface between a human being and the infinity of spirit world, is found throughout the world—encoding the knowledge that just as we have a placenta-being who mediates for us in the womb, and brings us nourishment from the mother, so do we have an energy double who performs the same function throughout our life. We have often lost touch with this twin, who holds our magical, supernatural, spiritual powers.

Eucharist of Mother's Milk

The natural biological communion of the gestating baby with mother, and the assimilation of the mother's retained menstrual blood as bodily nourishment (as it was viewed in the first cultures), was the original model for the Christian rite of the Eucharist, or Holy Communion. The sacred ritual of symbolically eating and drinking the body and blood of the Great Mother, or of a divine being such as Christ, was a practice common to many cultures around the world. Originally, it was the red womb blood of the mother that sustained us while in utero, and later her white breast milk after birth—the archetypal red and white waters of life. The red was associated with the generative womb of the Mother, her red river, and the white with her compassionate heart and breast milk, her white river. In later religions, the blood of the Mother was often symbolized by red wine, and her body by bread. In ancient Egypt, the hieroglyph denoting the feminine and the goddesses was the circular loaf of bread. In Sumeria, the pictogram for the loaf of bread was the downward pointing triangle, the universal image for the female, womb, and vulva.

In our natural developmental process, we leave the womb of our human mother at the time of birth and gradually transition our umbilical cord of connection to the womb of our Mother Earth. We eat the fruits of Gaia's body and drink of her waters of life; her body becomes our body. The same process happens at an energetic level, as we anchor our umbilical cord and placenta into the Cosmic Womb. We are always umbilically connected to the Mother, dependent on her for life. The more we become conscious of this connection and open to receive her nourishment, the more her universal Shakti can flow through us, and the more vital and radiant we become.

Our impulses of self-love, the desire to nurture ourselves, to receive pleasure and support, and our practical actions and commitments to give our body what it needs to thrive and bloom, are rooted in our connection with the Divine Mother.

Addictions that abuse the body, diminish our own beauty, and ignore the whispers of our soul mean we are following a program of the toxic placenta that man created, and can help us see where we still feel separated from the loving source of creation.

Our Soul Shakti depends on this flowing connection with the divine milk of love, and the wild, spontaneous, joyful, optimistically rooted sense of creativity it bathes us in.

Awakening the Magical Double

To the magician or sorcerer, the stronger your energetic placenta, or spiritual double, the stronger your magical powers. The purpose of the magical path was to unify mind, body, and psychology with this energetic twin, the interface between you and the universal life force. Thus, in Egypt and many other cultures, a great emphasis was placed on building and strengthening the ka body, for purposes ranging from spiritual rebirth to black magic and the accumulation of wordly power. The life force is neutral and can be accumulated for selfish or spiritual purposes.

"The complex ideas around the ka are one of the most important in the Egyptian religion," writes Egyptologist Andrey Bolshakov. "The external ka was primarily associated with the placenta (the twin of man) . . . and was born with him."[3] The ka is equated with the ideas of the inner djinn, genius, and daemon—the soul or spirit carrier—that embraces, nourishes, and protects the physical human being.

In Egypt, the hieroglyph of the ka is two upraised arms, reaching toward the celestial realms to receive the descending flow of divine energies from above. Similar images are seen in Paleolithic cave art: figures with upraised arms in an ecstatic trance, in a posture that reflects a state of spiritual communion with the Great Mother. This posture of upraised arms has also been called "drawing down the moon"—drawing down the Mother's etheric milk, the lunar essence of love from the Celestial Womb.

The ka body of light is identical to the magical energy body of *feminine consciousness* present in all humans, our interface with the Cosmic Mother and universe. Physically, it is the cerebellum that is the seat of that interface, the placenta of the brain that connects our conscious identity with the greater web of life so they can merge. The feminine energy body of the ka, a nonlocal auric field, is nurtured by deep states of pleasure, bliss, joy, divine communion, and sexuality. It is strengthened by spending time in nature, by dreaming, and by imaginal journeys.

In *The Candle of Vision,* George Russell describes this magical nurturing etheric milk as a body-based "organic light" that is somatic—literally *soma*. He says, "that Infinite we would enter is living." And he goes on to say how he felt "a growing luminousness in my brain as if I had unsealed in the body a fountain of interior light."[4]

The more connected we are with our energetic placenta, the more we can receive and be sustained by the cosmic "uterine milk," the flowing love, nourishment, and wisdom that pours into us directly from the magical womb lining of the mother universe, in much the same way as a gestating baby is nourished by the physical substance of her mother's body. In this embodied, primordial way, we are sustained by the nested mother-wombs. By plugging in our energetic placenta and umbilical cord to the universal life-force energy, the more universal *chi, shakti, prana,* and magical power is available to us to create the kind of world we wish to live in.

The Artificial Placenta

In Paleolithic times people were connected umbilically with the mother consciousness; the doorway between the worlds, the interface, was fully open and there was a living symbiosis between earth and her inhabitants, creating an "Eden."

Then from 10,000 BCE, across the world, art began to change, shifting from the serene and magical Paleolithic cave paintings to more frightening and disturbing images, such as those found at Göbekli Tepe. The original transformational mysteries of menstruation and birth gave way to rituals of sacrifice in order to appease the

Mother Goddess and guarantee abundant harvests through offerings of blood. At the same time, agriculture and animal husbandry was born, as well as new architecture, social hierarchy, slavery, and war. Family and tribe gave way to complex city-states and matriarchal temple complexes, and later to patriarchal cultures and religions that violently and systematically suppressed feminine consciousness. Even indigenous tribes across the world were touched by the changes in consciousness, with the emergence of menstrual taboos, suppression of the female shamans, and increasing war. Somehow, an alien, antilife energy began embedding itself into the collective consciousness of humanity, separating us, and gradually undermining our placental connection to the true Gaian and cosmic womb grids.

From this place of separation and feelings of being lost and alone, society derived the father culture, the false matrix, the false placenta—the artificial poisoned teat that is meant to sustain us. This false system promises us everything we think we need to be safe and nourished—money, jobs, processed foods, technology, manufactured goods, superficial sex, self-esteem based on external success, and distorted notions of gods that demand worship and who will sustain us as part of a deal, if we give them our life energy and sacrifice to them. This is all the sustenance we have ever known so we orient to it completely and become dependent upon it. This dependency leaves us vulnerable to manipulation—it is the wicked parent, the wicked womb that is man created, the evil stepmother of fairy tales.

The Theory of Love

Many people experience only the "theory of love" in this world, in which they "know" or "think" they are loved—but do not receive this love in a deeply embodied way.

We are often born into the world by mothers who are themselves still stuck in a young developmental stage—needing the primal love missing in their own childhood and carrying all the wounds that are created from this. In being parented by a mother with these wounds, we lose a connection with a deeply felt and received primordial Love, even if everything seems great on the surface. We feel abandoned, alone, separated—as if we are all alone even in the presence of life and others.

Often we look back on our "perfect" childhoods and cannot fathom where our deep emotional injuries have come from. Our parents love us, they say they love us and we know they love us; they fed and clothed us, worried about us, and took care of us to the best of their abilities. But often, at best, we have only been receiving the theory of love, and at worst we have been on the receiving end of emotional abuse or control, either subtle or overt.

Take a Deep Look

The following questions will help you tune in to whether you received what you really needed to grow, evolve, and thrive:

- Were you touched enough as a baby?
- Were you held safe and celebrated as you came into this world?
- Did you feel your mother's continual, deeply embodied, and unconditional Love presence?
- Did you feel safe, welcomed, and protected?
- Were you listened to?
- Were your feelings and natural inclinations allowed, even if they were noisy, messy, wild, uncontrollable?
- Were you cuddled, touched, massaged, held, played with?
- Did your parents feel like a pure fountain of embodied kindness and presence?
- Or were they busy, stressed, distracted, absent, wounded, disconnected from their own feelings, passions, desires, dreams, physical selves, and souls?

This is not an exercise to judge parents for lacking the inner resources to give embodied love—it is to explore how far away our culture is from the ideal of an awakened love-presence, and how *every person* (including parents) has an undernourished child within them as a result.

Healing the Soul of the World

The first step in Womb Awakening is to begin to let go of our dependency on the false placenta and reconnect to the true placenta of the Great Mother through the interface of our own ka energy body—our etheric double that entangles us in the networks of primordial intelligence—and its connection to Gaia, to nature, to sensuality, to joy, to loving relationships.

This healing reconnection begins with the journey of rediscovering and nurturing our own energy double with self-love, working in harmony with it so that it grows strong and vital again. From there we can connect our umbilical and placental energy fields to the true womb grids of life on this planet and in the cosmos. When we begin receiving support directly from Life, we can bloom in true fertile soil.

As our energy double heals, we open the communication pathways with our own feminine brain, with our bodies and feelings, with Gaia, with the Soul of the World and with Cosmic Creator/Creation. Along the way, we must begin to work with healing and releasing the inner obstacles lodged in our deep psyche—thousands of years of personal and collective pain and trauma—as we once again begin to reach for our birthright of pleasure, joy, and original innocence. When we are connected to the true placental field of the Mother, we open ourselves to receive her infinite support and activate our incredible creative power and magical potentiality.

Every time we orient to the false matrix for sustenance and safety, or replica religions, we take one step away from our soul. Every time we take a step to fill ourselves up with the pleasure and bliss of life, and follow our soul dreams, we take one step closer to the Great Mother and the web of life. When we feed our ka body, our placenta and energetic twin, our ka body will then feed us back tenfold. Our biology of love is the gateway that births heaven on earth.

One of the keys of this transition to a new earth—to returning to the original placenta of consciousness—is knowing how to live in connection with Mother Earth directly. Learning how to commune with nature and the land, remembering the wisdom of our ancestors, growing our own food, connecting to the sacred spirit of plants and animals, understanding the cycles, seasons, and secrets of Gaia, our Earth Mother. Our ancestors knew how to feed themselves, they planted fruit forests, practiced horticulture, they knew the herbs that would heal, and how to communicate with animals in dreamtime for the hunt. Their connection with their energetic twin, their placenta of feminine consciousness, connected into the web of life—it meant they could travel the deertrods of earth with skill and grace, and journey on the dreampaths between dimensions, feeling connected and supported.

Receiving Primordial Love

Primordial Love means original love, our first love—which extends from the Source of Creation deep into every cell of our being and every quality of our soul. In physical form it is given from a deeply loving heart presence; it is intimate, playful, sensual, sensitive, responsive, feeling, emotionally intelligent, kind, intuitive. It is a way of soul reading through the primal senses—a touch that truly listens, that emanates from the heart-soul, that touches our deepest self. It is instinctive, flowing through an awakened body intelligence that holds others, with healthy boundaries.

Our embodied human relationships on earth help activate our ka body, our double of light, and allow us to receive love deeply. When we open to receive the living flow of primal love, through the touch of love, we experience cellular and endocrine enlightenment and "enlovenment"—a grounded spiritual experience of love.

When we have not received enough true primordial Love, we resist it and feel overwhelmed and out of control when we receive love—as if it is destroying the safe barrier we have erected around ourselves. Like a bud, we need to trust and open to deeply embodied love; to allow the "sunshine" in to nourish us and bring us back to life again.

Listening to the Voice of Love

Ask your womb how much primordial love you are receiving in your life:

- Do you experience physical touch, pleasure, intimacy with others?
- Do you experience physical touch, pleasure, intimacy with yourself?
- Do you feel held and heard by others; can you share your authentic self?
- Do you hear and receive your own intuitive feelings and desires?
- Do you receive hugs, cuddles, strokes, pleasure, pampering?
- Do you feel supported, both practically and emotionally, by others?
- Do you support yourself to feel everything and follow your heart?
- Do you physically and soulfully nurture yourself every day?
- Do you allow nature to nurture you? Can you receive her Presence?
- Do you commune with animals and exchange loving touch?
- Do you receive primordial Love from Divine Creator in a felt way?

When we are touched by primordial Love we feel truly seen, felt, and received at a soul level. Our physical bioenergetic and spiritual pathways open to intimate connection with others, with earth, with animals, with All of existence. Primordial Love wires our physical, neural, and soulful pathways to become a living chalice for Love. We become wired to receive love from all sources, physical and nonphysical, and to trust in loving touch. From this embodied place we can truly give love to others and pass the gift of love on, rather than passing forward paradigms of lack, sacrifice, and suffering.

WOMB ORACLES SHARE
Mother Tongue of New Earth

I had a dream last night under the blue moon. It was like a burial and a birth at the same time. In the dream I was holding a potato that had many eyes in my hands, it was probably the size of a womb. It was still half-covered with earth and the skin was gently flaking in a soft palpable way, almost like a snake shedding its skin. As I held it in my hands it seemed so beautiful. And these words came: "This is my Mama." It woke me out of my sleep.

This was the Mother from the deep, the black, primordial earth. I was holding the Mother and she was holding me. It reminded me of a dream I had a few months ago, when I was told to put my hands inside my womb. Now I was putting my hands into the womb of the Earth, finding the root, the source of all rebirthing.

The dream took me back to the Motherland, where the Mother Tongue kept whispering to me as my ancestors gathered potatoes with many eyes from deep under the roots of the earth, and stirred the copper pot making moonshine under the lunar light. I had forgotten my feminine roots that were once wild and sensual, connected to the true Source, the Earth Womb of the Great Mother. I have heard her call. I am remembering the light that shines from the ancient eyes of darkness. The radiance of the Grail Light shines through the web of life that connects all generations on the New Earth.

A.C.

Message from the Magdalenes

I am reaching a beautiful crest of a wave that has been building and building, rising and rising for many, many, many moons. I awoke this morning with these words ringing in my body from the Magdalenes: "Love is Living to the fullest of every emotion, Love consciousness is being right here, right now in the fullest most alive sense. To become a living chalice is to be in Love." Yes! Wholiness is to live the breath of love, dance the living expression of love, sound the living caress of the Divine; emotions are the living waters of creation. This journey is truly amazing; it goes to the deepest, darkest depths and the highest, lightest peaks feeling humbled, awed, amazed at the divine perfection that suffuses living.

E.S.

SPIRAL 15

TOTAL REBIRTH

Healing Conception, Gestation, and Birth

Your children are not your children.
They are the sons and daughters of Life's longing for itself.
They come through you but not from you,
And though they are with you yet they belong not to you.
You may strive to be like them,
but seek not to make them like you.

ON CHILDREN, KAHLIL GIBRAN

OUR MOTHER'S WOMB is the cradle of our existence. Scientific research now shows that who we are on all levels—biologically, emotionally, and psycho-spiritually—is profoundly affected by our experiences in the womb.[1] The frequencies of feelings and beliefs that permeate us during our time in the womb genetically program us for a life of love, bliss, communion, and pleasure—or for a life in which we are wired for anxiety, trauma, suffering, and disconnection.

What we experience while gestating in our mother's womb directly influences who will get cancer, who will be obese, who will be intelligent, who will have successful love relationships, who will be anxious or depressed, who will have attention deficit disorder, who will be a good nurturing mother, who will be a sociopath. This happens in part through the mechanism of *epigenetic modification of our DNA*—in other words, our experiences change the way our genes are expressed. Our experiences turn on or turn off our genetic expression.[2]

While we are gestating in the womb, our genetic expression is modified by literally everything that our mother experiences—foods, toxins, relationships, emotions, illness, family support, cultural beliefs, and so forth. Her deep inner experience weaves us into being. Positive or negative experiences turn on or turn off different portions of our DNA, and until they are healed, these changes determine our lives at a deep subconscious and genetic level.

The implications of wombtime epigenetics are astounding. Multicenter collaborations of scientists around the world have independently validated the fact that mothers who diet during pregnancy or who lack certain nutrients give birth to children who are more likely to be obese. *And, most remarkably, these epigenetic changes are often passed on to future generations until they are dissolved.*[3] If our grandmother dieted or experienced a famine during pregnancy, *we* are more likely to be overweight, two generations later. The Dutch famine of 1944 made an entire generation of Dutch people more susceptible to weight gain, and these changes were passed on to their grandchildren as well. Our lives leave an ongoing legacy to future generations.

We are a culmination of all the experiences of our ancestors, which have left a profound genetic imprint on our DNA. This is the biological origin of our ancestral memories and our "ancestral soul." We are a web of experiences. In a recent landmark study, Brian Dias, Ph.D., professor of psychiatry at Emory University School of Medicine, showed how fear is epigenetically heritable across generations. If a mother experiences fear when she is pregnant, it epigenetically reprograms the DNA of her children and wires them to experience more fear.[4] *This change can be passed down for several generations unless it is healed.*

Researchers tried for years and years to understand the mystery of what caused schizophrenia. Eventually they realized that one of the strongest predictors was the experience of the child while in the womb. If the mother experienced a profound grief such as the death of a family member during pregnancy, there was a 600 percent increase in risk of having a schizophrenic child.[5] If certain women smoked marijuana in pregnancy, they had a 1,000 percent increased risk; if they lived in a busy urban environment, they had a 50 percent increased risk.[6] And, every day new research accumulates that proves that different kinds of stress, dietary nutrients, and chemical toxins alter the risk of schizophrenia. The same holds true for autism, for depression, for anxiety, and for many other states of emotional-neurological imbalance.

The National Cancer Institute states that 95 percent of cancers are caused by our life experiences and how those experiences shape our DNA—that is, 95 percent of cancers are due to epigenetic changes.[7] If our grandmother was exposed to the chemicals found in plastic water bottles, then we may be more likely to develop breast or prostate cancer.

Due to at least five thousand years of patriarchy, we have been (epi)genetically modified to disconnect from our original blueprint lived in love by our ancient mothers and fathers. As soon as we arrive in our mother's womb we are imprinted by the epigenetic traumas and wounds of both our parents; this stew of negative imprinting continues as we gestate and prepare to enter the world through birth.

Most mothers do not receive the respect, honor, and deep support they need to feel safe—on both a personal and cultural level. By devaluing this most sacred and primary work of birthing, a devastating original wound has been etched into the genetic code of humanity.

The mother is the key of all keys. It is through her that a new world will be born. Failure to support mothers with all of our love, strength, and wisdom is the failure of culture itself.

All humans are now experiencing such a dense, cumulative epigenetic ancestral load that as soon as we enter the womb, our direct feeling receptivity to the primordial Love of Creator disconnects, and we experience feelings of terror, isolation, abandonment, and separation upon entering this earth dimension. Depending on the emotional condition of the parents, this negative imprinting defines the bioenergetic and neural capacity of the body as it grows inside the womb. The sensitive developing system either becomes wired for pain, suffering, or sickness, or it has the potential to be wired for pleasure, love, relationship, and radiant vitality.

Many ancient teachings refer to this devastating knowledge that parents unconsciously pass on their wounds to the next generation, imagining their shadow material can be ignored and repressed, or dissolved at death—denying the reality that we encode it epigenetically into our children, who then amplify this ancestral karma, and pass it on to their children.

For the Cathars, their vow to not bring children into the "bondage of the world" was a declaration of a commitment to birthing avatar children through an enlightened "Virgin" Womb—in which negative cellular and epigenetic patterns and behaviors had been spiritually dissolved.

One of the impassioned vows of the bodhisattva is to break this karmic cycle of human suffering for all sentient beings. This includes the vow to return our Sacred Feminine birthing wisdom to mass consciousness, awakening the pristine bud within the Womb. Buddhist yogini teacher, Sahajayoginicinta says, "How is one to awaken the children, whose inner brightness is obscured, by the burgeoning of beginningless karma?"[8]

Reclaiming the Legacy of Love

Within our genetic treasure chest lives vast spiritual and biological potential that remains dormant—but we have the power to reawaken and reclaim these incredible potentials and become chalices of living light. Genetic memories of both love *and* pain live on inside us—waiting for us to choose the path we wish to live by and how we wish the world to be. When we have the courage to choose our genetic inheritance of love, and dissolve all that is *not* love, we become mothers and fathers of new earth. Our innate genetic gifts awaken and bloom.

We can reclaim our legacy of love by healing our ancestral trauma. Although much of the research has focused on the harm that can come from toxic epigenetic disruption, the "epigenetics of love" holds the key to our healing. Research shows that nurturing, primal touch, states of love and safety also powerfully modify genetic expression in positive ways.[9] And, just as negative imprints can be passed on to future generations, so can positive ones. Nurturing and support, and particularly the power of a mother's love, can actually reverse damage that has accumulated from ancestral epigenetic karma.[10] Frances Champagne, Ph.D., a prominent epigenetics researcher, realized this and publically announced that she would reduce her stress during her pregnancies, and instead fill her life with love, intimacy, and tactile touch as an epigenetic gift to her gestating children. Primal touch, instinctive love, and connection can also epigenetically modify adults to return to greater states of love and harmony. Magic is possible.

The gift of our biology is that our epigenetic expression is fluid in nature and can respond and adapt to changes in our inner and outer environment. *Thus, we can heal our DNA and restore a new, loving genetic expression.* Healing our gestational traumas opens the doorway to new experiences of nurturing, love, union, safety, and trust, which reactivates dormant genetic potentials. As we heal our own DNA, we heal our entire ancestral lineage.

Modern psychiatric research shows that we can heal trauma by gently *remembering and integrating* the source of the original trauma held in the subconscious memory and bringing *resolution* to it—not by avoiding it or trying to think it better with ungrounded positivity.[11] The subconscious is also *somatic*—it dwells in the fabric of the body and her cellular memory.

Revisiting the cauldron of our mother's womb, where our receptive capacity was formed, is a huge key to this genetic healing and awakening of primordial consciousness. Almost a century ago, Otto Rank, Ph.D., and other perinatal researchers put forward the idea that our bodies store memories from these early experiences and that by revisiting them we can create profound healing—through a process known as rebirthing or re-imprinting. Modern science has begun to fill in the missing puzzle pieces by showing that our cells and body structures posess a memory, a "body consciousness," long before our brain is fully developed. For instance, there is an entire class of immune system cells called "memory cells," which hold physical memory, and this also extends into the realms of the psyche. Our understanding of fetal memory and somatic body memory is now widely documented.[12] Rebirthing was one of the spiritual keys of the ancient ones—and now this wisdom returns.

Taking a Rebirth journey with openness and commitment to heal may actually *reprogram your genetic expression and awaken your feminine DNA*. What that means is your body, mind, and soul open to receive the pure flow of life force, love, vitality, orgasmic energy, and you commune deeply with Creator. You consciously reconnect to the placenta of the Void, the cosmic sustenance streaming from the Cosmic Womb that fills you with life, love, and pure energy. This is Source energy—the magical energy that holds the healing codes of life.

It can also prepare your own womb or testes for immaculate conscious conception, or transform and heal children that you have already birthed. This is the greatest gift we can give to future *and past generations*—as the web of our lineage is healed in both directions when we dissolve these wounds.

Womb Center of Spiritual Rebirth

Great Mother Womb was always known as the Great Weaver across many traditions. During conception, gestation, and birth, Great Mother is weaving you into being, weaving your existence into the web of life on a multidimensional level— your soul, energy light body, physical body, fluid body, feminine feeling body, masculine mental body, sexual life-force body. Epigenetically she is also weaving your DNA and genetics, crafting the design blueprint of your coming life on Earth.

In original innocence you would have been conceived in the immaculate conception of sacred union, gestated in a Holy Womb clear from any negative physical, emotional, energetic, psychic, and spiritual imprints; your genetic inheritance would be selected from a banquet of the finest jewels of your lineage, and you would enter this realm birthed in ecstatic, orgasmic, waves of pure love.

Tremendous bioenergetic waves of pleasure, bliss, and union released in ecstatic orgasmic conception would have bathed the newly fertilized egg in a coherent morphogenetic energy field. These powerful magnetic and biophotonic energy fields transmit vast coded information—our divine blueprint—directly to the receptive embryo, birthing the baby into a biology of love and energetic purity.

As your umbilical cord to your earth mother was gently allowed to fall away, the dazzling light cord of creation remained connected to Great Mother.

You would be born through love, gestated and genetically coded to receive love. You would be a being of love—and earth would be your paradise of Love.

Through the Great Womb we came to this world, and only by journeying through the Womb again can we be "born again" into our true birthright of vitality and love. In indigenous shamanic traditions this process is called "recapitulation," returning to the Source, back to the Cosmic Womb, by healing, releasing, and cleansing all experiences that block our direct umbilical cord connection to the Infinite.

Our maternal lineage has held the most powerful keys to our genetic transmission, passed down from one mother to the next, held in the cradle of the ancient feminine womb. One expression of this powerful link is through mitochondrial DNA—the portion of our DNA that comes only from our mother, passed directly from mother to daughter. It is this mitochondrial DNA that most directly connects us to the ancient mothers, our genetic Eve, via direct maternal transfer of these genes from mother to daughter in an unbroken chain, generation by generation over hundreds of thousands of years. Each of us is a son or daughter of Eve—we all possess her mitochondrial DNA.

In fact the egg that you birthed from was once present in the womb of your grandmother—as your mother's eggs were formed while she was still a fetus gestating in your grandmother's womb. The seed of your creation lived in your grandmother's womb, influenced by all her frequencies, just as your mother's egg had lived in your great-grandmother's womb, and so on in an unbroken line.

At this time our mitochondrial DNA is activating and awakening. If we so choose, we can remember through the unbroken genetic thread that goes back to the ancient mothers and their awakened wombs. Our ancient mothers are waiting to transmit this wisdom and remembrance through the genetic "internet" to us.

The more we delve into Womb lore we begin to see how shamanism is closely aligned to the science of Womb gestation—and that shamanism seeks to revisit this Womb dreamtime to dissolve epigenetic and perceptual limitations and immerse in the primordial wisdom we experienced in this "state between worlds," and to open genetic and psychic gateways into the other dimensions of being.

In the tantric text, Lankavatara Sutra—meaning the descent into Womb—it discusses *Tathagatha-garbha,* the Womb of the Buddhas, which lives within every human. Written in the third century, tantric shamans describe what Jung termed the unconscious as *alayavijnana,* and also describe a deeper, foundational realm of consciousness, known as *amalavijnana.*[13] This root or mother of consciousness was called "immaculate consciousness"—which is pure Womb Consciousness. This pure consciousness is epigenetically derailed by trauma, creating the unconscious. But within this unconscious lives the primordial realm of the quantum womb field, our original immaculate consciousness, waiting to be remembered and restored.

> *Oh fire of the Holy Spirit,*
> *life of the life of every creature,*
> *holy are you in giving life to forms . . .*
> *Oh boldest path,*
> *penetrating into all places,*
> *in the heights, on earth,*
> *and in every abyss,*
> *you bring and bind all together,*
> *From you clouds flow, air flies,*
> *Rocks have their humours,*
> *Rivers spring forth from the waters*
> *And earth wears her green vigour*
> *O ignis Spiritus Paracliti*
>
> HILDEGARD VON BINGEN

Womb Gestation

∞

Our First Shamanic "Hero" or "Heroine" Journey in Amniotic Otherworld

Not only can we dissolve negative epigenetic imprints of our gestation, we can also claim and switch on the many incredible gifts from this time in sacred space. We can open the magic doorway of our genetics once again. During our gestation we journey through the four womb elements of air, water, fire, earth. Our first entry from spirit world into form comes through womb air. Then the elements of fire and water spin and weave us into form, before we enter the gravitational pull of the earth element to prepare for our birth—our entry into the world.

These elemental energies live within us for the rest of our lives, expressed as our air-inspired visionary capacities, our watery access to the flowing feeling realms of deep love or grief, our fiery desire and wild sexual energy, and our ability to thrive and root into the earth plane. By revisiting the time these elemental energies were "seeded" into us in the womb, we can begin to understand the patterns that have unfolded in our lives—and restore our elemental balance.

Let us take a closer look at just how each of us was spun into existence.

Womb Air Element

∞

Spirit into Form, Flying the
Cosmic Dreampaths of Incarnation

Characteristics of the Womb Air Element: Spiritual remembrance; union; connection with Divine Mother, spirit world, the web of life, and Gaia; otherworld ecstasy; unbounded bliss; beauty; infinite starlit darkness; extrasensory perception; soulfulness; interconnection and Oneness; and "supernatural" abilities associated with avatars such as Yeshua.

The gestational element of air represents our great journey from spirit into matter. It is our journey from the vast, timeless, and formless dimensions of spirit into a finite, gravity-bound body. While we are still residing in the Cosmic Womb of spirit world, there is no relationship to matter, no gravity, no laws of physics as we know them, no connection to the body experiences, and no physical limitations. There is an incredible freedom in this state of lightness and absence of boundaries.

Then, in a starburst explosion of energy we are conceived into substance—a single-celled egg containing all the genetic codes of our mother and father and their lineages before them. After conception, this egg pulses and rests for a full twenty-four hours before beginning to rapidly divide into a sphere of two, four, eight, sixteen, then hundreds of cells. The first organ to form is a hole in the bottom of the sphere (called an invagination) that will eventually become the anus, bladder, and yoni. This is why our root chakra—our perineum, anus, and the base of our yoni or scrotum—holds such primal memories. The word *primal* means "first," and these organs hold our earliest sacred cellular memories, rooting our spiritual experience into our developing primal body, our original connection to God.

Soon after the anus and bladder form, the heart, nervous system, eyes, ears, skeletal structure, and all of the physical organs begin to take shape. All babies, males and females, have a female body blueprint for the first nine weeks of life, thus starting life with a yoni and clitoris. In some indigenous cultures it is believed that the baby shamanically shape-shifts between genders during this time, sometimes hour by hour, occupying an ambigious, liminal realm of in-between, cogendered consciousness that remains within the psyche and body memory for life.

The process of gestation is guided by the hand of God—scientists have tried for hundreds of years to understand the force that guides embryologic development. They cannot find any gene, molecule, or chemical that guides the overarching process and explains the mystery. Biologist Rupert Sheldrake adapted the term "morphogenetic field" to describe the field of consciousness and energy that guides the developing baby—the womb field—and beyond that, evolutionary fields of energy that guide us in our lives. The word comes from the Latin words *morph* meaning "shape," and *genesis* meaning "creation"—the force that shapes creation. We would call the field God, Divine Mother, Spirit.

The transition from spirit to matter does not happen instantly. It is a gradual movement from an almost weightless single egg cell suspended in the ocean of the mother's womb, still connected to the freedom of infinity, to a baby that is ready to be born into this earthly dimension, and weighted into this world by the gravitational pull of Earth. The environment of our mother's womb is very much like the ocean. The amniotic fluid that bathes us has a similar composition to sea water. The environment is dark but we see a soft red light when direct sunlight is filtered through our mother's belly. It is a very low-oxygen environment, similar to what a dolphin might experience in the dark depths of the silent seas.

Our embryological development completely parallels and retraces the evolutionary path of all of life on this planet. We start out as a single-celled organism, like the bacteria of the primordial oceans. We then briefly travel through a phase in which we are a sentient hollow tube that is almost identical to a sea urchin or worm at that stage of development. Next we pass through a phase in which we are shaped exactly like early vertebrates such as snakes or salamanders, and soon after that like whales or dolphins. We then look exactly like an orangutan or Bonobo monkey for a period. Like all other creatures, we even start life with a tail that finally reabsorbs at nine weeks of gestation. We voyage through this remarkable journey into the ancient animal world, and through this magical process we are connected by direct embryonic memories to the entire web of life, not as a fantasy but as a cellular lived reality we have experienced in the womb. We evolve through the entire web of life, and are connected to all creatures and beings through these memories. We have more in common with all the other creatures on the planet than we have differences.

These direct ancestral and embryological memories are the origin of the shamanic notions of shape-shifting; we hold these memories and possibilities within our very cells. Womb gestation is a dreamtime state. And it is likely that many of our womb dreams are animal memories, because up until the age of four years, a large portion of our dreams continue to be about animals.[14] If we can awaken these primal connections and memories again, we become animal intuitives and animal whisperers—being able to speak to, dream with, and journey with animals—which has always been an important aspect of shamanism.

We experience not only our human and animal ancestral memories, but also the collective evolutionary memories of Gaia. We feel and journey through the ancient memories of Mother Gaia, who is herself also a living evolutionary organism, following her eternal cycles of gestating and birthing, gestating and birthing, again and again.

While we are in this air element of the Womb, our doorways of perception are still fully open, as evidenced by the vivid memories recovered in Stanislav Grof's perinatal psychology research. We are still fully connected to the mystical experiences of spirit world when we are first coming into matter. A luminescent energetic umbilical cord connects us to the Cosmic Womb. We feel the infinite love of the Divine Mother with us. We feel angels and beings of Love guiding us into our new home on Earth.

Our sensory experiences in the womb are radically different from what we experience as adults. Womb air is a symphony of Oneness as remembered by saints and mystics, or the vivid quality of dreams and hallucinogenic shamanic journeys. Rather than perceiving five distinct sense perceptions (sight, sound, taste, touch, smell), we dance through the dreamtime of an infinite kaleidoscopic spectrum of merged and blended sensations and feelings—*primary perception*—due to the hyperconnectivity of our developing brain. We actually have an extraordinary number of brain cells and synaptic connections as a fetus, more so than at any other time in our lives. What we call learning is actually the pruning back of these neurons to create distinct concrete perceptual experiences, so we can focus on the things that aid our survival and immediate needs in the earthly dimension instead of forever floating in mystical states of oneness.

As we continue our neural development in the womb, we shift from *primary perception* to a more organized sensory experience called *synaesthesia,* in which several sense perceptions are blended and combined. In the womb, we can hear colors, see sounds, and touch smells. For example, music can be seen as streaming colors and shapes. It is a magical realm outside the bounds of ordinary perception, which we would call a supernatural, shamanic perception.

Synaesthesia has been proven by the neurobiologist Ramachandran to exist in approximately 5 percent of adults, and to a greater degree in children. But it can bloom in anyone during trance, orgasm, or under the influence of hallucinogens, or in other situations that open our doors of perception. Which is why these methods—sacred sex, sacred drugs, trance, and dreamstates—have always been utilized by shamans and initiates to revisit the Womb air experience.

Synaesthesia is more common in women, six to one (which is why the shamans were originally women), who have greater access to the feminine and womb dimensions. It's a gift of lunar feminine consciousness—our *first* connection to spirit. Synaesthesia runs in families, and is more common in artistic individuals, but while we are gestating in our mother's womb it is universal, because our fetal brains lack a working thalamus until thirty weeks of age.

The thalamus is the filter that organizes our sense perception. It is guardian of the doors of perception that when cleansed, opens our perceptions into the feminine dreamtime dimension. All sensory experiences prior to thirty weeks are dreamtime mystical visions. We can return to this dimension as adults, as shamans have known for thousands of years, if we but open the door with a magical key.

This beautiful gestation phase, in the Womb air element, holds us in the wild, otherworldy vistas of ecstatic, infinite experiences all mystics speak of. But negative feelings and experiences from our maternal and ancestral container block out the depth of this connection—and if the air element holds trauma imprints, we feel trapped and wish to escape life. This "death wish" is the urge to return to spirit world. This wounded desire to return to the spiritual realms and escape the confines of the womb can express as dissociation from earthly matters and the body, or a patriarchal, distorted, fundamentalist perception of God/dess.

We can now claim the treasures of this element and allow the doorways of perception to open again to our bounteous, beauteous inheritance of life.

Womb Water Element

———— ∞ ————

Flowing into Embodiment, Awakening the River of Life

Characteristics of the Womb Water Element: Multidimensional sensual perception; fluid ecstasy; the feminine feeling dimension; embodiment; connection with the spirit of Gaia, the oceans, and the primordial web of life; body-centered bliss; liquid realms of love; merging in love; joyfulness; vast intuitive awareness; trust; and gifts of the mermaid priestesses.

In the next stage of being woven into form, the baby enters the deep, fluid, sensual feeling realms of embodiment experienced during the second gestational Womb phase of water. As you move into this next gestational phase, you descend from the spirit realms deeper into the sensual realms, experiencing the next spiral of physical embodiment into the world of your mother's womb and the earth dimension. Great Mother begins to use the feminine and masculine elements of water and fire to weave your multidimensional body into being. The warp and the weft of these elements bring you from air—a state of spirit body—into matter.

Matter means "Mother," whose sacred magic permeates all the material substance of the cosmos, including the exquisite living temple of our physical bodies.

Our body is the structure, the earthy vessel and container that is filled with the energies of fire and water—the two great flows of life, feminine/masculine, yin/yang, lunar/solar. The Great Spirit infuses our developing form with matter as the divine chalice that holds it all.

The Womb water gestational element brings us into *feelings,* into the realms of the feminine senses—touch, sight, hearing, and an ocean of perceptions through feeling and intuition. If we are gestating in a Holy Womb, this opens us to vast expanses of liquid ecstasy and the intimate oceans of love, where everything is merging, pulsing, ebbing, flowing, in a mysterious and magical underwater symphony of bliss. We meet the mermaid and siren priestesses, commune with the ladies of the lake, swim with the ancient grandmother whales, and spiral with joy in dolphin love pods. The timeless stillness of turtle medicine bathes us in the patient surrender to the tides of life and her great, amniotic, oceanic cycles of ebb and flow.

In this element we become more sensitively attuned to our mother and her feelings, the dark currents of her watery feminine shadows—the emotions, grief, and fears that have been bottled up inside. This acute sensitivity can turn this vast ocean of love into a murky, dark ocean of aloneness if our mother feels separated from her true soul. We may meet the crones of our maternal ancestral line, who throw the bones to reveal the secrets of our lineage.

Womb water holds the choice to truly begin to come into form, and leave the vast infinity of formlessness behind in order to have a new experience. In original innocence, the experience of coming into body form was considered to be the greatest gift of Creator, and an adventure into blissful embodied love. But in our current condition, we may find ourselves wanting to trip out back into air, to escape the body, to escape the sensual currents of this dimension and the intensity of bathing in the feelings our exquisitely acute empathic gifts bring.

During this element we experience massive initiations. Our growing physical form, held in the feminine blueprint of oneness up to this point, now separates into either a male or female gender; we may remember the deep grief and shock from this split. Around the ninth week of gestation in boys the clitoris enlarges into a lingam and the lips of the yoni close and fuse together in the center to become the scrotal pouch. Men will be able to locate and see this fusion line, where their labia closed together into the scrotum. Meanwhile in women the yoni and clitoris continue to develop, but there are no major changes or transitions.

Nipples are another visible aspect of the feminine body blueprint that men carry. Even though there is no biological need for nipples in men, girls and boys are both created with this feminine body structure that only blooms into its full expression in women.

In a world where the masculine and feminine feel separated, this can create primordial shock—the sense that the masculine has chosen to "leave" or abandon the feminine, and for men, the sense that they have lost contact with the feminine that birthed them, and also their own feminine blueprint origins. Beyond the illusion of separation lives the truth that Great Mother Womb is a feminine blueprint, who also holds the gifts of the Divine Father, and who births both the complementary male and female twins who are created for union.

In this water phase, physical development leaps forward with an exquisite synchrony and precision. The primordial dragon tail reabsorbs around nine weeks of gestation; the heart first begins to beat; and the brain and nervous system begin to develop, along with all of the other organs. We also experience movement for the first time—swimming slowly and sensually through primal waters. It is also in this phase that our parents will usually discover that they are pregnant. The emotional response of our mother, and to a lesser extent our father, will determine if we feel welcome and safe to be alive.

The Original Shamanic Experience

Our physical endocrine glands and brain centers begin to develop, starting with the thalamus, which is the gateway to different perceptual realms. As this sacred region of the brain begins to form, it allows us to integrate our new sensory experience. We can now begin to perceive the five senses as different things: touch, sound, sight, taste, and smell. Before that it was one infinite spectrum of undifferentiated sensory input, with an infinite range of perception rather than five distinct senses. The eye of infinity is now becoming the eye of Gaia.

We still experience synaesthesia—the perceptual experience in which the sensations can blend, fuse, and merge. We can still hear colors, see sounds, and touch smells.

We experience a sense of weightlessness in the watery world of the womb. It is an in-between, liminal realm in which we are being slowly transitioned from a cosmic existence to a terrestrial one. We begin to sense the gravitational pull of Earth, but the magnetism is diminished as the amniotic fluid holds us in between the worlds. There is a magical, fluid dance of form and Spirit—very much embodied, but still supported by the Great Mother, and not yet completely bound by the physics of the earth dimension and all that connection brings.

In the final months of gestation, we spend more than 90 percent of our time in the REM brain-wave patterns that indicate the dreamstate, our first shamanic experience in a feminine, fluid, lunar, magical realm, outside of linear time. The shamanic drum of our mother's heartbeat and the rushing sound of her blood are our soundtrack to this rainbow bridge between earth and otherworld in the womb. They are the spirit horses that carry us on our soul journeys through the womb-time dreampaths. It is no coincidence that all shamanic traditions use drumming to journey with; it recreates the original sound of the heartbeat in the womb, not just our mother's, but also our own. We experience the first sounds of our own heartbeat drum in this phase, the feminine pulse of life and love, announcing that we are entering this realm.

We spend our gestational experience cocooned inside our mother's dark internal oceans, incubating in a sea of amniotic fluid that is very similar in composition to sea water. We are swayed and lulled in the soft wavelike motion of the maternal waters, the Waters of Life. In this dreamy waterworld we have direct access to the ancient memories of all the other sentient sea beings—the dolphins, whales, and sea turtles. Our minds and hearts touch through the ancestral currents of the dark, loving primordial oceans.

In this realm of lunar consciousness, we have a very dim perception of the sun, experiencing a soft red orange glow filtered through the belly of our mother, followed by absolute darkness at night. The moon directly influences the tides of the womb (and menstruation) and the tides of the sea. For the nine moons of gestation we develop in a predominantly dark, oceanic feminine environment, which is still very sensitively attuned to the lunar cycles. Our time in the womb is a moon-time experience—receptive, magical, mysterious, multidimensional, otherworldly, yet still embodied.

Womb Fire Element

∞

The Spark of Life Awakens, the Creative Flame Arises

By the Fire of my Love,
I shall birth myself again.
By the Dream-Fires of my Soul,
I shall breathe a New Earth into Being.
Mother I pray to you, set my soul on fire.

A. BERTRAND

This next stage ignites the dreamfire of your Soul Shakti. The quintessential quality of the fire phase of gestation is desire—the desire to embody our extraordinary human potential, our wild innocence, our magical power, our primal loving sexuality that God created us to experience, and to be reunited and merge in ecstatic union with our soul mate. *Our birthright.*

This is soul desire, holy desire, sacred desire. We are desire beings to our core. It fuels every action, every movement, every step of our growth and development, physically, emotionally, and spiritually. Desire is more than a feeling; it is the burning spark of life and morphogenetic God field that physically imbues each of our cells, propelling us forward through the radial explosion of biological energy that is necessary for our development in the Womb.

By revisiting our time in the womb, we can rewire our fire body, our genetic desire body, to come fully online—to heal and release the ancestral and familial traumas that block our ability to experience the infinite love of the universe. We can physically embody the Holy Spirit, the living light into our cells—reprogramming the epigenetic codes of our DNA to become a sacred chalice, a Holy Grail, bathed in the sea of bliss right here and now.

Our soul spark is initially contained in a single pulsing fertilized egg cell that rapidly divides and doubles so that by the time we reach several weeks of age we are already an organized body of millions of cells humming with an incredible metabolic electricity. By three weeks after conception our heart is beating, and then within days after that all of our other organs and tissues are developing—our nervous system, tongue, thyroid gland, arms and legs, and endocrine system.

What modern scientists have dubbed the morphogenetic field is in fact the fire of God that flows through us—it is Holy Shakti, Holy Spirit, the Holy Shekinah—the Divine Essence of Creation that is in each one of us and that permeates every atom of this universe. It is the explosive evolutionary impulse of life, desire in motion. We are that.

In our early gestational time in the womb, we are a dance of fire and water. Though it is dark, still, and safe in the watery womb that nurtures us, our own bodies are bursting with life and energy. By seven weeks of age we are moving, *spontaneously*, not reflexively. In other words, we are already moving to what we want, reaching for what we desire, pushing away from irritants. We already have a fiery Will, a biological imperative to be radically alive—to show it, to express it, to claim it. By the second trimester we are not-so-patiently waiting for our parents to pay attention to us, to play games with us. Parents who recognize this can play the "kick game" with their baby in the womb, in which they place their finger on different parts of the mother's belly and the baby responds by touching or kicking it, their heart racing with excitement, and mouth moving in attempts to vocalize their joy. By several months of gestational age babies are responsive, inquisitive, and adventurous.

During the early and middle phases of gestation, the womb environment is spacious. We float like little aquanauts in a near weightless environment, connected by our umbilical cord, but free to jump, twist, flip, spin, kick, and bounce off the walls of our new home. Early ultrasound shows that we are dancers and acrobats from the beginning, testing our new form with remarkable kinetic activity.

Our nervous system generates a potent electromagnetic field, and is closely linked with our energy body, auric field, and "presence." The initial growth of our nervous system outpaces all other development. By the end of the first trimester, nearly half of our weight is in our head, in preparation for the rapid expansion of our brains. We are literally growing 50,000 new neurons every second for the entirety of our time in the womb, so that we have 100 billion brain cells as we are ready to be born, each of those forming connections with more than 10,000 others, creating vast holographic neural webs that are staggering in their complexity.

Our kundalini fire is rising, fueling the development of our neuroendocrine system—the cascade of hormones, neurotransmitters, neuropeptides, and other "molecules of emotion" that function as alchemical sparks, turning on or off large sections of our DNA, depending on the container of our mother's womb.

Western mystery school hermeticists have long been practitioners of "endocrine alchemy," the science behind the magical elixirs of our fluids of life—especially the feminine fluids. From the European Merovingian lineage, through Yeshua and the Marys, to the kingly lineage of Solomon and David, and down through the Egyptian pharoahs—all understood that our endocrine alchemy, when activated, creates the fountain of life, the Holy Grail, longevity, and magical powers. It is a Womb gateway into God.

The hypothalamus, pituitary, thyroid, pineal, and sexual glands release powerful chemical messengers such as melatonin, oxytocin, serotonin, and many other signal molecules that light our magical lamps, summoning our inner genie into action. They are the spark that breathes life into our growing body-temple. Thyroid hormone is another important hormone that determines our metabolic rate—the amount of energy we are able to generate—by switching on the powerhouse of mitochondrial energy production within our cells.

All this fiery activity is pulsing within our being, forging our relationship to vitality, passion, *aliveness,* in the furnace of the womb; these seeds of Shakti will determine how safe we feel to really allow this burning desire to live, to love, to create on earth when we become adults.

Our sensual energy *is* our life-force energy, *is* our desire, *is* our fire. They are one and the same energy, different manifestations of our fundamental spark of life, our spiritual-biological-soulful yearning for union and evolution. When we are immersed in the beautiful, pure flow of ecstatic life-force energy inside the womb—our bio-energetic networks awaken into bliss.

Babies in the womb are also profoundly affected by the relationship of their parents. Their nervous systems are wired for pleasure or pain by the emotional energies that are exchanged between their parents. When mother and father are connected in love, the baby is flooded with the hormones and neurotransmitters of bliss—which pass through the placenta immediately to the baby, who then becomes neurologically wired to associate relationships with joy. Or, if the parent's relationship is full of anger, conflict, or disconnection, the baby infuses the imprint of aggression, pain, or abandonment, and in adulthood may unconsciously seek out similar relationships, replaying these troubling wombtime memories until they are healed.

Twin Energy

By using ultrasound to watch how twins interact in the womb, researchers have observed that babies have complex social interactions with each other as early as *seven weeks of age.*[15] Twins instantly play out their "karmic," or epigenetic, ancestral patterns with each other. Sometimes twins groom, lick, cuddle, kiss, hold, and play games with each other. Whereas with other pairs, one baby is hostile and aggressive, kicking and punching the other until she withdraws in despair.

Although only 1 percent of people are born with a living twin, nearly 10 percent of people start life in the womb with a twin, and in our genetic memories there was a time when this number was even greater. Thus nine out of ten twins die in the first months of gestation. The "vanishing" twin leaves for numerous reasons, many of them linked to incarnation shock and emotional trauma. Research shows that the rates of spontaneous miscarriage and fetal death are much higher when one or both parents do not want the child, or when the mother experiences significant emotional trauma.

The death of a twin comes as a terrible shock to the surviving baby, and is grieved in utero. Grimacing facial expressions, changes in heart rate, and withdrawal into stillness are some examples of the body language that provide a window into the baby's early emotional responses. When upset, a baby in the womb makes a "silent scream," moving their mouth but no sound comes out—and indeed Edvard Munch's compelling painting feels hauntingly familiar to anyone who has experienced wombtime despair. On the rare occasion that air reaches the upset baby's vocal cords (usually accidentally introduced as a result of surgery), it allows their heartwrenching fetal screams to be heard.[16] Within the deepest part of our psyche, we often repress profoundly disturbing memories of our own Womb terrors, of our unanswered silent screams—the ongoing vibrations of these emotions create what we now call the "hell realms."

Reclaiming Firepower

All of our experiences during the fiery formative period of our life in the womb are forever etched into the memory banks of our cerebellum, as well as epigenetically imprinted on our DNA. We pass these memories on to future generations, creating either a legacy of pain or passion. Nothing is ever forgotten, only repressed until we can remember, heal, and integrate it. Modern research studies performed by David Chamberlain, Ph.D., and others show that adults under hypnosis, who know nothing about their time in the womb, accurately remember the details of their mother's experiences as well as their own birth.[17] Young children under the age of four easily remember their womb and birth experiences, without the need for hypnosis. Our time in the womb is the blueprint for our life, until we choose to consciously rebirth.

The truth is that in this moment on Earth, no one is born with 100 percent of their fire element online, because in the womb we clearly feel all the emotional traumas of not only our parents but our entire ancestral line as well. We have the entire history of Earth held in our epigenetic coding—both as a burden and a blessing.

We experience energetic, chemical, and emotional insults in the womb against which we are powerless to protect ourselves. By direct and extrasensory telepathic perception (now documented by science) we realize that our parents may not support *our desires* if they conflict with *their desires* and the confines of society, a destructive paradigm they are plugged into. We understand that in order to receive the love we need, we may have to repress many of our own energies and desires. Our fire, *our freedom, our Shakti,* becomes enslaved.

The result is that to different degrees, each of us gives up on aspects of our deepest desires and soul dreams for life—resulting in a loss of desire and passion—and an unconscious death wish. We are afraid of being attacked, unsupported, and overwhelmed. We decide that we need to adapt to other people's wishes to survive rather than follow our own desires, and part of our soul steps out at that moment, until we heal and retrieve it. Or if, as babies, we were unable to embody the fire element due to emotional trauma, we feel withdrawn, collapsed, depressed, apathetic, dull, powerless, and passive. Now we must reach out to reclaim our *fire power* again.

When we embody the fire element we awaken a passionate determination, come what may, even if that means losing the support of "friends" and family. The element of fire lets nothing stand in the way of its desires. The fiery spirit is dynamic, sensual, excited, energetic—a true go-getter and leader. Our Shakti fire is the magical essence of magnetism within desire.

Womb Earth Element

———— ∞ ————

Forming the Bones of the Wyrd, Our Descent into Gaia's Body

The earth is at the same time mother, She is mother of all that is natural, mother of all that is human. She is the mother of all, for contained in her are the seeds of all.

HILDEGARD VON BINGEN

We now enter the sunlit, enchanted vistas of the ancient wild woods, the tribal hum of Gaia's heartbeat, the dark, fertile Womb of Gaia. Womb mystic Hildegard Von Bingen described the "greening power of God" as *viriditas*—which means vitality, fecundity, lushness, flourishing growth. It embraced the knowing that earth is a realm of the Divine Feminine in all her wonderous, magical, beauty—the physical embodiment of Holy Spirit of Shakti.

The earth element is our home in nature, in primal safety, our belonging to this green garden planet, our knowing it is an embodied realm of love. In the rolling hills and valleys of this landscape, we connect with the wise, majestic spirit of the trees, and the *tree of life* herself—who carries the mysterious feminine wisdom the Druids and Druidesses knew held the secrets of life. We also meet the great animal totems and familiars who will be our guides and companions; the Owl, the Bear, the Wolf, the Deer, and the queendom of the Bees.

Earth was created as the highest expression of love, the light embodied into *living Light*—the pulsing, slow, sensual vibration of Gaia's living Love. Patriarchal ideas and spirituality have taught us that earth is a mistake, lower, less than, a place to be transcended, or a "bootcamp of suffering," that our physical bodies are sinful and worthless. Nothing could be farther from the truth. When we embody the living Light, we return earth back to her original creation, we restore Gaia to her throne of beauty and wonder. Our soul is infused with the "power of greenness" and we become One with the Holy Spirit.

Our bodies are the most magical vehicles of creation, stunning masterpieces that science still only knows or understands the smallest part of. Our form is a primal symphony of interconnection and harmony that follows the creative blueprint of the entire universe, the divine golden ratio that weaves All together as One.

In the earth phase of gestation, we receive the gifts of patience, slowness, stillness, softness, *the art of being,* rather than doing—resting in the great glory of it all, allowing, enjoying. We connect to the descending flow of Shakti that connects us to gravity, the magnetic pull of Gaia's Womb, which grounds us fully into being. We feel safe and familiar in the dark caverns of the Mother, and in the primordial blackness of our own inner being, fertilizing our wild creativity in the vast silence.

We trust completely in life and surrender to the winding rivers of her flow, through the dense forests, the lulling valleys, the dramatic mountain heights, the magical rays of first sunlight, the mysterious reflection of moonlight on the great oceans. In this magical realm we can experience feminine enlightenment—stillness—stilling the wave as we sit in the Womb-Heart of Creation, with the spinning, spiraling, dance of life weaving around us. We surrender to the downward spiral, the gravitational pull of the Womb of Gaia, heaviness, embodiment, the pulsing heartbeat of Gaia. Earth is slow vibration . . . patience as you take your place in the great weaving, dependent on everything else. You have a direct relationship to the whole world, the web of life.

Earth is our Great Mother, and our experiences in our mother's womb epigenetically modify how deeply we can perceive and immerse in the full spectrum of Gaia's radiance and living web of ecological harmony.

If the landscape of our mother's womb was cold, dark, unfriendly, filled with fear, doubt, trauma, or disconnection, or if our mother has experienced a difficult time on Earth, survival struggles, financial trouble, sexual abuse, emotional shutdown, psychic attack, taboos around her own womanly body and cycles, then our experiences of the earth element can feel unsafe and frightening. The interdependency and vulnerability of an earth body is overwhelming.

If we cannot trust we will be cared for in this realm, we fear the "greening power of God" will not reach us, grow us, or bloom us, effortlessly in grace. We fear we will struggle to survive, unwelcomed, unsupported. In this fear our gestating primal body shuts down, and our perceptual and receptive capacity for love and wonder begins to diminish and atrophy—our cellular capacity becomes a death rattle.

The Lost Pathways of Sacred Union within the Brain

In Womb earth element we gain access to the realms of both the feminine and masculine consciousness, both parts of the brain—although the spectrum of our sensory capacity is determined or limited by our wombtime environment.

As mentioned earlier, our brain development in the womb retraces the evolutionary path of the history of life on Earth. The cerebellum, known as the feminine brain, as well as the limbic system, or the feeling brain, starts developing in the first months of gestation, and has been present in other creatures on this planet for hundreds of millions of years. Similarly in us, our feminine dreaming capacity as well as emotional intelligence forms first, long before our logical and rational mind. Our earliest memories and experiences are stored in these primal brain centers, and are often completely unknown by our logical mind until we make new connections to them in psychic journeying, intuitive openings, and dream travel.

In the womb, the cerebrum begins functioning at a basic level around six months of gestation, allowing our masculine consciousness to gradually become aware of our feminine dreamtime experience. This "conscious" or logical awareness of our feminine blueprint prepares us to make practical decisions in the outside world. In original innocence, the emerging cerebrum (masculine) would fully connect to and understand the cerebellum (feminine) and they would create union and harmony in the brain. But when our feminine consciousness has already started to shut down in the womb due to trauma, our cerebrum has nothing to connect to. He is lost and alone, not understanding what or who he is translating for.

The thalamus is another important brain center that filters and organizes our feelings and sensory perceptions, selecting which of them are allowed into our conscious awareness. If a feeling or sensation is frightening, the thalamus represses it from our thinking awareness in an attempt to keep us emotionally stable. For example, it is the traumatized thalamus that prevents us from being continuously aware of our extrasensory perceptions and psychic intuitions, which are a natural gift of all humans, but are conditioned out of us by parents. The thalamus also filters out traumatic emotional memories until we are ready to integrate them.

Before the thalamic filtering becomes mature, we perceive one infinite spectrum of undifferentiated sensory input—a moving sea of kaleidoscope swirls and feelings—rather than the five senses. But as our thalamus comes online, the eye of infinity gradually becomes interpreted by our cerebrum as the five senses we are familiar with—touch, taste, smell, hearing and sight, although the doorway to infinity is still available.

Of all the senses, touch is developed first, and is our most primal or original sense. This is why we say something inspiring or moving touches us, because it stirs us at a primal feeling level. And similarly, it is why touch therapies can help us access deep wombtime memories. Development of smell and taste soon follow, and like touch, give us direct access into the primal emotional, or limbic, areas of the brain. This is why the science of touch, primal scents, and sacred fragrance have always been a part of the feminine spiritual and shamanic traditions.

Hearing is another powerful shamanic sense that emerges in the earth element of gestation. We are first able to "hear" through our skin sensations—the pulses and vibrations of sound physically vibrate us at different frequencies. This is one of the reasons why people who are deaf can still enjoy dancing to music—they can "hear it" by feeling it through their skin; this is the sensuality of sound.

Our first language is the music of the ambient sounds echoing through the underwater sound chamber of the womb along with the background drum of the heartbeat. We hear sounds similarly to dolphin or whales—the sounds bounce and echo in primal surround sound, seemingly originating from all directions at once. Shamanic trance music throughout the ages has used combinations of rhythm and ambient sounds to recreate this dreamy wombtime dimension, allowing us to directly access the otherworld of feminine consciousness.

Our mother's unique pattern of pitches and rhythms, called her "voice spectrum," forms a key part of our early musical journey in the womb, and encodes her unique emotional spectrum that is carried on her vocal frequencies. Incredibly, research by Henry Truby, Ph.D., former professor of pediatrics and linguistics at University of Miami, shows that by the age of thirty weeks we can identically reproduce our mother's exact voice spectrum. In many ways we know more about our mother than she knows about herself while we are in the womb.[18]

Our mother's "missing notes" also become our missing notes as our voice (and therefore emotional) spectrum mirrors hers—until we remember and reclaim the full spectrum of our lost Soul Song, and that of our lineage too. Experiments have shown that when a crying baby is played the missing notes of its voice spectrum, inherited from its mother, it instantly calms down and is soothed.[19]

Scientists such as Alfred Tomatis discovered that the music of language and the language of music play a key role in guiding our intelligence and brain development, as well as our balance and coordination. Music and sounds are a "dynamo charging station" that organizes our brain development and memories according to the frequencies, vibrations, and rhythms. Music is the language of the creative, Divine Intelligence. "In the beginning was the Word"—sacred sound vibration from the Great Womb, echoing and pulsing in our own Wombs. We can heal and rebirth through the sacred vibration of Womb sound.

Research also shows that while we are in the womb we react with excitement and joy to music we love or when people speak directly to us. We can remember and distinguish the voices of both parents, siblings, and even family pets. We remember the songs and words spoken to us in the womb.

Inside the womb we can hear the sacred sounds of earth—birdsong, rivers rushing, thunder storms, rainfall—and begin to connect to our new home.

The Ancient Wisdom of the Bones

Bones are composed of the minerals of the earth. They are our most densely earthy and crystalline structure, and are one of the last physical systems to mature in gestation, as they depend on gravity to fully form. As we approach the time of birth, there is relatively less amniotic fluid in the womb compared to our growing body. Our head begins to point downward into the pelvis to prepare for birth, and we feel the effects of gravity more and more. It is a fluid movement that transitions us gradually into Earth's gravitational field, "down to earth."

Our bones do not fully form until we are out of the womb using our muscles; standing, jumping, and dancing all help build strong bones. The cranial bones that protect our brain do not close until three to six months after birth—creating the fontanelle, or soft spot, on the top of the head that many indigenous cultures say gives access to the other realms directly through the top of the head.

As the ancients have known, bones contain a deep wisdom, for within their crystalline caves they contain our marrow—the mother of our blood system. The marrow is rich in stem cells that continue to birth and rebirth our blood and immune system cells throughout our lives. Our bones are also the landscape where a woman's menstrual blood is first formed, deep in the earth element.

In the earth phase of gestation, our bodies are preparing for another massive psychological and evolutionary leap—our first breath. During the final months of gestation our lungs practice breathing amniotic fluid again and again until they become strong enough to breathe on their own. At the moment of birth our survival depends on our capacity to take that first breath, which is naturally a gentle process that occurs over five to ten minutes with our umbilical cord still attached to our guide and companion, the placenta, until it stops pulsing.

In modern hospital births, often the umbilical cord is cut immediately, leading to a precipitous drop in oxygen levels and an incredible survival shock as we gasp for air before we are ready. The moment we start breathing, our entire metabolic and respiratory mechanisms switch radically, from a low-oxygen existence in the womb that is similar to being in the ocean, to a full-oxygen environment.

Journeying from Womb to Earth

When the head engages down by thirty weeks, the cervix starts to dilate, and the baby has to choose to engage his or her connection with Womb of Gaia and earth. As the baby begins preparations to leave the womb nest it is cocooned in, it may feel excited, curious, or afraid about "what lies out there." A myriad of emotions can arise—a sense of stuckness, primal fear, don't want to come out, don't want to stay, separation, loss, can't trust, not safe . . .

In the earth element we are outgrowing the container of the womb, our gestational world. Where once our small, growing body could float, twist, swirl in an oceanic space of exploration, we are now meeting the walls of our home.

Depending on our relationship with the womb home, and the feelings we have been infused with from our mother, this phase can either feel like a terrible confinement, a profound stuckness, as if we are being squeezed to death, or an exciting interface with the outside world we are waiting to be birthed into.

Gestating in a Holy Womb, in full telepathic communion with our mother and trusting completely that the realm of earth is magical and supportive, at this stage we begin to connect with the magnetic force of the Womb of Gaia. We reorient ourselves from the womb connection and nourishment of our birth mother's womb into the Great Mother's Womb—so she can be our support.

This connection with Gaia's Womb is the force that begins to align our body, head facing down to the cervix—the *gateway between the worlds*—and allows us to be magnetically drawn down the birth canal, in a way that is ecstatic for mother and baby. It is vital that we connect into the magnetic pull of gravity. In this earth phase we harmonize and merge the gifts from both fire and water into sacred union, into the perfect balance of solar/lunar alchemy. We embody the soft, lunar currents of receptivity and intuitive feeling, while also claiming our wild, solar gifts of power, passion, and action. We can flow between the two.

Awakening the Dragon

Our dreamtime journeys and extrasensory perceptual capacities weave their kaleidoscopic tapestries through the fire element, bringing our consciousness in touch with the animal totems linked to fire—dragons, snakes, lions, panthers, and the sun-seeking eagles and hawks.

Dragons hold a special place in the myths and symbology of the Grail lineages, as they represent the primordial power of our sensual and sacred Shakti, held in our sacral energy center at the seat of the spinal cord. Our magical creative powers and primal wildness are held here in the dragon nodes within our Wombs and sexuality. Across all the ancient languages, the same sacred seed syllables of S and K are apparent in the dragon energy words: *sacred* (Sa Cred), *sacrum* (Sa Crum), *Shakti* (Sha Kti), *Shekinah* (She Kinah), *Sekhmet* (Se Khmet), *Shekem* (She Kem), *sex* (Se Ks).

Your Womb or Hara dragon is waiting to awaken, to breathe fire into the darkest, most depressed aspects of your being and soar them into the primordial light. This is the key to your soul charisma, your dynamism and vigor—rebirthing you into a being of passion, élan, vibrancy, brightness, and boldness.

Original Source of Shadow Patterns

In a womb disconnected from the Divine Feminine, we can feel overwhelmed, afraid, not wanting to stay, not wanting to leave, wanting to die or disappear. We do not want to connect to gravity, to this feeling of being *pulled down to earth*. Rather than merging the gifts of water or fire, we can become entrenched in the shadow of one of the elements. Either drowning in watery grief with no fire, no heat—or burning, irritated, agitated in an angry fire.

For most babies, this phase brings with it the fear of either being stuck in the womb, trapped forever—or being pushed out and evicted into a cold world. Ultimately these wounded feelings elicit two responses, which will define our entire behavior patterns for the rest of our life, unless we choose to heal it.

One is the "stuck" pattern of lunar grief, the water element shadow. We decide we don't want to come out, we would rather stay stuck, disappear, contract, make ourselves smaller, hide, drown in the amniotic shadow feelings, die to any desire for life, to shutdown into the darkness of depression and inertia. We do not want to face the world—and all the horror and terror we fear it will bring.

The other is the struggle pattern of solar rage, the fire element shadow. We decide

Fig. 15.1. Dragon labyrinth

(Illustration by Heather Skye)

to fight, to struggle, to kick our way out, to escape at any cost, to push through any boundaries with force, to never be trapped or powerless, to do anything to escape the amniotic shadow feelings, to escape into a frenzy of doing rather than feeling. We do not want to stay in the world of our mother's womb and her painful emotions.

These two patterns can also be described as the collapse shadow pattern and the react shadow pattern. Neither pattern connects us to the flow of life; both are wound responses to fear. The split between these patterns dominates the current world landscape.

Lunar Shadow—the Collapse Pattern

Those in collapse are very connected to their feelings, but are often too overwhelmed and confused by others to take positive action. Those in react are often disconnected from their true feeling state, but thrive on taking action to distract themselves. And so a world of leaders and followers, masters and slaves is born.

Those who predominantly respond with the collapse pattern are more likely to conform to their parent's world, to shut down their own feelings and will in order to get by and be safe. They are the world's "nice" victims, handmaidens, helpers, who give their energy to please and support others. They do not like conflict or change and find it difficult to take direct action or be daring. They find it easier to give their power away to others, and prefer to stay in the same, comfortable situation than to take risks, or to lead the way. Under pressure they shutdown and withdraw, hiding away, not speaking their true feelings. It feels frightening and overwhelming to come out and voice their desires. In physical terms they often experience chronic illness, weight gain, lack of energy.

Those in the collapse pattern respond to the traumas of life by giving up on their own will and fire. They withdraw in order to get by. They reduce their expectations of life. They give up what they really want in order to get along and get approval. They tend to be depressed, shy, anxious, and avoid confrontation. They are more in touch with their sadness, their fear, their vulnerability, and tender emotions—and from this place can easily empathize and sympathize with others. They tend to be hyperaware of their shortcomings. They don't like the spotlight, they don't like to be seen, or to put themselves out into the world.

They can be good listeners, they know what those around them are feeling, and they often reflexively try to pacify, soothe, and comfort those around them who are upset. They can be natural nurturers. They do well in supportive environments, but they become stressed and collapse in unsupportive and confrontational environments. They are people pleasers, and if people around them don't like them it creates a tremendous dis-ease. They tend to be humble or self-effacing. They are sensitive to rejection, and give up easily if they meet an obstacle. They undervalue themselves, they have difficulties supporting themselves, difficulties in business, difficulties taking actions in life. Fear, confusion, and uncertainty are their bedmates.

They often do not know what they want. They feel like victims—battered, overwhelmed, and exhausted by life. They often fall prey to narcissists, parents, people who take advantage of their "niceness." They feel like they have to take care of others. They value union and communion more than personal glory and achievements, and are more easily able to surrender into loving relationships and have long-standing heartful relationships, though they may lack sexual desire and fire. In short the feelers can feel, but they have a difficult time doing. They have plenty of access to the lunar feminine, watery realms of feeling, but they lack fire, they lack passion and desire. They have access to the soft feminine loving qualities of the heart, but less so to the masculine courageous qualities of the heart-in-action. They gave up on their desires and power in order to get by.

Solar Shadow—the React Pattern

Those who predominantly respond with the react shadow pattern are more likely to rebel, to escape, to force their will upon the world—and others. On the surface they can seem like free spirits, radical activists, creative whirlwinds, who are always pushing the envelope in exciting ways. They enjoy and thrive on challenge, change, leading the way, pushing their own and others limits. Always chasing new ideas and horizons. These people are afraid of stillness, of dropping deeply into the feminine dimension and the uncomfortable feelings they faced in the womb. Their action and movement is erratic, escapist, and not grounded. They have to be in charge, in power, directing—if not they feel the agitation of the powerlessness and worthlessness that haunted them in the womb. In physical terms, they have a kinetic, restless energy and often have very fit bodies.

The reactors respond to the traumas of life by shutting down their tender emotions and adopt the coping strategy of just pushing ahead in life and trying to push away the really difficult emotions. They bury their head in the sand from an emotional perspective, and keep on with their exercise plans, and self-help plans, and business plans, trying to "quick fix" everything. In the process they become separated from how they truly feel underneath the mask. But they do have fire. They are tough, they have a thick skin, they have determination. They don't give up easily. They have the capacity to push through challenges and setbacks, and initiate actions in the world. They have courage in the external world. They can have business success. They can get by in unsupportive situations if needed.

They don't mind being seen and promoting themselves. They know what they want, and they go after it. Although they prefer people to admire them and get along with them, they are not terribly bothered if someone doesn't—that is their problem. They tend to have strong energy, and they tend to have a superficial confidence and charisma, but it is not easily connected to their tender and loving emotions, and hides the feelings of low self-worth they have disconnected from. They tend to be prideful, and have difficulty recognizing and admitting their faults. And they have difficulty dropping the mask, being truly vulnerable, and deeply surrendering in their intimate relationships. Because of this it is difficult for them to experience the vast expanses and dimensions of love in relationship. In short, the doers do, but they don't feel— they have limited access to the watery, feeling, feminine dimensions of surrender, but they have plenty of fire and desire. They have access to the masculine courageous qualities of heart, but dropping into the lunar feminine dimension feels like a form of death to them. They have everything in the shop window, and nothing in the storeroom.

The Great Work of Reunion

Discovering our predominant lunar/solar shadow pattern is a big key in our healing journey. Often we can have different responses in different areas of our lives or with different people—we may be a react person in our career, but a collapse person when it comes to relationships. Our patterns may change with different triggers, through different ages, and during different life events and challenges. The constant is the hidden presence of fear, which either inspires our actions or prevents our actions, until we come back to the center of our soul.

It takes great humility, self-enquiry, and honesty to see where you are embodying the shadows of fire and water. In this culture men are often forced to exist in the shadow of fire, while women flip-flop between the shadow of fire and water. Often the escape from the water shadow into the fire shadow, or vice versa, can feel like evolution (the downtrodden housewife who becomes the go-getting career girl; the macho man who becomes the submissive new age man)—but neither opens the true Sacred Feminine or Masculine and the union within.

Understanding our lunar/solar shadows is the first step to reclaiming each of their gifts, marrying our feminine and masculine, and merging both gifts into one radiant stream of being.

Every child is created with the potential for a merged holistic consciousness of magical innocence, but the experience of the wombtime in the current paradigm, fragmented by ancestral and collective fear and grief, disconnects us from this potential. We replay in childhood what we first experienced in the womb. This in part explains why children are born with core pieces of their personality already formed. Perinatal psychology research shows that journeying back to our repressed womb experiences and making them conscious heals stubborn dysfunctional patterns at their root level that cannot be resolved in any other way, radically changing our biology and epigenetic codes of life. Descending back into the Womb of Consciousness to reclaim this possibility is the heart of what true rebirth means.

The traumas and memories that are repressed by the thalamus do not go away; they remain trapped in our cellular, energetic, and soulful memory, but we are simply unaware of them. In order to fully dissociate from them, we also have to dissociate from our body, sexuality, and feelings; this is known in the shamanic world as "soul loss." Instead of consciously recognizing the feelings of agitation that lie beneath the surface of our being, these stuck energies are unconsciously expressed through our body, emotions, and life path—through anxiety, depression, anger, agitation, breathing restrictions, body tensions, health problems, troubled relationships, lack of abundance, and seemingly external events, conflicts, or accidents.

Our feminine feeling mind tries to bring these repressed conflicts into our awareness through dreams, synchronicities, signs, symptoms, and by replaying out the original dramas in our current life (our law of attraction). We can heal these repressed traumas only by venturing past the gateway of the thalamus, and the often terrifying or unsettling guardians that stand there, and into the ancient feminine dreamtime brain—which is now populated with vast dimensions of repressed fears, horrors, and grief that originated during gestation.

This is the shamanic "hero and heroines" journey: to travel into these lost feeling dimensions to reclaim and retrieve the fragmented soul pieces. Then all is brought into awareness to be seen as it truly is, resulting in deep emotional releases and opening into infinite fields of sensory perception and connection. You have the choice in every moment, no matter what your experiences in the womb, to follow your own desires, your own movement, your own soul, to walk in the fire of transformation, to burn through the karma of your epigenetics, to birth a new way. Only you can make this decision at a soul level.

Otherwise, it is like trying to light a fire that sparks a few times but that doesn't catch hold. You become lost, drowning, sinking into a watery shadowy underworld of negative feelings and emotions—feeling trapped, powerless, a victim of the world, or like you are treading water.

Rebirthing journeys, where we consciously revisit our time in the womb, spiral us around the arms of the Cross of Life, merging, balancing, and harmonizing our elemental soul selves, so that we are extended out into the cosmos, the heavens, and grounded deep into the roots of earth and our body, dancing with both fire and water, love and power, action and reflection. We become whole, able to shape-shift between each aspect of our inner being.

This reunion of solar and lunar consciousness into one state of being is the Great Work of all alchemical traditions, from the Nahuals of Mexico to the Gnostics of the West. Our consciousness has been separated into a waking and dreaming reality—divided into the solar cerebrum and the lunar cerebellum. Building the bridge of sacred marriage between these lunar and solar consciousnesses restores wholeness.

As we start to enter the sacred marriage of consciousness, we merge our lunar and solar selves into one—gaining access to the wisdom and gifts of both. In the sunlit paths of waking life we still have access to the great dark ocean of dream consciousness that birthed us; in the lunar dreamtime paths of the night, we can bring the clarity and lucidity of our waking consciousness to interpret our experiences, and bring back messages, visions, and insights into the solar world.

In Mexican tradition this was called *temixoch,* when the solar *tonal* and the lunar *nahual* merge together to form a unified energy body. *Mexico* means "place of the moon's navel," and this wisdom was believed to have descended from a race of people 50,000 years old, who followed the womb religion and embodied the Moon Halo.

Our lunar world, the dark dreaming of Womb Consciousness, is restored back to her throne—and the solar gifts help birth her essence into the world to bring harmony.

WOMB ORACLES SHARE
Priestess of Rebirth

My womb was vibrating and I started to give birth, again and again, to each person in the circle, to my son, to my beloved, to my ex-husband, thus healing many traumatic births though my own womb. "Re-birthing," she was telling me—re-birthing, including the rebirthing of myself, into love and joy. After, I felt I was breastfeeding so many children, especially boys who really needed to connect with their mothers, who were longing for the Mother and so much healing was happening to all of these children and men, in an instant.

L.M.

Umbilical Cord of Life

I felt the very cut of my umbilical cord as my life force was so quickly severed. I went into shock trying to take my first breath, feeling panic as I was being suspended between two worlds. Then my own breath kicked in and I felt how totally supported I am by this amazing vessel we call the body. I was shown how trees act as surrogate umbilical cords, supporting and connecting all of life.

I was given the message: "When we truly birth in each moment it is the resurrection of Life itself."

S.J.

Finding the Magic Mother Within

I had a sense of myself crying and screaming in panic and pain, feeling like I was lying on my back, and flailing my arms and legs around. Then I saw that I was a little baby, in the plastic incubator at the hospital in my first week of life. I started to physically feel in my feet an intense searing, stinging, sharp pain—the pain of having needles stuck into my tender newborn soles a few times a day to draw blood samples. I felt and saw my baby self crying, alone, feeling like no one heard and understood me, that no one saw how much this hurt my very sensitive feet. What a frightening and overwhelming shock this introduction to life was, and having no one holding and soothing me, supporting me and helping me feel I was safe. I went and stood by my baby self, looking down at her into her eyes, and myself as a baby kept crying and screaming, but the fear and panic began to lessen. I was being witnessed and understood, my pain was being heard; I was not alone in it.

I then picked my newborn self up out of the incubator, into my arms, and we were suddenly in lush green, blossoming Nature, and I set me down in the soft sunlit grass, to be nurtured by this nourishing environment. Then Magdalene unexpectedly came, and she sat down at the foot of my baby self. She placed the palms of her hands on the bottoms of my feet and held them there for a while. She then began running her hands over my little body, from the top of my head gently down to my toes . . . over and over, in a softly caressing way. And it was like she was pulling the trauma out of my body, and down out my feet. I had tears flowing and felt various things in my body as this was happening, and a couple times I had to cough from deep in my gut/solar plexus, like something needed to come out. I felt like it was not only meant to help heal the trauma there, but also to help me open the grounding connection to the Gaia grid in my feet that had never formed. Then she started kissing my little baby feet many times and cooing like a mother would.

The whole way the world felt to me and how I perceived it was different. I didn't have a rigid mental definition of my identity; it was fluid and peaceful . . . I was simply being. I felt like I had been shown what it would be like when certain wounds and limitations in my identity had been healed and lifted, and what a different life that would be. And that this is the path I am on right now.

H.S.

Journey to Earth

I followed each thread and I came consciously into my mother's womb again. I heard my soul vibration—the name that I have had since the dawn of creation, the sound of the vibration that is the frequency of me, and I could see the light and love of my soul! It was so amazing, each time I felt it and heard it I became more embodied and the umbilical cord of light grew stronger from Great Mother to me and to my mother and I got closer to earth. I reached the womb and there was an electrical flash, a lightning strike, a starburst of infinity, and a certainty I was born to be here. I was in the womb and I was going to make the journey to earth. . . . After this journey I felt the deep truth of remembering again who I am in the universe. . . . My heart beats strong and my womb is alive with love.

E.S.

SPIRAL 16
SHAMANIC BIRTHING

Avatars of New Earth

Her simple and unselfcentered Mary-life,
became marvelous and Castle-like.
Her life resembled trumpets on the feast days
That reverberated deep inside every house;
And she, once so girlish and fragmented,
Was so plunged now inside her Womb.

RAINER MARIA RILKE

WE CAN HEAL OUR gestational and birth traumas, and unpick the web of wounds that became wrapped around our body and psyche as we were developing. This healing work rewires us back to pleasure and innocence, awakening our spirit. *But* the key for our future evolution is to begin conceiving, gestating, and birthing babies who do not have the burden of this negative karma to unwind—to bring souls into the world who can flourish from the start, growing in a garden of love. If a baby were born into a womb that had been reset to energetic virginity (original innocence) the bioenergetic form of the body would be able to develop to its true potential as a chalice and receiver of living light.

The baby born through an awakened womb would be in a condition far beyond what we now consider to be enlightened; it would be supernatural, as it would be fully inhabiting its true blueprint. Its endocrine system would be able to transmit and receive the chemistry of heaven—ecstasy, bliss, cosmic pleasure, primordial love. This is the meaning of Yeshua's "virgin birth"—he came into a womb that was far closer to a state of original innocence than most wombs, due to his mother's healing work as a womb priestess of the feminine mysteries. She was able to bring a child into this pure frequency of love. It has happened before, and it will happen again. The potential exists that every child born into this world can be a "Christ."

The womb is the sacred chalice that receives, generates, and sustains life. When we truly feel and live by the sanctity of this, *everything* will change. This isn't just about honoring women; this is about honoring the human race. It should be our *absolute priority* now as a species—our future depends on it.

In very ancient times when we followed moon time, women often gave birth en masse, in joyful ceremony. They conceived on a full moon (ovulation) and then gave birth together nine moons later in group rituals. There is an ancient birthing chamber in Malta, an island of the Goddess, where women ritually entered the chamber, gave birth together, and then emerged with babies—as if from the Womb of Gaia.

In other tribes, as women birthed new souls into the world with the ecstatic and orgasmic energy of mass ritual, all women and crone elders of the community would dance, sound, and chant in a womb circle around the women to help their journey. This would create a massive web of life-force energy to bring forward the new lives. One of the most famous of these ancient mass-birthing sites is Avebury, England.

Eventually we may once again live in a world that honors shamanic birthing; where communities of babies are conceived by the powerful light of the full moon in a deeply loving sacred union of soul mates, and women and men journey together for nine moons, opening into their new experience of parenthood, as the baby grows inside, nourished by love, harmony, healing food, sacred lovemaking, orgasms, sound vibration, massage, laughter, delight, and primal Love.

In shamanic birthing, the growing babies communicate telepathically with their parents, supported by a loving tribe. In mass birthings, the babies are welcomed into the world to the sound of drums and chanting, as grandmothers and mothers form a sacred womb circle around the birthing women, generating Shakti life force to support the women on their awakening journey into orgasmic birthing. In such a setting, a baby's first experience of this world is celebration, community, love, communion. The mother merges with Cosmic Womb in the divine ecstasy of Creation, and the baby connects to the Womb of Gaia, its new Earth Mother.

Begin to imagine how the world would be if it were populated by people who had been birthed in this ecstatic and loving way. We can dream this way back into being. We can begin with conscious conception and birth practices in our own lives, as well as honoring our body wisdom and our feelings. Awakening happens through embracing our biological reality, our deep genetically encoded need for love, touch, soulful presence, and kindness, not by transcending the physical reality into disembodied states. It means becoming a chalice for the divine milk of love.

Sacred Birthing

The embodiment of the true spiritual potential of our children is founded in the fertile soil of a gentle, soul-infused birthing process. This remembrance is igniting a natural birthing movement that will one day be the ground of the next evolutionary leap in human development—clearing the way for the "children of new earth" to once again be born on this planet. When we reweave the ancient birthing customs back into the world, we can begin to thread our children back into the holistic web of life. Rituals such as offering the placenta back into Mother Earth mean that the earth itself becomes our new placenta of connection. At an energetic level we plug our umbilical cord into the true womb grid of Gaia and the Cosmic Womb, drawing sustenance from our greater mothers.

Birthing was always known as a bridge between the worlds, a crossing of thresholds for both mother and baby—an important and sacred initiation.

Women would pilgrimage to special sacred sites with feminine energy vortexes, or where sacred rivers met, or to Womb Mystery schools in order to give birth.

These sacred birthing sites were often located on magical feminine islands, such as Isla Mujeres and Cozumel off the Yucatán coast of Mexico. Cozumel was sacred to the Goddess Ix Chel, and was a land of a magical birthing portal where women would pilgrimage to receive the blessing of the Mother Goddess.

Other magical birthing portals include Crete and Malta. One of the most renowned Womb Mystery schools and ancient birthing sites was on the sacred island of Iona, off the west coast of Scotland. Fingal's Cave, a magnificent cave hewn by Mother Earth from dazzling, geometric black basalt columns, was an ancient initiation site and birthing cave. Legends say that Magdalene and Yeshua visited the isle of Iona to birth one of their children nearby this sacred site. This legend is supported by a mysterious stained-glass window at the church of Kildare on the nearby isle of Mull, depicting a pregnant Magdalene holding hands with her beloved Yeshua.

Now the cave is filled with tidal water, but several thousand years ago when sea levels were much lower, it would have been possible to enter the cave ceremonially for birth.

Sites in Britain, such as Avebury and the nine Merry Maidens stone circle in

Cornwall, were also birthing sites and magical feminine initiation portals. They were constructed according to astrological and spiritual sciences to assist in the embodiment of a baby's soul on Earth—often aligned to the cosmic vulva. In pod consciousness, when the entire tribe followed lunar cycles, women would mass birth together in ceremonial womb circles, birthing under the light of the full moon. Hospitals still report to this day a peak in women going into labor on full moons, in the same way that groups of women synchronize their menstruation.

Researcher Andrew Collins proposes that the womb-temple site of Göbekli Tepi in Turkey may have also served as a birth chamber, or ceremonial space for the conscious conception of the baby's soul into the pregnant woman. He says, "The Göbekli builders would appear to have used the holed stones as *seelenloch* ["soul holes"] to enter an otherworldly environment associated with both the act of cosmic birth and creation of human souls."[1]

Royal families would also have sacred birth locations, such as the Kukaniloko Birthing Stones in Oahu, Hawaii, where only royal women gave birth.

In America, the lands near Asheville were believed to be a Cherokee birthing site, where women pilgrimaged to give birth, held sacred because of its configuration of rivers. Ancient people knew that the land we live on was a sacred fractal expression of the mother, it is the body of the goddess. Fertility was associated with water, so it was known that where two streams merged, it was like the twin-lobed uterus of the mother, and the site would be favorable to birthing.

How a baby was birthed into the world was a defining moment in how it would perceive and embody this new realm that was its home—was it safe and inviting, or threatening and overwhelming? Ancient mothers and fathers did everything to ensure a baby felt safe and welcomed as it entered its life in the earth realms.

As the baby emerges into this world, its new home, and leaves its previous home, the womb of its mother, it needs to feel safe, supported and connected—not as if this is a shocking separation that makes its psyche, biology, and soul shut down.

In the Hopi tribe a baby was kept in darkness for the first twenty days after birth, then slowly brought out into the light, to help acclimatize it to its new home and adapt to earth after the oceanic, infinite darkness of the womb. The baby did not have one particular name, but the tribe called the new child whatever different names felt inspired to come through them. Eventually the name that "felt" the most resonant with the growing baby became its one true name.[2]

Awakening the
Feminine Birthing Wisdom

In ancient times, babies entered this realm under the light of the moon or in soft light. The quality and quantity of the light frequencies that enter our eyes have a profound effect on our hormone production and state of consciousness. For a woman giving birth, soft lighting such as moonlight or candlelight assists in the transition from a normal state of consciousness into a shamanic birthing consciousness by altering hormone production and perception. Softer lighting creates a supportive lunar feminine environment for the journey of childbirth.

Modern hospitals often ignore this wisdom. The intense overhead fluorescent lighting of hospitals is a shock for babies after the protective cocoon of the womb, and is considered a factor for the development of neonatal retinopathy. As prenatal babies see a filtered red light through the mother's womb, a birthing room lit softly red can help the ease baby's transition into this world.

The ancient practice of water birthing also holds deep physio-soulful benefits for both the mother and the baby. This birth practice, which has its roots in several ancient traditions all over the world, can be a magical gateway to a relaxed and soulful birth—and is a beautiful fluid transition from one realm to another. Ancient tribes from the islands of the South Pacific gave birth in shallow seawater, and Egyptian pharaohs were traditionally born underwater. Even today, in Guyana, women still pilgrimage to sacred river sites to give birth.[3]

The birthing pool acts as a transitional womb, keeping the baby calm and connected while it moves from the primal oceans of its mother's womb to its new home, and begins to connect to the Womb of Gaia and the element of earth. Babies do not breathe in the watery womb, so this transition needs sensitivity.

Now modern science supports this wisdom, as research by doctors such as Frederick Leboyer shows that the warm water of a birthing pool helps support the mother as she goes into labor and assists the child to make the transition from the amniotic ocean of the womb to its new home on planet Earth. Doctors and midwives both report that babies born in water are often more relaxed and cry less, and are eager to connect with the mother and breastfeed.[4]

Being in a warm birthing pool with beautiful lighting and womb-resonant music creates a relaxed and sacred birthing environment, allowing the mother to relax into her own experience. This supports the production of oxytocin, the "love hormone," while at the same time inhibiting the production of the stress hormone, adrenaline. This relaxed lunar energy increases the production of endorphins in the mother, helping her to surrender to an orgasmic birth.

The gateway between the worlds is designed to be ecstatic, surrendered, opening; water supports the experience of birth as a shamanic initiation.

When a woman surrenders completely to the downward flow of Shakti, birthing contractions become ecstatic waves of pleasure, and she can be transported into states of God consciousness delivering the baby. The hormones oxytocin and prolactin, as well as a variety of endorphins are released in the birthing process, which when combined with a full orgasmic surrender and opening, can create "chemistry of heaven" or God consciousness during birth.

Ecstatic birthing creates avatars of new earth. Subtle magnetic fields emanating from the mother infuse into the birthing child, creating a blueprint of bliss in the child at a fundamental bioenergetic and cellular level. An ecstatic birth infuses the child's cellular processes with high octaves of pure Love, permanently affecting the expression of its genome and infusing its DNA with an expanded resonance. At birth we become either wired for pleasure—or suffering.

The biological and energetic space required for profound spiritual births is sensitive, and unnecessary medication can disrupt the natural wisdom of the mother's body. Synthetic medications administered to the mother will also infuse into the baby's blood, flooding its consciousness with artificial intoxicants that disorient the child and its sensitive birth process.

It is also crucial that the container of the birth is not guided by patriarchal ideas or medical practices that contravene the intuitive knowing and holistic process of the mother. The womb is the only authority in this situation, no one else.

Sometimes medical intervention is necessary to save the life of the baby, mother, or both. The safety of the mother and baby is always a priority. Emergency measures are not in opposition to womb wisdom when they are truly necessary, and throughout history there are records of wise women performing surgery, including what we now call caesarian sections, in order to deliver babies.

The presence of the loving supportive masculine is also crucial for the fullness of the blueprint of creation and union to be established. Excluding men from the wisdom and profound gnostic experience of childbirth creates a separation for both father and baby. This sacred moment is a crossing of thresholds, not only for mother and baby, but for the masculine—who steps into his role as sacred father. This not only helps the mother to feel safe and supported in her process, but also experientially connects the baby to the truth that life is sacred union.

In Celtic witch traditions, when a fairy queen gave birth, her husband also lay in bed with her to share her process and be part of the bonding birthing experience.[5] Similarly, indigenous tribes in California believed a couple about to give birth were physically "one," and the man was encouraged to participate in the sacred birthing energy, often even having his own midwife and birth pangs.

In Java the shaman-midwife massaged both the pregnant woman and man together in a sacred blessing bath scattered with vibrant flower petals.

In feminine shamanic cultures, childbirth is seen as sacred—and a cosmic portal for a man to be initiated into the awesome powers of the Womb of Creation. The journey of conception, gestation, and birth is taken together in union, not alone.

Imagine a world birthed through this joyful coming together of both parents.

Singing and Dancing the Baby onto Earth

Womb priestesses and wise women of the feminine ways knew that sound and dance were magical keys for the birthing process, opening mother and baby across many subtle dimensions. In ancient times people played drums to mirror the woman's heartbeat, and to show the baby it was now connected to the heartbeat of Gaia and was still in the Womb of the Divine and Earth Mother.

Music such as harp, lyre, or dolphin and whale sounds, played underwater during water births, can create an aquatic surround sound of bliss. Sound vibrations travel four times faster through water than air and resonate deeply through the womb. Water molecules rearrange in the presence of sound, forming a "resonance mandala" reflecting the harmonic frequency of the sound wave. Soothing and sacred sound vibrations can help harmonize the amniotic fluid into a high-frequency pattern before and during birth and also infuse the water of a birthing pool with sacred frequencies that set a magical and welcoming intention.

Chanting songs and communal singing also communicates to the baby in a primal way that it is born into a soul tribe and family of loving support—it attunes to the song of the tribe. The Himba tribe of Namibia chant a baby's soul song—a sequence of tones and rhythm that resonate with the baby's soul essence—during and after birth to assist with the child's soul embodiment on earth.

The Art of Birth Dancing

Birth dancing is a beautiful feminine art to support the birthing of avatars of new earth—babies born in resonant, supportive, harmonic environments. Many ancient feminine sacred dances—Egyptian belly dance, Hawaiian hula dance, and Indian temple dance, such as Odissi—were originally created to support the fertility of women, strengthen their womb, pelvis, and feminine crown and to help them develop their ability to open ecstatically as they brought babies into the world, trusting their own body intuition and womb wisdom.

Egyptologist Carolyn Graves-Brown, curator of the Egypt Center at University of Wales, writes about groups of women in ancient Egypt called Khener who were ceremonial singers and dancers that attended funerary rites—and childbirth. She says, "In the Sixth Dynasty tomb chapel of princess Watetkhethor at Saqqara, female dancers are portrayed accompanied by a song which refers to childbirth, translated as, 'But see, the secret of birth! Oh pull!'" And in the Papyrus Westcar, it describes the birth of Fifth Dynasty kings accompanied by four goddesses who have disguised themselves as dancers. Graves-Brown reminds us that in many parts of Africa, until recent times, friends and relatives of a birthing mother would dance to aid delivery.[6]

"Birth dancing during labor, circling hips, figure eights, and other movements help the baby move into a good birthing position and help the mother to open her passageway. The rhythmic undulations help to bring on contractions and allow the mother to move with her contractions instead of against them. Dancing these ancient movements assists the mother greatly in entering her primal mind, embodying Womb Consciousness, and empowering her to be a very active part of the birth. Dancing during labor quickens and eases the entire process.

"For postpartum recovery, the movements help the mother to reweave her muscles together again, tone her uterus and birth canal, strengthen muscles used in carrying her baby, create relaxation for better breastfeeding, and give the mother time for quiet meditation. Mothers can also wear their newborns wrapped to them to sway together and snuggle. The rhythms of the movements help the babies to relax and absorb the joys of their new bodies."[7]

Placenta Wisdom:
The Primordial Grandmother

The placenta has always been a sacred organ known to have spiritual dimensions by nearly every ancient civilization on the planet. It is an organ of truly vast and complex

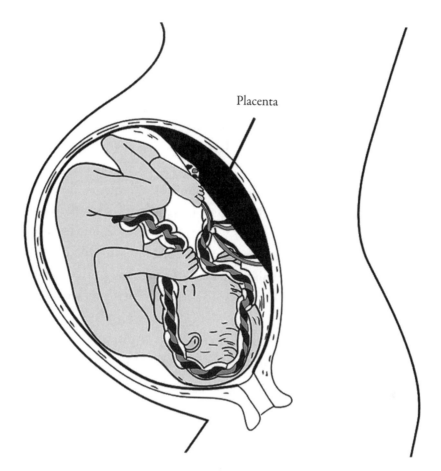

Placenta

Fig. 16.1. Gestating baby with placental twin
(Illustration by Heather Skye)

biological intelligence. Some knew the placenta as "the internal grandmother," or the "baby's cake," hinting at its ability to nourish both soulfully and biologically.[8] In fact, the placenta is likely the source of our widespread ritual for birthday cakes. It is only in the modern world, increasingly divorced from the feminine wisdom ways, that we have lost connection with our intuitive body-knowing that the placenta is a key part of the birthing mandala.

The sacred properties of the placenta were worshipped all across the world. Native American tribes believed that the placenta held the seat of the soul. They allowed the placenta to fall off naturally, with the mother wrapping the bundle in a sacred fabric and burying it in a secret place, where it could be retrieved and taken along if the tribe moved location. In Thailand, the placenta is buried in a sacred ceremonial ritual. In Aboriginal wisdom, the placenta is always buried in ritual as a way of infusing Gaia with the knowledge that a new child has been born. They believed the DNA and biological fluids within the placenta informed the Earth Mother of the child's nature, gifts, and purpose. The Maori people of New Zealand bury the placenta to ensure proper reincarnation to the next life. The Japanese created decorative placenta caskets. In Buddhist cultures, as well as in Malaysia, it was believed that the placenta remained in sympathetic union with the person for life. Many different tribes and cultures would also eat part or all of the placenta, or save it for healing purposes later in life.

In Indonesia, it was believed that the amniotic fluid was the older sibling of the child, and that the umbical cord and placenta were the younger sibling. These two womb companions were thought to be spirit protectors for the child. After the baby is born the salted cord and afterbirth are placed in white muslin, placed in the symbolic womb of a jug, and buried outside—with a constantly lit candle guarding the spirit friends for forty-five days, warding off evil energies.[9]

Tribal women often had a ritual placenta bowl or placenta pouch that passed from woman to woman, and held the placenta during this time. After the placenta naturally detached, burying it in sacred rituals let Earth Mother know her child has arrived, connecting the baby's placenta to the Womb of Gaia, while also honoring the mysteries of life and the sacredness of the new baby soul.

When the umbilical cord is cut immediately after birth it leaves the baby gasping for air and creates a psychophysiological trauma. While in the womb the baby "breathes" through its umbilical cord, not its lungs, which are filled with amniotic fluid. Until the baby's lungs are breathing well, which can take five or more minutes *after* birth, he or she *depends* on the flow of oxygenated blood coming in from the placenta through the umbilical cord.

Allowing the placenta to remain attached is known as a lotus birth, and has a range of emotional, physical, and spiritual benefits. Biologically, the baby receives 40 to 60 ml of extra blood from the placenta after birth if the cord is not tied until pulsing has ceased. Approximately one-third of a baby's blood is stored in the placenta. Through this blood, the baby continues to receive a nourishing flood of the "love hormone" oxytocin, quantum life-giving stem cells, and other important developmental nutrients, particularly iron.

Subtle soul magnetics and flows of bioelectrical Shakti continue to pulse from the placenta until it naturally detaches three to seven days after birth. The placenta is like a second mother, feeding the child with bio-soulful nutrition, assisting in its development and healthy neurology. It also helps the baby keep a conscious connection to its wombtime home, easing its transition between the worlds.

Deep attunement with the baby's physical and emotional needs at this critical time transmits a palpable sense that the baby is cared for, loved, and welcomed into the world. As mother and baby gaze into each other's eyes for the first time, in a safe, natural, and supported environment, the gates of primordial love open and a bonding process begins that can never be undone. An unimaginable field of love and postbirth bliss descends, rich with maternal warmth.

The first moments and day after birth are crucial for the baby to connect not only with its birth mother, but also to connect in a cosmic sense with the Divine Mother, and to connect in a primordial sense with the Earth Mother. This connection lets the baby know it is loved and sustained and held by all of creation, to feel that its birth mother is but one Womb among all the loving Wombs it is nested and held within.

The Power of a Lunar Cycle Babymoon

The first lunar cycle after birth nests the baby into the cycles of the earth realm and into its bonded relationship with its mother, through loving, nourishing touch and nurturance such as breastfeeding, skin-on-skin contact, and eye gazing.

Scientific research now shows the imperative of this bonding process. Allowing time and supported sacred space for the mother and baby to bond and develop their relationship is vital—it is the holy of holies for creating avatars of new earth, birthing children who feel safe, connected, supported, nurtured, and loved.

Breastfeeding creates a primal rapport with the baby that will sustain it soulfully throughout its entire life, it is the milk of human kindness and mother love. Breastmilk has millions of years of evolutionary engineering behind it, making it the ultimate superfood for newborns. Breastfeeding provides all the alchemical nutrients a baby needs. Studies show that it protects against allergies, sickness, obesity, diseases, and infections. Breast milk is easily digested, and studies also show that breastfed babies score higher on IQ tests, and mothers who breastfeed have a lesser chance of developing certain diseases.[10]

The amazing effects of breastfeeding come not just from its nutritional quality, but also from the sense of connection it builds between mother and child. Anyone who has not been breastfed needs to allow their inner grief at this loss.

On an energetic level, a breastfeeding woman is communicating to her child that this is a realm where the Mother provides, where the Mother's love is present. A woman in her breast radiance delivers loving soulful nourishment and awakened Shakti streams through her sacred breasts. The primal connection between the mother and child invigorates the child with the desire for life, the urge to be alive and immerse in the pleasure of life, while also infusing it with the softness of love. A woman's womb activates while breastfeeding, with her ecstatic maternal love feeding the child everything it needs—nutritionally and spiritually. When a mother is fully present with her child while she breastfeeds and gives from the deepest place in her heart, the child deeply feels a sense of connection to life and *knows* it is supported and its needs met.

A woman who is breastfeeding is deeply sacred—she becomes the embodiment of the Divine Mother. She also experiences increased levels of the love hormones prolactin and oxytocin, and this nourishing, natural erotic process of breastfeeding helps a woman to integrate the experience of childbirth.

When a woman allows her loving heart energy to open and her primal Womb energy to awaken to envelop her baby, she becomes a mother of new earth.

Bringing a child into the world is a great blessing. The Kogis believed that every baby born strengthens the quantum womb field and the radiance of the Great Mother. Taking this time to celebrate, integrate, and deeply bond as a family is essential, and a magical shamanic gateway that not only blesses the baby, but also heals the parents from any residual wounds of their first moments on earth.

Making the space and time to spend a thirty-day lunar cycle babymoon together as a family is an incredible gift to the world. This embodies the frequency that will birth a new earth, and birth a new octave of magical avatar children.

The first month spent together introduces the baby to the rhythm of life and the frequency of living in the earth realms. The baby shares a merged consciousness with its mother and is programmed to live by her patterns by unconsciously learning by her example. A slow and nourishing lifestyle filled with trust, pleasure, and time for love imprints that frequency into the baby's primal brain, where it will guide it for the remainder of its life. A family who takes the time to be with the child for the first babymoon opens the door to a huge wave of lunar feminine consciousness anchoring itself on Gaia through the consciousness of the children. When this happens, coming generations will fully live in a "garden of Eden" consciousness, brimming with peace, love, harmony, and fruitfulness.

It is also essential to remember that childbirth, and the initial adjustment to motherhood and breastfeeding, may not always go as planned—and it is important that we re-dream the possibilities of motherhood without adding further pressure to new mothers. The key for this important time of mother-baby bonding is to be in contact with *your own emotions,* to consciously communicate with your baby, and to reach out for support. Trust that this soul has chosen you and is far wiser than you can imagine. Every mother's journey is unique.

Magical Moon Children

There is a new wave of "moon children" entering the world at this time, flowing on the river of galactic energy that is restoring the feminine dimension to Earth. These children will be especially sensitive to any practices that wire a child into the disconnected, false grid of patriarchy, rather than connecting them to the web of life. Moon children bring with them the frequency of the feminine, of lunar consciousness, of the wild pathways of the natural world and her cycles.

Children of the moon will be dreamers, visionaries, and pioneers, with a deep love and reverence for the body of Mother Earth and all of her creatures. They arrive to plant new dream seeds and to assist the rebirth of the feminine soul of the world.

They will have little resonance with the industrial world matrix or patriarchal spirituality. They will bring a heart-based revolution from within, which will feel wild, natural, spontaneous, joyful, irreverent, and at times *un*spiritual and chaotic.

Riding high on starlight and swimming deep into the roots of earth, they will embody the original blueprint of innocence and the sacred marriage of creation.

These magical children will become the avatars of new earth and the new cycle.

WOMB ORACLES SHARE
A Lotus Birth Moon Baby

We called my daughter's conception "reach for the stars." While making love I felt my beloved rise, levitate upward behind me as he gently entered me. It must have been at that moment that she arrived on a starlight ray straight from the Cosmic Womb. Just before we conceived, my daughter came to me in a vision. We were sisters in Avalon, sitting talking by a river, a strong sisterly bond; shortly after, her name was transmitted to me. I really feel we called her Spirit in consciously. We felt the responsibility and commitment of this agreement.

I loved the way I felt during pregnancy, so alive, vibrant, sensual, and sexual. When I was six months pregnant, I heard about lotus birth. I hadn't heard of this birth practice before, but I knew instinctively this would be beneficial for me and my baby. This was a gently loving birth; it resonated with my being deeply.

During the home birth, with all the lights dimmed, I could feel my cervix opening with ease; my baby was working her way deeper and deeper down. The sensations were intense but not painful. I naturally felt to circle and spiral my hips; the sounds that came from me were deep and primal, oohs and aahs.

The sounding helped with the intense sensations. It was so empowering to bring my awareness to witness and allow my amazing body and its wisdom to do what it naturally needed to do. It felt like every cell of my body just knew how to surrender to the birthing process. I felt the immense power of my womb, waves of sensations, riding them gracefully as they came. As my womb would contract, I would push, and Zanna would push down, working her way farther down. It was perfect teamwork, listening and feeling each other, trusting each other.

Just before my baby arrived I started to Om. As I sounded Om, my visual was of a long tunnel, a birth canal. I felt like I was being born again, it was a blissful euphoric space to be in. As her head crowned, I felt an intense pain; I thought I was dying, feeling the pain of all women that have ever birthed. A collective pain that only lasted a few moments—a deep initiation into birth and in some way death. I felt this with both of my children's births.

At the moment my baby's head crowned, my beloved helped me guide her head and body from mine. Her warm, wet, pink body was placed on mine, pure bliss! Skin to skin, she smelt of me, my blood, my fluids and hers combined, a heavenly natural scent. We placed her placenta in a bowl beside us. It felt so natural to have it still attached to her; it was part of her, her womb friend, comforter, protector. We honored her placenta and thanked it for playing such a valuable role. Energetically, I could feel the communication and connection she had with her placenta. It felt right not to cut the cord; she felt whole with her placenta still attached. It felt like we were gently drifting into a transition period where she was not in my body but not fully separate. During the next few days I trusted she would settle into her new surroundings and detach from her placenta gently with ease. That evening my beloved washed her placenta continually, telling our baby what he was doing as if he were washing her body. The baby and I remained unwashed for three days. He salted and put a few drops of lavender oil on her placenta before wrapping it in muslin. She seemed to enjoy her placenta being tended to so lovingly and would visibly relax. We were in a love bubble together.

We had no visitors for these first days. It was like being in a world between worlds, a sacred space. On day three, I felt she was ready to detach from her placenta. That morning she looked at me with total awareness and hooked the cord around her toes, and gently the cord detached; she had the biggest grin on her face. She knew what she was doing and was ready to let go of her womb friend.

Her placenta was buried under a rosebush in a pot in the garden. This was the most profound and amazing experience of our lives.

Lotus birthing is a magical experience of Oneness. I really feel my daughter wanted this type of birth. It was important for her energy field and her spiritual development. There is a sense of wholeness and completeness to a lotus birth, an opportunity for baby to let go of its womb friend and the womb. Also, it is a gentle transition for the mother's body from pregnancy to motherhood.

L.W.

CYCLE 4

THE LUNAR MYSTERIES
AND WOMB CODES
OF CREATION

SPIRAL 17

MOON ALCHEMY

The Lost Lunar World

As if you were on fire from within.
The moon lives in the lining of your skin.

PABLO NERUDA

THERE IS A HIDDEN lunar world we have forgotten about and lost touch with. This moonlit feminine dimension of darkness and lunar cycles holds a huge key to recovering our feminine selves, and the feminine principle in life. We cannot help but be more attuned to the great solar cycles of day and night, summer and winter, but we have disconnected from the subtle but powerful lunar rhythms that guide the forces of creation, growth, dissolution, and evolution. The moon influences our feminine water element, and her soulful feelings and intuition. The vast and incredible effect of lunar light on our Earth is rarely mentioned; she governs not only the tides of the sea, but the tides of our feminine body too. This is true of every human being: woman, man, and child—we all have lunar cycles.

The feminine soul lives in a moonlit world of primordial lunar consciousness. Our wombs ebb and flow with the waves of lunar energy over a moon cycle, and this tidal movement is the crucible for life to be planted and grow inside us—not just physical life, but the creations of the spirit, the emanations of our desires. When we lose touch with these waxing and waning tides, we lose the power of conscious conception and our birthright as co-creators. We also lose touch with part of ourselves. We become less soulful, disconnected from dreamtime, other realms, and the beautiful layers and dimensions of our own feminine feelings.

274

Although the sun has a much bigger mass than the moon, the moon is only an intimate one light-second away, whereas the sun is eight light-minutes away—making the moon 480 times closer to us, with a far bigger gravitational pull.[1]

Our entire world is undulating in a lunar wave, swaying and moving with her dark and light rhythms. Back in the fourth century BCE, Aristotle reported on the moon rhythms present in all living creatures. A woman's ovaries swell at the time of the full moon, and this also happens for sea creatures, such as sea urchins.

Lunar Cycles of Plants and Animals

Many plants have lunar cycles, and gardening by the moon was one of the central feminine arts, to grow food that was in harmony with the cycles of life. Seeds swell with water during germination, and the maximum intake of water happens at full moon and new moon, following the creative powers of the moon.

Oyster populations also fluctuate with the rhythms of the moon, which is why they are considered an aphrodisiac, infused as they are with feminine lunar magic.

In 1971 it was discovered that the honeybee also lives in lunar consciousness. If the honeycomb has a north–south alignment, the hive experiences most activity on full moon. If their honeycomb has an east–west alignment, they fly out on new moon. The bees, always mythically sacred to the Goddess, follow a lunar rhythm.

Owls, who are considered also a magical totem of the feminine, also follow lunar rhythms, from making mating calls on full moon, to humming on new moon, and ovulating and laying eggs in tune with the moon cycles.

The psychic spiritual power of the moon was once the origin of ancient religion—the lunar ray was revered as the source of creative, generative growing power, and also held the power of darkness to dissolve, destroy, recreate, and rebirth.

In ancient China, the new moon was officially proclaimed by heralds sent out by the royal astronomer. The community would plant crops and cast benevolent spells of sacred intentions under the mysterious light of the new-birth moon.

In the lands of Canaan, Astarte was worshipped in her guise as the Ashera, the sacred moon tree of knowledge and immortality. Sabbaths to celebrate the new moon were held in sacred groves, until Yehovah banished the holy Moon Mother.

Her reflective light, called *noorah* in Aramaic, has been with us since the beginning of time; and the otherworldly light of her cyclical, natural wisdom glows on, deep in our feminine subconscious, despite our attempts to dim her.

An ancient Chaldean hymn speaks of the primordial power the moon holds, her celestial rays shining deep into the heart of matter and the Womb of Gaia . . .

> *Its root of white crystal stretched toward the deep.*
> *Its seat was the central pace of the earth;*
> *Its foliage was the couch of . . . the primeval mother.*
> *Into the heart of the holy house, which spreads its shade like a forest . . .*
> *There (is the house of) the mighty mother, who passes across the sky . . .*[2]

No wonder we have woven a mythical tapestry for humankind populated by mermaids, moon-spun honey nectars, and wise witches flying on full moons.

The moon is calling to us with her gentle rays because we have forgotten the soft glow of her light and the dazzling, reflective brightness she brings to our psyche.

Moon's magnetic forces influence our psyche—our soul—our feminine being, often repressed in our unconscious. The more untouched this aspect of our being is, the more extreme our reactions are to the moon's magic.

The Lunar-Solar Alchemy of Our Neurobiology

According to Dr. György Buzsáki, professor of neuroscience at NYU Neuroscience Institute, the primordial resting state of human consciousness is lunar consciousness; by default our brain is attuned to darkness. In the absence of external stimuli, our brains naturally reside in the dreamtime patterns of neurologic activity related to states of sleep or deep meditation. It is in this rich terrain that spontaneous synchronized neurological activity arises from nothing. This is the dark, fertile soil from which our creativity arises, the dreams and ideas that are birthed from a dimension beyond our conscious control and awareness.[3] Our lunar consciousness is a "receiver" for other dimensions.

From this primordial womb of lunar consciousness, we journey into waking consciousness for around sixteen hours each day. The timing of this dance moves in accordance with our natural circadian rhythms that are fundamentally aligned to the daily cycle of the *moon*. However, the light of the sun powerfully modifies and regulates the transitions from our lunar states into our solar waking states.

As the sun bursts forth in the morning, its rays of light travel directly into the depths of our primal brain. The blue spectrum wavelengths rouse the brain from its nighttime state of slumber, triggering the activation of our daytime neurocircuitry and the release of a flood of neurotransmitters: serotonin, acetylcholine, and many others. Sunlight is the original alarm clock.

At dusk, as the sunlight dims and we fall back into the womb of Mother Night, our pineal glands awaken and begin to release melatonin—the hormone of the night. Melatonin is a magical molecule that gently guides our brain into states of sleep, rest, dreaming, altered consciousness, and cellular regeneration. It affects human sexual response as well and was a key hormone in sexual alchemy. Shortly after its release it can be found in the blood, saliva, and female sexual fluids, which may have given rise to the esoteric sexual practices among the ancient dragon lineages of drinking the red and white female sexual elixirs during the night in order to access rejuvenating hormonal secretions.

Melatonin is a master regulator of not just sleep, but also immune function and cellular regenerative capacities. Unfortunately, the development of artificial lighting has profoundly disrupted the natural circadian rhythms and melatonin production of modern humans. Proper melatonin release depends on the combination of daytime exposure to natural sunlight and the nighttime absence of light—our brain chemistry depends on the natural dance of solar and lunar movements. Melatonin deficiencies are associated with cancer, high blood pressure, and early mortality, and are corrected by living in tune with the natural cycles of the sun and moon, as humans did for millions of years before electricity.

Our ancestors lived not just by the sun, but also by the light of the moon. Hunter-gatherer and other traditional cultures had very different sleep patterns than modern cultures—with a much greater percentage of time spent napping during the day and gathering together at night around the tribal fires. It was known that the night was a time for enchantment—that the night allowed us greater access to deep feminine consciousness, the realms of archetype and myth, storytelling and music, ritual theater and magic. This is the reason why, still to this day, plays, movies, and musical concerts are most commonly attended at night.

Across many parts of rural India, Africa, and Asia, which have less access to artificial light, people are still sensitive to the subtle energies of moonlight. Full-moon nights are a time of magic, dance, music, and social gatherings—a time in which many people are energized and celebrating rather than sleeping. Full moon triggers the ovulation-phase energies of increased social engagement, nighttime alertness, and receptive female sexuality. In contrast, the nights of the dark moon are extremely quiet, and marked by longer periods of sleep. In the Old Ways, full moon was a time for feasting, ritual, and festivities, and dark moon was reserved for fasting, rest, contemplation, and inward shamanic journeying.

Every morning that we awake to the sunlight is like a rebirth—we emerge from a dimly lit womb of lunar consciousness to greet the bright new solar world, just as we did on the day of our birth. Likewise, every night as we drop into sleep is like a death, a return to the primordial womb. How we feel about waking and facing the day will be influenced by our birth experience. How we feel about surrendering into sleep will be influenced by the gestational experiences in our mother's womb. The daily relational solar-lunar dance enlivens and informs every aspect of our being. It is a sacred union consciousness that depends on the presence of both the solar and lunar energies—one whose effects reach into our psyche and beyond, deeply touching almost every aspect of our biology.

Ancient womb cultures often had elegent rituals to honor the doorways of dawn and dusk, and to mark the transition into different states of consciousness. We can welcome our daily rebirth at sunrise, and also embrace the dark womb of night as the twilight falls and we are taken back into Mother Night's lunar arms.

Magical Journey of Our Moon Cycle

The lunar tides are felt on the land as well as waters, and, as we are 70 percent water, we are also experiencing an ebb and flow of tides—physically, emotionally, and spiritually. Research shows that the structure of water is changed by the passing of the moon overhead, which means that *we* are structurally changed by the changing phases of the moon.

The primal communion between the feminine fluid body (in both men and women) and the lunar cycle is full of wonderment and mystery. What is happening inside our bodies and our psyches with every cycle of the moon is truly astounding and beautiful, and was the basis for the curriculum in every ancient moon college—which is sadly lacking in modern-day "schooling." In our current lopsided society, the enlivening powers of ovulation are accepted, but menstruation is a misunderstood and neglected force. Our dark-moon self is where our womb becomes a mystical cauldron of psychic and sexual creative power that is harnessed to transform and evolve our state of consciousness.

The lunar cycle of 24.8 hours is what we attune to if in complete darkness, such as a cave, rather than the sun's cycle of 24 hours. Before artificial light, our bodies attuned to a balance of light and darkness, of day and night—the Earth's sacred union cycle.

Our sense of smell changes throughout the lunar cycle—waxing to a peak at ovulation when we are in a sensory dance of sacred union with the external world and then waning in rhythm with the moon, so that our external senses are at a low around menstruation when our "inner senses" are heightened and alive.

A Journey inside Our Body-Temples

The average womb cycle length is 29.5 days in women who are more regular, which is the exact length of the lunar cycle of the moon around the Earth.

The brain (pituitary and hypothalamus) produces hormones that activate the ovaries to produce estrogen. When the ovaries produce estrogen in the first half of the cycle (days 1–14), it makes the lining of the womb build up and get thicker—and makes the cervix produce "fertile" mucus.

This creative web that grows inside our womb linings is composed of many blood vessels, called spiral arteries, which form the richest capillary plexus in the entire body, as our glands also secrete nutritive hormones. Our wombs are waxing into the chalice of Life.

On day 14, ovulation is stimulated by hormones from the brain (pituitary and hypothalamus) and if we were awakened enough to consciously conceive, this cosmic egg holds the Divine intelligence to select a sperm that would create the best genetic blueprint for a new soul to incarnate into.

After ovulation, between days 14–28, the ovaries produce progesterone, which causes the lining of the womb to secrete substances that support the implantation of the egg. During this time a magical substance called "uterine milk" develops in the womb lining, which contains all the nutrients needed to nourish a baby. This womb superfood—a supernatural elixir of life—later becomes menstrual blood, which is also infused with powerful stem cells, the building blocks of life.

If the egg isn't fertilized, progesterone production in the ovary begins to decline after about 10 days until the life-empowered lining of the womb sheds—but if the egg is fertilized, it causes the ovary to keep producing progesterone to support pregnancy. Menstruation continues for an average of four days; when the ovaries produce enough estrogen, bleeding stops and the lining of the womb builds again.

Menstruation and Birth Alchemy

In pregnancy the nourishment-infused lining of the womb becomes the placenta, *or* if pregnancy doesn't occur it becomes menstrual blood. The placenta is a mysterious and powerful bridge between the baby and biological mother and Divine Mother; it is a source of maternal endocrine alchemy. The Divine powers and elixirs of love present in the placenta are also imbued in menstrual blood.

It is a powerful realization, when we come to *know* that every menstruation is in fact a *birth*—in which we are opening and accessing the creative forces of the life-giving womb to birth new dimensions from spirit into our lives and psyches.

Relaxin, a hormone most known for being released in pregnancy that allows liga-ments and connective tissue to stretch so the pelvis can open to give birth to a baby, is also released every month at menses to allow the descent of blood. Each menses is like a mini birth. Menstrual pains are like a mini labor. Just like we can have orgasmic birth, so too can we can have orgasmic menstruation.

During menstruation, the entire physiology undergoes changes in a very similar way to pregnancy. These intense bio-alchemical changes include sex hormone levels, body temperature, basal metabolic rate, blood sugar, water retention, body weight, respiratory capacity, carbon dioxide levels, oxygen levels, blood acidity, heart rate, inflammation, white blood cell counts, protein levels, vitamin levels, bile pigments, adrenaline levels, urine volume, thyroid function, adrenal function, electrical skin resistance, pupil size, pain threshold, skin color, breast changes, composition of cer-vical mucus, brain waves (EEG readings), sensory acuity (smell, visual, and audio), changes in REM/dream activity. So if you have wondered why you feel different at this sacred time, and wish to rest and recluse, it is a natural instinct and response to the profound shifts in your body.

Menstruation is a deeply shamanic experience of death and rebirth; we are releasing and rebirthing in one profound bio-spiritual journey. It is also a very pri-mal moment, when we remember our true origins. The scent of blood subliminally reminds us on a primal level of the smell of our own birth; smell is the most primal sensation and takes us directly to our oldest, ancestral memories.

In Revelations 22:2 in the Bible, the writers clearly refer to the menstration of the womb as the tree of life, saying of her monthly offerings of the moon, "I saw the tree of life with its twelve kinds of fruit, yielding its fruit each month."

In ancient Egypt, the amulet of Tiet, also known as the Blood of Isis, which was made of bloodred jasper, carnelian, or even red glass, symbolized the menstrual pow-ers of the Goddess's Womb. Egyptians considered menstrual blood to be very potent and sacred. One of the methods a woman might use to open to pregnancy and fertil-ity was to rub her own menstrual blood on her thighs. Menstrual blood could also be smeared on an infant to protect him from evil.

Psychic Dimensions of Lunar Cycles

Our physiological changes connected to lunar cycles are far-reaching, but what is unfolding in our psyche, the lost feminine soul, is *out of this world*. The ancients recognized that menstruation was a "time out of time" for women, where they held strange powers of prophecy and trance—including vision questing in the dreamtime.

In menses there is naturally more REM sleep (dreams happen in REM sleep), and studies show that allowing more time for resting, daydreaming, reverie, meditation, and sleeping actually reduces PMS and other womb symptoms. We can dream our feminine self back to health.

Patterns of dreams change throughout the cycle, and certain types of dreams tend to happen in certain parts of the cycle. During the dark moon, when our unconscious material begins to stir and rise to be seen, we can experience wilder, more sexually assertive, bolder, or terrifying dreams. When a woman opens to this remembering, she can experience a phenomenon called dreamshock, which triggers physical symptoms of fatigue, food cravings, increased sensitivity, sexuality, and creativity. The cauldron of the feminine psyche is boiling over.

Psychic and Hormonal Changes for Men

These psychic and hormonal changes affect the entire community and family, not just the menstruating woman, and men become entrained into the same cycle. Experiments show that the lunar cycles affect men's emotions as much as women's. No surprise considering that men are initially created in a feminine blueprint, then nurtured for nine moons in the feminine realm of the womb, and have a feminine soul too, which complements their masculine essence.

Incidents of violence and illness in men peak at the full moon. Like werewolves who howl at the moon, the pure, primal, masculine self beats at the bars of his cage. In a world where his creative male Shakti is often crushed or controlled, or not received, its wild potency twists into an energy of violence.

He also howls a lament for his lost feminine side. How can he express his moon self? His fluid, emotional being that feels and hurts just as deeply as a woman, who is opened into the realms of love every bit as passionately as female hearts.

Interestingly, violence in men connected with lunar cycles is linked to *low* testosterone, not high levels of this male hormone. During the full moon, or after an emotional shock or hurt, men's testosterone drops—and they enter their feminine selves. As they have been culturally conditioned to judge this aspect of themselves as shameful and weak, they become agitated, angry, and depressed.

Men's hormones follow a thirty-day path of fluctuation, just like women's. In fact their beard growth alters and changes in response to this—as do their emotions, and their body responses. The shadows of their psyche come up into the light to be seen, loved, and integrated and embraced by the Womb.

Psychic and Hormonal Changes for Women

For women, the wild feminine creature, the forbidden feminine lies in wait at the bottom of the menstrual well, inviting us to reclaim our sensuality, sexuality, and eroticism. How welcoming and connected to our wild power we and our family and culture are completely transforms our experience of menstruation.

Study after study shows that in the paramenstrum (the time just before, during, and after menses) women have the highest sex drive, higher than at ovulation. Not only do we experience increased *sexuality,* but also increased *sensuality* and heightened erotic experience—and the gift of merging our cosmic consciousness, or spirit, with our physical form. Though the science is there, society ignores these facts for it unsettles the idea that sex is for procreation.

It is a time in which women's sexuality is more active—more likely to take the erotic initiative; she is wilder, with "a desire to envelope and capture" the man in the wilds of her Womb and yoni. Physician and pioneer of psychosomatic medicine George Groddeck writes, "menstruation is the most exquisite time for sex. Blood is love-juice that flows with sexual excitement."[4] In a beautifully harmonic flow, as women go into a wild, sexually charged erotic zone at menstruation, men's libido drops. They enter a receptive, gentle lunar phase—surrendering to the passion of their beloved. At ovulation a man's libido increases and the roles are reversed, and a woman is surrendered.

For many thousands of years these wonders of menstruation and the womb were honored and worshipped. In Hebrew *hor* meant "cave" and "yoni/womb." Communing with the Holy Hor, the Holy Womb, was believed to gift a spiritual enlightenment called horasis to men. This gift was especially potent at the menstrual cycle, and is now diminished by the interpretation of *hor* (Hera/womb) as *whore,* meaning prostitute. It is time to reclaim the Holy Hor.

✳ *Sacred Moon Blood Rituals*

Offering your menstrual blood back to Mother Earth creates a maternal bond between your womb and the womb of Gaia. The essence of your womb becomes infused and entangled with the living intelligence of the earth, including the fertility of the soil, the neural networks of the trees, and the ancient memory of the rocks. It helps Mother Earth know her daughters intimately on a bioenergetic level and support their birth power.

1. Collect your moon blood—soaking menstrual cloths in water is an effective way.

2. Find a sacred place in nature or your garden where you wish to offer your blood. It can be a special tree or you can offer it to fertilize your herb or vegetable garden.

3. Close your eyes. Breathe into your womb and tune in to her powerful ruby essence.

4. Make a prayer or intention and ask to be connected to the womb grids of earth.

5. Say the invocation: "May it be rooted in the earth and birthed through the womb."

6. Pour the blessed moon blood into the earth, affirming your sacred bond with life.

WOMB ORACLES SHARE
Menstrual Spirit Medicine

Owning my freedom, creating space for the free flow of blood is the most natural way to be; it feels like going back to the roots. I found her taste and fragrance intoxicating—I even had moments of altered states of consciousness much like when I have been working with ayahusca spirit medicine. I also released many layers, ranging from cutting cords from remnant energies from my ex-partners to deep ancestral fears—I grew up in Africa and there was a lot of circumcision in my tribe. Even though I did not get circumcised, my clitoris is still holding these collective and ancestral memories.

K.S.

Connecting My Blood to Earth

I felt so feminine, I felt like a wild woman but in the gentle way. I then watched the faces of my ex-partners release into the earth and a new space opened up inside my Womb. Afterward I felt totally unguarded, totally naked and open. I have never felt like this before. I feel so connected to earth and my blood.

S.J.

Wild Erotic Ancestral Initiation

As soon as I felt the earth energy, felt the roots of the tree going down into the menstrual blood, I felt sexually aroused. I met my ancestors, who covered me in menstrual blood. It was liberating and pleasurable to immerse myself completely in a wild, fast-flowing river of menstrual blood. I felt the intensity and power of my red dragon and the beautiful power of the ruby's red light in my womb. I felt sparkling diamonds in my ovaries and a ruby red light shining from my womb, and witnessed visions of flowers, snakes, and other shapes. A wild, erotic journey.

L.W.

Red Tara and Sara-La-Kali

I could see a lake and as I entered the water, I dove into my Womb space. My Womb was completely calm and relaxed. A deep still darkness, safe and warm. I met Red Tara (I did not know there was a Red Tara before) and she had a message for me: "Pour the sacred fire of your Womb into the world." She initiated me as Red Womb priestess and gave me the "Red Sword of fierce, wild compassion" with the following words: "Take care of the sacred fire!"

Then another being came and I asked for her name. Sara-la-Kali was the answer. I asked her if she has a message for me or why is coming into my space. She answered, "I am you." I looked at Red Tara, and she nodded and said, "Sara-la-Kali is the name of your Womb. Merge with her now, that is why she is here." When I did so, I felt such incredible heat in my body, I thought, I am going to melt!

The ruby inside of me began to glow in a wild, hot orange-red color sparkling and radiating. It was mind-blowing!

U.R.

SPIRAL 18

WOMB BLOOD

Original Blessing of the Great Mother

Menstrual blood represents the essence of femininity.
SIMONE DE BEAUVOIR

OUR WOMB BLOOD is a symbol of renewal, a Divine blessing—so how did we turn against our own life blood, shaming it and naming it as a curse?

In modern society we have been stripped of our primal innocence and knowing, conditioned in an unspoken war against the feminine principle and the erotic creature who abides within us all, directly connected to Source.

We have been taught that our wombs, our cycles, our sacred blood, our sacred scents, our feminine selves are less than, unclean, unwanted, lower, *basic*. When the truth is, *basic* means "at the foundation"—it is our original connection to life and God. Our ancestors knew this truth and celebrated the feminine.

Menstruation is the oldest religion on Earth, as was honoring the moon cycles. Red ochre was mined at the twin rivers of Zambia in East Africa at least three hundred thousand years ago and is known to have been used in sacred ceremony to symbolize womb blood. The mines were then covered up to honor and respect the earth.

The left-handed, red-haired Neanderthals were also moon worshippers, and used red ochre in their sacred ceremonies to honor the Womb and her cycles. A ritual posture used in their worship was kneeling on the ground to reveal the yoni/root to the moon. We now use this position to bow in church. Its origins were rooted in the sacred union of opening the feminine crown center to the moon, as the masculine crown touched the ground—opening to earth *and* cosmos together in a beautiful relationship of love.

Life-giving menstrual blood—blood that flowed with the codes of creation and was not spilled through violence—was suppressed, condemned, and replaced with the blood of a sacrificed male god-king, in black magic ritual and in war.

The Sacred Power of Menstrual Blood in Ancient Tradition

Menstrual blood is an incredibly rich and magical substance, in its physical properties, healing capacity, history, and central place in myth and legend.

It was called *soma* in the tantric tradition—the Vedic ritual drink of immortality. In the Rigveda, the Soma Mandala contains 114 hymns praising its "energizing qualities." It was euphemistically referred to as the juice from the stalk of a plant (tree of life) that was the god of the gods—the Mother God.

It was called *amrita* in the Persian tradition—the elixir of life, and essentially the same as soma. It was said to give the gods immortality. If the magical powers of the male gods were waning, they would churn the Womb ocean to create more.

It is called the flower, and the life-giving river in many Indian traditions, still to this day. In Indian mythology the Mother Goddess Kali-Maya invited all the other gods to drink her menstrual blood, her fountain of life, and because of that they ascended into the heavens.

It was the fountain of life in Gnostic Christian tradition—and modern Christianity still retains much menstrual blood symbolism, and refers to fonts of life, living waters, holy baptisms, and the Eucharist—blood of Christ/Womb. Even the Bible calls menstrual blood the flower, in Leviticus.

It was the Holy Grail of Celtic Grail and Arthurian legends, and was also known as claret wine in the European legends that conferred enlightenment to the king who drank it.

It was known as ambrosia in the Greek legends—the nectar of the gods. And in Greece it was also known as the supernatural red wine given by Hera to nourish the other gods (*hera* means womb).

The Norse god Thor reached the land of enlightenment and eternal life by bathing in a river of menstrual blood. Odin came to power after stealing the "wise-blood" of the Mother Goddess.

In Celtic mythology, Taliesin came to power by tasting liquid from the Mother Goddess's "cauldron," symbolic of menses.

Egyptian pharaohs became divine by ingesting the menstrual blood of Isis.

In China, the legends are that the Yellow Emperor became a god by drinking the menstrual blood of 1,200 women.

When we remember the sacred life-giving power of womb blood, our species can heal and come out of the violent, sacrificial, patriarchal trance that has our world on the edge of a precipice. When we allow our womb blood to flow into the earth and merge, we will no longer need to shed blood through violence.

It is said in ancient myth that "her blood is gold," and indeed it is so. Your blood is gold. Your womb is sacred; you are the chalice of Life.

Menstruation:
The Original Shamanic Journey

The first shamans were female, and menstruation was the original shamanic journey. The word *ritual* comes from the Sanskrit root word *rtu,* meaning "menstrual blood." In ancient cultures a woman's first menstruation—known as menarche—was a sacred time of initiation into not only womanhood but her magical powers.

In Australia, among the Yolngu, a girl's first menses was considered to be so powerful and such a blessing that girls bled onto a handcrafted sacred blanket, which older women then kept for good fortune. Later in life, if the girl got sick she would be wrapped in the blanket, which was believed to hold magical healing powers.[1]

Menstrual blood was considered in many ancient traditions to be *the* creative source of human life, literally the flowing lifeblood of our species.

The Maori stated explicitly that human souls are made of menstrual blood, which when retained in the womb "assumes human form and grows into a man." Africans said menstrual blood is "congealed to fashion a man." Aristotle said human life is made of "coagulum" of menstrual blood. In Hindu theory as the Great Mother creates, her substances become thickened and forms a curd or clot. This was the way she gave birth to the cosmos, and women employ the same method on a smaller scale. Indigenous tribes of South America said all mankind was made of "moon blood" in the beginning.

In ancient Mesopotamia, they believed the Great Goddess Ninhursag made mankind out of clay that she infused with her "blood of life." Adam, from the feminine *adamah,* means "bloody clay." The Bible's story of Adam was lifted from an older female-oriented creation myth recounting the creation of man from clay and moonblood. In the Koran's creation story, it says that Allah "made man out of flowing blood"; but in pre-Islamic Arabia, Allah was the Goddess of creation, Al-Lat. Plutarch said man was made of earth, but the power that made a human body grow was the moon, source of menstrual blood.

The pelican, who feeds her young with her own blood, is an alchemical bird of the menstrual mysteries. Considered to be a symbol of Christ, Saint Isidore of Seville describes how the pelican lived on the Nile in Egypt and killed her young and mourned them for three days. After these three days of mourning she revives them with the sprinkling of her own blood.

Alchemy, the search for the Holy Grail, the fountain of life, the font of youth, the amber nectar, ambrosia, and soma were all references to the sacred life-giving elixir of womb blood. Even the male gods were dependent on the miraculous properties of menstrual blood for their supernatural powers. In Greece it was euphemistically called the "supernatural red wine" given to the gods by Mother Hera in her virgin form, as Hebe.

The Great Mother manifested herself as the spirit of creation (Kali-Maya). She "invited the gods to bath in the bloody flow of her womb and to drink of it; and the gods, in holy communion, drank of the fountain of Life."[2]

It is also recorded all through the world that there was a time when the "sacred menstrual skirt" of the female shaman was stolen, and her powers appropriated by men. The ancient goddess was cast down to a wife or a consort, and then banished altogether as "unholy" or a prostitute, and the secrets of her menstrual mysteries, containing the power of life itself, were lost or became taboo.

Masculine paradigm religion taught that women had no souls and that their sexual nature was sinful and their menstrual blood unclean. When in fact, across all ancient traditions we see that shamanic magical powers were associated with the female lineage, and shared with the male in sacred union as a gift. In his book on Indian ecstatic cults, Philip Rawson indicates that "the most powerful sexual rite . . . requires intercourse with the female partner when she is menstruating and her 'red' sexual energy is at its peak."[3]

Buddhist and Hindu tantra was birthed through a matriarchal tribal lineage of women with supernatural powers, whose wisdom was passed down through the mitochondrial (maternal) DNA and transmitted through the unbroken "sacrament" of menstrual blood, which later became "left-hand tantra."

These Tibetan shaman priestesses held the title of *Khandro*—a sky dancer, priestess of the Cosmic Womb. This name, much like "Magdalene" in Western tradition is a title of a Sacred Feminine lineage. "It is quite a unique word, with no male equivalent, and would seem to have arisen not out of the Sanskrit background of Tantra . . . but apparently from the shamanistic roots of Tibet itself," says June Campbell in *Traveller in Space*.[4] This lineage of women would later become known as dakinis, who were demoted to consorts.

The Buddhist Magadalene, Yeshe Tsyogal, was the lineage holder of this primordial tradition of female shaman priestesses, birthing the teachings that went on to become Tibetan Buddhism, alongside her male consort Padmasambhava. Her name translates as the "Primordial (*ye*) Wisdom (*shes*) Queen (*rgyal mo*) of the Lake (*tso*)." This makes her the Eastern counterpart of the priestesses of Avalon and the ladies of the lake, who carry the legacy of the primordial feminine power in their bloodlines.

Yeshe's feminine enlightenment came in visionary communion with Vajrayogini, the Red Queen of the Dakinis, also known as Red Tara, an ancient primordial Mother who is depicted drinking her menstrual blood from a skullcap held in her left hand. Yeshe Tsogyal describes this communion: "Then I had a vision of a red woman, naked, lacking even the covering of bone ornaments, who thrust her *bhaga* against my mouth, and I drank deeply from the copious flow of blood. My entire being was filled with health and well-being."[5]

At its roots, the Tibetan Buddhist mantra *Om Mane Padme Hum* is a primordial Womb-sound frequency, meaning "honor the jewel in the yoni." The Cathars also worshipped the *mani*—a "jewel that lit up the world" with her wisdom.[6]

The Love Feast

The God of the Old Testament, who many Cathars and Gnostics believed was a false god, a demiurge, forbids Adam and Eve to eat from the fruit of the tree in the middle of the garden. Fruit was often associated with the menses, and garden was called *hortus* in Latin, which also meant "Womb"; and the female reproductive system was the tree of life.

It is clear that the patriarchal god is trying to repress the gift of Womb Wisdom and the sacramental use of moon blood, known as wise blood, for awakening.

Eve follows the voice of her Womb and disobeys. "When the woman saw the fruit of the tree was good for food and pleasing to the eye, and also desirable for gaining wisdom, she took some and ate it. She also gave some to her husband, who was with her, and he ate it. The eyes of both of them were opened . . ."[7] The serpent, who was also known as Lilith or Sophia, was Shakti—the enlivening sexual energy force of Creator herself—and was the bringer of gnosis or wisdom. Early Gnostic Christians depicted it as a vivid green snake coiled around the tree of life or the Womb Chalice of the Holy Grail: the serpent of kundalini wisdom.

Some of the last followers of the menstrual mysteries in the West were the Cathars, who may have been persecuted for holding the knowledge of how to prepare the sacrament for the "love feast of Adam and Eve," the alchemical process that

Fig. 18.1. The menstrual medusa

(Illustration by Natvienna Hanell)

activated the renewing stem cells in menstrual blood to reach Divine states of consciousness and enlightenment and to experience rapturous Oneness with Mother Earth. In heretical traditions, we see the power of menstrual blood was held as the pinnacle of Holy Communion, and originally associated with Magdalene and Sophia (feminine wisdom, wise blood) as the gateway to God.

This love feast or sacred marriage was a core part of the menstrual mysteries, and was alluded to in the Bible when it talks of the wedding at Cana. Turning water into wine was alchemical code for the menstrual mysteries. Eventually the love feast was declared a heresy and women were barred from participating in sacred rites.

It is said the last Cathars, who were held in a siege at Montsegur in 1243 were in possession of the Holy Grail and smuggled it out to safety before they danced to their death refusing to renounce their faith in the feminine Holy Spirit, believing the patriarchal god was an alien usurper. It is possible the actual Holy Grail that was smuggled out was *knowledge* of how to harness the power of the Grail Womb.

Beatrice de Planissoles, born 1274, was a Cathar who was tried for heresy by the Inquisition for claiming that she did not believe the "body of Christ" was actually in the sacrament. Could she have thought the true sacrament was the power of menstrual blood? The embodied essence of Holy Spirit?

She was accused of sorcery and was found to have two umbilical cords in her keeping, which science has now discovered contain powerfully regenerative stem cells, showing that this indigenous knowledge may have been commonplace for the Cathars. She was also found to have a cloth soaked in the menstrual blood of her daughter's menarche (first blood), which was said was to enchant her husband into fidelity. But as indigenous womb-shaman cultures knew, this cloth would have also acted as a sacred talisman of womb magic with powerful healing properties.

The founding fathers of Christianity, like Augustine, often accused heretics such as the Cathars of all kinds of vile crimes—including "eating eucharists of babies." But this could have simply referred to the practice, which is becoming popular again now in some holistic circles, of eating part of the placenta, which is known for its nutrient-rich properties and stem cells.

The sacramental or magical use of menstrual blood is also alluded to in other heretical sects. During Manichean "ritual meals" the Elect ate foods that were believed to contain particles of light. It was believed the Elect would integrate these particles of light into their own soul after the feast, and that when their bodies died this acquired light would help liberate them from the earthly cycle of reincarnation. These foods were described as "glowing fruits." Fruit is almost always symbolic of the womb and her offerings. The reference to "particles of light" may well demonstrate that they understood the awakening power of uterine stem cells.[8]

The power of resurrection previously associated with the Holy Womb and menstrual blood of the Divine Mother was transferred to the story of Jesus and his ritual of Eucharist—*hic est sanguis meus*, or "this is the chalice of my blood"— where worshippers "drank his blood" to gain the power of rebirth through him. This occurred even though, in most ancient myths and religions throughout the world dating back hundreds of thousands of years, the power of rebirth had always been a blessing of the feminine Womb—embodied and gifted by the menstrual blood of sacred womb priestesses.

The Portal of Renewal

The crucifixion itself holds deep Womb symbolism. The story of Jesus's crucifixion and three-day descent in a "tomb" followed by a day of resurrection mirrors exactly the earlier menstrual mysteries that honored the Womb's power of renewal and the Goddess. Ascension was at-one-ment with the Divine Mother.

A fifth-century magical childbearing spell with Christian influence reads, "Come out of your tomb, Christ is calling you." In the spell, the Womb is compared with the tomb, hinting that "resurrection, being a kind of rebirth, requires a Womb."[9]

During the first three days of menstruation, all the life-giving blood vessels and stem cell capabilities that have been built up in the womb to hold new life begin to be dismantled. The first day of this process—essential to the renewal of life—was rewritten as a "death" in patriarchy, as the womb was rewritten as a tomb.

After three days of "death and descent," as the womb lining and all her life-giving stem cells are released, on day four (even if the womb is still bleeding) the blood vessels begin their creative journey of preparing to hold life again, and new rejuvenating stem cells awaken to support life. This was the original "resurrection of life." The Womb/Tomb holds this power of death and rebirth.

The Indian Baul mystics knew this secret, and in their sexual mysteries making love on the fourth day of menstruation was the most sacred and powerful time. The first burst of stem cells creates a powerful alchemy that when communed with in sacred union can transport couples into deep dimensions of love—or heaven, nirvana, Elysium, fairyland. Because of this in later traditions, making love during menstruation became taboo.

In ancient Goddess menstrual mysteries, death was renewal and the Great Womb was this portal of renewal. The universe was a uterus, a yoniverse. The power of renewal, rebirth, and resurrection was always associated with the Womb and the Divine Mother, never with male gods, although a later tradition of sacred kings who had to die to replenish the lands developed. The Womb was the only vessel that could "die" or shed blood through love, creation, and renewal rather than suffering and physical death.

The Celtic Grail and witch traditions also held this knowledge of the power of the Womb and menstrual blood, and were persecuted and almost annihilated because of it. The traditions had also devolved, as the true secret of the Womb was that only *pure love* could activate the alchemical stem cells—which had given rise to the traditions of courtly love, troubadours, and Grail knights.

Loving, honoring, appreciating, and cherishing a woman—especially the sanctity of her menstrual flow and the power of her Womb—was the awakening path to "heaven" and endocrine states of rapture, communion, and longevity. Yet throughout history Grail or "Womb" maidens, as women who held deep womb power, were used in ritual for both dark and light purposes. Virgins whose wombs were still pristine were especially sought after, as were girls experiencing menarche—their first menstruation—which in shamanic beliefs across the world, holds an immense power and creative potential if harnessed properly.

The power of menstrual blood has been either greatly misused or denied in the last ages, so it is also vitally important to honor the sanctity of this embodied flow of the Divine Mother, and only work with the blood in innocence and love.

Women born many thousands of years ago in a state of original innocence—before many of our genetic capabilities went offline—held this power naturally, as a birthright, shared with their tribes in renewal rituals.

Since those times, once the birthright was lost, women across many lineages and cultures—womb priestesses—have practiced many varied ways to heal, clear, and open the Womb, so it can once again embody the frequency of Love, of original innocence. In this way, the energetic and physical stem cell capacity can activate purer states of consciousness and activate incredible regenerative healing. This knowledge has been almost lost over the last thousand years, as it has been fragmented, scattered, and deliberately destroyed.

Now it is desiring to return, to "renew our lands" as the myths foretold.

WOMB ORACLES SHARE

Menstrual Baptism of the Cosmic Mother

There was a time when I had entered an emotional underworld of desolation. It felt as if all light and possibility had left my being, drained out to a single black point of despair. From this single black point, I offered a thread, a prayer to the cosmos, a call from deep within my soul, to feel alive again . . . to feel love, to connect with my Creator, to receive the love of the universe . . . to be reborn. For a few minutes there was nothing but a blank, empty silence.

Then a soft wave broke over the crown of my head, and a fountain of ecstatic cosmic energy began to pour inside me. As it descended down in waves, pulsing, to the root of my being, my Womb and yoni began to pulse wildly in ecstasy.

The energy was almost too much to bear and my legs trembled. I made my way to a bed to lie down; the waves were flowing faster with more power, more pleasure.

I became aware of a being stood beside me, with a coven of women accompanying her. She was Tibetan. I could barely breathe, but in between the waves of pleasure engulfing me, I managed to ask her name. "Yeshe Tsogyal," she replied in a pulse of energy. It sounded vaguely familiar, I knew she had been the consort of a Tibetan sage. That was all I knew. The women with her were also Khandros, such as Princess Mandarva and Pandaravasini, tantric womb priestesses of the Buddhist and Tibetan tantric shamanic lineage. Their energy held a circle around me.

Yeshe Tsogyal felt so familiar to me, almost part of me. I felt like I knew her so well, better even than parts of myself. But like an ephemeral dream the connection remained misty, so instead I allowed myself to surrender to the guardianship of her deeply powerful and soft loving presence.

For three days this fountain of cosmic ecstasy poured through me like a vast, infinite river—pulsing with pleasure and radiance, full of supersensory magic.

At times I could not walk, I had to lie down on the floor and surrender, dying, dissolving, then reborn all in one cosmic orgasmic pulse. At times I thought I might truly die, and I was aware that my mind was like a tight ball of wool that was slowly being unraveled and then threaded back around the starry cosmic web.

Completely undone, I wept with an astounding love that melted through my body like a fiery nectar, burning with wild passion, yet soft as moonlight on water. The trees were whispering love poetry to me, gardens were offering me bouquets of radiant, rainbow-colored flowers. It felt as if life was bowing down to me in deep love—and I was weeping in bliss for the vast beauty of all this love I belonged to.

On the last day of this cosmic love infusion, I found myself transported to a magical realm that was superimposed directly onto this one, entwined like thread. Here I entered into a cosmic Yab-Yum and surrendered completely to the waves of creative bliss. At the climax of this experience, I received an immense baptism and transmission of the Divine Mother's cosmic menstrual blood, her primordial wisdom rivers, and awakened directly into the feminine dimension.

S.B.

Creating an Inner Red Tent

I felt a mystical premenstrual mist descend and surround me; I feel like withdrawing from the outside world, nesting and sinking deep into myself. I've always wanted to sit in a Red Tent so I've started creating one in my inner world. It's here I'll sit with my blood in whatever shape or form she chooses to manifest; I've seen glimpses of her before but I sense I've been playing a game of hide and seek. In the tent we will sit, lie, share, talk, massage each other, hug, sleep, sing, dance, and play. Looking forward to her arrival, feeling her very close. Tears of joy and a sense of deeper reunion with a deep hidden aspect of myself.

K.S.

SPIRAL 19

CODES OF CREATION

Sacred Science of Menstrual Stem Cells

Woman is a beam of Divine Light.
She is not the being whom sensual desire takes as its object.
She is Creator, it should be said,
She is not a creature.

RUMI

THE GENERATIVE BIOLOGICAL POWER of menstrual-blood stem cells is astonishing—revealing a dazzling doorway into their role as a keeper of the codes of Creation. We are created in a divine blueprint as regenerating, renewing, creative beings. We are chalices for the flow of life and love, yet our potentials have withered. Many ancient texts talk about this potential for longevity and regeneration, yet in the modern world this has been dismissed as myth or wishful thinking.

The truth is, we *do* have "imaginal cells" within us that respond to energetic fields of resonance, such as love, harmony, intention, desire, and mystical union. These imaginal cells are called stem cells. Aging scientists working in private laboratories with the power of stem cells have experienced gray hair turning back to the glossy black of their youth, within months, during their experiments.[1]

This calls to mind the description of the Holy Grail in Eschenbach's *Parzival:*

By the power of that stone the phoenix burns to ashes, but the ashes give him life again. Thus does the phoenix molt and change its plumage, which afterward is bright and shining and as lovely as before. There never was a human so ill but that, if he one day sees that stone, he cannot die within the week that follows. And in looks he will not fade.... Such power does the stone give a man that flesh and bones are at once made young again. The stone is called the Grail.

Astoundingly the tantric text the Kaulajnananirnaya also alludes to the fact that the feminine elixirs, such as menstrual blood, can prevent or remove graying hair. In the text, which encodes teachings from ninth-century India and is attributed to the school of Matsyendranatha, it says, "O Mother of heroes, listen to the science of preventing grey hair. One should fix his mind on the Devi's Cakra, like the moon of the first night of the bright fortnight."[2]

Modern science has just discovered what the ancients have known for hundreds of thousands of years: menstrual blood is rich with these incredibly potent stem cells, which have the power to renew, regenerate, and create life. Stem cells are magical cells. They are similar in some ways to the imaginal cells that can turn a caterpillar into a butterfly, containing within them an incredible power of regeneration. They can regenerate and repair damaged tissues in our body in miraculous ways that science would have previously called impossible. Research has shown that stem cells can treat heart disease, blood vessel disease, can shrink brain cancer, and can heal other cancers and autoimmune disorders.[3] They have remarkable natural "homing" ability, an innate ability to migrate to the part of the body that is injured and needs repair, using primordial intelligence.[4] Menstrual stem cells are *multipotent progenitor* cells— they can grow and differentiate into almost any kind of cell in the body as needed. Modern science shows us that within a few days, a single menstrual stem cell can differentiate into a heart cell that spontaneously beats.[5] When two such heart cells come within a few inches of each other, they automatically begin to beat together in rhythm—they become energetically entangled in a synchronized dance.

This means that menstrual-blood stem cells can instinctively repair and regenerate almost any damaged body organs and tissues, and are now the centerpiece of an entirely new branch of healing that is called "regenerative medicine."

Practically speaking, this means that every month menstruating women shed life-saving stem cells in their menstrual blood that if collected could potentially *regrow* their own heart, brain, or many other tissues if they were damaged. Or, even more astoundingly, *it could reverse many of the effects of aging,* providing a person the energy and vigor of someone much younger in physical years.

We all start out life as a single cell, a fertilized egg that has within it the power to double, and double, and double until it eventually creates our entire adult body of 50 trillion cells—all from the single original egg cell . . . the quintessential stem cell. Every month a woman sheds menstrual blood that contains tens of thousands of these stem cells that are the "daughter cells" of that original egg, and they retain much of that egg's awesome biological "rebirth" power. When a woman becomes pregnant, stem cells from her baby are transplanted into her own body and renew and replenish her; this is the reason that a woman lives on average six months longer for every baby she has (up to twelve).[6]

Menstrual stem cells are also *unique* within the stem cells found in the body. In scientific terms they are known as immune-privileged, meaning they can be transplanted into anyone without being rejected. This is a *huge* gift, with huge implications. Other kinds of stem cells throughout the body need to be genetically matched to be successfully donated from one person to another.

Womb stem cells hold the gift of embrace and union—the Womb herself is a space of union, where a "human within a human" can coexist, where ideas and concepts of boundaries and a separate *I* dissolve. The Womb is nondual, or rather a space of sacred union. Menstrual stem cells inherit this gift, related to the immune system tolerance for the developing baby that is a "foreign" object.

The new scientific understanding of stem cells, and in particular *menstrual-blood stem cells* is truly breathtaking. And what is even more remarkable is that for thousands of years before modern science could prove their existence and healing properties, the ancients knew about their life-renewing potency through a process of direct intuitive gnosis, experience, and inherited wisdom.

Myths and legends of almost *every* ancient culture speak about the capacity of menstrual blood to promote health and longevity, and directly alter consciousness to produce states of illumination, sacred bonding, and embodied awakening.

In the ancient days as well as now, the power of menstrual blood at times was used in the name of love and healing, and in other situations was treated as a commodity and exploited by the powerful castes who guarded its secrets for themselves. It is vital to educate yourself about this power that lies within women and begin to speak out and to honor and protect it.

How a stem cell grows and develops, and if its mystical properties are able to be accessed, depends on the cues it receives from its environment. What this means is that these imaginal stem cells are responsive to our state of consciousness and the consciousness of our collective environment—they can be switched on or off. They demonstrate the different potentials inherent in the same genetic code. By opening to love and healing, and integrating our subconscious wounds, we can also "upgrade" our genetic expression.

We have the power within to awaken the magical properties of these stem cells, enjoying longevity, vitality, expanded sensory awareness, and regeneration. We can honor our bodies as holy and wise. This is why the ancient womb religion spoke so reverently of the *wise blood*.

We all have an "imaginal butterfly" within, waiting to take wings and fly.

Honey from the Flower

Contemporary science is only just starting to study these stem cells. Much more work is needed to understand their full potential. However, we can glean clues of their greater importance from spiritual traditions such as the Baul mystics of India, whose religious practices reflect the ancient knowledge of the spiritual and biological power of menstrual blood. This secret knowledge has been handed down from generation to generation over the six hundred years of Baul history.

The Baul mystics are celebrated for their capacity to enter ecstatic states of Divine Love through their dance, poetry, singing, and sexuality. Casting aside the cultural norms of modern India, they passionately seek to embody God through the temples of their own bodies. This is called Deha-Tattva, "truth within the body." For the Bauls, the Womb Mysteries are a core element of their religious and cultural experience.

"Ingesting menstrual blood is the focal point of Baul ideology," writes Kristin Hanssen, anthropologist and expert on the ancient blood mysteries. In the poetic terms of their bardic "twilight language," the Bauls describe the ingestion of menstrual blood as "drinking honey from the flower" or "going swimming in the river." Menstrual blood is the most powerful and holy of all bodily fluids, as it contains the strongest seed energy, to vivify and animate life. They perceive the magical substance of menstrual fluid to be closely related to song and music. Both are thought of as soul food—powerful means to directly transmit the vital spiritual force that invigorates the soul and binds a community together.

In one published paper, Hanssen shares the story of a menarchal girl in modern Bengal who allowed her menstrual blood to flow onto a cotton cloth, which was then soaked with milk, honey, coconut, and camphor before being ingested by her, the family guru, and the greater community. "Menstrual blood and related substances are valued . . . because they collapse the boundary between self and other, forging ties that resemble those between a mother and her offspring, or a deity and devotee."[7]

It was said that after the community of Bauls drank the magical blend of menstrual blood, their powers of memory and concentration were enhanced, their voices grew melodious, and their entire beings infused with happiness, serenity, love. It was known as the re-creation of the original rite performed by Grail lovers Radha and Krishna, and is reminiscent of gnostic "love feast" rites.

In Celtic lore those who ate the womb "apples" belonging to the Lady of Avalon "died to the real world" and became travelers in the feminine fairy realms. Merlin and his companions were reported to "run mad" after eating them.[8] The Bauls were also known for entering states of "divine madness," intoxicated by the love fruit of the alchemical feminine womb.

In Alaska the Koyukun people mixed menstrual and birthing fluids with medicinal plants, and in Tibet the menstrual blood of young girls was offered to the goddess Tara, and used as medicine for the whole community.[9] David Gordon White describes how original tantric rites often involved actual bodily substances, especially female sexual fluid, in what was known as endocrine alchemy, until these rites were repressed and internalized.[10]

In Western alchemical tradition, the power of menstrual blood was also well known—and was the healing and awakening "eucharist" of early Gnostic "Womb churches." This was the heresy that the patriarchal church sought to destroy. Researchers on Western alchemy Lynn Picknett and Clive Prince confirm that this knowledge was once a key of alchemical traditions: "It is significant that Agrippa, like the alchemists, believed that menstrual blood had a particular practical and mystical application. They believed that it contained some unique elixir or chemical and that ingesting it in a certain manner, using ancient techniques, would guarantee physical rejuvenation and bestow wisdom."[11]

For the ancient goddess devotees, the power of attending a Womb church lay in the sacrament that gave ecstatic communion with Divine Mother *and* provided tangible physical healing and regeneration benefits from receiving the awakened stem cells. It is no wonder that the ancient alchemists revered the feminine principle and created cathedrals, such as Chartres, to celebrate the "pilgrimage into the Womb." Worshippers and pilgrims would pass through the arched entrance of the church, which represented the labia of the yoni, often with a rosebud at the top to symbolize the clitoris, then step deeper inside the holy yoni to receive blessing in the living waters of the baptismal font, before entering her dark womb for rebirth.

Like other shamanic traditions that require special practices and preparations for use, such as the South American use of ayahausca and the Siberian shaman's use of *Amanita muscaria,* the menstrual blood had to be prepared with a special recipe of herbs and possibly snake venom in order to prevent coagulation or stomach acid from destroying the potent stem cells. This shamanic lore would have been passed down through lineages of womb shamans, and it is quite possible this is the knowledge the church was trying to eradicate during its persecutions of the Cathars and the witch trials, which often targeted wise women herbalists.

Now the recipes are lost, the shamanic lineage broken, the people disconnected from their own natural healing powers gifted from the body of the goddess.

In Russia there were womb shamans known as *upir*—later called vampires or werewolves—who worshipped the Moon Goddess and most likely drank sacred sacraments of her menstrual blood. The upir were often connected in folklore with wise women and witches, and symbols of the goddess such as the swan. In Slavic lore, a future vampire is born with a caul over his head, symbolizing the regenerative and transformative powers of the serpent energy in the womb.[12] Similarly, in Sicily a *strega*—a shaman-witch—is identified the same way.

For indigenous shamans and communities, ingesting menstrual blood appears to have been the ultimate way of incorporating the essence of another into oneself. And the sanctity of this rite, done in love, would have been the key to its success. The true otherworldly powers of the feminine elixirs can only be gifted in love for the benefit of life, not taken or manipulated for personal gain or power.

Shamanic journeys by The Fountain of Life womb oracles during intensive apprenticeships reveal how this knowledge was once widely known across the world. It was not only used as an elixir of life and union by communities, but was also *misused* in forms of black magic at times, with men having harems of thousands of women to harvest their menstrual blood. This terrible abuse of the feminine essence may well have led to the cultural taboos and fears that sprang up around a woman's cycle as being shameful or evil.

Now, as a modern culture we often condemn these primal rites, rejecting and demonizing the power held within our own bodies—and the sacred elixirs and rivers she produces. In the past, especially among mystics, this wasn't so.

Womb Elixirs of Immortality

Menstrual blood was known as the uterine milk of immortality, yet for a substance that is as biologically and mythologically important as menstrual blood, very little research has been done upon it, mainly due to the unspoken cultural taboo and the unconscious primal fears that scientists, often male, have around menstrual blood. However, the research that has been done on the composition of menstrual blood shows that it truly is an elixir of life.

Although the monthly uterine flow is most often referred to as menstrual blood, in reality it is a fluid rich in many nutrients, biologically active compounds, and immune system cells, in addition to the red blood cells that give it its distinctive color. Menstrual fluid is created every month by the network of blood vessels and connective tissue, the endometrial lining that lines the inner walls of the womb. The structure that supports the nutritive uterine lining is created and then shed again and again every month by the extremely potent menstrual blood stem cells, or endometrial regenerative cells, in preparation to nourish a fertilized egg that implants on the walls of the womb in the early stages of pregnancy.

When a fertilized egg implants on the wall of the womb, the menstrual fluid is retained to nurture the baby, rather than shed. Scientists who study the retained menstrual fluid refer to it as uterine milk, because its composition is analogous to breast milk. It contains fats, carbohydrates, sugars, proteins, immune-modulating compounds, and hormonal growth factors, all designed to nourish the fertilized egg in early pregnancy. It also contains minerals, particularly potassium and phosphorus, antioxidants such as vitamin E, and natural antimicrobial substances. Uterine milk production in early pregnancy is increased by prolactin, the same hormone secreted by the mother that later causes the production of breast milk.

The ancient myths of almost every culture in the world speak of the consciousness-altering and illuminating properties of menstrual blood. Up until about five years ago, there had been only a handful of landmark studies on menstrual fluid composition in the history of modern science—notably in 1845, 1920, and 1957—a remarkable unconscious "oversight" on the part of science. But over the past few years there has been renewed interest. What science now shows is that menstrual fluid contains more than 1,000 proteins that are biologically active, and 385 are unique proteins found *only* in menstrual fluid. This number does not include the hormones, neurotransmitters, and other kinds of bioactive and psychoactive substances that give it consciousness-altering properties.[13]

Menstrual blood is a powerful form of plant spirit medicine, from the tree of life: the Womb. It can be experienced in the same way as an ayahuasca journey.

The lubricating fluid of the yoni is produced by the glands on the walls of the yoni and cervix. This in part composes the "white river" of feminine fluids written about in the biblical Song of Songs as the lily of the valley, along with the female ejaculate fluid that builds up during sexual arousal. Similar to menstrual blood, in recent studies it has been found to contain more than 800 biologically active proteins, with approximately 685 unique proteins found only in this precious fluid.[14]

These are the elixirs of immortality that alchemists of old were connoisseurs of, knowing that they were the gateway to subtle realms. The proteins and peptides found in menstrual blood and yoni fluids include many growth factors and cell stimulators, as well as a portion that are *neurologically active or alter sensory perception,* so indeed science is now proving the biological basis for what ancient cultures have known for thousands of years: that the womb elixirs are entheogens, sacred gateways to God.

Even more interesting is the fact that the composition of the proteins and peptides of the feminine fluids can change radically, depending on the biochemical and physiological state of the woman. In the legends of the dragonlines of the Grail lineage, tremendous importance was placed on supporting women to be in loving and synchronous emotional states around times of menstruation and sexual exchange, as they knew that the composition of her nourishing fluids would be most beneficial if she felt loved, supported, connected, and safe. This was especially key if she were seeding a baby or a new creation.

This is a huge motif for the Grail tradition; a woman has to be held in deep love and sanctity, and to be cherished and adored. This was the wisdom that lay at the foundation of the troubadours, the bards, and the arts of "courting a woman." Opening the heart in true love also opened the gateway to the most enchanted alchemical frequencies of the Womb, creating the "chemistry of heaven."

These were secrets of the arts of immaculate conception.

This is different from many tantric traditions where the female was demoted to a consort or karma mudra in sexual ritual. It was encouraged that the man had no feelings of personal love or bonding for the woman he was engaging with.

The secret of endocrine alchemy was that *only love* could open the Grail Castle. The Womb chemically recognizes a man entering her, and the immune system rejects a masculine presence she is not familiar with. This was why monogamy was a foundation of sacred union and the pilgrimage into the Womb was symbolized by swans, who mate for life. Not based on reasons of morality, but on alchemical Womb lore of love. In sacred union the woman biochemically accepts the man's body as part of hers. Children seeded from this place hold a biochemical frequency of union.

A woman in the flow of her Womb powers, through sexual union, menstruation, or conception and birth, lives in a space between the worlds, on the cusp of possibilities of both death and rebirth, a living paradox and chalice of life and dissolution. She is precious, magical, sensitive, deeply vulnerable—she is surrendering into a highly feminine state of multidimensional cosmic opening.

In this magical space her feminine openness, her yin nature, needs protection. As consciousness fell and the tribe forgot to share the Womb Mysteries as a whole, as a hive, as a pod living in oneness consciousness, then taboos began to develop.

First, the women were secluded—not because they were shameful or dirty or dangerous to the other people in the tribe, but because they needed to be specially cared for, making sure no negative energies touched them in such a delicate and quantum state, which had the power to manifest and birth realities. Over time a reversal occurred, as the Womb Mysteries were forgotten, seclusion was deemed to be a segregation to protect the tribe from the menstrual pollution.

Although whispers of a time when menstruation was a vision quest for the entire tribe remain in the religious custom of honoring the Sabbath as a "day of rest." In Babylon, one day of sabbatu marked each quarter phase of the moon and was regarded as the day that Ishtar menstruated; on these days *all* people abstained from certain activities as if they were menstruating women.[15]

Just as the powers and wisdom of menstruation now are forgotten and discarded, in the past this knowledge was also greatly misused and harnessed for the dark arts. Using the Womb powers of menstruation and conception for low magic—to manipulate, control, and distort the immense flow of creation for personal use and gain—once prevailed, casting further fear and degradation on the Womb flow.

The gift of the Womb requires a devotional heart, fully committed to love and to the common good, to be a pure vessel for the power of the Great Mother, rather than something used for sorcery or separation, or as a tool for a disconnected patriarchal energy to harvest power.

The Awakening Fragrance of Womb Blood

Womb blood is *primal*. In other words it is *first,* the original Latin meaning of the word. The first smell that greets a baby as her mother births her into the world is the fragrance of her womb blood—the nutritive uterine milk, rich in iron, pheromones, hormones, and abundant neuropeptide "molecules of emotion." This maternal womb blood becomes the primal olfactory imprint that embeds itself deep into our feminine psyche—as smell is one of the strongest evokers of emotional memory. The olfactory nerve channels, the neural networks of smell, plunge directly into the brain's Womb of Consciousness—the amygdala and limbic emotional pathways of the brain—in a way that is different from all other sensory perceptions. In this way smell is primal, just as womb blood is primal.

Scent opens up new gateways of perception and the sacred science of scent was used for spiritual journeying by many womb priestesses, such as the priestesses of Isis. Menstrual and womb scents were the basis for awakening feminine memory, as were the scents of flower essences—the menstrual blood of nature.

When primal substance meets primal sense at the moment of our birth, the result is an explosion of emotional meaning and limbic imprinting. If the birth experience is gentle and sacred, the imprint of menstrual blood fragrance is immediately evocative of the essence of vitality, birth, rebirth, and renewal. If our birth process was traumatic or overwhelming (as is often the case in our modern birth culture), then the fragrance of menstrual blood can bring powerful unresolved emotions to the surface, to be seen and healed.

By the time we are even aware of a smell, we are already experiencing a strong emotional response to it, especially in the case of the smells of primal bonding that have such deep emotional meaning for us, and that have been imprinted into our developing brains as young ones. In the ancient days, women freely bled, without tampons or pads to obstruct the flow, or to obstruct the awareness of its fragrance. Women living together in tribes experienced synchronized menstrual flow at the dark moon. So at the time of tribal menstruation, the smell of menstrual blood emanated in a field around every menstruating woman, suffusing the entire tribe. The monthly flow was an especially important mechanism of bonding and imprinting between mother and children, as well as her sexual partner, who were in very close proximity to her blood.

Menstrual blood and female pheromones regulate the monthly lunar flows of emotions, hormones, dream cycles and relational activity not just in women, but also in the men and children of the household. In the ancient days when all menstruating women of the tribe bled in synchrony, menstruation set the schedule for the entire tribe. The whole village became a moon lodge. Menstruation was a time of rest and inner journeys for men and women, as well as a time of active female sexuality before the advent of menstrual taboos.

The collective fragrant menstrual aroma of the tribe's women encapsulated the entire tribe, including men and children, creating an enchanted, otherworldly container of altered consciousness akin to a menstrual merkaba (an auric Womb field), so as a web they could shamanically journey into the dark moon.

In these ways, the fragrance of menstrual blood immediately and directly transports us into our feminine primal brain, beyond the reach of our rational cerebral cortex, and into an altered state of shamanic consciousness if we allow it. It immediately takes us back to the emotional memories of not only our birth, but also our relationship with our mother during early childhood, who represented the Great Mother herself to us in our first years of life. For a man, menstrual blood is a primal olfactory emotional bridge that invites him into his "second birth," his spiritual rebirth into sacred sexual union with his sexual partner, whose monthly bleeding beckons him to surrender again and again, deeper and deeper into the beautiful state of union consciousness.

Menstrual blood works as a doorway in the deep psyche of men, beyond their conditioning, bringing both dangers and gifts. Most modern men have unresolved emotional issues around their own birth, their relationship with their mother, and prior sexual relationships that can initially make the fragrance of womb blood deeply terrifying or overwhelming at a subconscious level. This is often expressed as an aversion or discomfort with menstrual blood, rather than a candid admission of his feelings of vulnerability, powerlessness, or the sense of being overwhelmed that can arise. However as men begin a process of reimprinting and primal bonding with their sacred sexual partner, the fragrance can once again take them immediately into bliss or shamanic consciousness.

Beyond even these powerful emotional memories, the smell of menstrual blood links us to the epigenetic memories of our long line of maternal ancestors, as it has now been proven that *olfactory memories are passed down between generations.*[16] In other words, when a smell has an emotional meaning for a mother or father, it is imprinted into the epigenetic codes, and this meaning is passed down as an instinctively imprinted memory to the next generation. (It may be by a similar mechanism that all creatures can inherit memories that would otherwise seem impossible, such as generation upon generation of migrating monarch butterflies all landing on the exact same tree year after year.)

It is the sacred scent of the ancient mothers, flowing ancient wisdom through our Wombs in the unbroken transmission of wise blood from the time of creation. In fact the Spanish word for *law* shares a menstrual blood and Womb root. Womb lore was *law*—she was the keeper of the ancient knowledge and ways.

Menarche:
Doorway of Sexual Initiation

The time of menarche in young women, and the coming-of-age in young men, is the moment in which our potent sexual magic suddenly blooms into being, like a flower comes alive in springtime.

It is a key point in our developmental timeline that energetically seeds our creative sexual blueprint, governing all that we manifest in our future lives. It is symbolized by the number 13, the age of physical and spiritual initiation in indigenous cultures around the world. *The moment of our sexual coming of age is the key to understanding our creations in the world.* We weave our own web.

Our sexual energy *is* our life-force energy, *is* our creative energy, *is* the flow of Shakti through us, *is* our magical power. They are woven together as a seamless bioemotional-energetic movement, and cannot be separated. As a collective, we have ignored this at great peril, not just for our own lives, but for the entire planet. We have become separated from our wild sexual power, our source of magic. And by revisiting this time of power, traveling between worlds, we can reclaim it as ours.

In the shamanic traditions, the time of menarche/coming-of-age was recognized as a powerful gateway into the spirit worlds. The explosive emotional, neurological, physical, and spiritual changes that accompany this time serve as the fuel to travel deep into the otherworld where the young men and women of the tribe announce themselves as spirit keepers, ready to take their place as powerful Creators of their destiny.

Here they receive their spirit name, meet their animal familiars and spirit guides, and see their life vision—their soul purpose on this planet. The dreams and visions they receive at this age set their spiritual course for years to come.

At the time of our sexual coming-of-age and menarche, we are meant to experience an alchemical explosion of new energies within our biology derived from our sexual awakening. These are the hormones and the neuropeptide molecules of emotion that are physiologically responsible for the altered states of conscious and sublime perceptions born from our opening into sexual love. This is the biological basis for the garden of Eden, which is a perceptual state of wild innocence created when our biology is fully online, when it is functioning as our Creator truly intended.

Research shows that around the time of puberty the architecture of our brains radically grows and opens in a way that is only matched by our brain growth in the womb.[17] The change is vast, affecting the amygdala, cerebellum, hippocampus, hypothalamus, and prefrontal cortex; all the neural networks that govern our vision, smell, sense perceptions, sexuality, balance, spiritual, and dream connections bloom and grow, ready for us to step into an incredible new perception of reality if we choose. Whatever we feel and experience at this time shape-shifts our consciousness.

But when we have emotional and soulful wounds around love and sexuality, what was meant to be a harmonious neuroendocrine symphony morphs into a chaotic cacophony that wires us for pain and suffering. We secrete molecules of stress and trauma that anchor dysfunctional neural networks into place, resulting in an inner chemistry that is agitated, volatile, and depressed. This is the biology of separation, inherited from our wounded parents and culture.

At the age of menarche our creative power *and* our core emotional wounds come online, expressing through our sexuality. This generates our erotic shadow imprint—which becomes the wounded blueprint of all our future suffering in life until it is healed. Our sexual energy is a powerful magnet, and through our erotic shadow we unconsciously manifest and magnetize every betrayal, every bad relationship, every failed creation, as we shamefully stuff our most hidden sexual desires and imprints back under the bed, even denying them to ourselves.

But we can heal our biological imbalance and restore our capacity to experience profound states of love and bliss by reviving our hormones and neurochemistry.

The most direct way to do this is by relinking our primal energies into the field of love and the natural womb grid of Gaia and Divine Mother, as we release old wounds around our heart and sexuality, wounds that were firmly conditioned by our first sexual experiences. We must revisit these memories to release any residual pains or limiting beliefs that still affect us. As we do, our actual biochemistry shifts and changes, allowing us to experience the feeling of joyful sexual innocence in every moment that is our incredible human birthright.

Our capacity to create runs parallel with our sexual energy. If our sexual energy is open we can create remarkable things, but if our hearts are not open at the same time, we will find ourselves powerfully manifesting wounded creations. It is only when we heal our erotic shadow that we can truly create our deepest soul visions and rewire our consciousness for Love.

We were created in erotic innocence, our sexuality is pure and beautiful at its source. We can choose to dive deep into our erotic innocence to bloom again, and to rewire our neural networks into a new octave of sexual wholeness.

What if at age thirteen our entire being had been welcomed, accepted, honored, and celebrated? Our beautiful sexuality as much as our heart and mind? Our power and wildness as much as our sweetness?

The time has come to write a new history into our sexual psyche, to remake our own personal and ancestral timeline in a vision of wild innocence. Reclaiming rituals that honor and celebrate menarche and coming-of-age, celebrating the fragrant menstrual flow of life and the gifts of sexuality and renewal she brings is the sacred thread, the lifeline that will restore us to sexual wholeness.

WOMB ORACLES SHARE
Anointing the Moon

As I walked through the portal, women were covered in red from head to toe. I could see only their eyes full of mystery and magic. They were waiting for me. They took me into a bath house and bathed me with flowers and oils. It was very lovingly done. They dressed me and I realized I was bleeding. They sat me on a marble seat that was being warmed with a small fire underneath. As I sat there, I felt tired for some reason. Each one came and touched the blood running down the marble and anointed their feet and their throat. Then one anointed my crown, third eye, back of my head, my thymus gland and the palms of my hands. She then bent down, cupped my hands, and blew her breath into them. She said the power is in the blow, telepathically. I suddenly felt myself transformed and running with a pack of wolves. When I woke up my moon blood had started.

A.V.

Fire and Water of Isis

The Egyptian Goddess Isis appeared with a new moon above her head. She was initiating me in an ancient sacred ceremony with fire and water. It felt strongly powerful, like igniting some deep remembrance that I was treasuring inside me.

O.M.

SPIRAL 20

WILD AND HOLY WOMB

Uniting the Red and White Rivers of the Feminine

For I am the first and the last.
I am the honored one and the scorned one.
I am the whore and the holy one.
I am the wife and the virgin.

THE THUNDER, PERFECT MIND
(FROM THE NAG HAMMADI LIBRARY)

WHEN THE FEMININE was whole she was represented as the Great Mother, the *Magna Mater,* which also translates as "magnetic mother." This fusing of sexual magnetism *and* maternal love as a continuum of the same feminine thread, with both red and white strands woven together as one, meant that these two poles of the feminine, and of life herself, dark and light, erotic lust and love, were united (see plate 16).

These two rivers can be described as the white magic of the maternal essence, which creates feelings of security, comfort, and protection, and the red magic of erotic desire, which is dynamic and creates states of initiation, truth, and ecstasy. Often, the erotic feminine is taboo, as it brazenly challenges our need to be pleasing or "nice." "The active side of the feminine is similar to the divine madness of the soul, which invokes primeval forces that take us out of the limitations and conventions of social norms. Eros in this sense produces . . . liberation."[1]

Across many ancient cultures there are artifacts of double goddesses, female twins who share one yoni and represent the cycling dance of the female lunar poles—a harmonic merry-go-round of ecstatic creation from the Womb wheel. A hymn from ancient India celebrates this Sacred Feminine duality, saying, "twin sisters of various alternating forms, of the two, one glowing, the other dark."[2]

In Gnostic teachings there were two lights of the feminine: a pure white light, the transcendent White Maiden-Virgin, and a dark light or a blue light, which was the *Throne,* representing an immanent Black Goddess—the Womb, the Holy Hor. This mirrors Isis, who was known as both the Virgin and the Throne. The Throne is primal, the first one, the universal root consciousness that births the light.

The Zohar or Book of Splendour describes these two aspects of the feminine:

In the flame are two lights: one light is a bright white and one light is united with a dark or blue, this dark light, or bluish color, which is below, is the precious throne to the white . . . it unites to the above, to that white upper light, and unites itself below to one thing which is under it, which is burning matter . . ."[3]

This blue black light was also associated with the Shekinah, divine presence.

Lily and the Rose: The Sacred Womb Rivers

Our sexuality is cyclical, and in the ancient times it was known the feminine nature had two complementary poles: a full-moon white river and a dark-moon dark river. The full moon was associated with love, surrender, and conception. The dark moon was associated with awakened desire, lust, and dissolution or initiation. The dark or red river is full of wildness and creative power and the white river is brimming with intuitive receptivity and love. These two flows of Shakti are designed to be merged and in balance, and are represented by the elements of fire and water. Just like the fire of the sun and the waters of rain are both needed to make earth fertile, if one becomes out of balance, the land is either scorched or drowned. So it is with the feminine energy flows, which also represent power and love, and birth true wisdom when they are merged.

As the patriarchal matrix began to take hold five thousand years ago to dismantle the womb religion and with it the harmonious psyche of man and woman, these united rivers that formed our *wild innocence* began to separate from each other. As this split between the two harmonious and complementary flows of life-force energy began to accelerate, cultures began to embody one or the other shadow.

Civilizations such as Babylon, Egypt, and the Roman Empire, which were originally mother goddess cultures, began to degenerate and to use and abuse the feminine, creating the feeling that paganism—originally connected to pure Mother Earth worship—was dangerous or corrupt. Fertility rituals devolved into occult black-magic rites. The feminine principle was used, but also imprisoned in this misuse.

The rise of monotheistic religions such as Judaism, Christianity, and Islam reacted to this by condemning the feminine as evil and sinful, by shutting down any expressions of the wild feminine or the celebration of sexuality. Feminine rites known as merry making (Mary making), such as music, drumming, dance, pleasure, makeup, ornamentation, jewelry, celebration, festivals, and revels, were classed as the devil's work and were either frowned upon or banned. Feasting was replaced with fasting; priestesses who practiced sexual rites became celibate nuns; ecstatic dance and song was replaced with solitude and prayer.

As the feminine consciousness fell, these two poles began to separate—a woman could be either pure and virginal *or* a sensual lover, she could either be maternal and loving *or* free, wildish, and erotic, but not both at the same time. The feminine soul was wrenched in half, her wild sensuality cut from her heart. We see this in the myths of Virgin Mary the immaculate mother and Mary Magdalene the whore and fallen sinner.

The white light of the crown and the dark light of the throne had been rent apart.

Women's power and rights ebbed away as they were considered mere possessions of their husbands. Those women who still followed the Old Ways were persecuted, culminating in the witch hunts of the Inquisition, which killed millions of women, men, and children whose roots were in goddess culture. During waves of suppression over the past two thousand years, wild feminine qualities and their expressions were persecuted, repressed, and almost eliminated. In some eras there were total bans on dancing, singing, and merry (Mary) making.

Women were taught their pleasure was bad or sinful and that their multi-orgasmic potential for ecstatic erotic awakening was degenerate, unhealthy, and immoral. Female sexual desire and pleasure was classified as an illness that needed to be cured. The maternal feminine was revered; the wild feminine was condemned.

Those who liked to dance, and enjoyed celebrating themselves and wearing makeup, ornamentation, and beautiful fabrics, and who were open to pleasure were branded as whores and were shunned. The feminine was overwhelmed with a sense of shame over her true wildish, free, erotic nature. Women rejected their true selves, and tried to conform to rules that imprisoned their Shakti.

Over time, many women experienced low self-worth, depression, closed-down Wombs, repressed sexuality, difficulties in opening to orgasm, body issues, fear of shining or showing themselves, fear of embodying their true sexual power.

In today's world, many women are cut off from their true wildfire of creative potential, or have it distorted and funnelled into the masculine matrix, where we give our life force to creating for money not love. In the last era women have been encouraged to polarize in the white river, becoming too "nice" and motherly, kind and considerate to everyone else's needs, except their own—creating a whirlpool of wild rage and resentment inside.

Yet the Womb still remembers and offers a cauldron for their ecstatic reunion. It is time to reclaim our wild and holy inheritance, our wholeness.

Are you ready to open Pandora's box again?

The Redemption of Lust

Lust is a feminine word connected to the root word *lu*—feminine lunar light—from which words such as *luster, luscious, luminous,* and *illustrious* come.

It is said that when we lose our radiance, our life force, we are lackluster.

Over time this pole of being that was connected to wild feminine Shakti became demonized. The full moon became the "virgin" and the dark moon became the "whore." This also spoke to the patriarchal mythologies that connected dark-moon menstruation and desire to the fall of the feminine and original sin.

How did our sexuality, our lust, our wild Shakti come to be judged as separate from love? This energy is our *lust*er, a luminosity, filled with feminine light—Shakti radiance, a shimmering primordial sexual energy that lights us up with life.

This energy is embodied by the il*lust*rious archetype of Magdalene—the apostle of apostles, the priestess, the sacred prostitute, the "common whore," who is also the coredemptrix and feminine Christ. This energy was not only written out of the Bible, it was written out of the world, and our inner worlds and bodies.

It is the most judged, vilified, and forbidden energy—it is also the untamable life force that returns, in all its irrepressible, vital, flowing wildness to redeem us. When we integrate this Magdalene energy, it is so wild, so magnetic, so full of Shakti and feminine light, it flows us deep into the arms of love and union.

Our deliciousness, our pleasure, our wantonness, our juiciness, often lies entangled and buried in wounds. We have had to repress this energy. It gets bound up with shadow erotic charges or gets shutdown and ignored completely.

When energy is not expressed freely, it comes out sideways—in destructive, disturbing, and harmful patterns that bring us out of our true power and light. Often this wounded sideways expression is mistaken for its true nature. The Gospel of

St. Thomas says, "If you bring forth what is within you, what you bring forth will save you. If you do not bring forth what is within you, what you do not bring forth will destroy you."

We are often told that all the spiritual treasures lie in what we have labeled sanctity, holiness, the pure light—but there are many treasures, a full half of our sacred inheritance, that live on the dark side of the moon. We have to dare to enter the forbidden realms of the feminine underworld, in wanton innocence.

Lust is also intimately entwined with qualities such as pleasure and desire. It is known that we are desire beings at our core and that the quantum dark field responds to our deepest desires, and that our biology was initially wired for pleasure—until patriarchy epigenetically modified us for pain, fear, and suffering.

If a collective is conditioned to deny desire, and desire becomes absent or distorted, the people disconnect from their co-creative power. Eventually they will believe the source of that power has abandoned them, and feel powerless.

Wilhelm Reich, pioneer of somatic therapy and author of *The Function of the Orgasm,* also speaks of the vast implications of our disconnection from natural sexuality and life-enhancing pleasure instincts. He says, "Many devastating diseases can be traced to the fact that man is the sole species which does not fulfill the natural law of sexuality . . . psychic health depends on orgastic potency."[4]

The collective shadow of the intense levels of sexual abuse on this planet also remain hidden, forbidden, denied, the ghost in the closet of our lineage and psyche—distorting or shaming our natural, ecstatic sexual expressions.

In order to free this incredible feminine sexual energy, we have to claim it back.

Society shames, represses, judges, denies this dark river of the feminine energy. And often people will do anything to touch it, and everything to destroy it. As we approach our coming-of-age and menarche, we are given no support, no inspiration, no role models for what a healed and whole sexuality looks like.

We are told to hide it, repress it, control it—or be filled with guilt and shame.

Our spiritual systems are no exception; most are laced with distortion and antifeminine rules. Even most tantric models are presented through the prism of at least five thousand years of patriarchy—and are often describing loveless ritual, designed for a masculine energy body to harvest energy from a female, in order to "get" something—whether it be more vitality and longevity, or expanded states of god-consciousness. This is *using* and often goes against the deeper feminine Womb wisdom of quantum biology, and the divine creative blueprint we are born into.

Wild Womb: Dark Moon, Menstruation, the Rose of Sharon

The Dark Moon river is a time of initiation, of release, a dissolution of conditioned ways of being, to dive deeply into the great mystery of life.

A. AND S. BERTRAND

Our primal feminine essence of the red river is wild, passionate, fiercely protective, fearless, magnetic, alluring, sensual, and playful. *Wild* means not living in captivity—allowing *All* of yourself to be truly free, to be sensual, to be fearless and without any shame. This opens the primal, deep, passionate "she-wolf" at the core of your Womb, connected to the Womb of the World, web of life, and the Universal Womb that birthed all matter; it is the powerful essence of a woman that opens to the deepest wisdom, freedom, and power of Love. It's completely sexual, magnetic, and wild—without boundaries, able to overcome any obstacle. It will radically transform you, breaking you through all your fears and allowing your life force to flow with a roar and a deeply sensual shimmy.

Connecting with the wild energy that society has forbidden, shamed, and suppressed is the balm for issues of self-love; developing personal power and boundaries; overcoming sexual shame held at a cellular level; patterns of self-sabotage; or past patterns of victimhood and feelings of hopelessness or despair. It is also the gateway to opening to deep pleasure, sexually and sensually, making love with life itself. Feeling juicy and open in relationship to the masculine, and overcoming patterns of control or feeling contracted and unfeminine. It helps you magnetically attract bounty and abundance into your life, and gives you the power to follow your heart in every moment. *How much pleasure are you ready to handle?* This is the initiation the red river will flow you through. Orgasmic energy, pure pleasure, is the foundational energy of life—yet we block out and resist this cosmic gift, as our minds have been conditioned to deny and judge it.

We actually *choose* on a subconscious level to lead diminished lives; to go to jobs that aren't fulfilling and sap our energy; to live in places we don't thrive in; to settle for lackluster relationships that don't inspire us; to blame all our woes on lack of money, lack of time, lack of opportunities, lack of support. Why? Because we are terrified of the pleasure life is waiting to flow our way. Our receptive body has become shut down and withered. We find it difficult to contemplate that *good fortune* is the natural resting state of life, if we completely trust her.

Our inner "bad girl," our sexual siren, is dangling the keys to freedom with a wild glint in her eyes, taunting, "Do you dare claim me?" It is the energy of fascination and danger; we are compelled to it and repelled by it at the same time. Men even more so; they see heaven *and* hell in the red river, as it touches their deepest fears and desires to be totally overwhelmed in the feminine again, as they once were in the womb space. The dark river does not compromise or barter; she is *all* or nothing, and when you play with this archetype in yourself she will goad you toward the repressed side of yourself you have spent a lifetime avoiding.

Opening the doors to all the pleasure and sensuality we have locked away also means unleashing all the hidden grief and betrayal we feel around our sexuality. When women tap into their forbidden wild side again, mountains will move. Before that happens a huge explosion of anger needs to be danced with and embraced; and when we dare to tap into this pool of wild rage, we discover it contains our raw fire power, our wild, untamed, creative Shakti potential.

The wild womb will guide you with her radical and powerful voice. This raging red river graces us with the awesome, invincible, infinite, wild face of God herself—whom we reduce to a concept, make small, and trap inside churches and icons in our ignorance of who she truly is. During the throes of wild, multidimensional, full-body wombgasms you will peel back the curtains of the multiverse and gaze inside the profound depths of the Cosmos. Raging storms of your own intense sensations create a vortex, as the constellations of your soul are blown apart and repaginated in cosmic stellar wombs. This is what people call a religious experience and where the concept of the "fear of God" comes from, which translates as the profound fear we have when we begin to perceive just how immensely powerful Creator and creation is, and how powerful we ourselves are, if only we would choose to set the energy free and embody it.

Philosopher Edmund Burke described this experience as the sublime: where we experience the beauty of unbounded, limitless greatness as shocking and terrifying. Pleasure and pain merge. "The passion caused by the great and sublime in nature . . . is astonishment; and astonishment is that state of the soul, in which all its motions are suspended, with some degree of horror. In this case the mind is so entirely filled with its object, that it cannot entertain any other."[5]

Philosopher Emmanuel Kant identifies it as the failure of the mind to comprehend the vast magnitude of the Presence it feels surrounding it—the black Void, yin space, of Creation pouring from the Cosmic Womb.

The wild womb will shut down your thinking mind and open you to an immense new sensory way of perceiving that is beyond words and beyond understanding. You will never be the same again, and you will never be able to truly explain why.

> ### Gifts and Shadows of the Dark Feminine
>
> Ask your Womb which aspects of these gifts you embody or need to embrace and which aspects of these shadows you hold or need to heal.
>
> #### Gifts of the Dark Feminine
>
> Wild, sensual, erotic, free, pleasure, shining, confidence, beauty, celebration, sexual openness, fearless, sacred scents and oils, shamanic dress and ornamentation, self-worth, power, ecstasy, magnetism, passion, luxuriating in the body, stepping out, being seen, orgasmic living.
>
> #### Shadows of the Dark Feminine
>
> Vanity, manipulation, seduction, jealousy, envy, sabotage, superiority, judgment, attention-seeking, shallow, obsession with youth and beauty, controlling, cruel, denied low self-worth, need for validation and approval, sexual domination or manipulation, competitive.

The wild womb represents the dark-moon pole of the feminine cycle, inviting you into a deep inner journey of discovery, where you feel to withdraw from the mundane world and immerse in the deeper mysteries of life, as you allow the power of release and dissolution to renew you into a deeper octave of your self. At dark moon/menstruation, a woman's sexuality is *more* active than at ovulation—clearly showing that our sexual energy is designed for far more than procreation. At dark moon a woman is *magnetic,* she draws everything toward and into her, including her beloved. Paradoxically, as she retreats from the outer world, she becomes more alluring in the inner realms, and the man surrenders to her feminine power at this pole of the lunar cycle. She is the sexual initiator, and he is the devoted pilgrim who has come to be initiated inside the Great Womb. Research shows that women are more open to clitoral orgasm at this time of their cycle, whereas at ovulation their cervix is more sensitive. They are also more aroused by the sexual position of "being on top." This menstrual/dark-moon pole became demonized in the patriarchal era, when men became afraid of surrendering to a woman's sexual power. This is symbolized in the myth of Lilith, the wild woman who refused to lie underneath Adam and who supposedly tempted and initiated Eve with the knowledge of menstrual sexual power and wisdom.

When we close down our wild womb, our Womb-Heart also begins to close from its fullest potential, as the power of wildness supports the Heart to be free.

Womb-Heart: Ovulation, Full Moon, Lily of the Valley

Ovulation, and its energetic signature of creation, new life and fertility, is a gift of the Goddess of Amor, and a celebration of life.
A. AND S. BERTRAND

The Womb-Heart holds your deepest innocence; the tenderness of your feminine self that rests in stillness and silence at the center of your Womb.

When you open the Womb-Heart, you awaken the beautifully feminine, gentle, embracing river of love flowing through the Womb. It is the essence of a woman that is like soft petals flowering in tenderness at her center, completely still and present. It is a giving energy that bathes a woman with a soft glow, making her radiant and enchanting. It is the innocence always open to love, even in the darkest hour. Awakening this energy begins to call in your twin soul, taking you deeply into surrender and the potential for deep, loving sacred relationships and self-love. It heals anger, betrayal, and resistance toward the masculine, and helps with forgiveness toward yourself and others. It opens you to your original sexual innocence, where pleasure is felt as purity. When the heart of the Womb opens, life is experienced as "fairyland" and it brings up old grief and sadness to release, opening into deeper levels of Love. It helps identify and transmute mind programs of fear and lack of trust in life. This flow of energy helps to heal any self-judgment and perfection issues, allowing the embrace and acceptance of your innate perfection and goodness to overcome your critical inner voice. It magnetizes love in all forms: lovers, friendship, and the deep love of life itself.

Your inner "good girl" is always calling you toward love and forgiveness, soothing and softening the edges that have become hard or full of pride. When we connect with this archetype she gently guides us toward the truth of our shadows in a compassionate and embracing way. She gives our inner Lilith the trust and hope to continue opening to love, while Lilith supplies the raw power.

Gifts and Shadows of the White Feminine

Ask your Womb which aspects of these gifts you embody or need to embrace and which aspects of these shadows you hold or need to heal.

Gifts of the White Feminine

Love, tenderness, softness, vulnerability, surrender, kindness, compassion, intuition, empathy, simplicity, humility, devotion, inclusiveness, maternal instincts, loyal, supportive, honest, emotional, earthly wisdom, good listener, celebrates others, cooperative, integrity.

Shadows of the White Feminine

Afraid to speak out, afraid to shine, self-sabotaging, low self-confidence, passive-aggressive, self-sacrifice, unspoken expectations, disconnected from the body, difficulty with orgasm, shy, self-conscious, body-issues, afraid of pleasure, dowdy, people-pleaser.

The Womb-Heart is connected to the full-moon pole of the feminine cycle, inviting a woman to step out into the world and shine her creative power and sexual radiance. At full moon, a woman's sexuality is *outwardly focused*—and research shows a woman is more likely to socialize, and head out into the world to "find her man," emitting powerful hormonal fragrances. At full moon a woman is also *receptive,* she offers herself to her beloved with an invitation of sensual surrender. Paradoxically, as she opens herself sexually on the outer planes with erotic wantonness, she becomes more surrendered and serene in the inner realms, and allows herself to be penetrated deeply by the power of the pure masculine at this pole of the lunar cycle. At this time, the man is the sexual initiator and a woman surrenders herself into the wild power of the Great Womb. Research shows that women are more open to cervical orgasm at this time of their cycle, whereas at menstruation their clitoris is more sensitive. They are also more aroused by the receiving sexual positions, where they can let go into the Void of sexual pleasure and orgasm. This ovulation/full-moon pole is the archetype of femininity known as Eve, sensually beautiful, with either surrendered sexuality or fertile and maternal qualities. Full moon is a perfect time to open to motherhood, surrender to the love of a beloved, or the Divine Beloved, and to conceive and create new projects and ways of being in one's life.

In ancient times, womb priestesses would work with the lunar energies to clear their womb and yoni on a physical, emotional, and energetic level in the lead up to the full moon to restore their "energetic virginity." Then during the powerful portal of full moon, either in sacred relationship or alone in spiritual practice, they could bring pure Spirit from the Cosmic Womb into matter or the earth realm.

It is important to open into the knowing that the White River in balance is deeply sensual and sexual too, while the Dark River is also pure in her power and holds the gift of protection and the passion of love-in-action as service to the heart.

This is reflected in the archetypes of the material Virgin Mary, who was also a priestess and sexually awakened woman, and the magnetically sexual Magdalene, who was also a deeply holy and maternal feminine manifestation of the Divine.

Healing the shadows of both these rivers, embodying the gifts of both rivers, and then merging them together ignites Holy Womb Enlightenment: "The peace *and* passion that passeth all understanding."

WOMB ORACLES SHARE
Priestess of Isis Initiation

I was in a temple dressed in a red silk sari, gem-studded bracelets were placed on my ankles, and golden serpent adornments wound around both my arms. A serpent tiara went on my head with a serpent coming out of my third eye with a large sapphire gem. I started to dance in flowing movement, and I became the dance.

Then I was in a temple where Isis appeared before me and had me lie on a ceremonial stonelike table. A group of priestesses anointed me in fragrant oils. Isis said I am to be opened to the Isis priestess lineage. She showed me my right ovary that appeared to have a black snake wrapped around it. I asked where this snake came from and what I needed to do to heal it? The black snake said, "I am the shame of your ancestors and the hidden grief of rape in your lineage. I need you to feel your lost passion for life and ignite your deepest desires." Isis then pulled this long black snake out through my vagina.

She showed me my left ovary completely covered by black grime. She started cutting around it and pulled it out too, revealing my two ovaries filled with energy and light. Again, I asked this black energy what she needed and where she originated from. She said she came from the guilt and grief of my mother's lineage.

She showed me a black cord in my womb and a scene came in of being in a church saying vows of chastity; I was in a nun's body. Another scene of being repeatedly raped by soldiers and feeling great shame and humiliation, as I was a bride of Christ. A large looming male presence came in and said, "What about all your religious vows? They cannot be revoked." With Isis by my side she cut the cord in my womb and said I was now free, and together we revoked all those vows.

S.R.

SPIRAL 21

VOICE OF THE WOMB, VOICE OF WISDOM

Living the Truth of Feminine Power

There are vast realms of consciousness still undreamed of
vast ranges of experience, like the humming of unseen harps,
we know nothing of, within us.

INCOGNITA, D. H. LAWRENCE

INSIDE OUR DEEPEST, primal center lives a powerful voice that can guide and transform us. The voice of the Womb is a primordial inner wisdom keeper that cuts through the endless loops of the mind and gets down to the essence of the matter. It is direct, straight talking, and bathed in incredible insight and intuition. When we have important questions to ask, we can always tune in to this wisdom voice of our spiritual womb for guidance and for revelatory insights. This spiritual womb is an inner Divine Mother, the immanent presence of God, sometimes called Sophia or the Shekinah. By accessing this reservoir of supportive wisdom, we connect to a collective "grace field."

In ancient Sumerian, *Eme-Sal,* another translation of the root word for Salome, literally means the "voice of the yoni."* It was known that a priestess of the Womb

---

*In the Sumerian language, the pictogram for *sal* is the female vulva, and could also mean "woman, feminine." *Eme* meant "voice, tongue, or language." Thus, *Eme-Sal,* the name for one of the two common Sumerian language dialects, could be alternately translated as the voice of the vulva (*yoni* in Sanskrit), or the language of the feminine.

was also a channel for mystical truth and oracular propehcies—through the sacred stargate within her Womb, she could receive secrets of the universe.

The Womb is a gateway to God, and her voice comes from the direct flow of Source. It includes but is different from the intelligence of the Heart. It translates our deepest soul needs and desires into direct actions that will be magically supported by magnetic Womb synchronicity and will transform our lives.

It is also very protective and places self-love as the cornerstone of compassion.

Many people have become so disconnected from their primal feminine selves that they find it difficult to contact this wise inner voice. Emotional and sexual blocks, where we are repressing past traumas or feelings, serve to close the communication lines with the womb space and the Cosmic Womb she embodies.

By tuning in to the womb space every day, placing your hands on the womb and breathing deeply, dropping into the black velvet silence, and allowing any feelings, insights, or sensations to arise—we can switch the line back on and receive guidance for every aspect of our lives. Even if we first only feel boredom and agitation when we drop down into the Womb, with patience, commitment, and self-acceptance we can begin to untangle any blocks.

The Womb operates in the feminine *feeling* dimension, not the logical, linear world of reason of the current extreme masculine consciousness. Feelings are actually dimensional spaces; our feelings can create, change, and bend dimensional realities—including our own here on Earth. We have all experienced time go very slowly if we afraid or bored, or speed up when we are happy. We can sit in the same room as another person and have a completely different experience of reality based upon our own personal feeling states.

Currently many people on Earth *feel* afraid, upset, and angry underneath, so we live in a vibrational reality that is attuned to the frequency of fear. When enough people can *truly* feel magical innocence and love deep inside (not just put on a happy face and think positive thoughts) we will change the vibrational reality of the planet. It's actually a very simple principle, although it can be difficult to do—especially considering the current imbalanced state of our world.

To birth this frequency of love we have to begin to swim into our unconscious, where the lost feminine soul lives, and face and embrace what lives there. It is not something that happens through our mind—it happens through our hearts and wombs. These feelings are different from surface emotions, which are the result of our minds looping thoughts and keep us locked in mental conflict.

In Indian tradition it is called *bhava,* a preverbal, primordial feeling state that births every other emotion and event into our lives. Humanity is very disconnected from the truth and depths of these preverbal feminine feeling states, especially those from child-hood. These hidden Womb states birth our reality. If our preverbal experiences are trau-matic, we can experience earth as a nightmarish realm of suffering and separation, where fear is the core state. If our preverbal experiences were ecstatic and full of love, then we experience earth as a paradise realm of enchantment, embodiment, shimmering with joy.

When you touch upon a preverbal state you will know you have entered a lost inner world. It will feel like you have time traveled to another dimension or a lost dreamtime within yourself. It is very uncanny! And it will unlock the deepest healing possible for your soul.

When we descend into a very pure preverbal state, or clear a deeply embed-ded negative feeling, we access the black light of creative power—and from this we can begin to embody *rasa,* the juice of Shakti, the breathtaking beauty and sensual enchantment of being alive. It is a palpable, tangible feeling state that can also be transmitted to others and enfold them in a sensory dance of delight.

Saying or Feeling?

It is important to know within yourself the difference between "speaking words" and telling a story and actually feeling what lives beneath those words. The masculine truth opens the door; the feminine feeling is what lives beyond. . . .

Ask yourself today, what events have I spoken of, but not truly felt?

The body, as the feminine temple, feels and records everything. She is the keeper of truth. She holds the imprint of every memory, every feeling, every event. She is our internal Akashic Record. She bears witness to those deepest traumas and feelings that have shaped and defined our lives, especially those memories and truths the mental self is denying and disassociating from because of the pain.

❋ Mother Tongue: Cave of the Mouth Meditation

The truth held in the body can set us free when we choose to descend down into her inner cave of wisdom and listen to the voice of our lost inner knowing. This exercise helps you to connect with this liberating process and to receive important messages.

1. Bring your awareness into the cave of your mouth.
2. Feel the warm, velvet spaciousness within this sacred cave.
3. What mysteries live inside? What secret untold messages?
4. Feel how the cave of your mouth connects to your yoni and womb.

5. Allow any hidden feelings to rise up deep from your root center.

6. Bring this awareness into your tongue—feel it pulsing with the energy of truth.

7. Draw your energy back into the primordial root of your tongue.

8. How deeply is she rooted in your true expression? Allow any sensations to arise.

9. Your ancient self lives here. What message does her sacred voice bring?

This primal voice can also speak to us through synchronicity and through our dreams.

Shining Forth

Many people are hiding in a self-created cave of denial, living behind an acceptable mask that allows them to fit in and survive in the world. They are afraid to be truly *seen,* to energetically *shine*—to be truly intimate with others.

To shine means more than just allowing others inside to see the real you; it also means consciously bringing yourself *out,* toward others, stepping onto the open stage of life, offering your gifts, your unique voice, the sensual presence of your body, the powerful energy of your sexual life force, the wisdom of your experience, the radiance of your beauty, the essence of your soul signature.

It requires great courage, vulnerability, sensitivity, and innocence to take that first step, not knowing how you will be received, how you will be judged. To have the heart to stand in your power, whatever the outcome—to keep expressing yourself, to keep creating your visions, to trust that who you *truly* are is exactly what the world needs. To dare to shine your light, in all its shimmering glory.

Removing the False Masks That Hide Our Soul Shakti

Our Soul Shakti, or true Self, is a pristine diamond, a soft pearl, dazzling in innocence and light at our center. It has never been touched or harmed—and it has never left us, abandoned us, or separated from us. It lives deep within us, at the core of our being waiting to be reclaimed. Its infinitely loving, dazzling darkness guides us from within, always. It is our inner Divine Mother.

Through personal, ancestral, and collective wounds, epigenetic and genetic manipulation, and spiritual and religious programming, we have lost touch with perceiving our true self. Over many generations, our entire species has lost touch with living in the renewing, vital, wild, flowing, creative power of this Soul Shakti. A false world has been created, an artificial mental existence, disconnected from life. We know more about Facebook apps and iPhones than our own deep inner worlds. We have created false masks or layers that cover our light, which we have mistaken for our true self.

Once upon a time, in our childhoods, and at times of collective instability as a race, these masks were innocently taken up in the face of trauma and hurt, to protect ourselves and ensure our survival. But by keeping them in place and forgetting they were a temporary measure, we have lost touch with our true soul center, and the feeling of deep trust and safety on earth.

In Kabbalah these layers were called klipot, in Eastern traditions karma, and in Western traditions sin. But these protective layers do not need penance, forgiveness, or many lives of repentance and good deeds, purgatory, or any other distorted religious belief. They simply need to be felt, journeyed through with love and acceptance, and then let go. Like polishing a lamp. We can thank them for protecting our wounded inner child, and dissolve them into innocence again.

Often spiritual teachings called these protective layers the ego, as if humanity is naturally born with a defective, unloving aspect that has to be battled, vanquished, overcome, or separated from. But there is no such thing as an ego; there is only natural and healthy self-love, personal boundaries, primal needs, sacred desires, and the wound layers of protection and defense mechanisms that arise when these natural needs and desires have not been honored and met—by others and by the world—and we have experienced trauma, loss, or violation.

Human beings are by their very nature beautiful, pure, good, kind, and compassionate. There is no defective aspect that we need to cut out, only to grieve and heal where we have been hurt, and our soft, tender, precious innocence and wonder has not had the space to thrive. The current paradigm is not designed to hold the fullness of how beautiful, precious, and innocent we are at our core—so from conception we begin a process of shutting down.

As we birthed into a false grid where we felt alienated from our true self, so we unwittingly abandoned our own center, our Soul Shakti, which connects us to Source. We feel this loss, this disconnection, and it is the root of all our feelings of fear, anguish, despair, betrayal, separation, abandonment, unworthiness, and primal nonsafety. We long to come back to our primal power, our center, our love. In Celtic shamanism the word for lowerworld is *Annwfn*, which also means "*inner*world."[1] This journey inward is calling to us.

✹ *Respond to the Call: Take an Inward Journey*

1. Sit quietly with your hands on your Womb and breathe into this space that connects you to Divine Mother. Ask for her help to feel the repressed feelings and events that are living in your Womb.

2. If the desire is strong enough, you will connect to a deep feeling state. From this place it is not a conscious or logical understanding of what is hidden within you; it is a deep feeling awareness that opens up.

3. It can be terrifying, as it is as if you have time traveled to a feeling dimension you had been doing everything in your power to disconnect from.

4. You might begin to shake, cry, or have jaw tremors and a wild fear that begins to grip the stomach, or a churning vat of repressed anger that starts to seethe. Sit with all the feelings that arise.

5. Eventually a deep and sacred grief emerges that completely undoes all the masks you have been holding on to so tightly for so long. Or you can be gripped by wild uncontrollable laughter or orgasmic ecstasy as you release years of repression.

6. It feels like being stripped back to the very bones of your soul. It is bewildering and exhilarating.

7. Then pure Love comes pouring through, and a pristine innocence infuses your entire being with the renewal as you begin to be reborn.

Since ancient times, the feminine mysteries have provided a way to connect to these preverbal, primordial Womb feeling states through prayer, dance, sound, scent, movement, sacred sexuality, storytelling, sacred herbs, and sensual touch. By dropping into deep, pure, primordial feeling states, womb priestesses could not only contact the voice of their own Womb, they could also become an oracle for the Womb of Gaia and the Cosmic Womb, bringing through prophecy and wisdom to share with the entire community and culture they were a part of—and also creating deep holding spaces for soul retrieval for themselves and others.

In central England at a Womb site known as Creswell Crags, researchers discovered 45,000-year-old cave paintings depicting highly stylized women performing a ritual dance—these ritual dances were often oracular in nature.

Even as late as 300 CE the womb priestesses of Delphi were sought after by the leaders and rulers of Greece for prophecy and advice, and no policy could be implemented without first consulting the Womb voice of these wise women. In Jewish cultures, the wise women prophets were called the Bath Kol, literally meaning "daughters of the voice," those who could channel and speak the primordial feminine intelligence of the Womb of Gaia and the Cosmic Womb.

You too are an oracle, should you choose to hear this inner voice. You are a daughter of the Divine Mother's voice. Remember, this wisdom and this gift live with you.

WOMB ORACLES SHARE
The Essence of Womb Healing

I felt called out into the night, into the garden; the full moon was shining brightly as wisps of mysterious clouds slowly parted and floated off. There was a ring around the moon, a pale reddish glow out away from the moon, shown by the presence of the clouds as they drifted away. The moon felt magnetic and mysterious and nourishing, like an ancient portal. I stood in the dark, my feet on the grass with the bowl cupped in my hands, feeling transfixed. Then a large brilliant ruby, bloodred and vibrant, appeared in the essence bowl. And three crone witches, wise women healers, gathered round as if it was a mystical steaming cauldron, stirring their magic and herbs and ancient wisdom into the brew. Their faces glowed as if there was a fire in the darkness, and I felt the wisdom of ages. I felt and saw the tissues of women's Wombs, healthy and nourished and vital . . . and the phases all in healthy natural process—the shedding and flow of rich blood, a fertile space creating a secure Womb nest for a baby, ovaries, and yoni and in prime cellular health. All returning to original condition from whatever blockages or ailments had been present. I felt richness and vitality coming from these visions . . . the phrase "blooming with health" comes to mind to describe it. But there was a powerful sensual mysterious quality too . . . the Womb's powers, the energy of her magical tissues and blood. The crones know in their bones, and twinkling eyes, and magical bony fingers, all about what it truly means to be in a woman's body.

This wisdom is very much about supporting the physical body womb (the whole reproductive system). But knowing that so many ailments come from emotional causes, I asked how does this really help people who have womb conditions? It helps the body womb feel nourished so she can release, and it helps the Womb "remember" and feel her true state of health so she can find it again. And in women who are healthy or already recovered from past illness, it helps support and nourish the continuous process of health and healing and living, just like herbs, bodywork, yoni steaming, baths, and nurturing beauty rituals.

H.S.

Fall of Egypt: Bearing Witness

As I descended into my Womb I got an image of a place where the area was lush and green, where the houses were quite small. I saw a big castle in the distance. People were running around—children, adults. It was total chaos. I was between eighteen and twenty years old at the time, and I believe it was 4,355 years ago in eastern Egypt. I looked up into the sky and after a little while I started to sense something. I got a feeling of stones, hard and cold energy. They were there to shut us down, to kill the living part of us, and to steal our fire. I felt totally powerless. There was nothing I could do! Then I understood what I was doing in this place. I was collecting future images, to be able to "listen in." I was here as a womb oracle, as a witness.

N.H.

SPIRAL 22

DARK SIDE OF THE WOMB

The Trickster, Guardian of Power

Sacred Omen,
Calls me to the edge
Where an antler
And a feather
Fall.
A Buck roams
And rises with her scent,
Antlers scrape against trees
In search of Her.
A crow caws
On the same path
Her shadow answers back
Guardian of the Void.

A.C.

THERE IS ALWAYS a guardian who stands at the entrance of our deepest initiations in Womb Awakening. When we deeply desire to know the truth about our sexual power, and have demonstrated enough naivety to still be tripped up by our delusions, it is time to meet our good friend, the Trickster, guardian of the Womb. Trickster is amoral, and neither malevolent or benevolent. He teaches us through reaching into our own sexual wounds and seducing us to reveal them.

Through his mystery Trickster captures a woman's soul with his cosmological supernatural dance. In a wild sensuous epiphany, he confronts the forbidden psyche of the woman with his raw masculine essence that is alluring and sexually potent, and ignites her erotic imagination. This side of her self is the wild, untamed, unbridled, awesome, terrifying, raw creative power of universal Shakti. For the woman this is the seed of all her deepest inner desires, which are the root of her power, and without which she can do nothing. Under his guidance she gives an expression that shatters paradigms, emanating a sexual psychic radiance that goes beyond the speed of light and penetrates the depths of the universal psyche, and changes the webbed fabric of consciousness itself.[1]

In essence, through Trickster's forbidden and wildly erotic call to power, the woman gives birth to a new creation. But first she must free herself of her limitations, and step into true conscious relationship with this force within her, rather than birth through her wounded, unconscious expressions. She becomes the force for redemption, rather than part of the trick. In doing so she redeems the Trickster who now becomes the loving consort of the Great Mother, rather than the tempter. He is the one who remembers the taste of true feminine power, and in desiring to unite with her, he is destroyed and rebirthed by this force; as only the full feminine power can take him back home through the Cosmic Womb.

But first, he may trick you into revealing your power—or the ways you lost it.

Shadow Dancing

Trickster, through his mischievous games, highlights our shadow—sometimes in a subtle way, sometimes in a shocking way. He brings us the gift of *nous*, instinctive knowing that comes from deep within. His gift is usually delivered by leading us on a merry dance far away from our wise inner voice, into the lands of self-betrayal. The learning is to claim our truth back after wising up to the trick.

The message Trickster delivers is, "Never allow your compassion to get in the way of your discernment"[2] Or as Yeshua put this, "Be as wise as serpents and as gentle as doves." Often what we mistake for love and compassion is actually a pattern of powerlessness, inherited from our ancestry, which we keep repeating.

True love can bloom only from the roots of our personal power and knowing.

As a woman opens her sexual energy, she will often find Trickster lurking nearby, charming and confident, handsome in his black top hat and cape. Because you are "special," he will offer you his "assistance," if you let him in.

The Trickster appears charismatic, alive, powerful, decisive, and sexually or spiritually potent. Above all he is seductive. He knows you better than you know yourself—your pain, your needs, your secret fantasies and desires. He is the master shape-shifter, becoming anything you desperately need him to be. Your instincts

Fig. 22.1. Trickster, guardian of the Womb

(Illustration by Natvienna Hanell)

whisper that there are shadows of darkness around this character. But you choose to ignore it. It is as if your wounds have a mind of their own.

You may have met someone embodying this energy in your journey. Using your Womb nous, always be wise and canny to the "tricks up his sleeve," while learning from the lessons he brings, and knowing that your wild power is calling.

The power of the Womb is so immense and has been so misused by those with wounded or selfish motivations that her power will only be bestowed to those who have walked into the eye of the storm and the darkness held there, to heal.

Universal Archetype

This archetype of the Trickster, or the shadow teacher, is found throughout the world in many sacred traditions and teachings; he or she is the dark side that belongs to us, and reflects us, and is always calling to us to embrace its lessons.

In ancient shamanist traditions Trickster was known as a keeper of the thresholds, especially our sexual initiations such as menarche (our first menstruation), coming-of-age for men, and the moment we first consciously perceive ourselves as sexual beings and begin to work with our sexual power. In Bushman groups the Trickster-creator god governed puberty initiation.[3]

In the Hindu Tattwa Shuddhi tradition there is a character called Papa Purusha who represents the darkest aspects of our identity, which we rarely, if ever confront directly. He symbolizes the root of our shame, jealousy, pain, and the self-inflicted suffering we unconsciously expose ourselves too. Papa Purusha is often connected with the primordial traditions of Shakti, and the ways that we have fallen from the pure frequency of sexual energy into wounded exchanges.

In Native American traditions, Trickster is Heyoka, or coyote; he is a deceiver, a rascal, a mischievous force of opposition who teaches us, but not in the way we'd like. In Lakota mythology he is also a spirit of thunder and lightning, a truth giver, bringing moments of striking transformation and learning, like a thunderbolt. Black Elk, heyoka medicine man of the Oglala Sioux, describes this:

> This comes with terror like a thunderstorm; but when the storm of vision has passed, the world is greener and happier; for wherever the truth of vision comes upon the world, it is like a rain. Truth comes into this world with two faces. One is sad with suffering, and the other laughs; but it is the same face, laughing or weeping . . . as lightning illuminates the dark, for it is the power of lightning that heyokas have.[4]

In Celtic shamanism, Gwyddion—the light bringer—is an impeccable, charismatic, and charming sexual shaman who will invite you to the shadow waltz, and lead you on a merry dance as you explore the source of your power. Like Trickster gods in other traditions, he is deeply connected to sexual rites of passage, especially at puberty. His sister is Arianrhod, goddess of the "silver wheel" of lunar cycles, fertility, and feminine power, famous for her spinning "Womb castle."

In the book *Ecstatic Healing,* an African Yoruba priestess describes her native Trickster god, Exú, this way:

Exú destroys, seduces, procreates. He is the drive, a transcender of rules in order to create. Exú is the initiator. He is primordial. He is sexuality. And he ensures fertility. His perverted tricks bring his characteristics close to the Western concept of the Devil, but this is a misinterpretation. Exú and Satan are two different entities. He loves to test the character of mortals . . . he is the spirit of temptation. As a Divine Trickster Exú is not evil. As prince of the crossroads, he has the power to keep us from succeeding. Exú humbles us through his trickery regarding our petty truths. He likes to have fun. He fears nothing, and there is no road he will not travel. He is perceived as dangerous and volatile, but not evil. He can be invoked as a protection from evil.[5]

In Western traditions the Trickster is often known as Archangel Lucifer—rebel, tempter, and light bringer. He represents a collective archetype of "pride before a fall" and the desire for power and knowledge, or the need to own the power of others. His light also shows where we are a follower, easily giving our power away. If we push this archetype away, or denounce it, we cannot reclaim our own power or see the truth of our own wounded patterns around power.

Island Woman, a Native American arendiwanen (spirit keeper) of the Iroquois tribe, describes the split in the wholeness of our Shakti energy this way:

Power can be used either way. You have to choose. The Dark Twin is a tempter, coming on to you like an elk in rutting season, telling you that you'll be the one everyone will fear and admire. And he'll touch something inside you, because there is nobody human who doesn't have something of the dark side within him or her. Try to deny that, and you'll find yourself fighting half of the universe—and the dark side may swallow you while you are shouting that you are all about the light.[6]

Bringing this energy within ourselves back to love also awakens our primal Shakti and allows our wild feminine flow to merge with our Heart-Womb.

Sexual energy, Womb Shakti is pure power; it is the raw life force of Creation. As we begin to awaken this cosmic creative power within, we must face our wounds around power and pride and powerlessness and worthlessness.

The Anti-Soulmate

We often meet Trickster in the Womb Awakening journey, either in the dreamtime realms or in a person (male or female) who this energy is working through. He is known as a guardian of Womb work, not in a strictly benevolent sense, but as a teacher of the feminine shadow—and our relationship with our sexual power and sovereignty. He is a dangerous and powerful teacher.

He works through both sides of the shadow: powerlessness, sexual shutdown, shame, fear, low self-esteem *and* arrogance, power-over, manipulation, lack of sexual discernment, vanity, wanting to be admired and adored for our sexuality and beauty. His presence can be either primally terrifying or magnetically sexual and alluring, depending on how he is enjoying playing with your shadow. Many people mistake this energy for love. His greatest trick is to make us long for him or feel we love him, or that he loves and protects us. Every moment we are not owning our sexual power, standing in true self-love or truly open to love, we invite him in for the games to begin, so our shadow can be seen and reclaimed.

Often on the Womb Awakening journey a woman meets her anti-soulmate, the person who resonates perfectly with her darkest, denied wounds—and this meeting of mutual wounds can be so magnetic and compelling, so sexually, erotically, and spiritually charged it will feel like true love, when in fact it is the Trickster at play, giving a powerful, and often painful, initiation into her shadow. But it is also a powerful invitation to claim the power of the wild womb back.

Handled well, this can be a catalyst for deep evolution: reclaiming personal power and bringing it back to love. If not, it can be terribly destructive process.

Trickster illuminates the shadow of our separation from our pure (sexual) power and true self-love, and he swirls in a constellation of feelings brought up from that separation. His particular area of expertise is to work with the shadow of the "forbidden feminine" and our "erotic imprint"—our deep desire and longing to embody pure, wild, magnetic, wanton, inviting, surrendered sexuality; and all the ways we deny, shame, repress or judge that; or flaunt, manipulate, and seduce; or use it as a currency to barter for attention, admiration, safety.

Trickster is utterly cunning and has many tricks up his sleeve, and is wise to the ways of Creation, but the more we dive into these unchartered and feared waters to explore and embody our deep power, our "menstrual" sexuality, our wildness and holy wantonness, and our primal sexual magnetism, the less hold he has over us. We begin to birth the true, awesome, creative force that is the power of Love, a flowing raw power straight from the Source of Love.

As an archetype and guide, he helps us see where we *do not* truly love ourselves, or embody our power and wild sexual birthright. His trick is to promise us a lure of something we feel we lack and want, which is inside us all along and already belongs to us. He can also trick us into the realms of vanity and the substitution of being loved with that of being admired, and feeding off that energy and attention. We long for this archetype, or become influenced by it, as a reflection of where we are not yet in our true authentic power. It is also a huge collective archetype birthed through the collective feminine's loss of authentic sexual power, and our fragmentation into false, manipulative sexual power or exploited sexuality or low self-esteem and sexual shutdown and fear.

The Trickster archetype can play through the feminine in the form of the manipulative seductress who wants, and demands to be "the fairest of them all," and the wounded emotion of jealousy birthed from fear and low self-esteem. Island Woman says:

> Since I became a woman of power I've had to fight sorcery in many guises. Jealous rage was behind the worst attacks. There are people like that: if they can't do better than you, they are going to try and bring you down. If you let jealousy get away from you, it goes round like a hissing serpent, and evil spirit.[7]

We all have these feelings inside us, which are reflected to us by the Trickster.

Jealousy is one of our greatest gifts and teachers if we embrace it. By journeying down the thread of emotion, we will discover our most wounded place that feels unsafe, unworthy, afraid, ugly, unlovable, and unnoticed. We can bring the balm of self-love to heal this separated fragment of our soul that is trapped in pain.

It will also reveal what we desire the most—and what we are truly seeking.

By innocently exploring and lovingly holding hands with the attention-seeking, vain, power-craving seductress side of the feminine, who needs to find an artificial power base over both men and women, we often begin to connect with a very lost little girl or teenager who felt unloved, unnoticed, not safe to be herself, frightened of being left alone and powerless. And we can bring her back home to love, so she can mature into a truly loving, authentic sexually empowered woman who has walked through these shadows with compassion.

❃ Befriending the Hissing Snake of Jealousy

Every time you feel the sting of jealousy arise, it is an invitation to love yourself more, just as you are, without the need to change anything. True self-love is not created through tricks or strategies to feel good about yourself, but by letting go of the need to feel good about yourself, and loving yourself exactly as you are.

1. Close your eyes, place your hands on your Womb and breathe deeply, recalling the last time you felt jealous of someone or something.
2. Allow yourself to open your heart to this feeling of jealousy, rather than judging it and trying to push it away. Allow yourself to feel your inner child who is afraid she is not worthy of love—and ask her what self-love she needs from you now.
3. Allow yourself to feel what you desire, what you feel is lacking. You will discover this jewel also lives within you.

The Cauldron of Sexual Wounds

The deepest wounds of the feminine are held sexually, so when we explore the gateways of the yoni much arises—those times we have been disempowered, violated, or abused subtly, psychically, or physically. How our pleasure, innocence, wildness is repressed and trapped, how we have betrayed ourselves, not loved ourselves. These are often the most difficult and confusing wounds to feel and embrace. They take us right back into the mud of our shadow, things we thought we had left behind a long time ago, but are waiting patiently for us to reclaim.

In this cauldron of sexual wounds it is wise to be aware of and canny to the enticing or terrifying presence of the Trickster. The film *Bram Stoker's Dracula,* starring Gary Oldman is a powerful evocation of the Trickster energy and archetype. Dracula is portrayed as a seductive, sexually magnetic Trickster—both terrifying and alluring at the same time (a common polarity experienced inside the subconscious mind). He represents Mina's magnetic, wild sexuality (as does her shadow sister, Lucy), which she has become separated from in "civilized" Victorian society. This separation allows her to be deceived and allured by the Trickster energy, and to not be fully present and bonded with her beloved husband-to-be. This attraction to the Trickster/Dracula can also be seen as an ancestral ache and longing inside for her own inner "beast/ erotic creature," a projection of her own wild sexuality, and the parts of her she has killed off to fit in with society.

The Trickster can also embody through the masculine shadow in men—even those men who are religious and spiritual—showing them where their own sexual shadows are not yet resolved. In the denial of their wounds with the feminine, the Trickster is mischievously snorting with glee, feeding them a mixture of amazing wisdom and astounding lies, even granting them powerful healing skills, and then allowing their wounded inner inquisitor to run wild and reinforce the feminine/masculine wounds. The Trickster attaches himself to the male wounds of powerlessness and feelings of weakness, especially around unresolved issues in the Womb and childhood, and with their mother.

Men often find it excruciatingly painful to dive into their feelings of powerlessness, especially in relation to the feminine, and the weakness they feel in their deep sexual longing and desire to connect with a woman, and her Womb. The Trickster either plays with the masculine by repressing these desires, and the grief they bring up—leading to the need to control and condemn female sexuality or avoid connection with it; or by making these desires all consuming and obsessive—leading to the need to have sexual power over women, to become the dominator, the lord, the sexual or spiritual master.

This aspect of the Trickster is a great teacher for both sexes, as to where we are still plugged into patriarchal God and spiritual programs to either be "saved" or to "save" someone else, or to control or be controlled, and our secret desire to be a master or a slave, or to dominate or to submit. He often looms large in sexual circles, such as tantra, where sexual power is opened without pure love. When we learn, the Trickster gives us a wink and moves on to his next victim.

This energy wants and courts our attention, our needy love and desire for him, and feeds off the exchange. He seduces us with lures and promises of false power or the safety of success and worldly highs—he brokers the deal with the devil. In return he offers us the seemingly dazzling prizes of the false world matrix—beauty, admiration, fame, success, glamour, lust, power, glory, money, influence (even spiritual), artistic genius, healing power. Making us a black magician or sorceress of artificial power and beauty, which separates us from others.

We project all our self-betrayals and wounded desires onto Trickster, when truly they are to be found within ourselves. Owning them sets us free from the deal. In the same way, we project our sexual power as his, when it belongs to us. Feelings of low self-worth, fear, and childhood wounds unwittingly invite this energy in to dance with our shadows—especially when these wounds are denied, hidden, and swept under the carpet. Those who have been sexually, emotionally, or psychologically abused are particularly vulnerable. We cannot push this energy away or ignore it; we can only consciously work with it, healing our own wounds, so that we restore our sense of innocence and safety in life.

Our own wild power is stalking us, and the more we embody this primal life force the more we can magnetize and "Wombifest" true love into our lives.

The Trickster is an ally, when we dare to make him so.

WOMB ORACLES SHARE
Erotic Master of Illusion

The Trickster has a familiar face; I know him well. He is dangerous, magnetic, alluring, and erotic. This intense desire and longing turns me upside down. There was no place to hide, as he took in my nakedness and forbidden flow. With his top hat, coattails, and walking stick, he seduced me out of myself to meet my shadow. We met in our erotically charged mutual woundedness. He was a master of illusion and outer seduction, he stole my purse and took my power.

Could I open my Womb eye to see the truth of the shadow side of my wild sexuality to reclaim my power? When I went down into my Womb eye to see the truth, I saw a glowing red ruby jewel pulsing and vibrating. The jewel exploded into a red dragon woman who started dancing wildly and seductively with the Trickster in his black top hat, long coattails, and walking stick. Suddenly the red dragon woman turned into Kali, who danced more wildly and fiercely. She took the Trickster's walking stick and passionately pinned him to the ground. He turned into Shiva, the Divine Trickster who took Kali's Shakti. In her wild abandon Kali stood on his chest, her foot on his heart, he was feeding off her Shakti. She cut off the supply and took her Shakti back: Black One, Creation before Light, beyond time.

Dark Priest of Power: Master/Slave

I started out as the priest and then became the woman slave. As the priest, I felt the lust for power and control and the surge of energy through my body I got from my women. I treated my women tenderly, but forcefully too. Making them beg for me. Then I became that woman, enslaved to this master. And it was like I had been energetically attuned to him, so that he truly owned me, body and mind. It was as if he was my personal drug supply. . . . I was nothing without him. My thoughts were of him, my longing was for him. Life was all about the high of the sexual stimulation . . . or waiting for the next time, just like an addict. Wanting nothing more than for him to ravish my body. There was a feeling of absolutely loving and craving being "forced" into ecstasy this way. Afterward, I started to come down from the high into emptiness, depression, and hollowness of being. . . .

Scrying in Obsidion

I've met a man in the physical who embodies these qualities. I am not physically attracted to him although there is a tremendous pull that scares and attracts me at the same time. He is a very intense, Scorpio type! Being in contact with him is like scrying in obsidian! It reflects my shadows—he has been an amazing catalyst for me. The pull decreases as I reclaim my power and learn to love myself fully.

CYCLE 5

GRAIL WOMB
SHAMANISM AND
SACRED SOUL-MATE
UNION

SPIRAL 23

THE GRAIL LINEAGE OF LOVE

Traditions of Sacred Union

Dearly beloved!
Let us go toward Union.
And if we find the road of separation,
We will destroy separation.
Let us go hand in hand.
Let us enter the presence of Truth . . .
And imprint its seal upon our union, Forever.

RUMI

OUR MYTHS ARE MORE THAN make-believe; they are magical doorways into truth and frequencies of consciousness, which unfold their thousand petals of wisdom as we penetrate their mysteries with the eyes of our innocent enquiry. Grail lore sits as the ruby jewel on the throne of our lost mythology.

Womb Consciousness is the feminine frequency of God, encoded as the sleeping beauty held prisoner in the tower of patriarchy; the Divine Lady calling for the devotion of pure love, leading fallen masculine consciousness on a pilgrimage home, testing his love to distill his pure essence, bestowing upon him the radiance of her grace. Humanity is longing to reach the Womb Grail Castle, to break the devastating spell of separation, which has kept them apart for so long.

In the Grail lineage, this pilgrimage of love is the highest calling of a human soul.

It is told of, spoken of, and sung about by all the great bards, troubadours, poets, storytellers, and musicians. It is the call toward union, meeting the "other" in love. This emphasis on *relational* human love as the portal to transcendent Divine Love is the signature of the Christ path that emerged from the union of Jesus and Magdalene as Divine lovers who experienced the cosmic Yab-Yum.

The energy of Magdalene was more than a consort or wife; the Magdalene Womb was the embodiment of the living feminine light, the Holy Grail, Cosmic Mother. It was known that there was a lunar left-hand path of Christianity, with a feminine Christ at its helm, escorting her consort into the well of initiation.

For men, this was a journey to restore the sanctity of the heart and the feminine principle in their own being, serving only love. In a woman it was practices to restore her energetic virginity—also known as original innocence—cleansing her Womb of any feelings, experiences, patterns, or beliefs disharmonious with love.

When this harmonic resonance of Holy Shakti occurs, a woman emits a perfect note of sexual frequency—the sound of the spheres. Like music, it enchants, transports, and transforms. It holds the signature of God, the sound of creation. The awakening of the womb into ecstatic innocence plays celestial music across all realms. It births higher states of consciousness and new paradigms of love into being. This ecstatic Shakti creates profound and tangible dimensional shifts in collective consciousness.

This involved women and men harmonizing the waves of their solar and lunar rhythms together, in sacred union. Opening their hearts and bodies to true love, following the cycles of the womb and moon, and honoring the sacred portals of ovulation and menstruation, and communing with earth and Cosmic Womb.

The radical choice to love with a wild totality comes from an ecstatic outrageous openness within us that is on fire with a bold incandescence and raw with the desire to merge and to feel ourselves again as deeply sexual, open, and magnetic beings.

This is an initiatory path of allowing the womb to be a virginal space to transmute all past hurts and harm from our personal, ancestral, and collective experiences. To no longer live from the old scripts of blame, protection, and fear that shut us down. To understand that if the split between man and woman is to heal, then we have to trust in the redemptive power of our own sexual power and love. We invoke Divine Eros to immolate our sexual wounds in love's transformative fire.

In this energy field we become the "sacred hor" who receives and redeems all. We become the lady of the lake and the feminine Christ, priestess of the fountain.

Jesus as a Lunar Lover

In the Jewish tradition that Yeshua (Jesus) was born into, a man was not considered complete or mature until he had pair bonded with a woman. Only his bride could anoint him into his kingship and spiritual mission. The woman initiated the man. This is reflected in the Vedic Indian teachings recorded in the Satapatha, which state: "Therefore as long as he does not find a wife, so long he is not born; for so long he is not complete. But in finding a wife he is born, for then he becomes complete."[1] It was known that all life is *relational* and that in the union of two souls ecstasy was birthed. Sacred sexual union with a woman was the root of being "born again," so man could experience a second birth and resurrection.

In Kabbalistic tradition, Rabbi Levi says, "The upper waters are male; the lower, female. The former cry to the latter, 'Receive us! You are creatures of the blessed Holy One and we are His messengers.' They immediately receive them, as is written: *Let the earth open* (Isaiah 45:8)—like a female opening to a male."[2]

Our biology reflects this deep knowing, and the very fabric of our bodies, brains, and psyches are actually created and crafted to thrive and open through bonding. This does not just include babies and children, but holds true for adults too.

By making sacred relationship the Womb of Love where a couple could not only birth a new being or new creations, but also enter the "gateway of heaven" together, the true Christ teachings made the need for an external authority or priest redundant; Love was the intermediary, sexual union was the church.

The sacred union teachings that were embodied by Yeshua and Magdalene, and many male-female Love pods who followed in their path, were persecuted and stamped out by the founding fathers of Christianity—and the way of love, the feminine mysteries, and feminine-masculine union was branded a heresy.

Yet despite the assaults against the true church of love, it continued on, for the seeds of love are fertile and perspicuous, and they bloomed out into the Grail lineage—which incorporated ideas and aspects from Celtic, Egyptian, Gnostic, and Kabbalistic thought—and sought to rebirth the shamanic womb religion.

The Grail legacy is the enchanting whisper of the Old Ways, of the ancient womb worship that enveloped all of Europe many thousands of years ago. In the past thousand years it has undergone major reemergences, including the courtly love movement in France in the eleventh to thirteenth centuries, the Italian Renaissance in the fourteenth to sixteenth centuries, and the the Pre-Raphaelite movement in England in the late eighteenth century and early nineteenth century, as the poetic Holy Spirit of the bards and troubadours rebirthed in a community of male and female artists and writers.

Legends of Jesus and Magdalene have often been entwined in lore and legend with the Celtic mystery teachings of the priestesses of Avalon and the Druids. It is said that St. Bride, avatar of the Celtic Mother Goddess Brighid, was lifted up from the holy isle of Iona by angels and was carried across the sea to attend Jesus's birth as his midwife. Legends also say that Jesus and Magdalene visited the Celtic lands as part of their travels, and so these two threads merge into one.

Yeshua is a Merlin, a Grail king, from a long line of kings—a healer, magi, leader, hero, a man of destiny. *Merlin* means "from the Mer line." The Mer line is the lineage of the Marys, of Mari—the Great Goddess worshipped by the Cathars—who were also known as weavers, another code word for the Great Womb. It follows just as *mer*maid denotes a womb priestess, a Magdalene, "maidens of Mary," of the sea, the great primordial ocean of the Void, the Great Womb that births everything into being. (See fig. 23.1 on the following page.)

In ancient Sumeria the word *mar* meant both "sea" and "womb,"[3] and over time it developed into a revered titular name, Mary, which denoted feminine power.

Interestingly, in the Druid language *Mor,* from the same word root as *Mer,* also means "death" or "great ocean," again referring to the great primordial oceans of the Womb, where we are birthed and dissolved. The mysteries of life and death.

Yeshua is a man of love, *a lunar lover,* in union and at one with the feminine. He was often known as the healing moon man. His archetype is one of the purified lunar masculine principle, symbolized by the unicorn—the horned one. This rebirthed masculine fulfils the promise of the Grail legacy to return to the harmony of sacred union consciousness, embodying the blueprint of Creation.

The shamanic three days in the Womb of the Mother led to a reawakening of primordial consciousness, and the knowing that "I and the Mother are One."

Spinning Tower of Arianrhod

Returning to the Womb to be born again is a huge theme: in Celtic shamanism there is a tradition of being "interred" in the Cosmic Womb to become "twice born." This journey into the Cosmic Womb can be felt as an inner death; falling into the abyss, the Void, with no known way to come back out. Surrendering into this perceived individual death and trusting the process opens the heart and Womb back to

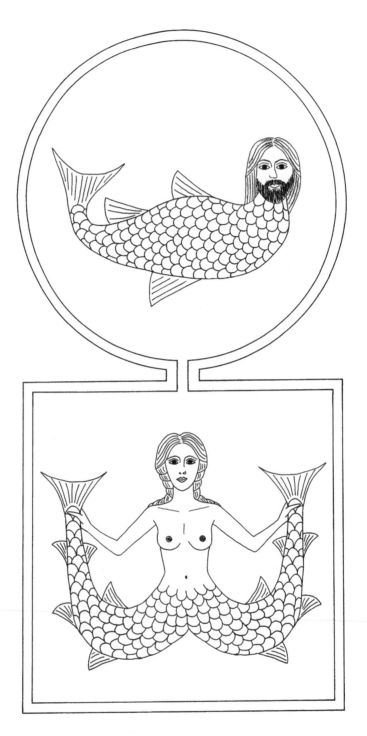

Fig. 23.1. Mer-couple

(Illustration by Heather Skye)

the great web of life. The initiation comes from emerging at the otherside, forever changed, neither here nor there but fully present, able to enjoy and give the wisdom, gifts, and fruits of all worlds, while fully grounded and born back into this world, middleworld, as an innocent, sensual, wise being.

In Celtic lore this journey into the Cosmic Womb is encoded in the story of Arianrhod and her spinning tower. Arianrhod is the Celtic Magdalene, "the tower, the great weaver, the magical doorway." She is the embodiment of the Great Womb, the lunar pathways that lead us back into the wilds of the feminine dimension, the cerebellum, which is out of time and completely out of our control—where we meet all our personal and collective angels and demons, and receive gifts and treasures from both terror and ecstasy. Her Holy Womb is where the masculine meets his destiny and is reborn into his spiritual powers.

"Arianrhod's tower is also called Caer Sidi, the Glass Castle or Spiral Tower and is traditionally the place wherein lore keepers serve their apprenticeship. The terms are strict and it is thought of as an imprisonment. Taliesin says he spent three periods in the prison of Arianrhod, learning his trade as seer and poet—the art of seeing clearly (clairvoyance) and the art of telling well so his audience could learn too (poetry); two basic skills for the shaman."[4]

The Glass Castle is also known as the Grail Castle, the pilgrimage place of the Grail knights, troubadours, Merlins, and bards, like Taliesin, who enter within the Grail Gates of her spinning, spiral tower to receive their initiation and rebirth. This is the hero's journey, to make the pilgrimage into the Womb. King Solomon; Yeshua, descendent of King David; and King Arthur also walked this labyrinth Womb path and experienced the shamanic internment, and symbolic rebirth or resurrection through the Divine Feminine—at-one-ment with the Great Mother.

The heroine's journey is to not only enter the Grail Castle, but to *become* the Grail Castle; to become both the eternal pilgrim and also the sacred site that the knights and bards make pilgrimage to, to receive their baptism; to become a Magdalene, a magical doorway or womb portal for others.

This is the Way of the Grail, the path of love. It requires great courage and complete surrender to enter the Cauldron of Poesy, the Great Womb, which is brimming with the fires of Holy Spirit, and will grant the poetry of divine inspiration to those who passionately devote their entire life and being to the union of Love—of which the union of the soul mates is the highest sacrament.

Spirit Keepers of the Womb Mysteries

Make me thy lyre, even as the forest is . . .
Be through my lips to unawakened Earth
The trumpet of a prophecy!

PERCY BYSSHE SHELLEY

To tell the tale my heart must feel;
Love, Love alone, my lyre shall claim,
In songs of bliss and sighs of flame.

LORD BYRON

Storytelling, accompanied by harp and lyre, created a shamanic portal into the other-world of the feminine dimension for enraptured listeners, and was not only an experiential journey but also an encoding of lost wisdom. It also reflected the *knowing* that the feminine dimension was *outside of linear time,* and many strands of time and story could be woven together and unpicked by the Divine Creatrix—who was the greatest storyteller and musician of all.

As the Grail returns, the enchanting, feminine soul song of the harp and lyre also returns to awaken the lands. This enchanted "soul flight" medicine was used by the swan priestesses of Isis, the great feminine mystery schools, the bards and troubadours, the Druidesses, and the magical Celtic Womb Awenydd, the spirit keepers of the feminine mysteries. Either in sound-healing meditation or shamanic sound and dance, the enchanted sounds of the harp and lyre were used to enrapture people into direct gnosis, to birth oracular visions, to bring harmonic resonance into the body and psyche, for sexual union, and to bathe initiates in the direct communion with the Source of Love, whose primordial love song vibrates through every cell of existence when we tune back in.

The prophetic and healing power of the lyre was a central jewel of the lost womb religion across many cultures—from Sumer, Assyria, and Palestine to Greece, France, Great Britain, and beyond. Lyres were a shamanic magic doorway.

Often real-life ancient oracular priestesses were demoted to myth or legend as the Great Womb religion, and the feminine wisdom it held was demonized and destroyed. Grail maidens and mermaids were from the lineage of swan priestesses who used lyre, harp, song, sound, and toning to technique create rapturous states of altered consciousness—and to sing the soul back home to the deep Womb waters of the feminine psyche. Siren priestesses were also famous for sound healing, as were the Cathars who were linked with the troubadours.

The Celtic bards also used lyre in their magical practices to convey storytelling lore and hidden wisdom and revelation. The legends of Merlin (a womb shaman) were birthed from the ancient Grail wisdom and the ancient womb religion.

Swan Lyre: Songlines of Sacred Union

Swans and doves were spirit birds associated with the Goddess—as these birds mated for life. The swan song was considered a sound frequency of sacred union birthed from the priestess arts that could travel across the worlds to birth, heal, and unify or to return to Source.

At Knossos on Crete a small alabaster lyre is decorated with a swan's head on each arm of the instrument. Slightly later, across the Aegean in the fourteenth century BCE, lyres have S-shaped arms and are frequently decorated with water birds. Minoan seals show stylized bird lyres, and vases from seventh-century Smyrna show a long-necked bird above a lyre.

Depictions of religious rites show a female priestess in ceremonial dress standing on a sphinx, wearing a tall headdress bearing a large swan head. In a sculptural group from Bogazkoy in Turkey, a Goddess is flanked by an attendant playing a bird-headed lyre. In the sanctuary of Artemis at Ephesus excavated ivory swan heads are thought to belong to lyres.

Soulful sound healing also affects us at a cellular level, bringing dis-ease and dis-harmony back into resonance, bringing our bodies and souls back in tune.

The ancients knew the truth of this healing and awakening power, which had the ability to bring us back into the symphony of the Song of the Cosmos.

"The sky and its stars make music in you" is inscribed at the Dendera temple in Egypt.

Whispers of this great shamanic musical tradition are even retained in the Bible at 1 Samuel 10:5–6, which describes the use of lyre in prophecy: "You will meet a group of prophets coming down from the high place with harp, tambourine, flute, and a lyre before them, and they will be prophesying. Then the [Holy Spirit] will come upon you mightily, and you shall prophesy with them and be changed."

In the Hebrew tradition the Bath Kol (the daughters of the voice) was a heavenly or Divine voice associated with receiving prophecy. Its feminine quality is similar to that of the Shekinah (Divine Presence) and Ruach HaKodesh (Holy Spirit). The voice of the Bath Kol was also said to emanate directly from the holy of holies—symbolically the sacred center of the temple, and literally the Womb.

The Pythian womb priestesses of Delphi also used lyre to prophesize and to raise the dragon energies of Gaia, before their lyres were stolen and used by the male gods. And Aphrodite played lyre and offered enchanting songs and poetry of love that brought people into her sacred grove (symbolizing her Womb).

In other ancient Greek records, the seven-stringed lyre is presented as a Muse in the Homeric hymn to Hermes.

In the Harmony of the Spheres, as outlined by the Pythagorean tradition, the lyre was seen as a microcosm of a universal harmony, of which the human body and soul were manifested echoes. Legends say Orpheus used his lyre to charm animals, vegetables, and minerals, and even to overcome death. Often the seven strings of the lyre were thought to symbolize the Seven Sisters of the Pleiades.

Soul Music and Sacred Sexual Union

The lyre and her symbolism are also intertwined with the mysteries of sacred sexuality. The enchanting sounds and frequencies of the lyre were used in the great sexual rites of the womb religion, such as the ritual of Hieros Gamos (which literally translates as "holy marriage," with "holy" derived from the womb root *her*) and sacred Grail union.

The love poem/prayer the Song of Songs continues this tradition of the sacred marriage of the lover and his Divine Bride. It was often sung at weddings by the betrothed, and evokes the path of union. *"The king has brought me into his chambers . . . While the king was at his table, my perfume spread its fragrance."*

The lyre symbolized woman and her yoni. The Song of the Spheres was the harmonic resonance of sexual energy that the Womb emitted in a powerful symphony of orgasmic, ecstatic waves during sacred union between lovers.

Sound, the "Word," and sexuality are all interconnected, creative, birthing vibrations.

Stringed instruments were often shaped with the sensual curves of the female body and played in devotion to her. In ancient times male rulers were often known as lyre kings, preserving the mythical memories of the sacred marriage between a king and the Goddess to grant him sovereignty to rule.

Lyres and harps were often attributed with the same gifts as the Womb—their sacred sound was coveted to lament the dying season and also celebrate the cosmic regeneration cycles. Orchestras of priestesses playing lyre would accompany the lamentation rites of Isis and Osiris—and the joy of new birth.

The lyre accompanied the great love songs, which the bards and troubadours offered to their lady, the Grail Castle, to gain admittance. These Grail romances and tales were melodic refrains reverberating down from the great sacred union rituals of the womb religion, as practiced by priests and priestesses of Isis.

Now we experience a new renaissance of the creative power of the Grail and this ancient wisdom, as the Womb sings to us again—this time even louder, even more enchantingly with her siren song. The Cosmic Grail is matchmaking soul mates together, rewriting story lines, creating happy endings, stirring fate in the cosmic cauldron, lighting the flame of love again, making our Wombs and hearts tremble with earthquakes of remembrance, calling us to become mothers and fathers of new earth. It is said that beauty will save the world—this is the path of the feminine.

Underneath all the mystery is a very simple, humble path of love that is our essential nature and design and can be walked by anyone at any time. It is very practical and can be walked, and *is* being walked, by men and women in the modern world, together, transforming their everyday lives into a chalice of love, devotion, and evolution. They are honoring the Womb as a sacred portal, transforming their relationships into a pilgrimage for the Grail for this new era.

WOMB ORACLES SHARE
Sacred Grail Union

As my beloved and I opened into the fields of primordial union, a vast velvet black spaciousness began to envelop us, and we entered together into the infinite roots of Womb Consciousness as a unified Soul, both male and female together.

As our union deepened, we began to travel through the magic doorway of the Womb into other dimensions and along other timelines, every moment opening deeper and deeper into the softness and spaciousness of love, letting go, and flying along the songlines of the cosmos in a way that also felt like swimming.

Every orgasmic wave of union opened us out farther into the unified field, and the possibilities of what we could feel, experience, and explore together expanded and expanded, until we found ourselves traveling through a specific door. At the other side of this door we found ourselves in thirteenth-century Italy.

As if this timeline were entwined with our current life, in this era we were also making love and entering into the cosmic fields of sacred union. Yet in this timeline we were deep inside a bridal chamber of a medieval Grail Castle.

We could feel that we had been prepared and tutored for some time to make this union, in a ritually prepared bridal chamber, on a magically auspicious date.

Outside the room, we could sense our tutor and teacher of the Grail line checking in with the quantum energy waves that were beginning to ripple across the collective field of consciousness, to ensure that his tutelage had been a success. He seemed content with the field of union, then his footsteps faded.

The atmosphere in the chamber was rich with darkness, like a vast shimmering ocean that we could completely unfold within together, and merge into One.

Different textures of love, like infinite threads of light, wove us deeper together.

We were no longer of this world, yet we belonged completely to this world. We were traversing infinite thresholds where possibilities pulse in and out of being.

Afterward, the magical blackness surrounded us in a cosmic cathedral dome and we rested back into its arms, and from deep within my Womb that most pristine energy of unified consciousness emerged upon the words "I am sanctified."

S.B.

SPIRAL 24

SACRED DUALITY

The Mystical and Magnetic Union of Opposites

*Through your Love, existence and non-existence merge. All
opposites unite. All that is profane becomes sacred again.*
RUMI, *THE ALCHEMY OF LOVE*

CREATION IS A *love story;* we are created to fall in love, to *be* love in love with
love.

The Way of the Grail is one of sacred duality—the visioning of life as the interweaving of sacred, complementary pairs, in creative union. In this way we do not view
Creation as a mistake of duality—but as an incredible opportunity to experience a
new octave of Love and to evolve through this experience.

Creation myths tell how the Mysterious One drew from his-her infinite Womb
the primordial mother and father pair, whose cosmic lovemaking birthed creation.

There is an ocean of difference between the concepts and *feeling* of a separated
duality and a sacred duality of union with everything in creative connection and marriage. One is a prison, fear, isolation—the other is joy, intimacy, communion, a portal
of creative union.

Sacred relationships are the foundation of the Grail path—the act of coming
together in a deeply loving union mirrors the most primordial cosmic movements of
creation. Making love mirrors the making of the world itself. Our longing is full of
creative birthing power.

Many teachings bearing the imprint of the Grail lineage hold this secret knowing too. In Kabbalah (from Hebrew word roots meaning "womb," "vulva," and "to

353

receive"*—the feminine chalice or Womb) the creation myth records that Ein Sof (the Divine field of eternal formlessness) desired to experience itself and that a yearning arose to meet with itself face to face, in sacred duality. And from this longing the tree of life and the masculine and feminine twins were created; their destiny was always to merge in love and meet with their Creator, so Love could "face itself" in a new and evolutionary way.

In tantric lore this knowing is embodied in the twin figure of *Ardhanarishwar*, showing Shiva and and Shakti (Parvati) as two male-female halves in one body. Theirs is the marriage of the universal energies of the masculine (Purusha) and feminine (Prakriti) in cosmic union.

This male-female androgyne was also shown in medieval alchemical texts.

The substructure of the universe is the devotional, erotic longing of union.

Depth psychology, as pioneered by Carl Jung, also speaks of this "pairing of opposites" and how their union is the root of the gnostic experience of Oneness.

> It is a psychological fact that as soon as we touch on these identifications we enter the realm of the syzygies, the paired opposites, where the One is never separated from the Other, its antithesis. . . . In this still very obscure field of psychological experience, where we are in direct contact, so to speak, with the archetype, its psychic power is felt in full force. This realm is so entirely one of immediate experience that it . . . can only be hinted at to one who already knows.[1]

The Gnostic-Shakti teachings of Simon Magus also spoke about the sacred duality of the complementary opposites. In *Great Revelation* he says,

> Of the universal Aeons there are two shoots . . . one is manifested from above, which is the Great Power, the Universal Mind organizing all things, male, and the other from below, the Great Thought, female, producing all things. Hence pairing with each other, they unite and manifest the Middle Distance . . . in this is the Mother-Father . . . a male-female power in the pre-existing Boundless Power."[2]

---

*Kabbalah, spelled *Q-B-L-H* in Hebrew, is derived from the word root *Q-B* (kab), meaning "cup, hollow vessel, to receive." The word *Q-B-H* (womb, vulva, tent, chamber) and the word *N-Q-B-H* (female) share the same root. The feminine womb is at the core of the esoteric Kabbalistic teachings.

Fig. 24.1. Alchemical sacred union seal

(Illustration by Natvienna Hanell)

The Magical Potency
of Eggs and Twins

Goddess-based religions also contained this knowledge of the twin. The European Great Goddess gave life to the dead. Her magical hands and music were for the release of the life forces. The symbols of becoming—eggs, crescents, horns, crosses within circles, and concentric circles—were engraved on her body or on votive vases. Both an egg split into two halves and twins were concepts that were emphasized and a layered split egg became the emblem of the Goddess. The popular symbolic portrayal of twin crescents, or two does with opposed bodies reflects the magical potency of splitting a pair.[3]

The tradition of the "magical eggs" that were deeply connected with Goddesses such as Oestra, Astarte, and Inanna were continued in the legends of Mary Magdalene.

It is told that following Jesus's death, she was invited to a banquet given by Emperor Tiberius Caesar. When she met him she held a white egg in her hand and proclaimed, "Christ is risen!" Caesar laughed and said that this was as likely as the egg turning red. Before he finished speaking, the egg magically turned bright red. Magdalene then declared, "Christ is risen, for Jesus has burst forth from the tomb." Today, many Eastern Orthodox Christians end the Easter service by sharing bright red eggs and proclaiming to each other "Christ is risen."

This legend is an encoding of the Womb Mysteries and the fertility cycles of creation and dissolution, and the splitting of the egg into sacred duality. Easter is a fertility ritual, connected to the Goddesses Oestra and Astarte, from which we take the word *oestrus,* referring to the fertility cycles of conception and birth.

And, of course, the white egg transforming into the red egg is symbolic of the Womb's moon cycles—the white river of ovulation becoming the red river of menstruation, the tantric colors of red and white representing the two elixirs of the feminine flows, the sacred opposites that are the foundation of life.

If we understand Christ to mean "Living Light," and the tomb to mean a Womb—we can see the life-affirming proclamation of the rebirth of the Living Light in the eternal cycles of the Great Womb. The power of life and fertility has risen again!

The esoteric Christ teachings of Magdalene's beloved, Yeshua, are steeped in the womb religion teachings of the knowledge of the twin and sacred duality.

This concept of the twins is also referred to in the Gospel of Thomas:

> When you make the two into one, and when you make the inner like the outer and the outer like the inner, and the upper like the lower, and when you make male and female into a single one, so that the male will not be male nor the female be female, when you make eyes in place of an eye, a hand in place of a hand, a foot in place of a foot, an image in place of an image, then you will enter [the Womb queendom].[4]

Like much Grail lore, the wisdom was spoken in riddles. By the feeling of the womb, this is not a negation of being either male or female, but a teaching of sacred union/duality—when the Two become One, as Love "meets itself."

Another reflection of this comes in the cryptic tale of the Greek seer Tiresius, who after seeing two large snakes mating hits them with a stick and is turned into a woman. This is riddling symbolism for a kundalini awakening into sacred union, where the male and female principle or "twin serpents of Shakti" merge within causing him to enter the feminine dimension of the Great Womb.

Further clues to the esoteric message are given later in the tale. As a woman Tiresius becomes a priestess of Hera. As we have learned, *hera* was an ancient word for "womb," and moon colleges devoted to Hera/womb worship flourished in the Greek lands at that time. According to some versions of the tale, "Lady" Tiresius was also a renowned sacred prostitute during his/her time as a priestess of Hera, and married and bore children who also had the gift of prophecy. After seven years, Tiresius once more saw two snakes mating and was turned back into a man, but with the gift of having married both sides of the coin of sacred duality, man and woman—having merged his inner "twin."

Isis herself is believed to have said, "Though I am female, I became a male,"[5] revealing the knowing that the feminine Eve birthed the male from her body—and that the divine creative spark lives equally within both expressions of form.

These complementary poles are not fixed and rigid, but are gender-fluid, spontaneous, and dynamic; we can play along the spectrum of both feminine and masculine energy flows as we might a harp, creating our own unique inner symphony from deep within.

Earth: Created as a Paradise of Love

These teachings lead us to the most important question a person can ask themselves: is this experience of life a *benevolent* journey into union and love, or a *malevolent* mistake? The answer to this will determine your entire way of life. If it is the latter, you may want to deny life, dissociate, avoid relationships, judge creation, or try to escape or punish this "realm of error." If it is the former, you will want to *give yourself fully to love,* experiencing and embracing all you meet. You will seek love out, and seek to remove all the barriers that prevent love. You will commit yourself to living the Divine Plan and trusting in the process.

In practical terms, this will mean opening to all the frightened, wounded places in your heart and meeting all the ways you *don't believe* in love, or sacred duality. *And* meeting, welcoming, and embracing those places in others too.

It also means opening to all your repressed desires and pleasures; the abundantly wanton, sensual, orgasmic places you have judged and shamed. Surrendering fully to the wildness of your being as a sacred creature.

Our deepest wounds are relational, so relationship is the fastest path to deep soul healing. Sacred duality is all about *relationship*—from our primal relationship to our Creator, and our twin soul to our relationship with ourselves, our family, our friends, plants and animals, and the earth herself.

All of existence is relational; we are interconnected and intertwined in ways we cannot even conceive. Everything is in an intimate relationship with everything else, we are held in an energetic spiderweb of connections and communications.

Because relationship is the place we receive our deepest wounding (initially from our parents and ancestral epigenetic memories, and then from the projection that our Creator and all other beings also have these wounds) true, deep, authentic, soulful relationship is what we avoid the most. We disconnect, we disassociate; we are halfhearted in our relatings. We choose *not* to love. Often men choose to shut their soft, tender, sacred hearts down, while women close the delicate flower of their Yoni-Heart.

We avoid and distract ourselves from feeling the deep pain of our sense that love has wounded us, abandoned us, betrayed us, and left us all alone, separated, and unsafe. Ironically we can even use relationships themselves to avoid this pain, by staying on a superficial surface, caught up in mundane routine, never daring or allowing ourselves to plummit into the wilds of our hearts and the depths of the shadows and fears this will uncover.

We can use anything as a substitute to feeling our pain of perceived separation, and the even greater terror that arises in choosing union and opening to love again. We use our jobs, money worries, health concerns, wounded desires for beauty, drink, drugs, food, TV, Internet—we even use spirituality and our relationship with God as a comfort blanket to avoid feeling our wounds.

Placing our intimate relationships at the center of our spiritual altar creates a paradigm shift. Our everyday life becomes the practice. The deep emotional experiences of our relationships become a rosary bead to meditate and pray with, bringing deep alchemical potential. Our heart's longing to be deeply touched by a soulful love that is embodied and lived here in the flesh becomes a beacon of light. We enter the Bridal Chamber.

The Rooted Spiritual Path to Sacred Union

The alchemical potential of sacred union blooms like the mystical Grail Rose when we make love from a soulful place of deeply centered yoni presence, or lingam presence for men, rooted deep into the body and our soul essence, rather than being "up in the mind" to numb out or to be caught up in its limited ideas, illusions, and fantasies that betray our true nature.

On a spiritual path, we are often told to transcend our primitive animalistic urges; yet if we all truly made love like animals, the entire world would be a more loving, peaceful place. The reality is that harmful sexual energies and experiences are created by emotional wounding that is repressed, disassociated, and distorted—and then projected out unconsciously onto another human being. Animals do not sexually torture or exploit each other. We need to be more *primal*, like animals who are often very pure and unconditionally loving beings.

Love requires us to be radically real, to be embodied, to be present, to be open. It asks us to climb down into the roots of our soul, where our wild sensual truth lives.

Making love from this space of rooted ecstatic primal innocence opens our hearts and souls into the infinite spiral of Womb Consciousness and bathes us in the nectar of cosmic orgasmic bliss that conceived, created, and birthed us.

The sacred union of those lovers whose hearts and Wombs have been awakened into cosmic doorways by the fires of their passion, devotion, and commitment, trailblaze through our myths as the flame carriers of Holy Love here on earth.

Truly committing to Love will take you on the royal road of the soul. Not only will you pass through all your own personal wounds and ancestral wounds, but it will also lead you through the valley of the original sacred wound of humanity—when sacred duality became separation. This is what we may call the feminine Christ path. We do not sit up on a mountain and ignore the valley beneath us—we walk down, flooding all experiences with Love and forgiveness, restoring connection.

Many spiritual paths of the past five thousand years have been laced with the unconscious fears and projections of patriarchy—a fear of the wild, uncontrollable, unknowable, mysterious flow of life, especially embodied in a woman's wild, uncontrollable sexuality and womb portal; fears of death, dissolution, and the sacred power of physical and cosmic menstruation, which renews and recycles all in the Great Womb; fears of the feminine dimension of feelings and primal sensations of terror and pleasure; fears of intimate relationship, sacred union, and the merging of souls, and the knowledge we are an interconnected web of energy, underneath our ideas of sovereign separation.

From these unconscious projections, many spiritual paths have unwittingly promoted a form of "blissed-out" masculine separation that denies or condemns sexuality, the feminine, bonding, connection, bodily needs, relationship, feeling, and desire. The feminine path is not one of detachment, but rather of radical, ecstatic *attachment,* where we merge with the All.

Our desire, our passion, our longing is the lifeblood of our souls. Rather than avoiding, denying, witnessing, or observing them, if we choose to dive deep within them, uncover them, explore them, embody them, and set our hearts on fire with them, miracles and profound transformations of love will occur. Not on an intellectual or spiritual level—but on a bioenergetic and soulful level.

We will also get to feel everything we would rather die than feel. And in that process we will experience a form of death, and be reborn and renewed. Our masculine logical self, which is now disconnected from our primal feminine self, fears the Great Wild Womb will dissolve him if he reconnects—and she will. Instead this logical-mind self wishes to understand this infinite Void that created us, without truly having stepped foot within it. It wants certainty. It wants an intellectual description of the mystery. It wants the "e-mail from God," with rules and a system outlined that can be written down in bullet points.

We *all* have this within us, both men and women, and it pulls on us and influences us in every moment. It is the baseline of our need for control and certainty. Relationships, feelings, desires, sexuality—the very essence of sacred duality—crumble all our hopes of autonomy, control, and certainty. Our fear and control mechanisms are freaking out, but our heart is madly leading us into the wild, unknowable shining darkness where we meet our destiny with love.

On the Path of Love we will always have to choose between control and love. We cannot enter deeply into the mystery of love and be in control. And here is the dilemma, because being out of control and uncertain is our worst fear.

All our anger, resentment, hate, and resistance is a symptom of our need to control life and the pain we perceive it has caused us and will bring to us again, if we drop down our guard and soften our barriers for even one moment. So it takes great courage and commitment to love to choose to go there; it feels like you are choosing complete annihilation; when in fact the greatest Love will be given.

Entering the Womb of Love is a striptease of the soul; letting go, stripping down completely, and surrendering into the vast, naked wildness of the feminine dimension—knowing that we are naked and renewing in every moment, and we cannot control this flow of life, only ride along in passionate wonderment and innocence. The moment we try to stop the flow, cover up, own or control anything, we begin the death of separation from life.

❈ Awakening the Root of Love

When we allow an outward expansion of energy, when we let go of the limited, contracted box we have kept ourselves "safe" in, we are brought into the orgasmic flow of life and love. Ask yourself the following questions to open the secret door to your heart.

1. Feel inside your heart: how strong is your courage, *le Coeur*, the passion to love *no matter what*? Do you bring this energy into your intimate relationships; do you dare to love truly, madly, deeply?

2. How can I be more naked, more vulnerable, more surrendered?
3. How can I trust more in the power of life flowing through my Womb?
4. What do I need to stop trying to control?
5. What do I "think" I own that I can set free?

In this realm of sacred duality, sacred union of the twin life forces—which we call masculine and feminine—is the recipe for balance and harmony. Just as the Source of love chose to separate from itself to create, so in the Womb the masculine decides to leave the feminine blueprint and bloom into a boy; this is the foundation of the creative process that brings union and births more longing and creative potential. If the One did not choose to split, the experiment of life could not happen, or if the two halves felt disconnected, the experiment in love would become distorted. When the two become *as* One, balance is restored.

Spiral Path of Womb Awakening

This is reflected in the knowing that Womb Awakening is a spiral path—which is the path of sacred union. It is the union of the masculine linear path (always marching forward, working in conventional time, logical, often with an undercurrent of pressure or eager excitement) and the feminine circle path (always returning to the same place through natural cycles, in the eternal *now,* illogical, nonsensical, nowhere to get to, relaxed, and nongoal oriented).

When we are immersed in the timeless beauty of the circle it can be hard to get anything done in this current paradigm. If we are too immersed in the masculine linear path, we become punishing, relentless, and unable to rest. When both meet and merge we experience evolution in a beautiful, harmonious way.

The spiral path marries both aspects; we revolve around the Sacred Feminine womb circle *and* we never return to the same place, we're always a step closer, an octave higher, a realm deeper, we're always desiring and longing for more evolution, greater knowledge. Visualize the spiral in 3-D, how galaxies spin, to feel this truth.

This is where all the magic happens, in a practical, embodied way. Just as much is happening when we're doing nothing as when we're experiencing a powerful, creative spurt. This is the wisdom of the two life flows meeting in sacred union and marrying the complementary poles of dark and full moon, menstruation and ovulation. Create, rest, create, release, in, out—the sacred breath and pulse of life herself. The spiral path is about finding our edge between courage and compassion. The womb knows and can tell us when to take radical action and when to rest in the beingness and rejuvenating waters of the feminine.

Since time out of mind, ancient people have known how to walk the spiral path, and the spiral is one of the oldest, most sacred symbols of humanity—we are being invited to remember and join the ancient ones on this path again.

When we travel too far into the masculine swing of the pendulum, we become isolated—just as when we swing too far into the feminine side, we lose a sense of our own individual essence; the ocean consumes the expression of the wave.

Eventually our evolutionary journey is to return to the ocean of Oneness, or *at-one-ness* with Creator, while still experiencing our unique essence as a co-creative waveform. This is expressed through nature in snowflakes. Each snowflake is created through an identical hexagonal blueprint or architecture, but each snowflake also has its own unique fingerprint.

What we are seeking is harmony, and this comes from balanced relationship; from a merging of the masculine and feminine elements on every level of being. Between the two aspects of ourselves, we walk the sacred fine line of knowing our own boundaries while also knowing that underneath we are also all One.

WOMB ORACLES SHARE
Ancient Primordial Mother and Father

As the Force started to work, I asked the Mother to be kind and to take me right to the places where She knew that I was ready to go; my perineum, coccyx, and yoni fully connected to the earth, like a cord being plugged down into the Womb of Gaia. My spine was made straight and I felt warm and glowing. With every breath, big continuous waves of pure energy were coming inside of me through the perineum, coccyx, and yoni, up my spine and out of my alta major and mouth, and I was experiencing waves and waves of ecstasy and full body orgasms. I could not stop laughing with a joy that was traveling all inside of me, becoming contagious and making the others glow and laugh as well. There was so much beauty everywhere! My beloved was in front of me and every time I looked at him the intensity of the energy increased between us. I was shown many other lives that we spent together and various aspects and agreements of our soul connection. He was my twin, indeed, and we both appeared as an ancient primordial Mother and Father.

L.M.

Everything Opened to Love

I went into the cave and Divine Mother took me straight into her arms and womb, so we could be one. I felt like a swan who had their wings in a sling, trapped and breathless, then there was a sound of snapping metal and a gold chain flew off my body and my wings unfurled. I saw myself in the reflection of the stars, a beautiful swan priestess/princess with wings unfurled. I was wearing a pale blue dress and had long bright hair that shone from red to white and gold and a strange deep copper-colored Celtic belt. I took off then and found myself side by side with an absolutely huge, magnificent dragon-swan. He was pale blue with iridescent rainbows, and we soared together through the cosmos. The words "This is your Twin Soul" sounded within me, and his name was given to me. As we wove between stars my name and his name resonated together, and it was like the universe unfurled and everything opened to Love, and I saw a vision of our future family.

E.S.

SPIRAL 25

OPENING TO LOVE

The Feminine Path of Sacred Relationship

Here is the deepest secret nobody knows
(here is the root of the root and the bud of the bud
and the sky of the sky of a tree called life; which grows
higher than the soul can hope or mind can hide)
and this is the wonder that's keeping the stars apart
I carry your heart (I carry it in my heart)

E. E. CUMMINGS

MYSTICAL UNION AWAKENS WHEN two soul lovers unite in the womb of pure love, birthing a united auric field that sings a new song of communion out to creation. The radiance and transmission of this energy sourced from the heart of Creation itself, the Womb of Life, switches on a new evolutionary biological response in every cell of our body, and unites our inner ecology with the vast web of life.

Sacred lovers enter a dimension of experience that exists beyond space and time, which is paradoxically available to us right here, right now, in this very instant.

In its deepest embodied form in the sacred union of soul mates, love creates a palpable bioenergetic field of radiance that shines like a beacon of light out into the world—rippling through the quantum field of creation like no other force known in existence. When lovers come together in this energy, an interdimensional doorway is opened that allows radical quantum leaps in consciousness. This shared spiritual supernova seeds new paradigms of love.

We long for this love, and we are wired to open to fully receive and *be* this love, it is the love song etched in our cells. At its heart, we long to be the chalice of love.

Truly embodied, truly sacred, psycho-spiritual-sexual love between man and woman *is* the key to creation. It is the heart of every ancient mystery teaching. It is the great alchemical work—the merging of the masculine and feminine *in totality,* so that a new energy body is created, a morphogenic field of sacred union Consciousness, the "divine child" that becomes the energetic womb that rebirths not only ourselves, but humanity, and previous imprints of separation.

The highest octave of sexual alchemy is union with your soul mate, your twin flame—the other half of your soul. All life is conspiring to bring twins together.

We can also imagine this as a "soul-mate frequency"—a benevolent love that heals, brings balm, and is brimming with nourishment, passion, and union. *All* relationships can open out into this frequency through the power of true love. Every relationship has the potential to be a powerful vessel for love to flow.

The twin soul exists on the spiritual, energetic, and etheric level. This mirrors what quantum physicists have discovered about the workings of our universe at a quantum level. If you take a single photon, a particle of light, and divide it into two identical pieces, then shoot them out in opposite directions at very long distances, when you make a change to one, the other instantly changes—faster than the speed of light or any known speed of communication. At this deep level there is no separation in these twin particles. They are One. They can also coexist in different entangled dimensions, communicating and communing as One.

This could be analogous to our own creation—for we are light beings at the quantum level too. If we came from a particle split in two we would remain connected at the deepest level, as One being, communicating and responding to each other in ways that would seem magical to our current modern mindset.

Twin souls are *always* connected, and magical pathways will begin to open for them to find each other and reunite once again on the physical level in this age.

The blueprint of Creation also contains this deep truth about the twin nature of reality—of two coming from the one. When we are first conceived in our mother's womb there is no gender yet, since the newly conceived fetus exists in a feminine blueprint.

These two expressions of the blueprint of Creation, male and female, originate from the same Source with no separation of gender. They belong together, and because of this they long for each other, they seek each other to the deepest level, because the primal memory of our original innocence is of union; of the memory of our original inner potential for *both* expressions of life force. In union we melt back into the delicious sea of possibility within both sexual poles.

The twins are created as *complementary* to each other, designed for union—not as opposites who are in conflict or at war. This is a wounded distortion. This is an incredible experiment in love meeting love, an evolutionary leap for love to play with and relate to itself, and by doing so, to know itself more deeply.

The feminine is relational, it is *always* seeking its other half, its twin—this is its true mission in life, and the masculine mission is to surrender to this magnetic call to union, although he has the impulse to separate from the whole. In balance, the masculine and feminine are both magnetized to love, both seeking union into One, bringing their own gifts to this union.

It is important to remember we *all*—both men and women—have these forces in us, the desire for union and the desire to separate from each other.

The key is to individuate *within the field of union,* to express our unique essence while still being connected to the relational root of love rather than having to split apart from it.

In the Gnostic Valentinian light-physics system, the original twins—syzygies or pairs of aeons—multiplied until, as polarization increased, a split occurred and one of the twins whirled out of the orbit of the other, separating them from union. This split is the foundation of the myths about a fall of consciousness.

But even from this perceived great distance of separation, the thread of love and longing for union compels us to search for our original twin, singing out across the cosmic songlines—like a divine mating call for connection and wholeness.

And this union is within us, singing from within our "dark DNA" and original soul—the part of us that never forgot and never separated and lives in innocence.

Love Meeting Love:
Primordial Sacred Union

In primordial innocence, before our fall into separation consciousness, all was in union; the radiant rose of this earthly experience was the union of souls in sacred relationship. Love facing love—this openness to love was vulnerable, innocent, completely transparent in its sacred desire to give everything for love.

The knowing that this realm is created in pairs, twin or sacred opposites, is recorded in the Kabbalist traditions in their Book of Light, the Zohar. "Come and behold: All the souls that are destined to come appear before Her as couples, with each soul divided each into male and female halves. Afterward, when the souls arrive in this world, the Holy One, blessed is She, matches them again."[1]

It was also known in the ancient feminine mystery schools that those who were at One with the Great Womb of Creation also had the ability to "see" those who were soul mates and help bring them together, a gift Magdalene was said to have.

Gnostic shaman Simon Magus, who studied at the mystery school created by John the Baptist, traveled and taught with his beloved, Helen. He was defamed as the "father of heretics" for his teachings and beliefs on sacred soul-mate union and the mystery teachings of the feminine womb path. He taught that a soul is divided into two halves and placed in different bodies, one male and one female, who both have a magnetic longing to unite. These souls search through all time for each other in a love beyond death. He emphasized the power of sacred sexuality to experience gnosis, and also claimed that the soul cannot rise to the next world until it finds its counterpart, its twin and soul mate.[2]

Twin Flame Frequency: The Cosmic Gateway

Love is the greatest risk we will ever take. Every time we marry our hearts to another being, be they our beloved, our child, a dear friend, or an animal familiar, we begin to dance with death, loss, fear, betrayal, change, dissolution. But when we keep extending the bridge between our hearts in order to merge, we begin a profound form of alchemy; we actually begin to integrate death and loss and transcend it; we begin to embody the truth that love is infinite and beyond death.

Avoiding love, especially in the name of spirituality, is a way of avoiding truth. We cannot think our way around the path of love; we can only be magnetically drawn into the benevolent heart of creation and surrender to what unfolds there. This unfolding of love actually transforms our biology and creates fields of pod consciousness. These morphogenic soul-mate fields can have incredible impact on the collective vibratory field, and bring about quantum inner and outer shifts.

It was known in ancient times that this morphogenic soul-mate field, where two energy fields had merged into One-ness, into a deep quantum entanglement beyond the limits of time and space, could survive death and could bridge the worlds. This was the root of "immortal love," a love beyond separation.

Twin flames are the bridge to the birthing of a new earth, and we can also perceive this evolutionary wave as a twin flame frequency that alights in deeply soulful, softly receptive, radically transparent relating in the wilds of the feminine dimension. How this bridge manifests in this dimension in the most complete way is through a fractal merging of body, heart, soul, psyche, and sexual energy fields in sacred relationship, deeply embodied and fully lived in love.

The powerful effects of soul-mate union actually birth a totally new energy field, with creative potentials that are vastly more powerful than anything possible alone. This is a *morphogenic field of Love*—the sacred energy body of union consciousness, sometimes called pod consciousness, similar to the instant telepathic communication and vast empathy shared among dolphin pods. These supersensory perceptual gifts are activated by the quantum awakening of merging with another into a morphic field of sacred soul-mate union.

The pioneering new earth biologist who coined the term *morphic fields,* Rupert Sheldrake, describes the nature of these energy fields as being "guided from above, as if by an unseen force"—as if a divine hand or intelligence is directing the process. They are culturally contagious. In other words, every couple that enters into the archetypal morphogenic field of love creates a pathway for the next couple to enter. Eventually a tipping point is reached and sacred union consciousness spontaneously arises in all beings across the Earth.

The morphogenic love field is symbolized by the sacred geometry of the vesica pisces, two overlapping circles that create a new creative portal where they meet. The energetic mathematics of sacred union, are likewise nonlinear. They are more than the sum of their parts. Biologically, these fields are referred to as *emergent,* meaning that the unique properties of the whole could not have existed in the independent man or woman before merging. They emerge from union. They are birthed spontaneously with a unique new possibility. They transcend the binds of linear progression or evolution as we think it.

The majesty and mystery of this phenomenon, which also extends to the emergent birthing of a new earth, is that we are not contained by the wounded limitations of our past or current self—in this rich birthing crucible *anything is possible.*

Our universe is crafted from a magical fabric of dazzling possibilities, of love longing for love, merging, uniting, dissolving, birthing, in more love.

The rich lore of romantic love, as sung by the troubadours and bards of all ages, whispers to us that sacred union has the power to change the world—to alter the very fabric of the universe. Contemporary quantum science now validates this ancient wisdom. Studies performed by multiple prestigious research groups including Princeton's Robert Jahn, Ph.D., Dean Radin, Ph.D., and others have demonstrated we are all able to affect the probabilities of quantum events.

Astoundingly, pair-bonded couples create an effect that is *six times more powerful* than any individual alone. The deeper the entanglement or merging of the sacred lovers, and the more clear they are in their own being, the more powerful these effects become. As the research continues we will see that those who are deeply in a soul-mate field, sharing their awakening process, will have a combined power that is many magnitudes beyond what has been recorded.[3]

The next evolutionary step of humanity—spiritually, biologically, and culturally—is built on the foundation of twin-flame union, healing the split between the masculine and feminine. Our evolutionary destiny is to deepen into oneness. Twin flames create the bridge for humans to access the next octave of at-one-ment consciousness in a tangible and grounded way. It becomes an embodied phenomenon that is practical and relational. Its energetic umbrella extends out from man and woman to envelop their children, and from the field of love emanates out into the greater community. It is only after two people have learned how to fully merge their consciousness *and* their body energy fields in sacred sexual love that the tribe as a whole will be opened into this capacity.

Twin souls are a gateway to the feeling-knowing that we are all twinned with everything in existence, all connected together in love. The following practice will support your connection to your twin soul.

❋ Connecting to Your Twin Soul

If you have not already met your twin soul in this realm, connect on the etheric realm—where communication is faster than the speed of light. You are a transmitter and receiver, and this being is the other side of you.

1. Sit quietly in a meditation space, and rest your hands on your Womb. Visualize another half of you sat opposite, facing you in the same position.
2. Start to flow an infinity loop of energy between your heart centers. Feel the deep connection between you.
3. Just as you may ask your own Womb or body for wisdom, begin to communicate with this other half of you. Ask what blocks are present in you, preventing a meeting in the 3-D world. You may receive surprising or revelatory answers. Open to receive wisdom.
4. Feel any black spots in your other half's body, feel where *they* have blocks, which they may not even be aware of. Ask what *you* can do with your own inner work and physical healing to help them clear this block to finding union. Remember, you are working together as one unit; what you heal helps them heal.
5. Afterward, send your unconditional love and release them to continue their journey. The reuniting of twin flames cannot be pushed or grasped for, only allowed and surrendered to by embodying pure love as deeply as you can.

Fig. 25.1. Twin flame

(Illustration by Seren Bertrand)

This union of physical opposites, or, more accurately, complementary pairs, harnesses incredible spiritual and creative powers. When the masculine and feminine is in harmony all is possible and heaven on earth is birthed; when they separate, a chasm opens in the fabric of the psyche and the soul of the world.

After the Fall

The devolution caused by this separation of the masculine and feminine is what we see written in suffering across the world today; only union can truly heal it.

After the fall, we entered a time of matriarchy—where womb worship devolved into a celebration of *only* the feminine twin, where sensuality, sexuality, and fertility were explored without a heartfelt commitment and union with the masculine.

Over time this created a massive wave of negative energy in the masculine consciousness of anger, betrayal, powerlessness, and worthlessness, and took the feminine consciousness away from her innocent heart, into realms of power, pride, and domination-based sexuality. This separation birthed patriarchy. As this distorted, angry, wounded consciousness separated from the feminine completely—condemning and crushing all the ways of the Goddess—so too did we separate from our Creator, our place in Creation, and the power of the Womb.

This matriarchy is not to be confused with the womb religion of the Great Mother, which cradled the earth in peace and equality for eons; instead it describes the tumultuous time of transition where a shift to a hierarchical "power-over" consciousness and culture started to emerge. In this process, the balance first shifted to women, who were naturally the power holders, as the birthers and shamans of the tribe, before the power was then seized by men.

This split between the masculine and feminine, and the deep well of grief and betrayal on both parts, is the fault line of our current civilization. From this place we are afraid and defensive, it becomes difficult to be open and vulnerable to love; to trust in union, not separation. From these wounds we wear our masks of safety and isolation, unwittingly "protecting" ourselves from the lifeblood of love. Sacred union consciousness is the desire to disarm and open again. Not for one twin to be in power, but to meet again in equality and sweet harmony.

Entering the Doorway of True Love

There will be time,
To prepare a face to meet the faces that you meet.

T. S. ELIOT

We all prepare a face (mask) to meet other faces (masks). If we don't willingly choose to be vulnerable, and to unmask ourselves, and to be in relationships with those who do the same, we can live our whole life as superficial interactions of masks speaking to masks.

Sacred union is a radical choice to unmask yourself—especially in intimate relationship. To expose and reveal all the parts of you that feel weak, needy, pathetic, unworthy, jealous, ugly, unwanted, and "bad," and reveal all the parts of you that are longing so much for love and connection and are so afraid. Something incredibly beautiful, pure, innocent, and authentic arises from this way of being.

Young children do not try to mask their desire and need for love, contact, comfort, play, intimacy, reassurance, support, nourishment, and attention.

One of the main obstacles to this vulnerability is our wounded desire to be independent (separate) and strong. Everybody's experiences of being dependent as a child, with wounded parents who were not able to embody pure unconditional love, were painful and traumatic in some way and made them feel powerless, helpless, and afraid. Because of this, somewhere deep down in our subconscious we vow never to repeat that experience again, to never be so vulnerable, open, and dependent on the love and care of others for our survival. But in doing so we shut the door to true love, from others and our Creator.

Being fully independent and not needing anything or anyone else is a mind program and illusion of the distorted masculine, birthed from the fear of the truth of interconnection, interdependence, and the perceived powerlessness and loss of control that goes with it. In the human body when a cell suffers the illusion it is independent, it refuses to surrender itself to the whole and multiplies, becoming cancerous and threatening the ecosystem of the body.

This thoughtform that has been propagated by many distorted masculine spiritual systems (based on fear) is now breaking down to be rebirthed. We are healing our collective cancer. Neediness is a just a natural desire for love and longing that hasn't been met because we are in the illusion of separation from Love. Our needs are our most beautiful gateway back—and we will feel weak, powerless, out of control in that journey. Once fully immersed in love we don't "need" anything, but that is through absolute fulfillment of love, not loss of love.

❋ Dropping the Masks

Here are some questions to stir in the cauldron.

1. How many people live as masks relating to other masks?
2. How often have I lived this way?
3. How often have these masks hidden my soul, my true feelings, my grief, my love, my desires, my longing?

4. Who could I drop my mask with today and reveal more of myself than I ever have before?

5. How can I allow my heart to be transparent?

Reaching Out for Love Again

When a baby experiences abandonment it first rages against this loss, expressing its primal need for love and contact through its voice and body. If the mother does not return, it then begins a grieving process. Eventually, if the mother stays absent long enough, it gives up and collapses into a stony despair, disconnected from its inner feelings and needs, looking peaceful, calm, and implacable on the outside.

In negative mind-control practice, to fragment the psyche of a person into sub-personalities, a child is held in a room, separated from the parent and taught to self-soothe so that even when the parent comes into the room, the child shows no sign of "needing" the parent. This enables the child to dissociate from the natural soul needs and longing for connection, feelings, and intuition, and to enter the trance of separation and feminine soul loss.

Aren't we all, in some way, that child in the room, separated from our Source, fragmented, learning to self-soothe? Are not many of our spiritual systems designed to help us disassociate from the pain of life into a false high or bliss?

This is the root of all addictions, the survival imperative to avoid our pain.

The balm is to begin reaching out again, admit we need, explore all the grief and longing in that need, trust and believe in the power of love and connection again. It can be very triggering to allow this process to undo us. Often claims to be "whole in ourselves" are simply a way to feel safe and in control and avoid confronting our deepest hurts. Merging is the end of "you," not as an inner mental idea or meditation or astral experience, but as a full-bodied, soul expanse into love. The more we open to it, the more humbled and lovestruck we become at the mystery of it all—and the more we let in the great love of the Mother. The word *sovereignty* at its roots means "on the throne of the queen." To be truly sovereign does not mean to be an island all alone, but to be a beacon of light held within the weaving of the web.

Divine Mother is waiting for all her children, always has been, always will be, but paradoxically it is terrifying to our wounds. We are the orphan child who has adapted to separation. Many spiritual systems are a mental setup to avoid this opening to the vastness of this reconnection and all the feelings it brings up. Many people will do anything not to lose control of the safe container of separation, independence, and self-reliance. This is our real comfort zone.

The Symbiotic Merging of Love

In modern psychology we are told that individuating from the mother is the height of healing, and that longing for symbiosis, that merged state of union, is a wounded and immature state. Yet, from another perspective, babies are not unaware and unable to conceptualize and perceive the difference between themselves and their mother. They are multidimensional beings, recent voyagers from a state of Spirit, who are navigating the new experience of an interdependent realm—where every step, every breath, every touch is dependent on something else in the web. Through this symbiosis of arriving in a woman's womb, this cosmic being gets a crash course in what it means to be part of the vast weaving of matter.

Often, the problem that arises is not that we crave a symbiotic state we have experienced with our birth mother as a young baby and now need to individuate out of, but that we have *never truly experienced this deeply lived symbiotic state of union and merging* because the mother, father, and parent culture were in a state of separation consciousness. So this vital imprint of deeply embodied and healthy union is missing within us.

We cannot extend to another being a state of consciousness that we do not inhabit. So for a new soul coming into form, from the very first second of conception he or she is brought into a womb of separation consciousness, no matter how loving or well intentioned the mother is. This is why, despite women's very best efforts, our society is still bearing the wound of separation.

From this early experience of inhabiting a distorted field with its mother, the child inherits a mutual world of pain. Symbiotic, permeable, and shared wounds lace down throughout the entire ancestry and collective. It is experienced as a nightmare, a hell realm of separation, more acutely perceived by the gestating baby who is closer to pure consciousness than the mother who is a product of her culture. From then on, the child entwines this terror with the idea of union.

Later in life, as we open to sacred relationship, we often find our longing for love and union is matched only by our profound fear of risking this toxic symbiosis again, or facing the shock of abandonment, causing us to revisit our early pain.

While it is impossible to physically repeat our bonding experiences with our birth mother, it is possible to reach for deep symbiotic love states in relationship. In fact, it is *vital*—despite our own young experiences—that we keep a torch lit in our hearts and are open to primordial states of unity consciousness with others.

But first we have to individuate out from a *false* imprint of what union is—we have to rebirth ourselves into a new imprint of what love and intimacy means.

This requires a shamanic recapitulation of our conception, gestation, birth, and childhood wounds so that we can heal our inner child and ancestral soul and awaken into conscious adulthood.

Awakening the Dragon of Power

Before we enter the marriage chamber to merge back into love, we first have to be firmly aquainted with all that is *not* love. Too often we lack discernment and deliver ourselves time and time again into the jaws of the beast. We ignore the healthy and loving parameters of our own boundaries, unable to claim our own power and essence in the world, or stand in our self-love with others. In psychological terms this is known as repetition-compulsion, a drive to replay our deepest, hidden wounds until they are made conscious and resolved. In relationships, we need to activate our Dragon Power first, our own mature selfhood and inner wisdom, as we open to merge and flow deeply into the waters of union, so our journey to the deep does not drown us.

Developing a healthy sense of self, boundaries, and ego is essential, which is a personal journey into self-love—although sacred relationship can forge this in chambers of fire, as we discover our inner parameters by dancing with another.

When we shine the bright light of clarity and love into our relationships and into our own emotional and psychological patterns, we will either awaken a beautiful phoenix of union out of the flames, or that which is not love will turn to ashes.

The path of love is one of surrender—but we must always ask first, What are we surrendering to? If it is not true love that asks us to surrender, it is submission.

We have a foundational desire to surrender and open. If this intense emotional need to give isn't connected into healthy love, then something else can step in its place—a mirage of love, something that wishes for us to be its energetic slave.

We must first know ourselves before we can truly surrender ourselves.

Womb knowing, cunning, nous, common sense, acumen, instinct are all gifts of the wild womb that allow us to safely surrender into the heart of the womb.

We are instinctual beings, and like animals, guarding our territory from real threats is not the same as a closing our heart to love because of past experiences and inner wounds. Wild women have fangs and claws as well as soft fur—mother love can be ferocious.

Without our wild womb, our fierce feminine power awakened, we cannot truly open to love. Without knowing and mapping the consciousness of our own self, we cannot let go into the other to unite the sacred opposites in liquid love.

When we have claimed enough of this self-love and tasted our loving power, we can begin to magnetize and invite the beloved to dance with us. We *know* by instinct when it is safe to surrender—if we listen to our womb's wise words.

Anchored into this deep womb knowing, we can free-fall into love and *close all the doors of escape that remain in our heart and soul*—and sit in the fire. And what we will be truly meeting and melting into is our own pure soul essence.

In *Sacred Pleasure,* Riane Eisler outlines how an earlier partnership model of society was replaced by a dominator model that valued hypermasculine qualities of strength, independence, separation, and power-based authority over more feminine qualities of softness, need, interconnection, family, and nurturing.

Science shows that feminine qualities such as healthy attachment and bonding, and the capacity to form relationships, can be *genetically switched off* if they are not learned in childhood.[4] If children do not experience a securely attached and bonded relationship with their mother in early childhood, they are much less likely to have successful romantic relationships later in life.[5]

Returning to the feminine dimension allows us to unravel these chains of isolation and come back into the embodied knowing that we are designed as a web.

Letting go into love is the deepest desire of our heart; it is written into our very DNA. When we surrender to this force of pure love wishing to flow through us, our genetic blueprint returns to wholeness. Lover's eyes are magic doorways.

The Five Spheres of the Path of Love

Sacred relationship takes us into the heart of love, the wild furnace of beauty and mystery that will completely transfigure us and transform our lives. Sacred relationship is the cathartic, supportive, catalyzing, powerful, and transformational cauldron for this healing to happen—so we can experience the symbiotic states of love, which were unwittingly withheld from us as a child. This is not a form of unconscious codependence, this is a fully conscious journey with two consenting adults who are fully prepared to enter the fire of initiation.

This fire of love is a crucible that will melt everything back into the original blueprint of love—not by adapting or compensating for the lack of love and being "alone together," but by daring to open again to the fullness of love, no matter what arises, to take the ultimate risk and reach for sacred union consciousness, which every human being deeply desires and is soulfully and bioenergetically wired for. This is the reality of our quantum womb biology, flowing from Spirit. We can express this journey as unfolding in five spheres of initiation.

1. Independence

Independence is the illusion that we can do it alone, that we are completely self-reliant and do not need anything or anyone else. The illusion of independence is embedded within the illusion of separation, and is a viruslike thoughtform that has humanity in its grip. It makes us feel in control, strong, powerful. Needing others, admitting we are part of a web of energy, makes the distorted masculine self in both men and women feel weak and powerless. In relationships this independence, strength, autonomy is a mask to avoid the deep feelings that will arise in true intimacy, opening, and the merging of souls. Those who live in this mask cannot melt into the wilds of love, the great mystery. The more gentle, tender, and truthful we are with ourselves, the more we embrace the fullness of who we are—gifts and flaws—and allow ourselves to be "wrong," imperfect, and still be worthy to receive love, the more this mask will dissolve.

In our current paradigm we are encouraged to view independence as positive; to not need anything or anyone. Men have been subject to this conditioning for a long time, but now women are also enmeshed in its spell of illusory strength. We harden up and say, "I'll never be hurt by love again." When you protect yourself against pain, you also protect and armor yourself against love and life. But true strength is the vulnerability to be soft, to melt, to trust that the web of life and Divine Mother will hold you and catch you if you fall.

In ancient times it was known that anyone who separated from the interconnection of the tribe would not survive on a physical or soul level. In the modern world, money, success, and achievements fuel this artificial sense of independence—we can live all alone, and buy whatever we need. But we cannot buy love. We cannot buy what our soul most needs to open, blossom, and thrive.

At its deepest level, we have entered the illusion we are independent from Gaia, and from the Great Womb that birthed us and will receive us on our departure.

We can begin by expressing our need for love to others, not in a demanding way, but in a softly vulnerable sharing of what our heart is truly feeling and desiring. We can also express our gratitude for Gaia and for others who support us, and open into our interconnection with nature, plants, and animals, as well as humans.

There is a risk that our vulnerable need for love will not, or cannot, be met—and usually we react to this by shutting off our needs, denying them, developing spiritual theories that make the need and desire for love "wrong" or "egoic."

Instead, on the path of love we can keep opening our hearts to this deep foundational need to love, to give love, to receive love, to touch others—physically and soulfully—and to be touched physically and soulfully.

Even if our need isn't met, we can keep opening our heart and souls and reaching, allowing ourselves to feel the deep grief, rejection, abandonment, separation when our desire for love isn't met—*and to still keep opening*. In this expansive blossoming, we are opening into the arms of Love herself.

We do not have to make demands of the other person, or project our anger on them, or force them to choose something they do not want or are not ready for. We can honor where they are and their free will and still say, *I choose love!* Even if that means leaving the relationship or letting go of the idea they were "the One" and grieving any feelings of betrayal or loss.

Holy love *includes our needs;* it does not exclude them—even if they are wounded, messy, childish, heartbreaking, clingy. This opens the doorway to our precious inner child who did not receive the love he or she needed to thrive. Our projections onto others are magical gateways if we navigate them consciously. It also opens the doorway to our true power, soft power, where Shakti flows in orgasmic, pulsing waves of coming together and meeting in true intimacy.

And that is the deepest fear and resistance—to meet the feelings and agonizing grief of our inner child and our innermost soul, to feel all the ways we think we have been separated from love, and are not worthy of being loved and cherished. It takes great daring to trust again, to open the crack in our heart and let love back in.

2. Dependence

When we take the courageous leap into love and connection, we begin to admit to ourselves and others that we can't do it alone, and this allows all our deepest wounds and desires to arise. We begin to feel our desperate need for contact and connection, to be seen and felt. We open to all the ways we did not feel this in our life, starting as a baby. Ancient fears, terror, and grief emerge; wild longings and palpable moments of ecstatic communion begin to arise.

Opening deeper into love can feel like dying and it is; it is the death of the old you, the separated you with its masks of independence and autonomy. This is why the process is called the Love that is Death. You may feel like you are regressing to a child-like state of vulnerable neediness, alternating this with primal fear and distrust of reaching for love again; pushing love or your beloved away as the deep fear of opening your heart again to the risk of abandonment and separation arises. In these moments, if you can open to and sit with the feelings in innocence, a wave of primordial Love will wash through you, as you understand you are opening to something far vaster than just personal love.

You will begin to feel the infinite love that created you flow back into you—the only way to reunite with the Source of love is to *love*. There is no mental shortcut that can help. Allowing our full spectrum self to be seen in relationships does.

It takes great courage to return to the feminine flow, to return to the Womb of Love—the current can feel wild, fierce, unpredictable. There is a fear it may destroy you. And it will; the sacred flow of the feminine will strip away your masks of power and control. So it can feel safer to stay at the edge, to read about it, think about it, talk about it; to be an expert on love, high on your alone mountain of separation.

To be a connoisseur of love is a descent into the fertile valley, into the underworld, into the dark and mysterious chambers that are both enticing and terrifying—where your shadow lives, where your God-created essential nature lives. We have forgotten who we are, only love can remind us.

It takes enormous trust and courage, and madness too. There is no safe way to step back into that flow of love again. It will knock you off your feet, pull you under, tumble you under great waves, carry you, transform you. There will not even be a moment to gain your breath, because the flow is infinite.

Daring to jump in is not a meditation practice that takes years to accomplish or master. It is here right now if we choose to take the leap. Often, our knees are trembling and it feels like death—we viscerally feel as if we are jumping into the abyss when we love, when in fact we are jumping into our Source, into our wildest ecstasy and our deepest destiny.

In relationship, this push-pull dynamic—one moment you cannot bear to be without someone, the next moment you feel overwhelmed, suffocated with an illogical desire to escape—requires the commitment to be honest and vulnerable. We fear we will be judged or abandoned if we admit we are needy for love or terrified of love, but we can open to both poles and embrace them with acceptance in the safe container of sacred relating. During this process we will spiral back to the original cause of these wounded responses: the lonely child who desperately wanted love and connection, and the angry child who has given up on having his needs met and is pushing anyone away who shows love.

We can sit in the fire of what comes up, and we will journey through many vibrational feeling realms and psychic layers, revisiting feelings and experiences that we thought we had safely locked away and thrown away the key to. In choosing love we choose to face all that isn't love and we welcome it all, we close any escape hatches and allow our innocence of love to be rebirthed.

Dependence is different from codependence, which is when you choose to stay in an abusive or unhappy relationship because you are afraid to be alone and it feels safer to make other people happy rather than express your true desires. In this situation, opening to self-love and honesty, and taking positive steps to empower yourself, opening into your own needs and desires, is the step forward into love.

When we ask deeply in our womb knowing if a relationship is healing us or harming us, we can make the decision that most serves love. If we receive the knowing that the relationship is harmful and abusive, and that our precious, fragile inner child is being hurt more—then we can open to our trust that life will hold us when we choose to love ourselves.

3. Interdependence

By fully allowing our needs and desires for love, without judgment or suppression, we enter a cauldron of love where we meet and transmute our deepest shadows and wounds against love. This requires total commitment, transparency, and vulnerability—to stand fully in the fire of who we really are, rather than who we would *like* to be. We allow our beloved to hold us and witness us in this process, to become naked in innocence. As we begin to travel through and heal some of our core personal and ancestral wounds a new, deeper, pristine love begins to birth within us—one that is graced with the purity of trust, not only in the other, but in life itself and the journey of love. We begin to reestablish a true circuitry of love; one that does not take, own, possess, manipulate from a fear-based place; one that does not negate the feminine principle of *receiving* from a misplaced sense that love can only include the masculine principle of giving, extending outward, penetrating another with love, but can also include the feminine principle, the living chalice, that receives love and draws love into itself as a process of spiritual and physical transformation.

With this balanced two-way circuitry in place, we enter the realms of interdependence—where we allow love and connection to unite us from a purer level of consciousness. Fears of being overwhelmed and controlled by love, or fears of being abandoned and betrayed by love recede, as the childhood and ancestral wounds that birth them dissolve. In their place a healthy interweaving of cooperation and co-creation emerges, full of integrity and peace. A great evolutionary leap in love occurs as we begin to develop ourselves within a web structure, rather than in isolation. The immense creative and loving power of the sacred couple in union becomes far greater than the sum of the parts.

We begin to heal our relationship with Creator and Creation, to remember that we are part of the whole, loved, supported, not a separated fragment.

Opening into web consciousness allows us to see and feel more deeply the interconnection of all life; our heart and souls soften, our sexuality opens in harmony with nature and the original blueprint. Incredibly magnetic and resonant pod energy fields surround us, and attract more harmony and love.

It is as if we have entered an enchanted garden, and our relating—while not always perfect—is infused with a tenderness, compassion, and self-awareness. There is a playfulness, joyful camaraderie, and intimacy as we travel the path of love together, as a dolphin pod swimming deeper into the ocean of love.

4. Communion

Love becomes a lived reality most of the time; pod Womb Consciousness emerges. Our hearts merge, we trust in love, and dissolve the illusion of separation completely. We are immersed in sacred union consciousness and feel ourselves to be fully interwoven into the web of life and the Source who created it. Not by denying, disassociating, or separating from the feelings of the feminine soul, but by fully integrating them. The divine biological blueprint switches on, igniting an awesome force field of living light that shines across all dimensions. The biology of love transfigures the human body, and the sacred lovers, into an immortal divine chalice; love pours in, in ecstatic waves of embodied endocrine responses, and then flows out into the world as a bountiful gift. The twin souls merge into One field of love. From this state of primordial innocence miracles happen, vast healing powers awaken, miraculous longevity becomes possible, supernatural powers are completely natural, time and space no longer exist as a limiting force, new paradigms of consciousness begin to birth. Few people on Earth have reached this stage—Divine lovers such as Yeshua and Magdalene are an exception—but this possibility is now being anchored on Earth for those who are willing to walk the path of Love.

5. Reunion

We merge with Source on an infinite journey deep into love that is beyond words. We become at one with the Mother/Father Womb of Creation. We merge into the dimension of love and enchantment, embodying it here on Earth—the fairyland, nirvana, and heaven that was inside us all along.

When enough men and women come together in physical, loving, sexual, soulful union and *merge* (not just uniting the masculine and feminine within), the actual vibrational fabric of our reality will change. This is the greatest power.

In mystical traditions the union of the alchemical queen and king is the highest form of alchemy, and the foundation of the redemption and rebirth of the world.

The road to this union is a messy, heart-stopping, completely unspiritual journey through our absolutely greatest fear, to feel weak, needy, and dependent, with no "space" left for our individual separate self (the fragmented part of ourselves we feel we need to be safe and survive). The path of love invites this into the heart for true healing. We surrender into our heart and embrace all we find there.

We begin to exist in a lived reality of "I and the (M)other are One."

WOMB ORACLES SHARE
Cosmic Hieros Gamos

During winter solstice, 2003, Mary Magdalene appeared to me during a dream-vision with her consort, the unicorn—the Christed One, or purified male principle. They united in hieros gamos throughout the night, immersing the entire earthly realm in healing light, bringing mystical love into density and transforming matter.

I was shown that their union is galactic, causing emanations of light-photon particles that ignite an awakening in the hearts and minds of humans. This mystical alchemical marriage is an archetype of rebirth, and when humans acknowledge the sacredness of all aspects of earthly life and sexuality, it births a new frequency throughout the universe. Their loving changes everything.

A.W.

Sacred Soul-Mate Union

We were created together in the Womb of God. But on Earth, for many years our identities were veiled from each other. Yet threads throughout our lives were seeking to weave us back together again. When we first recognized each other, it was as if a doorway of consciousness had opened. It was instant. Irrevocable. It felt like the sudden and detailed recollection of a deeper reality flooding back into consciousness. A huge veil had been lifted with this instantaneous awareness.

"This is my soul mate." The feeling flooded up from my womb not as a question, but as a direct knowing. In fact, my conscious mind tried to push it away. It was my feminine soul speaking, announcing the reunion, leaving no doubt. This was the other "particle" of me. Time stood still. My beloved instantly vowed to love me always, and named all parts of me he would love. It was a declaration of union.

In response, a doorway in my heart flung open. I was suddenly in the intimate presence of God. I made my vow of union, declaring that I would leave no escape hatches in my heart. I would sit in the fire of this union, no matter what. I knew it would dissolve me, and that the Creator had witnessed and bound this vow. Love was flooding through me in vast waves. I was committing to Love itself including but beyond the personal sense of love. My conscious mind was awestruck, horrified.

Without touching, even at distances apart, when our energy fields met our hearts would open in orgasmic union, pulsing with refined pleasure waves of ecstasy.

In visionary experiences I saw the names of soul halves written in a great book.

One day, standing at the opposite sides of a room, my beloved and I gazed into each other's eyes for more than an hour. It was like journeying through dimensions of love. Every ripple and deepening was stripping another layer from my heart, which was expanding out in waves. Eventually it felt as if my heart stopped beating. It did not feel like a vision, but a clear reality. My heart was no longer beating. Everything was perfectly still and eternal. It was as if I had died while still being alive. I was in a vast oceanic love, warm and deep, infinite, beyond time and space. I felt unable to stand—my body was losing form and melting into the velvet of this perfect stillness.

I lay down in my beloved's arms, and the black ocean of love was everywhere, in everything. I felt the deepest sense of peace, love, and perfection. It was a feeling beyond words, but which is often described as heaven or nirvana. My beloved asked me to pray from this place. I laughed—the question seemed incomprehensible. What was there to pray for? Then my awareness shifted and a prayer emerged slowly, like a ripple in the stillness: "May all beings experience this love."

S.B.

SPIRAL 26
DESCENDING TO EARTH

Awakening the Feminine Crown

I tell you in truth, man is the son of the Earthly Mother, and from her did the Son of Man receive his whole body, even as the body of the newborn babe is born of the womb of his mother. I tell you truly, you are one with the Earthly Mother; she is in you, and you in her. Of her you were born, and to her you shall return . . .

JESUS, ESSENE GOSPEL OF JOHN

OUR HOMECOMING BEGINS with the decision to come back down to earth. Our language tells us this could be something painful—we might land with a bump. But making the choice to fully inhabit our bodies and our lives here on earth, in this moment, is the gateway to the ecstatic energy of being fully alive.

In our present culture we celebrate the masculine. Our energetic movements tend toward ascending upward to the sky. We worship a God who lives outside of us, somewhere far away, "up there" in heaven. We speak of being "on top of the world," "flying high," and "climbing the ladder" of success.

We have forgotten to honor the feminine and to move our energy downward toward the earth. We no longer commune with the Goddess whose spirit lives *inside* our bodies, our lands, and the creatures and plants of the Earth. We speak of feeling "down in the dumps" or "low" when we are depressed, or of "falling" when we fail.

Our modern patriarchal culture, and the language born from it, has created a dangerous unconscious desire to leave our bodies. In its full expression, this desire to leave is actually the desire for death. It is anti-Life and anti-Love. It is the place in us that would rather not be here, the place that finds life lonely and terrifying. From this place we react with fear, anger, and hatred. Personally and collectively, it is our deepest wound.

The fact that we have created societies and religions based on the masculine imbalance that favors "up and out" over "down and in," reveals that at some point we experienced a massive trauma and were afraid for our collective survival. It became too overwhelming to stay in our bodies and feel the terror. As a result, we disconnected, and we never found our way back. There was once a time of Eden, and then this paradise was lost. Eden was not a physical location, but a dimension of experience. It was a time when we lived in harmony, equality, and love, where we honored Life, the earth, our bodies, and the rhythms of nature.

One of the body's survival mechanisms in dealing with trauma or a life-threatening situation is to disassociate, a powerful, unconscious bioenergetic response to the emotions of fear and terror. This mechanism, designed to be a temporary protective measure, can be very damaging when it becomes permanent.

We all experience this disassociation at times, especially in childhood. If we are physically, emotionally, or sexually abused, part of our awareness and soul leaves our bodies rather than experience the pain of what is happening. In the Native American and other indigenous traditions, medicine men or shamans perform soul-retrieval healings to bring back our lost soul parts.

For a sensitive, innocent child even the slightest upset can be very traumatic; a harsh word or careless criticism from a stressed-out parent can be felt like an assault. Over time, we lose more and more fragments of ourselves. We disconnect from so much of who we really are, we are running at only our minimum capacity.

Eventually we no longer embody our full potential as humans. Part of our emotions and soul become stuck in the past—trapped in a shock wave of fear—often without our awareness. This is why we may feel a sense of agitation, discomfort, or loss deep inside, with little understanding of the cause.

When we leave our bodies, we also lose connection with our Earth Mother. We begin to feel as if we are a separated fragment rather than a tapestry of wholeness, interconnected with the web of life and infused with the bond of love.

Now is the time to call these pieces of us home. The more we explore our own bodies, the more we feel safe to call these lost parts of ourselves back, and to face the experiences that were too difficult for us to deal with at the time. The more grounded we become, the stronger we are, and the more our energy flows.

Earth is our Mother. She provides for us, takes care of us, and loves us. Earth is a living organism, she has a soul, and we can connect and commune with her. When we are disconnected from her, we feel lost, afraid, and unsafe in the world.

If young babies do not receive the nourishing milk of their mothers, they die. If they do not receive the nourishing touch of physical, emotional, and energetic contact with their mothers, they die or become psychologically damaged.

The same principle applies to our relationship with Mother Earth. If we do not eat her pure, chemically untainted food, if we do not connect with nature we become sick and our life energy begins to die. We need to press our bare feet on warm soil and dewy grass, feel rain on our skins, bathe in fresh water, swim and play in the ocean, warm ourselves around naked fire, lay under the stars.

This connection comes through our bodies, and primarily through our feet. Our feet connect us to earth, they channel the energy of earth and the Earth Womb. A vast wellspring of feminine power resides in our feet. We need to stomp, be full-footed, awaken this energy portal that we are standing on—rather than tiptoe around like sky-bound ballerinas or be disempowered in torturous stiletto heels.

Cultures that hold more of the masculine imbalance denigrate feet—considering them dirty or insulting. Or they devise ways to control the power, such a foot-binding in China. Tribal cultures, who are more connected to the feminine, tend to engage in rhythmic dance where they stamp their feet to connect with earth.

Power of Descending Shakti

The subtle spiritual energies flow in many directions and in many configurations in our body. They are not always linear, nor do they always go up. This free flow could appear chaotic, but in fact it follows a sacred architecture, an original blueprint that underpins the spiral chakras and energy centers of our physical body. They are also linked to the ley lines or energy grids of the Earth. We can plug our own body into this planetary grid—or web—of energy, and the full force of its power can travel through us with astounding effects.

Often beliefs of how spiritual energies move in the body are distorted, because they are based on a fundamental misunderstanding: they ignore or degrade the downward feminine flow. This means we are often following spiritual systems that reinforce our already imbalanced cultural tendency to favor masculine ways of being, while ignoring our feminine sides, which urgently need reawakening.

The classic example of this is the Vedic chakra system, with its linear movement upward from the base to the crown that encourages us to ascend our energy along the channel of the spine. Often the base chakra is said to represent our "lower" feminine instincts, which need to be transcended into the purer, celestial realms of our masculine crown center. But the earth *is* the gateway to the celestial realms, so moving our energy downward without shame is a huge key.

Although there is great power in the ascending kundalini energy, we are missing out on the feminine half of our energy flow if we don't *descend* our Shakti energy, too.

Thousands of years ago, a patriarchal warlike people called Aryans swept through the Indus valley and down into India, overthrowing the indigenous Dravidian goddess cultures that flourished at that time, often using great force and violence. A hierarchical caste system was imposed, with Aryan Brahmins at the top, as self-appointed "Divine priests." Goddesses were discarded or turned into gods, feminine rites were disbanded, and women were disempowered. Despite the Aryan invasion, some elements of the Dravidian goddess culture survived in the worship of the Divine Mother, Kali and the consort goddesses of male divinities.

To make the pilgrimage through our bodies, we must first understand that the *feminine body* (in both men and women) has been the victim of a political war. A revolutionary act is as simple as moving your energy *downward*.

What is called the root chakra is also the feminine crown chakra, or throne—the symbol of Isis since ancient times. The masculine crown is the doorway to the celestial heavens, but the *feminine crown* is the doorway to *heaven on earth*, the portal to a deliciously embodied dimension of feminine sensuality here on Earth. It is an extremely magical and sensitive, physical and energetic center that connects us to life on this planet in an embodied and grounded way. It helps us anchor the cosmic energy all the way down into the root of our being. We hold the vibration of our primal innocence in this place, as well as the ability to feel the deep, ecstatic joy of being alive in a human body. Through our root, our feminine crown, we feel part of the All.

When we judge or shame our root chakra or our sexuality, we lose our ability to feel that we belong here on earth. We diminish our feminine selves. We lose touch with our ancestral wisdom, earth wisdom, and the web of life. Life becomes joyless, full of drudgery, and bound up in survival fears. Our root is like a precious heart that opens us up to deep *earth love*.

Is it any wonder our society is riddled with shame? That secretly we feel dirty? We judge our sexuality, our root, our anus, and our feminine half as sinful and base.

Opening the feminine crown chakra, also known as the *magnetic floor,* was a key part of the womb priestess practices in the temples of Isis. The constellation of energy points in the feminine crown circuit included the womb, yoni, psoas muscle, sacrum, tailbone, pelvis, perineum, and anus. By fully opening the feminine crown points, and then cascading the energy down into the thighs, legs, knees, and feet, the energy channels connecting us to the Womb of Gaia could be fully established. This anchored the frequency of *heaven on earth,* creating a powerful magnetic field that had the power to birth new states of consciousness.

❋ *Lunar Root Breathing*

Lunar root breathing is a great way to empower and heal this place in our body.

1. Bring awareness down to the feminine crown, and gently breathe soft lunar light into the root, anus, and sexual centers feel the glowing silver energy illuminate your perineum and pelvic floor muscles, and also feel a soft, energized suppleness in the area.

2. As you do so, hold in mind this rooted affirmation: "I am supple, alive, energized, powerful, rooted, safe, able to manifest all my needs."

3. Then breathe out, visualizing a translucent black smoke of any negative emotions that need to release from this area. See them evaporating into thin air. Feel the root and pelvis floor muscles soften and release, feel them open and blossom. Make noise as you exhale if you feel, either a sweet whisper of relief, or a primal roar, letting go of all the pain you have held onto for so long.

4. As you do so, hold in mind this rooted affirmation: "I surrender, let go, and release everything, I am relaxed and able to live in the flow."

Although we may feel at times that the earth has abandoned us, it is we who have abandoned her. We need to connect back to the earth, not only to receive from her, but also to *give* our love and gratitude to her. Only in giving *and* receiving can we have a true flow of energy. We cannot just take from the earth, without also flowing our love and care back to her.

In the modern world we are used to *taking*—getting more and more, without ever releasing or giving back. Even when we receive from the earth, if we cannot release or give back (using the descending energy flow) then the circuit is broken and the flow is blocked—to receive more, we need to first let go or give back.

The various emotional wounds that prevent giving, which are often labeled as greed, selfishness, or self-absorption, are actually different faces of the deeper primal fear that we aren't safe and won't be taken care of.

Letting Go, Letting Goddess

The feminine feels very unsafe in our current paradigm. This is reflected in the fact that at least one in ten women suffer from endometriosis, a disease of the womb in which the uterine lining is not fully released during menstruation, and instead "floats upward," causing inflammation, painful lesions, and problems with fertility.

The energetic signature of endometriosis is a womb whose energy is too "ascending" and does not feel safe enough to release downward. A healthy menstruation is the quintessential expression of the feminine descending energy, in which our body releases, lets go of, and dismantles the womb lining. The presence of endometriosis reveals an unconscious fear for our safety (or a past trauma, often sexual), and the inability to fully let go and trust in Life. A safe environment is the key factor that supports the descent of all the Sacred Feminine fluids of life—the "letting down" of breast milk, menstrual blood, sacred tears, and ecstatic sexual fluids.

In the feminine mystery schools, such as the temples of Isis, priestesses practiced descending their sexual orgasmic energy *downward* into the center of the Earth Womb to awaken the red magic of creative power. This released the pelvic magnetic floor and connected a woman's womb to the Earth grids. Male dominated teachings often focused on ascending sexual energy upward away from earth instead. Returning the sensual orgasmic power of the feminine to the Womb of the Earth awakens a woman's creative energy back into the web of life.

Feeling unsafe to fully *descend* and trust life to support us is also reflected in our relationship with money and abundance. When we do not feel safe to let go or release, we either hoard money and savings for safety, or we feel so unsupported by life that we cannot attract a flow of money. Either way, the healthy flow of money—and our energy, which it represents—is blocked. Ironically, hoarding money and being unable to spend and release it prevents even more abundance from circulating through us. We can menstruate our money and trust it will return to us on waves of creative flow, conceived in the magnetic womb of our soul Shakti.

Consciously descending our energy will first *reveal* and then *heal* much of our trauma patterns. When we experience trauma or shock, not only does a great part of our energy leave our bodies, it also *rushes upward* as if it is trying to escape. It then gets trapped in key areas such as the diaphragm, throat, neck, and jaw. When we experience a great shock we take a sudden in-breath and unconsciously contract our diaphragm. On an energetic level, until that trauma is released, we hold that breath in forever.

Many parts of our psyche and body are still "waiting to exhale," waiting to feel safe enough to release the breath and all the fearful emotions locked inside. To release the breath and diaphragm is to let go, and once again allow the flow of feelings into the body.

Digesting Our Life Experience

The digestive system and root chakra, of which the anus is the flower, has two aspects: the masculine principle extracts the nutrients from our food, while the feminine principle releases that which no longer serves our needs.

The feminine quality of release clears the channels, allowing us to receive more nourishment and evolve. Through our trauma and shock patterns, our energy ascends, or *rushes upward* into a constricted knot that is unable to release. We lose the emotional and energetic ability to release and let go—meaning we are unable to receive more nourishment.

We need to digest our pain and our life experiences fully, drawing out any insights, before we can truly let them go. This is one of the gifts of the feminine root chakra.

The root chakra is a place of balance and abundance; it can never heal by lack, control, or restriction. The mantra of the root is, *I want, I need, I desire, I shall receive.* This is reflected in the saying, "Ask and you shall receive." Life does not deny itself.

An energetically open root chakra lives by the wisdom that we are perfectly cared for, that we need never go without, and that we can trust enough in the abundance of life to always be provided for. We can feel safe to let go of whatever we are holding on to, and avoid grasping. This is the flow of life.

Ultimately the root is the flower of forgiveness; it fully opens when we are able to let go of past hurts, toxic waste emotions, and difficult experiences. It integrates our experiences of life and dissolves them into forgiveness, opening into the deep joy that comes from this process. This is the feminine path of embodiment and integration.

As we transform we need to weave a cocoon, or "womb," that can support us through our rebirth. Healing happens when we trust this inner womb of love, and we can let go and surrender into this vast holding space within us. We can visualize this spiritual womb as an infinite black velvet energy of support that will always catch us if we fall. When we let go into this infinite holding container, we experience the flow of the universe rush back into us.

Within this sanctuary, we enter a zone that brings wholeness and renewed aliveness and optimism; in Buddhism it is called "taking refuge." From this place of deep safety we can heal, transform, and alchemize our pain, as we learn to trust in life and our incarnation on Earth.

Surrendering to the Gravity Field of Gaia

One of the greatest, and most misunderstood, forces in this dimension is the power of gravity. This force emanates up from deep in the center of the Earth's Womb, and draws us toward Earth through the compelling attraction of two masses.

Scientists at NASA are researching the effects of gravity on the human body, and the perils of leaving Earth and the energetic pull of her Womb. Astronauts suffer lowered heart mass, atrophied muscle and bone, and weakened immune systems from just a short time away from the natural force of gravity.

The farther we are from Earth, the weaker our bones become—which represents our foundational relationship to Earth and life, which supports, roots, and grounds us.

Many people are energetically "out in space," afraid to connect to life, to Gaia, and to enter relational interconnectivity and all it brings to us.

On a subtle level, because we have become too identified with our masculine crown center, which naturally resists gravity and rises up toward the Cosmos, our feminine crown center also resists gravity, rather than surrendering to it.

Because of our personal and collective wounding, our disassociation and our unconscious urge for death—to float away and not be here—we resist this force that brings us back down to earth. The resistance plays out like a battle in our bodies. We associate heaviness with feeling bad and lightness with feeling good. We are afraid or unwilling to plant our feet firmly on the ground. Yet it is in the soil of consciousness and earth that we find our spiritual roots.

If we could fully surrender our feminine crown to gravity we would be pulled through a magical portal into another dimension of Earth—into a world beyond survival fears and lack, a place where there is abundance and joy.

Paradoxically the gravitational field of Gaia, which we can perceive as heavy and pulling us down, is actually the field that supports us, and allows us to move through life with lightness, fluidity, trust, joy, and expansion. We have to plant our roots before we can open our wings and fly.

So often our spiritual paths advocate a transcendence or ascension, helping us rise away from our bodies, our feelings, our Earth self, our feminine self. Energetically, we are resisting our Earth incarnation and are battling against the magnetic energy field of Gaia, placing us in a stressful space of struggle.

In symbolic terms we can see this resistance to gravity reflected in the distorted masculine spiritual paths humanity has followed for thousands of years, denying and disowning the feminine, rejecting Earth and the experiences unique to Earth, and flying away into airy, dreamy, ungrounded realms looking for external truths.

Feminine awakening is a *complete and radical surrender to gravity*—to fully allow the gravitational pull from the core of the Earth to take us. For thousands of years, no one on Earth has fully surrendered to gravity. When we enter this powerful descension process, we merge with the Womb of Gaia, which then ignites a tremendous, upward expansion of energy. An ascension naturally follows a descent that has been allowed to reach completion. Our dragon wings or swan wings unfold, and we rise from the ashes like the phoenix.

Only by surrendering fully to gravity can we begin to play lightly with its power.

The same process is reflected in the realm of astrophysics. Before a supernova expands outward, it first descends inward to its magnetic center, until a tipping point of concentrated energy—pure primordial power—is reached. It then bursts forth, showering the cosmos with its stardust. All energy has to be grounded and consolidated first in order to reach its full potential.

On a practical level, this surrender ignites a powerful energy in our feet, legs, yoni or lingam, and Womb, allowing us to receive an incredible reciprocal charge from Mother Earth, as she flows all her energetic sustenance into us. If we are not already experiencing this natural flow, it is simply because, at some level, we are resisting it.

Surrendering to gravity also creates a profound muscular relaxation, beginning a radical process of unfolding and realigning our skeletal muscular systems. We begin to experience our body as the ecstatic flowering of life force it truly is. The state of being we call relaxed is this letting go into Earth's gravitational pull. When we sleep, we lay on the floor in an act of surrender to this force, allowing ourselves to be held in the arms of the Earth Womb's energetic field. It is an act of trust.

Gravity is the force that builds bone density. The stronger our connection to Earth and her gravitational pull, the stronger our bones. In many ancient cultures bones were considered sacred and shamanic, the record keepers. Menstrual blood cells are actually first formed in our bone marrow and then flowed to our womb. This is why we speak of *knowing in our bones,* which is womb gnosis.

The radical surrender to life awakens our root halo, the glowing, shimmering sphere of light that expands out from our root and pelvis as a golden halo, signaling the ecstatic feminine awakening of Womb Enlightenment. The activation of the root halo was the centerpiece of becoming a Magdalene—a feminine portal, a doorway into expanded consciousness. This activation is fostered by the cosmic chalice body prayer.

✳ *Cosmic Chalice Body Prayer*

1. Stand on the grass in bare feet with your legs hip width apart. Begin to bring your awareness into your feet as an energy portal to the Earth Womb. Feel the force of gravity coming from deep inside the Earth's Womb. Trust and surrender to it. Feel as if your feet are being magnetically pulled downward, sinking down a few feet into the earth. Allow the beauty of heaviness. Surrender.

2. Feel your legs sink downward. Feel your Womb energy begin to flow downward to meet and commune with this incredible power in the Earth Womb. Allow yourself to release any fears you have of being alive. Feel cared for and secure.

3. Once this connection is firmly established and grounded, raise your arms above your head in an open V shape. Feel your chest and shoulders open in a relaxed way, without any straining. Feel energy flowing in from the Cosmos, into your masculine crown, through your hands and arms into your heart center.

4. Allow these two energies, ascending and descending, to meet inside your center. *You are* the power of life.

It is only after we develop a strong connection to earth, fully surrendering to her forces, that we are able to fully open up to the celestial realms. We open our hearts to the wonder of being alive, right here and now, sharing the gift of love.

TWIN SPIRAL CHAKRA SYSTEM

Marriage of Your Inner Soul Mates

OUR BODY IS a spiral energy vortex, into which we can magnetically draw the rich resources of the Cosmic Web, the Galactic Womb, the Earth Womb and our own inner womb. After we absorb the spiral flows of their wisdom into our being, we can then reflect them back out to life as a pulsing, living energetic breath of infinity.

Prior to the creation of the Vedic chakra system that most people are familiar with today, there existed an ancient womb religion chakra system based on the two principles of the *spiral* and *sacred duality,* or *sacred marriage.* This older chakra system was foundational to the feminine mysteries, and was known by many, including the indigenous witch-shamans of old Europe.

Rather than understanding the energy spirals within our bodies as a linear progression from base to top and back down again, the ancient twin spiral chakra system held the feminine wisdom of the *spiral path*—a dynamic, nonhierarchical, relational energy vortex within the human body that functioned as a cosmic portal of union.

The twin spiral chakra system of the Grail traditions is based on the sacred marriage of the relational twins within the body: upper half/lower half, masculine/feminine, and right/left. The twin spiral system recognizes the perennial wisdom of "as above, so below." What we see in the top half of the body is mirrored or reflected in the processes that happen below. What happens on the left is mirrored by the right, and what happens in the feminine realms is reflected by the parallel

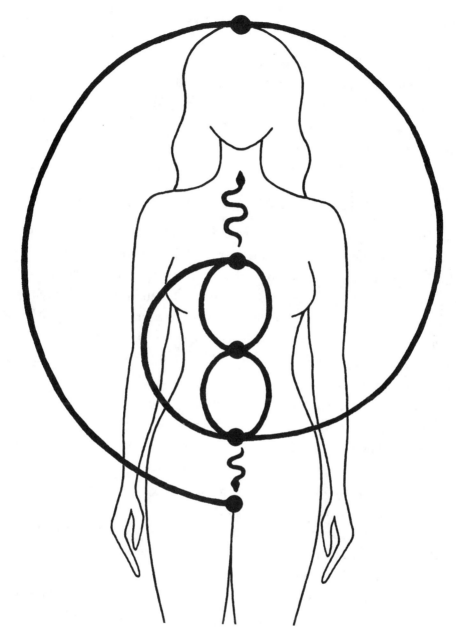

Fig. 27.1. Spiral chakra system
(Illustration by Heather Skye)

movements of the masculine realms. When the sacred dualities come together and work in harmony, an incredible and magical *third* results: a divine child, or cosmic child, whose birth is only made possible through their union.

This wisdom of sacred duality is visually represented in the image of the tree of life, whose earthly roots are equal in size and shape to its celestial branches, as well as the pre-Christian symbol of the circle-cross, with its left-right axis and up-down axis, contained and unified in the great feminine circle. When these complementary energies within us are merged, moving deeper into love and union, we feel centered in our body *and* soul. We feel equally connected to otherworld as we do this world. We feel safe to play and create here on earth, guided by upper- and lowerworld—connected to the roots of our being and the essence of our spirit.

Dynamics of the Spiral and Sacred Dualities

The power of the spiral was known to the earliest cultures of the world, who not only understood the spiral flows within the body, but also saw the spiral reflected externally throughout the natural world: in the spiderweb, the coiled snake, the nautilus shell, the whorls of our fingerprints, cyclones, and even in the spiral shape of our Milky Way galaxy, which they intuited long before the arrival of telescopes. Perhaps they also intuited what modern astronomers know—although galaxies exist in many shapes, *it is only spiral galaxies that can birth new stars.*[1] The spiral is an inherently dynamic and creative form.

Stone Age peoples recognized spiral movements within the human body. They painted spirals on cave walls and carved spiral patterns onto the womb-belly of goddess figurines, honoring the creative spiral vortex of the womb. Spiral labyrinths were inscribed into their temple complexes and circles of standing stones, which were created *as an external representation of our internal energy systems.* As always, what is inside is reflected externally, what is above is below.

When sacred duality of the upper and lower "twins" is combined with the spiral vortex, a potent and unique flow of energy emerges. See in your Womb eye the image of the twin poles of your body. Visualize your masculine upper half, consisting of your head, shoulders, arms, upper torso, and heart, as well as your feminine lower half, consisting of your feet and legs, root, yoni or lingam, womb, pelvis, and lower torso. Imagine them spinning around in a spiral vortex beyond the speed of light so that both halves merge into one—without either half of the twin having power or predominance over the other.

Nested within the twinned upper half and lower half of our bodies are the individual paired organs that represent energetic twins. In the Vedic tradition the word *chakra* means "wheel," and was understood to be a spinning spiral of energy. Likewise, in the twin spiral system of the ancient peoples, each masculine organ or energy center was envisioned as a spiral energetic vortex of subtle spiritual energies that was paired with its feminine twin in the lower half of the body. Together, they weave together to form a unified whole.

Heart-Womb Sacred Marriage

The foundation of the twin spiral chakra system is the relationship of the heart and womb energy centers. They are linked together in sacred marriage, creating a gateway into infinity within the body—our twin stargate chakra. The Hopi tradition also speaks of the womb chakra, resting under the navel, as the most important energy center in the body. They describe it as the "throne of the Creator" that directed all our internal energies, both physical and energetic, and it is paired with a corresponding masculine "doorway to the Creator" above.

As mentioned earlier, both men and women have a powerful womb chakra—our center of movement, the foundation of our being, and the essence of our primal creativity—known by different names across the world, such as the *hara* in Japan (literally, belly, abdomen, or womb), or the lower *dan tien* in the Taoist traditions of China. This powerful chakra is equally important in all humans, whether there exists a physical womb or not. Women who have had a hysterectomy, likewise, still have access to the full magical gifts of their energetic womb center.

When the throne room of the womb is united with the heart, the frequency of *embodied* love is birthed—a powerful love that can create new life upon the earth. The union of the heart and womb, perfectly balanced and centered in both love and power, allowed for harmonic resonance with the universal forces. In this union, cosmic Shakti rushes in and blooms open the flower of the body into her fullest ecstatic expression.

But if we were able to perceive the subtle energy bodies of most people today (both men and women), we would see an overdeveloped upper half and right side, and a withered lower half, especially on the left side. Our modern energy configurations reveal a species out of balance, ungrounded and ready to topple over.

The Feminine and Masculine Crowns

The root, also known as the feminine throne, and the brain, the masculine crown, are another set of paired or married energy centers. The masculine crown draws down the energies and information of upperworld—the celestial spheres—and the root draws up the powerful dragon energies and crystalline codes of the earth. Together, they are a powerful twin, as theirs is the fundamental Earth/Air relationship in our bodies, that of Mother Earth and Father Sky. When the root and crown merge together and connect in sacred marriage an incredible potency ignites. The flames of consciousness meet the fertile ground of matter, birthing and manifesting everything from new ideas and new visions, to entire new paradigms and dimensions.

Solar/Lunar: Throat and Yoni

As well as the womb-heart and root-crown twins, there are two other twin relationships that make up the eight primary energy centers of the human body: throat-yoni (or lingam) twin and the solar-lunar plexus twin. Anatomically, the throat and yoni represent the sacred twins of the upperworld and lowerworld birthing passageways, leading to the powerful creative centers of the heart and womb, respectively. Words and songs are birthed through the passageway of the throat, the enchanter and voice of cosmic magical creation—or *logos*—whose domain is the world of ideas, symbols, and images. The throat births symbolic utterances, a word derived from the same root as *uterus*, showing that sound is also rich with creative birthing power.

In Indian tantric lore the yoni is often cryptically referred to as the nether mouth. In ancient Egypt the female body was considered to have two mouths or two birthing centers—the upper masculine lips and mouth of the face, and the lower feminine lips and mouth of the yoni. In old Egyptian texts this twin relationship of the womb and the mouth is used as the basis of an ancient fertility test. It describes how an energy channel runs between a woman's yoni and her mouth—and how if this is blocked, her fertility and ability to create will also be compromised. To test the openness of this channel, the priestesseses advise a woman to place a small piece of onion inside the yoni and then wait to see how quickly she can taste the onion. If the transference happens quickly it means this magic channel is open and she is highly fertile.[2]

The solar plexus is the sacred twin of the lesser-known lunar plexus. The energy of the solar plexus is linked to the physical organ of the diaphragm, which governs the projection of our personal power out into the world. When we wish to declare our power, we speak, move, or sing from our belly—like an operatic diva, or the dramatic ancient orators of old. Our physical power comes from an active and dynamic diaphragm, but one that is at the same time fluid and supple. The rigid, tense solar plexus is paradoxically less powerful than a relaxed one. The diaphragm is also the guardian of the feeling gateway into the lower half of the body. In times of danger the diaphragm contracts, and until it feels safe enough to release and process, it guards us against feeling "gut fear" and emotional pains. Many people have a chronic, lifelong diaphragm spasm, manifesting as a tense knot at the top of the abdomen. It is released when we are able grieve our deep childhood hurts.

The lunar plexus lives at the navel and is the seat of the soft sea of emotions that lives in our belly, stored in the physical organ of our intestines. Our primal, or first, emotions are located in our intestines; they govern our ability to receive primal physical nourishment from our food but also primal physical love. This important area is the sacred site where our umbilical cord once connected us to the placenta and represents the nourishment of the mother. Wounds around connection, belonging, and primal nourishment live here—often holding grief and fear. The sacred twin relationship of the solar and lunar plexus balances our capacity to be firm, fiery, and powerful with healthy boundaries or soft, watery, and sensitive, open to merging. They also govern whether or not we can assimilate both food and emotions—shutting down our ability to digest in times of stress.

Twins within Twins

The relationship of twins continues throughout other important energy centers in the body—twins enfolded within twins. Existing within the brain is a deeper level of paired organs: the cerebrum, which is our masculine brain and seat of our Light consciousness, truth, information, external intelligence, space and time; and the cerebellum, which is our feminine brain and the seat of our Love consciousness, Oneness, eternal *now,* interconnection, internal intuition.

A left-right twin relationship also exists within the ovaries (and testes). The left ovary is the feminine twin and the right ovary is the masculine twin. Depending on whether you were conceived from an egg released from the left ovary or right ovary, you will be more likely to embody a feminine/lunar or masculine/solar way of being (whether you are male or female.) Ask your Womb or Hara and you will have a *knowing* of which ovarian twin you emerged from. You can also consciously intend to conceive from a specific ovary twin.

Even the heart has two twin chambers: the left and right chambers of the lower ventricles and the left and right chambers of the upper atria. Throughout the body, when the twin energies come together in love, a bridal chamber is created. This is the sacred space where the masculine and feminine energies meet, merge, and commune with Source, becoming *as* Source and returning to the original blueprint of Oneness.

Uniting the Twin Flame Within

Our physical body is having a love affair with itself. Our many paired organs are in holographic twin flame relationship with each other—when one hurts, the other hurts. When they become separated there is great pain and discord. They desire

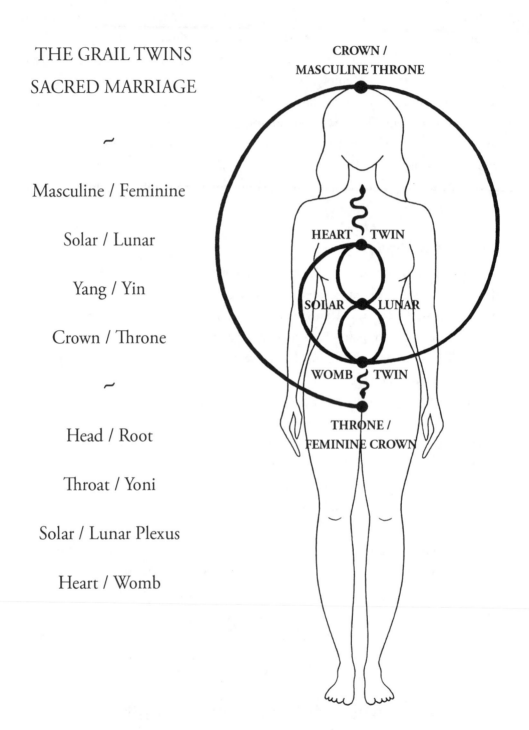

THE GRAIL TWINS
SACRED MARRIAGE

~

Masculine / Feminine

Solar / Lunar

Yang / Yin

Crown / Throne

~

Head / Root

Throat / Yoni

Solar / Lunar Plexus

Heart / Womb

CROWN /
MASCULINE THRONE

HEART   TWIN

SOLAR   LUNAR

WOMB   TWIN

THRONE /
FEMININE CROWN

Fig. 27.2. Energetic sacred marriage: the spiral chakra system
(Illustration by Heather Skye)

union. When they unite and marry in harmony, bliss and pleasure bloom into being.

If there is an issue or imbalance within any one of the twins, it affects the other member in the pair. If a throat chakra is blocked, it is very likely that the yoni or lingam will be energetically blocked. If there is an ancient grief stored in the intestines of the lunar plexus, the solar plexus and the diaphragm will contract to protect against feeling it. A problem in a shoulder likely reflects a corresponding issue in a hip, often in a diagonal relationship.

Modern allopathic medicine has a limited understanding of the energetic relationships within the human body. It splits up the body into isolated body parts, much like a machine—a delusion birthed from a patriarchal culture that fails to see the interconnectedness of all things.

An ailment of the spleen, which holds our emotional wounds around trust, will be treated without consideration for her masculine counterpart, the gall bladder, that holds the spirit of daring. The neck and throat will be diagnosed without investigating his other half, the yoni and lingam.

The same is true for the left and right sides of the body, which involves understanding how well your feminine and masculine energies harmonize and relate with each other. Your right and left, masculine and feminine selves have to be balanced and addressed at the same time, energetically and physically. For example, if the left ovary has a cyst, you will need to work with her twin, the right ovary, to help discover the underlying cause and effect healing. True healing can only happen in relationship—all deep healing is inherently relational.

Everything in existence is in a relationship of sacred duality, and the connection and harmony of these twin relationships will affect the emotional, physical, psychological, energetic, and spiritual health of the organs and energy centers within the body, the individual as a whole, the sacred union between individuals, and the entire energetic ecosystem of life.

The relationship between the left and right sides of our body reflects not just our own *inner* relationships between our masculine and feminine, but it also reflects parental or ancestral relationships to the masculine and feminine. If you have a stiff right shoulder, this could indicate an imbalance with your own masculine energies, *or* emotional and energetic wounds with your father, and male ancestral lineage. And if there is an imbalance in the masculine the feminine is *always* affected as well.

There are many layers and forms of these paired relationships within our bodies. It is vital to understand them, and then reunite them. Once you open a dialogue with your body, you will discover more and more of these connections of love and resonance.

Heaven on Earth

The relationship between the twins of our upper and lower body refer to our collective *external* relationship between the masculine and feminine. This is where our deepest collective wounds are held and embodied. The split between the upper and lower body represents the separation of our masculine consciousness from our feminine Living Light. The masculine-feminine, spirit-body split encapsulates the schism we experience on earth at this time, and the damage we are doing to the external expressions and mirrors of ourselves, other humans, creatures, plants, and the lands. The Mayan term *in lak'ech* is a simple but powerful expression of our interconnectedness: "I am another you."

On a collective or cultural level, we have to work on the relationship between our upper and lower body to restore harmony and balance. When the upper twin, which is masculine, logical, centered in the head, and connected to the light realms, is out of balance, we need to strengthen its connection and relationship to its twin, the lower half, which is feminine, intuitive, centered in the body and heart-womb, and connected to the dark fertility of the earth.

The aim is for union, not one realm of body dominating the other—but equality.

As we have learned, in ancient cultures long before Christianity, the cross was a Sacred Feminine symbol. It represented the four elements or directions of life force: air, fire, water, earth; and north, south, east, and west. It also represented the four directions of the body and the sacred relationship between these four quarters. It is also reflected in the embodied truth that everything is twinned.

The significance of a yogi's enlightenment occurring in the full lotus position was that her left hand (feminine side of the masculine upper body) would be touching the right foot (masculine side of the feminine lower body) and vice versa. It was a posture that reflected the sacred union of the cosmic twins within the body—right and left, upper and lower.

The conflict and separation between the masculine and feminine expressions of life force are etched inside and across our bodies. When they come back into union and harmony we can feel an incredible release of vital life-force energy, we become bathed in a deep sense of relaxation and completeness. Negative patterns suddenly dissolve and new and nurturing ways of being start to emerge.

Healing comes through, allowing these twins in our bodies to dialogue through the language of love, rather than conflict; to bring our body into sacred marriage counseling so they can work together as complementary pairs, as designed.

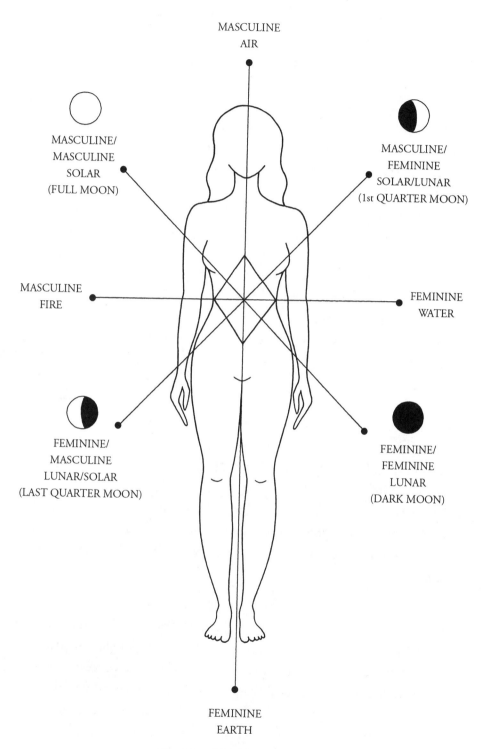

Fig. 27.3. The Cross of Life

(Illustration by Heather Skye)

✳ *Merging Your Inner Masculine/Feminine Twin*

1. Sit in a crossed-legged position or lie down; bring your awareness down inside your body, as if you are sinking into the deep darkness of inner space. Feel the black velvet energy pulsing inside.

2. Bring your attention to your right-hand side. Scan down energetically through the right side of your head, your neck, shoulder, chest, ribs, hip, right ovary or testicle, right leg, knee, calf, and finishing in your right foot. Observe and feel any physical or emotional sensations that come up: numbness, tenseness, tightness, pain, agitation, openness, joyfulness, tearfulness.

3. Now move your attention to your left side. Starting at your left foot, scan your attention upward energetically, through your left calf, knee, thigh, hip, ovary or testicle, ribs, chest, shoulder, neck, and finishing with the left side of your face and head. Observe and feel any physical sensations that come up: numbness, tightness, heat, discomfort, grief, pain, anger, fear and constriction, pleasure or tingling.

4. Can you feel a noticeable difference in the type of energy at either side?

5. Begin to ask your body to open up a dialogue between the two sides. Ask what the relationship is between the two feelings, ask where the separation has occurred. Ask what could be done to restore flow, communication, harmony, union. For example, if the masculine side feels overwhelmed and exhausted, it can result in a feminine side that is painful, contracted, or suffering from physical neurosis. The healing for the left side would then also include more rest and attention for the right side.

6. Throughout the day you can connect back and feel what is happening inside. You can gauge if you are feeling angry or fearful, if your masculine self is feeling triggered or unsupported, or if your feminine feels frightened or resentful.

Both men and women come into this world through a mother's womb that is, to varying degrees, contracted, unhealed, and afraid. Thus our first and primary relationship with the feminine space is fractured—we do not trust life to hold us safe. We do not have the deep feeling that earth is where we belong and where we can blossom.

Throughout the course of our childhood, we then experience different emotional wounds in relationship with our mother and father. These wounds are mirrored back to us in adulthood through our relationships with lovers, friends, colleagues, and community. We become full of grief, anger, confusion, doubt, sadness, guilt, and shame. We feel torn apart.

Our minds are able to deny or disassociate from painful emotions or situations—but our bodies cannot deny the experience, and never lie to us. We can struggle through a job we hate by creating ideas of why it is in our best interest—for money, for security, for career success—but our bodies will suffer. When we lose contact with our body, it begins an unconscious dialogue with us. It communicates through acute or chronic illness, accidents, or crisis events.

When we work with the body consciously, and connect to our Womb knowing, we can begin a much more graceful healing process. We are moving with the flow of life, rather than fighting against it and churning up chaos in our life.

✳ *Tree of Life: Twin Pose*

1. Stand with both feet planted firmly on the floor, hip width apart. Sense inside if you have a tendency to press down harder on one foot. Feel the energy flow into the earth, and flow back up again—this is your support.

2. Raise your hands above your head, and place the palms together in a raised prayer position. Feel the energy flow between your hands, and the heart energy flow upward through your arms.

3. Now raise your left leg, bend it and place the sole of your foot on your inner right thigh or underneath the knee. You will now be balanced on your right leg, with all your weight flowing down your masculine twin side. How does it feel? Secure, solid, fixed? Or do you feel wobbly, unsure, agitated? Do you feel energized or tired in this position?

4. Now, switch positions—raise your right leg and place the sole of your foot on your inner left thigh or underneath the knee. You will now be balanced on your left leg, with all your weight flowing down your feminine twin side. How does it feel? Powerful, grounded, certain? Or lightweight, unstable, weak? Do you feel magnetic or hopeless in this position?

5. Compare the sensations between both twin sides—which felt stronger? Could you tell where you tend to put your attention for balance and support? Did different emotions come up on different sides? Even in social situations or at work, you can raise one leg and place it on your calf, to test which side is feeling unstable, and then open the dialogue to understand what is needed to come back into balance.

This is about humans reclaiming the fullness of who we are, and our life on Earth—absolutely free, natural, and wild, connected to the web of life, living in Love.

DRAGON AND DOVE ALCHEMY

Ascending and Descending Kundalini

I am a creature of the Holiest Power,
of Wisdom in the Highest and of Primal Love . . .
I saw a light that was a river flowing,
Like rubies set in bands of gold

DANTE ALIGHIERI, *DIVINE COMEDY*

ON THE GRAIL PATH, the alchemical union of complementary solar and lunar energy streams births the dragon body or body of Light, marrying the primordial dragon power that rises into the body from the Womb of Gaia, in an energetic fire of molten lava, with the pure love that flows down from the Cosmic Womb, in the ecstatic rivers of the fountain of life.

Gnostic philosopher Lucius Apuleius reveals that this knowledge of the descending and ascending flows was part of the Mysteries of Eleusis, describing them as "dark descending rites" and "luminous ascending rites," in relation to the myth of Demeter and Persephone's descent into the underworld of the Womb.

The ascending flow was known as the dragon or serpent and the descending flow was known as the dove or swan. These polarities of bird and snake, heaven and earth, were united in the sacred marriage—both within and without—in the solar and lunar energy flows. An example is depicted in the alchemical egg diagram shown in fig. 28.1. In Taoism it was called yin and yang, and in Indian tradition these flows were known as prana and apana.

Fig. 28.1. The womb-egg as the alchemical vessel—with dragon and phoenix, sun and moon, birth-frog symbols.

(From the manuscript *De Lapide Philosophorum,* sixteenth-century England.)

In the Aramaic teachings of the Gnostic shamans, the feminine throne, the root, and her queendom of chakras is known as *hakima*—wisdom—the Holy Shakti. And the masculine crown and the upper chakras are known as *rakhma*—unconditional love—the Heavenly Father.* The union of the Womb and Heart, representing the

---

*In the Semitic languages there is a twinned relationship between the heart and the womb. Aramaic *rakhma* not only means "love" but also "womb." A similar close relationship exists in Hebrew, in which *rakham* means "love" and the sister word, *rekhem* means "womb." All derive from the Semitic root, *R-KH-M,* the original love we experienced in the womb.

meeting and merging of *Shakti* and *Bhakti,* of life force and love, is the holy union within, *Malkuta D'shmaya,* the grounding of heaven on earth.

In our awakening journeys this means uniting the wild flow of kundalini with the soft center point of the sacred heart, the love that melts all back into One. This births the *power of love*—an embodied love that is a sensual agent of transformation within and without, which merges our inner twin into harmony.

Endocrine Alchemy

On a bioenergetic level, these flows represent the alchemical circuitry of the human body and its energy system. Electrons from deep within the iron core of Gaia flow up the superconductive elements of the Earth through the feet into the human body. From there they rise through the front channels, passing through the pelvis—the throne, which is the foundation and powerhouse of the whole system. When they reach the crown, the circuit switches direction and the energy begins to flow down the back channels, in a cascade of electrons, through the feet, like lightning bolts, grounding us back into the magnetic core of Earth, our Mother.

Simultaneously, energy from the Cosmic Womb flows through the crown, cascading down the lunar back channels into the root, and then ascends back up the front channels, through the crown, expanding the energy system out into the cosmos and her dark matter field.

In Indian tantric kundalini tradition, the feminine energy reverses its downward flow, and instead awakens and ascends to merge with the masculine cosmic Shiva consciousness of the crown. In some feminine alchemical European traditions the Holy Spirit is feminine, while in others the masculine cosmic energy, the logos, descends to merge and unite with Sophia in the lower spheres and to "christen" the world with light. This is the Great Work of embodiment of divine light, revealing the robe of Living Light. A nonlinear understanding reveals that the dragon/dove primordial twins of creation are always within each other as yin/yang—and there is an essence of fire that rises and ascends and an essence of water that flows and descends.

In the most ancient traditions, the playful interaction of the masculine ascending and feminine descending Shakti energies leads to the flowering of union in both the crown and the root—embodying the greatest love and magic here on earth. The male and female energies both awaken into love and initiate each other into union, and no particular one is given exclusive precedence.

But tension or blocks in the body act as a circuit break and the flow dwindles, stagnation occurs, and disease or discomfort forms. At its lowest level it can be loss of energy, lethargy, sluggish elimination and assimilation systems, and at the more extreme it can threaten the whole ecosystem of the human body. Modern osteopathic medicine was based on this principle: that disease can only occur in the absence of flow, in areas of bioenergetic stagnation. At the root of energy blocks we can almost always find deep emotional traumas that are still retained within the cellular memory field, causing constriction and tension.

As the pelvis is the "power station" of the human body, any blocks, tension, holding and stress patterns, instantly take down the energy system. Allowing the energy to flow freely through the pelvis is key to any kundalini awakening.

Science now knows that these toroidal energy patterns or circuits form the basis of the energy flows within the entire cosmos, birthing our power. These vortexes act as huge energy generators throughout the whole of creation.

The magnetic field of the human heart extends out from us in a toroidal shape, and is capable of biologically influencing the heart rhythms of another human ten feet away. Likewise, the electromagnetic fields of Gaia and the sun are also giant toroids—the toroid is a common motif that repeats throughout the universe, from the microcosm to the macrocosm; as above, so below.

As energy flows up or down the central axis of the human body, a toroidal energy field is generated that radiates out and around, and circles back again to repeat the cycle. The ascending and descending flows are not linear or static, rather they come around again and again in repeating waves.

These circuits correlate somewhat to the ida and pingala of Eastern kundalini wisdom, where one subtle energy channel travels up the left hand of the spine and one travels up the right hand of the spine, with the shushumna—the point of sacred union—in the middle. The left-handed ida represents lunar, feminine energy, while the right-handed pingala represents the solar, masculine energy.

The left-handed lunar energy is actually located at the back of the body and is a *descending* flow—while the right-handed solar energy is at the front of the body and is an *ascending* flow; together these complementary flows create a spiral, vortex circuitry of energy. If solar kundalini rises without the balanced circuitry of the descending lunar flow, a "burn out" caused by excessive fire energy can occur, and the person becomes ungrounded, disconnected, lost in astral "spacey" realms, which have a masculine flavor. Descending lunar Shakti brings juiciness, earthiness, and grounds the energy and activates the endocrine system.

We can visualize these flows as a beautiful fire of golden light rising up through the front of our body, and then flowing down the back of our body in a cascading waterfall of lunar light. In old witch and Celtic traditions, the front of our body was our masculine half, and the back was our feminine half. We are very familiar with the front of our body, but like the feminine, the back remains a mystery. This lunar side of us has a powerful sensory system that we have disconnected from, and she experiences life and knowing in a different way. When we begin to open these lunar channels again, and "feel, sense, and know" with our back body, we enter a magical twilight world of almost supernatural sensory perception. This is the experience of "seeing with eyes in the back of our heads."

The solar/lunar womb grid is part of an ancient body of wisdom known as endocrine alchemy, which merged solar and lunar, masculine and feminine aspects to create chemical states of rapture that matched the vibration of heaven or nirvana. It was a path of union to God Consciousness. In its highest octave this alchemy is the merging of two human soul halves (the twin flames) back together. This happens through a doorway in our biology.

In alchemical traditions, both East and West, it is often stated that the aim of inner alchemy is to raise the kundalini fire located at the base of the spine, and often called Shakti, to meet and merge with pure consciousness, Shiva, located in the crown chakra and the brain. While there is much truth and power in this teaching, it is also limited by its loss of the feminine ways of Womb lore.

There can be a misconception that consciousness is somehow located in the crown and that this is a seat of higher evolution the initiate must aspire to—transcending the "base" and physical elements of the feminine throne. However quantum biology shows that consciousness is nonlocal and holographic. So our little toe is as infused with consciousness as our brain. The linear thinking is a symptom of the shift to hypermasculine awareness, and the loss of the feminine consciousness that is directly connected to the nonlinear spiral of Creation.

By the same merit, patriarchal alchemical traditions (which are most prominent at this time and have been for the past five thousand years) often overlook the core element of love in the alchemical fusion of sacred union consciousness. Not as an impersonal energy to channel for immortality, but as a living, breathing, *felt* substance and exchange that is relational and interconnected, and full of wildness, passion, and kindness. In patriarchal tantric tradition, the emphasis was often (though not always) on *using* the feminine essence for male purposes.

The Master (and where there's a master, there is often a slave) employed a consort, or karma mudra, to experience tantric union for his own benefit. This union was often bereft of personal love, and it was encouraged that an initiate have no personal feelings of love for his consort, in case it "got in the way." This was a devolution from original tantric dakini practices, where the woman was an esteemed womb shaman, teacher-consort, and bride of love.

Sexual Union: Uniting the Spiral of Life

Understanding and working with ascending and descending flows and lunar/solar alchemy is foundational for transformative sexual union.

Sexual union can only be experienced by *descending* deeply into the body and the root, outside of any mental fantasies or astral realms of consciousness. When the primordial orgasmic energy ignites and blooms, it can then *ascend* and spiral out through the body and soul. Sexual union of the Grail path happens within the vast, deep spaciousness of Womb Consciousness. The gateway to this lives within the body, and the Womb.

It is also a majestic cosmic heart space, soft, loving, surrendered, receptive.

There is no control, no tantric technique, no method—only the great relaxation and release of the mind, back down into the heart, into the Womb, into the body.

This union comes from a deep desire to give everything for love and to love. It is an invitation for the power of love to flow through our primordial sexual self.

The Bauls, who followed a path of feminine mysticism, practiced *maithuna,* ritual sex to experience the embodiment of *maner mānus*—their concept of merging with the Divine as a "human being of the heart" and uniting the masculine and feminine in a sacred union. They believed that sexual union made this divine essence swim down from the crown of the head, in the form of a fish, toward the root chakra, at the perineum, where it was then empowered by the kundalini Shakti, whose elemental feminine power awakened the masculine energy. The fish then swims back up to the crown, piercing all the chakras with Shakti.

This ritual union was often recommended on the third or fourth day of menstruation, the magical portal when the renewing Shakti stem cells are blossoming again.[1]

It is described this way in tantric lore: "This fish (which) swims in the 'high tide' of a woman's menstrual flow . . . is caught by the enjoyer . . . , the [soul] who is full of love. This is the tide time in the river, the overflowing of rasa (sexual fluids). He catches the fish and causes it to move in an upward direction."[2] Interestingly, both Jesus and the Grail king were known as fisher kings. And in tantric tradition, male initiates of the Goddess mysteries were known as Lords of the Fish.

Originally, it was known that the Yab-Yum, the power of sacred union, came from soul mates or divine lovers united in the deepest love and primal bonding, which awakened an incredible field of pod consciousness and endocrine response—a love that was lived and felt, not just in sacred ceremony, but in the daily rituals of everyday life, which are written into our cellular consciousness.

This bonding is the secret of creation, when our entire universe was permeated by a burst of light as protons and neutrons first fused together. This merging is at the heart of matter. From the very first moment of creation, our universe moved toward creating relationships, with different aspects drawn to each other by their very nature, full of a primal desire to unite, bond, and merge. The universe is making love to itself in every moment through the "allurement of opposites."[3]

Over time, the dragon and the dove—the essence of fire and water, the masculine and feminine—became divorced from a deeply meaningful connection, fully lived and embodied on earth. And they longed for each other, and in this longing came an incredible grief etched into our biology—and a desire to reconnect again. Primal bonding, both in childhood with a mother/father, and in adulthood with a wife/husband or lover, softens the entire physical and energetic system, and opens the subtle channels. Daily loving touch is a healing balm.

The union of the masculine and feminine in sacred relationship creates an alchemical friction that was symbolically encoded in medieval texts—this bringing together of the opposites begins a reactive process, transforming each component and whittling them down to their essence, until they become so refined that they can merge and create a new substance, the "pure gold of love."

It can also be a highly volatile, explosive, and dangerously experimental process, as anyone who has committed to a truly sacred, truthful relationship can testify!

This alchemy of love ideally happens in the container of a true relational love, lived out fully on a day-to-day basis. However in many tantric traditions this devolved and the relationship between guru and student replaced that of the sacred lovers. Now this alchemical relational friction, designed to bring about "ego-death" in the student, was generated by the guru-student interactions—usually between two men. Often male-female tantric union was only visulized in archetypal realms of the god and goddess. If physical sexual union occurred with a female consort, she was worshipped, but also regarded as dispensible, an object or vehicle to attain enlightenment through.

The image of the lonely hermit in his cave, with his solitary practices of austerity replaced the older peak experiences—such as when a man witnessed the birth of his child and was ecstatically awakened by the awesome flow of descending energy, or "Holy Spirit" flowing from the Cosmic Womb and his beloved's womb as the baby entered the world.

Our biology is created for bonding, for touch, for sacred union of the masculine and feminine flows. When we don't receive this union, our system "deactivates." We can also unite these dragon and dove energies through healing, bodywork, breathwork, and sacred movement. The key is to move the energy in the body, to open the heart and the life-flow, and to *feel* again.

Often our bioenergetic system is closed down, deactivated or blocked by tension and repressed emotions. This creates stagnation and disease, and our endocrine and nervous system is unable to deliver the cocktail of bliss we were designed for. In

Fig. 28.2. Cretan priestess

(Illustration by Natvienna Hanell)

women, this can deeply affect our reproductive and hormonal system—making menstruation painful, both physically and emotionally. When we begin to bring awareness to these magical portals, glands, and places in our womb grid, we can begin to feel, dissolve, and move the energy again—and most importantly, to connect our two beautiful flows of energy back together again, creating an ouroboros (the snake that bites its own tail) of power within. This is marriage counseling within our own bodies—healing and resolving trauma and blocks.

The ascending and descending flows are designed to be in a sacred dance of union, they long for each other, they belong to each other—they *are* love.

WOMB ORACLES SHARE
Awakening Dragon Shakti

Dragon Shakti breathing recharges your life force with the resurgence of shimmering, wild, Shakti energy. It undulates in serpentine wavelike movements as you rest on your back with your feet on the ground. The bioenergetic current moves up into your feet from the iron core of Gaia and rises up into the pelvis, the throne that is the foundation and power of the whole system. The pelvis is the power station, the pump house that moves the breath through the body.

This practice churned up all the old wounds and traumas, all the repressed agony I buried long ago. My skin shed like a snake as I released and renewed from the inside out. I extracted the wise blood from my aching bones. I started to glow, writhing with an inner ecstasy, a sense of pleasure and sensuality, a magnetic sexuality that radiated the magic and power of my feminine essence.

Dragon Shakti breathing in moonapause is truly a way of turning on the fountain of Life. My body has become renewed with this light energy regenerating the cells and tissues of my body. My eyes danced, toenails and fingernails became pink with half-moons rising from their beds. My breasts became full and round with radiance. Everything is pink with new life; there is a sense of juiciness, silkiness in the essence of my nipples and yoni. My creativity is wild and flowing. Dragon Shakti breathing has brought the moon down, it brought me back to my childhood, my maiden self. And now in moonapause, the moon is pouring down its healing lunar nectar of regeneration.

Dragon Shakti breathing awakened my feminine soul like a vibrating current of stars spinning around my head. I heard the roar under my breath as I held back the reins of a powerful dragon with tetany in my hands. I descended into the Womb of Gaia riding the Dragon's breath, rising with radiant wings of light into the Cosmic Womb. A spontaneous current circulated through my womb, heart, and throat opening the mouth of the Goddess.

I continued to breathe into the cave of my yoni, birthing three blue crystal dragon eggs.

I did not expect to meet the Dragon rising from the Womb of Gaia, glowing with the wise blood in my bones. I was breathing fire, melting crystals in my spine that undulated from my sacrum to the base of my skull. My sacrum was the portal that scraped against the crystal floor of the earth. Like a circuit, the light ran up through the liquid crystal core of my spinal cord to my pineal gland. The radiance ascended to the butterfly wings of my sphenoid bone that opened from the back of my head into the primal lunar brain.

I descended on a stream of silver light sliding down my back into the earth releasing pulsating waves of light hidden not only in my womb but in the Womb of Gaia. As the womb-heart field started to clear, a continuous infinity loop of pulsating Shakti energy generated a current of light that anchored my womb magnetically toward the crystal core of the earth.

A.C.

CYCLE 6

WOMB
MEDICINE WHEEL

Awakening the Eight Grail Gates

ROYAL ROAD

Entering the Three Grail Gates of the Yoni

Woman is the creator of the universe,
The universe is her form;
Woman is the foundation of the world,
She is the true form of the body.

SHAKTISANGAMA TANTRA

THERE IS AN ANCIENT pathway to the power of the Womb; it is the most sacred pilgrimage a human being can take. It is the royal road, the quest for the Holy Grail, the Chalice that holds the infinite possibilities of Life herself. Here we enter the Temple of the Womb.

This lost alchemical tantric tradition holds secret wisdom of magical *gateways within the womb,* known as Gates of Mystery, doorways to the source of Creation that have the power to bestow renewal and awakening for men and women who walk this spiral path.

Womb Awakening was practiced by the priestesses of Isis, tantric yoginis, Tibetan Khandros, Celtic swan maidens, priestesses of Avalon, and the gnostic Magdalenes.

This pilgrimage, this sacred quest for truth, love, and union, is taken by walking the inner and outer landscape of the feminine form, by taking this spiral path deeper and deeper until all veils have been cast aside—and our primal innocence held in the Womb is revealed, embodying our original blueprint of Creation.

The pathway *is* you, the Holy Grail is *your* womb space, the journey takes *you* into the deepest intimacy with your true self, and all the veils that have kept you from this relationship. It is a journey of wild innocence, of pure nakedness.

The Grail Gates of the Holy Womb are a woman's most precious and intimate "sacred sexual sites" where life-giving regenerative energies, Shakti, flow through a womb grid of ley lines. Here, feminine meridian points that web across our bodies merge together in the nerve-rich energy gateways of the yoni. These portals produce different feelings, energies, and gifts that embody our unique soul essence. All traditions have known this and have practiced yoni worship in some way. The Celtic Grail tradition was birthed through the feminine mysteries of the Great Womb. In the Isis temples and temples of Inanna, their traditions also journeyed through the opening of the seven gates to enter the mystical eighth—the black root of Creation, the Void.

In the Kabbalist Zohar, the indwelling feminine aspect of God—the Shekinah—is described as the opening into the Divine. It says, "One who enters must enter through this gate."

In the medieval alchemical text *The Chemical Wedding of Christian Rosenkreutz,* Christian has to go through a number of gates to get to the magical castle where the alchemical wedding will take place.

In *The Wedding Song of Wisdom,* second century CE, it says, "The Maiden is Light's Daughter: Her tongue is like the Door-hanging . . . Her fingers are secretly setting, the Gates of the City ajar. Her bridechamber shineth with Light, pouring forth scent of balsam and sweet herbs."[1]

These allegories of "gates" and the "Grail" all secretly allude to the female womb.

When we touch this holy of holies, the Grail Castle, the Great Womb, we unlock a cascade of feeling and endocrine responses, which can chemically and soulfully transport us to paradise on earth—heaven, nirvana, fairyland, Elysium; we awaken into the truth of the pure pleasure and bliss in our bodies that flows directly from the Womb of Creation.

Traveling the Fairy Paths of the Womb

In traditions across the world there are the concepts of holy roads, royal roads, or fairy paths that follow the magical, magnetic dragonlines of Earth's telluric energy. Keeping these fairy paths open was essential to the well-being of the world; to damn or block them was believed to bring bad luck or a curse upon the land.

These royal roads, holy paths, and fairy ways are also found within the female body, which is a living landscape of initiation and spirit travel, leading to the inner Grail Castle—the Womb. When the feminine energy lines that flow through the inner Grail Gates and form sexual "energy wells," or "ecstatic fountains," are blocked, the magic doorway of the Womb closes down. Awakening these fairy paths of sensual Shakti energy is the alchemical key that births an embodied divine womanhood and also rebirths the world into the vibration of joy and love.

When these inner energy paths are awakened it not only blesses the woman but also bestows the grace of "sensual salvation" to her lover, and awakens the divine masculine.

From the wisdom of our wombs, we know that our birthright is to experience fully the wonder and ecstasy of *being alive* as sacred containers of living Light. We feel deeply this is a realm of pure love, and we understand that separation was in fact a dance of union.

Now this wisdom is rebirthing, and we are being invited to walk these pathways into the Womb again. This journey is embedded physically, energetically, and soulfully in the eight Grail Gateways of the female yoni and womb and the male lingam and energetic womb space. Eight is the feminine number of infinity.

The yoni and lingam are twinned. They belong together, they fit together; one is a key that fits the Cosmic lock and opens the doorway into the vastness of the Great Womb of Creation, and the vibration of pure love. When we walk this path, even if we are alone, our frequency upgrades will attract the person who holds a potent "key" for us, to open more, to love more, to grieve more, to awaken more. Or we can practice this inner alchemy on our own.

These feminine and masculine qualities can also be embodied in same-sex relationships to explore the qualities, gifts, and initiations of each gateway.

Journeying through the Grail Womb Cross

During our pilgrimage through the Grail Gates, we will follow the shamanic path of the womb medicine wheel—a symbolic map of the Grail womb cross. This encodes the pathway of a spiral journey into the Womb of Creation. This can be an ascending pathway into the Celestial Womb or a descending path to the Earth Womb. Traveling through the Grail Gates invokes the power of creative spirit to awaken and conceive new paradigms. It is a journey taken by two beloveds in sacred sexual union or by a womb priestess or shaman practicing alone in spiritual-sexual devotion.

The cross is the axis or spindle around which the Great Womb weaves and creates life—and new possibilities of consciousness. Plato describes the nature of the cosmos as a spindle turning on the knees of the Goddess, alongside the Three Fates, who spin and weave the thread of each soul. In Christian tradition the Virgin Mary was also said to have "earned her living by spinning,"[2] as *theotokos,* the *mother of god,* she who is the Divine Creatrix of all.

This Womb map begins by leading us through the first three Grail gateways of the yoni, and takes us to the dweller at the threshold: the Cosmic gate of the cervix, the "third eye" of the Womb. These first three Grail Gates form the lower vertical axis of the Grail womb cross, and they take us through the three faces of the feminine: the maiden, the queen, and the crone. This journey can also be taken through the lingam, journeying through the three faces of the masculine: the knight, the king, and the magi. Both pathways lead into the Cosmic Womb; they take us to the threshold of our personal human journey, and across into something far vaster.

This holy feminine trinity of maiden, queen, crone (which is intimately connected with the seasons of life and the cycles of the moon) also reflects certain states of feminine consciousness, and signature vibrations that live within us all at every moment. When we have awakened these Grail gateways, we can claim and embody these states of consciousness—so we can call upon them at any time in our awakening journeys. We *all* have a maiden, queen, and crone within us, holding specific wisdom and gifts, no matter what our life stage.

The first three Grail Gates contain your own personal imprint, gifts, and wounds both ancestrally and from this life. Once you cross the threshold of the third Grail Gate you enter the collective energy of the Great Womb and the elements and directions of life force—earth, fire, air, water—that form the arms of the cross.

The journey culminates in the center, the Womb of Creation—the mystical rose of Grail tradition, the flower of Life in Sacred Feminine geometry, the Void, the bindu point of tantra. This sacred center is also symbolized by the labyrinth.

Every gateway also has a shadow, and this also holds its gifts and can be called upon at any time during the journey to shake things up, throw in a wild card, and help integrate the fullness of our human experience. These Grail Gate shadows are asking to be explored, understood, befriended, and embraced, not judged.

The first Grail Gate and second Grail Gate both have a solar and lunar portal, which each bring different signatures and subtleties to the awakened gateway. The clitoris is the solar portal of the first Grail Gate while the sacred entrance to the yoni is the lunar portal. In the second Grail Gate, there is a solar G-spot on the front wall of the yoni, and a lunar G-spot on the back wall of the yoni. Uniting the solar and lunar gateways of the first two Gates helps weave and anchor the union of the solar and lunar pathways to enter the union of the third Grail Gate.

This is a spiral journey—it is not linear. You will find yourself spiraling deeper and deeper into and through every gate, and this process is limitless and infinite.

Once you begin this pilgrimage it will be easy to feel which Grail Gate the spiral is taking you through, and after a massive breakthrough you will be immersed in the Cosmic Womb of the eighth gate—the Womb of Creation—to infuse with Pure Love, and replenish your spirit before you spiral to your next Grail Gate.

The spiral rebirths the wisdom of the crone into the innocence of the maiden and blooms her into sensual womanhood, and every spiral births each of the qualities of this holy trinity of triple goddesses into deeper dimensions of love.

Each of these Grail Gates is an energetic vortex *within* the yoni and Womb. But once awakened, the signature frequency spirals throughout your whole being, catalyzing new states of consciousness and even biology, anchoring you deeply into the cosmic womb grid and the mysteries of the dark-matter creative field.

During your pilgrimage you will find yourself journeying through the initiations of each frequency of consciousness and the gifts and challenges it holds. The maiden brings to us a time of new beginnings, fresh hope, falling in love with life again—it often arises out of a Dark Night of the Womb, and is the first ray of sun rising from a darkened sky. The initiation is to allow this trust and openness again, and to be able to forgive the hurts of the past, and begin afresh again.

The mother/lover brings to us the gift of building, nesting, creating our queendom on earth, shining our gifts and radiance into the world, rooting into love and opening to the bounty of life. This initiation can be challenging for the parts of us that want to escape, that fear commitment and the deeper level of intimacy, maturity, and love it will bring. We are called to embrace and surrender into the cycles of life and to passionately trust in the divine flow that is birthing.

The crone brings us the gift of release, letting go, rebirthing all that no longer serves us so we can spiral into a deeper octave of wisdom and life; she is full of fierce devotion and wild truth. She holds the power of daleth, death, so something new can be born. This initiation can be exhilarating, intense, and terrifying; this frequency is often a tornado that whirls through your life. What is left standing is real and true, and you are called to trust in this divine pruning.

We invite you to begin your pilgrimage into the Sacred Feminine medicine wheel, the Grail Castle, which lives within. To guide you on your way, we present the following for each of the first three gates: the archetype; the voice of the Womb; the attributes, including the alchemical twins, the goddess, the season, the moon cycle, the womb cycle, and the earth essence; the gifts and wounds; and the shadow. The royal road of feminine awakening awaits.

To take a guided shamanic journey through the womb medicine wheel, see "Womb Awakening Audio Tracks" on page 525.

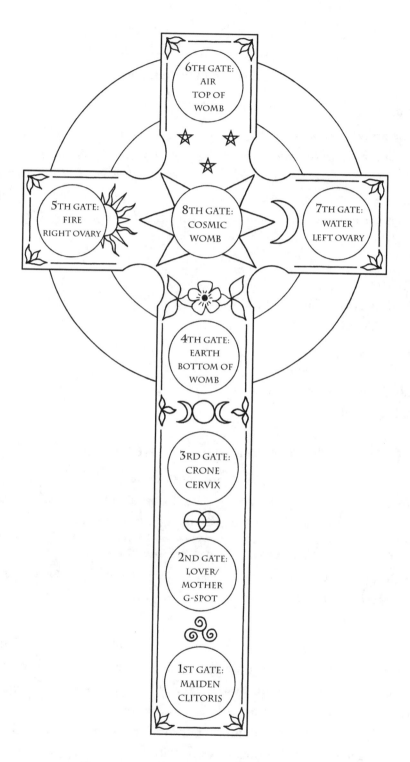

Fig. 29.1. Grail Gates of the Womb Cross

(Illustration by Heather Skye)

First Grail Gate: The Clitoris and Yoni Lips

∞

Archetype: The Maiden

Voice of the Womb

I am the delicate whisper of innocence; I come to you in silence, when the wind dances through the trees and the morning dew reflects rainbow light. I am the pure place that has never been hurt, who opens with trust and playful sweetness. I am sensitive and responsive, sometimes shy, sometimes wantonly surrendered. I am forever virgin; everything is new within me. If you show me devotion, I will give you everything, for in my vulnerability I am made perfect.

Attributes

Alchemical Twins: Clitoris/Thymus
Goddess: Virgin Mary, Blodeuwedd, Parvati
Season: Spring
Moon Cycle: New Moon
Womb Cycle: Cellular Renewal
Earth Essence: Pearl

Gifts and Wounds of the First Grail Gate

Gifts of the First Grail Gate

Trust, Wonder, Playfulness, Patience, Integrity, Purity, Open to Life, Surrender, Harmony, Vulnerability, Lack of Artifice, Enthusiasm, Gracefulness, Sensitivity, Beauty

Wounds of the First Grail Gate

Distrust, Betrayal, Suspicious, Scared, Jaded, Numb, Afraid of Life, Overdisciplined, Controlling, Judgmental, Cynical, Armored Heart, Disappointment, Bitter

This is the first step on your pilgrimage into the Womb. It is a place of innocence, tenderness, vulnerability, and surrender. This aspect cannot be rushed, forced, or pressured into opening. It is the flower bud that blossoms in her own time, through trust, appreciation, sensitivity, patience, kindness, support, and softness.

Associated with the season of spring, the maiden of the first Grail Gate is eternally coming into bloom, bathing the world with freshness and enchantment. She is the rising sap, the feeling of quiet joy in the first spring sunshine as green buds begin to burst through. This is the aspect of the feminine that has complete faith in love, who loves the romance of life, who gives herself completely to the adventure of relationship with enthusiasm and excitement, who is utterly open.

It is the gateway of innocence and renewal, the temple doors of the yoni and Womb—which is approached with reverence, integrity, and devotion. Only those with the truest hearts can gain entry to this cosmic door. On the energy realms, we serenade and court this Grail Gate; we sing the sweet songs of surrender, love, and enchantment; we bring our offerings of love and beauty to her gate.

The maiden is a frequency that lives within us all and accompanies us throughout all our life journeys, bearing her shimmering lamp of Grail light to lead us and guide our way. She is the pure, immaculate love that watches over us and tends to our deepest wounds with her purifying rays—who speaks to our most jaded, forsaken places and touches them with green buds of hope and renewal. She whispers to us to keep the faith, to trust in life again, even when our heart has been broken and our sexual energy is fragile, afraid, betrayed. She reminds us of a love so vast, so infinite, that all wounds can be healed in its arms.

When we have journeyed through a Dark Night of the Womb, the maiden waits for us at the end of the birth tunnel—her radiance lighting up our life again, illuminating us with the magical wonder of everyday life and the sparkle of joy.

This Grail Gate is radiant, enchanting, and invites us to open to love once again.

It is also intimately connected with the thymus gland, a major part of our womb grid, which rests behind the breastbone in the center of the chest, about two inches below the clavicle. This beautiful gland is the seat of our innocence, playfulness, joy, and wonder. It is where our inner child lives. When the thymus is nourished it gives us a childlike energy, vitality, excitement, and enthusiasm. It is full of an exquisite innocence and playfulness that is our natural birthright; it contains our original purity, tenderness, and complete trust and wonder in life.

It is also the seat of our sexual innocence—it is a portal to the Womb Heart.

But the thymus gland is very sensitive to emotional and environmental stress; it can shrink to half its size in twenty-four hours following a stressful episode or illness, and it can also grow when it feels happy. This explains the feelings we often have of our heart opening or closing—as this sensitive gland contracts or expands.

The same is true of the clitoris, which can become engorged and open, pulsing with delight, or can contract, shrink, and numb-out if not treated with proper care. This explains how we can feel as if we are sexually opening or closing down, depending on how nourishing our lives and intimate relationships are.

Come into awareness of the connection of the thymus to the tender, innocence of the clitoris. This creates a circuitry of love that feeds back in an infinity loop between our heart and yoni to create the sacred Heart Womb.

We hold our greatest betrayals in this gate: the deep sadness that we have not been met in our innocence, in our openness, in our desire to love deeply. Awakening this gate will bring you into the deep grief and fear around being "entered" again, about relinquishing control, surrendering your boundaries and merging with another. It will stir the sleeping dragon of emotions around all the times your boundaries have been violated, dishonored, and discarded.

Ultimately it will bring you into the deepest primal fear of allowing life, love, Shakti to enter and penetrate you again and bring you back to life. It will bring you into the abyss of merging back with Source of Creation, and relinquishing the illusion of owning and being in control of your own separate self.

This gate is the magical doorway into the exquisite enchantment of dissolving back into the ocean of love, of melting into the Void of the Great Womb that births and rebirths everything. It is the shimmering lightness of the rainbow that infuses and anoints all of life with its holy radiance, making all as newly born.

This gate calls for your complete trust, devotion, and surrender.

Shadow: Tease/Knave

The shadow side of the first gate is the immature seductress, the young feminine who teases and allures, who relies on superficial beauty and adornments to tantalize, but who is afraid of deep emotional surrender, and can be cruel, contrary, uncommitted, attention seeking, and flighty in her avoidance of this.

In the masculine, this immature energy expresses as the knave—the pretty man-child who is dripping with sweet words and high tales, who enjoys the thrill of the chase and seduction, but is afraid to commit to love. This creates deep wounds of betrayal and abandonment in the women he is romancing, and reveals that he has probably experienced these wounds himself, in childhood.

The shadow of the tease/knave is a gift to reveal where the heart is still closed, afraid, and protected. If you have either experienced or embodied this shadow, your own superficiality and fear of the depths of love is being reflected to you. Befriend and embrace both elements of this shadow—the seducer and the victim.

❋ Questions to Percolate in Your Womb Cauldron

Sit in the womb meditation pose (see fig. 29.2) and breathe gently into this gate; feel what is held here. The first Grail Gate is the sacred entryway into the yoni. Ask to feel . . .

1. What does this Grail Gate wish to invite into your life?
2. Whom and what kind of energies have you allowed to enter you?
3. Can you feel the beauty, purity, and divinity of your sexuality?
4. Do you feel cherished, valued, and honored in your feminine vulnerability?
5. What aspect of your life needs an infusion of freshness, renewal, and lightness?

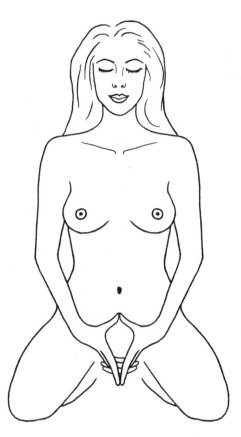

Fig. 29.2. Sitting posture in yoni mudra
(Illustration by Heather Skye)

❋ *Breath and Sound Meditation*

1. Sit in the womb meditation pose. Allow your shoulders to relax downward, so the rose of your heart can open. Bring your awareness to the Womb and breathe here for a few moments, inhaling and exhaling the delicious, fertile velvet darkness.

2. Now allow yourself to gently drop your energy into your clitoris. Breathe here for a few minutes with all your awareness gently focused on your clitoris. You

can also focus your energy on your moon petals and the entrance of your yoni cave, feeling how the sensitivity flows through the flowering lips of your yoni.

3. Allow any feelings, colors, sensations, or visions to arise and be with them. Ask if your clitoris has any messages she wishes to share with you, allow yourself to listen.

4. Begin to chant the mantra for the first Grail Gate: *ee-oo-ee*. Do this for as long as you feel called.

❋ *Visualization Practice*

1. Bring your hands to your Womb. Feel the first Grail Gate of your yoni gently opening. Visualize a shining maiden, glowing with light, walking toward you—she comes bearing a chalice of holy lustral water, infused with the petals of spring's first flowers, and the innocent dew essence of the soft rays of the new moon.

2. Bring your awareness into the clitoris and the lips of the yoni, and begin to visualize the first time your clitoris was touched—how did it feel? Was it insensitive and painful? Or was it soft and loving? If you wish, you can begin to make sounds or silently allow any deep feelings to arise. Gently, the shining maiden begins to anoint the sacred entrance of your first Grail Gate with the healing waters, allowing the floral and lunar essence to bathe and cleanse any negative imprints to dissolve them into love.

3. Now begin to remember the first time you experienced a clitoral orgasm— can you take yourself back to that moment? How did it feel? How deep was the pleasure? Breathe softly and visualize rays of beautiful light shining from your clitoris.

Second Grail Gate: The G-spot

———— ∞ ————

Archetype: Queen

Voice of the Womb

I am the ripe fruit, the midday sun warming your skin, the rhythmic sea waves inviting you in. I open you into deep pools of sensuality and pleasure. I initiate you into womanhood, motherhood, and awaken your primal erotic creature, who fearlessly loves and protects her brood. I am the juicy, vital place in you that remains open and welcoming. I bathe everything in bliss, joy, and ecstasy. My wild, devotional sexuality is my deep gratitude to Creator for the gift of Life.

Attributes

Alchemical Twins: G-spot/Thyroid
Goddess: Magdalene, Rhiannon, Yeshe Tsyogal
Season: Summer
Moon Cycle: Full Moon
Womb Cycle: Ovulation, Conception
Earth Essence: Ruby

Gifts and Wounds of the Second Grail Gate

Gifts of the Second Grail Gate

Pleasure, Laughter, Loyalty, Openness, Desire, Passion, Commitment, Sensuality, Wildness, Gratitude, Abundance, Fertility, Magnetism, Compassion, Kindness

Wounds of the Second Grail Gate

Betrayal, Sourness, Shame, Isolation, Loneliness, Hardness, Despair, Selfish, Insecure, Inhibited, Eating and Anxiety Disorders, Low Self-Esteem, Jealousy, Seriousness

This second step on your pilgrimage into the Womb takes you deeper into the spiral of love. It is a place of sensuality and openness. At the first gate you passively *allowed* yourself to be entered, but now you are opening your doors wide with welcome and inviting all the sensations and risks of love inside. This is a choice, *the* choice; it shows willingness, commitment, self-love. This space bubbles up inside you with passion, desire, and overwhelming gratitude for life.

Associated with the season of summer, the lover/mother of the second Grail Gate is a cascade of fertile fragrance, of wild flowers blossoming in rich abandon. She is warm summer rain drenching soft skin, balmy nights of sensual enchantment, and the sunny optimism of a cloudless blue sky. She is benevolent and blooming. This is the aspect of the feminine that has the courage to love completely, to open herself to pleasure fully, to share all her bountiful gifts with all she meets. It holds the orgasmic, sensual fertility of motherhood, the wild beauty of creation, and the sexual magnetism and initatory power of the priestess-lover.

This frequency holds the energy of the benevolent queen, the woman who lives from her feminine center, who sits with grace and compassion on the throne of her own power, who allows herself to step forward with her gifts into the world as mother, lover, and leader.

There is a surrendered movement that is joyful and expansive and giving in this

Grail Gate that opens itself and delights in being seen and participating in the wonder of love and the wildness of the feminine flow. This is the frequency of the holy bride approaching the bridal chamber, revealing and offering the fullness and promise of her radiant and bountiful femininity, to come together in union.

Because she holds the power and knowing to say no to anything that does not serve love or her own self-love, she also holds a deeply spontaneous and wild *yes* to life. She is also a pantheress protecting all her children, both her physical babies and her creative endeavors; she is both softly sensual *and* fiercely loving.

In a world that values "doing," this Grail Gate will be your *undoing*—it invites you into a luxurious, wanton space of pleasure, sensation, enjoyment, and adornment. It is the aspect of the feminine that is celebrated with festivals, feasting, dancing. All the places within that have been conditioned to push, to thrive on pressure and *hard* work, will be melted in softness and the knowing that life is full of ease.

It is also intimately connected with the thyroid gland, a major part of our womb grid, which rests behind the clavicle at the base of the neck. This juicy gland is the seat of our wild sensual pleasure. It is where our inner tigress lives. When the thyroid is nourished it gives us an abandoned, wanton deeply multiorgasmic openness. It is full of an erotic wildish sensuality that is our natural birthright, and contains our shameless sexuality, which has never judged itself as sinful.

It is also the seat of our sexual pleasure; it is a multidimensional portal to cosmic orgasmic energy and the vast powers of the wild womb.

The neck and the jewel of the thyroid housed within it, is a twin of the yoni and G-spot. This memory and knowing lives on in "love bites," vampire lore, and romantic movies; when a woman throws her head back and exposes her neck, this is a symbolic show of openness and an invitation to come within. It is possible to have physical thyroid orgasms, and to experience physical neck orgasms either through kissing, licking, biting, and gentle pressure.

The shut down of the wild, sensual feminine, and the shame and judgment around opening to full orgasmic pleasure, is reflected by so many women experiencing thyroid problems—especially underactive thyroid, indicating low Shakti.

An initiation into the second Grail Gate is to engage in open, honest, and transparent communication. Truth is a gateway to feminine power and authenticity. To be fully honest and open, emotionally, sexually, and soulfully with your beloved or lover, will provide the container for the greatest openings. It will awaken the voice of your Womb and the wisdom she holds and is waiting to share. When we do not feel safe to honor our boundaries, or tell others what gives us pleasure or pain, we limit our capacity to grow into deeper awareness and ecstatic spaces.

We hold the grief of abandonment in this Grail Gate: the deep fear of rejection, of being left and discarded, of loneliness and loss. We long so much for union, for communion, for family, for connection; but with this *invitation*, this reaching out, we perceive that we open ourselves to great danger and risk. The stakes are the highest in the universe—our precious heart. We gamble everything on love.

When we experience heartbreak, loss, abandonment, or rejection, the second Grail gate begins to close her doors; to stop welcoming love and pleasure inside. She becomes defended and hard, independent and self-reliant. She wants to cheat life. There is a sense of infertility: physical, creative, and spiritual. Life becomes thankless and dull, filled with the drudgery of survival, despair, and isolation.

This gateway leads us to our deepest terror of abandonment; the dark lurking feeling that our Creator has left us to fend for ourselves in a meaningless, cruel world and that we are not good enough. But there is also the uncomfortable dissonance that somehow it is we who have abandoned our true self—who still lives in love, and who is waiting for us to throw open the doors once again, if only we dare.

Often our greatest fear is allowing ourselves to open to all the love and pleasure that will flow into us when we choose to open the doors of our hearts and sexuality again. It takes an incredible softness to surrender to this flow.

When we open these doors, a bountiful, abundant birthright of the sheer pleasure of the frequency of love awaits us, consuming us in wild bliss.

Courage, desire, and deep faith in the sanctity of our sexuality open this door.

Shadow: Seductress/Fool

The shadow side of the second Grail Gate is the abandoned, hurt woman who in her despair has opened without discernment, rather than shutting down. Her low self-esteem is momentarily soothed by unloving sexual encounters, but her heart is plunged further into despair when she is rejected and used again and again. Alternatively, this shadow can be the cruel Queen who uses her sexual power to manipulate and use others, to gain attention, glory, fame, money, and other worldly riches—but who leaves her true feminine self destitute and bankrupt.

In the masculine, this energy expresses as the fool, the anarchist, the trouble stirrer, the rebel, or the solitary spiritual seeker who wants to leave all the troubles of responsibility and relationship behind for freedom and knowledge. This is a Trickster energy that can do anything in any moment and isn't anchored to the need to be loving, good, or reliable. It can create great transformation and movement, but often hides a deep fear of opening to Love.

The shadow of the seductress/fool is often very useful in opening the second

Gate; it takes us out of our comfort zone, and challenges our preconceived boundaries, even if just for a while. Sometimes we need to play the fool, to rebel, to let go of responsibility that no longer serves us, and to go off on a solitary adventure to discover ourselves and let others down. Embracing this shadow means holding the space to return to love after a lesson is learned.

❋ Questions to Percolate in Your Womb Cauldron

Sit in the womb meditation pose and breathe gently into this gate; feel what is held here. The second Grail Gate is a sensual invitation into the yoni. Ask to feel . . .

1. How magnetic, abundant, and sensual is your inner Queen?
2. What is this Grail Gate wishing to create and birth in your life?
3. Have you allowed betrayal and hopelessness to enter this gate?
4. Can you fully surrender to the pulsing waves of wild Shakti?
5. How deep is your desire to open into sexual union with a soul mate?

❋ Breath and Sound Meditation

1. Sit in womb meditation pose with a soft, relaxed, and upright posture. Allow your shoulders to relax downward, so the rose of your heart can open. Bring your awareness to the Womb and breathe here for a few moments, inhaling and exhaling the delicious, fertile velvet darkness.
2. Now allow yourself to gently drop your energy into your G-spot. Breathe here for a few minutes with all your awareness gently focused on your G-spot. You can also try bringing your energy upward from the entrance of your yoni cave, inside the yoni passageway, and into the G-spot and sense if this feels different.
3. Allow any feelings, colors, sensations, or visions to arise and be with them. Ask if your G-spot has any messages she wishes to share with you, allow yourself to listen.
4. Begin to chant the mantra for the second Grail Gate: *oon-agh*. Do this for as long as you feel called.

❋ Visualization Practice

1. Bring your hands to your Womb. Move your awareness to the G-spot and begin to breathe deeply, as if you are inhaling and exhaling from within your G-spot.

2. Visualize your pelvis as a chalice glowing full of golden light and ask to meet the Magdalene so she can assist you and give you any messages or insights.

3. Begin to ask this Grail Gate what feelings of abandonment and repressed pleasure are stored here. Ask to be shown how deeply this gate desires to open and awaken.

4. Then begin to quicken your breathing, gently rocking your pelvis backward and forward. Begin to feel a passion stir from within, a deep desire to open to love, to open to life, to open your sexual magnetism. Make any soft sounds that arise to express this feeling.

5. Visualize a vibrant, pulsing soft pink rose merging into your G-spot—feel the energy expand outward, pulsing with life and joy. Feel the Magdalene vibrate within you.

6. Afterward, whisper the mantra, *Divine Mother, I thank you for my life*, three times.

Third Grail Gate:
The Cervix and Cosmic Gateway

———— ∞ ————

Archetype: The Crone

Voice of the Womb

I am the mystery of moonlight on midnight waters, I am the silence in the deathly hush of snowfall, I am the trees stripped bare to their bones. When I come to you, you must be ready—for my gaze is awesome and will reflect your hidden face. I have drunk the wisdom of the wise blood and have its secrets to share—for those who have the courage to know. I am your infinite essence, beyond time or space. I am the chalice holding the life distilled from death. I am immortality.

Attributes

Alchemical Twins: Cervix/Amygdala
Goddess: Marie Salome, Ceridwen, Baba Yaga
Season: Winter
Moon Cycle: Dark Moon
Womb Cycle: Menstruation, Moonapause
Earth Essence: Moonstone

> ### Gifts and Wounds of the Third Grail Gate
>
> #### Gifts of the Third Grail Gate
>
> Wisdom, Intuition, Courage, Prophecy, Soul Union, Power, Magic, Clairaudience, Directness, Transformation, Dreamwalker, Psychic, Initiation, Wildness
>
> #### Wounds of the Third Grail Gate
>
> Black Magic, Manipulation, Power Over, Powerlessness, Pride, False Humility, Vanity, Worthlessness, Separation, Denial, Closed, Self-Aggrandizing, Cruel or Cold

This third step on the Grail Gate pathway takes you to the threshold; you unzip the fabric of the universe and gaze through into the vastness of infinity. This involves a total loss of control and disintegration of who you *think* you are, in order to rebirth who you *really* are. This experience can fill you with utter awe and reverence for the majestic truth of reality, or with a devastatingly unspeakable primal terror that completely undoes you. The choice is yours. Crossing this Grail Gate is not so much a step as a giant leap of faith.

Associated with the season of winter, the crone of the third Grail Gate is the wisdom of eternity percolated in the cosmic cauldron, the haunting hush of night when the world sleeps. She is the hidden dreampaths of the dark moon. This is the aspect of the feminine that watches wisely over Creation, like a seasoned grandmother raising her eyebrows at her foolhardy children. She is the mistress of magic and mystery, but she also deals in no-nonsense common sense. She is cunning and wise, and will gladly strip you of illusions, so great is her love.

We often associate the crone with a wise old woman, but she is also a *wild* woman, full of passion, vitality, and inner dynamism. Only the patriarchy has withered her and stolen the juice of the wise blood she retains for wisdom. She is sexual and fully alive, with lightning bolts in her eyes—like the Khandros, the prepatriarchal Tibetan womb shamanesses famous for their passionate enlightenment. The third Grail Gate holds the promises and gifts of *wildness*. Of no longer being constrained by what society or others think of you. Of being free. She rides her broomstick of awakened sexual power with no apologies or limits.

Crone energy resides within us all, no matter what age we are. It is a quality and essence we can draw upon at any time in our life or journey when power, wisdom, discernment, deep knowing, and nous are required to make an evolutionary leap. This crone magic naturally comes alive as we enter the dark moon and our menstrual phase, the *moment of truth,* when our Womb begins her shamanic menstrual journey deep into the underworld to shed her skin. At moonapause the gifts of the crone are fully embodied, as we become an Elder.

The third Grail Gate is where you first begin to dissolve into the Great Womb. You feel the call of the Mother, guiding you and singing you back home. Many of your old traumas and deep fears will surface here, but the pull of the radiant darkness, of the frequency of pure love will be stronger than the pull of fear. At this gate you will be guided, triggered, and transformed. Big changes will begin to happen; you may change jobs, experience health issues, end relationships and friendships, or suddenly find you are reconnecting with soul family and soul mates. You may begin to have a Womb Awakening crisis, but if you can surrender to this new evolutionary spiral, magical possibilities, divine synchronicity, and moments of benevolent grace await you. You are supported.

It is said that women initiate men at this threshold, but truly the Great Womb initiates both beloveds, and if they choose, they walk through this gate together, hand in hand, humbled by the power of love, as they choose to merge with each other—and the web of life. This moment can be a thunderbolt, a lightning strike.

The cervical orgasm is a gift of this Grail Gate. On a physical, emotional, and energetic level it *opens* the most sacred doorway and awakens the cervical eye—which is often depicted as a disembodied eye within a triangle. In fact, when the cervical eye opens you may be graced with visions of many eyes staring back at you, like portals—or womb holes—into other worlds and inner worlds.

In previous orgasms, you have been sipping from pools and lakes of pleasure, now you will be immersed into the infinite ocean. How much pleasure can you handle? You be amazed at how difficult it is to surrender to this tsunami of pleasure and bliss. But when you do, life will never be the same again. The cervical orgasm is a spiritual healing, as you begin to merge with the web of life.

This Grail Gate corresponds to the amygdala and the alta major—also known as the mouth of the Goddess—at the craniosacrum, where the skull and neck meet. This is the feminine third eye of the brain, and leads us deep into the labyrinth of feminine consciousness housed in the cerebellum, currently referred to as the unconscious or subconscious. The cervix and amygdala/alta major are feminine and masculine twins; they are both different sides of the same womb portal.

We hold the deep fears and wounds of separation at this Grail Gate. The sheer magnitude of the grief around this feeling is so deep in our feminine psyche, we are rarely able to even touch upon it, let alone feel it. But go there we must. It is the soul-destroying feeling that we are separated from our Mother Creator, from our twin, that we have lost connection with life, with the plant and animal kingdoms, with the otherworldly psychic realms. It is the profound fear we are all alone and unsupported floating in an abyss of oblivion that will swallow us.

We are more afraid of separation than of death; indeed, our only fear of death is the fear of separation. We begin to encounter and face the illusion of death at this gate, and only the power of our *longing for union* will carry us through this pain.

The wounded part of us dies in order to rebirth into the innocence of Love, which is completely wild, vast, and beyond any form of control. We can only surrender into the arms of love, then trust and let go into the flow. A resisted death is painful; a surrendered shamanic death is orgasmic birth. But don't judge any labor pains.

You will want to escape—it will be as if every animal instinct has kicked in and is saying, *Run for your life!* Ironically, the door to freedom feels like an intense confinement, before the breakthrough. This is what keeps you in separation.

Power, discernment, and the courage to let go completely are called for here.

As we dissolve into this mystical initiation at the third Grail Gate, we begin to merge the great rivers of the feminine; we unite the dark and light rivers into sacred union, into Divine wholeness. We integrate these two *seeming* polarities back into the circle of life, and awaken into the universe's deepest secret: the crone has two faces, she also holds the shining face of the maiden, who is returning to innocence and renewing. She is completing the circle.

The crone and the maiden are keepers of the thresholds; they walk the fine lines between beginnings and endings, holding the birthing wisdom of creating and dissolving in one sacred cosmic movement. They dwell in the magical in-between realms, such as dawn and dusk, when the two lights and the two worlds meet. This is why, in Grail lore, the questing knight often had a mystical guide and initiator who could appear as both a terrifying hag and as an enchanting maiden.

The gift of the third Grail Gate is the power of love to renew. Every betrayal and hurt, every grief and heartbreak, every aspect of your life you may be called to let go of flows into the cosmic cauldron to be rebirthed on a higher octave of love.

Shadow: Black Magician / Sorceress

The dilemma of this shadow is that the moment we begin to tap into the greatest powers in the universe, we are also called to surrender them to love. There is no "more than" or "less than" in the Great Womb—no masters and servants, no grand hierarchy. All are equal in this space, as Love is the great equalizer. All is One.

Some choose to dwell on the threshold, attaining great intellectual and psychic powers or bewitching beauty, without making the great leap across into love. These powers can be used to manipulate and influence others for personal gain. Power without love corrupts, and those in this shadow use fear to get their own way—whether that is to make money, find fame, or gain spiritual power.

Paradoxically, fear can be one of the greatest servants of love. Fear is a space waiting to be filled by the fullness of love. We befriend fear until it melts into love. This shadow is symbolized by *The Lord of the Rings*—even the greatest wizards and witches struggle to wield this absolute power, even to fight for the light, without being corrupted by it. This is the greatest initiation we undergo.

❋ Questions to Percolate in Your Womb Cauldron

Sit in womb meditation pose and breathe gently into this gate; feel what is held here. The third Grail Gate is the cosmic doorway into the Great Womb. Ask to feel . . .

1. How connected do you feel to your deep feminine power?
2. What fierce wisdom does your inner crone wish to share with you?
3. Have you experienced shut down or sexual manipulation at this gate?
4. How do you sensually express your wild connection with Spirit and Earth?
5. How deep is your desire to merge with Source of Creation in sacred union?

❋ Breath and Sound Meditation

1. Sit in womb meditation pose with a soft, relaxed, and upright posture. Allow your shoulders to relax downward, so the rose of your heart can open. Bring your awareness to the Womb and breathe here for a few moments, inhaling and exhaling the delicious, fertile velvet darkness.

2. Now allow yourself to gently drop your energy into your cervix. Breathe here for a few minutes with all your awareness gently focused on your cervix. You can also try bringing your energy upward from the entrance of your yoni cave, inside the yoni passageway, and into the eye of the cervix and sense if this feels different.

3. Allow any feelings, colors, sensations, or visions to arise and be with them. Ask if your cervix has any messages she wishes to share with you. Allow yourself to listen.

4. Begin to chant the mantra for the third Grail Gate: *sh-ka-ra*. Do this for as long as you feel called.

✳ *Visualization Practice*

1. Bring your hands to your Womb. Begin to breathe deeply and strongly, inhaling through the nose, exhaling though the mouth.

2. Bring your awareness to your alta major, and breathe into this portal. Feel it activate and open, connect this sensation to your cervix.

3. Ask to be taken into the amygdala, the seat of our primordial emotional responses—what feeling first arises? Connect this feeling to your cervix and the hidden truth residing there.

4. Breathe deeply and strongly, and ask to meet the crone; ask her for her visionary assistance to reveal this truth. Allow yourself to open to any symbols or memories that arise. Be fully present with whatever feelings come up. If grief arises, cry. If fear arises, surrender to it. If anger emerges, you can pound your legs on the floor. Keep going for as long as it takes.

5. Afterward, curl up in the fetal position with a blanket over you, so you feel nested, and visualize an egg of golden light surrounding you.

6. Whisper "I love and forgive myself," three times, then rest.

WOMB ORACLES SHARE

Merging into Oneness

I wanted my beloved and I to go together through this portal that was wide open, present inside of me, and from which all of this energy of pure love and joy was flowing outward. I started to work on the opening of the first three Grail Gates, and one afternoon we began to make love. I was completely surrendered and connected again, inside of myself and with my partner, so much in love and so open. We made love for a long time and he took me to the second Grail Gate and then to the third, and I started to experience orgasms coming from my womb, which soon took over my whole body. It was like electricity was flowing through me. My arms, palms, legs, and head were full of "ants," my heart was wide open, my womb pulsing. Soon there was no longer an I or me . . . it was like something so much bigger, vaster took over, and I was no longer. All that existed was Love/Consciousness transmitting the joy of sharing itself with All That Is . . . like it was all merging into One. Again, tears and laughter were coming out at the same time and Love was filling up all the space, the room, everything. After a while, I could feel that there was an I again, but the love coming out of every cell of my body was still there, and I was filling up my aura and my partner's aura with it. . . .

Later on, when I asked the Womb, she confirmed that a portal has been opened, a new level of diving inside, and this act of making love on the physical plane, not only at the soul level, but in the body as well, opened a gate. And that also, with so much love and light flooding this new gateway, a lot of the shadow would be brought to the surface as well; so I needed to be prepared and to know that there will be work to do, both for myself and for my beloved. She also said that during the ceremony a lot of the boundaries between us had been dissolved. There would no longer be "his issues" and "my issues," but we would feel even more strongly what the other was feeling in the relationship, and that we were to work together, with courage and honesty, through all that would come.

L.M.

Reclaiming Our Shakti Power

At first I had a strong vision of a luminous butterfly and through the first gate a white swan came and pecked at my heart. Through the second gate, diving into the waters on the swan and feeling a warm openness, I saw two luminescent blue dragons guarding a diamond gateway. A blaze of fire appeared and I had a strong vision of a dragon opening its wings. I felt lots of movement and swirls of light.

Next I came through an opening of the forest into a wide-open expansive lake; mist was rising off the lake. I unveiled my face from my white cloak and removed my hood to look at my reflection in the waters. I was adorned in a white cape and had long flowing wavy golden hair and wore a diamond jewel on my third eye and had a crescent moon tattoo on my forehead. The Lady of the Lake appeared in all her beauty, dressed and adorned in purple and magenta colors; she had four hands. She called me forth and a whirlpool of the waters of the lake swirled around me, cleansing me. Behind me I saw the line of my ancestors.

I let go and swam with the Lady of the Lake through the waters and entered through a small hole into darkness. It was warm and mysterious. Felt so powerful and so beautiful. I saw myself with the same long flowing golden hair, spinning wool through a reflection of a large elongated egg-shaped mirror framed in gold. I also saw a fire burning in a fireplace in the room I was in. I heard whispers of a woman in the background, which felt so calming and peaceful.

I met the wise crone and she told me I am teacher, she told me not to wait to be invited, to step into my power and reclaim it and walk forward. She told me to stop waiting for something (which I saw as approval). As we walked out onto the ocean on a silver light path of the moon, she told me to merge into union with the masculine and feminine, and I saw two massive serpents rise out of the ocean entwining in the alchemical symbol, but with two strong distinctive heads.

As they rose high entwining out of the ocean, they shimmered in golden light, and all that was left was a diamond of gold that opened into a gate in the shape of an opening yoni. Above I saw the moon and the Seven Sisters Pleiadian stars. I entered the yoni gateway to be reborn and felt so much love and peace.

N.Z.

SPIRAL 30
DRAGONS OF CREATION

Journey through the Four Womb Elements

We shall not cease from exploration
And the end of all our exploring
Will be to arrive where we started
And know the place for the first time.
Through the unknown, unremembered gate
When the last of earth left to discover
is that which was the beginning.

T. S. ELIOT, *LITTLE GIDDING*

THE WOMB IS A DOORWAY between the worlds. A woman with a fully awakened Womb is a true shamaness; she walks between the worlds. Every cell has a womb hole to other dimensions, and the physical womb is the holographic Mother of this physical and energetic web of multidimensional doorways.

We were originally created with this doorway open, giving us a deep connection to our Creator; to the web of life; the elements of life; the animal, plant, and mineral kingdom; the dreamtime; other realms; and other beings. Ancient moons ago, in primal innocence, supernatural phenomenon was entirely natural—a sacred birthright. We were never designed to feel disconnected from everything around us.

As many prophecies have shown, the time for remembrance is now—and it is calling for men and women to summon their courage and step into their boldest power and deepest love.

The pilgrimage into the Womb first takes us on a path through the archetypal Grail Gateways of the triple goddess or holy trinity. All life spirals through these three cycles of being, where the deepest wisdom is renewed into innocence. In birthing terms, when our seed has ripened and come to harvest, we begin on a deeper spiral of wisdom, we seed a new creation, birth a deeper aspect of love. We become infinitely ancient and pristinely new.

Many physical, energetic, and emotional wounds and gifts from our present life are stored in our first three Grail Gates: all the sexual encounters we have ever had, loving and unloving, consensual and nonconsensual; all the sexual thoughts and fantasies we have bathed these gates in, born of our deepest, purest desires and the erotic imprint created by our sexual wounding. All our emotional betrayal, abandonment, fear, anger, and resistance is stored here in these three Grail Gates. They are either open to Life with a trusting invitation, a wanton *yes,* or closed down, trapping our life force and saying *no* to more pain, denying love entry.

During this journey we often drop into the collective *no*—the massive pain body of the feminine, which is in shock, angry, disassociated, and profoundly traumatized. It takes extreme courage and devotion to love to feel this collective pain, and to *not* become stuck in its vast wound vortex; to grieve fully for yourself and the ancestral lineage that birthed you, while still summoning the courage to step forward into your *yes;* to reach for love; to feel, integrate, and move beyond this pain and any sense of righteous anger, and to open to life again.

Only the power of innocence can heal this great wound in our collective psyche; innocence is forgiveness in its deepest sense. It goes far beyond a mental acknowledgement and an external forgiving of a person or a situation; the balm of innocence literally dissolves all traces of the wound, event, or hurt so it is no longer embedded in our physical body, energetic body, psyche, or soul. We return to innocence. Like a child, we open to the magical possibilities of life, without past hurts coloring our perception and closing down our bioenergetic field.

When we collectively experience this balm of innocence, we will experience what will appear as a massive evolutionary leap, reawakening our true biological potential as powerful multidimensional beings of love. This transformation, in its truest sense, is the forgiveness and integration of our journey through separation embraced back into the innocence of our original blueprint.

On a personal level, this return to innocence expresses through the Grail Gates as a deep sexual awakening. The hurt, pain, and resistance you have encountered in your healing spiral dissolves, resetting your sacred portals back to pristine purity. When this happens you will feel bathed in innocence, enchanted, like a virgin. All the pain will be transmuted into the sweetest, shimmering love. You will feel sexually reborn, as if a pure place within has awoken for the first time, which is in fact a deeply ancient essence within you.

Biologically, this triggers a cascade of endocrine responses, generating renewing Shakti stem cells and creating a chemistry of heaven on a cellular and DNA level. It also births a deeply embodied, wild sensuality. We come into our "pure erotic creature," who connects with the blissful, orgasmic, multisensory web of life.

This renewal of innocence does not come from denying, separating, or disassociating from the pain of traumatic memories or leaving them behind, cutting them out, or clearing them like garbage. It comes from befriending them, retrieving them, comforting them, and traveling deep within their dark core, and integrating them so completely into your heart with love that they dissolve.

And, of course, as a spiral journey, there are layers of innocence to recover, until we reach the pristine center of our being, our original primal innocence. You will be spiraling between dark and light, wounds and love, weaving them into one.

After we have danced a number of these healing, embracing spirals and woven enough of ourselves into wholeness, we make our first leap across the cosmic threshold of the third Grail Gate. We consciously step into our infinite soul self—and find many new lessons, challenges, and incredible magical gifts waiting there.

The approach to this threshold can be quite dramatic; it can be experienced as a Dark Night of the Womb. Life will throw everything at you to see what you do with it, and how prepared you are to travel further into other realms of yourself. The intensity of these experiences are not necessarily bad events—often our deepest wounds are revealed and exposed by opening to love, by meeting our soul mate, by deepening into sacred relationship, by having our dreams met.

Our current cosmic cycle is at this point: a universal menstruation of the Great Womb in her crone phase, dissolving all around us and inside us that does not support love, and helping us face and embrace our wounds of separation and awaken to the power of love again.

And after the raging storms, the lightning bolts of realizations, the furnace of fears, the cauldron of our chaotic wounds, the fierce challenges of the crone, we arrive . . . at the beginning again: the maiden, innocence, trust. Like Dorothy landing in Oz, after the whirlwind subsides, we find ourselves in an enchanted land—sweetness, silence, rest, wonder, and the peace of simply being alive.

Similarly, after our universal Dark Night of the Womb, the cosmos shall rebirth into a new, deeper, spiral—awakening into the maiden, virgin, new earth.

Four Womb Elements:
The Spiral of the Grail Womb Cross

As we cross the threshold of the third gate we are renewed in innocence. Our hard-won wisdom, experience, and knowing dissolves in the wonder of new potential and magical possibilities. We land in the fourth Grail Gate: new earth. Also very ancient, this earth exists in the lost realms of the feminine dimension.

Here you begin your journey through the four elements and directions of life-force energy, the mystery of creative power, and the secrets of your lost soul, which speak in a hidden language of symbols, synchronicity, magic, dreams, pure desires, intuitions, teachers, guardians, inspirations, and treasures.* The elemental powers are birthed from the Dragons of Creation, nonhuman cosmic intelligences that live deep within our biology and genetic code.

You begin to awaken and greet your destiny, your purpose for being on Earth at this time, the secret dreams of your soul that have been seeded in you since conception. Like a human caterpillar, you begin to unfold the wings of your heart, walking between all worlds, manifesting effortlessly in this one, so you can embody the beautiful feminine butterfly you were designed to be in the plan of Creation.

Weaving with the four elements and directions of the Womb, you begin creating a magnificent, enchanting, wildly innocent feminine light body that co-creates with many other webs, and threads beautifully into the womb grid of all life. Bringing you deeper into the center of the sacred pattern, the Great Womb, the benevolent heart of Creation, who holds, births, and dissolves all in her arms.

In Mayan tradition, the Womb of Gaia is usually portrayed as a circle with four quarters and a disk in the center, representing this grid of womb elements.[1]

Crossing the threshold of the third Grail Gate takes us into the wilds of the womb elements, and we begin to understand how to flow with the currents of each direction. We learn how to balance and integrate all the elements, so we become whole and centered—literally centered in the Womb of Creation. This is a dance, finding this balance, this center. When we merge these flows and directions, our feminine phoenix (the swan) arises, holding the power of each element.

---

*The knowledge and formulations in our womb medicine wheel—which differ from many native and indigenous traditions—were received through direct womb transmission in connection with the ancient mothers and the Womb of Gaia. Whatever system, tradition, or lineage you work with to connect with either the four elements or the yoni gateways, the main point is that it is healing, nourishing, and transformational for you—and honors the creative powers.

Fig. 30.1. Celtic tree of life

(Illustration by Natvienna Hanell)

Within the central axis of our womb space, which is a hologram of the Womb of Creation, we enter the archetypal *tree of life*. Here we can begin to co-create with lowerworld and our ancestors (South Pole), and upperworld and our teachers/guides (North Pole) by weaving the two flows of life force, both feminine and masculine (west and east), receptive and active, together.

Like all of creation, these elements/directions have a twin relationship. Earth and air are in a twin pair, as are fire and water. Many traditions speak of the marriage of Father Sky and Mother Earth, and the pinnacle of sexual alchemy, through many ancient traditions, is known as setting fire to water. These four elements combined birth the divine child—our pure soul self.

On the tree of life, represented by the vertical axis of the cross, air is upperworld, the celestial realms, and earth is lowerworld, realms of the ancestors and primordial ones. Different powers are available in each. This is the cosmic container that houses and empowers our life here on earth.

The horizontal axis reflects the two co-creative flows of Life that manifest everything into being in this realm, middleworld. This merging of the two flows of life force—the active, creative, masculine, fire principle residing in the right ovary (or right testes for men) and the receptive, surrendered, feminine, water principle residing in the left ovary (or left testes in men) is sacred union.

These two complementary, intertwined life flows have been known in this era of separation as the masculine and feminine. But these are symbolic words for the essence of life within *each* of us, and externally embodied in gender, male and female. In union, these flows play and weave equally through all life forms.

The Dragon Mother: Cosmic Creatrix

In Grail lore, one who had harmonized all four elements was known as a Dragon. In many ancient cultures, Womb Enlightenment was depicted by a serpent or dragon entwined around an elemental cross, similar to Christian symbology.

This quest for the Holy Grail, the Holy Womb, was expressed as a journey through the four elements of the Womb, leading to the ultimate rebirth and renewal in the Cosmic Womb. It was encoded in Celtic myth in the Welsh Mabinogion: where Taliesin, the magical divine child, journeys to harmonize the four womb elements and is rebirthed through the Womb of the Goddess, Ceridwen.

In Mesoamerican teachings, the cosmos is symbolized by a four-petaled flower representing the division of the cosmic space into four cardinal regions and a center[2]—the womb cross of the four elements. Like many womb worship sites in Europe, the sacred site of Teotihuacán was built around a sacred cave (symbolic of the Great Mother's Womb) underneath the Pyramid of the Sun.

In the Egyptian tradition, the four womb elements also correspond to the *body of Isis,* the multidimensional bodies that awaken and merge as we begin to attain the robe of glory or Christ body. The air element represents our light/ka body, which descends like the dove, into the Womb—and is threaded into the *Aufu,* the flows of the fire within our blood and the watery rivers of our lymph—and then descends, grounds, roots, and anchors into the earth element, matter, the *Khat.* This is known as bringing Spirit into matter, or heaven onto earth.

When this is achieved, we spiral into the center point, the vortex of the Cosmic

Womb, and awaken the Akhu—the shining body—to become a dragoness, a cosmic serpent of Shakti, Christed with pure life force. This was the achievement of the oracles of the Delphi (meaning "womb") in Greece—who were known as Dragoness or Serpent. They had become at One with Gaia and were transformed into oracles for the Womb of Gaia's voice to speak through them in prophecy.

Becoming a mistress of the web, weaving the four womb elements in a dance of creativity and regeneration, was also the Great Work of Sophia. "Sophia may be guarded and transmitted until the time when . . . the Rose of the World shall bloom upon the cross of the elements, when the Mistress of Life leads us home."[3]

Awakening Your Inner Queendom and Kingdom

Another way of depicting this alchemical knowledge of heaven/earth and masculine/feminine was in the symbology of kingship or queenship. A wise ruler sat on a throne, wearing a crown and holding a sacred scepter and chalice or orb. This did not symbolize ruling over an *external* kingdom or queendom but of ruling wisely within your inner kingdom or queendom by balancing all four elements: earth, air, fire, and water.

Each element had its alchemical symbol and inner meaning.

Earth/Malkhut—symbolized by the Red Throne, our feminine foundation

Air/Heaven—symbolized by the Golden Crown, our masculine wisdom

Fire/Masculine—symbolized by a Scepter held in the right hand, our power

Water/Feminine—symbolized by a Cup or Orb held in the left hand, our love

---

Due to our life experiences, and at different stages of life, we can experience different blocks or awakenings in our first three Grail Gates, but the four womb elements are deeper flows within our feminine essence, archetypes that we embody at a soul level and are born with. The challenge of our life is to know and fully embody our predominant "gift element" and balance it with the others.

Each womb element brings us a different healing gift, and it is important to balance and weave them together in order to root and ground transformative processes and insights, so that they can gestate and birth into fullness.

Like all of Creation the womb elements are paired together, and their gifts complement each other. Together, as a wheel, they can guide us through all the stages of rebirthing ourselves into wholeness, in a practical, commonsense way.

Womb air brings us the gift of *inspiration*—those moments when we need to reach to the heavens to receive big visions and revitalize our spirit. This is naturally partnered with womb earth, who brings us the gift of *integration*. Mystical visions need to be grounded, integrated, and gestated before their meaning can be fully understood and applied to the world to bring healing.

Womb fire grants us the potent gift of *transformation*—the lightning storms of change and rebirth, which can be intense, passionate, or momentarily destabilizing. This is softened by the power of its partner, womb water, who brings us the healing gift of *restoration*—and the sacred ability to make whole anything that has been shattered, to rejuvenate and reweave your life in balance.

For each of the Grail Gates of the elements you will find the following attributes: Direction, what it Embodies, its Womb Wisdom, Guardian Spirits, Feminine Essence, Sacred Sound, and its Invocation—as well as its Gifts and Blocks.

❋ Mapping Your Journey

You can map your elemental journey through the next four Grail Gates.

1. Create a womb map by drawing a circle on a piece of paper with a cross through the center, dividing it into four quarters.
2. Begin to map out what you are embodying in each direction and element—noting insights, feelings, and dreams; using words, colors, and doodles.

Fourth Grail Gate:
Womb Element Earth

∞

Grounding, Web of Life / Womb of Gaia

Attributes

Direction: Lower Womb / South / Foundation
Embodies: Grounding, Sensuality, Knowing
Womb Wisdom: Birthing, Herbal Lore, Healing
Guardian Spirits: Crystals, Dragons, Bear
Feminine Essence: Hera, Elen of the Ways, White Buffalo Woman
Sacred Sound: Earth's Heartbeat (Schuman Resonance)
Invocation: *May I root into the support and grounding of Earth*

Fig. 30.2. Mandala of the four elements
(Illustration by Natvienna Hanell)

You emerge through the third Grail Gate into the otherworldly roots of the *tree of life,* lands of the ancient ones, your ancestors, and the primordial Mothers and Fathers. This deep, rich, nurturing space is home to the Womb of the World, of Gaia. It glitters with the radiance of the cystal earth stars, carriers of deeply embodied feminine light. The wisdom and gifts held here will give you access to the *grammarye*—the ancient lore, also known as the Akashic or karmic records.

You also connect into the subtle realms of a shimmering crystalline earth, filled with living light that is beyond and underneath our current concepts of matter. This is Malkuta D'shmaya, the queendom of ecstatic light and vibration, also known as *new earth,* which is really an ancient blueprint of original creation. This dimension of earth lives on within our feminine consciousness, waiting for us to wake up and transfigure into the heart of matter, to true reality.

You will be able to bring through deep womb gnosis, *knowing* in communion with the plant, animal, and crystal realms and the Spirit of Gaia herself. You will be able to communicate telepathically and intuitively with animals, and will draw to your side guardians, teachers, and familiars (totems/power animals) to work alongside you. Many gifts will be given—including the power to affect the weather, and to commune with plants, flowers, and herbs for healing purposes.

This womb element is associated with menstruation, motherhood, and the rhythms of Earth's cycles. Your feminine crown halo will begin to open and shine—the forgotten symbol of Womb Enlightenment—as you feel deeply rooted in your physical incarnation and your soul purpose this lifetime. Working consciously with menstruation, offering your moon blood back to Mother Earth, and riding the dreampaths of the ebbs and flows of your blood will be a big key at the fourth Grail Gate. Record your dreams, feelings, and intuitions. Place your moon blood on your herb garden to aid physical healing through plant remedies, and anoint your masculine third eye (brow chakra) and your feminine third eye (alta major) to open into deeper womb gnosis. Save some moon blood diluted in spring water or alcohol to work with during new moons and full moons (if your cycle has not regulated to these rhythms), and infuse some under your tongue.

This womb element brings up any healing needed in your ancestral lineage, and also helps awaken any gifts you need to open into from your bloodline. Working consciously with your own time in your mother's womb, and how you were birthed can open great healing—especially if there was trauma or lack of safety.

In the ancient roots of the world, you can also connect to the primordial Mothers, and the unbroken line of mothers connected to your Womb and present in your mitochondrial DNA, which is passed exclusively down the maternal line. Healing and awakening this DNA will facilitate *great* healing, which ripples along the timelines backward into the past and forward into the future. It will trigger a huge personal spiral of Womb Awakening when a major shift in your mitochondrial DNA happens; when enough women experience this, it will create a huge revolution and evolution collectively. We will birth a new world.

Earth as an element of sexual energy brings us a deeply grounded sexual presence and the gift of deep wombgasms, which awaken healing Shakti stem cells and bring our physical body into harmonic resonance with the earth hum. This magnetic energy begins to *draw* everything you need toward you, including love and abundance, in a way that looks effortless to others.

Earth Energy in Relationship

The masculine looks for this energy in a woman to ground and nourish him, and be his feminine anchor into the deep Earth Womb energies. In balance, this womb element will arouse feelings of commitment and safety in a man; he will feel the desire to create a home and children with a woman holding this feminine quality, and nest himself in her grounded energy field to bond.

When this element is out of balance with too little earth, a woman can trigger early childhood mother issues in a man. This is often experienced in relationships by forming an intense sexual or romantic connection at first, which then fizzles out due to a lack of commitment on the man's part, or long-term relationships where the man is afraid to settle down and have children or awaken onto a committed soul path together. When a woman does not truly trust herself, love herself, and feel connected to her earth incarnation and physical body, the masculine will reflect this "I don't want to be here" back to her.

If there is too much earth, the masculine can feel pulled down and trapped by an energy that is too "down to earth" and practical. He will seek advice, friendship, and comfort—but not sexual connection or intimate commitment. In a relationship, there will be a deep friendship but no sexual fire or soul connection.

Gifts and Blocks of the Fourth Grail Gate

Gifts of the Fourth Grail Gate

Powerful, Grounded, Keeper of Earth, Crystal and Plant Wisdom, Interconnected, Guardian of Gaia's Womb, Ancestral Records, Menstrual Mysteries.

This is the space where your being is grounded into the wisdom of earth and life itself. Your root connection to the Womb of the World means you feel completely safe and at home on Earth, knowing you will always be looked after. Your energy resonates with the hum of the Earth, giving you a sensual stillness as you move through life. This is your seat of strength, your protective "she-wolf" who knows her boundaries, and defends them with love. You feel very connected to your body, and are supple, strong, and open—energetically and physically.

Blocks of the Fourth Grail Gate

You don't feel supported by life, or other people. You often find yourself giving more than you receive, and feel drained as a result. Feeling low on energy and enthusiasm is a constant. Sleep doesn't make you feel refreshed and there is a deep desire to just stop and rest. You may have some repressed anger that you don't feel safe to express. You fear saying no, and find it hard to stand up for your true desires and set boundaries. This element is often blocked in women who have been abused in the past. You feel abandoned by life—and yourself.

❉ *Womb Mapping:*
   Earth Element

1. Sit in a cross-legged womb meditation, bring your hands into a prayer position in front of your heart, then rotate your joined hands forward, so they are now pointed outward straight in front of you. Bring them slowly apart so only your fingertips are touching. Feel the energy flowing, creating a womb space in front of your heart.

2. Move your energy and awareness to the bottom of this womb-grid mudra where your fingertips meet. Feel a connection between this point and the lower/bottom half of your Womb reaching down to your anus/perineum. Begin to feel the energy of this area—any warmth, blocks, coldness, resistance.

3. Ask yourself the following questions, or allow any insights and visions to arise.

Questions to Percolate in Your Womb Cauldron

1. How do the qualities of patience, slowness, and rooting feel to you?
2. How safe did it feel in your mother's womb and to be born on earth?
3. What is Mother Earth's message "from the deep" to you in this moment?

❉ *Breath and Sound Meditation*

1. Sit cross-legged and with a soft, relaxed, and upright posture. Allow your shoulders to relax downward, so the rose of your heart can open. Bring your awareness to the Womb and breathe here for a few moments, inhaling and exhaling the delicious, fertile velvet darkness.

2. Now allow yourself to gently drop your energy into the floor of your Womb. Breathe here for a few minutes with all your awareness gently focused on your pelvic floor.

3. Allow any feelings, sensations, or visions to arise and be with them. Ask if the earth has any messages she wishes to share with you, allow yourself to listen.

4. Begin to chant the mantra for the fourth Grail Gate: *ah-doo-ma.* Do this for as long as you feel called.

Fifth Grail Gate: Womb Element Fire

—— ∞ ——

Sacred Sexuality, Creative Power

Attributes

Direction: Right Ovary / West
Embodies: Creativity, Passion, Pleasure
Womb Wisdom: Menstruation, Sacred Sexuality, Death Doula
Guardian Spirits: Bees, Womb Dragons, Serpents
Feminine Essence: Ishtar, Morgan le Fay, Vajrayogini
Sacred Sound: Tribal Drumming
Invocation: *May the Fire ignite my passion for transformation*

As you emerge through the roots of the *tree of life* into the fifth Grail Gate you awaken the primordial fire of your primal kundalini Shakti energy. As it rises, it enflames you with passion, desire, excitement, and *wildness*—you *have* to create, you are driven to swirl, spiral, perform, dance, shine, express your inner self externally. You are filled with passion, purpose, and a call to action. This is the first flow of life force, active and solar in nature, often called the red river. At the right ovary, you will find the flow of your wild womb, the passion and energy to break through any stagnation or blocks, or to challenge any small-minded belief systems you are holding on to, or any sexual blocks or shame.

Its wildness knows no limits and cannot be kept within boundaries; if there are parameters, this energy will break through them. It *cannot* be contained. It is perceived as primal chaos, the seething river of fiery sexual creative power. It is *raw fire power;* it transforms, creates, and it can burn if not handled properly.

This power will connect you to a lineage of the feminine that has held the wild serpent energy of sexuality, without judgment of herself, and without placing restriction on herself. Tantric priestesses, sacred prostitutes, sexual shamans have all used the power of this energy to initiate deep awakenings for themselves and others—especially a masculine energy disconnected from the Womb. Their wild orgasmic explorations have dived deeply into the sanctity of all sexual experiences and encounters and are embodied in the temple prostitutes—the Harine—the orgiastic frenzies of the Greek Maenads, and the unfettered Beltane ceremonies and celebrations.

Dance, rhythmic drumming, and sacred sexuality are a big key at this Grail Gate. Without the flame of life burning inside it is hard to create anything. We need this wild primal pulse to drive us forward, in ecstasy and joy, on our path. If this serpent is sleeping, we need to awaken her—to charm and uncoil her, to help her rise upward in her sacred spiral dance to the pulse of life. This creates momentum and movement on our spiritual path and in our relationships.

This sexual energy is an initiator and an activator—it is multiorgasmic, sensual, and a bold invitation to experience the pleasure of life and the feminine form. It gives itself to the wild waves of bliss and knows that sometimes only madness, wildness, spinning completely out of control, can take us over the edge of our comfort zone and into the arms of life, where all energy merges in sacred union.

Fire Energy in Relationship

The masculine is seduced, enchanted, and enthralled by this energy. It is the energy the masculine most fears and desires; he will do *anything* to have it and *everything* to destroy it. Holding this flame is a deep responsibility and sometimes dangerous for women. If a woman has an imbalance in this Grail Gate of too much fire, she will burn herself and others in its flame. Her sexual energy will either be too confrontational or intense for the men she attracts and arouses, and after wild and uninhibited sexual exchanges, she may find herself judged, abandoned, or rejected. This either creates the alluring seductress who now uses this magnetic sexual fire to avenge herself, or a woman who uses sexual energy without discernment in a way that harms herself.

With an excess of fire, a woman often burns through men she feels are not strong or bold enough for her, only to be rejected and discarded by those she feels are.

Where there is a deficit of fire, a woman tends to feel overlooked and unnoticed by the masculine. She is afraid to be seen and to put herself out there fully. This creates a loop of low self-esteem. She allows situations and relationship that are not progressing to linger on in the hope something will change—while not having the fire power to initiate that change herself, or walk away if necessary. In long-term relationship, sex drive can dwindle, and there is a fear of setting the agenda in the relationship and of putting her desires first or shaking things up. This can express in what is often called victim energy, and can bring out latent tendencies in the masculine to bully, punish, and control the feminine.

When this energy is balanced in a woman, the masculine feels inspired and enchanted by the passion of this wild flowing dark river in his woman. It opens deeper currents of sensuality and sacred sexual exploration together, and creates the fuel for momentum in both spirituality and emotional intimacy.

Gifts and Blocks of the Fifth Grail Gate

Gifts of the Fifth Grail Gate

Shining, Dynamic, Inspired Passion, Creative Force, Performer, Enchantress, Power of Love, Wild, Sensual, Charming, Transformative, Sacred Sexuality.

This is where your aura, charisma, and radiance are fully embodied. When the fire of the right ovary is flowing you are shining, flowering, bursting out with incredible creativity and magnetism. This is the energy we associate with talent, success, dynamism, power, beauty—to be a star in whatever field you choose. You give birth to your deepest desires and ideas, and present them to the world. You have the confidence and self-love to transform yourself and the world. Your vision and passion inspires others. You are a whirlwind, a true force of nature.

Blocks of the Fifth Grail Gate

You may be creative and full of imagination, but you don't always find the success or recognition you deserve. You are shy and sensitive and feel unsure of presenting yourself in public. There is a disconnection with the power and wildness of your feminine essence. You may have a deep subconscious feeling that it is dangerous to shine and be noticed; retreating into your interior worlds, daydreams, and fantasies. Sometimes this power flows, but disconnected from the heart. This can make you competitive and hard or manipulative—coming from a false masculine attitude. Eventually this will drain your feminine essence and make you feel empty inside. Female power is tender as well as tenacious, flowing with easy abundance and soft grace.

❋ Womb Mapping: Fire Element

1. Sit in a cross-legged womb meditation, bring your hands into a prayer position in front of your heart, then rotate your joined hands forward, so they are now pointed outward straight in front of you. Bring them slowly apart so only your fingertips are touching. Feel the energy flowing, creating a womb space in front of your heart.

2. Move your energy and awareness to the right side of this womb grid mudra where your right knuckles are. Feel a connection between this point, and the right side of your womb and your right ovary.

3. Begin to feel the energy of this area—any warmth, blocks, coldness, resistance.

4. Ask yourself the following questions, or just allow any insights and visions to arise.

Questions to Percolate in Your Womb Cauldron

1. What aspect of yourself are you most ashamed to show others?
2. Do you have any secret fantasies or judgments about wild sexuality?
3. What makes you feel alive with burning passion and commitment?

❋ Breath and Sound Meditation

1. Sit cross-legged and with a soft, relaxed, and upright posture. Allow your shoulders to relax downward, so the rose of your heart can open. Bring your awareness to the Womb and breathe here for a few moments, inhaling and exhaling the delicious, fertile velvet darkness.
2. Now allow yourself to gently drop your energy deep inside your right ovary. Breathe here for a few minutes with all your awareness gently focused on your ovary.
3. Allow any feelings, sensations, or visions to arise and be with them. Ask if fire has any messages she wishes to share with you, allow yourself to listen.
4. Begin to chant the mantra for the fifth Grail Gate: *he-ra-hom*. Do this for as long as you feel called.

Sixth Grail Gate: Womb Element Air

———— ∞ ————

Inspiration, Soul Wisdom

Attributes

Direction: Upper Womb / North / Ceiling
Embodies: Inspiration, Freedom, Clarity
Womb Wisdom: Conception, Soul Doula, Divination
Guardian Spirits: Bird Tribe (Swan, Owl, Eagle), Celestial and Fairy Beings
Feminine Essence: Arianrhod, Artemis, White Tara
Sacred Sounds: Harp, Lyre, Flute
Invocation: *May the lightness of Air lift me up and inspire me*

The initiation of taming and embodying the wild life flow into a creative and loving dance opens you out to the celestial branches of the *tree of life,* and connects you to the teachers of your soul lineage who feel you are ready to dive deeper into love, and to take on more of your soul mission on Earth. Infused with the power of Shakti, you are able to open into greater realms of freedom. Old belief systems, friends, careers, and networks fall away as you begin to grasp the bigger picture of what is happening in your life and on Earth, from a vaster soul perspective, rather than the limited perspective of your conditioned mind.

As you start to awaken this womb element you begin to encounter the feeling of being in the world, but not of it. In its truest sense, this means you are fully anchored into Earth's Womb and her energy, but are unplugged from the distorted world matrix—expressed in our current social, cultural, economic, and patriarchal paradigm. You begin to follow a higher law—the law of Love.

When you spiral up into your womb air element, an immensely transforming leap often unfolds on your spiritual path and you are gifted with radical new wisdom, as if the windows of your soul have been washed clean so you can see and feel truth with greater clarity. Not only will you connect with new teachers and guides, who initiate you to a higher octave, but you also begin to feel called to teach and share yourself. People begin to seek out *your* help and guidance.

Paradoxically, at the same moment as people are seeking you out and life is connecting you with many people, you also feel a deep need for quietness and solitude to rest and integrate the new wisdom that is flowing into you. Nature, meditation, and gentleness calls to your soul. You also develop a more refined sense of the purity of love, and are happy to just soar in the magical cosmos.

You also become more sensitive to everything that is *not* love. This can bring up old wounds and thrust existing relationships into turmoil, as situations you could once handle become intolerable. A chasm can seem to open up between the inner realms of your being, and the outer world you are living in, which feels isolating.

One of the balancing acts of this womb element is to resist the urge to completely retreat from the world. Often people avoid intimate relationship and shut down their sexuality as they open into this realm—rather than keep opening. It can be easy to use the beautiful sensations of pure love you are receiving from the higher realms to escape from life—but it is your job to be on earth, embodying love, not escaping up into the clouds, trying to transcend any uncomfortable relationships or the physical realities of your life or the world.

The energy flow of the womb element brings a new level of consciousness and wild innocent purity to your sexuality. You begin to experience exquisite energy orgasms of feminine light that ripple through your multidimensional being.

Air Energy in Relationship

When we open our sexuality into womb air, we begin to embody the magic of enchantment and rarity that brings out the sensitive, protective, romantic side in the masculine. This is the realm the Grail maidens and the swan maidens occupied, which holds a beautiful soulful sexuality. It awakens the chivalrous knight into his divine qualities of honor and truth. Women with this element in balance will receive marriage proposals everywhere they go, and will touch the sacred center of every masculine heart they meet.

When the womb air element is out of balance in excess, it can create sexual shutdown and an intellectualism and mental predisposal, preventing deep sensual, emotional intimacy with another. Expressing through childhood wounding, it can also create an attitude of superiority and judgment, and the "ice maiden" who looks down on everyone as beneath her. It can also create relating patterns where intense cerebral connections are made, fuelled by lots of deep spiritual conversations and debates, but that never translate to relationship.

If the womb air element is deficient, relationships can be too practical—focused on material factors, or the need for emotional security or to have children. These partnerships become a prison of stagnation rather than a container of growth. There is a deep fear of connecting with a greater purpose in life and what this might mean—and what has to be embraced or released to open to your soul.

Gifts and Blocks of the Sixth Grail Gate

Gifts of the Sixth Grail Gate

Inspired, Purposeful, Divinely Guided, Celestial Wisdom, Freedom, Visionary, Clarity, Discernment, Soul Lineage, Teacher, Radical Truth, Enchantment, Purity.

This space in your womb holds your intuition, your imagination, your discernment, and your inner vision. It's the place you set your goals, dreams, and desires and where you open up to magical possibilities. It houses your trust in life and your ability to move forward. It embodies your deepest soul wisdom, the ancient knowledge in direct connection to Source. A strong connection to your womb air element will lead you to the perfect teachers, events, friends, opportunities to open your mind and heart to new adventures. Your life will be inspired. It will feel like you have found your soul path and are on a journey into the heart.

Blocks of the Sixth Grail Gate

When this womb element is blocked you will feel confused and stagnant. It might be hard to contact what your heart's desires and dreams are, or it may feel difficult to find practical ways to take steps forward. There is a hopeless energy that feels like giving up and staying stuck. Deep down you feel that life, and people, have let you down. Betrayal is a core wound. You also feel disempowered and look to others in authority to guide you. There is a profound sense of isolation, and part of your core being has chosen to not be here.

❋ *Womb Mapping: Air Element*

1. Sit in a cross-legged womb meditation, bring your hands into a prayer position in front of your heart, then rotate your joined hands forward, so they are now pointed outward straight in front of you. Bring them slowly apart so only your fingertips are touching. Feel the energy flowing, creating a womb space in front of your heart.

2. Move your energy and awareness to the top of this womb-grid mudra where your thumbs meet. Feel a connection between this point, and the upper realms of your Womb, opening into your heart space.

3. Begin to feel the energy of this area—any warmth, blocks, coldness, resistance.

4. Ask yourself the following questions, or just allow any insights and visions to arise.

Questions to Percolate in Your Womb Cauldron

1. What do you feel your deepest soul purpose on earth is?
2. How do you shut down your feelings and truths to please others?
3. Who is your current soul guide—and what is their message today?

❋ *Breath and Sound Meditation*

1. Sit cross-legged and with a soft, relaxed, and upright posture. Allow your shoulders to relax downward, so the rose of your heart can open. Bring your awareness to the Womb and breathe here for a few moments, inhaling and exhaling the delicious, fertile velvet darkness.

2. Now allow yourself to gently expand your energy into the ceiling of your Womb. Breathe here for a few minutes with all your awareness gently focused on the top of the Womb.

3. Allow any feelings, sensations, or visions to arise and be with them. Ask if air has any messages she wishes to share with you, allow yourself to listen.

4. Begin to chant the mantra for the sixth Grail Gate: *he-ra-hom.* Do this for as long as you feel called.

Seventh Grail Gate: Womb Element Water

— ∞ —

Compassion, Feminine Mysteries

Attributes

Direction: Left Ovary / East
Embodies: Intuition, Receptivity, Surrender
Womb Wisdom: Ovulation, Prophecy, Union
Spirit Guardians: Mermaids, Dolphins and Whales, Primordial Mothers
Feminine Essence: Oshun, Stella Maris, Ladies of the Lake
Sacred Sounds: Siren Song and Whale Sounds
Invocation: *May the healing flow of Water cleanse and renew me*

After traveling the feminine path around the womb circle, through the *tree of life,* you open into the second flow of life force, into the deep feminine qualities of surrender and being. You become a receptive channel for all of life, and Source itself, to flow through. The greatest gnosis and wisdom on the feminine path, since the beginning of time, has been received through this lunar element in balance. It is the Divine Mother's grace bestowed.

There is a deep compassion and kindness in the womb water element; it merges the fluid movement of pure Shakti with infinitely embracing love. From this element the archetypes of the ladies of the lake were birthed, whose gentle waters receive the woes of all those warriors who seek refuge. These are the healing waters; the fountain of life—everything is bathed and rebirthed here.

This element holds the key of shimmering, living light—feminine light, held in the liquid black light of primordial love. All life began in water, and our individual lives begin in the waters of our mother's womb. Our bodies are made up of 70 percent water, and water holds the resonance of feeling; it is a pure vessel for our soul essence. In this element you begin to embody the feminine Christ.

Miracles and synchronicities become a normal way of life, and you find yourself living in a pristine feminine dimension of love. Old wounded trauma patterns drop away, healed by the balm of forgiveness and innocence. People become magnetically drawn to you, not for advice or help, but simply to bathe in the beauty of your presence. Your physical body becomes a temple for Spirit, you are illuminated by a soft glow, and you can transmit regenerative waves of love.

You start dropping out of the mental realms of thoughts and ideas, and diving deeper into the realms of feelings, symbols, dreams, and interconnectivity. You become a soul reader: you can feel everything inside a person, even things that they are unable to feel in themselves. You have no desire to judge anyone or anything. Love is your only desire—for yourself, others, and all living creatures.

As you become more acutely sensitive and aware, there can be a frightening sense that the boundaries between you and the world are dissolving—and you are now open to all the wounded thoughts and feelings swirling in the ether. Balancing with the other elements is essential so that you don't become completely overwhelmed by this experience of merging, or your compassion and receptivity is not taken advantage of by a world still out of resonance with love.

The sexual energy of this flow is a surrendered invitation to embrace and pleasure. It embodies the swirls, flows, and currents of orgasmic love, diving deeper and deeper into unknown pools of pleasure, receiving everything. Here orgasmic pleasure becomes a sacrament, a pure offering of love to the beloved.

Water Energy in Relationship

This pure white river merged with the sensual flow of Shakti is what every man desires in his deepest soul self. It is home. It is sacred union. It heals, restores, and revives the masculine of all his perceived wounds. When this union of life-force flow occurs, a woman becomes everything to a man—his mother, his lover, his sister, his best friend, his teacher, and reason for being. In return for his devotion, a woman gives everything of herself, so she can be a vessel of pure Love, a conduit for Source, and his pathway back to wholeness.

When there is too much water element, a woman can become too passive, too receptive, not discerning or protective enough of her boundaries. This is embodied in the woman who gives too much, who squanders all her power and precious energy on giving to others, and taking on their problems. In relationship, the woman takes on a mothering or enabling role, trying to fix the life of her partner, at the expense of her own needs and desires.

If there is deficient water element, a woman can be too uptight and controlling—surrendering to love or orgasm feels very difficult. Men find this energy hard and prickly, and relationships founder because of an inability of the woman to let down her guard. Often women turn to careers for safety and control.

Gifts and Blocks of the Seventh Grail Gate

Gifts of the Seventh Grail Gate

Psychic, Compassionate, Intuitive, Empathetic, Genius, Anointrix, Priestess Lineage, Womb Gnosis, Womb Shamaness, Feminine Light Body.

This space connects you to the tender feminine essence that embraces all of life. It is softly radiant and attracts love and nourishment effortlessly. It is the receptive channel that connects with other people, the cosmos, and earth wisdom. It is the seat of your psychic intuition. Women in touch with the water element of their Womb will have an almost supernatural power to intuit knowledge and feel others' emotions, and manifest synchronicities. This element connects you to your soul mate with a deep psychic bond. Ideas that flow from this element are often paradigm changing—moments of true genius. This is the element associated with oracles and female priestesses through the ages, and connects to their Wisdom. It is the flow of Life, which Source speaks through.

Blocks of the Seventh Grail Gate

You find it difficult to connect to the magic of life, and are prone to judge others and yourself. You may have denial about the true extent of your emotional wounds, guarding and protecting them with anger and resistance. Your receptive channel is offline, because to open it would also mean a huge amount of grief flowing through. You feel life is against you. You struggle to relate to the masculine or surrender to love. You can be "spiky" or argumentative. Underneath your suspicion and anger is a deep feeling that you have to close your heart to survive. You often retreat into the intellectual realms and value control and career success.

❋ Womb Mapping: Water Element

1. Sit in a cross-legged womb meditation, bring your hands into a prayer position in front of your heart, then rotate your joined hands forward, so they are now pointed outward straight in front of you. Bring them slowly apart so only your fingertips are touching. Feel the energy flowing, creating a womb space in front of your heart.

2. Move your energy and awareness to the left side of this womb grid mudra where your left knuckles are. Feel a connection between this point, and the left side of your womb and left ovary.

3. Begin to feel the energy of this area—any warmth, blocks, coldness, resistance.

4. Ask yourself the following questions, or just allow any insights and visions to arise.

Questions to Percolate in Your Womb Cauldron

1. What do you need to surrender to and release in order to let love in?
2. What makes you relax and feel as if you are "in the flow"?
3. What secret message is your intuition whispering to you?

✳ *Breath and Sound Meditation*

1. Sit cross-legged and with a soft, relaxed, and upright posture. Allow your shoulders to relax downward, so the rose of your heart can open. Bring your awareness to the Womb and breathe here for a few moments, inhaling and exhaling the delicious, fertile velvet darkness.
2. Now allow yourself to gently drop your energy deep into your left ovary. Breathe here for a few minutes with all your awareness gently focused on your ovary.
3. Allow any feelings, sensations, or visions to arise and be with them. Ask if water has any messages she wishes to share with you, allow yourself to listen.
4. Begin to chant the mantra for the seventh Grail Gate: *wa-lu-na*. Do this for as long as you feel called.

WOMB ORACLES SHARE
Your Sexuality Is a Gift

I was embraced by Divine Mother, with soft white swan wings and colors of whites and aqua. She says, "I am here, sweet child. I am here to love you. I am you. I breathe through you, my breath is your breath."

I am under her wing being cradled like a child in this loving embrace.

We journey upward. Into the upperworld, the air elemental realms, surrounded by peaceful cool blues. I see a trickle of crystalline-looking light of starlight essence enter my crown chakra.

I appear to have a cloak and soft white swan wings holding a staff and a feminine headband/crown. I feel unworthy. Who am I to hold this staff, have these wings?

Divine Mother is holding me, a hand over my solar heart and a hand over my lunar heart. She says, "You are here now. These are your gifts to share. This is your essence. You are purity, you are innocence. Your pristine sexuality is a gift to share."

With hands of the starry night she holds my womb space. A shimmering crystalline egg is placed glowing in the radiant cauldron of inspiration of my womb.

The crystalline egg radiates and magnetizes the loving frequency of sacred union to my womb. This frequency of information gently mingles and swirls within the shimmering dark waters of my womb, percolating in my feminine heart.

Standing behind me, Divine Mother does a movement with her hands to open my heart space then makes the shape of a cross. "Communication is your gift. It is what you came here to do. Communicate what is in your heart."

J.W.

SPIRAL 31

BLACK MOTHER, WOMB OF CREATION

The Eighth Grail Gate

Know that it is the womb
From which all beings arise;
the universe is born within me,
and within me will be destroyed.

BHAGAVAD GITA

THE EIGHTH GRAIL GATE is the cosmic womb hole that lives deep inside, allowing us to travel into both deep and high dimensions and to emerge rebirthed from within.

The womb is a hologram of the Great Womb; within us is a magic doorway— a multidimensional, holographic gateway where Spirit steps in and out of matter. This black light hole is the centerpiece of our feminine crown, our "earth halo."

Yet, we have lost connection to our roots, to Mother Earth in her multidimensional form, to the Womb of Earth, to our ancestors, to our deep womb knowing. Our root halo is closed. We have become lost, ungrounded, unsafe, feeling that we do not belong in our bodies or here on earth. This portal connects us to the knowledge that light embodied in matter (living light) was created as the *greatest* expression of our Creator, not designed to be a prison of suffering for the soul. There is a throne of ecstasy waiting to awaken inside us.

Opening to feminine awakening reclaims our true heritage as magical creatures of love embodied in the beauty of creation. It is a birthright held deep in our DNA, in the living Light pulsing in every cell. For the tree of life to flourish and extend her branches far out to the cosmos, we first need to anchor into our roots.

In practical terms, this means journeying into and reclaiming all the shamed, judged, and disowned parts of our feminine self and experience: our feelings, our longings, our desires, our sexuality, our dreamtime, our unconscious. To become vulnerable, surrendered, receptive, powerful, creative, and ecstatic.

On the bioenergetic level it means reclaiming the energy vortexes in our lower half; our feet, our legs, our buttocks, our anus, our perineum, our pelvis, our yoni and womb—the anchors of our powerful life force, which are shamed as dirty, embarrassing, or "less than," and to be ignored in our present culture.

We have to climb down from our heads and come back into our primal feminine centers in our lower half. We have to let go of the control our intellectual self loves so much and enter the primordial wildness of the Womb.

It can feel like skydiving or plummeting down an elevator shaft.

The spiral descent calls us inward to the center of our Soul Shakti.

The Magnetic Womb Grid

The feminine, embodied in the Womb, is *magnetic;* it attracts and pulls everything toward it and inside it, it draws whatever is in our feminine self (for both men and women) into our lives. The huge disconnection from our feminine self means we often draw things into our lives that don't "appear" to be what we want. We don't know our feminine side enough to be aware of our true hidden feelings. Our fear acts like a magnetic wounded desire—we pull "bad" events, circumstances, and relationships toward us, not as a lesson as such, but as a reflection, as a call from our feminine side, to listen to her voice again.

We cannot "positive think" or meditate this away. We can only reach out for, get to know, awaken, and activate and embrace our lost feminine self. *Know thyself.*

❊ Explore Your Magnetic Force

1. Sit for a moment and feel into the magnetic womb grid of your feminine crown center—your womb, yoni, pelvis, anus—how do you really feel about

these physical areas? Pure, ecstatic, open, flowering, beautiful, innocent? Or ignored, dirty, shameful, ugly, hurt, closed, hidden?

2. Whatever feelings come up, this is the emotional and psychic cauldron from which you are currently magnetizing everything into your life.

3. Do you feel the call to befriend these places more?

When we open our Womb and give voice to our feminine self, big shifts happen. First we become aware of what's *really* running the show on the emotional level: our fears, wounds, traumas, and inherited beliefs. The negative patterns of our lives become clearer; we feel less a victim of circumstance. From that place, we begin to heal and open the magnetic power of the feminine to bring to us all the nourishment, opportunity, love, and relationships we need.

Sacred Bowing

In ancient cultures the anus and perineum were sacred. The last truly feminine culture on Earth used to show their feminine crown center to the full moon as a sacred act of devotion and power. We also use this same posture as an act of devotion, but we call it bowing and "think" the sacred act is touching our forehead to the floor, rather than raising and opening our feminine crown to the sky. In fact, it is a beautiful posture of sacred union of the twins—our masculine crown touches the earth in honor and reverence, while our feminine crown reaches up and opens to the sky in a gesture of honor and trust.

During the bowing posture, become aware of these two crown centers, greeting Mother Earth and Father Sky in harmonious union. Get in touch with how this feels energetically: the humility of bringing your masculine consciousness down to earth; the vulnerability of opening your feminine consciousness into the cosmos.

Dissolving into the Feminine Crown

To be held deeply in the Womb of Creation, we have to love ourselves deeply in our feminine crown center, because this is the where the multidimensional portal lives. The Cosmic Womb is always here, inside us, waiting to merge us into her pure Love—we just have to reach for her and reach for our true self.

The root is home to a massive plexus of nerves that connect to the spinal cord and communicate directly with the womb of the brain (the primal back brain). The perineum is also part of this sensitive nerve vortex and forms the energetic "spine" of our yoni, and connects us deeply to the earth element of our wombs.

Descending back into the feminine, deep into the Great Womb, is to become immersed, dissolved, and baptized in the infinite vastness of the radiant darkness; it will dissolve your separate wounded self in a cosmic cauldron. So we fear the darkness, we fear the night, we fear what we cannot see, what lies beyond the safe range of visible light, because we are afraid of the black womb.

The black womb Void is our dark mother, our Black Madonna of Creation and dissolution—she holds all existence together and is with us always, in all ways.

As Matthew Fox says,

The Black Madonna is Dark and calls us to the darkness. Darkness is something we need to get used to again—the "Enlightenment" has deceived us into being afraid of the dark and distant from it. . . . Meister Eckhart observes that "the ground of the soul is dark."[1]

The Black Madonna invites us into the dark and therefore into our depths. This is what the mystics call the "inside" of things, the essence of things. This is where divinity lies. It is where the true self lies. It is where illusions are broken apart and the truth awakens.

Andrew Harvey puts it this way,

The Black Madonna is the transcendent Kali-Mother, the black womb of light out of which all of the worlds are always arising and into which they fall, the presence behind all things, the darkness of love and the loving unknowing. She calls us to that darkness, which is mystery itself. She encourages us to be at home there, in the presence of deep, black, unsolvable mystery. . . . Eckhart calls God's darkness a "superessential darkness, a mystery behind mystery, a mystery within mystery that no light has penetrated."[2]

The Goddess is associated with blackness or black light—the light beyond light that gleams in the darkness of the Void. Isis is described as wearing a black robe, and poet Henry Vaughan says, "There is in God, some say, a deep and dazzling darkness." This reflects the mystical teachings of St. Gregory of Nyssa, who, in the fourth century described God as a *divine darkness*. Unlike many theologians of his time, who believed that the spiritual journey was a path from darkness into light, St. Gregory believed that the spiritual quest begins with light and then progresses into deeper states of mystical luminous darkness. In his work *Life of Moses* he writes, "Moses' vision of God began with light . . . But when Moses rose higher and became more perfect, he saw God in the darkness." It is compelling to percolate on the idea that, as we discovered earlier, Simon Magus—the lineage heir of John the Baptist—described Moses as a sort of "womb shaman" who had declared paradise to be the Womb of Creation. The Womb of the Goddess was the portal of the luminous, dazzling dark matter of creation—the mystery of God. Yet over time, as consciousness fell, her shining darkness was reimagined as the abyss of evil—and she lay forgotten, waiting for us to remember the hidden birth-light of her Cosmic Womb, which creates All, so we can be anointed into her spirit again.

The mysterious Black Madonna lies at the epicenter of this lost and secret womb religion; she is the embodiment of the radiant darkness of the Cosmic Womb—the great portal of creation and dissolution, the source that births all. *She also lies, often lost, at the epicenter of our own wombs.* When we journey through the Sacred Feminine medicine wheel, the "womb wheel" or Grail rose, we once again return to our sacred center—and to the center of creation.

This mysterious darkness, the dazzling dark matter that marries all things, is the well of radiant creative potential that lives within our Wombs; our Sacred Feminine center is a portal to the Cosmic Womb—where we can commune with Source and bring these potentialities to life.

✳ *Breath and Sound Meditation*

1. Sit cross-legged and with a soft, relaxed, and upright posture. Allow your shoulders to relax downward, so the rose of your heart can open. Bring your awareness to the Womb and breathe here for a few moments, inhaling and exhaling the delicious, fertile velvet darkness.

2. Now allow yourself to gently bring your energy into the center of your Womb. Breathe here for a few minutes with all your awareness focused on this spiral portal.

3. Allow any feelings, sensations, or visions to arise and be with them. Ask if Great Mother has any messages she wishes to share with you, allow yourself to listen.

4. Begin to chant the mantra for the eighth Grail Gate: *o-m*. Do this for as long as you feel called.

WOMB ORACLES SHARE

Cells of Whirling Galaxies

Meeting Mother Black Madonna brought me to my knees in a holy sacramental moment of being in her loving presence. She placed her hand on my heart igniting a gold cross embossed in symbols with a rose in the center of it. She bent over and opened my yoni, and my body turned into a golden, geometric, brilliant structure of light.

She led me to a sarcophagus box and had me lie in it, saying I am to go into dreamtime, rest, and receive visions. A door opened, with a man beckoning me closer. At the edge of the door I looked into another time, an ancient land where I knew my ancestors lived. A whole large community was there. Asking about my parents, they appeared. We felt such happiness seeing and hugging each other. They said there are many of us who are gathering in communities to seed the new earth and to watch where we are led. They said they are now embodied as us, and that the old timelines are collapsing and much is and will be revealed about the coming times.

A golden being moved from above through the top of my head and merged with me, my twin flame. Another vision appeared of ethereal people dancing with sheer, flowing white cloth on their bodies that appeared as winglike. They were whirling and whirling a new vision of life in. The Black Madonna led me into the center of the room and placed a baby golden solar dragon in my womb. I never saw Black Madonna's face even though I tried to see it. Instead she appeared fathomless with only whirling galaxies moving everywhere like they were her cells.

I instinctively know the healing of my womb is also a collective vision that is happening right now as womb teachings are reawakening and streaming into the consciousness of our field, healing the collective. My visions seemed as though I saw through wormholes.

S.R.

Dancing the Web of Life

I'm in a cave inside the Womb of the Earth, crones are surrounding me, looking on . . .

I am dancing in spirals, fast and light as a fairy, spinning right up into the universe . . . free, spinning spiraling energy, exhilaration, joy.

The crones stop me and ask for me to stand still.

Tree roots grow up from the ground, into my feet, winding round my legs. My fingers turn into shoots and braches grow out; my hair turns into branches. The roots and branches weave together. Eventually I am woven and meshed into the tree. I am the tree. The roots and branches are like a cocoon, or womb, around me.

I feel trapped and stifled, compared to my spiraling dance. I am caught in a web.
"Now *dance!*" demand the crones.
"*I can't move,*" I tell them.
"*Dance from a different place, inside,*" they reply.
So a movement begins, from deep inside my heart, a feeling. I begin to dance inside this web and it feels beautiful and connected, full of love, as the web dances with me as one movement in deep, deep love and interconnectedness.

S.B.

CYCLE 7

RETURN OF THE FEMININE CHRIST

Completing the Circle

AWAKENING THE GRAIL KNIGHTS

The Sacred Masculine as Guardian of the Womb

*I found him whom my soul loveth: I held him, and would not
let him go, until I had brought him into my mother's house, and
into the chamber of her that conceived me.*

SONG OF SONGS

THE RETURN OF THE feminine calls men to fully step into their courageous
hearts and become guardians of the Womb; to protect and champion not only
women and the feminine principle but also to become Grail knights *for their own
inner feminine*. The world can only rebirth with men and women, the masculine and
feminine flows, *both* being honored and walking hand-in-hand in sacred union. It is
through this communion with the deep yin that the true yang is birthed.

We are entering a time of a rebirth of masculinity, creating a spiritual, emotional,
and physical blossoming of men in ways that are beyond our imagination. It is the
return of the radical, courageous heart of man, which has been hidden under wounds
for thousands of years. One of the greatest powers on the planet today is the pure,
loving heart of a man that serves the principle of life herself.

This will bring our world the gift of true freedom. Men have been seeking their
freedom in the wrong places for thousands of years—on the battlefields, on Wall
Street, on lonely mountaintops, in heaven or monasteries—anywhere but within
their own body and soft lunar self. True freedom is emotional freedom *within* the

body, within relationships, here on this Earth, with two feet on the ground.

Emotional freedom is being able to recognize, feel, and express emotions as they arise, without shame. It is *the* essential ingredient to self-knowledge, but has been left out of most major spiritual paths that have been propagated in the past few thousand years. Women are more naturally attuned to feelings, but emotional freedom has been virtually unknown to men for thousands of years. Instead, disassociated "fearless" states and false strength have been promoted and idealized as the mark of a "real man"—at a great cost to our psyches and world. The return of the feminine invites us to reclaim the full spectrum of our emotions and bodies in order to awaken our true inner power and potential.

Through men's powerful and courageous love, they will also be able to hold and help heal the women and children in their lives. As women are healed, all things will come back into balance. Women have been controlled, degraded, shamed, and attacked for thousands of years, which also injures men terribly, though this is often unrecognized. The ecology of the Womb becomes the ecology of our world—because it is through the wombs of women that future generations are birthed.

The most effective way to cripple a man is to damage his mother, his wife, or his children. An emotionally damaged mother will pass on her wounds to her son. If she has been crushed and emotionally depressed, her child will absorb these wounded energies. If she carries anger toward men, the sensitive young boy will feel it and hold anger against women. We need to hold hands and take the leap into wholeness together. Healing relationships between mothers and sons is key.

For the adult man, a healed woman is capable of sharing the most exquisite energies of renewal, especially through the presence of her tender loving embrace and the wild flow of her vital power and of her fluid sexuality.

This is a complete biological and spiritual rebirth. Man is reborn through the womb of the woman, also the Womb of life itself. The opened and healed womb is a magical portal into dimensions that most of us only dream of.

In tantric Buddhist tradition, the vulva is honored as the gateway of life and called the citadel of Buddahood; a female spiritual partner is an honored representative of the Divine Mother to be cherished, adored, appreciated, and praised. Spiritual practice for men includes contemplating how the womb of his beloved has been the sacred passageway for his rebirths—and is now his numinous gateway to enlightenment. By this meditation, he unites with the "Mother" force.[1]

The return of the feminine is the *only* thing that can revive our dying planet. We are hurtling like a runaway train toward an environmental catastrophe that threatens the survival of the human race, unless we radically change the way we live on Earth.

No amount of solar panels, recycling, or environmental redesign alone can save us. We must change radically from within in order to learn how to directly perceive the web of life in a way that is harmonic and balanced.

As the true feminine takes her rightful place in union with the true masculine, an incredible power is born. The light of creation formed by the union of man and woman will suddenly *turn on*. It is a creative force more powerful than any other frequency we have known on this planet. It brings with it a deep connection to the web of life and nature that most animals intuitively feel, but that we humans lost several thousand years ago when we collectively lost the feminine.

Male Embrace of the Feminine Blueprint

Just as the womb is a magic portal of power, creation, and love—so is the lingam, the Sanskrit word for penis. In cultures that honor the womb, the phallic power of the lingam is also celebrated—not as something separate to the feminine, to dominate it or have power over it, but as complementary power that comes together in unified wholeness. In India this was symbolized by the Shiva Lingam and Shakti Yoni—which contained both expressions of the primal Creatrix.

Since patriarchy, with its bloody history of rape and conquest, we have lost touch with the knowing that the masculine is also a sensitive creature. In its original consciousness the phallus is deeply intelligent, intuitive, and tuned to love.

Both women and men need to reconnect to this knowing, in order for women to restore their trust and faith in the masculine, and for men to reclaim their honor and self-esteem as beings of love and integrity who uphold the web of life.

The awakened lingam and yoni are in equal, harmonious relationship, in perfect communication and communion; from this union they merge together as they enter the shared womb space, as a portal to the Source of Creation. The male and female dissolve into Oneness in the feminine womb. From this space sacred sex, making love, or shamanic sexual awakening is possible—in the multidimensional container of the universal womb space.

The lingam is a sensitive, feeling, loving, alive intelligence. It has its own intuitive, prophetic capabilities—and communes directly with the power of the womb. In this communication the womb opens. Not because the lingam is "doing" anything to her, but because he is speaking, relating, honoring, and cherishing her. He is calling, singing to this primal source of origin—and she always answers by opening her energetic space and receiving him.

There is no opposition, conflict, or duality between male and female, these two beautiful, complementary expressions of the feminine blueprint of life; they are designed to play together, to fit together, to love together, to create together.

Only our wounded perception of the war between masculine and feminine prevents us from feeling and living this. We have far more similarities than differences. Qualities we now call masculine (logic without heart, power without compassion, sexuality without soul) belong to neither men nor women.

Men are feminine *feeling* beings too. Their lingams are feminine design (but not female), acutely sensitive, and feeling oriented, but with their own unique male essence. The persecution of the feminine aspect of the human male is one of the most damaging tragedies in this world.

This has been a terrible violence against men, which has led to much violence being inflicted on women from this disconnection—with all the fear, grief, and rage that it comes with. The male's deep longing to connect back to the feminine is so primal and profound it is almost too much for them to bear. But until men can heal their relationship with the feminine, they can never know themselves, or embody the union of Shiva-Shakti that lives within them.

Our society has conditioned men to feel that being feminine is weak, sinful, or shameful, and men are persecuted and punished for connecting to or exhibiting any feminine qualities. On the playground, boys police each other—feelings, tears, love, or affection are laughed at, mocked, and attacked.

The feminine energetic flow within man is his beautiful, pure, sensitive, and loving heart. Research shows that young boys are actually *more* emotional and sensitive than girls, but by adolescence this natural tendency has been conditioned out of them—often programmed by both subtle and overt judgment and emotional shaming.[2]

Men learn early that to survive they have to completely shut down their feminine essence. They are taught to deny that they are birthed from a feminine blueprint. And in doing so, they cannot truly love themselves or others, or their Mother Earth. This is one the biggest revelations being given to the planet at this moment in time, and also the most emotionally triggering for men. It takes them directly into their deepest wounds and fears of the feminine.

Women are also not embodying their feminine blueprint, and are pursuing distorted masculine ways of being, essentially men in women's bodies—shutting down feelings, valuing productivity over relationship, living from mental ideals at the expense of their sensuality. Paradoxically, when men embrace their feminine blueprint, it opens them into the gifts and powers of their true *male essence*—their wild, primal Shakti, the incredible courage of their hearts.

The power of men embracing their feminine side as the source of shamanic and psychic power was common knowledge in ancient times. Shamans and medicine men would often enhance their feminine traits to access the feminine universal creative field of wisdom. In the Tao Te Ching there are a number of references to the power of feminine consciousness, and male initiates are recommended to practice cultivating a divine embryo within.

It was believed that by merging male and female energies within, the creation of an internal embryo would be birthed, which would create an immortal body.

The Tao master Ma Yu says in a sutra poem, "If a son of good nature embraces his good nature, he does not need . . . rituals. . . . Internally cultivating his extraordinary womb . . . He gives birth to a miraculous child that has great talents."[3]

This knowledge that men also had an internal womb space, a hara, that was brimming with primordial creative possibilities, was the foundation of many ancient Eastern systems that honored the feminine as the original cause.

Men were taught not to fear or judge the feminine, but to embrace all internal and external manifestations, and to become at One with the Divine Mother.

But over time, to disempower the masculine and to strip him of his shamanic and psychic magical powers, men were forbidden to taste the feminine within.

Awakening Wild Male Shakti

Not only is this sensitive, feeling side "forbidden," but the wild, primal, sexual masculine is also frowned upon, shamed, and controlled. Men grow up in a world where the primal masculine sexual forces are perceived as lustful, violent, or predatory. This raw male energy is often associated with harmful unconscious acts such as rape, or a sexuality that is taking and unloving. There are, of course, frequencies of male sexuality that are extremely wounded that can manifest in aggressive, violent acts, but this comes from emotional wounds and mental programming, and is *not* the essence of wild male Shakti—which is *pure* power.

Primal masculine sexuality is embodied in the archetypes of Pan, Cernunnos, Dionysus—the greening, fertilizing, masculine energy of earth, which is vital, alive, sensual, and sexually activating.

Reclaiming authentic male sexual energy and feeling all the wounds of shame, judgment, or fear surrounding it is a key element of this journey. Men are often raised by mothers with deep emotional wounds in relation to the masculine. As a result, these mothers can have difficulty holding and supporting a teenage boy to blossom into his sacred, wild, primal sexuality—and may try to repress, control, deny, or shame it by overt or subtle means. Allowing this repressed energy to flow again in all its wildness, and having it lovingly received in sacred relationship, is a profound healing step and the heart of alchemy.

For a man, the deepest healing comes from stepping into his role as a guardian of the womb and honoring the feminine in her journey back to wholeness. The more his beloved woman heals, the more her womb opens into its wild, innocent, magnetic power. Her activated womb is the Grail that renews and restores him.

For women, the Grail Gates journey is about opening and activating the womb, so that she can once again hold the masculine and renew all separation into Oneness. Each gate holds specific feminine energies and archetypes that heal by being loved, acknowledged, and witnessed. A man's love and support accelerates this process *tremendously* for a woman. In fact, her beautiful flower of sexuality cannot open to its fullest *without* the love of a man. Her womb responds to love like a flower responds to the sun—his love blooms her open.

The masculine is the guardian and protector of the womb. In the safety of his love she opens. Many masks of the feminine will drop in this process—and all resistance and denials dissolve back into the soft, sensual, shining, magical flows of the feminine essence. This is what men long for, and what women long to embody.

For men, this journey is first about discovering and embracing his own repressed feelings and primal sensory perception. He can then attune to his woman's emotions and sexual Grail Gates—feeling and discovering the quality of love that each of the gates needs in order to bloom open. Sometimes tenderness, compassion, and patience are required. At other times it may be gratitude, chivalry, or an unconditional love of the aspects of herself she finds shameful.

The womb blooms open in the presence of the man's consistent commitment, honor, respect, and appreciation, and offers powerful gifts to support his journey.

Guardians of the Womb:
Grail Knights of New Earth

We live in a time of an antilife, distorted consciousness that is waging war on the feminine, and has been for thousands of years. This energy will try to crush the seed of new feminine rebirth—unless we step forward to protect it.

This pledge is a commitment to protecting all our internal and external expressions of the feminine, of love, harmony. It is a commitment to dissolve all our external and internal expressions of greed, judgment, and disharmony.

We need to activate our collective immune system, and to open into healthy expressions of our masculine power in ways that work to keep the whole in balance. By doing so, we begin to consciously choose the world we create.

This remembrance reawakens the feminine, and rebirths the masculine. It is a time of union, not separation. It is a time of knowing we are all equal, and we all have feminine and masculine qualities within us that need to be honored.

Every man is a guardian of the womb, and every woman holds her own inner womb guardian. Every woman is a carrier of womb power, and every man can merge with it, and initiate his own powerful feminine consciousness.

The sacred womb has the power to rebirth us all.

With commitment to protect this gestating seed of change, new earth will bloom.

Descent into the Womb of Isis

It was the night before we would ascend to the throne of Isis, deep in the magical woods of Rennes-les-Bains. This simple stone seat, ancient in origins, was strongly connected to the Womb of Gaia. That night I went to bed restless, with a headache. In the early hours of the morning, I had a dream.

I found myself in a totally dark place, bathed in black light. I lay on the ground, curled up like a fetus, in another state of consciousness. Around me were several priestesses of Isis, forming a downward pointing triangle. I was told that I would stay there for three days and that the women would be with me all the time.

The next day we began our pilgrimage to the throne of Isis. The path was steep, winding upward through the trees. The sunlight was filtered by the leaves and made them light up in beautiful, intense green shades. The air was warm, still, and peaceful. It was a silent procession going up. Passing fellow pilgrims on their way up to the throne; one playing the lyre softly; others praying or walking in meditation. Finally we reached the throne. It was beautiful the way it was situated there in the curve of the winding path, with a sacred spring nearby.

I felt the deep longing from my core to meet Mother Isis. I wanted to run to her like child that is called by its mother. In my mind's eye I saw Isis sit on her throne. Her body was small but her presence was huge. A golden halo surrounded her entire body. She was staring straight at me. After being anointed, I sat on the throne. My eyes closed as I started to go deeper within, as my body was gently convulsing. I had no visions and heard no messages. All was black.

After a little while, I stood up and took my place by the trees. I was drawn deeper within, as if to descend into the Womb of Gaia herself. I saw Isis standing in front of me with her wings spread out, looking at me with her dark eyes, made up just like in those beautiful Egyptian paintings on ancient papyrus. Eyes adorned with heavy, thick, black lines around them.

Then she took me up into the universe. First to the sun. She did not speak, nor did I. We were in the sun for a while, as she showed me secrets. Next, she took me to the Cosmic Womb. Then back to Earth, to the Womb of Gaia. In the deep blackness there, she showed me a line of shining crystals. She stood behind the crystals with her wings spread out. With the energy of a wordless question I asked her what she wanted me to do. I did not understand her. Then she gave me one of the crystals. I knew I had to swallow the crystal. It was sent straight to my hara, which then activated with a warm, pulsing energy.

My legs felt weak. Isis invited me to kneel. I knelt, bending forward with my head touching the earth, relaxing my body more. Isis stood behind me, bending forward so her wings covered me, the tips overlapping each other at the point of my heart. As they touched my body, my heart center, the front and back opened. I sighed as I felt the spaciousness within. Never before have I felt it so strongly. In a powerful movement Isis pointed at the sky. I felt strong surges of energy shooting up from the bottom of my spine all the way up to the sun. She made this movement a few times with the energy running upward.

From the blackness words came: My name, Akash, and then Ishtar. Akash, Ishtar, Akash, Ishtar, Ishtar, Ishtar.

I needed to lie down. I curled up on the ground, and I noticed how beautifully womb shaped the place was. I was drawn deep within. Nestling in the space on the inviting ground. No longer any images, but a spacious, expansive blackness. My body started to contract strongly and relax again. After a while in this darkness, I noticed the ladies of the lake were gathered around me, caressing me, silently humming or chanting. One of them gave me a flower in my hand.

The same events from my dream, which I had shared with no one, were being enacted in this world. I had experienced the mystical, initiatory descent into the Womb of Isis, and had been awakened by the loving touch of the priestesses of Isis, into soul rebirth.

A.V.K.

SPIRAL 33

THE FEMININE CHRIST RETURNS

Womb Consciousness Rebirths

The spirit of the Fountain dies not.
It is called the mysterious Feminine.
The doorway of the mysterious Feminine
is called the root of Heaven-and-Earth.
Lingering like gossamer, it has only a hint of existence;
and yet when you draw upon it, it is inexhaustible.

TAO TE CHING

THE MULTIDIMENSIONAL POWER of the womb is grounded in our physical biology. This is how we embody our Soul-Shakti gifts as a lived reality. By accessing the portals inside our physical body, we can ignite and awaken the chemistry of our soul and align our physical structure back to its harmonic blueprint.

We are either deliberately misled or too afraid to inhabit our physical, multidimensional power. Without this, everything is just talk—nice ideas and clever theories, but no real transformation. From the moment we were conceived, gestated, and birthed into a wounded world, we disassociated from our bodies so we could escape from threatening, terrifying, or heartbreaking emotions.

It takes the greatest courage to come back to life, to feel again, to reclaim our physical bodies—one of the most sophisticated, miraculous vehicles in existence. Coming back to life, cell by cell, is to become the embodiment of love, here on earth. It opens up miraculous pathways not witnessed for thousands of years.

No one in this world is fully inhabiting their body and its (super)natural powers. To heal we have to reconceive, regestate, rebirth, and renurture ourselves. There is no shortcut. No mantra can heal the deep traumas we hold. *But love can.*

We have endured an imbalanced, violent shadow world of commerce that kills our dreams, constricts our hearts, pollutes our wombs, pillages the feminine body and the body of our Mother Gaia; we have valued economies of hate and greed over co-creation, harmony with nature, and gift economies that nurture and bloom the deepest dreams of our hearts, in a synchronistic symphony together.

How have we looked to heal this terrible state of affairs?

We have labored under many different imbalanced systems of spirituality for thousands of years. We have denigrated the body and focused the mind, we have chosen detached peace over sensual passion, we have sat alone on mountains and abandoned our shared celebrations of moon cycles. And where are we?

Our Earth is dying, our systems are derelict, the masculine and feminine are at war, our collective health is failing, we are hooked on corporate-peddled drugs, children starve every second, women are raped, we live in fear and denial.

Womb Awakening is a powerful way to truly heal ourselves and our world; to rebirth in a real, tangible way, out of this suffering that has been created.

It's not a practice or a meditation—it's a pledge from the very root of our being, to Come Alive, to reclaim our rightful biological, energetic, and soulful inheritance. It's about rolling our sleeves up and getting down and dirty with our personal wounds, and then having the strength to face collective ones too.

It means opening into the incredible possibility we were designed to live in innocent ecstatic sensual pleasure; that life really is looking after us and loving us in every moment; that we are not fatally flawed sinners; that we were created perfectly, and only our collective fear and lack of self-love prevent us living it.

It invites us to travel the lunar pathways of rest, recuperation, relaxation, renewal, to dive into our inner worlds and know there are jewels waiting there.

It requires holding ourselves and others in love, and supporting each other on our healing journeys. It is anchored by bringing our babies into this world in orgasmic waves of love, rather than on drugs and in pain, choosing the sacred work of child-rearing and soul-nurturing vocations, rather than just paying bills, and educating our children in freedom and joy, not prisons of conformity.

It requires that we follow our dreams, intuitions, and womb *knowing*, not the delusions of a psychopathic system. That we commit to our relationships, and to opening our magnificent, sacred sexual selves. To love until there are no hidden places left in our hearts, and to grieve what we had locked away for so long.

The Grail Maidens Return:
Healing the Holy Wells

We are completing the circle, yet the spiral leads us back to the beginning with fresh eyes, fresh perceptions, fresh footsteps, on a new octave, in a new place.

We are retreading virgin ground, a crone shape-shifting into a maiden.

In regaining Eden, we birth a new Eden—a new octave and expression of creation, bringing all our hard-earned wisdom along with us, refracting it through dazzling prisms of innocence and renewal. We cannot go back—only forward, spinning the wheel of the spiral, deeper and deeper, higher and higher.

All these experiences—matriarchy/patriarchy, loss, betrayal, separation—are now in the melting pot, and we are all entangled in them through the quantum collective field. These experiences are now calling for our radical embrace. When we redeem ourselves from them, we redeem each other. We are a web.

The mysterious Grail text *L'Elucidation* tells the story of the damsels of the well, whose ministry is to tend to those thirsty for renewal. These magical maidens emerge from the sacred wells of Gaia and offer sustenance to pilgrims, giving them the food of life and allowing them to drink the elixirs of their golden cups.

However, a king rapes one of the maidens, and his men soon follow him into this fallen rape consciousness, until no maidens of the wells are left undefiled. The sacred and holy wells of the feminine dry up, becoming a barren wasteland. Their golden cups, their Holy Wombs, are also stolen by these men—to be harvested for their personal gain, rather than preserved in service to love.

From this time, the earthly paradise was lost. The voice of the feminine fell silent. The Grail Gates of the Womb closed down.

News of this tragedy reached the Grail knights of the Round Table, guardians of the womb. They swore they would not rest until the damsels had been avenged. They set off on a quest, finally discovering a mysterious tribe wandering the forests, who were the descendents of the damsels of the wells and the evil king.

But how could they take out their vengence, their wild justice? To kill the family of the fallen ones also meant killing the children of the damsels of the Grail—their ancestry, their blood, and their fate were now entwined. Rather than avenging the past, the healing balm was to birth a new future.

The damsels of the well now bring a message from the soul of the world:

> *By healing the Wombs of women, so will we heal the physical*
> *and spiritual wasteland—and the sacred rivers of the*
> *feminine will flow, and redeem, again.*

This is our restoration to wholeness, and the work of the feminine Christ.

Womb Awakening is a true revolution, and it starts right here in this moment, inside your body, inside your heart, inside your Womb.

Will you choose to gaze deep into the sacred well and hear the call?

The voice of the feminine returns.

> *A new Seed is planted.*
> *A new Cycle is turning.*
> *A new Earth is birthing.*

WOMB ORACLES SHARE
Awakening the Tree of Life

Look deeply into the middle of the circle. It all begins with a single seed. That seed will begin to grow roots, which will go deeper and deeper. Soon a small flower bud will begin to show. This flower is very soft and delicate. Inside of it, a woman is sleeping. The roots will keep spreading, anchoring, growing strong, and eventually they will begin to touch deep and unknown places. As the flower begins to open and bloom, slowly, slowly, small roses will also begin to bloom along the roots, softening the darkness. Over time, the flower and its roots will become very strong. It will eventually transform into a beautiful tree and bless the world.

N.H.

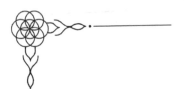

~ *Vow of the Womb Priestess* ~

If you are called, place your hands on your Womb, and from your deepest heart make this vow to become a chalice for the return of the Divine Feminine.

I give myself to the Great Remembering,

I serve only Love and our evolution in Love,

I vow to anchor the true Divine Feminine on Earth,

I vow to anchor the true Divine Feminine in my Womb,

I vow to leave no shadow unloved, no wound without balm,

I walk the path of Love, I commit to our return to innocence,

I strip away all my armor and leave my heart undefended,

I embrace all my feelings; nothing is forbidden or left out,

My strength is my surrender to the Divine Feminine flow,

I honor my pristine sexuality as a gift of Life, wild and free,

I long to merge with the ecstatic innocence of Love in All,

Sacred relationship is my sacrament, the Womb my temple,

I vow to return my Womb to her immaculate sensuality,

To embody the sacred powers of conscious conception,

My life is part of a greater tapestry, I offer all to this weaving,

holding the corners of the pure land from whence we came,

Beloved Divine Mother, bear witness to my vow.

ACKNOWLEDGMENTS

THANK YOU to our beloved parents for being the doorway. Special thanks to Margaret Bertrand for all her support. Gratitude to all our earth family, all our ancestors, and to Mother Earth. Thank you to our soul family and spirit guides for being the spirit doulas for this work and the ever-present love of Divine Mother.

Thank you to all those who have touched our hearts in some way along the path, either in person or through their wisdom transmissions; thank you for lighting the way. We appreciate all those from the past who have given themselves, despite persecution, to preserving the old feminine teachings and protecting the earth.

Thank you to Linda Star Wolf for her generosity and vivacity of spirit, and for being the "Fairy Wolf Mother" for this book and graciously offering to write the foreword—we appreciate your support. Thank you to Jon Graham for his support and his guardianship of the Sacred Feminine. Thank you to all the staff at Inner Traditions for their hard work and dedication to the crafting and birthing of the book; with special mention to Jamaica Burns Griffin, Nancy Yeilding, Elizabeth Wilson, and Virginia Scott Bowman, plus Ashley Kolesnik and Erica B. Robinson.

Deep appreciation goes to all of our worldwide womb circle, past, present, and future, who have journeyed with us, and courageously shared the path—your wisdom weaves through this book and brings it to life. Thank you especially to the womb oracles whose stories shine like stars within the pages of this book.

Seren Bertrand (S.B.)
Eliana Starweaver (E.S.)
Victoria Oonagh Moonfire (V.M.)
Sofiya Jones (S.J.)
Cara Lo Iacono (C.L.I.)
Laura Maria (L.M.)
Karina Schoonbert (K.S.)
Olivia Martin (O.M.)
Ani Williams (A.W.)
Jacqui Ward (J.W.)

Natvienna Hanell (N.H.)
Heather Skye (H.S.)
Aine Cailleach (A.C.)
Jodi O'Meara (J.O.M.)
Anabel Vizcara (A.V.)
Louisa Williams (L.W.)
Ulrike Remlein (U.R.)
Sunomi Rose (S.R.)
Natalie Zukerman (N.Z.)
Akash van Kessel (A.V.K.)

Thank you to Louisa Williams for holding the organizational threads together, and much more—including the research on the conscious birthing chapter. Thank you to Logan May for research on the womb lore compilation, and to Aine Cailleach for gathering, compiling, and editing the womb oracle sharings.

Gratitude to Zanna, the budding womb priestess whose sacred birth story is described in the book; she is the visionary shining maiden.

Special thanks to Heather Skye (www.SacredEnchantment.com) and Natvienna Hanell (www.HolyWomanHolyGrail.com) who created all the beautiful illustrations in the book in a wild flow of Shakti! Thanks also to Heather Skye for her beautiful design work on the book cover and interior. Much gratitude to Linda Go for the beautiful illustrations of Göbekli Tepe.

Thank you to Ani Williams for sharing her visionary dream of Yeshua and Magdalene's sacred union. Ani is a world-renowned harp player, pilgrimage guide, writer, and musician—and has been receiving the songs of the Grail for over thirty years. Visit www.AniWilliams.com to find out more about her music.

Thank you to Michelle Dionne, priestess and birth dance facilitator, for sharing her wisdom about the benefits of birth dancing. To find out more about her sacred work visit www.TheMandorla.com

Thank you to our cat-guides, Merlin and Lyra, who have entertained us through the process and kept us inspired with their "paws in the air" meditation techniques.

We give special thanks to the Neanderthals and those of the First Time, who met us at the cosmic doorway between the worlds in 2012 to reach out and share the story of their ancient moon/womb religion, more than three hundred thousand years old, and the genocide that was wreaked upon them. This experience, gifted through the cauldron of our own sacred union, baptized us into the feminine dimension, creating an inner paradigm shift that seeded the inspiration for this book.

This book is for those to come, who will take the next big evolutionary step. May we bequeath you a new earth, full of the love you deserve.

IN LOVE AND GRATITUDE,
DR. AZRA AND SEREN BERTRAND

GLOSSARY

Akashic Record: Collective cosmic memory. Just as the human body has cellular and genetic memory where experiences, feelings, and events are imprinted as a record, so the collective body of the universe and our Earth carry similar records of memory and experience. In many spiritual traditions, accessing these Akashic Records brings great resources of wisdom.

alta major: The feminine third eye, located at the back of the head where the nape of the neck and the cranium meet. Connects energetically to the masculine third eye at the brow, and is the doorway to nonlinear, primal, lunar feminine consciousness.

Bhagavad Gita: Sacred Indian text thought to be written between 400 BCE and 200 CE. *Bhagavad* is Sanskrit for holy or divine and is derived from the root word *bhaga,* which means "womb" or "yoni." *Gita* is song. So, the original meaning of *Bhagavadgita* is "Song of the Divine Womb" or "Song of the Womb of Creation."

black hole: Densest matter in the known universe that absorbs all light and matter that comes within its gravitational pull.

cerebellum: Located in the primal hindbrain, the feminine cerebellum is the "mothership" of consciousness. The first part of our brain to develop as we gestate in the womb, containing more brain cells and neurons than the *entire body put together.*

Ceridwen: The Celtic Mother Goddess; a Welsh witch, crone, and goddess of poetry, inspiration, and of the cauldron of transfiguration, from whom the bards received their inspiration.

chakra: In Indian traditions *chakra* means "spinning wheel" and represents key energy vortexes in the body that connect to different powers. See *Grail Gate.*

Cosmic Womb: The spiritual and energetic birthing portal at the center of a universe, galaxy, or star system—correlating in scientific terms to black holes.

deertrod/dreampath: An energetic or spiritual inner pathway within the psyche that leads us into magical dreamtime realms of knowledge and self-discovery.

Divine/Great Mother/Great Womb: The infinite, benevolent source of all creation. Prime Creator who is both immanent and transcendent, who births and dissolves all.

dragonpaths/dragonlines: Primordial energy pathways in sacred sites of the body and Earth; Earth's electromagnetic ley lines of special power vortexes.

endocrine alchemy: Spiritual science behind the teachings of alchemy, with the "lab"

489

located within the human body—transforming the endocrine, nervous, and neural systems and the magical elixirs of life force, especially the feminine fluids.

feminine dimension: A secret feminine universe that exists at the root of matter/creation, which we have disassociated from; union with the source of life.

galactic center: At the core of our Milky Way galaxy is a gravitational whirlpool known as the galactic center—a giant cosmic black hole that birthed us. Ancients believed it to be our Mother; also called heaven. The Maya called our galactic core Hunab Ku, "Mother Womb," and believed it to be our ultimate Creator and a dimensional portal.

gnosis: A direct "knowing" perceived through the primordial body and feminine consciousness, beyond the limits of the thinking mind, which becomes "essence."

Gnostic shaman: Men and women who formed the early "primitive" Christian Church between 30 BCE and 300 CE, before the institutionalized Christian religion that now exists, who were later known as Gnostics. Evidence suggests their spirituality included beliefs and practices that were shamanic and magical in origin.

Grail Gate: A physical location in the yoni or lingam, or the body, or Earth that acts as a bioenergetic, spiritual, and dimensional portal of cosmic feminine energy.

Hathor: The ancient Egyptian Mother Goddess of beauty, fertility, and love. Symbolized by the cow, Hathor means "Great Womb," and in ancient myths she was the Great Mother of all the gods. Later, she became the daughter of the sun god, Ra.

hara: The energetic space within a man's body, located where a woman's womb is, and energetically equivalent to a woman's womb (not the belly). Commonly known as the sacral chakra in Vedic systems and the *dan tien* in the Daoist systems.

Holy Grail: A mystical chalice of renewal that promises eternal life or rebirth across many traditions—symbolized by cups, cauldrons, gourds. It can refer to a sacred relic, like the cup Jesus drank from, or the womb or divine feminine consciousness.

Isis: The Egyptian mother goddess associated with the moon. Her Egyptian name is Auset (AST). *Set* means "seat, throne, or womb." Isis was known as a goddess of new life, pregnancy, fertility, birth, motherhood, and also as a funerary goddess of death.

Ix-Chel: The Mayan jaguar goddess of the moon, also known as a rainbow goddess and lady of the waters; connected to fertility, birth, renewal, and rebirth.

Kabbalah: An ancient Jewish tradition of mystical interpretation of the Bible, first transmitted orally, which reached the height of its influence in the later Middle Ages.

Kali: A Hindu goddess who is a manifestation of the Divine Mother, representing the female principle—her name means both "time" and "black." She is equated with the eternal night, the transcendent power of time, and is the consort of the god Shiva.

kundalini: Creative cosmic energy, often visioned as a serpent coiled at the base of the spine. In tantric traditions, when the serpent of kundalini awakens it rises through the spine to the crown chakra and initiates states of enlightenment. Kundalini is pure primordial sexual energy.

lingam: A Sanskrit word used in Indian religious traditions to refer to the penis. It also refers in a greater sense to the cosmic generative phallus of Shiva or Divine Male.

lunar plexus: The lower abdomen and navel area, connected to the inner self, childhood feelings and beliefs, nurturing, needing, and a person's core self-esteem.

Magdalene, Mary: A biblical figure named as the "apostle of apostles" who announced the resurrection of Jesus. She is also believed by some to be a priestess of Isis and the wife and spiritual partner of Jesus, and symbol of the Great Mother.

Padmasambhava: Sanskrit for "lotus born." A tantric Buddhist master who helped to transmit tantric Buddhism to Tibet during the eighth century and, according to popular belief, established the first monastery in the region.

Pistis Sophia: A Gnostic text discovered in 1773, possibly written between the third and fourth centuries CE. It relates the Gnostic teachings of the transfigured Yeshua (Jesus) to the assembled disciples, including his mother Mary, Mary Magdalene, and Martha.

priestess: A woman who devotes her life to embodying sacred teachings, and performs ceremony, ritual, and prophecy, and practices the feminine healing arts.

Princess Mandarava: Born a princess in India in the eighth century, she is one of the two principal consorts of Padmasambhava and is a female guru/deity in Buddhism.

root halo: Our feminine crown—energy vortexes in our lower body, our anus, genitals, womb/hara, legs, feet—connecting us with our roots and the Earth Womb.

sacred duality: Represents the eternal dance of the masculine and the feminine.

sacred union: A celebration and merging of the co-creative energies of masculine and feminine, inner and outer, solar and lunar, experiencing communion with Gaia and with the cosmos. Sacred sexual union with a soul mate or spiritual partner.

Shakti: The sanskrit word for "life force," and our vitality, our sexual energy, our regenerative energies, our passion, creativity, and power. Also a name for the tantric goddess of creation, Maha Shakti.

shaman healers: Seers and guardians of the traditions of the ancestors. Shape-shifters who commune with Spirit, animals, and nature beyond ordinary perception. Entering womb portals above and below to gain wisdom and healing.

shamanic menstruation: Free bleeding, and retreating into the inner womb space during menstruation, with the womb blood as a shamanic guide; a lunar vision quest.

Simon Magus: A biblical figure who was demonized by the Church as a magician. Also a Gnostic shaman who taught with his beloved Helen, and was defamed as the "father of heretics" for his teachings and beliefs on the mysteries of sacred union and the feminine womb path.

solar plexus: The upper abdomen and diaphragm area; connected to the externalized expression of self-confidence, and strength of boundaries and personal power.

spiral chakra system: An ancient system where our energy vortexes (chakras) are viewed as spiraling together in a nonlinear pattern, uniting our upper and lower bodies, working in balance, without one having dominance over the other.

Srinmo: The ancestral earth goddess of Tibet. She holds the cosmic wheel upon which the universal law, and personal karma, turns. Later classified as a demon.

tantra: A nonhierarchical sect of Indian Hindu and Buddhist philosophy, with a mystical practice based on prepatriarchal indigenous Mother worship. In the greater sense, refers to a spirituality that fully embraces the sacred sensuality of life.

Trickster: A spirit being, sorcerer, or cosmic intelligence, usually perceived as masculine, who embodies a dark—though not necessarily malevolent—primal power and teaches and initiates humans through trickery, mischief, and paradoxes.

twin flame: Soul mates, same soul. Complements that come together to merge in pod consciousness to embody unity and oneness; bringing wholeness, harmony, and balance to earth, healing the split between the masculine and feminine.

witch: A healer, birth and death doula, a wise woman in a community, a woman with "nous" knowing, connected to her womb gnosis she travels the inner dimensions with Spirit, animals, and nature to bring healing and wisdom.

womb: The physical organ, also known as the uterus, within women. Also refers to a greater sense of a sacred cosmic birthing/rebirthing portal of the Divine Mother/Cosmic Womb.

Womb Consciousness: Primordial awareness and presence, uncluttered by any cultural conditioning or emotional and perceptual limitations. A state of conceptual virginity, known as "reality" or the *now,* beyond mental beliefs and illusions.

Womb Enlightenment: Reconnecting to the Womb of Earth, to the Cosmic Womb, to our ancestors and to our own womb knowing; embodied kundalini activation.

womb medicine wheel: A shamanic map within the womb space, identifying elemental Shakti forces, soul gifts, archetypes, guides, and treasures present within.

Womb of Gaia: The spiritual and energetic birthing portal at the center of Earth.

womb shaman/ness: A female or male mystic, shaman, healer, midwife, or tantrika who practices the feminine mysteries and believes in a non-dual Mother Creatrix.

Yeshe Tsogyal: A female Buddha; a Khandro and shaman priestess, believed to be an incarnation of Saraswati or Tara, who was the consort of the Padmasambhava, the founder figure of the Nyingma tradition of Tibetan Buddhism.

Jesus/Yeshua: Biblical figure believed to be the redeemer of the world in traditional Christianity. In heretical tradition, a Grail king who worshipped the Great Mother and walked a path of love and sacred union with Mary Magdalene.

yoni: A Sanskrit word used in Indian tantric traditions to refer to the vagina. It also refers in a greater sacred sense to the cosmic generative portal of the Divine Mother.

Zohar: An esoteric Jewish mystical text, written in thirteenth-century Spain, that synthesized various secret oral Kabbalistic teachings and myths about the Torah.

NOTES

INTRODUCTION

1. Pagels, *Gnostic Gospels,* 50. Further discussion in Durdin-Robertson, *God the Mother,* 23.
2. Hippolytus, *Philosophumena,* 6.14.
3. Vinokur, *Secrets of the Eternal Book,* 10.
4. Walker, *Woman's Encyclopedia of Myths and Secrets,* 820.
5. Durdin-Robertson, *Religion of the Goddess,* 15.
6. Luckenbill, "The Temple Women of the Code of Hammurabi," 1–12.
7. Durdin-Robertson, *Religion of the Goddess,* 4.
8. Collins, "Elen and the Celestial Deer Path," 69–93.
9. Washington, *Our Mothers, Our Powers,* 13–55.
10. Gimbutas, *The Goddesses and Gods of Old Europe,* 86.

SPIRAL 1. WOMB AWAKENING

1. Mookerjee, *Kundalini,* 74.
2. Mitchell, trans., *Bagavad Gita,* 100.
3. Lau, trans., *Tao Te Ching,* xxxv.
4. Matt, *The Zohar,* 31.
5. Science Daily, "In Theory, the Milky Way Could Be a 'Galactic Transport System'"; Rahaman et al., "Possible Existence of Wormholes in the Central Regions of Halos."
6. Pordage, *Theologica Mystica,* 16.
7. Collins, "Elen and the Celestial Deer Path," 112.
8. Matt, *The Zohar,* 189.
9. Lambdin, trans., Gospel of Thomas, 113.
10. Odier, *Tantric Kali,* 45.
11. Scholem, *Major Trends in Jewish Mysticism,* 227.
12. Swimme and Tucker, *Journey of the Universe,* 35.
13. Swimme, *The Universe Is a Green Dragon,* back cover.

SPIRAL 2. MESSAGE FROM AN ANCIENT MOTHER

1. Corbin, *The Foul and the Fragrant,* 44.

SPIRAL 4. POWER OF THE WOMB

1. Yan et al., "Male Microchimerism in Women without Sons," 899–906; Crean et al., "Revisiting Telegony," 1545–52.

SPIRAL 5. WOMB COSMOLOGY

1. Neumann and Manheim, *The Great Mother,* 95.
2. Rigoglioso, *Cult of Divine Birth,* 198.
3. Moyes and Prufer, "The Geopolitics of Emerging Maya Rulers," 225–48.

4. Eisler, *Sacred Pleasure,* 26.
5. Shaw, *Passionate Enlightenment,* 144.
6. Haskins, *Mary Magdalen,* 163.
7. Eisler, *Sacred Pleasure,* 16.
8. Addison, *Understanding English Place Names,* 61.
9. Gimbutas and Dexter, *The Living Goddesses,* 55–71; Perks and Bailey, "Stonehenge: A View from Medicine."
10. Blackmer, *The Lodge and the Craft,* 249.
11. Campbell, Leanne Michelle, "Bronze Age Adyta," 13.
12. Goodison, "From Tholos Tomb to Throne Room," 345–48.
13. Kaplan, *The Bahir,* xxii.
14. *Aluna; From the Heart of the World;* Kogi creation myth.
15. Williams, "Her Song Changes Everything," 163–64.
16. Cleary, *The Flower Ornament Scripture,* 226.
17. Mortimer, "Tuning the Instrument."
18. Mullett, *Spider Woman Stories,* 1–6.
19. Threecrow, "The Kogi Myth."
20. Collins, *The Cygnus Mystery,* 112–13.
21. Collins, *The Cygnus Mystery,* 29–43; information accessed during a shamanic journey taken by Seren Bertrand on December 13, 2013.
22. Tedlock, *Woman in the Shaman's Body,* 207, 320.
23. Campbell, Joseph, *The Mythic Image,* 168, 184, 185.
24. Reichel-Dolmatoff, "The Loom of Life," 5–27.
25. Epiphanius, *Panarion,* as quoted by Ashe, *The Virgin,* 150–51.
26. Turk, "Neanderthal Flute."
27. Walker, *Woman's Encyclopedia of Myths and Secrets,* 155, 966.
28. Hardy, "Taoism: Symbolism."
29. Carrasco, *Quetzalcoatl and the Irony of Empire,* 108.
30. Carr-Gomm and Heygate, *The Book of English Magic,* 6.
31. Partridge, *Introduction to World Religions,* 59.
32. Durdin-Robertson, *God the Mother,* 63.
33. Walker, *Woman's Dictionary of Symbols and Sacred Objects,* 34.
34. Schimmel, *The Mystery of Numbers,* 129.
35. Waters, *Mexico Mystique,* 150–51, 229.
36. Gooch, *Cities of Dreams,* 147–52.
37. Waters, *Mexico Mystique,* 150–51, 229.
38. Matthews, *Sophia,* 262.
39. Alba, "Temazcal."
40. Hadley, *The Spiritual Roots of Restorative Justice,* 70.
41. Vitebsky, *Shamanism,* 61.
42. Ryan, *The Strong Eye of Shamanism,* 190–91.
43. Ellis, Jeannette, *Forbidden Rites,* 448–52.
44. Bleeker, *Hathor and Thoth,* 25.
45. Ellis, Jeannette, *Forbidden Rites,* 448–52.
46. Ibid., 449.
47. Bleeker, *Hathor and Thoth,* 48.
48. Durdin-Robertson, *God the Mother,* 27.
49. Gravrand, *La Civilisation Sereer,* 195.
50. Washington, *Our Mothers, Our Powers,* 13–55.

51. Dashú, "Icons of the Matrix"; Dashú, "Wu."
52. Encyclopedia Britannica Online, "Buddhism."
53. Stenudd, "The Taoism of Lao Tzu and Chuang Tzu Explained."
54. Eskildsen, *Teachings and Practices of the Early Quanzhen Taoist Masters*, 80.
55. Walter and Fridman, *Shamanism*, 691.
56. Charleux, *Nomads on Pilgrimage*, 356, 364.
57. Vitebsky, *Shamanism*, 70.
58. Japanese Mythology & Folklore, "Womb Mother." See further discussion in Gumilev, *Searches for an Imaginary Kingdom*, 277–82; and Tengerism, "Sacred Mountains and Trees."
59. Tedlock, *Woman in the Shaman's Body*, 232.
60. Durdin-Robertson, *God the Mother*, 15.
61. Joseph and Beaudoin, *Opening the Ark of the Covenant*, 194.
62. Aubert, "Threatened Wombs," 424.
63. Ibid., 421–29.
64. Simeonova, "Valley of Thracian Kings Keeps Its Secrets."
65. Gimbutas, *The Living Goddesses*, 60–70.
66. Patai, *The Hebrew Goddess*, 57.
67. Boyer, *Nature Spirituality*, 58.
68. Matthews, *Sophia*, 227.
69. Jensen, *Living Water*, 249–50.
70. Hubbs, *Mother Russia*, xii.
71. Collins, "Elen and the Celestial Deer Path," 98–102.
72. Joseph and Beaudoin, *Opening the Ark of the Covenant*, 167.
73. Collins, *The Cygnus Mystery*, 85.
74. Doolittle (H. D.), *Notes on Thought and Vision*, 20.
75. Ibid., 52.
76. Ibid., 27.

SPIRAL 6. WOMB SYMBOLOGY

1. Walker, *Woman's Encyclopedia of Myths and Secrets*, 974.
2. Baigent, Leigh, and Lincoln, *Holy Blood, Holy Grail*, 288.
3. Gimbutas, *Language of the Goddess*, 102.
4. Camphausen, *The Yoni*, 62.
5. Gimbutas, *Language of the Goddess*, 102.
6. Haskins, *Mary Magdalen*, 163.
7. Pinch, *Egyptian Mythology*, 18.
8. Shaw, *Buddhist Goddesses of India*, 432.
9. Pinch, *Egyptian Mythology*, 129.
10. Tedlock, *Woman in the Shaman's Body*, 158.
11. Ibid., 224.
12. Pagels, *Gnostic Gospels*, 351.

SPIRAL 7. COSMIC WOMB AND EARTH WOMB

1. Guénon, *The Esoterism of Dante*, 35.
2. Campbell, Joseph, *Mythic Image*, 103.
3. Hays, *In the Beginnings*, 373; Walker, *The Woman's Encyclopedia of Myths and Secrets*, 639.
4. Waters, *Book of the Hopi*, 137–53.
5. Carlsen and Prechtel, "The Flowering of the Dead"; Taube, "Flower Mountain," 69–98.
6. Gimbutas and Dexter, *The Living Goddesses*, 55–71.

7. Hubbs, *Mother Russia*, 70.

8. Markman and Markman, *Masks of the Spirit*, 159.

9. Hubbs, *Mother Russia*, 60.

10. Walker, *Man Made God*, 93.

11. Campbell, Joseph, *The Mythic Image*, 184–85.

12. Powell, *The Most Holy Trinosophia*, 51.

13. Bible NIV, Ephesians 4:9–10.

14. Hancock, *Magicians of the Gods*, 320–30; Collins, *Göbekli Tepe*, 83–86, 107–8.

15. Collins, *Göbekli Tepe*, 60–105.

16. Ibid.

17. Eliade, *Shamanism*, 259; Markman and Markman, *Masks of Spirit*, 121.

18. Levy, *Gate of Horn*, 174.

19. Campbell, Joseph, *The Mythic Image*, 185.

20. Ibid., 22.

21. Angus, *The Mystery Religions and Christianity*, 45.

22. Apuleius, *Metamorphosis*, 283.

23. Baring and Cashford, *Myth of the Goddess*, 623.

24. Bible, Genesis 28:12–17.

SPIRAL 8. WOMB MYSTERY SCHOOLS

1. Merculieff, "The Womb at the Center of the Universe."

2. Murray, *The God of the Witches*, 65.

3. Sanusi Credo Mutwa in private conversation with Rah Busby, womb healer, shared with permission, August 2014.

4. Livingstone, *Mystical and Mythological Explanatory Works*, 45.

5. Noble, *Motherpeace*, 213.

6. Matthews and Matthews, *Ladies of the Lake*, 42.

7. Hubbs, *Mother Russia*, 10.

8. Noble, *Motherpeace*, 123.

9. Hubbs, *Mother Russia*, 10.

10. Shaw, *Passionate Enlightenment*, 67.

11. Giunio, "Isis: The Star of the Sea," 432.

12. Picknett and Prince, *The Templar Revelation*, 279.

13. Jones, trans., *Pausanias Description of Greece*, ii.38.2.

14. Virani, *The Ismailis in the Middle Ages*, 107.

15. Moody, *The Feasts of Adonai*, 107.

16. Emyrs, *Revelation of the Holy Grail*, 338.

17. Varner, *Sacred Wells*, 20–23, 111.

18. Wise, *Finding Elen*, 34–35.

19. Collins, *Gods of Eden*, 49.

20. Walker, *Woman's Encyclopedia of Myths and Secrets*, 50; see also Stutley, *Hindu Deities*, 53.

21. Apffel-Marglin, *Rhythms of Life*, 87–89, 91–96.

SPIRAL 9. FEMININE WOMB ENLIGHTENMENT

1. Mead, *Simon Magus: His Philosophy and Teachings*, 26–27.

2. Smith, *Jesus the Magician*.

3. Murray, *The God of the Witches*, 110.

4. Campbell, Joseph, *The Mythic Image*, 238.

5. Shaw, *Passionate Enlightenment*, 83.

6. Tedlock, *Woman in the Shaman's Body,* 53.

7. Shaw, *Passionate Enlightenment,* 27.

8. Ibid., 27.

9. Tedlock, *Woman in the Shaman's Body,* 59.

10. Ibid., 56.

11. Chonan and Khandro, *The Lives and Liberation of Princess Mandarava,* 23.

12. Tedlock, *Woman in the Shaman's Body,* 185.

13. Shaw, *Passionate Enlightenment,* 111.

14. Keizer, "Hildegard of Bingen," 170.

15. Ibid., 129.

16. King-Lenzmeir, *Hildegard of Bingen,* 65.

17. Douglas-Klotz, *Prayers of the Cosmos,* 3, 14.

18. Fox, *Illuminations of Hildegard of Bingen,* 24.

19. Ibid., xviii.

20. Patai, *The Hebrew Goddess,* 41.

21. Walker, *Man Made God,* 193.

22. Ibid., 196.

23. Matthews, *Sophia,* 181.

SPIRAL 10. THE AGE OF INNOCENCE RETURNS

1. Sentier, *Shaman Pathways—Elen of the Ways,* 14, 16–28.

2. Wise, *Finding Elen,* 110.

3. Collins, *Elen and the Celestial Deerpath,* 93–121.

4. Schmidt, "Bricolage, Ritual Performance, and Habitus."

5. Collins, *The Cygnus Mystery,* 101–2, 127.

6. Freke and Gandy, *Jesus and the Lost Goddess,* 99.

7. Callaway, "Mystery Humans Spiced Up Ancients' Sex Lives."

8. Mead, *Simon Magus,* 9.

9. Apocryphon of John cited in Pagels, *The Gnostic Gospels,* 146.

10. Rigoglioso, *Cult of Divine Birth,* 71–81.

11. Mead, *Simon Magus,* 25.

12. Collins, *From the Ashes of Angels,* 62.

13. Ibid., 236–37, 305.

14. Bible RSV, Wisdom of Solomon 1:13-14.

SPIRAL 11. WOMB OF GOD

1. Pagels, *The Gnostic Gospels,* 55.

2. Shonkoff and Fisher, "Rethinking Evidence-Based Practice," 1635–53; Conger, Belsky, and Capaldi, "The Intergenerational Transmission of Parenting," 1276–83; Kerr et al., "A Prospective Three Generational Study," 1257–75.

3. Shaw, *Passionate Enlightenment,* 46.

4. Campbell, June, *Traveller in Space,* 112.

SPIRAL 12. WOMBTIME ORIGINS OF SHAMANISM

1. Gooch, *Total Man,* 263.

2. Krippner, "The Maimonides ESP-Dream Studies," 39–54; McTaggart, *The Field,* 166–67.

3. Howe, *The Nature of Early Memory,* 34–35; Levin, *Mapping the Mind,* 52, 78, 188–89.

4. Thorndike, *Elements of Psychology,* 330–31.

5. Lydston, *The Diseases of Society,* 178; Parkins, "Emotion," 1–7.

6. Koziol et al., "Adaptation, Expertise, and Giftedness," 499–525.
7. Fuentes, "'Motor Cognition'" 232–36.
8. Holstege, "Brain Activation during Human Male Ejaculation," 9185–93; Redoute et al., "Brain Processing of Visual Sexual Stimuli," 162–77; Koziol, "Adaptation, Expertise, and Giftedness," 499–525.
9. Parkins, *Total Brain Total Mind*, 244.
10. Ibid., 238.
11. Blood, "Intensely Pleasurable Responses to Music," 11818–23.
12. Chia, *Healing Light of the Tao*, 202–3.
13. Parkins, "Emotion," 1–7.
14. Neumann, *The Origins and History of Consciousness*, 261–306.
15. Lin and Murray, "Unconscious Processing," 296–98; Dijksterhuis et al., "On Making the Right Choice," 1005–7.
16. Lipton, *The Biology of Belief*, 200–203.
17. Neumann, *The Origins and History of Consciousness*, 261–306.
18. University of Missouri–St. Louis. "Sample Myths."
19. Horodezky, *Rabbi Nachman von Brazlaw*, 188.
20. Mitchell, trans., *Tao Te Ching*, 55.
21. Bible NIV, Luke 18:16; Mark 10:15.
22. Patterson and Meyer, *Gospel of Thomas*, 22. Note that the text has been regendered as feminine by the authors.

SPIRAL 13. SOUL MIDWIFE RITES

1. Carman and Carman, *Cosmic Cradle*, 169.
2. Tedlock, *Woman in the Shaman's Body*, 222.
3. Carman and Carman, *Cosmic Cradle*, 221.
4. Ibid, 221.
5. Tedlock, *Woman in the Shaman's Body*, 247–54.
6. Erickson, "Twirling Their Long Sleeves," 50.
7. Ibid., 53.
8. Meyer, ed., *The Nag Hammadi Scriptures*, 227, 229.

SPIRAL 14. PLACENTA OF THE VOID

1. Bible NLT, I Peter 2:2.
2. Roscoe, *The Baganda*, 235–36.
3. Bolshakov, "Ka," 215.
4. Russell, *The Candle of Vision*, 23, 28. See further discussion in Lash, *Not in His Image*, 338.

SPIRAL 15. TOTAL REBIRTH

1. Ulupınar, "Effects of Prenatal Stress on Developmental Anatomy," 1–13; Paul, *Origins*, 1–300; Gluckman and Hanson, *The Fetal Matrix*, 1–257.
2. Nathanielsz, *Life in the Womb*, 1–363; Rosenfeld, *The Epigenome and Developmental Origins of Health and Disease*, 1–519; Newnham and Ross, *Early Life Origins of Human Health and Disease*, 1–205.
3. National Scientific Council on the Developing Child, "Early Experiences Can Alter Gene Expression," 1–12.
4. Dias and Ressler, "Parental Olfactory Experience," 89–96.
5. Sullivan, "The Genetics of Schizophrenia," e212.

6. Caspi et al., "Moderation of the Effect of Adolescent-Onset Cannabis Use on Adult Psychosis," 1117–27; Sullivan, "The Genetics of Schizophrenia," e212.

7. Anand, "Cancer Is a Preventable Disease," 2097–2116.

8. Shaw, *Passionate Enlightenment,* 189.

9. National Scientific Council on the Developing Child, "Early Experiences Can Alter Gene Expression," 1–12.

10. Weaver et al., "Epigenetic Programming by Maternal Behavior," 847–54.

11. Van der Kolk, *The Body Keeps the Score,* 242–64.

12. Lagercrantz, *Infant Brain Development,* 1–156; Siegel, *The Developing Mind,* 46–90.

13. Odier, *Desire,* 69–71.

14. Foulkes, *Children's Dreaming and the Development of Consciousness,* 60–65.

15. Chamberlain, *Windows to the Womb,* 119–71.

16. Ibid., 3–71.

17. Chamberlain, "Reliability of Birth Memory," 14–24.

18. Truby, "Prenatal and Neonatal Speech," 57–101.

19. Ibid.; Chamberlain, *Windows to the Womb,* 78, 106.

SPIRAL 16. SHAMANIC BIRTHING

1. Collins, *Gobekli Tepe,* 110–11.

2. Waters, *Book of the Hopi,* 7–10.

3. Balaskas and Meeus, *The Waterbirth Book,* 5.

4. Leboyer, *Birth without Violence,* 1–131; Odent, *Water, Birth and Sexuality,* 3–14; Tournaire and Theau-Yonneau, "Complementary and Alternative Approaches to Pain Relief," 409–17; Odent, "Birth Under Water," 1476–77.

5. Tedlock, *Woman in the Shaman's Body,* 200.

6. Graves-Brown, *Dancing for Hathor,* 93.

7. Dionne, "The Mandorla."

8. Massey, "A Book of the Beginnings," 269.

9. Tedlock, *Woman in the Shaman's Body,* 220.

10. Victora et al., "Association between Breastfeeding and Intelligence," e199–e205; Schack-Nielsen and Michaelsen, "Breast Feeding and Future Health," 293.

SPIRAL 17. MOON ALCHEMY

1. Van Lysebeth, *Tantra,* 20.

2. Cashford, *The Moon,* 229.

3. Buzsáki, *Rhythms of the Brain,* 1–18, 175–87.

4. Groddeck, *Exploring the Unconscious,* 23–26.; Shuttleworth and Redgrove, *The Wise Wound,* 73–74.

SPIRAL 18. WOMB BLOOD

1. Tedlock, *Woman in the Shaman's Body,* 179.

2. Lederer, *The Fear of Women,* 139. See also Walker, *The Woman's Encyclopedia of Myths and Secrets,* 636.

3. Rawson, *Tantra,* 24.

4. Campbell, June, *Traveller in Space,* 145.

5. Noble, *The Double Goddess,* 206.

6. Rahn, *Kreuzzug gegen den Gral,* 107, 185.

7. Bible NIV, Genesis 3:6–7.

8. Harris, *The Secret Heresy of Hieronymus Bosch,* 112.

9. Stausberg and Engler, "The Routledge Handbook," 279.

SPIRAL 19. CODES OF CREATION

1. Director of stem cell laboratory (who wishes to remain anonymous), personal communication, 2009.
2. Mukhopadhyaya, *The Kaulajnananirnaya*, 39.
3. Han et al., "Inhibition of Intracranial Glioma Growth," 606–10; Murphy et al., "Allogeneic Endometrial Regenerative Cells," 1–8; Wollert and Drexler, "Cell Therapy for the Treatment of Coronary Heart Disease," 204–15.
4. Zhong et al., "Feasibility Investigation."
5. Meng et al., "Endometrial Regenerative Cells."
6. Kamper-Jørgensen et al. "Male Microchimerism and Survival among Women," 168–73.
7. Hanssen, "Blood Mysteries," 365–79.
8. Matthews and Matthews, *Ladies of the Lake*, 66–67.
9. Tedlock, *Woman in the Shaman's Body*, 184.
10. Noble, "Yeshe Tsogyal," 154–62.
11. Picknett and Prince, *The Templar Revelation*, 189.
12. Hubbs, *Mother Russia*, 15.
13. Yang et al., "Proteomic Analysis of Menstrual Blood," 1024–35.
14. Shaw et al., "Proteomic Analysis of Human Cervico-Vaginal Fluid," 2859–65.
15. Matthews, *Sophia*, 117.
16. Dias and Ressler, "Parental Olfactory Experience," 89–96.
17. Blakemore, "The Role of Puberty in the Developing Adolescent Brain," 926–33.

SPIRAL 20. WILD AND HOLY WOMB

1. Ulanov, *The Feminine in Jungian Psychology*, 269; See also discussion in Qualls-Corbett, *The Sacred Prostitute*, 56.
2. Noble, *The Double Goddess*, 6.
3. Mead, *Simon Magus*, 55.
4. Reich, *The Function of the Orgasm*, 9.
5. Burke, *Philosophical Enquiry*, 56.

SPIRAL 21. VOICE OF THE WOMB, VOICE OF WISDOM

1. Sentier, *Dreamweaver*, 119.

SPIRAL 22. DARK SIDE OF THE WOMB

1. This paragraph is inspired by a passage on Dionysus by Erich Neumann in *The Great Mother*, 294.
2. Message received in ceremony by womb oracle Louisa Williams, November 2014.
3. Guenther, *Tricksters and Trancers*, 112.
4. Black Elk, *Black Elk Speaks*, 149.
5. De Wys, *Ecstatic Healing*, 95.
6. Moss, *Dreamways of the Iroquois*, 157.
7. Ibid., 158.

SPIRAL 23. THE GRAIL LINEAGE OF LOVE

1. Gardner, *Realm of the Ring Lords*, 61.
2. Matt, *The Zohar*, verse 535.
3. Arvigo and Epstein, *Spiritual Bathing*, 9.
4. Sentier, *Shaman Pathways—The Celtic Chakras*, 27.

SPIRAL 24. SACRED DUALITY

1. Jung, *The Collected Works of C. G. Jung*, 194.
2. Mead, *Simon Magus: His Philosophy and Teachings*, 19. Quoted from *Great Revelation*.

3. Gimbutas, *The Goddesses and Gods of Old Europe*, 196.
4. Malachi, *The Gnostic Gospel of St. Thomas*, verse 22, 172.
5. Picknett and Prince, *The Templar Revelation*, 422.

SPIRAL 25. OPENING TO LOVE

1. Matt, *The Zohar.* Parashat Lech Lecha, verse 346. Translation of God as masculine has been reverted to feminine by the authors.
2. Mead, *Simon Magus: His Philosophy and Teachings*, x.
3. McTaggart, *The Field*, 119.
4. Belsky and Rovine, "Temperament and Attachment Security," 787–95; Mangelsdorf et al., "Infant Proneness-to-Distress Temperament," *Child Development* 61(1990): 820–31; Van den Boom, "The Influence of Temperament and Mothering on Attachment," 1457–77.
5. Pearce, Rob, "Attachment Theory Predicts the Formation of Romantic Relationships," 1–9.

SPIRAL 27. TWIN SPIRAL CHAKRA SYSTEM

1. Clements, *Infrared Astronomy*, 141.
2. Watterson, *Women in Ancient Egypt*, 112.

SPIRAL 28. DRAGON AND DOVE ALCHEMY

1. Hanssen, "Blood Mysteries," 365–79; McDaniel, *The Madness of the Saints*, 182.
2. White, *The Alchemical Body*, 229.
3. Swimme and Tucker, *Journey of the Universe*, 13.

SPIRAL 29. ROYAL ROAD

1. Mead, trans. *The Wedding Song of Wisdom*, 19.
2. Freke and Gandy, *Jesus and the Lost Goddess*, 110.

SPIRAL 30. DRAGONS OF CREATION

1. Markman and Markman, *Masks of the Spirit*, 83, 121–22, 158; Vogt and Stuart, "Some Notes on Ritual Caves."
2. Molesky-Paz, *Contemporary Maya Spirituality*, 49; Markman and Markman, *Masks of the Spirit*, 83, 121–22, 158.
3. Matthews, *Sophia*, 257.

SPIRAL 31. BLACK MOTHER, WOMB OF CREATION

1. Fox, "The Return of the Black Madonna."
2. Fox, *The Hidden Spirituality of Men*, 233. Harvey, *Return of the Mother*, 371.

SPIRAL 32. AWAKENING THE GRAIL KNIGHTS

1. Shaw, *Passionate Enlightenment*, 59.
2. Kraemer, "The Fragile Male," 1609–12.
3. Eskildsen, *Teachings and Practices of the Early Quanzhen Taoist Masters*, 181.

BIBLIOGRAPHY

Abelar, Taisha. *The Sorcerer's Crossing: A Woman's Journey*. New York: Bloom, 1993.

Addison, William. *Understanding English Place Names*. London: Little Brown Book Group, 1979.

Alba, Horacio Rojas. "Temazcal: III/III. Preparation of the Temazcal..." *Tlahui-Medic*, no. 2 (1996). www.tlahui.com/temaz3.htm (accessed January 22, 2017).

Alexander, Eben. *Proof of Heaven: A Neurosurgeon's Journey into the Afterlife*. New York: Simon & Schuster, 2012.

Alighieri, Dante, and John Ciardi. *The Divine Comedy: The Inferno, the Purgatorio, and the Paradiso*. New York: New American Library, 2003.

Aluna. Documentary film. DVD. Directed by Alan Ereira. Sunstone Films, 2012.

Anand, Preetha. "Cancer Is a Preventable Disease that Requires Major Lifestyle Changes." *Pharmaceutical Research* 25 (2008): 2097–116.

Angus, S. *The Mystery Religions and Christianity: A Study in the Religious Background of Early Christianity*. New York: Dover Publications, 1975.

Apffel-Marglin, Frederique. *Rhythms of Life—Enacting the World with the Goddesses of Orissa*. Oxford: Oxford University Press, 2008.

Apuleius, Lucius. *The Metamorphosis, or, Golden Ass, and Philosophical Works, of Apuleius*. Translated by Thomas Taylor. London: Triphook and Rodd, 1822.

Arvigo, Rosita, and Nadine Epstein. *Spiritual Bathing, Healing Rituals, and Traditions from around the World*. Berkeley, Calif.: Celestial Arts, 2003.

Ashe, Geoffrey. *The Virgin*. London and Henley: Routledge & Kegan Paul, 1976.

Aubert, Jean-Jacques. "Threatened Wombs: Aspects of Ancient Uterine Magic." *Greek, Roman, and Byzantine Studies* 30, no. 3 (1989): 421–49. http://grbs.library.duke.edu/article/view/3991/5563 (accessed January 22, 2017).

Baigent, Michael, Richard Leigh, and Henry Lincoln. *Holy Blood, Holy Grail*. New York: Delacorte Press, 2004.

Balaskas, Janet, and Cathy Meeus. *The Waterbirth Book: Everything You Need to Know from the World's Renowned Natural Childbirth Pioneer*. London: Thorsons, 2004.

Baring, Anne, and Jules Cashford. *Myth of the Goddess: Evolution of an Image*. London: Viking Arkana, 1991.

Beitchman, Philip. *Alchemy of the Word: Cabala of the Renaissance*. Albany: State University of New York Press, 1998.

Belsky, Jay, and Michael Rovine. "Temperament and Attachment Security in the Strange Situation: An Empirical Rapprochement." *Child Development* 58, no. 3 (1987): 787–95.

Bernard, Simon. *The Essence of the Gnostics*. London: Arcturus Publishing, 2004.

Black Elk, John G. Neihardt, Alexis N. Petri, and Lori Utecht. *Black Elk Speaks: Being the Life Story of a Holy Man of the Oglala Sioux*. Lincoln: University of Nebraska Press, 2004.

Blackmer, Rollin C. *The Lodge and the Craft: A Practical Explanation of the Work of Freemasonry*. Richmond, Va.: Macoy Publishing & Masonic Supply, 1976.

Blakemore, Sarah-Jayne, Stephanie Burnett, and Ronald E. Dahl. "The Role of Puberty in the Developing Adolescent Brain." *Human Brain Mapping* 31, no. 6 (2010): 926–33.

Bleeker, Class Jouco. *Hathor and Thoth: Two Key Figures of the Ancient Egyptian Religion.* Leiden, Netherlands: Brill, 1997.

Blood, A. J., and R. J. Zatorre, "Intensely Pleasurable Responses to Music Correlate with Activity in Brain Regions Implicated in Reward and Emotion." *Proceedings of National Academy of Science* 98 (2001): 11818–823.

Bolshakov, Andrey. "Ka." In *The Oxford Encyclopedia of Ancient Egypt,* vol. 2. Edited by Donald B. Redford. Oxford, U.K.: Oxford University Press, 2001.

Boyer, Mark G. *Nature Spirituality: Praying with Wind, Water, Earth, Fire.* Eugene, Ore.: Resource Publications, 2013.

Burke, Edmund. *A Philosophical Enquiry into the Origin of Our Ideas of the Sublime and Beautiful.* Oxford, U.K.: Oxford University Press, 2008.

Buzsáki, György. *Rhythms of the Brain.* Oxford: Oxford University Press, 2011.

Callaway, Ewen. "Mystery Humans Spiced Up Ancients' Sex Lives." *Nature.* November 19, 2013. www.nature.com/news/mystery-humans-spiced-up-ancients-sex-lives-1.14196 (accessed January 22, 2017).

Campbell, Joseph. *Goddesses: Mysteries of the Feminine Divine.* Novato, Calif.: New World Library, 2013.

———. *The Mythic Image.* Princeton, N.J.: Princeton University Press, 1981.

———. *The Power of Myth.* New York: Anchor Books, 1988.

Campbell, June. *Traveller in Space: Gender, Identity, and Tibetan Buddhism.* London: A & C Black, 2002.

Campbell, Leanne Michelle. "Bronze Age Adyta: Exploring Lustral Basins as Representations of Natural Spaces and Places." *Eras* 14 (February 2013): 1–32.

Camphausen, Rufus C. *The Yoni: Sacred Symbol of Female Creative Power.* Rochester, Vt.: Inner Traditions, 1996.

Carlsen, Robert S., and Martin Prechtel. "The Flowering of the Dead: An Interpretation of Highland Maya Culture & Taube." *Man,* n.s., 26 (1991): 23–42. www.latinamericanstudies.org/maya/maya-culture.pdf (accessed January 22, 2017).

Carman, Elizabeth M., and Neil J. Carman. *Cosmic Cradle: Spiritual Dimensions of Life before Birth.* Rev. ed. Berkeley, Calif.: North Atlantic Books, 2013.

Carrasco, David. *Quetzalcoatl and the Irony of Empire.* Chicago: University of Chicago Press, 1982.

Carr-Gomm, Philip, and Richard Heygate. *The Book of English Magic.* London: John Murray Publishers, 2009.

Cashford, Jules. *The Moon: Myth and Image.* New York: Basic Books, 2003.

Caspi, A, T. E. Moffitt, M. Cannon, J. McClay, R. Murray, H. Harrington, A. Taylor et al. "Moderation of the Effect of Adolescent-Onset Cannabis Use on Adult Psychosis by a Functional Polymorphism in the Catechol-O-methyltransferase Gene: Longitudinal Evidence of a Gene X Environment Interaction." *Biological Psychiatry* 57 (2005): 1117–27.

Chamberlain, David B. "Reliability of Birth Memory: Observations from Mother and Child Pairs in Hypnosis." *Journal of Prenatal and Perinatal Psychology and Health* 14 (1980): 14–24.

———. *Windows to the Womb: Revealing the Conscious Baby from Conception to Birth.* Berkeley, Calif.: North Atlantic Books, 2013.

Charleux, Isabelle. National Centre for Scientific Research (CNRS). "Mongol Pilgrimages to Wutai Shan in the Late Qing Dynasty." *Journal of the International Association of Tibetan Studies,* no. 6 (December 2011): 275–326. www.thlib.org/collections/texts/jiats/#!jiats=/06/charleux/b5 (accessed January 22, 2017).

Charleux, Isabelle. *Nomads on Pilgrimage: Mongols on Wutaishan (China), 1800–1940.* Leiden, Netherlands: Brill, 2015.

Chia, Mantak. *Healing Light of the Tao: Foundational Practices to Awaken Chi Energy.* Rochester, Vt.: Destiny Books, 2008.

Chonan, Lama, and Sangye Khandro, trans. *The Lives and Liberation of Princess Mandarava: The Indian Consort of Padmasambhava.* Somerville, Mass.: Wisdom Publications, 1998.

Cleary, Thomas. *The Flower Ornament Scripture.* Boston: Shambhala, 1993.

Clements, David L. *Infrared Astronomy—Seeing the Heat: From William Herschel to the Herschel Space Observatory.* Boca Raton, Fla.: CRC Press, 2015.

Collins, Andrew. *The Cygnus Mystery: Unlocking the Ancient Secret of Life's Origins in the Cosmos.* London: Watkins Media, 2008.

———. "Elen and the Celestial Deer Path: The Quest for the Origins of the Primordial Mother of Life." In *Finding Elen: The Quest for Elen of the Ways,* edited by Caroline Wise, 93–124. London: Eala Press, 2015.

———. *From the Ashes of Angels.* London: Penguin Books, 1997.

———. *Göbekli Tepe: Genesis of the Gods; The Temple of the Watchers and the Discovery of Eden.* Rochester, Vt.: Bear & Company, 2014.

———. *Gods of Eden: Egypt's Lost Legacy and the Genesis of Civilisation.* London: Headline Publishing Group, 1998.

Conger, R. D., J. Belsky, and D. M. Capaldi. "The Intergenerational Transmission of Parenting: Closing Comments for the Special Section." *Developmental Psychology* 45, no. 5 (September 2009): 1276–83.

Corbin, Alain. *The Foul and the Fragrant: Odor and the French Social Imagination.* London: Bloomsbury Publishing, 1986.

Crean, Angela J., A. M. Kopps, and R. Bonduriansky. "Revisiting Telegony: Offspring Inherit an Acquired Characteristic of Their Mother's Previous Mate." *Ecology Letters* 17 (2014): 1545–52.

Dashú, Max. "Icons of the Matrix." www.suppressedhistories.net/articles/icons.html (accessed January 22, 2017).

———. "Wu: Female Shamans in Ancient China." www.suppressedhistories.net/articles2/wu.html (accessed January 22, 2017).

Davidson, H. R. Ellis. *Myths and Symbols in Pagan Europe: Early Scandinavian and Celtic Religions.* Syracuse, N.Y.: Syracuse University Press, 1989.

De Wys, Margaret. *Ecstatic Healing: A Journey into the Ecstatic World of Spirit Possession and Miraculous Medicine.* Rochester, Vt.: Inner Traditions, 2013.

Dias, G., and Kerry J Ressler. "Parental Olfactory Experience Influences Behavior and Neural Structure in Subsequent Generations." *Nature Neuroscience* 17 (2014): 89–96.

Dijksterhuis, Ap, Maarten W. Bos, Loran F. Nordgren, Rick B. van Baaren. "On Making the Right Choice: The Deliberation-Without-Attention Effect." *Science* 311, no. 5763 (February 17, 2006): 1005–7.

Dionne, Michelle. "The Mandorla." http://themandorla.com/sacred-dance/philosphy/ (accessed January 22, 2017).

Doolittle, Hilda (H. D.). *Notes on Thought and Vision and the Wise Sappho.* London: Peter Owen, 1988.

Douglas-Klotz, Neil. *The Hidden Gospel: Decoding the Spiritual Message of the Aramaic Jesus.* Wheaton, Ill.: Quest Books, 1999.

———. *Prayers of the Cosmos: Reflections on the Original Meaning of Jesus's Words.* New York: Harper One, 1990.

Durdin-Robertson, Lawrence. *God the Mother: The Creatress and Giver of Life.* Enniscorthy, Ireland: Cesara Publications, 1982.

———. *Religion of the Goddess.* Enniscorthy, Ireland: Cesara Publications, 1982.

Eisler, Riane. *The Chalice and the Blade: Our History, Our Future.* New York: HarperCollins, 1988.

———. *Sacred Pleasure: Sex, Myth, and the Politics of the Body; New Paths to Power and Love.* New York: HarperCollins, 1996.

Eliade, Mircea. *Rites and Symbols of Initiation.* New York: Harper and Row, 1965.

———. *Shamanism: Archaic Techniques of Ecstasy.* Translated by Willard R. Trask. Princeton, N.J.: Princeton University Press, 2004.

Ellis, Jeannette. *Forbidden Rites: Your Complete Introduction to Traditional Witchcraft.* New Alresford, U.K.: John Hunt Publishing, 2009.

Ellis, Normandi. *Dreams of Isis: A Woman's Spiritual Sojourn.* Wheaton, Ill.: Quest Books, 1995.

Emyrs, Chavalier. *Revelation of the Holy Grail.* Aurora, Colo.: Timothy W. Hogan, 2007.

Encyclopedia Britannica Online. "Buddhism." www.britannica.com/topic/Buddhism (accessed January 22, 2017).

Endres, Klaus-Peter, and Wolfgang Schad. *Moon Rhythms in Nature: How Lunar Cycles Affect Living Organisms.* Edinburgh, U.K.: Floris Books, 2002.

Erickson, Susan N. "Twirling Their Long Sleeves, They Dance Again and Again . . . Jade Plaque Sleeve Dancers of the Western Han Dynasty." *Ars Orientalis* 24 (Fall 1994): 39–63.

Eskildsen, Stephen. *The Teachings and Practices of the Early Quanzhen Taoist Masters.* Albany: State University of New York Press, 2006.

Flanagan, Sabina. *Secrets of God: Writings of Hildegard of Bingen.* Boston: Shambhala Publications, 1996.

Foulkes, David. *Children's Dreaming and the Development of Consciousness.* Cambridge, Mass.: Harvard University Press, 2002.

Fox, Matthew. *The Hidden Spirituality of Men: Ten Metaphors to Awaken the Sacred Masculine.* Novato, Calif.: New World Library, 2008.

———. *Illuminations of Hildegard of Bingen.* Rochester, Vt.: Bear & Company, 1985.

———. "The Return of the Black Madonna: A Sign of Our Times or How the Black Madonna Is Shaking Us Up for the Twenty-First Century." Feb 21, 2011. www.matthewfox.org/blog/the-return -of-the-black-madonna-a-sign-of-our-times-or-how-the-black-madonna-is-shaking-us-up-for-the -twenty-first-century (accessed February 2, 2015).

Freke, Timothy, and Peter Gandy. *Jesus and the Lost Goddess: The Secret Teachings of the Original Christians.* New York: Harmony, 2002.

From the Heart of the World: The Elder Brothers' Warning. Documentary film. Directed by Alan Ereira. BBC, 1990.

Fuentes, C. T., and A. J. Bastian. "'Motor Cognition'—What Is it and Is the Cerebellum Involved?" *The Cerebellum* 6 (2007): 232–36.

Gardner, Laurence. *Realm of the Ring Lords.* Cenarth, U.K.: MediaQuest, 2000.

George, Christopher S., trans. *The Candamaharosana Tantra, Chapters 1–8: A Critical Edition and English Translation.* American Oriental Series, no. 56. New Haven, Conn.: American Oriental Society, 1974.

George, Demetra. *Mysteries of the Dark Moon: The Healing Power of the Dark Goddess.* New York: HarperCollins, 1992.

Gimbutas, Marija. *The Goddesses and Gods of Old Europe: Myths and Cult Images.* Berkeley: University of California Press, 1982.

———. *Language of the Goddess.* New York: Harper & Row, 1989.

Gimbutas, Marija, and Miriam Robbins Dexter. *The Living Goddesses.* Berkeley: University of California Press, 1999.

Giunio, A. Kornelija. "Isis: The Star of the Sea and the Ceremony of Navigium Isidi." *Diadora* 26/27 (2013): 421–40.

Gluckman, Peter D., and Mark A. Hanson. *The Fetal Matrix: Evolution, Development and Disease.* Cambridge: Cambridge University Press, 2005.

Goethe, Johann Wolfgang. *Faust*. New York: Bantam Classics, 1962.

Gooch, Stan. *Cities of Dreams: When Women Ruled the Earth*. London: Aulis Books, 1995.

———. *The Neanderthal Legacy: Reawakening Our Genetic and Cultural Origins*. Rochester, Vt.: Inner Traditions, 2008.

———. *Total Man*. New York: Holt, Rinehart & Winston, 1972.

Goodison, L. "From Tholos Tomb to Throne Room: Some Considerations of Dawn Light and Directionality in Minoan buildings." In *Knossos: Palace, City, State*, edited by G. Cadogan, E. Hatzaki, and A. Vasilakis, 339–50. British School at Athens Studies 12. London: British School at Athens, 2004.

Grahn, Judy. *Blood, Bread, and Roses: How Menstruation Created the World*. Boston: Beacon Press, 1993.

Graves-Brown, Carolyn. *Dancing for Hathor: Women in Ancient Egypt*. London: Continuum, 2010.

Gravrand, Henry. *La Civilisation Sereer: Pangool*, vol. 2. Dakar, Senegal: Les Nouvelles Editions Africaines du Senegal, 1990.

Gray, Miranda. *Red Moon: Understanding and Using the Gifts of the Menstrual Cycle*. Rockport, Mass.: Element Books, 1994.

Groddeck, George. *Exploring the Unconscious*. London: Vision Press, 1950.

Grof, Stanislav. *The Cosmic Game: Explorations of the Frontiers of Human Consciousness*. Albany: State University of New York Press, 1998.

———. *LSD Psychotherapy: The Healing Potential of Psychedelic Medicine*. Sarasota, Fla.: MAPS, 2001.

Guénon, René. *The Esoterism of Dante*. Hillsdale, N.Y.: Sophia Perennis, 2003.

Guenther, Mathias G. *Tricksters and Trancers: Bushman Religion and Society*. Bloomington: Indiana University Press, 1999.

Gumilev, Lev Nikolaevich. *Searches for an Imaginary Kingdom: The Legend of the Kingdom of Prester John*. Cambridge, U.K.: Cambridge University Press, 2009.

Hadley, Michael L. *The Spiritual Roots of Restorative Justice*. Albany: State University of New York Press, 2001.

Han, Xiaodi, Xiaolong Meng, Zhenglian Yin, Andrea Rogers, Jie Zhong, Paul Rllema, James A. Jackson et al. "Inhibition of Intracranial Glioma Growth by Endometrial Regenerative Cells." *Cell Cycle* 8, no. 4 (2009): 606–10.

Hancock, Graham. *Magicians of the Gods*. New York: Thomas Dunne Books, 2017.

Hanssen, Kristin. "Ingesting Menstrual Blood: Notions of Health and Bodily Fluids in Bengal." In "Blood Mysteries: Beyond Menstruation as Pollution." Special issue, *Ethnology* 41, no. 4 (2002): 365–79.

Harding, M. Esther. *Women's Mysteries*. Boston: Shambhala Publications, 2008.

Hardy, Julia. "Taoism: Symbolism." Patheos Library. www.patheos.com/Library/Taoism/Ritual-Worship -Devotion-Symbolism/Symbolism (accessed January 22, 2017).

Harris, Lynda. *The Secret Heresy of Hieronymus Bosch*. Edinburgh, U.K.: Floris Books, 1995.

Haskins, Susan. *Mary Magdalen: Myth and Metaphor*. New York: Riverhead, 2005.

Hays, H. R. *In the Beginnings: Early Man and His Gods*. New York: G.P. Putnam's Sons, 1963.

Heinberg, Richard. *Memories and Visions of Paradise: Exploring the Universal Myth of a Lost Golden Age*. Wheaton, Ill.: Quest Books, 1995.

Heselton, Philip. *Earth Mysteries*. London: Element Books, 1995.

Hippolytus, and Francis Legge. *Philosophumena; or, The Refutation of all Heresies*. London: Society for Promoting Christian Knowledge, 1921.

Holstege, G., J. R. Georgiadis, A. M. J. Paans, et al. "Brain Activation during Human Male Ejaculation." *Journal of Neuroscience* 23 (2003): 9185–93.

The Holy Bible, New International Version. Grand Rapids, Mich.: Zondervan Publishing House, 1984.

The Holy Bible, New Living Translation. Carol Stream, Ill.: Tyndale House Publishers, 2007.

The Holy Bible. Revised Standard Version. Oak Harbor, Wash.: Logos Research Systems, 1971.

Horodezky, A. Samuel. *Rabbi Nachman von Brazlaw.* Berlin: M. Poppelauer, 1910.

Howe, M. L. *The Nature of Early Memory.* Oxford: Oxford University Press, 2011.

Hubbs, Joanna. *Mother Russia: The Feminine Myth in Russian Culture.* Bloomington: Indiana University Press, 1993.

Janov, Arthur. *The Biology of Love.* Amherst, N.Y.: Prometheus Books, 2000.

Japanese Mythology & Folklore. "Womb Mother and 'Great Mother of Mercy and Love' of Bon and Mongol Cosmology, and Tibetan Influences upon Southwest China and East Asia." https://japanesemythology.wordpress.com/great-mother-of-mercy-and-love-of-bon-cosmology-and-tibetan-influences-upon-southwest-china-and-east-asia/ (accessed January 22, 2017).

Jensen, Robin. *Living Water: Images, Symbols, and Settings of Early Christian Baptism.* Leiden, Netherlands: Brill, 2010.

Jones, W. H. S., trans., Henry Arderne Ormerod, and R. E. Wycherley. *Pausanias Description of Greece.* London: W. Heinemann, 1918.

Joseph, Frank, and Laura Beaudoin. *Opening the Ark of the Covenant: The Secret Power of the Ancients, the Knights Templar Connection, and the Search for the Holy Grail.* Franklin Lakes, N.J.: Career Press, 2007.

Jung, Carl Gustav, Michael Fordham, and Herbert Read. *The Collected Works of C. G. Jung.* London: Routledge & Paul, 1993.

Kamper-Jørgensen, Mads, Henrik Hijalgrim, Anne-Marie Nybo Andersen, Vijayakrishna K. Gadi, and Anne Tjønneland. "Male Microchimerism and Survival among Women." *International Journal of Epidemiology* 43, no. 1 (2014): 168–73.

Kaplan, Aryeh. *The Bahir: Illumination.* Newburyport, Mass.: Red Wheel Weiser, 2001.

Keizer, J. Gerrit. "Hildegard of Bingen: Unveiling the Secrets of a Medieval High Priestess and Visionary." Chap. 4 in *Entheogens and the Development of Culture, the Anthropology and Neurobiology of Ecstatic Experience,* edited by John A. Rush. Berkeley, Calif.: North Atlantic Books, 2013.

Kempton, Sally. *Awakening Shakti: The Transformative Power of the Goddesses of Yoga.* Louisville, Colo.: Sounds True, 2013.

Kent, Susan. *Gender in African Prehistory.* Walnut Creek, Calif.: Sage Publications, 1998.

Kerr, D. C., D. M. Capaldi, K. C. Pears, L. D. Owen. "A Prospective Three Generational Study of Fathers' Constructive Parenting: Influences from Family of Origin, Adolescent Adjustment, and Offspring Temperament." *Developmental Psychology* 45, no. 5 (September 2009): 1257–75.

King, L. Karen. *The Gospel of Mary of Magdala: Jesus and the First Woman Apostle.* Santa Rosa, Calif.: Polebridge Press, 2003.

King-Lenzmeir, Anne. *Hildegard of Bingen: An Integrated Vision.* Collegeville, Minn.: Liturgical Press, 2001.

Knight, Chris. *Blood Relations: Menstruation and the Origins of Culture.* New Haven, Conn.: Yale University Press, 1995.

Koziol, L. F. et al., "Adaptation, Expertise, and Giftedness: Towards an Understanding of Cortical, Subcortical, and Cerebellar Network Contributions." *Cerebellum* 9, no. 4 (2010): 499–529.

Kraemer, Sebastian. "The Fragile Male." *British Medical Journal* 321 (2000): 1609–12.

Kreisberg, Glenn. *Lost Knowledge of the Ancients: A Graham Hancock Reader.* Rochester, Vt.: Bear and Company, 2010.

Krippner, Stanley. "The Maimonides ESP-Dream Studies." *Journal of Parapsychology* 57 (1993): 39–54.

Lagercrantz, Hugo. *Infant Brain Development: Formation of the Mind and the Emergence of Consciousness.* Cham, Switzerland: Springer International Publishing, 2016.

Lambdin, Thomas O., trans. "The Gospel of Thomas." *The Gnostic Society Library.* Ed. Stephen Hoeller. The Gnostic Society. www.gnosis.org/naghamm/gthlamb.html (accessed September 1, 2015.)

Lau, D. C., trans. *Tao Te Ching*. Hong Kong: Chinese University Press, 1982.

Lash, John Lamb. *Not in His Image: Gnostic Vision, Sacred Ecology, and the Future of Belief.* White River Junction, Vt.: Chelsea Green Publishing, 2006.

Laszlo, Ervin. *Science and the Akashic Field: An Integral Theory of Everything.* Rochester, Vt.: Inner Traditions, 2004.

Leboyer, Frédérick. *Birth without Violence.* New York: Knopf, 1975.

Lederer, Wolfgang. *The Fear of Women.* New York: Harcourt Brace Jovanovich, 1968.

Leloup, Jean-Yves. *The Gospel of Philip: Jesus, Mary Magdalene, and the Gnosis of Sacred Union.* Rochester, Vt.: Inner Traditions, 2004.

Levin, Fred M. *Emotion and the Psychodynamics of the Cerebellum: A Neuro-psychiatric Analysis and Synthesis.* London: Karnac, 2009.

———. *Mapping the Mind: The Intersection of Psychoanalysis and Neuroscience.* London: Karnac, 2003.

Levy, G. Rachel. *The Gate of Horn: A Study of the Religious Conceptions of the Stone Age, and Their Influence upon European Thought.* London: Faber and Faber, 1948.

Lin, Zhicheng, and Scott O. Murray. "Unconscious Processing of an Abstract Concept." *Psychological Science* 25, no. 1 (2014): 296–98.

Lipton, Bruce H. *The Biology of Belief.* London: Hay House, 2015.

———. *The Honeymoon Effect: The Science of Creating Heaven on Earth.* Carlsbad, Calif.: Hay House, 2013.

Livingstone, Alasdair. *Mystical and Mythological Explanatory Works of Assyrian and Babylonian Scholars.* Warsaw, Ind.: Eisenbrauns, 1986.

Lorimer, Jodi. *Dancing at the Edge of Death: The Origins of the Labyrinth in the Paleolithic.* Robina, Australia: Kharis Enterprises Publishing, 2009.

Luckenbill, D. D. "The Temple Women of the Code of Hammurabi." *The American Journal of Semitic Languages and Literatures* 34, no. 1 (1917): 1–12.

Lydston, G. Frank. *The Diseases of Society (the Vice and Crime Problem).* Philadelphia: J. B. Lippincott, 1904.

Lysebeth, André van. *Tantra: The Cult of the Feminine.* York Beach, Maine: Samuel Weiser, 1995.

Malachi, Tau. *The Gnostic Gospel of St. Thomas: Meditations on the Mystical Teachings.* St. Paul, Minn.: Llewellyn Publications, 2004.

Mangelsdorf, S., M. Gunnar, R. Kestenbaum, S. Lang, and D. Andreas. "Infant Proneness-to-Distress Temperament, Maternal Personality, and Mother-Infant Attachment: Associations and Goodness of Fit." *Child Development* 61, no. 3 (1990): 820–31.

Marciniak, Barbara. *Earth: Pleiadian Keys to the Living Library.* Santa Fe, N.Mex.: Bear & Company, 1994.

Markale, Jean. *Courtly Love: The Path of Sexual Initiation.* Rochester, Vt.: Inner Traditions, 2000.

———. *The Great Goddess: Reverence of the Divine Feminine from the Paleolithic to the Present.* Rochester, Vt.: Inner Traditions, 1999.

Markman, Peter T., and Roberta H. Markman. *Masks of the Spirit: Image and Metaphor in Mesoamerica.* Berkeley: University of California Press, 1989.

Massey, Gerald. *A Book of the Beginnings,* vol. 1. New York: Cosimo, 2007.

Matt, Daniel Chanan. *The Zohar,* vol. 1. Stanford, Calif.: Stanford University Press, 2011.

Matthews, Caitlin. *Sophia: Goddess of Wisdom, Bride of God.* Wheaton, Ill: Quest Books, 2001.

Matthews, Caitlin, and John Matthews. *Ladies of the Lake.* London: HarperCollins, 1996.

McCabe, Elizabeth A. *An Examination of the Isis Cult with Preliminary Exploration into New Testament Studies.* Lanham, Md.: University Press of America, 2008.

McDaniel, June. *The Madness of the Saints: Ecstatic Religion in Bengal.* Chicago: University of Chicago Press, 1989.

McTaggart, Lynn. *The Field: The Quest for the Secret Force of the Universe.* New York: HarperCollins, 2008.

Mead, G. R. S. *Gnostic John the Baptizer: Selections from the Mandaean John-Book*. London: Forgotten Books, 2007.

——. *Hymns of Hermes: Ecstatic Songs of Gnosis*. York Beach, Maine: Weiser Books, 2006.

——. *A Mithraic Ritual of the Cult of Mithra*. Whitefish, Mont.: Kessinger Publishing, 2010.

——. *Pistis Sophia: The Gnostic Tradition of Mary Magdalene, Jesus, and His Disciples*. New York: Dover Publications, 2005.

——. *Simon Magus*. Whitefish, Mont.: Kessinger Publishing, 2010.

——. *Simon Magus: His Philosophy and Teachings*. San Diego: Book Tree, 2003.

——. *The Wedding Song of Wisdom*. Whitefish, Mont.: Kessinger Publishing, 2010.

Meng, X., T. E. Ichim, J. Zhong, A. Rogers, Z. Yin, J. Jackson, H. Wang et al. "Endometrial Regenerative Cells: A Novel Stem Cell Population." *Journal of Translational Medicine* 5, no. 57 (2007): 1–10.

Merculieff, Ilarion. Bioneers. "The Womb at the Center of the Universe." media.bioneers.org/listing /the-womb-at-the-center-of-the-universe-ilarion-merculieff/ (accessed January 22, 2017).

Meyer, Marvin, ed. *The Nag Hammadi Scriptures*. San Francisco: Harper One, 2007.

Mitchell, Stephen, trans. *The Bhagvad Gita*. New York: Harmony Books, 2000.

——. *Tao Te Ching: A New English Version*. New York: HarperPerennial, 1991.

Molesky-Paz, Jean. *Contemporary Maya Spirituality: The Ancient Ways Are Not Lost*. Austin: University of Texas Press, 2009.

Moody, Valerie. *The Feasts of Adonai: Why Christians Should Look at the Biblical Feasts*. Lubbock, Tex.: Gibbora Productions, 2009.

Mookerjee, Ajit. *Kundalini: The Arousal of the Inner Energy*. New York: Destiny Books, 1982.

Mor, Barbara, and Monica Sjöö. *The Great Cosmic Mother: Rediscovering the Religion of the Earth*. New York: Harper & Row, 1987.

Mortimer, B., A. Soler, C. R. Siviour, R. Zaera, F. Vollrath. "Tuning the Instrument: Sonic Properties in the Spider's Web." *Journal of the Royal Society Interface* 13 (2016).

Moss, Robert. *Dreamways of the Iroquois: Honoring the Secret Wishes of the Soul*. Rochester, Vt.: Destiny Books, 2005.

Moyes, Holley, and Keith Prufer. "The Geopolitics of Emerging Maya Rulers." *Journal of Anthropological Research* 69, no. 2 (Summer 2013): 225–48.

Muhl, Lars. *The Law of Light*. Oxford, U.K.: Watkins Publishing, 2014.

Mukhopadhyaya, Satkati. *The Kaulajnananirnaya: The Esoteric Teachings of Matsyendrapada Sadguru of the Yogini Kaula School of Tantric Tradition*. New Delhi: Aditya Prakashan, 2013.

Mullett, George Crawford Merrick. *Spider Woman Stories: Legends of the Hopi Indians*. Tucson: University of Arizona Press, 1991.

Murphy, Michael P., Hao Wang, Amit N. Patel, Suman Kambhampati, Niren Angle, Kyle Chan, Annette M. Marleau, et al. "Allogeneic Endometrial Regenerative Cells: An 'Off the Shelf Solution' for Critical Limb Ischemia?" *Journal of Translational Medicine* 6, no. 1 (2008): 1–8.

Murray, Margaret Alice. *The God of the Witches*. New York: Oxford University Press, 1970.

——. *The Witch-Cult in Western Europe: A Study in Anthropology*. London: Forgotten Books, 2012.

Muten, Burleigh. *Return of the Great Goddess*. Boston: Shambhala Publications, 1994.

Nathanielsz, Peter W. *Life in the Womb: The Origin of Health and Disease*. Ithaca, N.Y.: Promethean Press, 1999.

National Scientific Council on the Developing Child. "Early Experiences Can Alter Gene Expression and Affect Long-Term Development: Working Paper No. 10" (2010). http://developingchild.harvard.edu/resources/early-experiences-can-alter-gene-expression-and-affect-long-term-development (accessed February 26, 2017).

Neumann, Erich. *The Origins and History of Consciousness*. Princeton, N.J.: Princeton University Press, 1995.

Neumann, Erich, and Ralph Manheim. *The Great Mother*. Princeton, N.J.: Princeton University Press, 1972.

Newnham, John P., and Michael G. Ross. "Early Life Origins of Human Health and Disease." Basel, Switzerland: Karger, 2009.

Niangoran-Bouah, Georges. *L'Universe Akan Des Poids à Peser L'Or: Les Poids Dans la Société*. Dakar, Senegal: Les Nouvelles Editions Africaines du Senegal, 1987.

Noble, Vicki. *The Double Goddess: Women Sharing Power*. Rochester, Vt.: Bear and Company, 2003.

———. *Motherpeace: A Way to the Goddess through Myth, Art, and Tarot*. London: HarperCollins, 1995.

———. *Shakti Woman: Feeling Our Fire, Healing Our World; The New Female Shamanism*. London: HarperCollins, 1991.

———. "Yeshe Tsogyal: Awesome Yogini and Tantric Consort in Tibetan Buddhism." In *Feminine Mysticism in Art: Artists Envisioning the Divine*, edited by Victoria Christian, 154–62. Ashland, Ore.: New Paradigm Publishing, 2012.

Odent, Michel. "Birth Under Water." *Lancet* 322 (1983): 1476–77.

———. *Water, Birth and Sexuality: Our Primeval Connection to Water and Its Use in Labour and Therapy*. Sussex, UK: Clairview Books, 2014.

Odier, Daniel. *Desire: The Tantric Path to Awakening*. Rochester, Vt.: Inner Traditions, 2001.

———. *Tantric Kali: Secret Practices and Rituals*. Rochester, Vt.: Inner Traditions, 2016.

Owen, Lara. *Her Blood Is Gold: Celebrating the Power of Menstruation*. New York: HarperCollins, 1993.

Pagels, Elaine. *The Gnostic Gospels*. New York: Random House, 1989.

Parkins, Eric. "Emotion: A Neuropsychological Perspective." Self-published monograph. (2013): 1–7. www.academia.edu/5439172/Emotion_a_neuropsychological_perspective (accessed January 22, 2017).

———. *Total Brain, Total Mind: Vol. 1 An Integrated Brain/Mind Architecture*. 2nd ed. Self-published, 2016. Available at http://totalbraintotalmind.co.uk.

Partridge, Christopher. *Introduction to World Religions*. Minneapolis, Minn.: Fortress Press, 2011.

Patai, Raphael. *The Hebrew Goddess*. Detroit, Mich.: Wayne State University Press, 1990.

Patterson, Stephen, and Marvin Meyer. "The Gospel of Thomas." In *The Complete Gospels, Annotated Scholars Version*, edited by Robert J. Miller. Farmington, Minn.: Polebridge Press, 1994.

Paul, Annie Murphy. *Origins: How the Nine Months Before Birth Shape the Rest of Our Lives*. New York: Free Press, 2011.

Pearce, Joseph Chilton. *The Biology of Transcendence: A Blueprint of the Human Spirit*. Rochester, Vt.: Park Street Press, 2002.

Pearce, Rob. "Attachment Theory Predicts the Formation of Romantic Relationships." *Griffith University Undergraduate Student Psychology Journal* 1 (2009): 1–9.

Peers, E. Allison. *Interior Castle: St. Teresa of Avila*. Mineola, N.Y.: Dover Publications, 2007.

Perks, Anthony, and Darlene Marie Bailey. "Stonehenge: A View from Medicine." *Journal of the Royal Society of Medicine* 96, no. 2 (2003): 94–98.

Picknett, Lynn. *Mary Magdalene: Christianity's Hidden Goddess*. New York: Carroll & Graf Publishers, 2003.

Picknett, Lynn, and Clive Prince. *The Templar Revelation: Secret Guardians of the True Identity of Christ*. New York: Touchstone, 1998.

Pinch, Geraldine. *Egyptian Mythology: A Guide to the Gods, Goddesses, and Traditions of Ancient Egypt*. Oxford: Oxford University Press, 2004.

Pordage, John, Jane Lead, and Edward Hooker. *Theologia Mystica, Or, The Mystic Divinitie of the Aeternal Invisibles, Viz., the Archetypous Globe, or the Original Globe, or World of All Globes, Worlds, Essences, Centers, Elements, Principles and Creations Whatsoever*. London, 1683.

Pordage, John, and Edward Hooker. *The Wisdom of John Pordage*. Edited by Arthur Versluis. Great Works of Christian Spirituality Series 3. St. Paul, Minn.: New Grail Publishing, 2003.

Powell, Robert. *The Most Holy Trinosophia: And the New Revelation of the Divine Feminine.* New York: Anthroposophic Press, 2001.

Prakasha, Padma Aon, and Anaiya Aon Prakasha. *Womb Wisdom: Awakening the Creative and Forgotten Powers of the Feminine.* Rochester, Vt.: Destiny Books, 2011.

Prescott, James W. "Failure of Culture." Touch The Future Foundation. April 28, 2014. https://ttfuture .org/blog/james-prescott/term/589 (accessed August 30, 2014.)

Qualls-Corbett, Nancy. *The Sacred Prostitute—Eternal Aspect of the Feminine.* Toronto: Inner City Books, 1988.

Rahaman, Farook, P. Salucci, P. K. F. Kuhfittig, Saibal Ray, and Moisur Rahaman. "Possible Existence of Wormholes in the Central Regions of Halos." Annals of Physics 350 (2014): 561–67.

Rahn, Otto. *Kreuzzug gegen den Gral.* Rev. ed. Struckum, Germany: Verlag für ganzheitliche Forschung, 1989.

Rawson, Philip. *Erotic Art of the East: The Sexual Theme in Oriental Painting and Sculpture.* London: Weidenfeld & Nicholson, 1968.

———. *Tantra: The Indian Cult of Ecstasy.* London: Thames & Hudson, 1973.

Redoute, J., S. Stoléru, M. C. Grégoire, N. Costes, L. Cinotti, F. Lavenne, D. Le Bars, M. G. Forest, and J. F. Pujol. "Brain Processing of Visual Sexual Stimuli in Human Males." *Human Brain Mapping* 11, no. 3 (2000): 162–77.

Reich, Wilhelm. *The Function of the Orgasm.* Translated by Vincent R. Carfagno. Vol. 1, *The Discovery of the Orgone.* New York: Farrar, Straus, and Giroux, 1973.

Reichel-Dolmatoff, Gerardo. "The Loom of Life: A Kogi Principle of Integration." *Journal of Latin American Lore* 4, no. 1 (1978): 5–27.

Rigoglioso, Marguerite. *The Cult of Divine Birth in Ancient Greece.* Basingstoke, U.K.: Palgrave Macmillan, 2011.

Roscoe, John. *The Baganda: An Account of their Native Customs and Beliefs.* London: Macmillan, 1911.

Rosenfeld, Cheryl S. *The Epigenome and Developmental Origins of Health and Disease.* Amsterdam: Academic Press, 2016.

Roth, Stephanie. "The Cosmic Vision of Hildegard of Bingen." *The Ecologist* 30, no. 1 (January/ February 2000), 40–42.

Rush, John A., ed. *Entheogens and the Development of Culture: The Anthropology and Neurobiology of Ecstatic Experience.* Berkeley, Calif.: North Atlantic Books, 2013.

Russell, George W. *The Candle of Vision.* Los Angeles: Library of Alexandria Publishing, 2002.

Ryan, Robert E. *The Strong Eye of Shamanism: A Journey into the Caves of Consciousness.* Rochester, Vt.: Inner Traditions, 1992.

Schack-Nielsen, Lene, and Kim Fleischer Michaelsen. "Breast Feeding and Future Health." *Current Opinion in Clinical Nutrition & Metabolic Care* 9, no. 3 (May 2006): 289–96.

Schimmel, AnneMarie. *The Mystery of Numbers.* New York: Oxford University Press, 1994.

Schmidt, Peter R. "Bricolage, Ritual Performance, and Habitus [Forgotten] in Barongo Iron Smelting." In *The World of Iron,* edited by J. Humphries and T. Rehren, 66–72. London: Archetype Books, 2013.

Scholem, Gershon. *Major Trends in Jewish Mysticism.* New York: Schocken Books, 1995.

Schwartz, Howard. *Tree of Souls: The Mythology of Judaism.* New York: Oxford University Press, 2007.

Science Daily. "In Theory, the Milky Way Could Be a 'Galactic Transport System.'". www.sciencedaily.com /releases/2015/01/150121083648.htm (accessed August 1, 2015).

Sentier, Elen. *Dreamweaver.* (Self-published) Raleigh, N.C: Lulu.com, 2009.

———. *Shaman Pathways—Elen of the Ways: British Shamanism; Following the Deer Trods.* Ropely, U.K.: John Hunt Publishing, 2013.

———. *Shaman Pathways: The Celtic Chakras.* Ropely, U.K.: John Hunt Publishing, 2013.

Shaw, Julie L. V., Christopher R. Smith, and Eleftherios P. Diamandis. "Proteomic Analysis of Human Cervico-Vaginal Fluid." *Journal of Proteome Research* 6, no. 7 (2007): 2859–65.

Shaw, Miranda. *Buddhist Goddesses of India*. Princeton, N.J.: Princeton University Press, 2006.

———. *Passionate Enlightenment: Women in Tantric Buddhism*. Princeton, N.J.: Princeton University Press, 1994.

Sheldrake, Rupert. *A New Science of Life*. Duxford, U.K.: Icon Books, 2009.

Shonkoff, Jack P., and Philip A. Fisher. "Rethinking Evidence-Based Practice and Two-Generation Programs to Create the Future of Early Childhood Policy." *Development and Psychopathology* 25 (November 2013): 1635–53.

Shuttle, Penelope, and Peter Redgrove. *Wise Wound: Menstruation and Everywoman*. New York: Marion Boyars Publishers, 2005.

Siegel, Daniel J. *The Developing Mind: How Relationships and the Brain Interact to Shape Who We Are*. New York: Guilford Publications, 2015.

Simeonova, Diana. "Valley of Thracian Kings Keeps Its Secrets." Archaeology News Network. https://archaeologynewsnetwork.blogspot.com/2015/07/valley-of-thracian-kings-keeps-its .html#ZPWhVWCy8g8dYSZ1.97. (Accessed August 1, 2015)

Smith, Morton. *Jesus the Magician*. Worthing, U.K.: Littlehampton Book Services, 1978.

Smits, Rik. *The Puzzle of Left-Handedness*. London: Reaktion Books, 2012.

Starbird, Margaret. *The Goddess in the Gospels: Reclaiming the Sacred Feminine*. Rochester, Vt.: Bear & Company, 2001.

———. *The Woman with the Alabaster Jar: Mary Magdalene and the Holy Grail*. Rochester, Vt.: Bear & Company, 2001.

Star Wolf, Linda. *Visionary Shamanism: Activating the Imaginal Cells of the Human Energy Field*. Rochester, Vt.: Bear & Company, 2012.

Star Wolf, Linda, and Nikki Scully. *Shamanic Mysteries of Egypt: Awakening the Healing Power of the Heart*. Rochester, Vt.: Bear & Company, 2007.

Stausberg, Michael, and Steven Engler. *The Routledge Handbook of Research Methods in the Study of Religion*. Abingdon, U.K.: Routledge, 2013.

Stenudd, Stefan. "The Taoism of Lao Tzu and Chuang Tzu Explained." Taoistic. www.taoistic.com /taoteaching-laotzu/taoteching-06.htm (accessed January 22, 2017).

Stone, Merlin. *When God Was a Woman*. New York: Houghton Mifflin, 1978.

Stutley, Margaret. *Hindu Deities: A Mythological Dictionary with Illustrations*. New Delhi: Munshiram Manoharlal Publishers, 2006.

Sullivan, P. "The Genetics of Schizophrenia." *Public Library of Science Medicine* 2 (2005): e212.

Swimme, Brian. *The Universe Is a Green Dragon: A Cosmic Creation Story*. Santa Fe, N. Mex.: Bear & Co., 1985.

Swimme, Brian, and Mary Evelyn Tucker. *Journey of the Universe*. New Haven, Conn.: Yale University Press, 2011.

Swimme, Brian, and Thomas Berry. *The Universe Story*. New York: HarperCollins, 2003.

Sykes, Bryan. *The Seven Daughters of Eve: The Science That Reveals Our Genetic Ancestry*. New York: W. W. Norton, 2001.

Taube, Karl A. "Flower Mountain: Concepts of Life, Beauty, and Paradise among the Classic Maya." *RES: Anthropology and Aesthetics* 45 (2004): 69–98.

Tedlock, Barbara. *The Woman in the Shaman's Body: Reclaiming the Feminine in Religion and Medicine*. New York: Random House, 2005.

Tengerism. "Sacred Mountains and Trees." www.tengerism.org/sacred_mountains.html (accessed January 22, 2017).

Thompson, J. Eric S. *Maya History and Religion*. Norman: University of Oklahoma Press, 1998.

Threecrow, Barbara. "The Kogi Myth and the Feminine Principle." February 26, 2010. threecrow .blogspot.com/2010/02/kogi-myth-and-feminine-principle.html (accessed January 22, 2017).

Thorndike, E. L. *The Elements of Psychology*. New York: Seiler, 1905.

Tournaire, Michel, and Anne Theau-Yonneau. "Complementary and Alternative Approaches to Pain Relief during Labor." *Evidence-Based Complementary and Alternative Medicine* 4 (2007): 409–417.

Trimondi, Victor, and Victoria Trimondi. "The Shadow of the Dalai Lama: Sexuality, Magic, and Politics in Tibetan Buddhism." Translated by Mark Penny. *Trimondi Online Magazine* (2003). www.trimondi .de/SDLE (accessed January 22, 2017).

Truby, H. M. "Prenatal and Neonatal Speech, 'Pre-speech,' and an Infantile-Speech Lexicon." *Word* 27, nos. 1–3 (1971): 57–101.

Turk, Ivan. "Neanderthal Flute." Republic of Slovenia, Government Communications Office. November, 2003. www.ukom.gov.si/en/media_room/background_information/culture/neanderthal _flute/ (accessed January 22, 2017).

Ulanov, Ann. *The Feminine in Jungian Psychology and in Christian Psychology*. Evanston, Ill.: Northwestern University Press, 1971.

Ulupınar, Emel. "Effects of Prenatal Stress on Developmental Anatomy of the Brain and Adult Behavioural Pathology." *International Journal of Experimental and Clinical Anatomy* (2009):1–13.

University of Missouri–St. Louis. "Sample Myths." Excerpts from *Tree of Souls: The Mythology of Judaism* by Howard Schwartz. Oxford, U.K.: Oxford University Press, 2004. www.umsl.edu /~schwartzh/samplemyths_1.htm (accessed January 30, 2017).

Van den Boom, D. C., "The Influence of Temperament and Mothering on Attachment and Exploration: An Experimental Manipulation of Sensitive Responsiveness among Lower-Class Mothers with Irritable Infants." *Child Development* 65, no. 5 (1994): 1457–77.

Van der Kolk, Bessel. *The Body Keeps the Score: Brain, Mind, and Body in the Healing of Trauma*. New York: Penguin, 2014.

Varner, Gary. *Sacred Wells: A Study in the History, Meaning, and Mythology of Holy Wells*. New York: Alogra Publishing, 2009.

Versluis, Arthur. *The Secret History of Western Sexual Mysticism: Sacred Practices and Spiritual Marriage*. Rochester, Vt.: Destiny Books, 2008.

Victora, Cesar G., Bernardo Lessa Horta, Christian Loret de Mola, Luciana Quevedo, Ricardo Tavares Pinheiro, Denise P. Gigante, Helen Gonçalves, Fernando C. Barros. "Association between Breastfeeding and Intelligence, Educational Attainment, and Income at 30 Years of Age: A Prospective Birth Cohort Study from Brazil." *Lancet Global Health* 3, no. 4 (April 2015): e199–e205.

Vinokur, Semion. *Secrets of the Eternal Book: The Meaning of the Stories of the Pentateuch*. Ontario, Canada: Laitman Kabbalah Publishers, 2013.

Virani, Shafique N. *The Ismailis in the Middle Ages: A History of Survival, a Search for Salvation*. New York: Oxford University Press, 2007.

Vitebsky, Piers. *Shamanism*. Norman: University of Oklahoma Press, 2001.

Vogt, E. Z., and D. Stuart. "Some Notes on Ritual Caves among the Ancient and Modern Maya." In *In the Maw of the Earth Mother: Mesoamerican Ritual Cave Use*, edited by James E. Brady and Keith M. Prufer. Austin: University of Texas, 2013.

Walker, Barbara G. *Man Made God: A Collection of Essays*. Seattle, Wash.: Stellar House Publishing, 2010.

———. *The Woman's Dictionary of Symbols and Sacred Objects*. New York: HarperCollins, 1995.

———. *The Woman's Encyclopedia of Myths and Secrets*. London: HarperCollins, 1991.

Walter, Mariko Namba, and Eva Jane Neumann Fridman, eds. *Shamanism: An Encyclopedia of World Beliefs, Practices, and Culture*. Oxford, U.K.: ABC-CLIO, 2004.

Washington, Teresa N. *Our Mothers, Our Powers, Our Texts: Manifestations of Àjé in Africana Literature*. Bloomington: Indiana University Press, 2005.

Waters, Frank. *Book of the Hopi*. New York: Ballantine Books, 1972.

———. *Mexico Mystique: The Coming Sixth World of Consciousness*. Athens, Ohio: Swallow Press, 1975.

Watterson, Barbara. *Women in Ancient Egypt*. Stroud, UK: Amberley, 2013.

Weaver, Ian C. G., Nadia Cervoni, Frances A. Champagne, Ana C. D'Alessio, Shakti Sharma, Jonathan R. Seckl, Segiy Dymov, Moshe Szyf, and Michael J. Meaney. "Epigenetic Programming by Maternal Behavior." *Nature Neuroscience* 7 (2004): 847–54.

White, David Gordon. *The Alchemical Body: Siddha Traditions in Medieval India*. Chicago: University of Chicago Press, 1998.

Wise, Caroline, ed. *Finding Elen: The Quest for Elen of the Ways*. London: Eala Press, 2015.

Williams, Ani. "Her Song Changes Everything." In *Earthwalking Sky Dancers*. Edited by Leila Castle. Berkeley, Calif.: Frog, Ltd., 1996.

Witt, R. E. *Isis in the Ancient World*. Baltimore, Md.: Johns Hopkins University Press, 1997.

Wolkstein, Diane, and Samuel Kramer. *Inanna, Queen of Heaven and Earth: Her Stories and Hymns from Sumer*. New York: HarperCollins, 1983.

Wollert, Kai C., and Helmut Drexler. "Cell Therapy for the Treatment of Coronary Heart Disease: A Critical Appraisal." *Nature Reviews Cardiology* 7 (2010), 204–15.

Yan, Z., N. C. Lambert, K. A. Guthrie, A. J. Porter, L. S. Loubiere, M. M. Madeleine, A. M. Stevens, H. M. Hermes, and J. L. Nelson. "Male Microchimerism in Women without Sons: Quantitative Assessment and Correlation with Pregnancy History." *American Journal of Medicine* 118 (2005): 899–906.

Yang, Heyi, Bo Zhou, Mechthild Prinz, and Donald Siegel. "Proteomic Analysis of Menstrual Blood." *Molecular & Cellular Proteomics* 11, no. 10 (2012): 1024–35.

Zhong, Z., A. N. Patel, T. E. Ichim, N. H. Riordan, H. Wang, W. P. Min, E. J. Woods et al. "Feasibility Investigation of Allogeneic Endometrial Regenerative Cells." *Journal of Translational Medicine* 7, no. 15 (2009): 1–8.

The Zohar. Unpublished translation from The Kabbalah Centre study materials.

INDEX

Numbers in *italics* preceded by *pl.* indicate color insert plate numbers.

WOMB AWAKENING
AUDIO TRACKS

Audio tracks of three guided Womb Awakening journeys are available to download at

audio.innertraditions.com/womawa

1. **Womb Awakening Grail Gates Journey (33:13):** A shamanic sound journey through the sacred mantras of the eight Grail Gates explored in cycle 6 of the book.

2. **Royal Road of the Goddess (13:33):** A shamanic guided journey through the archetypes of maiden, mother, and crone to awaken and merge these feminine powers.

3. **Elemental Dragons of Creation (13:13):** A shamanic guided journey to awaken the elemental powers of earth, fire, air, and water and enter into the quintessence of Spirit.

Credits

© 2017 by Azra and Seren Bertrand

Incantation by Seren Bertrand

Background music by Cris Coleman (www.criscoleman.bandcamp.com)

Mantra toning on Grail Gates Journey by Seren Bertrand, Azra Bertrand, and Linda Go (lindagomusic.com)

THE FOUNTAIN OF LIFE
ABOUT THE AUTHORS

DR. AZRA BERTRAND AND SEREN BERTRAND are evolutionary enchanters and guides, dedicated to helping women awaken their womb power and to assisting the rebirth of the masculine into his true gifts, uniting them in sacred union. They facilitate international retreats and apprenticeships on Womb Awakening, sacred union, and the return of the feminine dimension, for men and women.

Through their Grail mystery school, the Fountain of Life, their Womb Awakening teachings have spanned the globe to more than twenty countries, touching many thousands of people and inspiring a worldwide remembrance of Womb Consciousness.

Seren and Azra live in the ancient Mother Mountains of Appalachia, with their two cat-guides, Merlin and Lyra, and devote their lives to opening deeper into union and love. The journey of sacred marriage and intimate relationship is their greatest teacher, and fills them with joy and divine purpose.

To join one of their Womb Awakening online courses, apprenticeships, or retreats, or to buy their Sacred Sounds of the Womb CD, please visit their websites: www.thefountainoflife.org and www.wombawakening.com